Discovering AutoCAD® 2006

MARK DIX

CAD Support Associates

PAUL RILEY

CAD Support Associates

PEARSON

Prentice Hall

Upper Saddle River, New Jersey
Columbus, Ohio

Library of Congress Cataloging-in-Publication Data

Dix, Mark, 1948-
    Discovering AutoCAD 2006 / Mark Dix, Paul Riley.
        p. cm.
    Includes index
    ISBN 0-13-171388-4
    1. Computer graphics. 2. AutoCAD. I. Riley, Paul, 1943- II. Title.

T385.D5895 2006
620′.0042′0285536—dc22

                                            2005053643

Executive Editor: Debbie Yarnell
Managing Editor: Judith Casillo
Editorial Assistant: ReeAnne Davies
Production Editor: Louise N. Sette
Production Supervision: Karen Fortgang, *bookworks*
Design Coordinator: Diane Ernsberger
Cover Designer: Keith Van Norman
Art Coordinator: Jill Horton
Production Manager: Deidra M. Schwartz
Marketing Manager: Jimmy Stephens

This book was set by *The GTS Companies*/York, PA Campus. It was printed and bound by Hamilton Printing. The cover was printed by Coral Graphic Services, Inc.

Certain images and materials contained in this publication were reproduced with the permission of Autodesk, Inc. © 2005. All rights reserved. Autodesk and AutoCAD are registered trademarks of Autodesk, Inc., in the U.S.A. and certain other countries.

Disclaimer:

The publication is designed to provide tutorial information about AutoCAD® and/or other Autodesk computer programs. Every effort has been made to make this publication complete and as accurate as possible. The reader is expressly cautioned to use any and all precautions necessary, and to take appropriate steps to avoid hazards, when engaging in the activities described herein.

Neither the author nor the publisher makes any representations or warranties of any kind, with respect to the materials set forth in this publication, express or implied, including without limitation any warranties of fitness for a particular purpose or merchantability. Nor shall the author or the publisher be liable for any special, consequential or exemplary damages resulting, in whole or in part, directly or indirectly, from the reader's use of, or reliance upon, this material or subsequent revisions of this material.

Pearson Education Ltd.
Pearson Education Singapore Pte. Ltd.
Pearson Education Canada, Ltd.
Pearson Education—Japan

Pearson Education Australia Pty. Limited
Pearson Education North Asia Ltd.
Pearson Educación de Mexico, S.A. de C.V.
Pearson Education Malaysia Pte. Ltd.

10 9 8 7 6 5 4 3 2 1
ISBN: 0-13-171388-4

CONTENTS

PREFACE

Get Active with *Discovering AutoCAD® 2006*

Designed for introductory AutoCAD users, *Discovering AutoCAD® 2006* offers a hands-on, activity-based approach to the use of AutoCAD as a drafting tool—complete with techniques, tips, shortcuts, and insights designed to increase efficiency. Topics and tasks are carefully grouped to lead students logically through the AutoCAD command set, with the level of difficulty increasing steadily as skills are acquired through experience and practice. Straightforward explanations focus on what is relevant to actual drawing procedures, and illustrations show exactly what to expect on the computer screen when steps are correctly completed. This edition features Web-based exercises and projects included in each chapter. These optional exercises both assess and reinforce a student's understanding of the material.

Features

The book uses a consistent format for each chapter that includes:

- Overview and lists of new commands and tasks to be completed
- Exercises that introduce new commands and techniques
- Exercise instructions clearly set off from the text discussion
- Lots of illustrations with AutoCAD drawings and screen shots
- Ten or more end-of-chapter Review Questions
- A conclusion with 4–6 realistic engineering drawing problems—fully dimensioned working drawings
- Optional Internet Projects at the end of each chapter
- Companion Website: **http://www.prenhall.com/dixriley**

High-quality working drawings include a wide range of applications that focus on mechanical drawings but also include architectural, civil, and electrical drawings.

Appendix A contains 18 drawing projects for additional review and practice, as well as 3D models of 36 objects drawn in 2D in earlier chapters.

Companion Website: http://www.prenhall.com/dixriley

This dedicated site is designed for both professor and student users of this text. It closely supports the book and serves as a useful tool that both complements and increases the value of the text. In particular, students will find multiple choice assessment questions for each chapter. These questions serve as checkups to see whether they have mastered new AutoCAD commands. Students can answer these questions as either check-up exercises or quizzes. They receive the results of these quizzes instantly and can email these directly to their professor. Chapters are also supported by an extended AutoCAD project. These extended projects complement the book and provide extra challenges for students. Finally, this website contains a Net search capability that helps lead students to different sites dealing with AutoCAD topics.

Professors can take advantage of this site's Syllabus Manager™ feature. Following a step-by-step interface, professors can use this tool to create a graphic Web page containing class information and assignments. Professors control access to this site and maintain it with their own user ID and password. Syllabus Manager makes managing your class in either a local or distance learning situation a snap.

Our Approach

AutoCAD 2006 contains dramatic new features that significantly change fundamental elements of the user interface. Elements such as the screen cursor and the coordinate display, which have not changed through many releases, have now taken on new looks and new functionalities. It has been a great pleasure to dig into this milestone version of AutoCAD and to continue to face the challenges that we have set for ourselves in each of our AutoCAD books; that is, to create an optimum learning sequence, to get students involved in drawing as quickly as possible, to keep the learning process active, and to give students a thorough and practical understanding of AutoCAD concepts and techniques. In teaching something as content-rich as the AutoCAD 2006 software package, it is often necessary to keep in mind that less is more, and that "coverage" can be the enemy of understanding. The AutoCAD world is full of books, many of which do little more than duplicate the function of the AutoCAD Command Reference. We have all seen them at the bookstore, huge books that grow larger with every new release. The job of teaching, however, is not to try to tell everything all at once, but to anticipate what the student will need at each new phase of the learning curve.

This book is designed as a teaching tool and a self-study guide and assumes that readers will have access to a CAD workstation. We also hope that many who use it will have access to the Internet and our exciting Companion Website at **http://www.prenhall.com/dixriley**, which adds a whole new dimension to the interactive possibilities of this teaching method. Web activities, including explorations, drawing projects, and self-scoring tests, are optional components of every chapter.

The book itself is organized around drawing tasks that offer the reader a demonstration of the commands and techniques being taught at every point, with illustrations that show exactly what to expect on the computer screen when steps are correctly completed. While the focus is on the beginning AutoCAD user, we have found over the years that experienced CAD operators also look to our books for tips, suggestions, and clear explanations of AutoCAD commands and principles. It has not been unusual for seasoned pros working with our books to recognize connections and concepts that they had not noticed or considered previously.

Our target audience, however, is the beginning AutoCAD student with a serious professional interest. We strive to present a highly efficient learning sequence in an easy-to-follow format. Topics are carefully grouped so that readers progress logically through AutoCAD commands and features. Explanations are straightforward and focus on what is relevant to actual drawing procedures. Review questions, drawing problems, and WWW activities follow new material. And, most important, drawing exercises are included at the end of every chapter so that students can apply newly learned techniques to practical drawing situations immediately. Retention and skill development are optimized as the level of difficulty increases steadily and facility is acquired through experience and practice. At the end of the book we have included additional drawing projects for those who want to go further.

All working drawings have been prepared using AutoCAD. Drawing exercises at the end of all chapters are reproduced in a large, clearly dimensioned format on each right-hand page with accompanying tips and suggestions on the left-hand page. Drawing suggestions offer time-saving tips and explanations on how to use new techniques in actual applications. The book is not a drafting manual, yet the drawings include a wide range of applications.

Online Instructor's Manual

An online Instructor's Manual is available to qualified instructors for downloading. To access supplementary materials online, instructors need to request an instructor access code. Go to *www.prenhall.com,* click the **Instructor Resource Center** link, and then click **Register Today** for an instructor access code. Within 48 hours after registering, you will receive a confirming email including an instructor access code. Once you have received your code, go to the site and log on for full instructions on downloading the materials you wish to use.

Bundle This Book!

To make the cost of purchasing several books for one course more manageable for students, Prentice Hall offers discounts when you purchase this book with several other Prentice Hall textbooks. Discounts range from 10 to 20% off the price of the two books separately.

To request more specific pricing information, to get ISBNs for ordering bundles, and to learn more about Prentice Hall's offerings in graphics and CAD, contact your Prentice Hall Sales rep. For the name and number of your sales rep, please contact Prentice Hall Faculty Services at 1-800-526-0485.

Autodesk Student Portfolio

Many students ask how they can get a copy of the AutoCAD software for their home computer. Through a recent agreement with AutoCAD's publisher, Autodesk®, Prentice Hall now offers the option of purchasing *Discovering AutoCAD® 2006* with either a 180-day or a 1-year student software license. This provides adequate time for a student to complete all the activities in this book. The software is functionally identical to the professional license, but is intended for student or faculty personal use only. It is not for professional use. For more information about this book and the Autodesk Student Portfolio, contact your local Pearson Prentice Hall sales representative, or contact our National Marketing Manager, Jimmy Stephens, at 1-800-228-7854, Ext. 3725 or at Jimmy_Stephens@prenhall.com. For the name and number of your sales rep, please contact Prentice Hall Faculty Services at 1-800-526-0485.

Reviewers

We'd like to thank the following reviewers who critiqued our last book.

Y.J. Lin, *University of Akron*
Thomas J. Siller, *Colorado State University*
Jesse D. Mireless, *Phoenix College*
Joe Gaiser, *Le Tourneau University*

PART I
BASIC TWO-DIMENSIONAL ENTITIES

1 Lines

COMMANDS

ERASE	SAVE
LINE	SAVEAS
NEW	U
OPEN	UCSICON
REDO	

OVERVIEW

Drawing in AutoCAD can be a fascinating and highly productive activity. AutoCAD 2006 is dramatically different from any previous AutoCAD release and it is full of features that will enhance your CAD performance. Throughout this book, our goal is to get you drawing as quickly and efficiently as possible. Discussion and explanation is limited to what is most useful and relevant at the moment, but this should also give you an understanding of the program to make you a more powerful user.

This chapter introduces some of the basic tools you will use whenever you draw in AutoCAD. You will begin to find your way around AutoCAD menus and toolbars and learn to control basic elements of the Drawing Window. You will produce drawings involving straight lines. You will learn to undo your last command with the U command and to erase individual lines with the ERASE command. Your drawings will be saved, if you wish, using the SAVE or SAVEAS commands.

TASKS

1.1 Beginning a New Drawing

The General Procedure that follows is for reference only. We offer these General Procedures throughout the book as a convenience and quick overview. *They do not substitute for the more detailed and specific exercises that follow them.*

GENERAL PROCEDURE

1. Close the current AutoCAD drawing.
2. Type Ctrl+N or select New from the File drop-down menu.
3. Ensure that acad.dwt is entered in the File name box.
4. Press Enter.

AutoCAD can be customized in many ways, so that the exact look and sequence of what you see might be slightly different from what we show you here. We assume that you are working with "out of the box" settings but take steps to ensure that your screens resemble ours and that you have no trouble following the sequences presented here. Your first task will be to begin a new drawing using the standard acad template. First, however, we have to load AutoCAD.

⌖ From the Windows Start menu, choose All Programs, then the AutoCAD 2006 program. Alternatively, if your system has an AutoCAD 2006 shortcut icon on the Windows desktop, double-click the icon to start AutoCAD.

⌖ Wait...

When you see the AutoCAD 2006 screen, as shown in Figure 1-1, you are ready to begin.

AutoCAD 2006 may open with a variety of different appearances, including some settings that can be customized and defined as "workspaces." With typical settings, you open in a drawing with a generic name like Drawing1.

For this exercise the first thing you should do is to close the drawing on your screen and open a new one to ensure that your screen resembles ours. Closing AutoCAD drawing files is similar to closing other Windows application files. You can select Close from the File menu or click the close button, labeled with an X in the upper right corner of the drawing window. (Be careful to choose the lower of the two X buttons. The top button closes AutoCAD. The lower button closes the current drawing only and leaves AutoCAD open.)

⌖ Click the close button to close the current drawing.

The drawing area of your screen will go blank and your screen should resemble Figure 1-2.

Now open a new drawing. In AutoCAD, you typically open new drawings with some form of template. Even simple drawings can be opened with the basic acad template. Template drawings are discussed in detail in Chapter 3. Until then, we suggest that you always open with the acad template.

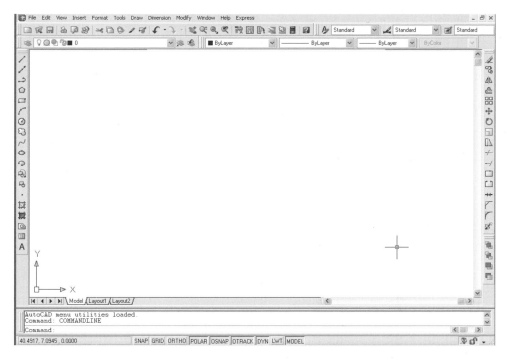

Figure 1-1

Figure 1-2

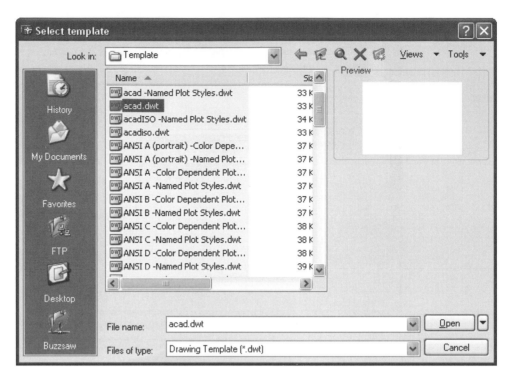

Figure 1-3

⊕ Hold down the Ctrl key and type N.

This opens the Select template dialog box shown in Figure 1-3. For now, all you need to do is look at the File name box near the bottom of the dialog box. It should read acad.dwt. Dwt is a file extension given to AutoCAD drawing template files. If your File name box has a different template, double-click in the box and type acad.

⊕ Assuming the File name box is now showing acad or acad.dwt, press Enter to complete the dialog.

1.2   Exploring the Drawing Window

You are looking at the AutoCAD Drawing Window with a new drawing based on the acad template. Elements of the drawing window are labeled in Figure 1-4. There are many ways that you can alter the drawing window to suit a particular drawing application. We explore these throughout the book. In this task we examine some of your basic tools.

The Screen

The AutoCAD Drawing Window has many features that are common to all Windows programs. At the top of the screen you will see the title bar, with the

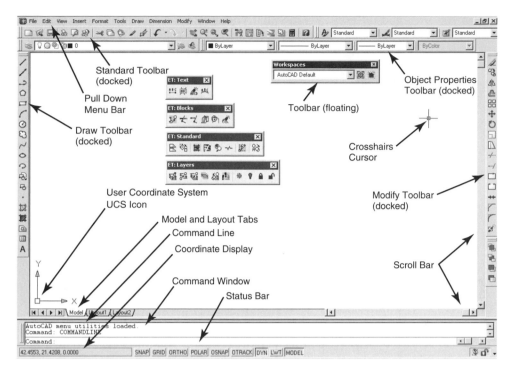

Figure 1-4

AutoCAD icon on the left and the standard Windows minimize, maximize, and close buttons on the right. To the right of the AutoCAD icon is the name of the current drawing.

Below the title bar you will see AutoCAD's pull-down menu bar, including the titles for the File, Edit, View, Insert, Format, Tools, Draw, Dimension, Modify, Window, and Help pull-down menus. Pull-down menus work in AutoCAD just as in other Windows applications and are discussed later in this section.

The next line down shows the Standard toolbar and the Styles toolbar. These are two of many that can be displayed in the AutoCAD Drawing Window. There are 30 toolbars available in AutoCAD 2006. Toolbars can be created and modified. They can be moved, resized, and reshaped. They are a convenience, but they can also make your drawing area overly cluttered. For our purposes, you do not need more than a few of the available toolbars. The use of toolbars is also discussed later in this chapter and in Chapter 3.

The next line shows the Layers toolbar and the Properties toolbar. These display the current layer and linetype. They also include tools for changing other object properties. Layers and linetypes are discussed in Chapter 4.

Below these toolbars you will see the drawing area with the Draw toolbar positioned vertically along the left side and the Modify toolbar and a vertical scroll bar along the right side. You might also see other windows or toolbars on your screen. If so, close each of these by clicking the X in its upper right or left corner.

At the bottom of the drawing area, you see arrows and tabs with the words Model, Layout1, and Layout2. These tabs allow you to switch among the drawing and different layouts that you create for printing or plotting. For the time being, you should always have the Model tab selected. We start using layouts in Chapter 6. To the right of these tabs, you see a horizontal scroll bar that works like the scroll bars in any Windows application. Clicking on the arrows or clicking and dragging the square sliders moves your drawing to the left or right within the drawing area. The vertical scroll bar moves the drawing up or down. We demonstrate these in a moment.

Beneath the scroll bar you will see the command prompt area. Typed commands are one of the basic ways of working in AutoCAD and we introduce them in the next task.

At the bottom of the Drawing Window is the status bar, with the coordinate display on the left, currently showing three four-place decimal numbers separated by commas, and nine mode buttons (Snap, Grid, Ortho, Polar, Osnap, Otrack, Dyn, LWT, and Model) in the middle. The coordinate display and mode buttons are discussed in the next task.

Finally, the bottom of your screen shows the Windows taskbar, with the Start button on the left and buttons for any open applications in the middle. You should see a button with the AutoCAD 2006 icon here, indicating that you have an AutoCAD window open.

> **Tip:** You can gain more room for your drawing area by using the autohide setting for the Windows taskbar. This is done by opening the Windows Start menu, selecting Control Panel, and then selecting Taskbar & Start Menu. This opens a Taskbar Properties dialog box. Click the Auto hide check box and the Always on top check box. Then click OK. With this setting, the taskbar only appears when you move your cursor to the bottom of the screen. It disappears again when you move away.

Switching to the Text Window

There are a number of features that can be turned on and off using the function keys on your keyboard. One is the Text Window.

⊞   Press F2.

This opens the AutoCAD Text Window. AutoCAD uses this window to display text that will not fit in the command area. All text entered at the command line in a single drawing session is saved and can be viewed in the Text Window.

⊞   Press F2 again.

This brings you back to the Drawing Window.

⊞   Press F2 to view the Text Window again.

1.3   Interacting with the Drawing Window

There are many ways to communicate with the Drawing Window. In this task, we explore the mouse, crosshairs, arrow, and other simple features. In the next task, we begin to enter drawing commands.

The Mouse

Most of your interaction with the Drawing Window will be communicated through your mouse. Given the toolbar and menu structure of AutoCAD and Windows, a two-button mouse is sufficient for most applications. In this book, we assume two buttons. If you have a digitizer or a more complex pointing device, the two button functions will be present, along with other functions that we do not address.

On a common two-button mouse the left button is called the pick button and it is used for point selection, object selection, and menu or tool selection. All mouse instructions in this book refer to the left button, unless specifically stated otherwise. The right button sometimes functions as an alternative to the Enter key on the keyboard, but most often it calls up shortcut menus as in other Windows applications. The menu that is called depends on the context. Learning how and when to use these menus can increase your efficiency. We show you how to use many shortcut menus as we go along, but most instructions are for the left button. If you click the right button accidentally and open an unwanted shortcut menu, close it by left-clicking anywhere outside the shortcut menu.

Your mouse may also have a scroll wheel between the left and right buttons. This wheel has a highly useful zooming function in AutoCAD, which we will demonstrate in Chapter 3. For now, if you happen to click the mouse wheel forward or backward, just click it in the opposite direction to reverse the zooming action.

> **Note:** In AutoCAD the right button can be set to perform in different ways. Our discussions of right-click behavior assume that you are using the default settings. If your right button does not function as described, you can return it to the default modes by typing shortcutmenu, pressing Enter, typing 11, and then pressing Enter again. This resets the shortcutmenu variable.

Crosshairs and Pick Box

You should see a small cross with a box at its intersection somewhere in the display area of your screen. If you do not see it, move your pointing device until it appears. The two perpendicular lines are the crosshairs, or screen cursor, which show you the point currently indicated by the position of your pointing device.

The small box at the intersection of the crosshairs is called the pick box and it is used to select objects for editing. You will learn more about the pick box later.

⊕ Move the mouse and see how the crosshairs move in coordination with your hand movements.

⊕ Move the mouse so that the crosshairs move to the top of the screen.

When you leave the drawing area, your crosshairs are left behind and you see an arrow pointing up and to the left. The arrow is used as in other Windows applications to select tools and to open menus from the menu bar.

> **Note:** Here and throughout this book, we show the AutoCAD 2006 versions of AutoCAD screens in our illustrations. If you are working with another version, your screen could have significant variations.

⊕ Move the cursor back into the drawing area and the selection arrow disappears.

The Coordinate Display and Dynamic Input

The coordinate display at the left of the status bar keeps track of screen coordinates as you move the pointer. The coordinate display is controlled using the F6 key or by clicking on the display itself.

⊞ Move the crosshairs around slowly and keep your eye on the three numbers at the bottom left of the screen.

The first two should be moving very rapidly through four-place decimal numbers. When you stop moving, the numbers show coordinates for the location of the pointer. These coordinates are standard coordinate values in a three-dimensional coordinate system originating from (0,0,0) at the lower left corner of the drawing area. The first value is the x value, showing the horizontal position of the crosshairs, measuring left to right across the screen. The second value is y, or the vertical position of the crosshairs, measured from bottom to top on the screen. Points also have a z value, but it is always 0 in two-dimensional drawings and can be ignored until you begin to draw in three dimensions (Chapter 12). In this book, we do not include the z value if it is 0, as it is until we get into 3-D drawings. Coordinates shown in this form, relative to a fixed coordinate grid are called absolute coordinates. As we shall see shortly, the coordinate display can also show polar coordinates, which are given as a length and an angle relative to a given point.

⊞ Carefully move the crosshairs horizontally and watch how the first value (x) changes and the second value (y) stays more or less the same.

⊞ Move the crosshairs vertically and watch how the second value (y) changes and the first value (x) stays more or less the same.

⊞ Press F6.

The numbers freeze and the coordinate display turns gray.

⊞ Move the crosshairs slowly.

Now when you move the crosshairs you can see that the coordinate display does not change. You also notice that it is still grayed out.

At this point, you probably will also see something new on your screen, as shown in Figure 1-5. This is the **dynamic input display**, new in AutoCAD 2006. We will have a lot to show you about this powerful feature in this chapter. In many ways the dynamic input display duplicates the function of the coordinate display, but it is easier to track because it follows your cursor. Dynamic input can be turned on and off using either the Dyn button on the status bar or the F12 key. Try this:

⊞ Press F12.

The dynamic input numbers on your screen disappear.

⊞ Press F12 again.

The dynamic input reappears.

Currently, the numbers in the dynamic display are x and y coordinates, just as in the coordinate display. The coordinate display on the status bar is static, while the dynamic display is still moving through values when you move your pointer. Take a moment to ensure that you understand these values. The x value is measuring horizontally, the y value is measuring vertically. The z value is set at 0.0000 on the status bar and is not shown on the dynamic input display.

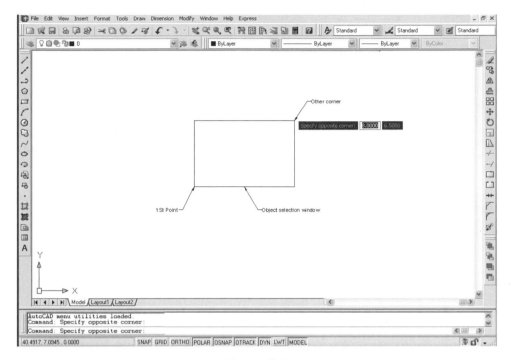

Figure 1-5

⊞ Move the crosshairs to another point on the screen.

AutoCAD opens a box on the screen, as shown in Figure 1-5. *You are not drawing anything with this box.* This is the object selection window, used to select objects for editing. It has no effect now because there are no objects on your screen. You can give two points to define the window and then it vanishes because there is nothing there to select. Object selection is discussed in Chapter 2.

AutoCAD prompts for the other corner of the selection window. You see the following in the command area and on the dynamic input display:

Specify opposite corner:

⊞ Pick a second point.

This completes the object selection window and the window vanishes. Notice the change in the static coordinate display numbers.

⊞ Press F6 to turn the coordinate display on again.

The status bar coordinate display actually has two different dynamic modes, but this is not apparent until you enter a drawing command such as LINE (Task 1.5), which asks for point selection.

Note: The units AutoCAD uses for coordinates, dimensions, and measuring distances and angles can be changed at any time using the UNITS command (see Chapter 2). For now, accept the AutoCAD default values, including the four-place decimals. In the next chapter, we change to two-place decimals. *The F-keys and status bar buttons are switches only; they cannot be used to change settings.*

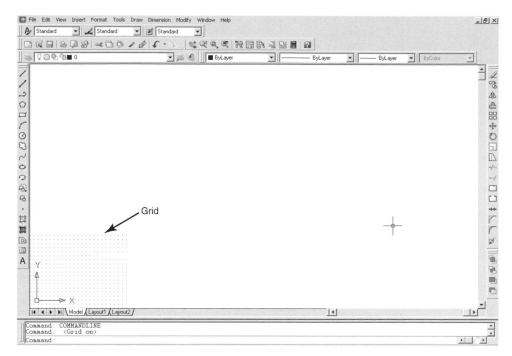

Figure 1-6

The Grid

⊞ **Press F7 or click the Grid button on the status bar.**

This turns on the grid as illustrated in Figure 1-6. When the grid is on, the Grid button will appear in the "down" position on the status bar, as shown in the figure. The grid initially appears in the lower left of the drawing area, as illustrated. We use a simple procedure with the ZOOM command to enlarge and center it. ZOOM is discussed in detail in Chapter 3.

⊞ **Type z and press Enter to execute the ZOOM command.**

Z is a shortcut for typing zoom. Such keyboard shortcuts, called aliases, are discussed in Task 1.4.

⊞ **Type a to zoom to the complete grid.**

Your grid should now be enlarged and centered in your drawing area, as illustrated in Figure 1-7.

The grid is simply a matrix of dots that helps you find your way around on the screen. It does not appear on your drawing when it is plotted, and it can be turned on and off at will. You can also change the spacing between dots using the GRID command, as we do in Chapter 2.

The grid is currently set up to emulate the shape of an A-size (12 × 9 inch) sheet of drawing paper, with grid points at 0.50-inch increments. There are 20 grid points from bottom to top, numbered 0, 0.5, 1.0, 1.5, and so on, up to 9.0. There are 26 points from left to right, numbered 0 to 12, including all 0.5-unit increments.

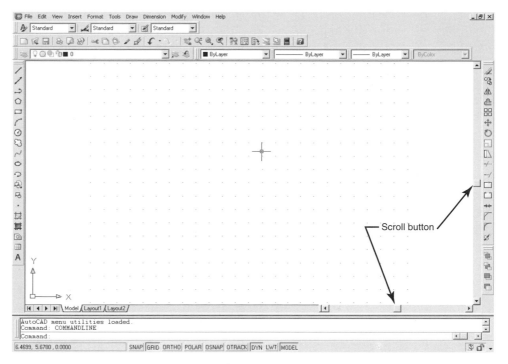

Scroll button

Figure 1-7

The AutoCAD command that controls the outer size and shape of the grid is LIMITS, which is discussed in Chapter 4. Until then, continue to use the present limits setting.

Model Space

You should be aware from the beginning that there is no need to scale AutoCAD drawings while you are working on them. That can be handled when you get ready to plot or print your drawing. You will always draw at full-scale, where one unit of length on the screen represents one unit of length in real space. This full-scale drawing space is called *model space*. Notice the Model button on the status bar, indicating that you are currently working in model space. The actual size of drawings printed out on paper might be handled in *paper space*. When you are in paper space the word PAPER appears on the status bar in place of the word MODEL. For now, all your work will be done in model space, and you do not need to be concerned with paper space.

Scroll Bars

⊕ Click the left arrow on the horizontal scroll bar at the bottom of the screen.

   Your grid moves a little to the right.

⊕ Click the left arrow again.

As you see, the movement is slight and the grid moves in the direction opposite to where the arrow is pointing. This might seem backward. Think about the scroll bars controlling the Drawing Window rather than the grid itself. As you move the window to the left, the drawing within the window appears to move to the right.

⊕ Click the left arrow and hold the mouse button down so that the grid moves continuously across the screen.

⊕ Work with the left and right buttons until the grid is again centered within the drawing area.

Notice that moving the grid in this way does not change the coordinate value of dots on the grid. The position of grid points has changed relative to the screen, but not relative to other points on the grid. Also notice that when the grid is centered the slider shown on the scroll bar should be centered in the bar. The vertical scroll bar works the same way to control vertical positioning of the drawing in the Drawing Window.

Snap

Snap is an important concept in all CAD programs. There are several AutoCAD features through which an approximate screen cursor location locks onto a precise numerical point, a point on an object, or the extension of an object. All of these features enhance productivity in that the operator does not have to hunt or visually guess at precise point locations. In this chapter, we show examples of several of these related techniques, but we leave in-depth discussion and demonstration for later chapters. The simplest form of snap is called incremental snap or grid snap, because it is conceptually related to the screen grid. Try the following:

⊕ Press F9 or click the Snap button on the status bar.

The Snap button should go into the down position, indicating that the snap mode is now on.

⊕ Move the crosshairs slowly around the drawing area.

Look closely and you will see that the crosshairs jump from point to point. If your grid is on, notice that is impossible to make the crosshairs touch a point that is not on the grid. Try it.

⊕ If your coordinate display is in the static mode, press F6 to switch to dynamic mode.

Move the cursor and watch the coordinate display.

Notice that the coordinate display shows only values ending in .0000 or .5000.

⊕ Press F9 or click the Snap button again.

Snap should now be off and the Snap button is in the up or off position on the status bar.

If you move the cursor in a circle now, the crosshairs move more smoothly, without jumping. You also observe that the coordinate display moves rapidly through a full range of four-place decimal values again.

F9 turns snap on and off. With snap off, you can theoretically touch every point on the screen. With snap on you can move only in predetermined increments. With the acad template default settings, snap is set to a value of .5000 so that you can move only in half-unit increments. In the next chapter, you learn how to change this setting using the SNAP command. For now, we leave the snap settings alone. A snap setting of .5000 is effective for the drawings at the end of this chapter.

Using an appropriate snap increment is a tremendous time-saver. It also allows for a degree of accuracy that is not possible otherwise. If all the dimensions in a drawing fall into 1-inch increments, for example, there is no reason to deal with points that are not on a 1-inch grid. You can find the points you want much more quickly and accurately if all those in between are temporarily eliminated, and the snap setting allows you to do that.

Tip: Incremental snap is more than a convenience. In most cases, it is a necessity. With snap off, it is virtually impossible to locate any point precisely. If you try to locate the point (6.5000, 6.5000, 0.0000) with snap off, for example, you might get close, but the probability is very small that you will actually be able to select that exact point. Try it.

Other Buttons on the Status Bar

All the status bar buttons are important and can be used to turn powerful features on and off. Some of the features are so powerful, however, that they can interfere with your learning and ability to control the cursor at this stage. For this reason, we encourage you to keep some features off until you need them. *In early chapters of this book, generally Snap, Grid, Dyn, and Model should be on and all other buttons should be off.* Dyn controls the dynamic input display. Ortho and Polar are discussed later in this chapter, and you can use them at your discretion. Osnap, which stands for Object Snap, is a very important feature that forces the selection of a geometrically definable point on an object, such as the endpoint or midpoint of a line. We leave Osnap alone until Chapter 6 so that you have the freedom to select points without the interference of an Object Snap selection. Otrack stands for Object Snap Tracking. Otrack is an outgrowth of Object Snap and we save it for Chapter 6 as well. LWT stands for Lineweight, which we introduce in Chapter 3.

The User Coordinate System Icon

At the lower left of the screen, you see the User Coordinate System (UCS) icon (see Figure 1-4). These two perpendicular arrows clearly indicate the directions of the *x*- and *y*-axes, which are currently aligned with the sides of your screen. In Chapter 12, when you begin to make 3-D drawings, you will be defining your own coordinate systems, which can be turned at any angle and originate at any point in space. At that time, you will find that the UCS icon is an essential visual aid. However, in two-dimensional drafting it is hardly necessary. If for any reason you wish to turn it off, you can do so by following these steps:

1. Type ucsicon and press Enter.
2. Type off and press Enter.

1.4   Exploring Command Entry Methods

You can communicate drawing instructions to AutoCAD by selecting items from a toolbar, a tool palette, a pull-down menu, a shortcut menu, dialog boxes, or a tablet menu. Each method has its advantages and disadvantages, depending on the situation, and most tasks can be accomplished in several different ways. Often a combination of two or more methods is the most efficient way to carry out a complete command sequence. The instructions in this book are not always specific about which to use. All operators develop their own preferences.

Heads-Up Design

An important concept in the creation of AutoCAD command procedures is termed *heads-up design*. What this means is that optimal efficiency is achieved when the CAD operator can keep his or her attention focused on the screen, in particular the drawing area and the objects being worked on. The less time and effort spent looking away from the screen, the better. Staying heads-up is certainly a valuable concept as a general rule, and we provide you with many techniques to support it as we go along. In AutoCAD 2006 a major innovation supporting heads-up technique is the dynamic input display. Because this display moves with the cursor, it allows you to stay focused on your drawing area.

We describe each of the basic command entry methods in this task. You do not have to try them all out at this time. Read them over to get a feel for the possibilities and then proceed to exploring the LINE command in Task 1.5.

The Keyboard and the Command Line

The keyboard is the most primitive and fundamental method of interacting with AutoCAD and it is still of great importance for all operators. Toolbars, menus, and dialog boxes all function by automating basic command sequences as they would be typed on the keyboard. Although other methods are often faster, being familiar with keyboard procedures increases your understanding of AutoCAD. The keyboard is the most basic, the most comprehensive, and changes the least from one release of AutoCAD to the next. It is literally at your fingertips, and if you know the command you want to use, you do not have to go looking for it. For this reason, some excellent CAD operators might rely too heavily on the keyboard. Do not limit yourself by typing everything. If you know the keyboard sequence, try the other methods to see how they vary and how you can use them to save time and stay screen-focused. Ultimately, you want to type as little as possible and use the differences between the toolbar and menu systems to your advantage.

As you type commands and responses to prompts, the characters you are typing appear on the command line after the colon. Also, if dynamic input is on, they may appear in the drawing area next to the crosshairs. Remember that you must press Enter to complete your commands and responses. The command line can be moved and reshaped, or you can switch to the text screen using F2 when you want to see more lines, including previously typed entries.

Many of the most often used commands, such as LINE, ERASE, and CIRCLE, have aliases. These one- or two-letter abbreviations are very handy. A few of the

COMMAND ALIAS CHART		
LETTER + ENTER		**= COMMAND**
A	⏎	ARC
C	⏎	CIRCLE
E	⏎	ERASE
F	⏎	FILLET
L	⏎	LINE
M	⏎	MOVE
O	⏎	OFFSET
P	⏎	PAN
R	⏎	REDRAW
S	⏎	STRECH
Z	⏎	ZOOM

Figure 1-8

most commonly used aliases are shown in Figure 1-8. There are also a large number of two- and three-letter aliases, some of which we introduce as we go along.

Pull-Down Menus

Pull-down menus and toolbars have the great advantage that instead of typing a complete command, you can simply point and click to select an item, without looking away from the screen. The pull down menus are always available and contain most commands that you use regularly. Menu selections and toolbar selections often duplicate each other.

Pull-down menus work in AutoCAD as they do in any Windows application. To use a menu, move the crosshairs up into the menu bar so that the selection arrow appears. Then move the arrow to the menu heading you want. Select it with the pick button (the left button on your mouse). A menu appears. Run down the list of items to the one you want. Press the pick button again to select the item (see Figure 1-9). Items followed by an arrow pointing to the right have cascading submenus that open automatically when an item is highlighted. Picking an item that is followed by an ellipsis (. . .) calls up a dialog box.

Dialog boxes are familiar features in all Windows applications. They require a combination of pointing and typing that is fairly intuitive. We discuss many dialog boxes and dialog box features as we go along.

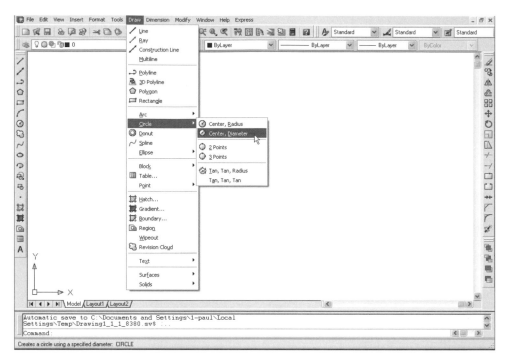

Figure 1-9

Toolbars

Toolbars are another standard Windows feature. They comprise buttons with icons that give one-click access to commands. Thirty toolbars can be accessed from a shortcut menu opened by right-clicking any open toolbar.

Once opened, toolbars can float anywhere on the screen or they can be docked along the edges of the drawing area. Toolbars can be a nuisance, because they cover portions of your drawing, but they can be opened and closed quickly. Beyond the Standard, Object Properties, Draw, and Modify toolbars, which are typically open by default, you probably only want to open a toolbar if you are doing a whole set of procedures involving that toolbar. In dimensioning an object, for example, you might wish to have the Dimension toolbar open. Do not use too many toolbars at once, and remember that you can move toolbars or use the scroll bars to move your drawing right, left, up, and down behind the toolbars.

> **Tip:** You can temporarily remove all open toolbars and tool palettes from the screen by typing Ctrl-0 (press the zero key while holding down the Ctrl key). Repeating this action will return the toolbars and palettes to the screen.

Tooltips

The icons used on the toolbars are also a mixed blessing. One picture might be worth a thousand words, but with so many pictures, you might find that a

Figure 1-10

few words can be very helpful as well. As in other Windows applications, you can get a label for an icon by allowing the selection arrow to rest on the button for a moment without selecting it. These labels are called *tooltips*. Try the following:

⊕ Position the selection arrow on the top button of the Draw toolbar, as shown in Figure 1-10, but do not press the pick button.

You will see a yellow label that says Line, as shown in Figure 1-10. This label identifies this button as the LINE command button.

When a tooltip is displayed, you also see a phrase in the status bar in place of the coordinate display. This phrase describes what the tool or menu item does and is called a *helpstring*. The LINE helpstring says, "Creates straight line segments: line." The word following the colon identifies the command as you would type it in the command area.

Note: In later chapters of this book, we illustrate most toolbars in a horizontal position even though yours might be in a docked vertical position on your screen. This is simply because vertical toolbar illustrations take up more text space. There is no reason your toolbars need to be in the same orientation as our illustrations. Also, when showing common toolbars, we often illustrate only a portion of the toolbar surrounding the tool you need.

Tool Palettes

Tool palettes were introduced in AutoCAD 2004. They are similar in many ways to toolbars, but provided access to drawing symbols, hatch patterns, and previously drawn objects. In AutoCAD 2005 this capability was expanded to include access to AutoCAD commands. This provides yet another way to enter commands. Tool palettes are introduced in Chapter 10 of this book.

Tablet Menus

If you are using a digitizer with a tablet (as opposed to a plain mouse), you might have a tablet menu available. Tablet menus were once very popular, but they are less common now because everything you need is accessible in menus and toolbars. With a good menu system, there should be a large number of commands and subcommands available on the tablet, and you do not have to search through submenus or toolbars to find them. The major disadvantage of the tablet menu is that it is the antithesis of heads-up design. To use it, you must take your eyes off the screen.

On a digitizing tablet, move the pointing device over the item you want and press the pick button. Also be aware that tablet menus can be turned on and off using the F4 key.

Now let us get started drawing.

1.5 Drawing, Undoing, and Erasing Lines

GENERAL PROCEDURE

1. Type L, select Line from the Draw menu, or select the Line tool from the Draw toolbar.
2. Pick a start point.
3. Pick an endpoint.
4. Pick another endpoint to continue in the LINE command, or press Enter or the right button on your mouse to exit the command.

Remember, the procedure just listed is a general list of how to enter and use the LINE command. It is for reference and clarity only. It does not substitute for the more detailed and specific exercise that follows.

⊕ In preparation, make sure that your status line resembles ours, as shown in Figure 1-11.

In particular, note that SNAP, GRID, DYN, and MODEL are in the on position (down), whereas ORTHO, POLAR, OSNAP, OTRACK, and LWT are

Figure 1-11

off (up). This keeps things simple and uncluttered for now. *This is very important.* Although features like Osnap and Polar tracking are very powerful, they also can get in your way when used at the wrong time. You will have plenty of use for them later on.

⊕ Type L or select the Line icon from the Draw toolbar, or Line under Draw on the pull-down menu. (Remember to press Enter if you are typing.)

As soon as you enter the command, the dynamic input prompt appears next to the crosshairs. Also, look at the command area. You should see the following in the command area and the dynamic input prompt, regardless of how you entered the command:

> Specify first point:

⊕ Move your crosshairs to the point (1.0000,1.0000,0.0000) and press the pick button.

AutoCAD registers your point selection and responds with another prompt:

> Specify next point or [Undo]:

This prompts you to pick a second point. The Undo option is discussed shortly.

Rubber Band

⊕ Move your cursor up toward the center of your drawing area and let it rest, but do press the pick button.

There are several other new things to be aware of here. The dynamic input display has become much more complex. With typical settings, there will be three new features on the screen. There is a line called the *rubber band,* a dimension with a dotted line above the line, and an angular dimension between the line and the horizon, as illustrated in Figure 1-12. The rubber band extends from the first point to the crosshairs on the screen. If you move the cursor, you notice that this visual aid stretches, shrinks, or rotates like a tether, keeping you connected to the starting point of the line. Rubber bands have various functions in AutoCAD commands. In this case, the rubber band represents the line you are about to draw.

Polar Coordinates

The two dimensions show a visual display of polar coordinates. Polar coordinates are given as a length and an angle relative to a starting point. In this case, you see the length of the line you are drawing and the angle it forms from the horizon, straight out to the right. Typically, the coordinate display will also show polar coordinates. If not, press F6 once or twice until you see something like 5.6569<45,0.0000 on the coordinate display.

⊕ Press F6 until the coordinate display shows polar coordinates.

There are three values in the polar coordinate display. For example, 5.6569, 45, and 0.0000. The first number (5.6569) is the distance from the starting point of the line to the crosshairs. The second (45) is an angle of rotation, measuring counterclockwise, with 0 degrees being straight out to the right. The third value (0.0000) is the *z*-coordinate, which remains at 0 in 2-D drawings.

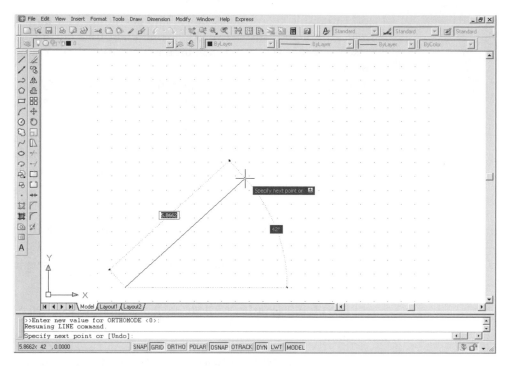

Figure 1-12

Notice that the coordinate display and the dynamic input display show the same polar coordinate values, as illustrated in Figure 1-12.

Working with Absolute and Polar Coordinates

The presence of the coordinate display with the dynamic display allows you to use absolute (x, y, z) coordinates and polar coordinates simultaneously. Try this:

⊞ Press F6 several times and watch the coordinate display.

As you do this you will notice that there are three coordinate display modes: static (values grayed out, with no change until you select a point), absolute *xyz* (*x*, *y*, and *z* values separated by a comma), and polar (length < angle, *z*).

⊞ Press F6 until you see absolute (x, y, z) coordinates in black.

With absolute coordinates showing, you can use the coordinate display to pick a point on your grid, while the dynamic display continues to show the polar coordinates of the line you are drawing.

⊞ Move the cursor to the point with absolute coordinates (8.0000, 8.0000,0.0000).

Notice that the dynamic input display shows that this line is 9.8995 units long and makes a 45-degree angle with the horizon.

⊞ Pick the point (8.0000,8.0000,0.0000).

Your screen should now resemble Figure 1-13. AutoCAD has drawn a line between (1,1) and (8,8) and is asking for another point.

```
Specify next point or [Undo]:
```

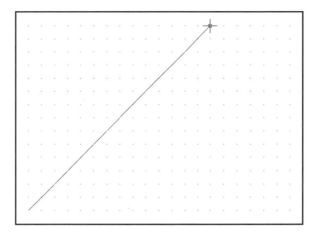

Figure 1-13

The repetition of this prompt allows you to stay in the LINE command to draw a whole series of connected lines if you wish. You can draw a single line from point to point, or a series of lines from point to point to point to point. In either case, you must tell AutoCAD when you are finished by pressing Enter or the spacebar.

Note: When you are drawing a continuous series of lines, the polar coordinates on either display are given relative to the most recent point, not the original starting point.

⊕ Press Enter or the spacebar to end the LINE command.

You should be back to the Command: prompt again, and the dynamic input display disappears from the screen.

Spacebar and Enter Key

In most cases, AutoCAD allows you to use the spacebar as a substitute for the Enter key. Although this is one of the oldest AutoCAD features, it is a major contributor to the goal of heads-up drawing. It is a great convenience, because the spacebar is easy to locate with one hand (your left hand if the mouse is on the right side) while the other hand is on the pointing device. For example, the LINE command can be entered without removing your right hand from your pointing device by typing the L on the keyboard with your left index finger and then hitting the spacebar with your left thumb. The major exception to the use of the spacebar as an Enter key is when you are entering text in your drawing (see Chapter 7). Because a space can be part of a text string, the spacebar must have its usual significance within text commands and some dimension commands.

Tip: Another great convenience provided by the spacebar and Enter key is that pressing either at the Command: prompt causes the last command entered to be repeated. We remind you of this feature frequently until it becomes habitual.

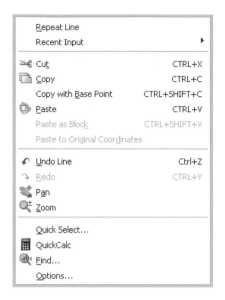

Figure 1-14

Right-Click Button and Shortcut Menus

The right button on your mouse can also be used in place of the Enter key some-times, but in most cases, there will be an intervening step involving a shortcut menu with choices. This, too, is a major heads-up feature, which we explore as we go along. For now, the following steps give you an introduction to shortcut menus.

⊕ Press the right button on your mouse. (This action is called right-clicking from now on.)

This opens a shortcut menu, as shown in Figure 1-14. The top line is a Repeat Line option that can be used to reenter the LINE command. (Remember, you can also do this by pressing the spacebar at the command prompt.) You have no use for the other options on this shortcut menu until later chapters.

Shortcut menus are context sensitive, so the menu that is called depends on the situation.

⊕ Move the cursor anywhere outside of the shortcut menu and left-click.

The shortcut menu disappears, but AutoCAD takes the picked point as the first point in an object selection window.

⊕ Pick any second point to the right of the first to close the object se-lection window.

There are many context-sensitive shortcut menus in AutoCAD. We do not attempt to present every one, but encourage you to explore. You will find many possibilities simply by right-clicking while in a command or dialog box.

Relative Coordinates and @

Besides typing or picking points on the screen, AutoCAD allows you to enter points by typing coordinates relative to the last point selected. To do this, use the @ sym-bol. For example, after picking the point (1,1) in the last exercise, you could have

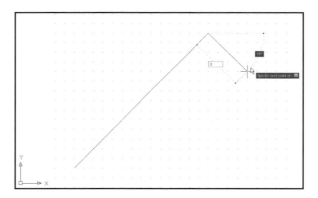

Figure 1-15

specified the point (8,8) by typing @7,7 as the second point is over 7 and up 7 from the first point. Or, using polar coordinates relative to (1,1), you could, in theory, type "@9.8995 < 45." All of these methods would give the same results.

Dynamic Input

You can also enter values directly to the dynamic input display. For example, you can pick the first point of a line and then show the direction of the line segment you wish to draw, but instead of picking the other endpoint you type in a value for the length of the line. Try this:

⊕   **Repeat the LINE command by pressing Enter or the spacebar.**

    AutoCAD prompts for a first point.

    Tip: If you press Enter or the spacebar at the Specify first point: prompt, AutoCAD selects the last point entered, so that you can begin drawing from where you left off.

⊕   **Press Enter or the spacebar to select the point (8,8,0), the endpoint of the previously drawn line.**

    AutoCAD prompts for a second point.

⊕   **Pull the rubber band diagonally down to the right, as shown in Figure 1-15.**

  Use the dynamic input display to ensure that you are moving along the diagonal at a 45-degree angle, as shown. The length of the rubber band does not matter, only the direction. Notice that the length is highlighted.

    Note: Be aware that in other contexts this angle, which is 45 degrees below the horizon, would be identified as negative 45 degrees to distinguish it from the angle that is 45 degrees above the horizon. This convention is ignored in dynamic input because the visual information removes any ambiguity.

⊕   **With the rubber band stretched out as shown, type 3.**

    Notice that the 3 is entered directly on the dynamic input display as the length of the line.

⊕   **Press Enter or hit the spacebar.**

    AutoCAD draws a 3.0000 line segment at the angle you have specified.

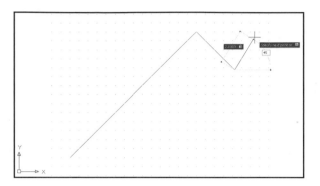

Figure 1-16

You can also use this method to input an angle. Try this:

⊕ With the length highlighted on the dynamic input display, type 2, but *do not press Enter.*

Pressing Enter will complete the line segment at whatever angle is showing, as you did in the last step. To move from the length value to the angle value, use the Tab key on your keyboard before pressing Enter.

⊕ Press the Tab key once.

The value 2.0000 is locked in as the length, as shown in Figure 1-16. You will see a lock icon on the length display and will notice that the rubber band no longer stretches, though it can still be rotated. Now you can manually specify an angle.

Note: Because you are now entering numbers rather than showing an angle on the screen, there is room for ambiguity here. If you place the rubber band above the horizon AutoCAD will draw the segment along the positive 45-degree angle. If you place the rubber band below the horizon it will draw the negative angle. You can also force a negative angle by typing –45.

⊕ Place the rubber band above the horizontal.

⊕ Type 45 and press Enter.

⊕ Press Enter or the spacebar to exit the LINE command.

Your screen should resemble Figure 1-17.

Undoing Commands with U

⊕ To undo the line you just drew, type U and press Enter or the space-bar, or select the Undo tool from the Standard toolbar, as shown in Figure 1-18. (Note that we do not show the complete toolbar, only the portion you need.)

U undoes the last command, so if you have done anything else since drawing the line, you need to enter it more than once. In this way, you can walk backward through your drawing session, undoing your commands one by one. As mentioned previously, there is also an Undo option within the LINE command so that you can undo the last segment drawn without leaving the command.

⊕ Click the Redo tool, which is to the right of the Undo tool on the Standard toolbar.

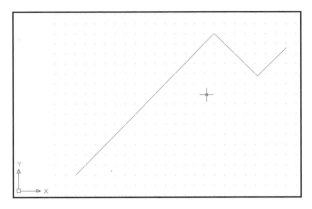

Figure 1-17

Figure 1-18

This redoes the line you have just undone. AutoCAD keeps track of everything undone in a single drawing session, so you can redo a number of undone actions.

Note: Typing U actually executes the simple U command, which undoes the last command. Selecting the Undo tool executes a command called Undo. Although the two commands often have the same effect, U is not an alias for UNDO, which has more elaborate capabilities. REDO can be used to reverse either U or UNDO. Also note that R is not an alias for REDO.

Erasing Lines

The ERASE command is explored fully in Chapter 2, but for now you might want to have access to this important command in its simplest form. Using ERASE brings up the techniques of object selection that are common to all editing commands. The simplest form of object selection requires that you point to an object and click the pick button. Try the following:

⊞ Move the crosshairs so that they are over one of the lines on your screen, as shown in Figure 1-19.

When your pick box crosses the line, it becomes thickened and dashed, as shown in the figure. *This is an AutoCAD 2006 feature called rollover highlighting.* As your pick box rolls over an object it is highlighted before you select it, so that you can be certain that you are selecting the object you want.

⊞ Press the pick button.

The line becomes dotted, indicating that it has been selected. You also see small blue boxes at the middle and at each end of the line. These are called grips, but you can ignore them for now. They are discussed in Chapter 2 as well.

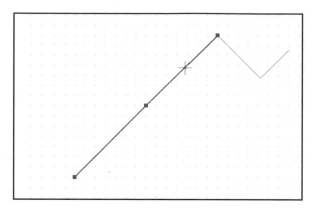

Figure 1-19

Now that the line is selected, you can enter the ERASE command to erase it.

⊕ Type e with the middle finger of your left hand and hit the spacebar with your left thumb.

The line disappears. Notice the left-hand alias and spacebar technique again.

⊕ Before going on, use U or ERASE to remove all lines from your drawing, leaving a blank drawing area.

Be aware that undoing ERASE causes a line to reappear.

Ortho

Before completing this section on line drawing, we suggest that you try the Ortho and Polar tracking modes.

⊕ Type L <Enter> or select the Line tool from the Draw toolbar.

⊕ Pick a starting point. Any point near the center of the screen will do.

⊕ Press F12 to turn off dynamic input.

Turning dynamic input off will make it easier to see what is happening with Ortho and Polar tracking.

⊕ Press F8.

F8 switches Ortho on and off. Notice that the Ortho button on the status bar is now in the down or on position. You can also turn Ortho on and off by clicking this button.

⊕ Move the cursor in slow circles.

Notice how the rubber band jumps between horizontal and vertical without sweeping through any of the angles between. Ortho forces the pointing device to pick up points only along the horizontal and vertical quadrant lines from a given starting point. With Ortho on, you can select points at 0, 90, 180, and 270 degrees of rotation from your starting point only (see Figure 1-20).

The advantages of Ortho are similar to the advantages of snap mode, except that it limits angular rather than linear increments. It ensures that you get precise and true right angles and perpendiculars easily when that is your

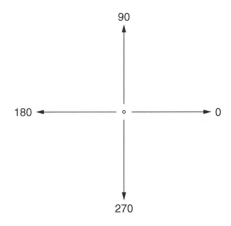

Figure 1-20

intent. Ortho becomes more important as drawings grow more complex. In this chapter it is hardly necessary, but it is convenient in Drawings 1 and 3.

Polar Tracking

Polar tracking is an AutoCAD feature that can replace Ortho for many purposes. Try it using the following steps:

⊕   Press F10 to turn on polar tracking.

Notice that Polar and Ortho are mutually exclusive. They cannot both be on at the same time. When you turn Polar on, Ortho shuts off automatically.

⊕   Move your cursor in a slow circle around the starting point of your line, just as you did with Ortho on.

With polar tracking on, when the rubber band crosses a vertical or horizontal axis (i.e., when the rubber band is at 0, 90, 180, or 270 degrees), a dotted line appears that extends to the edge of the drawing area. You also see a tooltip label, similar to the dynamic input display, giving a value like Polar 4.3835 < 0°. (See Figure 1-21.) The value is a polar coordinate. By default, polar tracking is set to respond on the orthogonal axes. In later chapters, you will see that it can be set to track at any angle. If your polar tracking is picking up angles other than 0, 90, 180, and 270 degrees, it means that someone has changed this setting on your system. For now, you should leave polar tracking off and focus on basic line drawing and point selection.

⊕   Press F10 or click the Polar button to turn polar tracking off.

Move the crosshairs in a circle and observe that polar tracking is no longer in effect.

Polar: 4.3835 < 0°

Figure 1-21

The Esc Key

⊕   While still in the LINE command, press the Esc (escape) key.

This aborts the LINE command and brings back the Command: prompt. Esc is used to cancel a command that has been entered. Sometimes it is necessary to press Esc twice to exit a command and return to the command prompt.

1.6   Saving and Opening Your Drawings

Saving drawings in AutoCAD is just like saving a file in other Windows applications. Use SAVE to save an already named drawing. Use SAVEAS to name a drawing or to save an already named drawing under a new name. In all cases, a .dwg extension is added to file names to identify them as AutoCAD drawing files. This is automatic when you name a drawing file.

The SAVE Command

To save your drawing without leaving the Drawing Window, select Save from the File pull-down menu, or select the Save tool from the Standard toolbar, as shown in Figure 1-22.

If the current drawing has been previously saved, AutoCAD saves it without an intervening dialog box. If it has not, AutoCAD opens the Save Drawing As dialog box and allows you to give the file a new name and location before it is saved.

The SAVEAS Command

To rename a drawing or to save a drawing in a new location, type Saveas or select Save As from the File pull-down menu.

Any of these methods open the Save Drawing As dialog box (see Figure 1-23). The cursor blinks in the area labeled File name:, waiting for you to enter a new file name. You can include a drive designation (i.e., A: 1-1) if you are saving your work on a removable disk. Or, if you prefer, you can open the directory list by clicking on the arrow next to the box at the top labeled Save in:. A list of drives and folders on your computer opens and you can select a location from the list.

SAVEAS also allows you to save different versions of the same drawing under different names while continuing to edit.

The Save Drawing As dialog box is one of several standard file selection dialog boxes. These boxes all have a very similar format. There is a File name and a file type edit box at the bottom, a list of places to look or places to save a file on the left, and a Look in or Save in list at the top. The places list on the left includes standard locations on your own computer. There is a History folder, a My Documents folder, a Favorites folder, a folder for File Transfer Protocol (FTP)

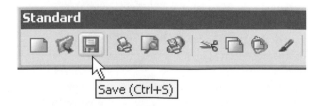

Figure 1-22

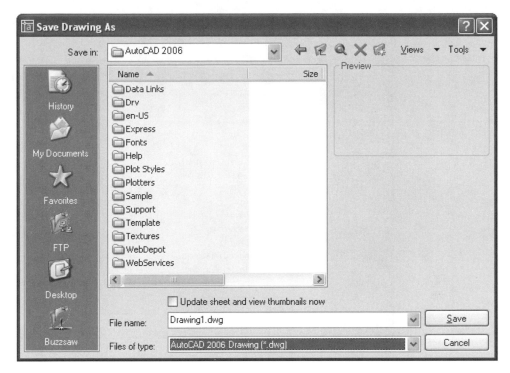

Figure 1-23

Figure 1-24

sites for downloading from the Internet, your computer's Desktop, and Autodesk's Buzzsaw website. Buzzsaw provides project sites where designers can make versions of their drawings available to others on a project team so that collaboration can be facilitated through Internet access.

Opening Saved Drawings

To open a previously saved drawing, type open, select Open from the File pull-down menu, or select the Open tool from the Standard toolbar, as shown in Figure 1-24.

Once you have saved a drawing you need to use the OPEN command to return to it later. Entering the OPEN command by any of these methods brings up the Select File dialog box shown in Figure 1-25. This is another standard file selection dialog box. It is identical to the Save Drawing As dialog box, except that Save in has been replaced by Look in. In this Select File dialog box, you can select a file folder or Internet location from the places list on the left or from a directory in the middle. When you select a file, AutoCAD shows a preview image of the selected drawing in the Preview Image box at the right. This way you can be sure that you are opening the drawing you want.

Figure 1-25

Exiting the Drawing Window

To leave AutoCAD, open the File pull-down menu and select Exit, or click the Windows close button (X) at the upper right of the screen. If you have not saved your current drawing, AutoCAD asks you if you want to save your changes before exiting.

1.7   Review Material

Questions

Before going on to the drawings, review the following questions and problems. Then you should be ready for Drawing 1-1.

1. What function key opens and closes the text window?
2. What are the three different modes of the coordinate display and how does each mode appear? What are two ways to switch between modes?
3. What is heads-up design? Give three examples of heads-up design features from this chapter.
4. Explain and describe the differences among absolute, relative, and polar coordinates.
5. Explain how dynamic input and the coordinate display can be used simultaneously to provide different types of information.
6. What function key turns dynamic input on and off?

7. You have just entered the point (1,1,0) and you now wish to enter the point two units straight up from this point. How would you identify this point using absolute, relative, and polar coordinates?
8. What is the value and limitation of having Snap on?
9. Name three different ways to enter the LINE command.
10. Name and describe three different methods of point selection in AutoCAD.
11. What does the U command do?
12. What is the keyboard alias for the ERASE command?
13. What key do you use to cancel a command?
14. What command would you use to save a new version of a drawing under a new file name? How would you enter it?

Drawing Problems

1. Draw a line from (3,2) to (4,8) using the keyboard only.
2. Draw a line from (6,6) to (7,5) using the mouse only.
3. Draw a line from (6,6) to (6,8) using dynamic input.
4. Undo (U) all lines on your screen.
5. Draw a square with the corners at (2,2), (7,2), (7,7), and (2,7). Then erase it using the ERASE command.

> ***Tip:*** For drawing an enclosed figure like the one in Problem 5, the LINE command provides a convenient Close option. Close connects the last in a continuous series of lines back to the starting point of the series. In drawing a square, for instance, you would simply type c in lieu of drawing the last of the four lines. For this to work, the whole square must be drawn without leaving the LINE command.

1.8 WWW Exercise 1 (Optional)

AutoCAD is a fully integrated Internet program. If you have Internet access you can access websites directly from within the AutoCAD program. You must first be connected to your Internet service provider. Once connected, you can move easily in and out of AutoCAD as you access all the resources available on the Web. AutoCAD drawings can be published to the Web, transferred as email attachments, uploaded, downloaded, and included as part of websites and home pages. Later in this book you learn how objects in a drawing can be designated as hyperlinks so that selecting them takes you directly from the drawing to an associated Uniform Resource Locator (URL). Also, you learn how common symbols and predrawn objects can be accessed and inserted into your drawings to reduce duplicated effort. To facilitate your learning, this book has its own companion website that you are encouraged to access. At this site you will find self-scoring tests for each chapter of the book, special Web projects related to the material in the chapter, and links to other important and interesting CAD-related websites.

In this chapter we show you how to access Autodesk.com and then take you to our companion website. Once there, take the test or go to the Web Project page for further instructions.

⊞   First, you must be sure that you are connected to an Internet service provider.

You might already be connected to the Internet, depending on your system. If you are not, you need to go through a sign-on procedure. In most cases, AutoCAD automatically initiates your sign-on procedure when you enter a Web command. If this does not happen, do not exit AutoCAD, but use the minimize button (the third button from the right at the top of the screen, with the minus sign) to temporarily leave the drawing window. We cannot give you specific instructions for connecting to the Internet from your system. For these, consult your Internet software documentation, instructor, or system manager.

⊕ Once you are connected to the Internet, click the AutoCAD icon on the Windows taskbar to return to the AutoCAD Drawing Window.

⊕ At the command prompt, type browser.

This is the BROWSER command, through which you can access Internet addresses, local network addresses, or locations on your own computer. AutoCAD prompts for an address:

```
Enter Web location (URL) <http:www.autodesk.com>:
```

The default location is shown within the brackets (< >) and might be different from the one shown here. It can be any valid location on your computer or on the Internet. In Chapter 2, we show you how to change the default location. As shown, the out-of-the-box default Internet location is Autodesk's own website, *http://www.autodesk.com*. Pressing Enter at this prompt takes you directly to this website.

⊕ Press Enter to accept the default website.

If your Internet connection is in order, you will see the Autodesk website home page, as shown in Figure 1-26, or whatever website is the default location on your system.

Note: All descriptions and illustrations of Web pages were current as of the writing of this book. Websites can and should change, so by the time you are reading this, things might look different.

Our Companion Website

This book has its own useful companion website. On the site, you will find self-scoring tests for each chapter of the book, special Web projects related to the material in the chapters, and links to other important and interesting CAD-related websites. To reach any website that is not the current default Web location, type the address at the command line.

⊕ Close the Autodesk website.

⊕ At the Command: prompt, type browser.

```
AutoCAD prompts for an address:
Enter Web location (URL) <http:www.autodesk.com.>:
This time, enter a different address.
```

⊕ Type prenhall.com/dixriley.

If you are properly configured and connected, this opens our companion website home page, shown in Figure 1-27.

⊕ Maximize the window, as shown, and enjoy your visit!

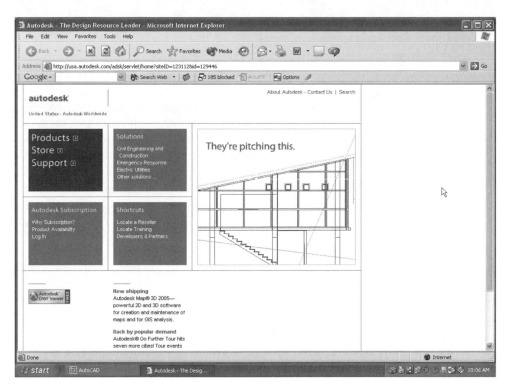

Figure 1-26

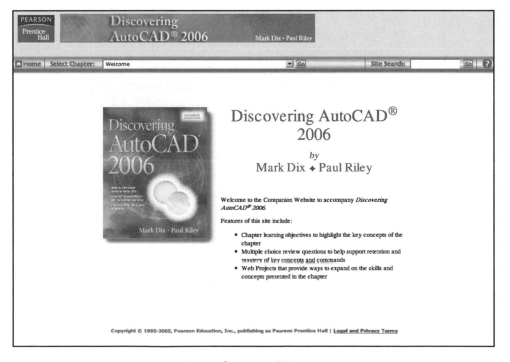

Figure 1-27

1.9   Drawing 1-1: Grate

Before beginning, look over the drawing page. The first two drawings in this chapter are given without dimensions. Instead, we have drawn them as you will see them on the screen, against the background of a half-unit grid. All these drawings were done using the default half-unit snap, but all points are found on one-unit increments.

Drawing Suggestions

- If you are beginning a new drawing, type or select New.
- Ensure that acad is entered in the File name box of the Select template dialog box and press Enter to complete the dialog box.
- Remember to watch the coordinate display or dynamic input display when searching for a point.
- Be sure that Grid, Snap, Model, and the coordinate display are all turned on and that Osnap, Otrack, and Lwt are turned off. Dyn, Ortho, and Polar can be on or off as you wish.
- Draw the outer rectangle first. It is six units wide and seven units high, and its lower left-hand corner is at the point (3.0000,1.0000). The three smaller rectangles inside are 4×1.
- The Close option can be used in all four of the rectangles.

If You Make a Mistake–U

This is a reminder that you can stay in the LINE command as you undo the last line you drew, or the last two or three if you have drawn a series.

- Type U and press Enter. The last line you drew will be gone or replaced by the rubber band, awaiting a new endpoint. If you want to go back more than one line, type U again, as many times as you need to.
- If you have already left the LINE command, the U command undoes the last continuous series of lines.
- Remember, if you have mistakenly undone something, you can get it back by using the Redo tool. You cannot perform other commands between U and REDO, but you can redo several UNDO commands if they have been done sequentially.

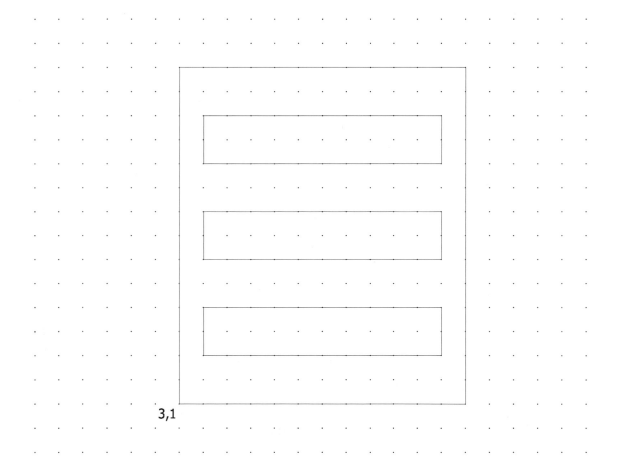

3,1

GRATE
Drawing 1-1

1.10   Drawing 1-2: Design

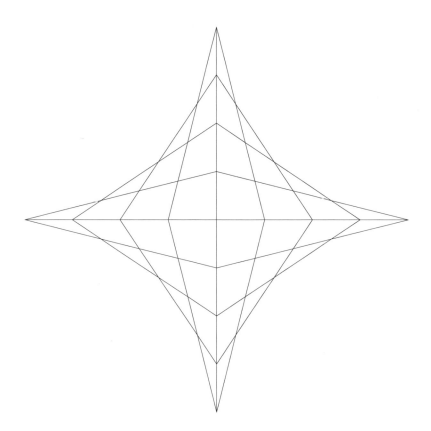

Drawing Suggestions

- If you are beginning a new drawing, type or select New, check to see that you are using the acad template, and press Enter.
- Draw the horizontal and vertical lines first. Each is eight units long.
- Notice how the rest of the lines work—outside point on horizontal to inside point on vertical, then working in, or vice versa.
- You will need to make sure Ortho is off to do this drawing.

Repeating a Command

Remember, you can repeat a command by pressing Enter or the spacebar at the Command: prompt. This is useful in this drawing because you have several sets of lines to draw.

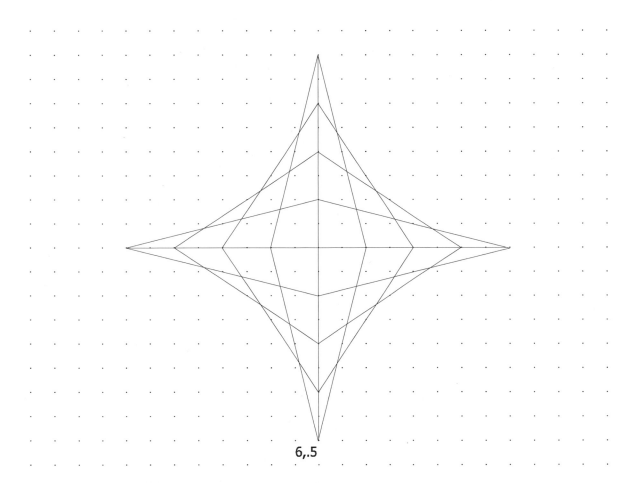

6,.5

DESIGN #1
Drawing 1-2

1.11   Drawing 1-3: Shim

This drawing gives you further practice in the LINE command. In addition, it gives you practice in translating dimensions into distances on the screen. Note that the dimensions are only included for your information; they are not part of the drawing at this point. Your drawing should appear like the reference drawing on this page. Dimensioning is the subject of Chapter 8.

Drawing Suggestions

- If you are beginning a new drawing, type or select New and open with the acad template.
- It is most important that you choose a starting point that positions the drawing so that it fits on your screen. If you begin with the bottom left-hand corner of the outside figure at the point (3,1), you should have no trouble.
- Read the dimensions carefully to see how the geometry of the drawing works. It is good practice to look over the dimensions before you begin drawing. Often the dimension for a particular line might be located on another side of the figure or might have to be extrapolated from other dimensions. It is not uncommon to misread, misinterpret, or miscalculate a dimension, so take your time.

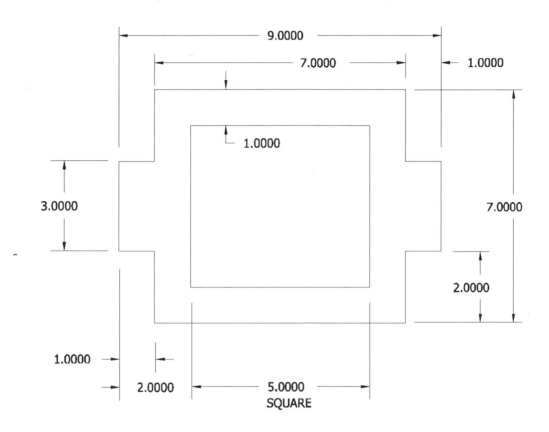

SHIM

Drawing 1-3

1.12   Drawing 1-4: Stamp

This drawing gives you practice in point selection. You can begin anywhere and use any of the point selection methods introduced in this chapter. We recommend that you try them all, including the use of dynamic input and the Tab key.

Drawing Suggestions

- If you are beginning a new drawing, type or select New and open with the acad template.
- Ortho should be off to do this drawing.
- The entire drawing can be done without leaving the LINE command if you wish.
- If you do leave LINE, remember that you can repeat LINE by pressing Enter or the spacebar, and then select the last point as a new start point by pressing Enter or the spacebar again.
- Plan to use point selection by typing, by pointing, and by dynamic input. Make use of absolute, relative, and polar coordinates.

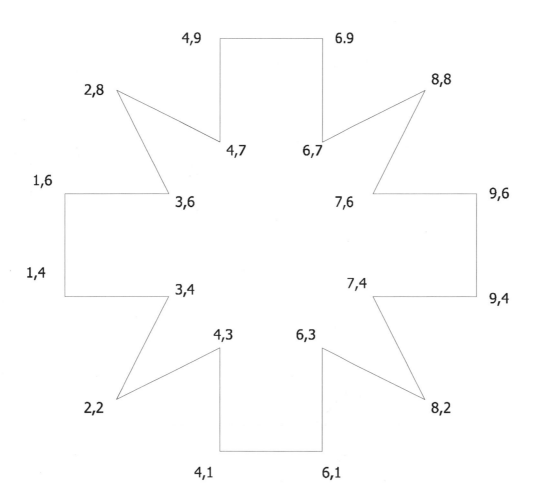

STAMP
Drawing 1-4

1.13 Drawing 1-5: Tiles

This drawing will give you lots of practice with the LINE command. All points are on the 0.50 grid and the dimensions on the drawing page give all the information you need to complete the drawing.

Drawing Suggestions

- Begin by drawing an 8 × 8 square.
- Be sure to make frequent use of the spacebar to repeat the LINE command.
- Add sixteen 2″ square tile outlines.
- Fill in the geometry in each of the 2″ squares.

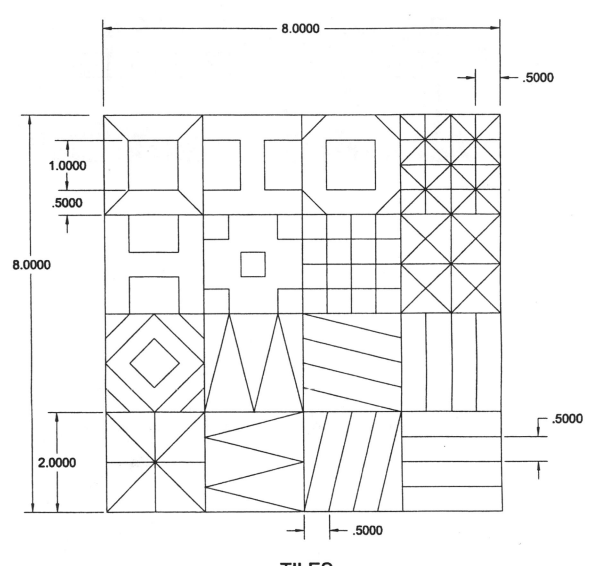

TILES

Drawing 1-5

2

Circles and Drawing Aids

COMMANDS

CIRCLE	ERASE	OOPS	SNAP
DDRMODES	GRID	PLOT	UNITS
DIST	HELP	RECTANGLE	

OVERVIEW

This chapter is loaded with new material and techniques. Here you begin to gain control of your drawing environment by changing the spacing of the grid and snap and the units in which coordinates are displayed. You add to your repertoire of objects by drawing circles with the CIRCLE command and rectangles with the RECTANGLE command. You explore the many methods of object selection as you continue to learn editing procedures with the ERASE command. You gain access to convenient Help features and begin to learn AutoCAD's extensive plotting and printing procedures.

TASKS

2.1 Changing the Grid Setting

GENERAL PROCEDURE

1. Type grid.
2. Enter a new value.

When you begin a new drawing using the acad template, the grid and snap are set with a spacing of 0.5000. In Chapter 1, all drawings were completed without altering the grid and snap spacings from the default value. Usually you want to change this to a value that reflects your application. You might want a 10-mile snap for a mapping project, or a 0.010-inch snap for a printed circuit diagram. The grid can match the snap setting or can be set independently.

⊕ To begin, open a new drawing by typing new or selecting New from the File menu.

⊕ Check to see that acad is in the File name box and press Enter.

> Once again, this ensures that you begin with the settings we have used in preparing this chapter.

⊕ Using F7 and F9, or clicking on the status bar, be sure that Grid and Snap are both on. Using the status bar, turn other modes off.

⊕ Type z and press Enter to enter the ZOOM command.

⊕ Type a to zoom all.

⊕ Type grid.

> We will no longer remind you to press Enter after typing a command or response to a prompt. Do not use the pull-down menu or toolbar yet. We will get to those procedures momentarily.

> The command area prompt appears like this, with options separated by slashes (/):

> `Specify grid spacing(X) or [ON/OFF/Snap/Aspect]<0.5000>:`

> If dynamic input is on, you also see part of this prompt next to the crosshairs. You can ignore the options for now. The number <0.5000> shows the current setting. AutoCAD uses this format <default> in many command sequences to show you a current value or default setting. It usually comes at the end of a series of options. Pressing the Enter key or spacebar at this point confirms the default setting.

⊕ In answer to the prompt, type 1 and watch what happens. (Of course, you remembered to press Enter.)

> The screen changes to show a 1-unit grid.

⊕ Move the cursor around to observe the effects of the new grid setting.

> The snap setting has not changed, so you still have access to all half-unit points, but the grid shows only single-unit increments.

⊕ Try other grid settings. Try 2, 0.25, and 0.125.

> Remember that you can repeat the last command, GRID, by pressing Enter or the spacebar.

⊕ What happens when you try 0.05?

When you get too small (smaller than 0.07 on our screen), the grid becomes too dense to display and you see this message in the command area:

Grid too dense to display

⊕ Before going on to Task 2.2, set the grid back to 0.5000.

2.2 Changing the Snap Setting

GENERAL PROCEDURE
1. Select Drafting Settings from the Tools pull-down menu, or right-click the Grid or Snap button and select Settings. 2. Enter a new snap value. 3. Click OK to exit the dialog box.

The process for changing the snap setting is really the same as changing the grid, but we use the Drafting Settings dialog box this time. Grid and snap are similar enough to cause confusion. The grid is only a visual reference. It has no effect on selection of points. Snap is invisible, but it dramatically affects point selection. Grid and snap might or might not have the same setting.

Using the Drafting Settings Dialog Box

Snap can be changed using the SNAP command at the prompt, as we did with the GRID command in the last section. Both can also be changed in the Drafting Settings dialog box, as we do in this task.

⊕ Type ds or open the Tools pull-down menu and click Drafting Settings, as shown in Figure 2-1.

This opens the Drafting Settings dialog box shown in Figure 2-2. DSETTINGS is the command that calls up this dialog box, and ds is the command alias. Look at the dialog box. It contains some common features, including tabs, check boxes, radio buttons, and edit boxes.

Tabs

At the top of the dialog box, there is an arrangement that resembles a well-ordered set of four tabbed index cards with the words Snap and Grid, Polar Tracking, Object Snap, and Dynamic Input on the tabs. Tabbed dialog boxes are common in Windows applications. With this tabbed arrangement, a single dialog box can provide organized access to a variety of related features. By clicking a tab, you can bring the related file card to the top of the stack so that it is visible in front of the others. We do not need to access the Polar Tracking, Object Snap, or Dynamic Input tabs at this time.

⊕ If the Snap and Grid card is not on top, click its tab to bring it up.

Check Boxes

Below the tabs you will see check boxes labeled Snap On (F9) and Grid On (F7). You can turn snap and grid on and off by moving the arrow inside the appropriate

Figure 2-1

check box and pressing the pick button. A checked box is on and an empty box is off. In your dialog box, check boxes should show that both snap and grid are on.

Panels

On the Snap and Grid tab there are four bordered and labeled areas. Most dialog boxes are divided into sections in this way. We refer to these labeled sections as *panels*. They are also sometimes referred to as *panes*. The four panels here are Snap, Grid, Snap type & style, and Polar spacing. In this task, we look at the Snap and Grid panels only.

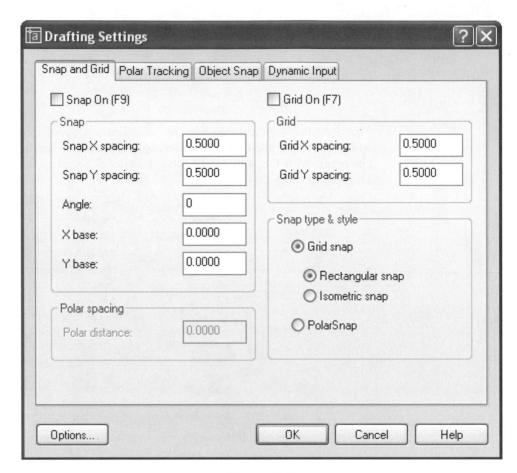

Figure 2-2

Edit Boxes

The snap and grid settings are shown in edit boxes, labeled Snap X spacing, Snap Y spacing, Grid X spacing, and Grid Y spacing. Edit boxes contain text or numerical information that can be edited as you would in a text editor. You can highlight the entire box to replace the text, or point anywhere inside to do partial editing.

To change the snap setting, do the following:

⊕ Move the arrow into the edit box labeled Snap X spacing.

> **Note:** The dialog box has places to set both *x* and *y* spacing. It is unlikely that you want to have a grid or snap matrix with different horizontal and vertical increments, but the capacity is there if you do. Also notice that you can change the snap angle. Setting the snap angle to 45, for example, would turn your snap and grid at a 45-degree angle. When you alter the grid or snap angle, you might also want to designate *x* and *y* base points around which to rotate. This is the function of the *x* and *y* base point settings.

⊕ Double-click to highlight the entire number 0.5000 in the Snap X spacing edit box.

⊕ Type 1 and press Enter.

Pressing Enter at this point is like clicking on OK in the dialog box. It takes you out of the dialog box and back to the screen.

Snap is now set at 1 and grid is still at 0.5. This makes the snap setting larger than the grid setting. Move the cursor around the screen and you will see that you can only access half of the grid points. This type of arrangement is not too useful. Try some other settings.

> **Tip:** Another way to open the Drafting Settings dialog box is to right-click while pointing at the Grid or Snap button on the status bar. This opens a shortcut menu with On, Off, and Settings options. Selecting Settings opens the Drafting Settings dialog box.

⊕ **Open the dialog box again by right-clicking the Snap button on the status bar and then choosing Settings from the shortcut menu.**

⊕ **Change the Snap X spacing value to 0.25.**

Move the cursor slowly and observe the coordinate display. This is a more efficient arrangement. With grid set coarser than snap, you can still pick exact points easily, but the grid is not so dense as to be distracting.

> **Note:** Commands that call dialog boxes, like other commands, can be repeated by pressing the spacebar or Enter.

⊕ **Press Enter to open the Drafting Settings dialog box again and set the snap to 0.05.**

Remember what happened when you tried to set the grid to 0.05?

⊕ **Move the cursor and watch the coordinate display.**

Observe how the snap setting is reflected in the available coordinates. How small a snap will AutoCAD accept?

⊕ **Try 0.005.**

Move the cursor and observe the coordinate display.

⊕ **Try 0.0005.**

You could even try 0.0001, but this would be like turning snap off, because the coordinate display is registering four decimal places anyway. Unlike the grid, which is limited by the size and resolution of your screen, you can set snap to any value you like.

⊕ **Finally, before you leave this task, set the snap back to 0.25 and leave the grid at 0.5.**

> **Tip:** If you wish to keep snap and grid the same, set the grid to 0 in the Drafting Settings dialog box, or enter the GRID command and then type s for the Snap option. The grid then changes to match the snap and continues to change anytime you reset the snap. To free the grid, just give it its own value again using the GRID command or the dialog box.

2.3 Changing Units

GENERAL PROCEDURE
1. Type Units, or select Units from the Format menu.
2. Answer the prompts.

Drop-Down Lists and the Drawing Units Dialog Box

The Drawing Units dialog box makes use of drop-down lists, another common dialog box feature. Lists give you quick access to settings, files, and other items that are organized as a list of options.

⊕ Type Units or select Units from the Format menu.

This opens the Drawing Units dialog box shown in Figure 2-3. This four-panel dialog box has five drop-down lists for specifying various characteristics of linear and angular drawing units, and a Sample Output area at the bottom. Drop-down lists show a current setting next to an arrow that is used to open the list of other possibilities. Your dialog box should show that the current Length Type in your drawing is decimal units precise to 0.0000 places, and Angle Type is decimal degrees with 0 places.

⊕ Click on the arrow to the right of the word Decimal, under Type in the Length panel of the dialog box.

A list drops down with the following options:

```
Architectural
Decimal
Engineering
Fractional
Scientific
```

Architectural units display feet and fractional inches ($1' - 3\frac{1}{2}''$), engineering units display feet and decimal inches ($1' - 3.50''$), fractional units display

Figure 2-3

units in a mixed number format ($15\frac{1}{2}$), and scientific units use exponential notation for the display of very large or very small numbers (1.55E + 01). With the exception of engineering and architectural formats, these formats can be used with any basic unit of measurement. For example, decimal mode works for metric units as well as English units.

Throughout most of this book, we stick to decimal units. Obviously, if you are designing a house you would use architectural units. If you are building a bridge, you might want engineering-style units. You might want to use scientific units if you are mapping subatomic particles.

Whatever your application, once you know how to change units, you can do so at any time. However, as a drawing practice you should choose appropriate units when you first begin work on a new drawing.

⊕ Click Decimal, or click anywhere outside the list box to close the list without changing the setting.

Now we will change the precision setting to two-place decimals.

⊕ Click the down arrow next to 0.0000 in the Precision list box in the Length panel.

This opens a list with options ranging from 0 to 0.00000000, as shown in Figure 2-4.

We use two-place decimals because they are practical and more common than any other choice.

⊕ Run your cursor arrow down the list until 0.00 is highlighted, as shown in Figure 2-4.

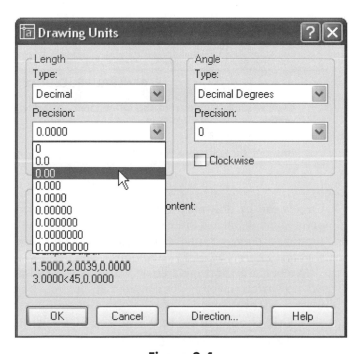

Figure 2-4

✛ Click 0.00.

The list closes and 0.00 replaces 0.0000 as the current precision for units of length. Notice that the Sample Output has also changed to reflect the new setting.

The area to the right allows you to change the units in which angular measures, including polar coordinates, are displayed. If you open the Angle Type list, you see the following options:

Decimal Degrees
Deg/Min/Sec
Grads
Radians
Surveyor's Unit

The default system is standard decimal degrees with 0 decimal places, measured counterclockwise, with 0 being straight out to the right (3 o'clock), 90 straight up (12 o'clock), 180 to the left (9 o'clock), and 270 straight down (6 o'clock). Leave these settings alone.

✛ Check to see that you have two-place decimal units for length and zero-place decimal degree units for angles. Then click OK to close the dialog box.

Tip: All dialog boxes can be moved on the screen by clicking the gray title area at the top of the dialog box, holding down the pick button, and dragging the box across the screen.

2.4   Drawing Circles Giving Center Point and Radius

GENERAL PROCEDURE

1. Type c, select Circle from the Draw menu, or select the Circle tool from the Draw toolbar.
2. Pick a center point.
3. Enter or show a radius value.

Circles can be drawn by giving AutoCAD a center point and a radius, a center point and a diameter, three points on the circle's circumference, two points that determine a diameter, or two tangent points on other objects and a radius. In this chapter, we use the first two options.

We begin by drawing a circle with radius 3 and center at the point (6,5). Then we draw two smaller circles centered at the same point. Later we erase them using the ERASE command.

✛ Grid should be set to 0.5, snap to 0.25, and units to two-place decimal.

✛ Type c, select Circle from the Draw menu, or select the Circle tool from the Draw toolbar, illustrated in Figure 2-5.

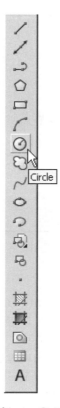

Figure 2-5

The prompt that follows looks like this:

```
Specify center point for circle or
[3P/2P/Ttr (tan tan radius)]:
```

⊕ Type coordinates or point to the center point of the circle you want to draw. In our case, it is the point (6,5).

AutoCAD assumes that a radius or diameter will follow and shows the following prompt:

```
Specify radius of circle or [Diameter]:
```

If we type or point to a value now, AutoCAD takes it as a radius because that is the default.

⊕ Move your cursor and observe the rubber band and dragged circle.

If your dynamic input display is not on, turn it on by pressing F12 or by clicking the Dyn button.

Dynamic input is a great feature for drawing circles. It will give you the radius or diameter of the circle you are drawing.

⊕ Watch the dynamic input display and move the crosshairs 3.00 away from the center point.

With snap on, you will find that you can only move exactly 3.00 if you are at 0, 90, 180, or 270 degrees.

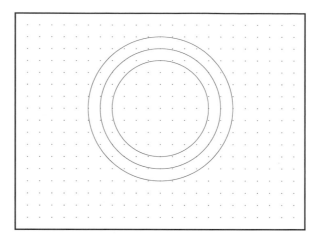

Figure 2-6

⊕ If your coordinate display is not showing polar coordinates, click it once or twice or press F6 until you see something like "3.00 < 0,000"

⊕ Move the crosshairs 3.00 away from the center point in any direction.

⊕ Press the pick button to show the radius endpoint at a distance of 3.00 from the center.

Your first circle should now be complete.

⊕ Draw two more circles using the same center point, radius method. They should be centered at (6,5) and have radii of 2.50 and 2.00.

The results are illustrated in Figure 2-6.

2.5 Drawing Circles Giving Center Point and Diameter

GENERAL PROCEDURE

1. Type c, select Circle from the Draw menu, or select the Circle tool from the Draw toolbar.
2. Pick a center point.
3. Type d.
4. Enter or show a diameter value.

We will draw three more circles centered on (6,5) having diameters of 1, 1.5, and 2. This method of drawing circles is almost the same as the radius method, except you do not use the default, and you will see that the rubber band and dynamic input display work differently.

⊕ Press Enter or the spacebar to repeat the CIRCLE command.

⊕ Indicate the center point (6,5) by typing coordinates or pointing.

⊕ Answer the prompt by typing d for diameter.

⊕ Move the crosshairs away from the center point.

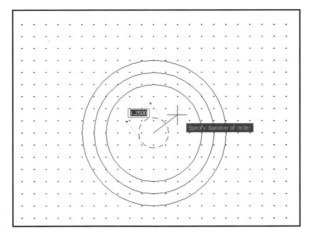

Figure 2-7

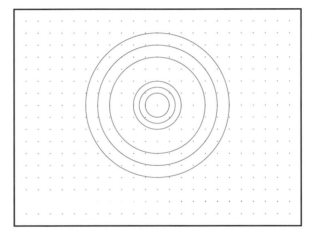

Figure 2-8

Notice that the crosshairs are now outside the circle you are dragging on the screen (see Figure 2-7). This is because AutoCAD is looking for a diameter, but the last point you gave was a center point. So the diameter is being measured from the center point out, twice the radius. Also notice that the dynamic input display has responded to the diameter specification and is now measuring the distance across the circle. Move the cursor around, in and out from the center point, to get a feel for this.

⊞ Point to a diameter of 1.00, or type 1.

You should now have four circles.

⊞ Draw two more circles with diameters of 1.50 and 2.00.

When you are done, your screen should look like Figure 2-8.

Studying Figure 2-9 and using the HELP command, as discussed in the next task, give you a good introduction to the remaining options in the CIRCLE command.

2 POINT

Pick two points.
The distance between points
defines the diameter of circle.

3 POINT

Pick three points.
The arc through all three points
is completed to from circle.
Circle is visible on screen after
second point is selected.

TANGENT, TANGENT, RADIUS

Select two objects on the screen.
Type or show radius length.
AutoCAD constructs the circle
that has the given radius and is
tangent to both objects.

Figure 2-9

Tip: Here are two ways to stay heads-up and avoid going to the keyboard to type d for the diameter option: (1) After entering the CIRCLE command and picking a center point, right-click to open a shortcut menu with the options Enter, Cancel, Diameter, Pan, and Zoom. Select Diameter. (2) If you enter the CIRCLE command from the Draw pull-down menu and select one of the options on the submenu, some of the command steps are automated. For example, if you select the Center, Diameter option, the command behaves as if Diameter is the default and you do not have to enter a d.

2.6 Accessing AutoCAD Help Features

GENERAL PROCEDURE

1. Press F1 or open the Help menu and select Help.
2. Click the Index tab.
3. Type the name of a command or topic.
4. Highlight the item you want.
5. Press Enter or click Display.

The AutoCAD HELP command gives you access to an extraordinary amount of information in a comprehensive library of AutoCAD references and information. The procedures for using HELP are standard Windows procedures and access the User's Guide, the Command Reference, the AutoCAD Driver and Peripheral Guide, the Installation and Licensing Guide, and the Customization Guide. In this task, we focus on the use of the Index feature, which pulls information from all the references, depending on the topic you select. For a demonstration, we look for further information on the CIRCLE command.

⊕ **To begin you should be at the command prompt.**

HELP is context sensitive; it goes directly to the AutoCAD Command Reference if you ask for help while in the middle of a command sequence. You should try this later.

⊕ **Press F1 or open the Help menu and select Help.**

This opens the AutoCAD Help dialog box shown in Figure 2-10. If the Contents tab is showing, you see the list of available references. You can browse through the contents of each reference but it is usually quicker to use the Index tab. You also see a Search tab and an Ask Me tab. Search is similar to index, but does not show you a list of topics until after you enter words as a search criterion. Ask Me is another way of searching for information. Instead of entering search words, you type questions or issues and Ask Me lists relevant pages.

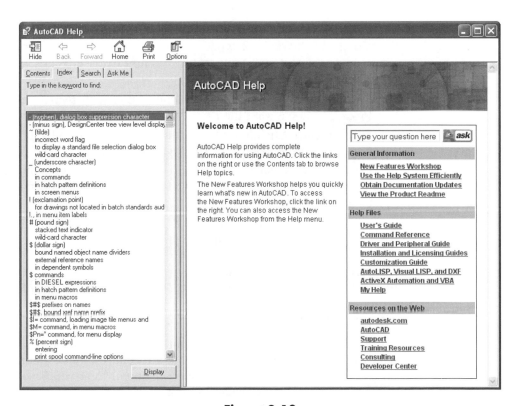

Figure 2-10

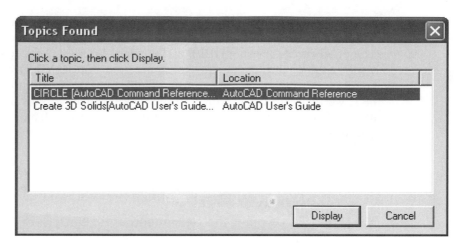

Figure 2-11

⊕   If necessary, click the Index tab.

You should see the Index as shown in Figure 2-10. The list of topics is very long, so it is rare that you use the scroll bar on the right. Most often you type in a command or topic. The list updates as you type, so you might not need to type the complete word or command.

⊕   Type Ci.

Do this slowly, one letter at a time, and you can see how the index follows along. When you have typed ci, the list shows entries beginning with Circle. Adding the rest of the letters rcle has no further effect.

⊕   Double-click CIRCLE command.

This opens a second smaller dialog box with two options, as shown in Figure 2-11. We want the first option.

⊕   Double-click CIRCLE again, press Enter, or click Display.

AutoCAD displays the CIRCLE command page from the AutoCAD Command Reference, as shown in Figure 2-12. Links to additional information on items on this page are available for words underlined and shown in bold.

⊕   Click Ttr (tan tan radius).

This adds the information for the Tangent, Tangent, Radius option of the CIRCLE command, shown in Figure 2-13.

Note: If you click the link that says "Display all hidden text on this page," you open a complete discussion of the CIRCLE command and all of its options. Try it.

Concepts, Procedures, and Commands

Before leaving the Help dialog box, notice the three tabs at the top of the Command Reference page, labeled Concepts, Procedures, and Commands. These give you access to further discussion of the command or topic you have reached through the index. For example, consider the following:

⊕   Click the Concept tab.

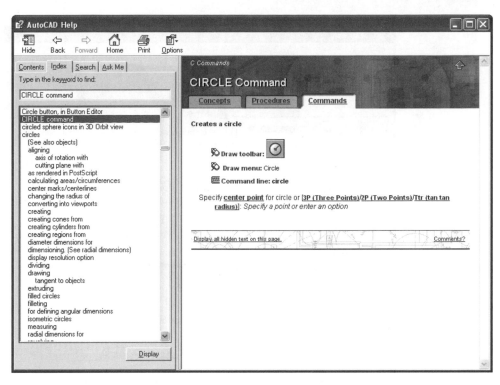

Figure 2-12

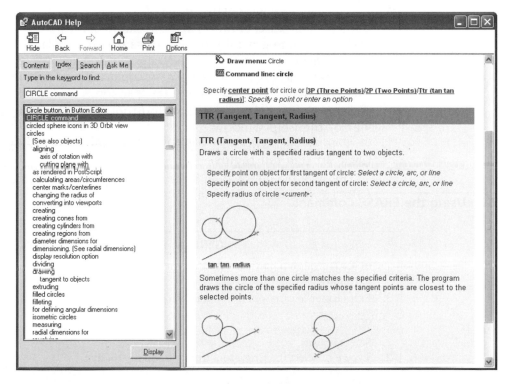

Figure 2-13

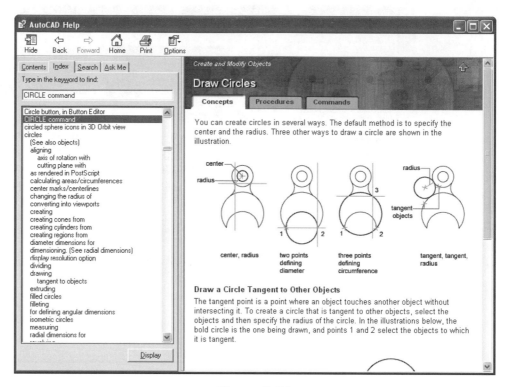

Figure 2-14

This calls up a page of discussion of concepts related to the topic you have chosen, in this case, drawing circles, as shown in Figure 2-14. The Procedures tab takes you to general procedures lists that are similar to the ones we use at the beginning of many of the sections in this book. Try it. The Commands tab shows you glossary-like entries for commands and system variables relating to the topic you have chosen. Try that, too.

⊕ To exit Help, click on the Close button, the X in the upper right corner of the Help window.

This terminates the HELP command and brings you back to the command prompt.

2.7 Using the ERASE Command

GENERAL PROCEDURE

1. Type e or select the Erase tool from the Modify toolbar.
2. Select objects.
3. Press Enter to carry out the command.

or

1. Select objects.
2. Type e or select the Erase tool from the Modify toolbar.

AutoCAD allows for many different methods of editing and even allows you to alter some of the basics of how edit commands work. Fundamentally, there are two different sequences for using most edit commands. These are called the noun/verb and the verb/noun methods.

In earlier versions of AutoCAD, most editing was carried out in a verb/noun sequence. That is, you would enter a command, such as ERASE (the verb), then select objects (the nouns), and press Enter to carry out the command. This method is still effective, but AutoCAD also allows you to reverse the verb/noun sequence. You can use either method as long as noun/verb selection is enabled in your drawing.

In this task, we explore the traditional verb/noun sequence and then introduce the noun/verb or "pick first" method along with some of the many methods for selecting objects.

Verb/Noun Editing

⊕   To begin this task you should have the six circles on your screen, as shown previously in Figure 2-8.

We use verb/noun editing to erase the two outer circles.

⊕   Type e or select the Erase tool from the Modify toolbar, as shown in Figure 2-15.

Erase can also be found on the Modify menu, but the other methods are more efficient.

The crosshairs disappear, but the pick box is still on the screen and it moves when you move your cursor.

In the command area and the dynamic input display you see the prompt

Select objects:

This is a very common prompt. You will find it in all edit commands and many other commands as well.

⊕   Move your cursor so that the outer circle crosses the pick box.

The outer circle will darken. This is the rollover preview introduced in Chapter 1.

Tip: In many situations, you might find it convenient or necessary to turn snap off (press F9) while selecting objects because this gives you more freedom of motion.

⊕   Press the pick button.

The circle will be highlighted (dotted). This is how AutoCAD indicates that an object has been selected for editing. It is not yet erased, however. You

Figure 2-15

can go on and add more objects to the selection set and they, too, will become dotted.

⊕   Use the box to pick the second circle moving in toward the center.

      It too should now be dotted.

⊕   Press Enter, the spacebar, or the right button on your pointing device to carry out the command.

      This is typical of the verb/noun sequence in most edit commands. Once a command has been entered and a selection set defined, a press of the Enter key is required to complete the command. At this point the two outer circles should be erased.

Tip: In verb/noun edit command procedures where the last step is to press Enter to complete the command, it is good heads-up practice to use the right button on your mouse in place of the spacebar or Enter key.

Noun/Verb Editing

Now let's try the noun/verb sequence.

⊕   Type u to undo the ERASE command and bring back the circles.

⊕   Use the pick box to select the outer circle.

      The circle is highlighted, and your screen should now resemble Figure 2-16. Those little blue boxes are called *grips*. They are part of AutoCAD's autoediting system, which we begin exploring in Chapter 3. For now, you can ignore them.

⊕   Pick the second circle in the same fashion.

      The second circle also becomes dotted, and more grips appear.

⊕   Type e or select the Erase tool from the Modify toolbar.

      Your two outer circles disappear as soon as you press Enter or pick the tool. Note that in this sequence the right mouse button calls a shortcut menu, so you should avoid it unless you have use for the options on the menu. Also note that you can use the Delete key on your keyboard in place of typing e.

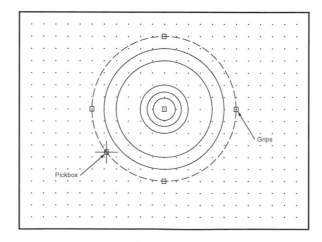

Figure 2-16

The two outer circles should now be gone. As you can see, there is not a lot of difference between the two sequences. One difference that is not immediately apparent is that there are numerous selection methods available in the verb/noun system that cannot be activated when you pick objects first. We cover other object selection methods momentarily, but first try the OOPS command.

OOPS

⊕   Type oops and watch the screen.

If you have made a mistake in your erasure, you can get your selection set back by typing oops. OOPS is to ERASE as REDO is to UNDO. You can use OOPS to undo an ERASE command, as long as you have not performed another ERASE in the meantime. In other words, AutoCAD only saves your most recent ERASE selection set.

You can also use U to undo an ERASE, but notice the difference: U simply undoes the last command, whatever it might be; OOPS works specifically with ERASE to recall the last set of erased objects. If you have drawn other objects in the meantime, you can still use OOPS to recall a previously erased set. However, if you tried to use U, you would have to backtrack, undoing any newly drawn objects along the way.

Other Object Selection Methods

You can select individual entities on the screen by pointing to them one by one, as we have done previously, but in complex drawings this is often inefficient. AutoCAD offers a variety of other methods, all of which have applications in specific drawing circumstances. In this exercise, we select circles by the windowing and crossing methods, by indicating last or L, meaning the last entity drawn, and by indicating previous or P for the previously defined set. There are also options to add or remove objects from the selection set and other variations on windowing and crossing. We suggest that you study Figure 2-17 to learn about other methods. The number of selection options available might seem a bit overwhelming at first, but time learning them is well spent. These same options appear in many AutoCAD editing commands (MOVE, COPY, ARRAY, ROTATE, MIRROR) and should become part of your CAD vocabulary.

Selection by Window

The object selection window was demonstrated in Chapter 1. Now we put it to use. Window and crossing selections, like individual object selection, can be initiated without entering a command. In other words, they are available for noun/verb selection. Whether you select objects first or enter a command first, you can force a window or crossing selection simply by picking points on the screen that are not on objects. AutoCAD assumes you want to select by windowing or crossing and asks for a second point.

Let's try it. We will show AutoCAD that we want to erase all of the inner circles by throwing a temporary selection window around them. The window is defined by two points moving left to right that serve as opposite corners of a

OBJECT SELECTION METHOD	DESCRIPTION	ITEMS SELECTED
(W) WINDOW	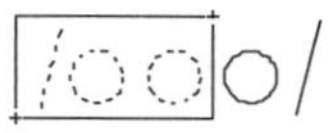	The entities within the box.
(C) CROSSING	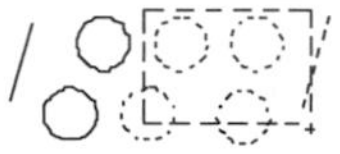	The entities crossed by or within the box.
(P) PREVIOUS	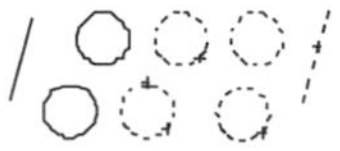	The entities that were previously picked.
(L) LAST		The entity that was drawn last.
(R) REMOVE	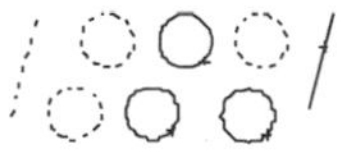	Removes entities from the items selected so they will not be part of the selected group.
(A) ADD	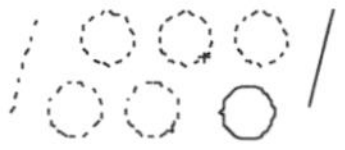	Adds entities that were removed and allows for more selections after the use of remove.
ALL		All the entities currently visible on the drawing.
(F) FENCE	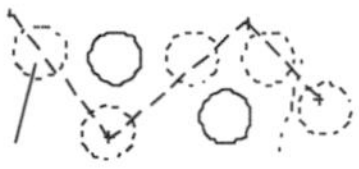	The entities crossed by the fence.
(WP) WPOLYGON	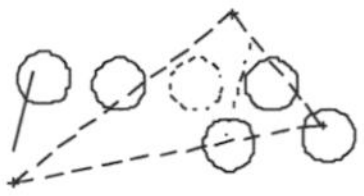	All the entities completely within the window of the polygon.
(CP) CPOLYGON	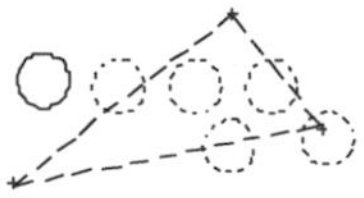	All the entities crossed by the polygon.

Figure 2-17

rectangular window. Only entities that lie completely within the window are selected (see Figure 2-18).

⊕ Pick point 1 at the lower left of the screen, as shown.

> Any point in the neighborhood of (3.5,1) will do.
> AutoCAD prompts for another corner:

> Specify opposite corner:

⊕ Pick point 2 at the upper right of the screen, as shown.

> Any point in the neighborhood of (9.5,8.5) will do. To see the effect of the window, be sure that it crosses the outside circle, as shown in Figure 2-18.

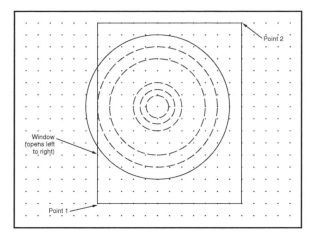

Figure 2-18

⊞   Type e or select the Erase tool.

   The inner circles should now be erased.

⊞   Type oops to retrieve the circles once more. Because ERASE was the last command, typing u or selecting the Undo tool also works.

Selection by Crossing Window

Crossing is an alternative to windowing that is useful in many cases where a standard window selection could not be performed. The selection procedure is the same, but a crossing box opens to the left instead of to the right and all objects that cross the box are chosen, not just those that lie completely inside the box.

   We use a crossing box to select the inside circles.

⊞   Pick point 1 close to (8.0,3.0), as in Figure 2-19.

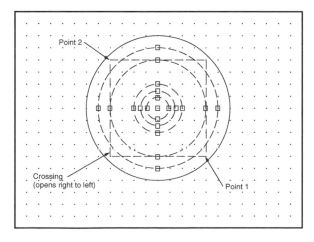

Figure 2-19

AutoCAD then prompts

Specify opposite corner:

⊕ Pick a point near (4.0,7.0).

This point selection must be done carefully to demonstrate a crossing selection. Notice that the crossing box is shown with dashed lines and a green color, whereas the window box was shown with solid lines and a lavender color.

Also, notice how the circles are selected: those that cross and those that are completely contained within the crossing box, but not those that lie outside.

At this point we could enter the ERASE command to erase the circles, but instead we demonstrate how to use the Esc key to cancel a selection set.

⊕ Press the Esc key on your keyboard.

This cancels the selection set. The circles are no longer highlighted and the grips disappear.

Selecting the "Last" Entity

AutoCAD remembers the order in which new objects have been drawn during the course of a single drawing session. As long as you do not close the drawing, you can select the last drawn entity using the "last" option.

⊕ Type e or select the Erase tool.

Notice that there is no way to specify "last" before you enter a command. This option is only available as part of a command procedure. In other words, it only works in a verb/noun sequence.

⊕ Type L.

One of the smaller circles should be highlighted.

⊕ Press Enter to carry out the command.

The circle should be erased.

Selecting the "Previous" Selection Set

The P or previous option works with the same procedure, but it selects the previous selection set rather than the last drawn entity. If the difference is not obvious to you now, don't worry; it will become clear as you work more with edit commands and selection sets.

Remove and Add

Together, the remove and add options form a switch in the object selection process. Under ordinary circumstances, whatever you select using any of the aforementioned options is added to your selection set. By typing r at the Select objects: prompt you can switch to a mode in which everything you pick is deselected or removed from the selection set. Then by typing a you can return to the usual mode of adding objects to the set.

Undoing a Selection

The ERASE command and other edit commands have an internal undo feature, similar to that found in the LINE command. By typing u at the Select objects:

prompt you can undo your last selection without leaving the edit command you are in and without undoing previous selections. You can also type u several times to undo your most recent selections one by one. This allows you to back up one step at a time without canceling the command and starting all over again.

Other Options

If you press any key other than the ones AutoCAD recognizes, at the Select objects: prompt, you see the following:

```
Expects a point or
Window/Last/Crossing/Box/All/Fence/WPolygon/CPolygon/Group/Class
/Add/Remove/Multiple/Previous/Undo/AUto/SIngle
Select objects:
```

Along with the options already discussed, All, Fence, WPolygon, and CPolygon are shown in Figure 2-17. Box, Multiple, AUto, and SIngle are used primarily in programming customized applications. Look up the SELECT command in the AutoCAD Help index for additional information.

2.8 Using the RECTANGLE Command

GENERAL PROCEDURE

1. Select the Rectangle tool from the Draw toolbar.
2. Pick the first corner point.
3. Pick another corner point.

Now that you have created object selection windows, the RECTANGLE command comes naturally. Creating a rectangle in this way is just like creating an object selection window.

⊕ To prepare for this exercise, erase all objects from your screen.

⊕ Select the Rectangle tool from the Draw toolbar, as shown in Figure 2-20.

AutoCAD prompts for a corner point:

```
          Specify first corner point or
      [Chamfer/Elevation/Fillet/Thickness/Width]:
```

You can ignore the options for now and proceed with the defaults.

Figure 2-20

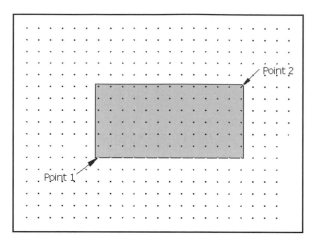

Figure 2-21

⊕ Pick (3.00,3.00) for the first corner point, as shown in Figure 2-21.

AutoCAD prompts for another point:

Specify other corner point:

Notice how the coordinate display and dynamic display work differently after you have entered the command. The coordinate display continues to show absolute coordinates relative to the screen grid. Dynamic input shows values relative to the first corner point of the rectangle so that you can see the dimensions of the rectangle you are drawing.

⊕ Pick a second point to create a 6 × 3 rectangle.

The dynamic input display will show 6.00 and 3.00, while the coordinate display will show that the second corner point is at (9.00,6.00), as shown in Figure 2-21.

⊕ Pick (9.00,6.00) for a second corner point, as shown in Figure 2-21.

As soon as you enter the second corner, AutoCAD draws a rectangle between the two corner points and returns you to the command prompt. This is a faster way to draw a rectangle than drawing it line by line. There are also some other advantages that we examine in Chapter 3.

Leave the rectangle on your screen for the plotting demonstration in Task 2.10.

2.9 Using the DIST Command

GENERAL PROCEDURE

1. Open the Tools menu, highlight Inquiry, and select Distance.
2. Pick a first point.
3. Pick a second point.
4. Read the information in the command area.

The DIST command is one of AutoCAD's most useful inquiry commands. Inquiry commands give you information about your drawing or objects within it. DIST works like a simple LINE command procedure, but it gives you distances instead of actually drawing a line. Let us say that you need to know the distance from corner point 1 to corner point 2, the diagonal in the rectangle you just drew. Try the following:

⊕ Select Inquiry and then Distance from the Tools menu, as shown in Figure 2-22.

AutoCAD prompts you to pick a point:

`Specify first point:`

⊕ Pick (3,3) again.

Notice that AutoCAD gives you a rubber band, just as if you were drawing a line. You are also prompted for a second point:

`Specify second point:`

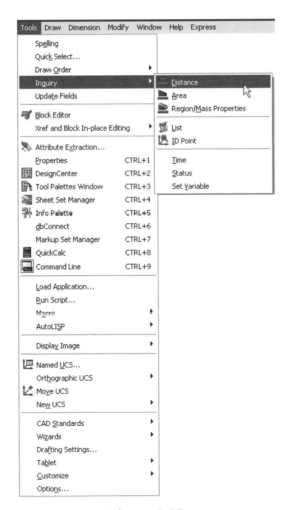

Figure 2-22

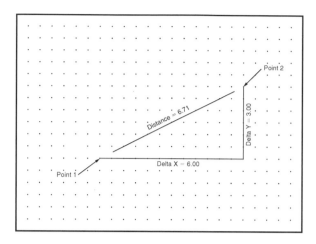

Figure 2-23

⌖ Pick (9,6) again.

You are returned to the command prompt and no line is drawn between the two points. However, you should see something like this in the command prompt area:

```
Distance = 6.71 Angle in XY Plane = 27, Angle from XY Plane = 0
Delta X = 6.00, Delta Y = 3.00, Delta Z = 0.00
```

All this information can be useful, depending on the situation. Distance gives the straight-line distance between the two selected points. Angle in XY Plane gives the angle that a line between the two points would make within the coordinate system in which 0 degrees represents a horizontal line out to the right. Angle from XY Plane is a 3-D feature and is always 0 in 2-D drawings. Delta X is the horizontal displacement, which can be either positive or negative. Similarly, Delta Y is the vertical displacement. Delta Z is the displacement in the *z* direction. It is always 0 until we begin to explore AutoCAD's 3-D drawing capabilities in Chapter 12.

Compare what is in your command prompt area with Figure 2-23.

2.10 Plotting or Printing a Drawing

GENERAL PROCEDURE

1. Type Ctrl+P, select the Plot tool from the Standard toolbar, or select Plot from the File menu.
2. Click Window.
3. Pick two points to define a window.
4. See that Fit to paper is showing in the Scale list box.
5. Prepare printer or plotter.
6. Click OK.

Figure 2-24

AutoCAD's printing and plotting capabilities are extensive and complex. In this book, we introduce you to them a little at a time. We try to keep you moving and get your drawing on paper as efficiently as possible. You will find discussions of plotting and printing in Chapters 2 through 8, before the review material and drawings in each chapter.

Plotting and printing in AutoCAD requires that you understand the relationships among model space, paper space, plot styles, page setups, and layouts. All these concepts are introduced as you need them. In this chapter, we perform the simplest type of plot, going directly from your current model space objects to a sheet of drawing paper, changing only one or two plot settings. Different types of plotters and printers work somewhat differently, but the procedure we use here should achieve reasonably uniform results. It assumes that you do not have to change devices or fundamental configuration details. It should work for all plotters and printers and the drawings in this chapter. We use a window selection to define a plot area and scale this to fit on whatever size paper is in your plotter or printer.

⊕ Type Ctrl+P, or select Plot from the File menu or the Plot tool from the Standard toolbar, as shown in Figure 2-24.

Any of these methods opens the Plot dialog box illustrated in Figure 2-25. You will become very familiar with it as you work through this book. It is one of the most important working spaces in AutoCAD. It contains many options and can be expanded to allow even more options by clicking the > button at the bottom right. (If your dialog box is already expanded, you can reduce it by clicking the < button.) In this exercise we will need only two settings.

But first, you need to specify a plotter or printer. The second panel from the top is the Printer/plotter selection area. Look to see if the name of a plotting device is showing in the Name list box.

⊕ If None is displayed in the list box, click the arrow on the right and select a plotter or printer.

Now look at the panel labeled Plot area at the lower left. The drop-down list labeled "What to plot" gives you the choice of plotting based on what is on the Display, the Extents or Limits of the drawing, or a Window you define. For our purposes, defining a window gives more consistent results than relying on the Display area, which might differ more from one system to another. Windowing allows you to plot any portion of a drawing by defining a window in the usual way. AutoCAD bases the size and placement of the plot on the window you define.

Before creating the plot area window, look at the Plot scale panel in the center of the dialog box. In the Scale list box, locate the Fit to paper check box. If your plot scale is configured to plot to fit your paper, as it should be by default, then AutoCAD plots your drawing at maximum size based on the paper size and the window you specify.

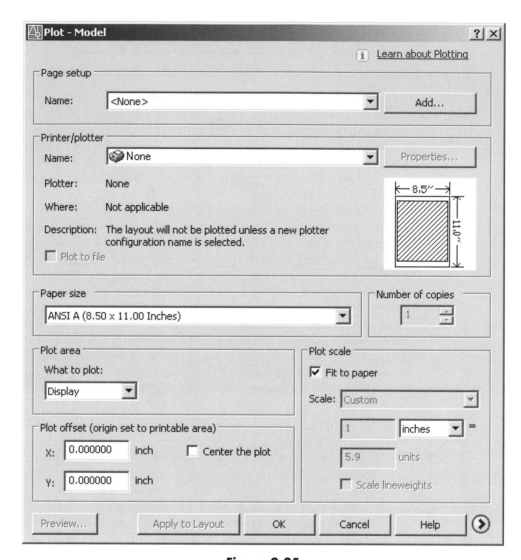

Figure 2-25

⊕ If for any reason Fit to paper is not checked, click in the box to check it.

On the Custom line below Plot scale, you should see edit boxes with numbers like 1 = 4.768. Right now the plot area is based on the shape of your display area and these numbers are inaccessible. When you use a window to create a plot area that is somewhat smaller, these scale numbers change automatically. When you use Scales rather than Fit to paper, these numbers will be accessible and you can set them manually or select from a list.

⊕ Select Window in the What to plot list.

The Plot dialog box disappears temporarily, giving you access to the drawing. You will see the crosshairs, but the pick box is absent. AutoCAD prompts for point selection:

```
Specify window for printing
Specify first corner:
```

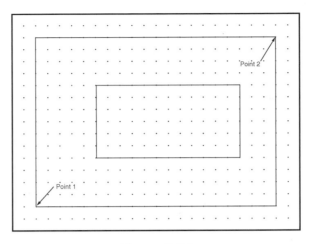

Figure 2-26

⊕   Select the point (1.00,1.00), as shown in Figure 2-26.

AutoCAD prompts

Specify opposite corner:

⊕   Select the point (11.00,8.00), as shown in Figure 2-26.

As soon as you have picked the second point, AutoCAD displays the Plot dialog box again with two changes. First, the Window radio button is now accessible and selected. Second, the Plot scale ratio changes to something like 1 = 0.9533. We use the phrase "something like" because there might be minor variations depending on your plotter.

You are now ready to plot.

⊕   If you want to plot or print the rectangle, prepare your plotter and then click OK. Otherwise, click Cancel.

Clicking OK sends the drawing information to be printed. You can sit back and watch the plotter at work. If you need to cancel for any reason, click Cancel.

For now, that's all there is to it. If your plot does not look perfect—if it is not centered on your drawing sheet, for example—don't worry; you will learn all you need to know about plotting in later chapters.

2.11   Review Material

Questions

1. Which is likely to have the smaller setting, Grid or Snap? Why? What happens if the settings are reversed?
2. Name three ways to open the Drafting Settings dialog box.
3. How do you switch from decimal units to architectural units?
4. Where is 0 degrees located in AutoCAD's default units setup? Where is 270 degrees? Where is −45 degrees?
5. How do you enter the CIRCLE command?
6. Why does the rubber band touch the circumference of the circle when you are using the radius option, but not when you are using the diameter option?

7. What does the dynamic input display show when you are drawing a circle using a diameter dimension?
8. What does the dynamic input display show when you are selecting the second point of a rectangle in the RECTANGLE command?
9. How does AutoCAD know when you want a crossing selection instead of a window selection?
10. What is the difference between a Last selection and a Previous selection?
11. What is the difference between noun/verb and verb/noun editing?
12. How do you access the AutoCAD Help index?

Drawing Problems

1. Leave the grid at 0.50 and set snap to 0.25.
2. Use the 3P option to draw a circle that passes through the points (2.25,4.25), (3.25,5.25), and (4.25,4.25).
3. Using the 2P option, draw a second circle with a diameter from (3.25,4.25) to (4.25,4.25).
4. Draw a third circle centered at (5.25,4.25) with a radius of 1.00.
5. Draw a fourth circle centered at (4.75,4.25) with a diameter of 1.00.

2.12   WWW Exercise 2 (Optional)

In this second voyage to the World Wide Web, we show you how to change the default Uniform Resource Locator (URL) so that you don't have to type a long, ugly address every time you go out to the Web.

We show you how to change the default Web location to the companion website for this book. Of course the general procedure works just as well with any other legitimate Web address or file on your computer. Whether or not you actually want to retain our website as the default, we encourage you to go there now, take the self-scoring review test, and try the Web project.

⊕   Type inetlocation at the command prompt.

INETLOCATION is a system variable that stores the name of the default URL. AutoCAD prompts

`Enter new value for inetlocation <http:www.autodesk.com>:`

Remember that the address within the arrows is the current default. This value is replaced by the address you enter.

⊕   Type www.prenhall.com/dixriley.

The new value is stored, and AutoCAD returns you to the command prompt. Now all you need to do is enter the BROWSER command and press Enter at the prompt.

⊕   Type browser.

The AutoCAD prompt shows the new default URL:

`Enter web location (URL) <prenhall.com/dixriley>:`

⊕   Press Enter to accept the default location.

Away you go. Good luck on the test.

2.13   Drawing 2-1: Aperture Wheel

This drawing gives you practice creating circles using the center point, radius method. Refer to the table following the drawing for radius sizes. With snap set at 0.25, some of the circles can be drawn by pointing and dragging. Other circles have radii that are not on a snap point. These circles can be drawn by typing in the radius.

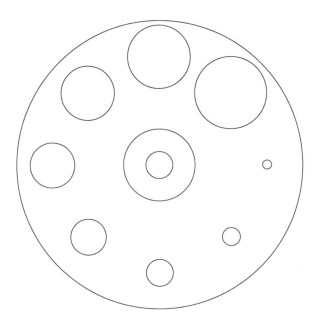

Drawing Suggestions

GRID = 0.50
SNAP = 0.25

- A good sequence for doing this drawing would be to draw the outer circle first, followed by the two inner circles (h and c) in Drawing 2-1. These are all centered on the point (6.00,4.50). Then begin at circle a and work around clockwise, being sure to center each circle correctly.
- Notice that there are two circles c and two h. The two circles having the same letter are the same size.
- Remember, you can type any value you like, and AutoCAD gives you a precise graphic image. However, you cannot always show the exact point you want by pointing. Often it is more efficient to type a few values than to turn Snap off or change its setting for a small number of objects.

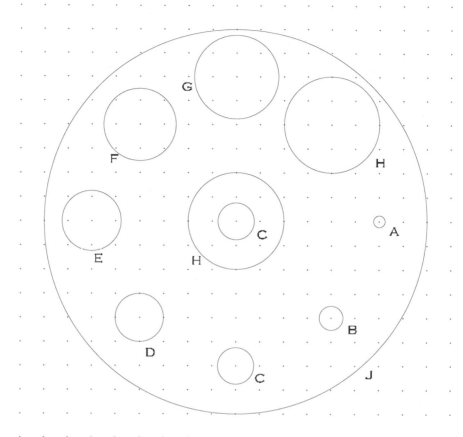

LETTER	A	B	C	D	E	F	G	H	J
RADIUS	.12	.25	.38	.50	.62	.75	.88	1.00	4.00

APERTURE WHEEL

DRAWING 2-1

2.14   Drawing 2-2: Roller

This drawing gives you a chance to combine lines and circles and to use the center point, diameter method. It also gives you some experience with smaller objects, a denser grid, and a tighter snap spacing.

> **Tip:** Even though units are set to show only two decimal places, it is important to set the snap using three places (0.125) so that the grid is on a multiple of the snap (0.25 = 2 × 0.125). AutoCAD shows you rounded coordinate values, like 0.13, but keeps the graphics on target. Try setting snap to either 0.13 or 0.12 instead of 0.125, and you will see the problem for yourself.

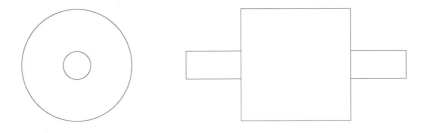

Drawing Suggestions

$$\text{GRID} = 0.25$$
$$\text{SNAP} = 0.125$$

- The two views of the roller appear fairly small on your screen, making the snap setting essential. Watch the coordinate display as you work and get used to the smaller range of motion.
- Choosing an efficient sequence makes this drawing much easier to complete. Because the two views must line up properly, we suggest that you draw the front view first, with circles of diameter 0.25 and 1.00, and then use these circles to position the lines in the right side view.
- The circles in the front view should be centered in the neighborhood of (2.00,6.00). This puts the upper left-hand corner of the 1 × 1 square at around (5.50,6.50).

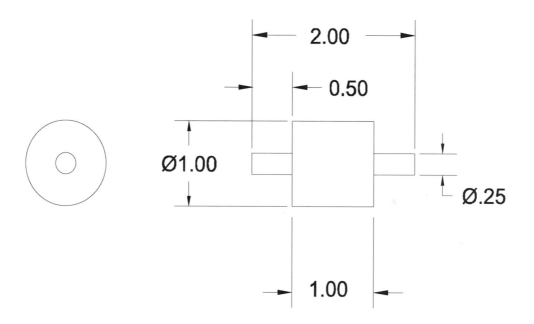

ROLLER

Drawing 2-2

2.15   Drawing 2-3: Fan Bezel

This drawing should be easy for you at this point. Set grid to 0.50 and snap to 0.125 as suggested, and everything falls into place nicely.

Drawing Suggestions

$$GRID = 0.50$$
$$SNAP = 0.125$$

- Notice that the outer figure in Drawing 2-3 is a 6 × 6 square and that you are given diameters for the circles.
- You should start with the lower left-hand corner of the square somewhere near the point (3.00,2.00) if you want to keep the drawing centered on your screen.
- Be careful to center the large inner circle within the square.

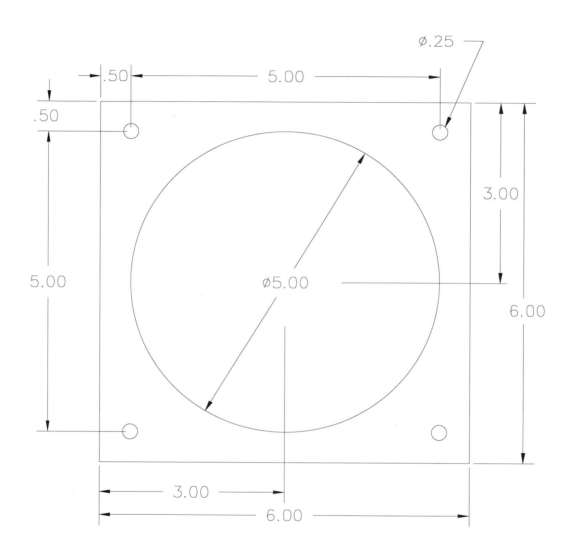

FAN BEZEL

Drawing 2—3

2.16   Drawing 2-4: Switch Plate

This drawing is similar to the last one, but the dimensions are more difficult, and a number of important points do not fall on the grid. The drawing gives you practice using grid and snap points and the coordinate display. Refer to the table that follows Drawing 2-4 for dimensions of the circles, squares, and rectangles inside the 7×10 outer rectangle. The placement of these smaller figures is shown by the dimensions on the drawing itself.

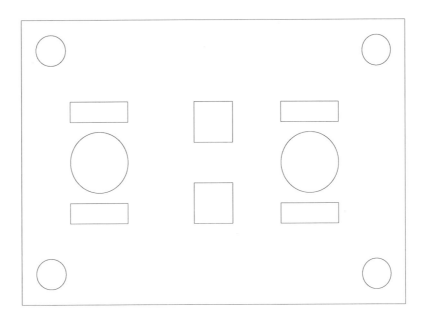

Drawing Suggestions

$$\text{GRID} = 0.50$$
$$\text{SNAP} = 0.25$$

- Turn on Ortho or Polar snap to do this drawing.
- A starting point in the neighborhood of (1,1) keeps you well positioned on the screen.

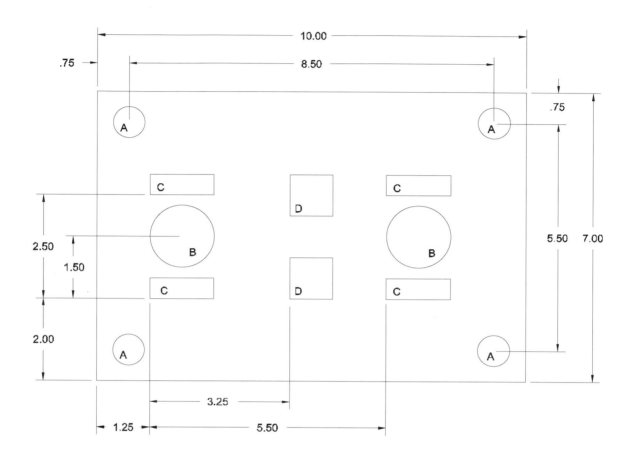

HOLE	SIZE
A	Ø.75
B	Ø1.50
C	.50 H x 1.50 W
D	1.00 SQ

SWITCH PLATE
Drawing 2-4

2.17   Drawing 2-5: Gasket

Drawing 2-5 gives you practice creating simple lines and circles while utilizing Grid and Snap. The circles in this drawing have a 0.50 diameter. With snap set at 0.25, the radii are on a snap point. These circles can be drawn easily by dragging the circle out to show the radius or by typing in the diameter.

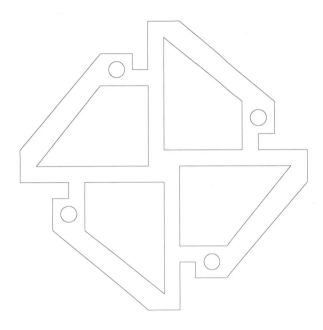

Drawing Suggestions

GRID = 0.50
SNAP = 0.25

- A good sequence for completing this drawing would be to draw the outer lines first, followed by the inner lines and then the circles.
- Notice that all endpoints of all lines fall on grid points; therefore, they are on a snap point.

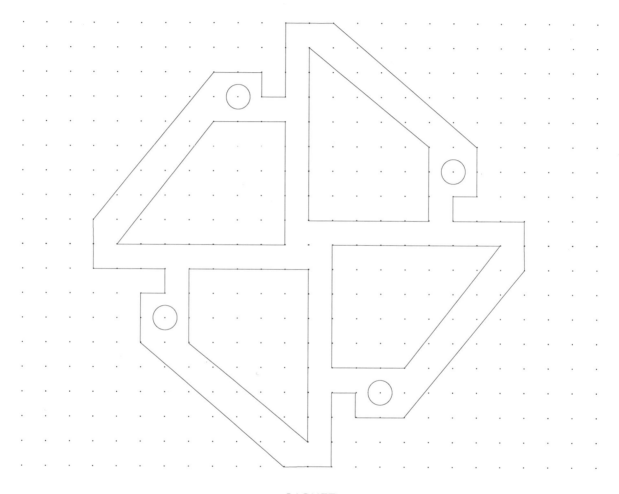

GASKET
Drawing 2—5

3

Layers, Colors, and Linetypes

COMMANDS

CHAMFER	LAYER	PAN	REGEN
FILLET	LTSCALE	PLOT	ZOOM

OVERVIEW

CAD is much more than a computerized way to do drafting. CAD programs have many powerful features that have no correlation in manual drawing. Layering is a good example. Layers exist in the same space and the same drawing, but can be set up and controlled individually, allowing for greater control, precision, and flexibility. In the first two chapters, all of your drawings were completed on a single layer called 0. In this chapter, you create and use three new layers, each with its own associated color and linetype.

The ZOOM command is another bit of CAD magic, allowing your drawings to accurately represent real-world detail at the largest and smallest scales within the same drawing. In this chapter, you also learn to FILLET and CHAMFER the corners of previously drawn objects and to move between adjacent portions of a drawing with the PAN command. You gain further control of the PLOT command by using partial and full previews. All of these new techniques add considerably to the professionalism of your developing CAD technique.

TASKS

3.1 Creating New Layers

GENERAL PROCEDURE

1. Select the Layer Properties Manager tool from the Object Properties toolbar or Layer from the Format pull-down menu.
2. Click the New layer icon.
3. Type in a layer name.
4. Repeat for other new layers.
5. Click OK to close the dialog box.

Layers allow you to treat specialized groups of entities in your drawing separately from other groups. For example, all of the dimensions in this book were drawn on a special dimension layer so that we could turn them on and off at will. We turned off the dimension layer to prepare the reference drawings for Chapters 1 through 7, which are shown without dimensions. When a layer is turned off, all the objects on that layer become invisible, although they are still part of the drawing database and can be recalled at any time. In this way, layers can be viewed, edited, manipulated, and plotted independently.

It is common practice to put dimensions on a separate layer, but there are many other uses of layers as well. Fundamentally, layers are used to separate colors and linetypes, and these, in turn, take on special significance, depending on the drawing application. It is standard drafting practice, for example, to use small, evenly spaced dashes to represent objects or edges that would, in reality, be hidden from view. On a CAD system, these hidden lines can also be given their own color to make it easy for the designer to remember what layer he or she is working on.

In this book, we use a simple layering system, most of which is presented in this chapter. You should remember that there are countless possibilities. AutoCAD allows a full range of colors and as many layers as you like.

You should also be aware that linetypes and colors are not restricted to being associated with layers. It is possible to mix linetypes and colors on a single layer. Although this might be useful for certain applications, we do not recommend it at this point.

⊕ Open a new drawing by typing new or selecting New from the File menu.

⊕ Check to see that acad is in the File name box and press Enter.

⊕ Press F7 to turn on the grid.

⊕ Type z to enter the ZOOM command and then a to zoom all.

The Layer Properties Manager Dialog Box

The creation and specification of layers and layer properties in AutoCAD is handled through the Layer Properties Manager dialog box. This dialog box consists of

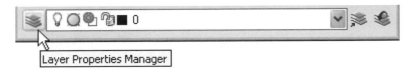

Figure 3-1

a table of layers. Clicking the appropriate row and column changes a setting or takes you to another dialog box where a setting can be changed.

⊕   Select the Layer Properties Manager tool from the Object Properties toolbar, as shown in Figure 3-1, or select Layer from the Format pull-down menu.

Either method opens the Layer Properties Manager dialog box illustrated in Figure 3-2. The large open space to the right shows the names and properties of all layers defined in the current drawing. Layering systems can become very complex, and for this reason there is a system to limit or filter the layer names shown on the layer list. This is controlled by the icons at the top left. With no filters specified, the layer list shows all used layers. Currently, 0 is the only defined layer. The icons on the line after the layer name show the current state of various properties of that layer. We get to these shortly.

Now we will create three new layers. AutoCAD makes this easy.

⊕   Click the New layer icon, just above the top left of the layer list.

A newly defined layer, Layer1, is created immediately and added to the Layer name window. The new layer is given the characteristics of layer 0. We alter these in Task 3.2. First, however, we give this layer a new name and then define three more layers.

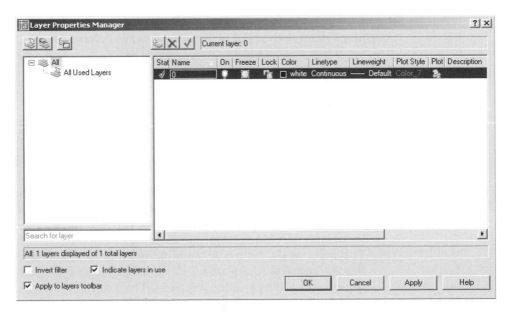

Figure 3-2

Layer names can be long or short. We have chosen single-digit numbers as layer names because they are easy to type and we can match them to AutoCAD's index color numbering sequence.

⊕ Type 1 for the layer name.

Layer1 changes to simply 1. It is not necessary to press Enter after typing the name.

⊕ Click the New layer icon again.

A second new layer is added to the list. It again has the default name Layer1. Change it to 2.

⊕ Type 2 for the second layer name.

⊕ Click the New layer icon again.

⊕ Type 3 for the third layer name and press Enter to complete the process.

At this point, your layer name list should show Layers 0, 1, 2, and 3, all with identical properties.

3.2 Assigning Colors to Layers

GENERAL PROCEDURE

1. Select the Layer Properties Manager tool from the Object Properties toolbar, or select Layer from the Format menu.
2. Click the color icon on the row for the layer you want to change.
3. In the Color dialog box, select a color from the index color chart or type a color name or number in the edit box.
4. Click OK.

We now have four layers, but they are all pretty much the same. Obviously, we have more changes to make before our new layers have useful identities.

Layer 0 has some special features, which are discussed in Chapter 10. Because of these, it is common practice to leave it defined the way it is. We begin our changes on Layer 1.

⊕ If for any reason you have closed the Layer Properties Manager dialog box, reopen it by selecting the Layer Properties Manager tool from the Object Properties toolbar or Layer from the Format menu.

⊕ Move the cursor arrow to the Layer 1 line and click the white square under Color.

Clicking the white square in the color column of Layer 1 selects Layer 1 and opens the Select Color dialog box illustrated in Figure 3-3. The three tabs in this dialog box show three ways in which colors can be defined in AutoCAD. By default, the Index Color tab is probably selected, as shown in Figure 3-3. The index color system is a simple numbered selection of 255 colors and shades. The True Color and Color Books systems are standard color systems commonly used by graphic designers. The True Color tab can be set to access either the Hue, Saturation, and Luminance (HSL) color model or the Red, Green, and Blue (RGB) model. Both of these systems work by mixing colors

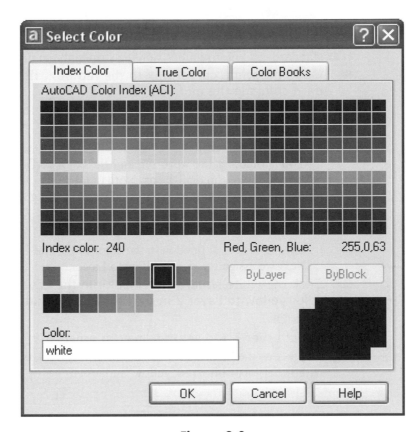

Figure 3-3

and color characteristics. The Color Books tab gives access to Pantone and RAL color books. These standard color sets are also numbered, but they provide many more choices than the AutoCAD index color set. In this book we confine ourselves to the Index Color tab.

⊕ **If necessary, click the Index Color tab.**

The Index Color tab shows the complete selection of 255 colors. At the top is a full palette of shades 10 through 249. Below that are the nine standard colors, numbered 1 through 9, followed by gray shades, numbered 250 through 255.

⊕ **Move your cursor freely inside the dialog box.**

When your cursor is on a color, it is highlighted with a white box.

⊕ **Let your cursor rest on any color.**

Notice that the number of the color is registered under the palette next to the words Index color. This is the AutoCAD index color number for the color currently highlighted. Notice also the three numbers on the right following the words Red, Green, Blue. This is the RGB color model equivalent. RGB colors are combinations of red, green, and blue, with 255 shades of each.

⊕ **Left-click to select any color in the palette.**

When a color is selected, it is outlined with a black box and a preview "patch" is displayed on the bottom right of the dialog box against a patch of the current color for comparison. The color is not actually selected in the drawing until you click OK to exit the dialog box. For our purposes, we want to select standard red, color number 1 on the strip in the middle of the dialog box.

⊕   Move the white cursor box to the red box, the first of the nine standard colors in the middle of the box.

Notice that this is index color number 1 and its RGB equivalent is 255, 0, 0, pure red with no green or blue added.

⊕   Select the red box.

You should see the word red and the color red shown in the preview area at the bottom of the dialog box. Note that you can also select colors by typing names or numbers directly in this edit box. Typing red or the number 1 is the same as selecting the red color box from the chart.

⊕   Click OK.

Layer 1 is now defined with the color red in the Layer Name list box.
Next we assign the color yellow to Layer 2.

⊕   Click the white square under Color in the Layer 2 line and assign the color yellow to Layer 2 in the Select Color dialog box.

⊕   Click OK.

⊕   Select Layer 3 and set this layer to green.

Look at the layer list. You should now have Layers 0, 1, 2, and 3 defined with the colors white, red, yellow, and green.

3.3   Assigning Linetypes

> **GENERAL PROCEDURE**
>
> 1. Select the Layer Properties Manager tool from the Object Properties toolbar or Layer from the Format menu.
> 2. Click in the Linetype column of the layer you want to set.
> 3. In the Select Linetype dialog box, select a linetype. If necessary, load linetypes first.
> 4. Click OK.
> 5. Click OK again to exit the dialog box.

AutoCAD has a standard library of linetypes that can easily be assigned to layers. There are 45 standard types in addition to continuous lines. In addition to continuous lines, we use hidden and center lines. We put hidden lines in yellow on Layer 2 and center lines in green on Layer 3. Layers 1 and 0 retain the continous linetype.

The procedure for assigning linetypes is almost identical to the procedure for assigning colors, except that you have to load linetypes into the drawing before they can be used.

⊕   If for any reason you have closed the Layer Properties Manager, reopen it by selecting the Layer Properties Manager tool from the Object Properties toolbar.

⊕   Click Continuous in the Linetype column of the Layer 2 line.

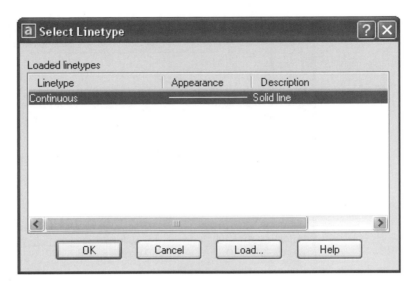

Figure 3-4

Note: Make sure that you actually click the word Continuous. If you click one of the icons in the Layer 2 line, you might turn the layer off or freeze it so that you cannot draw on it. These properties are discussed at the end of Task 3.5.

This selects Layer 2 and opens the Select Linetype dialog box illustrated in Figure 3-4. The box containing a list of loaded linetypes currently only shows the continuous linetype. We can fix this by clicking Load at the bottom of the dialog box.

⊕ Click Load.

This opens a second dialog box, the Load or Reload Linetypes dialog box illustrated in Figure 3-5. Here you can pick from the list of linetypes available from the standard acad file or from other files containing linetypes, if there are any on your system. You also have the option of loading all linetypes from any given file at once. The linetypes are then defined in your drawing, and you can assign a new linetype to a layer at any time. This makes things easier. It does, however, use up more memory.

For our purposes, we load only the hidden and center linetypes we are going to be using.

⊕ Scroll down until you see the Center linetype.

⊕ Click Center in the Linetype column at the left.

⊕ Scroll down again until you see the Hidden linetype on the list.

⊕ Hold down the Ctrl key and click Hidden in the Linetype column.

The Ctrl key lets you highlight two separate items in a list.

⊕ Click OK to complete the loading process.

You should now see the center and hidden linetypes added to the list of loaded linetypes. Now that these are loaded, we can assign them to layers.

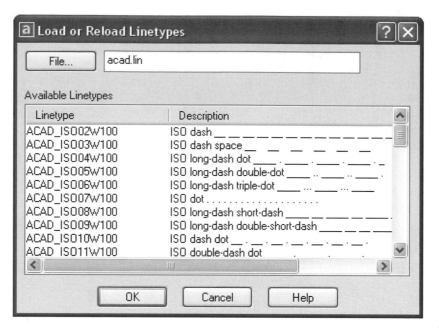

Figure 3-5

⊕ Click Hidden in the Linetype column.

⊕ Click OK to close the dialog box.

> You should see that Layer 2 now has the hidden linetype.
> Next assign the center linetype to Layer 3.

⊕ Click Continuous in the Linetype column of the Layer 3 line.

⊕ In the Select Linetype dialog box, select the Center linetype.

⊕ Click OK.

> Examine your layer list again. It should show Layer 2 with the hidden line-type and Layer 3 with the center linetype. Before exiting the Layer Properties Manager, we create one additional layer to demonstrate AutoCAD's lineweight feature.

3.4 Assigning Lineweight

GENERAL PROCEDURE

1. Select the Layer Properties Manager tool from the Object Properties toolbar or Layer from the Format menu.
2. Click the Lineweight column of the layer you want to change.
3. In the Lineweight dialog box, select a lineweight.
4. Click OK.
5. Click OK again to exit the dialog box.

Lineweight refers to the thickness of lines as they are displayed and plotted. All lines are initially given a default lineweight. Lineweights are assigned by layer and are displayed only if the LWT button on the status bar is in the on position. In this task, we create a new layer and give it a much larger lineweight for demonstration purposes.

⊕ If for any reason you have left the Layer Properties Manager dialog box, reopen it by selecting the Layer Properties Manager tool from the Object Properties toolbar.

First, we create a new layer because we do not want to change our previous layers from the default lineweight setting.

⊕ If Layer 3 is not highlighted, highlight it by pointing to the name 3 and pressing the pick button.

⊕ Click the New layer icon in the dialog box.

Notice that the new layer takes the characteristics of the previously highlighted layer. Our last action was to give Layer 3 the center linetype, so your new layer should have green center lines and the other characteristics of Layer 3.

⊕ Type 4 for the new layer name and press Enter.

⊕ Click Default in the Lineweight column of Layer 4.

This opens the Lineweight dialog box, shown in Figure 3-6. We use a rather large lineweight to create a clear demonstration.

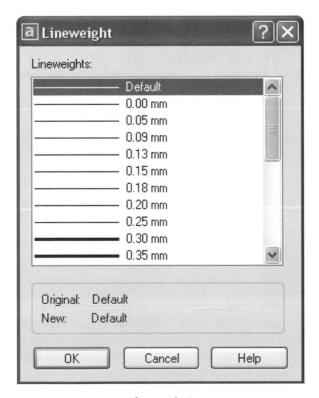

Figure 3-6

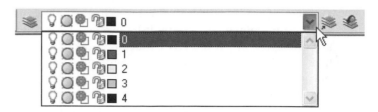

Figure 3-7

⊕ Scroll down until you see 0.50 mm on the list.

⊕ Highlight the 0.50 mm line.

Below the list you can see that the original specification for this layer was the default and is now being changed to 0.50 mm.

⊕ Click OK to return to the Layer Properties Manager.

It is now time to leave the dialog box and see what we can do with our new layers.

⊕ Click OK to exit the Layer Properties Manager.

Note: Do not exit the dialog box by clicking the close button. Exit only by clicking OK. If you use the close button, or if you cancel the dialog box, all of your changes, new layers, and so on, will be lost.

Before proceeding, you should be back in your Drawing Window with your new layers defined in your drawing. To verify that you have successfully defined new layers, open the Layer drop-down list on the Object Properties toolbar, as shown in Figure 3-7.

⊕ To open the Layer list, click anywhere in the list box.

Your list should resemble the one in Figure 3-7.

3.5 Changing the Current Layer

GENERAL PROCEDURE

1. Open the Layer list from the Object Properties toolbar.
2. Select a layer name.

or

1. Select the Make Object's Layer Current tool from the Object Properties toolbar.
2. Select an object on the layer you wish to make current.

In this task, we make each of your new layers current and draw objects on them. You can immediately see how much power you have added to your drawing by the addition of new layers, colors, linetypes, and lineweight.

To draw new entities on a layer, you must make it the currently active layer. Previously drawn objects on other layers that are turned on are also visible and plotted, but new objects go on the current layer.

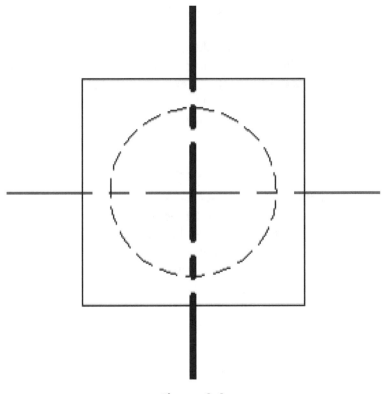

Figure 3-8

There are two quick methods to establish the current layer. The first works the same as any drop-down list. The second makes use of previously drawn objects. We use the first method to draw the objects in Figure 3-8.

⊕ Click anywhere in the Layer list box on the Object Properties toolbar.

This opens the list, as shown previously in Figure 3-7.

⊕ Select Layer 1 by clicking to the right of the layer name 1 in the drop-down list.

Layer 1 replaces Layer 0 as the current layer on the Object Properties toolbar.

⊕ Using the RECTANGLE command, draw the 6 × 6 square shown in Figure 3-8, with the first corner at (3,2) and other corner at (9,8).

Your rectangle should show the red, continuous lines of Layer 1.

⊕ Click anywhere in the Layer Control box on the Object Properties toolbar.

⊕ Click to the right of the layer name 2.

Layer 2 becomes the current layer.

⊕ With Layer 2 current, draw the hidden circle in Figure 3-8, centered at (6,5) with radius 2.

Your circle should appear in yellow hidden lines.

- Make Layer 3 current and draw a horizontal center line from (2,5) to (10,5).

   This line should appear as a green center line.
- Click the LWT button on the status line so that it is in the on position.
- Make Layer 4 current and draw a vertical line from (6,1) to (6,9).

   This line should appear as a green center line with noticeable thickness.
- Click the LWT button again to put it in the off position.

   With LWT off, the lineweight of the horizontal center line is not displayed.

Making an Object's Layer Current

Finally, we use another method to make Layer 1 current before moving on.

- Select the Make Object's Layer Current tool from the Object Properties toolbar, as shown in Figure 3-9.

   This tool allows us to make a layer current by selecting any object on that layer. AutoCAD shows the prompt

   ```
   Select object whose layer will become current:
   ```
- Select the red rectangle drawn on Layer 1.

   Layer 1 replaces Layer 4 in the Current Layer box.

Other Properties of Layers

There are several other properties that can be set in the Layer Properties Manager, or, more conveniently, in the Layer list box. These settings probably will not be useful to you until later on, but we introduce them briefly here for your information.

On and Off

Layers can be turned on or off with the light bulb icon. On and off status affects only the visibility of objects on a layer. Objects on layers that are off are not visible or plotted, but are still in the drawing and are considered when the drawing is regenerated. Regeneration is the process by which AutoCAD translates the precise numerical data that makes up a drawing file database into the less precise values of screen graphics. Regeneration can be a slow process in large, complex drawings. As a result, it might be useful not to regenerate all layers all the time.

Freeze and Thaw

Frozen layers are not only invisible, but are ignored in regeneration. Thaw reverses this setting. Thawed layers are always regenerated. Freeze and thaw properties are set using the sun icon, to the right of the light bulb icon. Layers are thawed by

Figure 3-9

default as indicated by the yellow sun. When a layer is frozen, the sun icon is replaced by a snowflake.

Freeze or Thaw in Current Viewport

The sun icon freezes or thaws layers in all viewports. Next to the sun icon is an icon with a sun and a square. The square represents a drawing viewport. Viewports are introduced in Chapter 6. This setting is off by default. It allows you to freeze a layer in the current viewport while leaving it thawed in other viewports.

Lock and Unlock

Next is the lock icon. The Lock and Unlock setting does not affect visibility, but does affect availability of objects for editing. Objects on locked layers are visible, but they cannot be edited. Unlocking reverses this setting.

Deleting Layers

You can delete layers using the Delete button in the Layer Properties Manager dialog box. However, you cannot delete layers that have objects drawn on them. Also, you cannot delete the current layer or Layer 0.

3.6 Editing Corners Using FILLET

GENERAL PROCEDURE

1. Type f, select the Fillet tool from the Modify toolbar, or select Fillet from the Modify menu.
2. Type r for radius.
3. Enter a radius value.
4. Select two lines that meet at a corner.

Now that you have a variety of linetypes to use, you can begin to make more realistic mechanical drawings. All you need is the ability to create filleted (rounded) and chamfered (cut) corners. The two work similarly, and AutoCAD makes them easy. Fillets can also be created between circles and arcs, but the most common usage is the type of situation demonstrated here.

We only work with the square in this exercise, but instead of erasing the other objects, turn them off, as follows:

⊕ If you have not already done so, set Layer 1 as the current layer.

⊕ Open the Layer list on the Object Properties toolbar, and click the light bulb icons on Layers 2, 3, and 4 so that they turn from yellow to gray, indicating that they are off.

⊕ Click anywhere outside the list box to close it.

When you are finished, you should see only the square. The other objects are still in your drawing and can be recalled anytime simply by turning their layers on again.

Figure 3-10

We use the square to practice fillets and chamfers.

⊕ Type f or select the Fillet tool from the Modify toolbar, as shown in Figure 3-10.

Fillet is also on the Modify menu, but the alias or the toolbar selection is quicker. A prompt with options appears as follows:

```
              Current settings: Mode=TRIM, Radius=0.50
        Select first object or [Polyline/Radius/Trim/Multiple]:
```

Note: As mentioned previously, we show the Modify toolbar in horizontal, floating position. Yours is probably in vertical, docked position as usual.

Polylines are discussed in Chapter 9, but we have something to show you about this option in a moment. Trim mode is discussed at the end of this exercise.

The first thing you must do is determine the degree of rounding you want. Because fillets are really arcs, they can be defined by a radius.

⊕ Type r.

AutoCAD then prompts

```
                    Specify fillet radius <0.00>:
```

The default is 0.00.

⊕ Type .75.

You have set 0.75 as the current fillet radius for this drawing. You can change it at any time. Changing does not affect previously drawn fillets.

The prompt is the same as before:

```
    Select first object or [Undo/Polyline/Radius/Trim/Multiple]:
```

Notice that you have the pick box on the screen now without the crosshairs.

⊕ Use the pick box to select two lines that meet at any corner of your square.

Behold! A fillet! You did not even have to press Enter. AutoCAD knows that you are done after selecting two lines.

The Multiple Option

We use the Multiple option to fillet the remaining three corners of the square. Multiple allows you to create multiple fillets without leaving the FILLET command.

⊕ Press Enter or the spacebar to repeat FILLET.

⊕ Type m for the Multiple option.

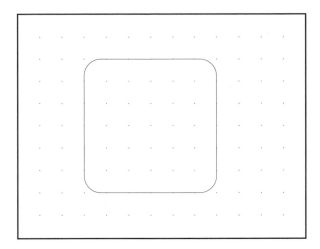

Figure 3-11

⊕   Select two lines to fillet another corner.

   You do not have to enter a radius value again because the last value is retained.

⊕   Proceed to fillet all four corners.

   When you are done, your screen should resemble Figure 3-11.

⊕   Press Enter to exit FILLET.

Trim Mode

Trim mode allows you to determine whether you want AutoCAD to remove square corners as it creates fillets and chamfers. Examples of fillets created with Trim mode on and off are shown in Figure 3-12. In most cases, you want to leave Trim mode on. To turn it off, enter FILLET and type t for Trim and then n for No Trim.

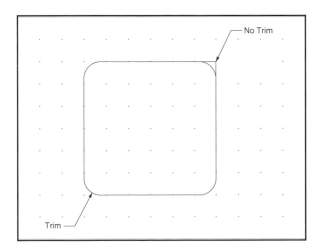

Figure 3-12

3.7 Editing Corners Using CHAMFER

GENERAL PROCEDURE

1. Select the Chamfer tool from the Modify toolbar, or select Chamfer from the Modify menu.
2. Type d for the Distance option.
3. Enter a chamfer distance.
4. Enter a second chamfer distance or press Enter for an even chamfer.
5. Select two lines that meet at a corner.

The CHAMFER command sequence is almost identical to the FILLET command, with the exception that chamfers can be uneven. That is, you can cut back farther on one side of a corner than on the other. To do this, you must give AutoCAD two distances instead of one.

In this exercise, we draw even chamfers on the four corners of the square. Using the Polyline option, we chamfer all four corners at once. We also take the opportunity to use a new shortcut menu.

⊕ Select the Chamfer tool, as shown in Figure 3-13.

AutoCAD prompts:

```
(TRIM mode) Current chamfer Dist1=0.00, Dist2=0.00
                Select first line or
[Undo/Polyline/Distance/Angle/Trim/mEthod/Multiple]:
```

You can type a letter to select an option, but there is also a shortcut menu.

⊕ Right-click anywhere in the drawing area.

This opens a shortcut menu with the Polyline, Distance, Angle, Trim, mEthod, and Multiple options in the middle panel.

⊕ Select Distance.

The next prompt is

```
Specify first chamfer distance <0.00>:
```

⊕ Type 1.

AutoCAD asks for another distance:

```
Specify second chamfer distance <1.00>:
```

The first distance has become the default and most of the time it is used. If you want an asymmetric chamfer, enter a different value for the second distance.

Figure 3-13

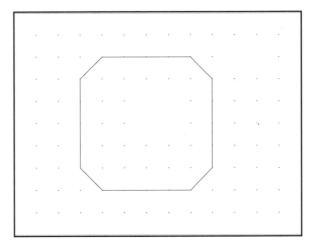

Figure 3-14

⊕   Press Enter to accept the default, making the chamfer distances symmetrical.

At this point, you could proceed to chamfer each corner of the square independently. However, if you have drawn the square using the RECTANGLE command, you have a quicker option. The RECTANGLE command draws a polyline rectangle. Polylines are discussed in Chapter 9, but for now it is useful to know that a polyline is a single entity comprised of several lines and arcs. If you have drawn a closed polyline and specify the Polyline option in the CHAMFER or FILLET commands, AutoCAD edits all corners of the object.

⊕   Type p or open the shortcut menu and select Polyline.

AutoCAD then prompts

Select 2D polyline:

⊕   Answer the prompt by pointing to any part of the square.

You should have four neat chamfers on your square, replacing the fillets from the previous task. Your screen should resemble Figure 3-14.

3.8   Using the ZOOM Command

GENERAL PROCEDURE

1. Type z or select the Zoom tool from the Standard toolbar.
2. Enter a ZOOM method or magnification value.
3. Enter values or points, if necessary, depending on choice of method.

The capacity to zoom in and out of a drawing is one of the more impressive benefits of working on a CAD system. When drawings get complex, it often becomes

Figure 3-15

necessary to work in detail on small portions of the drawing space. Especially with a small monitor, the only way to do this is by making the detailed area larger on the screen. This is done easily with the ZOOM command.

⊕   You should have a square with chamfered corners on your screen from the previous task.

We demonstrate zooming using the Window, All, Previous, and Realtime options.

⊕   Type z or select the Zoom Window tool from the Standard toolbar, as illustrated in Figure 3-15.

The prompt that follows includes the following options:

```
Specify corner of window, enter a scale factor (nX or nXP),
    or[All/Center/Dynamic/Extents/Previous/Scale/Window]
                        <realtime>:
```

If you have used the Zoom Window tool, the Window option is entered automatically. As in ERASE and other edit commands, you can force a window selection by typing w or selecting Window from a shortcut menu. However, this is unnecessary. The windowing action is automatically initiated if you pick a point on the screen after entering ZOOM.

⊕   Pick a point just below and to the left of the lower left-hand corner of your square (point 1 in Figure 3-16).

AutoCAD asks for another point:

```
                Specify opposite corner:
```

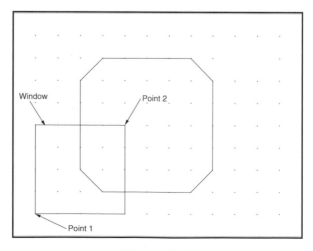

Figure 3-16

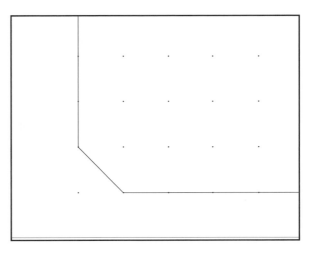

Figure 3-17

You are being asked to define a window, just as in the ERASE command. This window is the basis for what AutoCAD displays next. Because you are not going to make a window that exactly conforms to the screen size and shape, AutoCAD interprets the window this way: Everything in the window will be shown, plus whatever additional area is needed to fill the screen. The center of the window becomes the center of the new display.

⊕ **Pick a second point near the center of your square (point 2 in the figure).**

AutoCAD will zoom in dynamically until the lower left corner of the square is enlarged on your screen, as shown in Figure 3-17.

⊕ **Using the same method, try zooming up further on the chamfered corner of the square. If Snap is on, you might need to turn it off (press F9).**

Remember that you can repeat the ZOOM command by pressing Enter or the spacebar.

At this point, most people cannot resist seeing how much magnification they can get by zooming repeatedly on the same corner or angle of a chamfer. Go ahead. After a couple of zooms, the angle does not appear to change, though the placement shifts as the center of your window changes. An angle is the same angle no matter how close you get to it, but what happens to the spacing of the grid and snap as you move in?

When you are through experimenting with window zooming, try zooming to the previous display.

Zoom Previous

⊕ **Press Enter to repeat the ZOOM command, or select the Zoom Previous tool, as shown in Figure 3-18.**

⊕ **If you repeated the command by pressing Enter, type p.**

You should now see your previous display.

AutoCAD keeps track of up to 10 previous displays.

Figure 3-18

⊕ ZOOM Previous as many times as you can until you get a message that says

No previous view saved.

3.9 Zooming and Panning with the Scroll Wheel

GENERAL PROCEDURE
1. Click the scroll wheel forward to zoom in and back to zoom out.
2. With the scroll wheel pressed down, drag the image on the screen to pan.

AutoCAD 2006 has new options for zooming and panning using the scroll wheel on your mouse. Zooming in this manner is very convenient, but less precise than using the ZOOM command. You occasionally get unexpected results. On the other hand, panning with the scroll wheel works just as well as using the PAN command and involves fewer steps.

Zooming with the Scroll Wheel

In AutoCAD 2006 each click of the scroll wheel will cause a 10% magnification or reduction of the image in your drawing area. Clicking forward (away from your hand) will cause you to zoom in. Clicking back (toward your hand) will cause zooming out. Notice that clicking forward after clicking back does *not* exactly reverse the zoom. The 10% factor is always applied to the current view, so that clicking back after clicking forward will leave you with a slightly reduced image. (For example, your first zoom in will take you to 90% of the original view. The next zoom out will take you out by 10% of 90% and you will now be at 99% of the original view.) Also, when you use the scroll wheel to zoom, AutoCAD uses the position of the crosshairs to determine the line of the zoom, so you can get very different zooms from different crosshair positions. This can get a little unpredictable. You will have better control if snap is on and if you don't move the cursor too much between zooms. Try it.

⊕ Check to see that the Snap button is in the down position.

⊕ Place the cursor near the center of the chamfered square and click the scroll wheel one click forward.

Your screen image will be enlarged by 10%.

⊕ Click another click forward.

Your screen is further enlarged.

⊕ Click one click back.

⊕   Click another click back.

Notice that your current image is slightly smaller than your original view.

Panning with the Scroll Wheel

Panning with the scroll wheel is even easier than zooming and does not create any of the mathematical or other unexpected results encountered with zooming. To pan, press the scroll wheel down, just as you would press down on either of the mouse buttons. When the wheel is down you can drag your screen image around. It will continue to follow your cursor until you release the wheel.

⊕   Position the crosshairs near the middle of the screen and press the scroll wheel down.

The grid will disappear and the realtime scroll icon, which looks like a hand, will appear.

⊕   Hold down the scroll wheel and move the cursor diagonally up and to the right, as illustrated in Figure 3-19.

⊕   Release the pick button to complete the PAN procedure.

Try it again.

⊕   Press the scroll wheel and drag the image back near its original position.

In a moment we will explore AutoCAD's realtime ZOOM and PAN features. You will find that panning with the scroll wheel is very similar to realtime PAN. But first, let's go back to where we started.

ZOOM All

This is the option we have been using to enlarge our grids since Chapter 1. ZOOM All zooms out to display the whole drawing. It is useful when you have been working in a number of small areas of a drawing and are ready to view the whole scene. It also quickly undoes the effects of zooming repeatedly with the scroll wheel. You do not want to have to wade through previous displays to find your way back. ZOOM All takes you there in one jump.

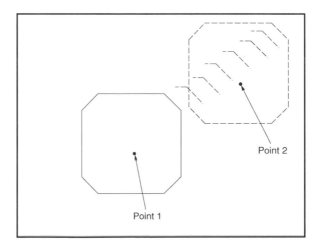

Figure 3-19

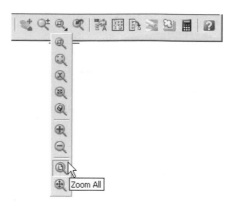

Figure 3-20

To see it work, you should be zoomed in on a portion of your display before executing ZOOM All.

⊕   Use the scroll wheel or the ZOOM command to zoom in on a window within your drawing.

⊕   Press Enter or type z to repeat ZOOM again.

⊕   Type a for the All option.

> **Note:** The Zoom Window tool also has a flyout that includes tools for all the ZOOM command options, including ZOOM All, as shown in Figure 3-20. Flyouts are toolbar features that make additional tools available. Any tool button that has a small black triangle in one corner opens a flyout. To open a flyout, hold down the pick button while the arrow is on the tool. Then run down or across the flyout to the tool you want. When the tool button is down, release the pick button.

3.10 Using Realtime ZOOM and PAN

GENERAL PROCEDURE
1. Pick the Pan Realtime or Zoom Realtime tool from the Standard toolbar.
2. Use the cursor to move objects (PAN) or increase or decrease magnification (ZOOM).
3. Press Enter or the spacebar to exit the command.

Like the scroll wheel, realtime ZOOM and PAN allow you to see changes in display and magnification dynamically as you make adjustments. As soon as you start to use ZOOM, you are likely to need PAN as well. Whereas ZOOM allows you to magnify portions of your drawing, PAN allows you to shift the area you are viewing in any direction.

You also have the option of panning with the scroll bars at the edges of the drawing area, but the PAN command provides more flexibility. In particular, it allows diagonal motion. We use the Pan Realtime tool first and then the Zoom Realtime tool.

Figure 3-21

✦ Type p or select the Pan Realtime tool from the Standard toolbar, as illustrated in Figure 3-21.

With either method, you see the PAN command cursor in the form of a hand icon, with which you can move objects on the screen. When the mouse button is not depressed, the hand moves freely across the screen. When you move the mouse with the pick button held down, the complete drawing display moves along with the hand. This action is similar to panning with the scroll wheel, but you are dragging with the left button instead of the wheel.

✦ Move the hand near the middle of the screen without holding down the pick button.

✦ Hold down the pick button and move the cursor across the screen.

✦ Release the pick button to complete the PAN procedure.

Experiment with Pan Realtime, moving objects up, down, left, right, and diagonally. Watch the scroll bars respond as you pan across the drawing area.

Realtime Zoom

When you are in either the ZOOM or PAN command, you can access a shortcut menu by right-clicking anywhere on the screen. Try it.

✦ Without leaving PAN, click the right button on your mouse.

This opens the shortcut menu illustrated in Figure 3-22. This menu allows you to switch quickly between realtime PAN and realtime ZOOM.

✦ Select Zoom from the shortcut menu.

The menu closes and the realtime ZOOM cursor appears. As illustrated in Figure 3-23, this is represented by a magnifying glass with a plus (+) sign above and a minus (−) sign below.

Figure 3-22

Figure 3-23

⊕ Without pressing the pick button, move the Zoom cursor near the bottom of the screen.

As with the Pan cursor, you are able to move freely when the pick button is not held down.

⊕ Press the pick button and move the cursor upward.

With the pick button pressed, upward motion increases magnification, enlarging objects on the screen.

⊕ Move up and down to see the effects of the Zoom cursor movement.

⊕ Release the pick button to complete the process.

When you release the button, you do not exit the command. This is important because it might take several trips up or down the screen to indicate the amount of magnification you want. Moving the cursor halfway up the screen produces a 100% magnification.

⊕ Continue to experiment with realtime ZOOM and PAN until you feel comfortable.

⊕ To exit, press Esc, the spacebar, or Enter.

You can also right-click to open the shortcut menu and then select Exit.

Transparent Commands

If you have used the toolbar or the menu to enter the ZOOM and PAN commands, you might have noticed that they place an apostrophe and an underline before the name of the command. If you select the Pan tool, for example, you see the following in the command area:

Command: '_pan

The apostrophe is a command modifier that makes the command transparent. This means that you can enter it in the middle of another command sequence, and when you are done you are still in that sequence. For example, you can pan while drawing a line. This is convenient if you already have selected the first point and then realize that the second point will be off the screen. A sample procedure using transparent PAN would go as follows:

1. Type l or select Line.
2. Pick a first point.
3. Type 'p (notice the apostrophe) or select the Pan tool.
4. Move the display as you wish.
5. Exit PAN.
6. Pick a second point to complete the line.

The underline character (_) you see after the apostrophe and before many commands that AutoCAD sends to the command line is added to commands in menu systems to ensure that AutoCAD interprets the commands in English. Foreign-language versions of AutoCAD have their own command names, but can still use menus developed in English, as long as the underline is there as a flag.

3.11 Using Plot Preview

GENERAL PROCEDURE

1. Type Ctrl+P, select the Plot tool from the Standard toolbar, or select Plot from the File pull-down menu.
2. Change parameters as needed.
3. Select Preview.

Plot preview is an essential tool in carrying out efficient plotting and printing. Plot configuration is complex, and the odds are good that you will waste time and paper by printing drawings directly without first previewing them on the screen. AutoCAD has previewing tools that help you know exactly what to expect when your drawing reaches a sheet of paper.

In this task, we are still significantly limited in our use of plot settings, but learning to use plot preview makes all your future work with plotting and printing more effective. As in Chapter 2, we suggest that you work through this task now with the objects on your screen and refer to it as necessary after you have done any of the drawings at the end of this chapter.

⊕ To begin this task you should have objects or a drawing on your screen ready to preview.

⊕ If you are using the objects drawn in this chapter, turn all layers on using the Layer list on the Standard toolbar.

⊕ Type Ctrl+P, or select the Plot tool from the Standard toolbar or Plot from the File menu.

This opens the Plot dialog box, familiar from the last chapter. The Preview button is at the bottom left of the dialog box. The button will call up a full preview image of your drawing on a sheet of drawing paper. Without going to a full preview, however, you already have a partial preview in the Printer/plotter panel. It shows you an outline of the effective plotting area in relation to the paper size, but does not show an image of the plotted drawing. This preview image will change as you change other plot settings, such as plot area and paper size. Let's look at a full preview.

Note: We address paper sizes in the next chapter. For now, we assume that your plot configuration is correctly matched to the paper in your printer or plotter. If you do not get good results with this task, the problem might be in this area.

⊕ Check to see that a plotter or printer has been selected in the Printer/plotter name box. If not, select one now.

The Preview button will not be accessible if you have not chosen a plotter.

⊕ Click the Preview button.

The dialog box disappears temporarily and you see a preview image similar to the one in Figure 3-24. This image represents your drawing on paper as it is

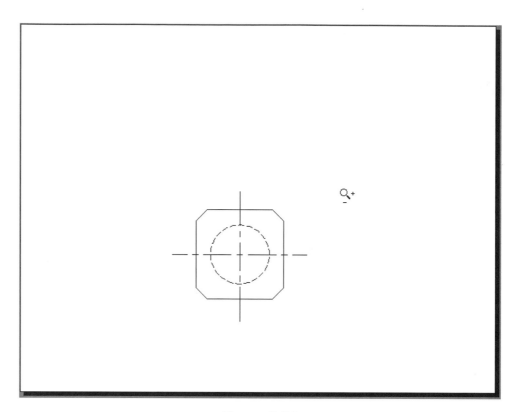

Figure 3-24

now configured for printing. The ZOOM Realtime cursor appears to allow you to zoom in or out on aspects of the preview. By clicking the right button, you can access the Zoom and Pan shortcut menu demonstrated earlier in this chapter. The scroll wheel also works here for panning and zooming. Panning and zooming in the preview has no effect on the plot parameters. You might want to experiment with this feature now.

⊕ When you are done experimenting with Zoom and Pan, press Esc, Enter, or the spacebar to return to the Plot dialog box.

This ends our initial preview of your drawing. In ordinary practice, if everything looked right in the preview, you would move on to plot or print your drawing now by preparing your plotter and then clicking OK. In the chapters that follow, we explore more features of the Plot dialog box and use full and partial plot previews extensively as we change plot parameters. For now, get in the habit of using plot preview. If things are not coming out quite the way you want, you can fix them soon.

⊕ To save your settings, including your plotter selection, click the Apply to Layout button.

⊕ Click OK to plot or print your drawing, or click Cancel to exit without printing.

Figure 3-25

Using the Plot Preview Tool

AutoCAD also has a Plot Preview tool on the Standard toolbar, as illustrated in Figure 3-25. This icon is similar to the Preview tool in other Windows applications and performs the same function as the Preview button in the Plot dialog box. It gives you a quick look at your drawing positioned on a drawing sheet, but you have to go to the Plot dialog box if you want to make changes in plot configuration. Try it.

⊞   Click the Plot Preview tool, as illustrated in Figure 3-25.

You see a full preview of your printed drawing, as shown previously in Figure 3-24.

Note: If you have not saved your settings by clicking Apply to Layout, you will see a message in the command area that says "No plotter has been assigned." In this case AutoCAD will not show a preview.

3.12   Review Material

Questions

1. What function(s) can be performed directly from the Layer list on the Object Properties toolbar? What functions can be performed from the Layer Properties Manager?
2. What linetype is always available when you start a drawing from scratch in AutoCAD? What must you do to access other linetypes?
3. How many colors are available in AutoCAD's Index Color system? What are the other color systems that are available in the Select Color dialog box?
4. How many different layers does AutoCAD allow you to create?
5. Name three ways to change the current layer.
6. You have been working in the Layer Properties Manager, and when you return to your drawing you find that some objects are no longer visible. What happened?
7. What is a transparent command? How do you make a command transparent when entering it at the command line?
8. What happens to the grid when you zoom way out on a drawing?
9. Name one limitation of scroll bars that the PAN command does not have.
10. Describe the use of the scroll wheel for panning and zooming.
11. What is the difference between a partial and a full plot preview?
12. What type of preview is created by the Plot Preview tool?

Drawing Problems

1. Make Layer 3 current and draw a green center line cross with two perpendicular lines, each two units long and intersecting at their midpoints.
2. Make Layer 2 current and draw a hidden line circle centered at the intersection of the cross drawn in Step 1, with a diameter of two units.
3. Make Layer 1 current and draw a red square of two units on a side centered on the center of the circle. Its sides run tangent to the circle.
4. Use a window to zoom in on the objects drawn in Steps 1, 2, and 3.
5. Fillet each corner of the square with a 0.125 radius fillet.

3.13   WWW Exercise 3 (Optional)

This time we demonstrate the use of the Web toolbar. Your task is to open the toolbar, use the Browse the Web tool to go to our website, take the test, and then do the Web project. The project for this chapter takes you deeper into the world of CAD on the Internet. The Web is full of interesting and informative CAD-related websites. There are sites maintained by professional journals, CAD newsgroups, CAD industry sites, sites with drawings that can be viewed or downloaded, sites with tutorials, sites with tips on CAD technique, and sites with information on CAD-related software.

Start by opening the Web toolbar using the Toolbars shortcut menu. This is the quickest way to open a toolbar.

⊕ Move the cursor so that the arrow is pointing anywhere inside of any of the currently visible toolbars.

⊕ With the arrow in this position, right-click.

This opens the Toolbars shortcut menu, shown in Figure 3-26. This long menu includes 29 toolbar selections.

⊕ Locate Web near the bottom of the list.

⊕ Select Web.

This opens the Web toolbar, shown in Figure 3-27.

⊕ Select the Browse the Web tool, as shown.

The Browse the Web tool executes the BROWSER command and automatically enters the default URL.

⊕ If you have not made our website the default, navigate to it from your default site, using the address www.prenhall.com/dixriley.

Away you go!

Figure 3-26

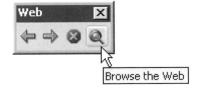

Figure 3-27

3.14   Drawing 3-1: Mounting Plate

This drawing gives you experience using center lines and chamfers. Because there are no hidden lines, you have no need for Layer 2, but we continue to use the same numbering system for consistency. Draw the continuous lines in red on Layer 1 and the center lines in green on Layer 3.

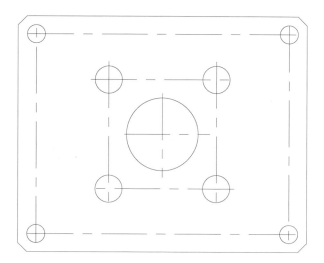

Drawing Suggestions

GRID = 0.5
SNAP = 0.25
LTSCALE = 0.5

LTSCALE

The size of the individual dashes and spaces that make up center lines, hidden lines, and other linetypes is determined by a global setting called LTSCALE. By default, it is set to a factor of 1.00. In smaller drawings, this setting is too large and causes some of the shorter lines to appear continuous regardless of what layer they are on. To remedy this, change LTSCALE as follows:

1. Type lts.
2. Enter a value.

For the drawings in this chapter, use a setting of 0.50. See Figure 3-28 for some examples of the effect of changing LTSCALE.

LTSCALE = 1.00

LTSCALE = .50

LTSCALE = .25

Figure 3-28

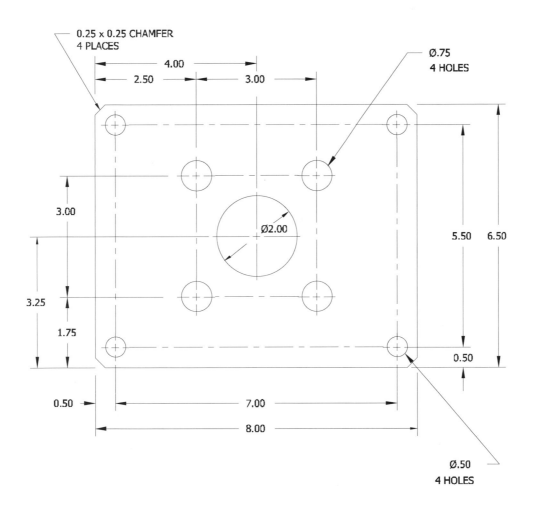

MOUNTING PLATE

Drawing 3-1

3.15   Drawing 3-2: Stepped Shaft

This two-view drawing uses continuous lines, center lines, chamfers, and fillets. You might want to zoom in to enlarge the drawing space you are actually working in, and pan right and left to work on the two views.

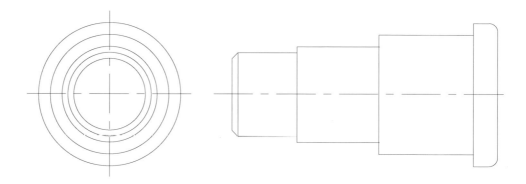

Drawing Suggestions

GRID = 0.25
SNAP = 0.125
LTSCALE = 0.5

- Center the front view in the neighborhood of (2,5). The right side view will have a starting point at about (5,4.12), before the chamfer cuts this corner off.
- Draw the circles in the front view first, using the vertical dimensions from the side view for diameters. Save the inner circle until after you have drawn and chamfered the right side view.
- Draw a series of rectangles for the side view, lining them up with the circles of the front view. Then chamfer two corners of the leftmost rectangle and fillet two corners of the rightmost rectangle.
- Use the chamfer on the side view to line up the radius of the inner circle.
- Remember to set the current layer to 3 before drawing the center lines.

3-D Models of Multiple-View Drawings

If you have any difficulty visualizing objects in the multiple-view drawings in this chapter through Chapter 11, you might wish to refer to the images in Section 14.18 at the end of Chapter 14. These are 3-D solid models derived from 2-D drawings done throughout the book.

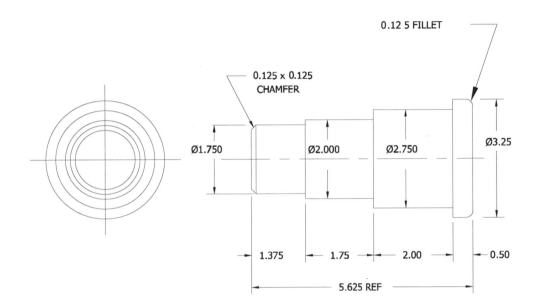

0.12 5 FILLET

0.125 x 0.125
CHAMFER

Ø1.750

Ø2.000

Ø2.750

Ø3.25

1.375

1.75

2.00

0.50

5.625 REF

STEPPED SHAFT

Drawing 3-2

3.16   Drawing 3-3: Base Plate

This drawing uses continuous lines, hidden lines, center lines, and fillets. The side view should be quite easy once the front view is drawn. Remember to change layers when you want to change linetypes.

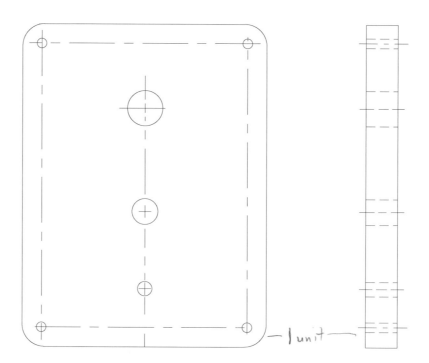

Drawing Suggestions

GRID = 0.25
SNAP = 0.125
LTSCALE = 0.5

- Study the dimensions carefully and remember that every grid increment is 0.25, and snap points not on the grid are exactly halfway between grid points. The four circles at the corners are 0.38 (actually 0.375 rounded off) over and in from the corner points. This is three snap spaces ($0.375 = 3 \times 0.125$).
- Position the three circles along the center line of the rectangle carefully. Notice that dimensions are given from the center of the screw holes at top and bottom.
- Use the circle perimeters to line up the hidden lines on the side view, and the centers to line up the center lines.

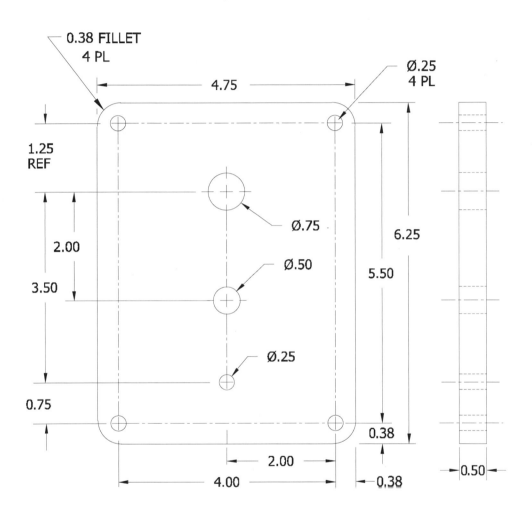

BASE PLATE

Drawing 3-3

3.17 Drawing 3-4: Bushing

This drawing gives you practice with chamfers, layers, and zooming. Notice that because of the smaller dimensions here, we have recommended a smaller LTSCALE setting.

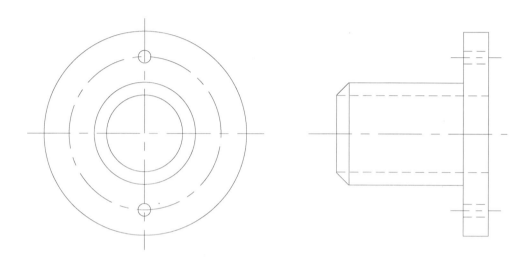

Drawing Suggestions

GRID = 0.25
SNAP = 0.125
LTSCALE = 0.25

- Because this drawing appears quite small on your screen, it would be a good idea to zoom in on the actual drawing space you are using and pan if necessary.
- Notice that the two 0.25-diameter screw holes are 1.50 apart. This puts them squarely on grid points that you should have no trouble finding.

Regen

When you change a linetype scale setting you see a message in the command area that says Regenerating model. Regeneration is the process by which AutoCAD translates drawing data into screen images. Regeneration happens automatically when certain operations are performed. You can also force a regeneration using the REGEN command by selecting Regen from the View menu.

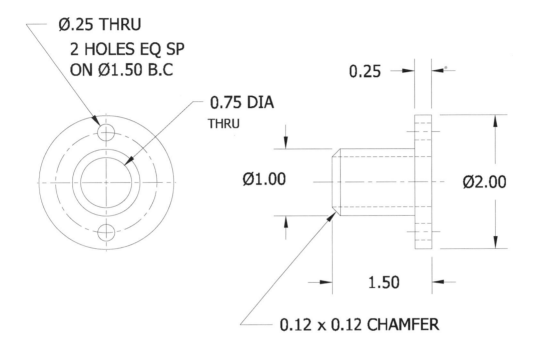

Ø.25 THRU
2 HOLES EQ SP
ON Ø1.50 B.C

0.75 DIA
THRU

0.25

Ø1.00

Ø2.00

1.50

0.12 x 0.12 CHAMFER

BUSHING
Drawing 3-4

3.18   Drawing 3-5: Half Block

This cinder block is the first project using architectural units in this book. Set units, grid, and snap as indicated, and everything falls into place nicely.

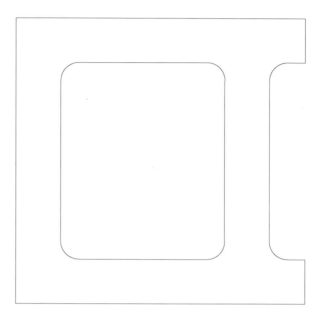

Drawing Suggestions

$$\text{UNITS} = \text{Architectural precision} = 0' - 0\tfrac{1}{4}''$$
$$\text{GRID} = \tfrac{1}{4}''$$
$$\text{SNAP} = \tfrac{1}{4}''$$

- Start with the lower left corner of the block at the point $(0' - 1'', 0' - 1'')$ to keep the drawing well placed on the display.
- Set the FILLET radius to $\tfrac{1}{2}''$ or 0.5. Notice that you can use decimal versions of fractions. The advantage is that they are easier to type.

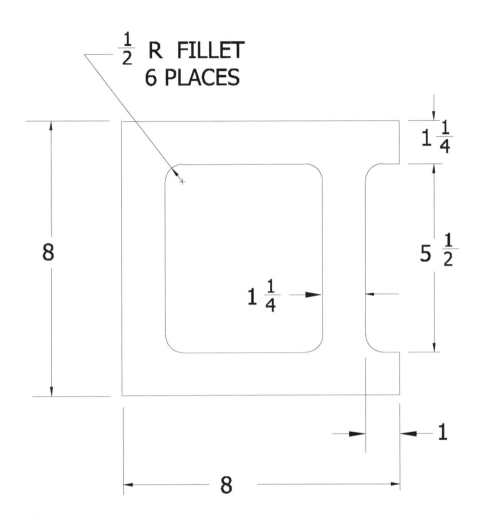

$\frac{1}{2}$ R FILLET
6 PLACES

8

$1\frac{1}{4}$

$5\frac{1}{2}$

$1\frac{1}{4}$

1

8

HALF BLOCK

Drawing 3-5

3.19   Drawing 3-6: Packing Flange

This drawing uses continuous lines, hidden lines, center lines, and fillets. The side view should be quite easy once the top view is drawn. Remember to change layers when you want to change linetypes.

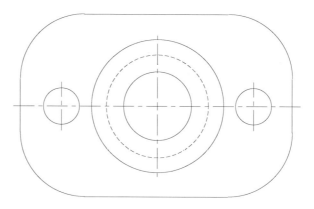

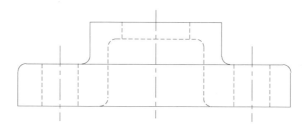

Drawing Suggestions

UNITS = Fractional
GRID = $\frac{1}{4}''$
SNAP = $\frac{1}{16}''$
LTSCALE = 0.5

- Study the dimensions carefully and remember that every grid increment is $\frac{1}{4}''$ and snap points not on the grid are exactly halfway between grid points. Notice that the units should be set to fractions.
- Begin by drawing the outline and then the three center lines in the top view. Then proceed by drawing all circles.
- The circles can be drawn using center and diameter. Position the center of the circle where the center lines cross and type in the diameter.
- Use the top view to line up all the lines on the side view.

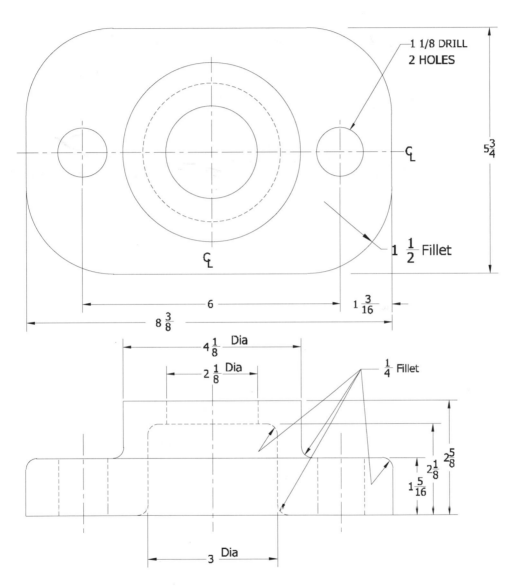

PACKING FLANGE
Drawing 3-6

4

Template Drawings

COMMANDS

ARRAY (RECTANGULAR)	LIMITS
COPY	MOVE

OVERVIEW

In this chapter, you learn some real timesavers. If you have grown tired of defining the same three layers, along with units, grid, snap, and ltscale, for each new drawing, read on. You are about to learn how to use template drawings. With templates, you can begin each new drawing with setups you have defined and saved in previous AutoCAD sessions, or with a variety of predefined setups included in the software.

In addition, you learn to reshape the grid using the LIMITS command and to copy, move, and array objects on the screen so that you do not have to draw the same thing twice. We begin with the LIMITS command, because we want to change the limits as part of defining your first template.

TASKS

126

4.1 Setting Limits

GENERAL PROCEDURE

1. Select Drawing Limits from the Format menu.
2. Enter a lower left corner.
3. Enter an upper right corner.
4. Zoom All.

You have changed the density of the screen grid many times, but always within the same 12 × 9 space, which basically represents an A-size sheet of paper. Now you will learn how to change the shape by setting new limits to emulate other sheet sizes or any other space you want to represent. First, a word about model space and paper space.

Model Space and Paper Space

Model space is an AutoCAD concept that refers to the imaginary space in which we create and edit objects. In model space, objects are always drawn at full scale (1 screen unit = 1 unit of length in the real world). The alternative to model space is paper space, in which screen units represent units of length on a piece of paper. You encounter paper space when you begin to use AutoCAD's layout features. A layout is like an overlay on your drawing in which you specify a sheet size and other paper-related options. Layouts also allow you to create multiple views of the same model space objects. To avoid confusion and keep your learning curve on track, however, we avoid using layouts for the time being.

In this exercise, we reshape our model space to emulate different drawing sheet sizes. This is not necessary in later practice. With AutoCAD, you can scale your drawing to fit any drawing sheet size when it comes time to plot. Model space limits should be determined by the size and shapes of objects in your drawing, not by the paper you are going to use when you plot.

Setting Limits

Limits can be set using the LIMITS command. We begin by opening a new drawing and changing its limits from an A-size sheet (12 × 9) to a B-size sheet (18 × 12).

⊕　Type new or select New from the File menu.

　　This brings you to the familiar Select template dialog box. At this point we continue to use the acad template. Once you have created your own template, it appears in this box along with all the others.

⊕　Press Enter to select the acad template.

⊕　Press F7 to turn on the grid.

　　You are now ready to proceed with creating new limits. Leaving your grid where it is at the lower left of your screen gives you visual feedback about what is happening when you change limits.

⊕　From the Format menu, select Drawing Limits as shown in Figure 4-1.

Figure 4-1

The LIMITS command works in the command area. You see this prompt:

```
Reset Model Space limits:
Specify lower left corner or [ON/OFF] <0.0000,0.0000>:
```

The on and off options control a feature called limits checking. They determine what happens when you attempt to draw outside the drawing limits. With checking off, nothing happens. With checking on, you get a message that says Attempt to draw outside limits and AutoCAD does not allow you to begin a new entity outside of limits. By default, limits checking is off.

The default value shows that the current lower left corner of the grid is at (0,0), where we leave it.

⊕ Press Enter to accept the default lower left corner.

AutoCAD prompts:

```
Specify upper right corner <12.0000,9.0000>:
```

Changing these settings changes the size of your grid.

⊕ Type 18,12.

Your grid is redrawn with larger limits, as shown in Figure 4-2. The usual Zoom All procedure enlarges and centers the grid on your screen.

⊕ Type z to enter the ZOOM command.

⊕ Type a to zoom all.

You should have an 18 × 12 grid on your screen. Move the cursor to the upper right corner to check its coordinates. This is the grid we use for your B-size template drawing.

You might want to experiment with setting limits using some of the possibilities shown in Figure 4-3, which is a table of drawing sheet sizes. It shows the two sets of standard sizes. The standard you use might be determined by your plotter.

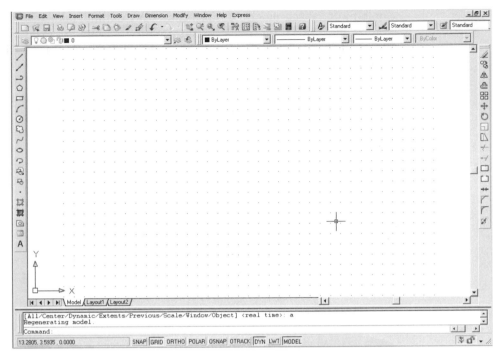

Figure 4-2

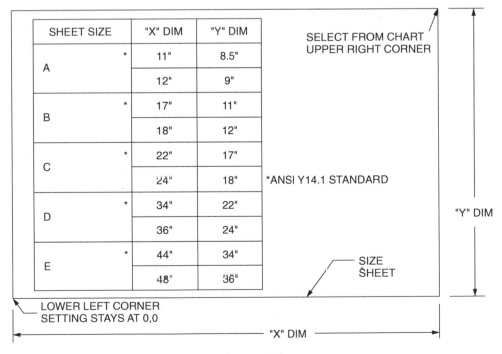

SHEET SIZE		"X" DIM	"Y" DIM
A	*	11"	8.5"
		12"	9"
B	*	17"	11"
		18"	12"
C	*	22"	17"
		24"	18"
D	*	34"	22"
		36"	24"
E	*	44"	34"
		48"	36"

SELECT FROM CHART
UPPER RIGHT CORNER

*ANSI Y14.1 STANDARD

"Y" DIM

SIZE
SHEET

LOWER LEFT CORNER
SETTING STAYS AT 0,0

"X" DIM

Figure 4-3

Some plotters that plot on C-size paper, for example, take a 24 × 18 sheet but do not take a 22 × 17 sheet. This information should be programmed into your plotter driver software and appears in the Plot Configuration dialog box in the preview image.

After you are finished exploring the LIMITS command, we will create the other new settings we want and save this drawing as your B-size template.

You are now in the drawing that we will use for your template, so it is not necessary to begin a new drawing for the next section.

4.2 Creating a Template

> **GENERAL PROCEDURE**
>
> 1. Define layers and change settings (grid, snap, units, limits, ltscale, etc.) as desired.
> 2. Save the drawing as an AutoCAD Drawing Template file.

To make your own template so that you can begin new drawings with the settings you want, all you have to do is create a drawing that has those settings and then tell AutoCAD that this is a drawing you want to use as a template. The first part should be easy for you now, because you have been doing your own setup for each new drawing in this book.

⊞ Make changes to the current drawing as follows:

GRID:	0.50 ON (F7)	COORD:	ON (F6)
SNAP:	0.25 ON (F9)	LTSCALE:	0.5
UNITS:	2-place decimal	LIMITS:	(0,0) (18,12)

Also, ensure that the Snap, Grid, and Model buttons on the status line are on, and that Ortho, Polar, Osnap, Otracking, and LWT are off. Dyn can be on or off.

⊞ Load all linetypes from the acad file using the following procedure:

1. Open the Linetype dialog box from the Format menu.
2. Click Load to open the Load dialog box.
3. Highlight the first linetype on the list.
4. Scroll down to the end of the list.
5. Hold down the Shift key as you highlight the last linetype on the list.
6. With all linetypes highlighted, click OK.
7. Click OK in the Linetype dialog box.

⊞ Create layers and associated colors, linetypes, and settings to match those in Figure 4-4.

Remember that you can make changes to your template at any time. The layers called text, hatch, and dim are not used until Chapters 7 and 8, in which we introduce text, hatch patterns, and dimensions to your drawings. Creating them now saves time and makes your template more complete later.

At this point, your drawing is ready to be saved as a template, which is the focus of the next task.

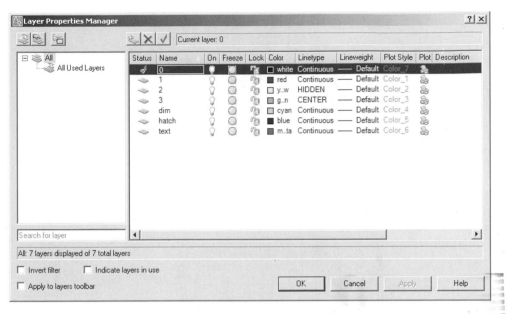

Figure 4-4

Note: Do not leave anything drawn on your screen or it will come up as part of the template each time you open a new drawing. For some applications, this is quite useful, but for now, we want a blank template.

4.3 Saving a Template Drawing

GENERAL PROCEDURE

1. Select Save As from the File menu.
2. Enter your template drawing name in the File name edit box.
3. Select AutoCAD Drawing Template File (*.dwt) in the Files of type list box.
4. Click Save.
5. Type a template description in the Template Description box.
6. Click OK.

A drawing becomes a template when it is saved as a template. Template files are given a .dwt extension and placed in the template file folder.

⊕ To begin this task, you should be in the drawing created in the last task. All the drawing changes should be made as described previously.

⊕ Open the File menu and select Save As.

This opens the familiar Save Drawing As dialog box shown in Figure 4-5. The File name edit box contains the name of the current drawing. If you have not named the drawing, it is called Drawing 1.

Below the File name box is the Files of type box, which lists options for saving the drawing.

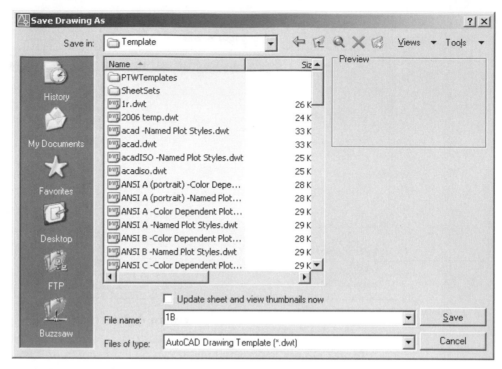

Figure 4-5

✦ Open the Files of type list by clicking the arrow to the right of the list box.

This opens the list of file-type options. AutoCAD Drawing Template file is fourth on the list in AutoCAD 2006.

✦ Highlight AutoCAD Drawing Template File (*.dwt) and click it so that it shows up in the list box.

This also opens the Template file folder automatically. You see the same list of templates you have seen often using the NEW command. There are many templates there supplied by AutoCAD that might be useful to you later. At this point, it is more important to learn how to make your own.

Note: The templates included in the AutoCAD software consist of various standard sheet sizes, all with title blocks, borders, and predefined plot styles. These are convenient. At this point, however, they can cause confusion because they are created in paper space and automatically put you into a paper space layout. You have no need for titles and borders until we cover text in Chapter 7.

✦ Double-click in the File name box to highlight the drawing name.

✦ Type 1B for the new name.

Tip: Because template files are listed alphabetically in the file list, it might be convenient to start your template file name with a number so that it appears before the acad and Ansii standard templates that come with the AutoCAD software. Numbers precede letters in the alphanumeric sequence, so your numbered template file appears at the top of the list and saves you the trouble of scrolling down to find it.

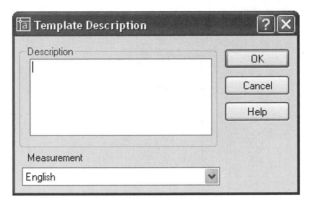

Figure 4-6

Once your drawing name (1B) is in the name box and the Files of type box shows AutoCAD Drawing Template File, you are ready to save.

⊕ Click Save.

This opens a Template Description box, as illustrated in Figure 4-6. This description is used if you select the template in the Create New Drawing dialog box. You can ignore it for now.

⊕ Click OK in the Template Description box.

The task of creating the drawing template is now complete. All that remains is to create a new drawing using the template to see how it works.

⊕ Open the File menu and select Close to close Drawing 1B.

⊕ Open the File menu and select New, or pick the New tool from the Standard toolbar.

This opens the Select template dialog box as usual. However, now 1B is at the top of your list.

⊕ Highlight 1B on the list of Templates.

Note: If 1B is not at the top of your list after the PTW Templates and Sheet Sets folders, it may be because your list is sorting in descending order. To reverse order, click on Name.

⊕ Press Enter or click Open.

A new drawing opens with all the settings from 1B already in place.

4.4   Using the MOVE Command

GENERAL PROCEDURE

1. Type m, select the Move tool from the Modify toolbar, or select Move from the Modify menu.
2. Define a selection set. (If noun/verb selection is enabled, you can reverse Steps 1 and 2.)
3. Choose the base point of a displacement vector.
4. Choose a second point.

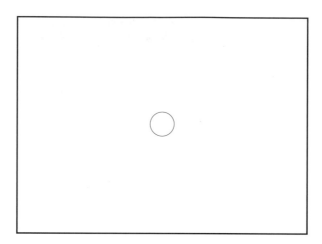

Figure 4-7

The ability to copy and move objects on the screen is one of the great advantages of working on a CAD system. It can be said that CAD is to drafting as word processing is to typing. Nowhere is this analogy more appropriate than in the cut-and-paste capacities that the COPY and MOVE commands give you.

⊞ Draw a circle with a radius of 1 near the center of the screen (9,6) as shown in Figure 4-7.

As discussed in Chapter 2, AutoCAD allows you to pick objects before or after entering an edit command. In this exercise, we use MOVE both ways, beginning with the verb/noun method. We use the circle you have just been drawing, but be aware that the selection set could include as many entities as you like and a group of entities can be selected with a window or crossing box.

⊞ Type m, select Move from the Modify menu, or select the Move tool from the Modify toolbar, as shown in Figure 4-8.

You are prompted to select objects to move.

⊞ Point to the circle.

As with the ERASE command, your circle becomes dotted.

In the command area, AutoCAD tells you how many objects have been selected and prompts you to select more. When you are through selecting objects, you need to press Enter or right-click to move on.

⊞ Right-click to end object selection.

AutoCAD prompts

        Specify base point or displacement:

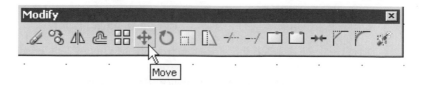

Figure 4-8

Most often you show the movement by defining a vector that gives the distance and direction in which you want the object to be moved. To define movement with a vector, all AutoCAD needs is a distance and direction. Therefore, the base point does not have to be on or near the object you are moving. Any point will do, as long as you can use it to show how you want your objects moved. This might seem strange at first, but it will soon become natural. Of course, you can choose a point on the object if you wish. With a circle, the center point might be convenient.

⊕ Point to any location not too close to the right edge of the screen.

AutoCAD gives you a rubber band from the point you have indicated and asks for a second point:

```
Specify second point of displacement or
<use first point as displacement>:
```

As soon as you begin to move the cursor, AutoCAD also gives you a circle to drag so you can see the effect of the movement you are indicating. An example of how this might look is shown in Figure 4-9. Let's say you want to move the circle 3.00 to the right. Watch the coordinate display and stretch the rubber band out until the display reads 3.00 < 0,0. (Press F6 to get polar coordinates.)

⊕ Pick a point 3.00 to the right of your base point.

The rubber band and your original circle disappear, leaving you with a circle in the new location.

Now, if Ortho is on, turn it off (press F8) and try a diagonal move.

⊕ Type m, select the Move tool, or press the spacebar to repeat the command.

AutoCAD follows with the Select objects: prompt.

⊕ Reselect the circle.

⊕ Right-click to end the object selection process.

⊕ Select a base point.

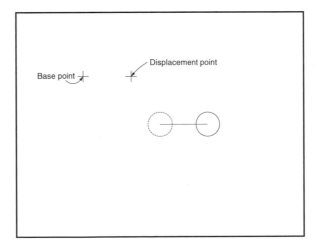

Figure 4-9

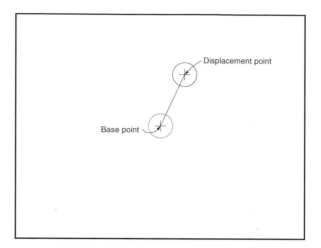

Figure 4-10

⊞ Move the circle diagonally in any direction you like.

Figure 4-10 is an example of how this might look.

⊞ Try moving the circle back to the center of the screen.

It might help to choose the center point of the circle as a base point this time and choose a point at or near the center of the grid for your second point.

Moving with Grips

You can use grips to perform numerous editing procedures without ever entering a command. This is probably the simplest of all editing methods, called *autoediting*. It does have some limitations, however. In particular, you can only select by pointing, windowing, or crossing.

⊞ Point to the circle.

The circle is highlighted and grips appear.

Notice that grips for a circle are placed at quadrants and at the center. In more involved editing procedures, the choice of which grip or grips to use for editing is significant. In this exercise, you will do fine with any of the grips.

Note: To remove grips and exit the grip edit mode without editing, press Esc.

⊞ Move the pick box slowly over one of the grips.

If you do this carefully, you notice that the pick box locks onto the grip as it moves over it. You can see this more clearly if snap is off (press F9). When the cursor locks on the grip, the grip turns green and the number 1.00 appears, indicating the diameter of the circle.

⊞ When the pick box is locked on a grip, press the pick button.

The selected grip becomes filled and changes colors again (from green to red). In the command area, you see

```
        ** STRETCH **
Specify stretch point or [Base point/Copy/Undo/eXit]:
```

Figure 4-11

Stretching is the first of a series of five autoediting modes that you can acti-vate by selecting grips on objects. The word stretch has many meanings in AutoCAD, and they are not always what you would expect. We explore the stretch autoediting mode and the STRETCH command in Chapter 6. For now, we bypass stretch and use the MOVE mode.

AutoCAD has a convenient shortcut menu for use in grip editing.

⊕ **Right-click.**

This opens the shortcut menu shown in Figure 4-11. It contains all of the grip edit modes plus several other options.

⊕ **Select Move on the shortcut menu.**

The shortcut menu disappears and you are in Move mode. Move the cursor and you see a rubber band from the selected grip to the same position on a dragged circle. Notice that the prompt has changed to

```
** MOVE **
Specify move point or [Base point/Copy/Undo/eXIt]:
```

⊕ **Pick a point anywhere on the screen.**

The circle moves where you have pointed.

⊕ **Press Esc to remove grips.**

Moving by Typing a Displacement

There is one more way to use the MOVE command. Instead of showing AutoCAD a distance and direction, you can type a horizontal and vertical displacement. For example, to move the circle three units to the right and two units up, you would use the following procedure (there is no autoediting equivalent for this procedure):

1. Pick the circle.
2. Type m or select the Move tool.
3. Type 3,2 in response to the prompt for base point or displacement.
4. Press Enter in response to the prompt for a second point.

4.5 Using the COPY Command

GENERAL PROCEDURE

1. Select the Copy Object tool from the Modify toolbar (not Copy to Clipboard, which is on the Standard toolbar).
2. Define a selection set. (Steps 1 and 2 can be reversed if noun/verb selection is enabled.)
3. Choose a base point.
4. Choose a second point.
5. Choose another second point or press Enter to exit the command.

The COPY command works much like the MOVE command. The main difference is that the original object does not disappear when the second point of the displacement vector is given and you can create multiple copies by picking additional displacement points. First, we make several copies of the circle in various positions on the screen.

⊕   Type co, select Copy from the Modify menu, or select the Copy Object tool from the Modify toolbar, as shown in Figure 4-12.

Notice that c is not an alias for COPY (it is the alias for CIRCLE). Also notice that there is a Copy to Clipboard tool on the Standard toolbar that initiates the COPYCLIP command. This tool has a very different function. It is used to copy objects to the Windows Clipboard and then into other applications or drawings. It has no effect on objects within your current drawing, other than to save them on the clipboard. We explore COPYCLIP in Chapter 10.

⊕   Select the circle.

⊕   Right-click to end the selection process.

⊕   Pick a base point.

As in the Move command, AutoCAD prompts for a second point.

⊕   Pick a second point.

Figure 4-12

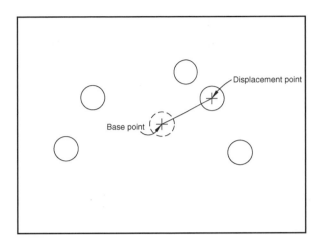

Figure 4-13

You will see a new copy of the circle. Notice also that the prompt to specify a second point of displacement has returned in the command area and that another new circle is shown at the end of the rubber band. AutoCAD is waiting for another vector, using the same base point as before.

⊕ **Pick another second point.**

Repeat this process as many times as you wish. If you get into this, you might begin to feel like a magician pulling rings out of thin air and scattering them across the screen. When you finish you should have several copies of the circle on your screen, as shown in Figure 4-13.

⊕ **Press Enter to exit the command.**

Copying with Grips

The grip editing system includes a variety of special techniques for creating multiple copies in all five modes. The function of the Copy option differs depending on the grip edit mode. For now, we use the Copy option with the Move mode, which provides a shortcut for the same kind of process you just executed with the COPY command.

Because you should have several circles on your screen now, we take the opportunity to demonstrate how you can use grips on more than one object at a time. This can be very useful if your drawing contains two or more objects that maintain the same relationship with each other at different locations in your drawing.

⊕ **Pick any two circles.**

The circles you pick should be highlighted, and grips should appear on both, as illustrated in Figure 4-14.

⊕ **Pick any grip on either of the two highlighted circles.**

The grip should change colors. This time we do not use the shortcut menu. In the command area, you see the grip edit prompt for the Stretch mode:

** STRETCH **

`Specify stretch point or [/Base point/Copy/Undo/eXIt]:`

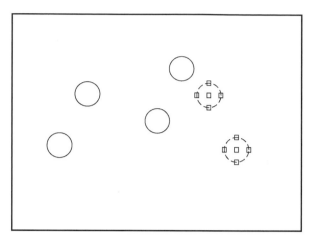

Figure 4-14

⊕   Press the spacebar.

This brings you to the Move mode prompt:

```
** MOVE **
```

```
Specify move point or [/Base point/Copy/Undo/eXIt]:
```

⊕   Type c to initiate copying.

The prompt changes to

```
** Move (multiple)**
```

```
Specify move point or [/Base point/Copy/Undo/eXIt]:
```

You will find that all copying in the grip editing system is multiple copying. Once in this mode, AutoCAD continues to create copies wherever you press the pick button until you exit by typing x or pressing the spacebar.

⊕   Move the cursor and observe the two dragged circles.

⊕   Pick a point to create copies of the two highlighted circles, as illustrated in Figure 4-15.

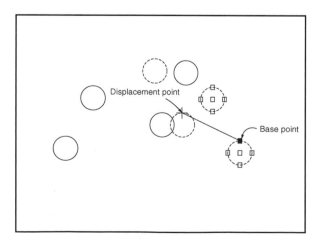

Figure 4-15

⊕　Pick another point to create two more copies.

⊕　When you are through, press Enter or the spacebar to exit the grip editing system.

⊕　Press Esc to remove grips.

4.6　Using the ARRAY Command—Rectangular Arrays

GENERAL PROCEDURE

1. Select the Array tool from the Modify toolbar or Array from the Modify menu.
2. Define a selection set. (Steps 1 and 2 can be reversed if noun/verb editing is enabled.)
3. Press Enter to end selection.
4. Select Rectangular in the dialog box.
5. Enter the number of rows in the array.
6. Enter the number of columns.
7. Enter the offset distance between rows.
8. Enter the offset distance between columns.

The ARRAY command gives you a powerful alternative to simple copying. An array is the repetition of an image in matrix form. This command takes an object or group of objects and copies it a specific number of times in mathematically defined, evenly spaced locations.

There are two types of arrays. Rectangular arrays are linear and defined by rows and columns. Polar arrays are angular and based on the repetition of objects around the circumference of an arc or circle. The dots on the grid are an example of a rectangular array; the radial lines on any circular dial are an example of a polar array. Both types are common. We explore rectangular arrays in this chapter and polar arrays in the next.

In preparation for this exercise, erase all the circles from your screen. This is a good opportunity to try the Erase All option.

⊕　Type e or select the Erase tool from the Modify toolbar.

⊕　Type all.

⊕　Press Enter.

⊕　Now draw a single circle, radius 0.5, centered at the point (2,2).

⊕　Type ar, select Array from the Modify menu, or select the Array tool from the Modify toolbar, as shown in Figure 4-16.

　　This opens the Array dialog box shown in Figure 4-17.

Figure 4-16

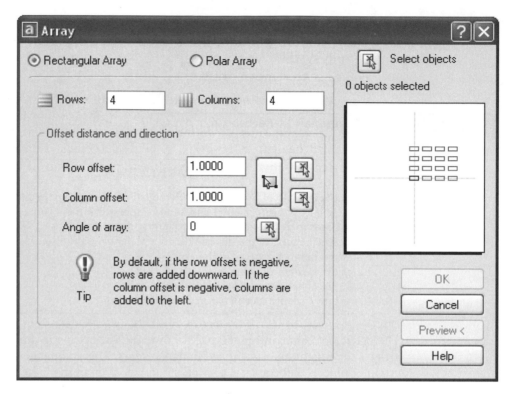

Figure 4-17

⊕ Click Select objects at the top right of the dialog box.

This step is not necessary if you use noun/verb editing and select objects before entering the ARRAY command.

⊕ Point to the circle.

⊕ Right-click to end the selection process.

AutoCAD returns you to the dialog box.

⊕ Make sure that the Rectangular Array radio button is selected at the top left of the dialog box, as it should be by default.

Next, you determine the number of rows in the array.

⊕ Type 3 in the edit box next to the word Rows.

Now you determine the number of columns in the array. Remember, rows are horizontal and columns are vertical, as shown by the gray and white icons next to the words Rows and Columns. What would an array with three rows and only one column look like?

We will construct a five-column array.

⊕ Type 5 in the edit box next to the word Columns.

Note: Do not press Enter after you enter numbers in these edit boxes. AutoCAD interprets this as an OK and constructs an array with whatever information you have provided so far.

Before your array definition is complete, AutoCAD needs to know how far apart to place all these circles. There are 15 of them in this example—three rows with five circles in each row. There are three ways to specify this information. First, you can enter row and column offset values directly in the edit boxes on the left. Second, you can show two corners of a window using the large button to the right of the edit box. Using this option, the horizontal width of the window gives the space between columns and the vertical side gives the space between rows. Third, you can show either of the offset values independently using the buttons on the right. In this exercise, we use the default values in the edit boxes.

⊕ Check to see that 1.00 is the value for Row offset. If not, change the value to 1.00.

⊕ Check to see that 1.00 is the value for Column offset. If not, change the value to 1.00.

We have now provided all the information we need. Use the Preview button to check out the results.

⊕ Click Preview at the lower right of the dialog box.

You should have a 3 × 5 array of circles as shown in Figure 4-18. You will also see a message box with three choices: Accept completes the ARRAY command, Modify takes you back to the dialog box where you can change or add information, and Cancel cancels the ARRAY command.

Notice that AutoCAD builds arrays up and to the right. This is consistent with the coordinate system, which puts positive values to the right on the horizontal *x*-axis and upward on the vertical *y*-axis. Negative values can be used to create arrays in other directions.

⊕ Click Accept to complete the ARRAY command.

The message box disappears and the array remains in your drawing.

We use the array now on your screen as the selection set to create a larger array. We specify an array that has three rows and three columns, with 3.00 between rows and 5.00 between columns. This keeps our circles touching without overlapping.

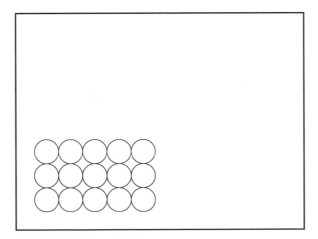

Figure 4-18

⊕ Press Enter to repeat the ARRAY command.

⊕ Click Select Objects in the dialog box.

⊕ Using a window, select the whole array of 15 circles.

⊕ Right-click to end the selection process.

⊕ Enter 3 for the number of rows.

⊕ Enter 3 for the number of columns.

⊕ Enter 3 for the row offset.

⊕ Enter 5 for the column offset.

⊕ Click Preview.

You should have a screen full of circles, as shown in Figure 4-19.

⊕ Click Accept to complete the command.

When you are ready to move on, use the U command to undo the last two arrays.

⊕ Type u to undo the second array.

⊕ Type u again to undo the first array.

Now you should be back to your original circle centered at (2,2). Notice that the U command works nicely to undo an incorrectly drawn array quickly. Be aware, however, that for other purposes, the objects in an array are treated as separate entities, just as if you had drawn them one by one.

Try using some negative distances and a noun/verb sequence to create an array down and to the left.

⊕ First, use the MOVE command or grips to move your circle to the middle of the screen.

⊕ Select the circle.

⊕ Select the Array tool.

This opens the dialog box. Because you have already selected the circle, you do not have to select objects now.

⊕ Enter 3 for the number of rows.

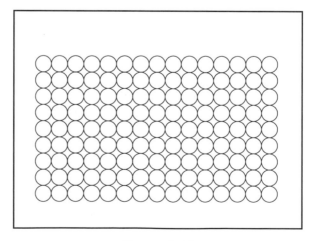

Figure 4-19

⊕ Enter 3 for the number of columns.

⊕ Enter −2 for the row offset.

⊕ Enter −2 for the column offset.

⊕ Click Preview.

Your array should be built down and to the left. The −2 distance between rows causes the array to be built going down. The −2 distance between columns causes the array to be built across to the left.

⊕ Click Accept or Cancel to exit the command, or click Modify to continue experimenting.

4.7   Changing Plot Settings

In the previous chapter, you began using plot previews. In this chapter, we explore more options in the Plot dialog box. We have used no specific drawing for illustration. Now that you know how to use plot preview, you can observe the effects of changing plot parameters with any drawing you like and decide at any point whether you actually want to print the results. We remind you to look at a plot preview after making changes. Plot previewing saves you a lot of time and paper and speeds up your learning curve.

⊕ To begin this exploration, you should have a drawing or drawn objects on your screen so that you can observe the effects of various changes you make. The drawing you are in should use the 1B template so that Limits are set to 18 × 12. The circles drawn in the last task are fine for this demonstration.

⊕ Select Plot from the File pull-down menu, or the Plot tool from the Standard toolbar.

This opens the Plot dialog box.

The Printer/Plotter Panel

One of the most basic changes you can make is your selection of a plotter. Different plotters will use different sheet sizes and will have different default settings. We begin by looking into the list of plotting devices and showing you how to add a plotter to the list.

⊕ Click the arrow at the right of the Name list in the Printer/plotter panel.

The list you see depends on your system and might include printers, plotters, and any faxing devices you have, along with AutoCAD's DWF6 ePlot, JPG, and PNG utilities, which can be used to send drawing and plotting information to the Internet.

The Add a Plotter Wizard

For a thorough exploration of AutoCAD plotting, it is important that you have at least one plotter available. If you have only a printer, you will probably be somewhat limited in the range of drawing sheets available. You might only have an A-size option, for example. For the exercises in this book, you can use the DWF6 ePlot utility to simulate a plotter, or you can use the Add a Plotter Wizard to install one of the AutoCAD standard plotter drivers, even if you actually have no such plotter on your system. To add a plotter, follow this procedure:

1. Close the Plot dialog box.
2. From the File menu, select Plotter Manager.
3. From the Plotters window, click Add a Plotter Wizard.
4. Click Next on the Introduction page.
5. Check to see that My Computer is selected on the Add Plotter-Begin page, then click Next.
6. On the Plotter Model page, select a manufacturer and a model, then click Next.
7. Click Next on the Import Pcp or Pc2 page.
8. Click Next on the Ports page.
9. Click Next on the Plotter Name page.
10. Click Finish on the Finish page.

When the wizard is done, the new plotting device is added to your list of plotting devices in the Plot Configuration dialog box.

⊕ If you have closed the Plot dialog box to install a plotter driver, reopen it by selecting the Plot tool from the Standard toolbar. Then open the list of plotting devices again.

⊕ From the list of plotting devices, select a plotter or the DWF6 ePlot utility to simulate a plotter.

Paper Size

Now that you have a plotter selected you should have a number of paper size options.

⊕ From the Paper Size list, below the plotter name list, select a B-size drawing sheet.

The exact size depends on the plotter you have selected. An ANSI B 17×11 sheet is a common choice.

Drawing Orientation

Drawing Orientation choices are found on the expanded Plot dialog box, as shown in Figure 4-20.

⊕ If your dialog box is not already expanded, click the right arrow button (>) at the bottom right of the dialog box.

There are basically two options for drawing orientation: portrait, in which the short edge of the paper is across the bottom, and landscape, in which the long edge is across the bottom. Portrait is typical of a letter or printed sheet of text, and landscape is typical of a drawing sheet. Your plotting device has a default orientation, but you can print either way using the radio buttons. Drawing orientation obviously has a major impact on how the plotting area of the page is used, so be sure to check out the partial preview any time you switch orientations. Try the following:

⊕ Click Preview to see how your current drawing orientation is interpreted.

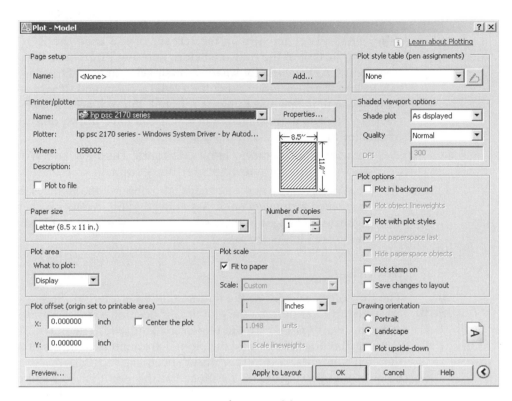

Figure 4-20

✦ Press Esc to return to the Plot dialog box.

✦ Switch from landscape to portrait, or vice versa.

✦ Click Preview again to see how drawing orientation changes the plot.

> **Tip:** On some plotters, you have a choice of different paper orientations. You might have an 11 × 17 and a 17 × 11 option, for example. In this case, there should be a correlation between the paper you choose and the drawing orientation. If you are plotting in landscape, select the 17 × 11; in portrait, select the 11 × 17. Otherwise your paper settings will be 90 degrees off from your drawing orientation and things will get confusing.

✦ For the following task, check to see that your drawing orientation is set to landscape.

> This is the default for most plotters.

Plot Area

Look at the Plot area panel at the left of the Plot Settings dialog box. This is a crucial part of the dialog box that allows you to specify the portion of your drawing to be plotted. You have some familiarity with this from Chapter 2, where you plotted using a window selection. Other options include Display, Limits, and Extents. Changes here have a significant impact on the effective plotting area.

The list box on the left shows the options for plotting area. Display creates a plot using whatever is actually on the screen. If you used the ZOOM command to enlarge a portion of the drawing before entering PLOT and then selected this option, AutoCAD would plot whatever is showing in your Drawing Window. Limits, as you know, are specified using the LIMITS command. If you are using our standard B-size template and Limits is selected, the plot area will be 18 × 12. Extents refers to the actual drawing area in which you have drawn objects. It can be larger or smaller than the limits of the drawing.

⊕ Try switching among Limits, Extents, Display, and Window selections and use plot preview to see the results.

Whenever you make a change, also observe the changes in the boxes showing inches = drawing units. Assuming that Fit to paper is checked, you will see significant changes in these scale ratios as AutoCAD adjusts scales according to the area it is being asked to plot.

Plot Offset

The Plot offset panel is at the bottom middle of the Plot Settings dialog box. Plot offset determines the way the plot area is positioned on the drawing sheet. Specifically, it determines where the plot origin is placed. The default locates the origin point (0,0) at the lower left of the plotted area and determines other locations from there. If you enter a different offset specification, (2,3), for example, the origin point of the drawing area is positioned at this point instead and plot locations are determined from there. This has a dramatic effect on the placement of objects on paper.

The other option in Plot offset is to center the plot. In this case, AutoCAD positions the drawing so that the center point of the plot area coincides with the center point of the drawing sheet.

⊕ Try various plot offset combinations, including Center the plot, and use plot preview to see the results.

4.8 Review Material

Questions

1. Name at least five settings that would typically be included in a template drawing.
2. Where are template drawings stored in a standard AutoCAD file configuration? What extension is given to template file names?
3. What is the value of using a template drawing?
4. What is the main difference between the command procedure for MOVE and that for COPY?
5. What is the main limitation of grip editing?
6. What do you have to do to remove grips from an object once they are displayed?
7. How do you access the grip edit shortcut menu?
8. Explain how arrays are a special form of copying.

9. What is a rectangular array? What is a polar array?

10. Why is it important to do a plot preview after changing plot area or plot offset?

Drawing Problems

1. Create a C-size drawing template using an ANSI standard sheet size, layers, and other settings as shown in this chapter. Start with your 1B template settings to make this process easier.

2. Open a drawing with your new C-size template and draw a circle with a two-unit radius centered at (11,8).

3. Using grips, make four copies of the circle, centered at (15,8), (11,12), (7,8), and (11,4).

4. Switch to Layer 2 and draw a 1 × 1 square with lower left corner at (1,1).

5. Create a rectangular array of the square with 14 rows and 20 columns, one unit between rows, and one unit between columns.

4.9   WWW Exercise 4 (Optional)

At Chapter 4 of our companion website, you will find a drawing project to complete in addition to the self-scoring chapter test. The drawing project challenges you to use edit commands in place of drawing commands. When you are ready, complete the following steps:

⊕   Make sure that you are connected to your Internet service provider.

⊕   Type browser or open the Web toolbar and select the Browse the Web tool.

⊕   If necessary, navigate to our companion website at www.prenhall. com/dixriley.

　　Good luck!

4.10   Drawing 4-1: Pattern

All the drawings in this chapter use your 1B template. Do not expect, however, that you never need to change settings. Layers stay the same throughout this book, but limits change from time to time, and grid and snap change frequently.

This drawing gives you practice using the COPY command. There are numerous ways in which the drawing can be done. The key is to try to take advantage of the repetition in the pattern by copying in an efficient manner. The following figures suggest one way to accomplish this:

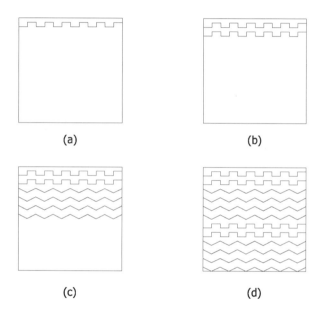

(a)   (b)

(c)   (d)

Drawing Suggestions

GRID = 0.5
SNAP = 0.25

- Begin with a 6 × 6 square. Then draw the first set of lines as in Reference 4-1a.
- Copy the first set down 0.5 to produce Reference 4-1b.
- Draw the first set of V-shaped lines. Then use a multiple copy to produce Reference 4-1c.
- Finally, make a single copy of all the lines you have so far, using a window or crossing box for selection. (Be careful not to select the outside lines.) Watch the displacement carefully and you will produce Reference 4-1d, the completed drawing.

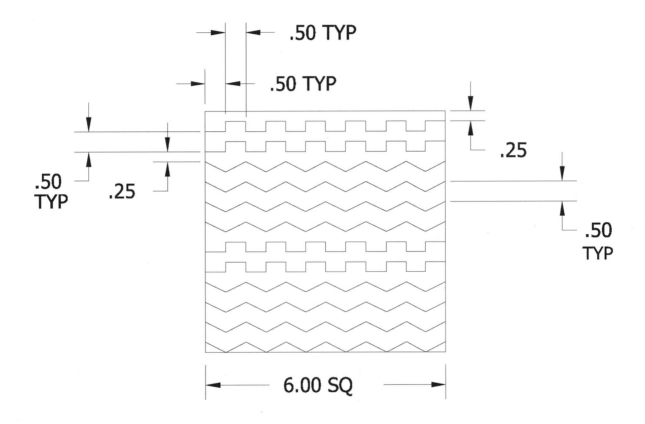

PATTERN

Drawing 4-1

4.11   Drawing 4-2: Grill

This drawing should go very quickly if you use the ARRAY command.

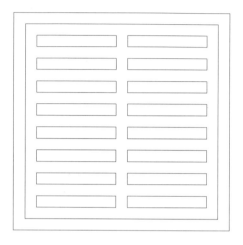

Drawing Suggestions

GRID = 0.5
SNAP = 0.25

- Begin with a 4.75 × 4.75 square.
- Move in 0.25 all around to create the inside square.
- Draw the rectangle in the lower left corner first; then use the ARRAY command to create the rest.
- Also remember that you can undo a misplaced array using the U command.

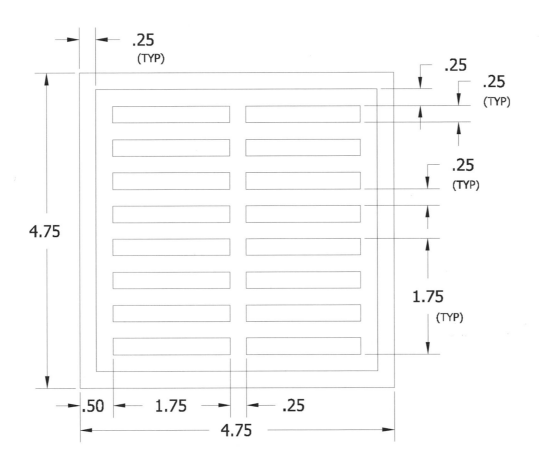

.25
(TYP)

.25

.25
(TYP)

.25
(TYP)

4.75

1.75
(TYP)

.50   1.75   .25

4.75

GRILL
Drawing 4-2

4.12   Drawing 4-3: Weave

As you do this drawing, watch AutoCAD work for you and think about how long it would take to do this by hand! The finished drawing looks like Reference 4-3. For clarity, the drawing shows only one cell of the array and its dimensions.

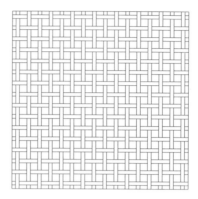

Drawing Suggestions

GRID = 0.5
SNAP = 0.125

- Draw the 6 × 6 square; then zoom in on the lower left using a window. This is the area shown in the lower left of the dimensioned drawing.
- Observe the dimensions and draw the line patterns for the lower left corner of the weave. You could use the COPY command in several places if you'd like, but the time gained will be minimal. Don't worry if you have to fuss with this a little to get it correct; once you have it right, the rest will be easy.
- Use ARRAY to repeat the lower left cell in an 8 × 8 matrix.

    If you get it wrong, use U and try again.

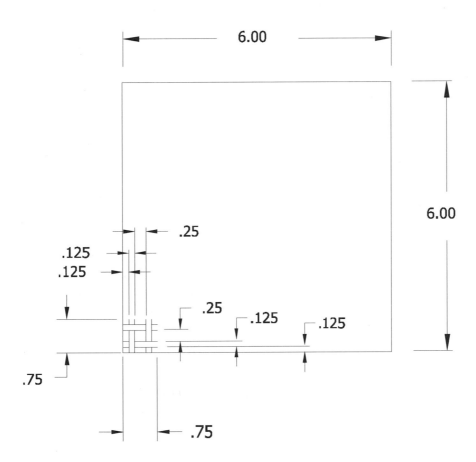

WEAVE

Drawing 4-3

4.13   Drawing 4-4: Test Bracket

This is a great drawing for practicing much of what you have learned up to this point. Notice the suggested snap, grid, ltscale, and limit settings and use the ARRAY command to draw the 25 circles on the front view.

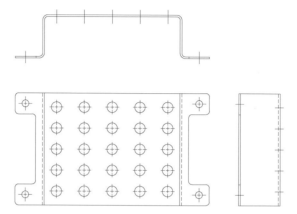

Drawing Suggestions

GRID = 0.25   SNAP = 0.125
LTSCALE = 0.50   LIMITS = (0,0)(24,18)

- Be careful to draw all lines on the correct layers, according to their linetypes.
- Draw center lines through circles before copying or arraying them; otherwise you will have to go back and draw them on each individual circle or repeat the array process.
- A multiple copy works nicely for the four 0.50-diameter holes. A rectangular array is definitely desirable for the 25 0.75-diameter holes.

Creating Center Marks with the Dimcen System Variable

There is a simple way to create the center marks and center lines shown on all the circles in this drawing. It involves changing the value of a dimension variable called *dimcen* (for dimension center). Dimensioning and dimension variables are discussed in Chapter 8, but if you would like to jump ahead, the following procedure works nicely in this drawing:

1. Type dimcen. The default setting for dimcen is 0.09, which causes AutoCAD to draw a simple cross as a center mark. Changing it to −.09 tells AutoCAD to draw a cross that reaches across the circle.
2. Type −.09.
3. After drawing your first circle, and before arraying it, type dim. This puts you in the DIMENSION command.
4. Type cen, indicating that you want to draw a center mark. This is a very simple dimension feature.
5. Point to the circle.
6. Press Esc to quit the DIM command.

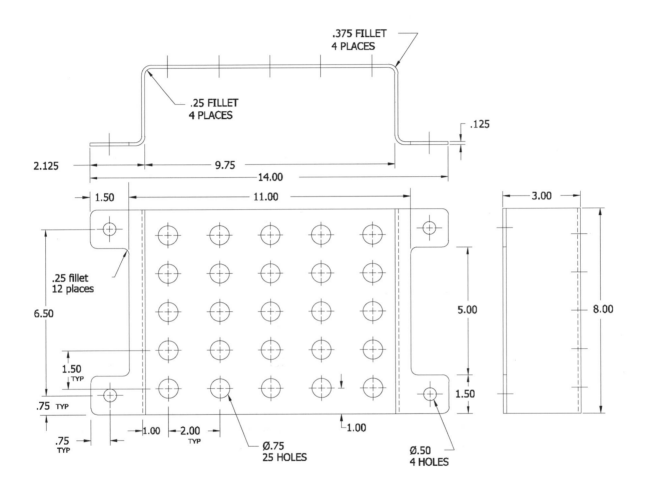

TEST BRACKET

Drawing 4-4

4.14 Drawing 4-5: Floor Framing

This architectural drawing requires changes in many features of your drawing setup. Pay close attention to the suggested settings.

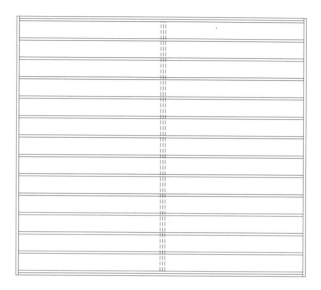

Drawing Suggestions

> UNITS = Architectural, Precision = 0' − 0″
> LIMITS = 36', 24' 24'
> GRID = 1'
> SNAP = 2'
> LTSCALE = 12

- Be sure to use foot (') and inch (″) symbols when setting limits, grid, and snap (but not ltscale).
- Begin by drawing the 20' × 17″ − 10 rectangle, with the lower left corner somewhere in the neighborhood of (4',4').
- Complete the left and right 2 × 10 joists by copying the vertical 17' − 10″ lines 2″ in from each side.
- Draw a 19' − 8″ horizontal line 2' up from the bottom and copy it 2″ higher to complete the double joists.
- Array the inner 12 × 10 in a 14-row by 1-column array, with 16″ between rows.
- Set to Layer 2 and draw the three 17' − 4″ hidden lines down the center.

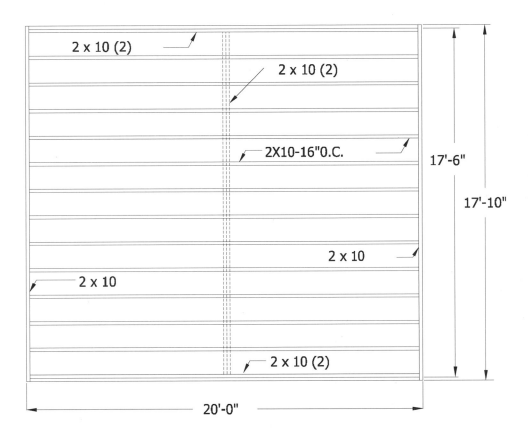

2 x 10 (2)

2 x 10 (2)

2X10-16"O.C.

2 x 10

2 x 10

2 x 10 (2)

17'-6"

17'-10"

20'-0"

FLOOR FRAMING

Drawing 4-5

4.15   Drawing 4-6: Threaded Shaft

The finished drawing should be the top and front views without dimensions, as shown in the reference drawing. Draw the circular view first. This is the top view. Use the top view to line up the front view.

This drawing includes a typical application of rectangular ARRAY and COPY commands.

Drawing Suggestions

GRID = 1/4
SNAP = 1/8
LIMITS = (0,0)(18,12)
LTSCALE = 0.5

- Draw the circles in the top view and use these to line up the horizontal lines in the front view.
- Pay particular attention to the detail drawing when designing the acme screw thread. Draw the outline of the zig-zag shape on each side for one thread and then connect the lines, creating the full thread. Be sure the zig-zag on opposite sides is offset by one thread before drawing the angular lines.
- Now that one thread is created, a simple array completes the whole shaft length.
- Complete the drawing by adding shaft lines and the square shape at the top end.

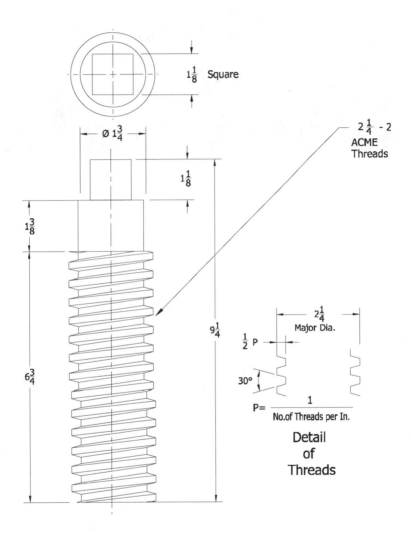

$1\frac{1}{8}$ Square

Ø $1\frac{3}{4}$

$1\frac{1}{8}$

$1\frac{3}{8}$

$6\frac{3}{4}$

$9\frac{1}{4}$

$2\frac{1}{4}$ - 2
ACME
Threads

$2\frac{1}{4}$
Major Dia.

$\frac{1}{2}$ P

30°

$P= \dfrac{1}{\text{No.of Threads per In.}}$

Detail
of
Threads

THREADED SHAFT
Drawing 4-6

5

Arcs and Polar Arrays

COMMANDS

ARC   MIRROR
ARRAY (POLAR)   ROTATE

OVERVIEW

So far, every drawing you have done has been composed of lines and circles. In this chapter, you learn a third major entity, the ARC. In addition, you expand your ability to manipulate objects on the screen. You learn to rotate objects and create their mirror images. You learn to save Plot settings as named Page setups. First, however, we pick up where we left off in Chapter 4 by showing you how to create polar arrays.

TASKS

5.1 Creating Polar Arrays

GENERAL PROCEDURE

1. Select the Array tool from the Modify toolbar or Array from the Modify menu.
2. Define a selection set. (Steps 1 and 2 can be reversed if noun/verb editing is enabled.)
3. Right-click to end selection.
4. Click Polar Array in the dialog box.
5. Pick a center point.
6. Enter the number of items to be in the array.
7. Enter the angle to fill (or 0).
8. Enter the angle between items.
9. Indicate whether to rotate items.

The procedure for creating polar arrays is lengthy and requires some explanation. The first three steps are the same as in rectangular arrays. Step 4 is also the same, except that you select Polar instead of Rectangular. From that point on, the steps are new. First, you pick a center point, and then you have several options for defining the array.

There are three qualities that define a polar array, but two are sufficient. A polar array is defined by any combination of two of the following: a certain number of items, an angle that these items span, and an angle between each item and the next. You also have to tell AutoCAD whether to rotate the newly created objects as they are copied.

⊕   Begin a new drawing using the 1B template.

⊕   In preparation for this exercise, draw a vertical 1.00 line at the bottom center of the screen, near (9.00,2.00), as shown in Figure 5-1.

   We use a 360-degree polar array to create Figure 5-2.

⊕   Select the line.

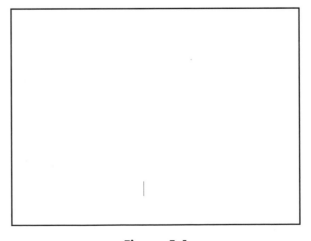

Figure 5-1

Figure 5-2

Figure 5-3

⊕ Type Ar, select Array from the Modify menu, or select the Array tool from the Modify toolbar, as illustrated in Figure 5-3.

⊕ This opens the Array dialog box, familiar from the last chapter.

⊕ Click Polar Array.

Clicking Polar Array changes the dialog box, as illustrated in Figure 5-4. To define a polar array, you need to specify a center point. Rectangular arrays are not determined by a center. Polar arrays, however, are built by copying objects around the circumferences of circles or arcs, so we need to define one of these.

Below the Polar Array button is a line labeled Center point. There are two edit boxes with the *x*- and *y*-coordinates of a default center point, and a Pick Center Point button on the right that takes you out of the dialog box so that you can pick a point.

⊕ Click the Pick Center Point button.

⊕ Pick a point directly above the line and somewhat below the center of the screen.

Something in the neighborhood of (9.00,5.00) will do. As soon as you pick the point, the dialog box returns with the coordinates of the point entered in the X and Y edit boxes.

Below the Center point edit boxes is a list box labeled Method. If you open this list, you can see the three possible paired combinations of total number of items, angle to fill, and angle between items. We take these in order:

⊕ If necessary, select Total number of items & Angle to fill.

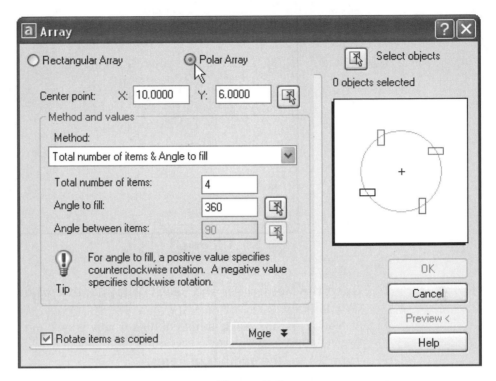

Figure 5-4

With this selection, notice that the Angle between items edit box below is grayed out (unavailable).

⊕ Type 12 in the Total number of items edit box.

This time around we construct a complete 360-degree array. This is the default, but if it has been changed you might need to enter it on your computer.

⊕ If necessary, enter 360 in the Angle to fill edit box.

Notice the Tip, which tells us that if we give a positive value for angle to fill, the array is constructed counterclockwise; if we give a negative angle, it is constructed clockwise. Get used to this; it comes up frequently.

AutoCAD now has everything it needs. Notice the check box at the bottom left of the dialog box labeled Rotate items as copied. With this box checked, as it should be by default, copied objects in the array are rotated around the center point rather than retaining their vertical/horizontal orientation.

⊕ If necessary, check the Rotate items as copied check box.

⊕ Click Preview.

Your screen should resemble Figure 5-2, except that there will be a message box with the options Accept, Modify, or Cancel. Click Modify so that we can return to the dialog box and try some other arrangements.

⊕ Click Modify.

We use the same center point, but define an array that has 20 items placed 15 degrees apart and not rotated.

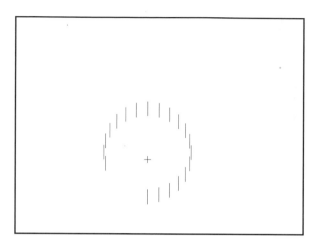

Figure 5-5

⊕ Open the Method list and select Total number of items & Angle between items.

    Notice that the Angle to fill edit box is now grayed out and the Angle between items box has become accessible.

⊕ Type 20 for the number of items.

⊕ Type 15 for the angle between items.

    All that remains is to tell AutoCAD not to rotate the lines as they are copied.

⊕ Clear the Rotate items as copied check box.

    Notice how the general preview image at the right of the dialog box changes as you change your selections.

⊕ Click Preview to view a true preview.

    Your screen should now resemble Figure 5-5.

⊕ Click Modify to return to the dialog box.

Try one more and then you are on your own with polar arrays. For this one, define an array that fills 270 degrees moving clockwise and has 30 degrees between each angle, as shown in Figure 5-5:

⊕ Open the Method list and select Angle to fill & Angle between items.

⊕ Type –270 for the angle to fill.

    What does the negative angle do?

⊕ Type 30 for the angle in between.

⊕ Select the check box to rotate items as they are copied.

⊕ Click Preview.

    Your screen should resemble Figure 5-6.

⊕ Click Accept to close the dialog box and return to the command prompt.

This ends our discussion of polar arrays. With the options AutoCAD gives you, there are many possibilities that you can try. As always, we encourage experimentation. When you are satisfied, erase everything on the screen in preparation for learning the ARC command.

Figure 5-6

5.2   Drawing Arcs

GENERAL PROCEDURE

1. Type a, select the Arc tool from the Draw toolbar, or select Arc from the Draw menu.
2. Type or show where to start the arc, where to end it, and what circle it is a portion of, using any of the 11 available methods.

Learning AutoCAD's ARC command is an exercise in geometry. In this section, we give you a firm foundation for understanding and drawing arcs so that you are not confused by all the available options. The information we give you is more than enough to do the drawings in this chapter and most drawings you encounter else-where. Refer to the AutoCAD Command Reference and the chart at the end of this section (Figure 5-9) if you need additional information.

AutoCAD gives you eight distinct ways to draw arcs (11 if you count variations in order). With so many choices, some generalizations are helpful.

First, notice that every option requires you to specify three pieces of information: where to begin the arc, where to end it, and what circle it is theoretically a part of. To get a handle on the range of options, look at the list of options from the Arc submenu.

⊕   Erase any objects left on your screen from the previous section.

⊕   Open the Draw menu and highlight Arc to open the cascading sub-menu illustrated in Figure 5-7.

Notice that the options in the fourth panel (Center, Start, End, etc.) are simply reordered versions of those in the second panel (Start, Center, End, etc.). This is how we end up with 11 options instead of eight.

More importantly, Start is always included. In every option, a starting point must be specified, although it does not have to be the first point given.

The options arise from the different ways you can specify the end and the circle from which the arc is cut. The end can be shown as an actual point (all End options) or inferred from a specified angle or length of chord (all Angle and Length options).

The circle that the arc is part of can be specified directly by its center point (all Center options) or inferred from other information, such as a radius length (Radius

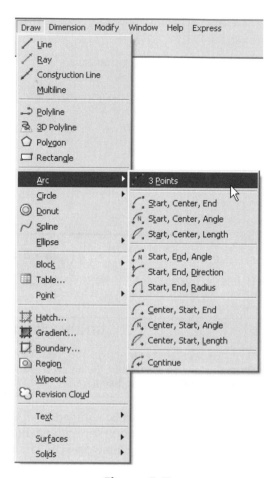

Figure 5-7

options), an angle between two given points (Angle options), or a tangent direction (the Start, End, Direction, and Continue options).

With this framework in mind, we begin by drawing an arc using the simplest method, which is also the default, the three-points option. The geometric key to this method is that any three points not on the same line determine a circle or an arc of a circle. AutoCAD uses this in the CIRCLE command (the 3P option) as well as in the ARC command.

⊕ Select 3 points from the Draw menu, type a, or select the Arc tool from the Draw toolbar, as shown in Figure 5-8.

Figure 5-8

AutoCAD's response is this prompt:

`Specify start point of arc or [Center]:`

Accepting the default by specifying a point leaves open all those options in which the start point is specified first.

If you instead type c, AutoCAD prompts for a center point and follows with those options that begin with a center.

⊕ Select a starting point near the center of the screen.

AutoCAD prompts

`Specify second point of arc or [Center/End]:`

We continue to follow the default three-point sequence by specifying a second point. You might want to refer to the chart (Figure 5-9) as you draw this arc.

TYPE	APPEARANCE	DESCRIPTION
3-point	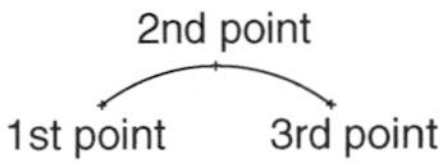 2nd point / 1st point / 3rd point	Clockwise or counterclockwise
S, C, E (start, center, end)	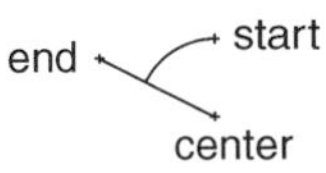 end / start / center	Counterclockwise Radial rubber band indicates angle only, length is insignificant
S, C, A (start, center, angle)	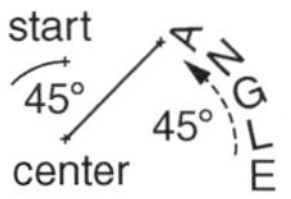 start / 45° / center / 45° / ANGLE	+ angle = CCW − angle = CW Rubber band shows angle only, starting from horizontal
S, C, L (start, center, length of chord)	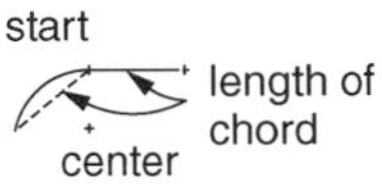 start / length of chord / center	Counterclockwise "Chord" rubber band shows length of chord only, direction is insignificant
S, E, A (start, end, angle)	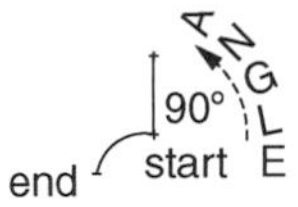 end / 90° / start / ANGLE	+ angle = CCW − angle = CW Rubber band shows angle only, starting from horizontal
S, E, R (start, end, radius)	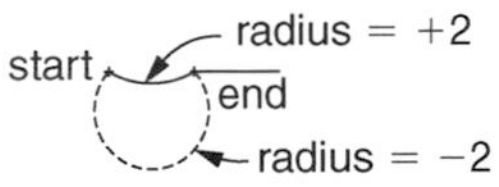 start / radius = +2 / end / radius = −2	Counterclockwise + radius = minor arc − radius = major arc Rubber band shows + radius values only, For − radius (type value)
S, E, D (start, end, direction)	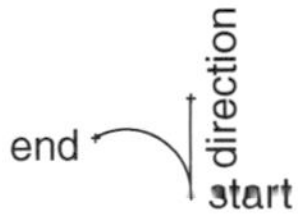 end / direction / start	Direction of rubber band is a line tangent to the arc being constructed and runs through the start point
CONTIN: (continuous from line)	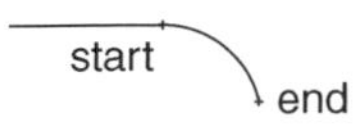 start / end	Arc begins at end point of previous line or arc and is tangent to it; Rubber band is a chord from start point to end point

Figure 5-9

⊕ Select any point one or two units away from the previous point. Exact coordinates are not important right now.

Once AutoCAD has two points, it gives you an arc to drag. By moving the cursor slowly in a circle and in and out, you can see the range of what the third point will produce.

AutoCAD also knows now that you have to provide an endpoint to complete the arc, so the prompt has only one option:

<pre>   Specify end point of arc:</pre>

Any point you select will do, as long as it produces an arc that fits on the screen.

⊕ Pick an endpoint.

As you can see, three-point arcs are easy to draw. It is much like drawing a line, except that you have to specify three points instead of two. In practice, however, you do not always have three points to use this way. This necessitates the broad range of options in the ARC command. The dimensions you are given and the objects already drawn determine what options are useful to you.

Next we create an arc using the start, center, end method, the second option illustrated in Figure 5-9.

⊕ Type u to undo the three-point arc.

⊕ Type a or select the Arc tool.

⊕ Select a point near the center of the screen as a start point.

The prompt that follows is the same as for the three-point option, but we do not use the default this time:

<pre>   Specify second point of arc or [Center/End]:</pre>

Specify the Center option.

Tip: If you choose options from the Draw menu, some steps are automated. If you select Start, Center, End, for example, the c is entered automatically.

⊕ Type c or right-click and select Center from the shortcut menu, if necessary.

This tells AutoCAD that we want to specify a center point next, so we see the prompt

<pre>   Specify center point of arc:</pre>

⊕ Select any point roughly one to three units away from the start point.

The circle from which the arc is to be cut is now clearly determined. All that is left is to specify how much of the circle to take, which can be done in one of three ways, as the following prompt indicates:

<pre>   Specify end point of arc or [Angle/chord Length]:</pre>

We specify an endpoint by pointing. First, however, move the cursor slowly in a circle and in and out to see how this method works. As before, there is an arc to drag, and now there is a radial direction rubber band as well. If you pick a point anywhere along this rubber band, AutoCAD assumes that you want the point where it crosses the circumference of the circle.

Note: Here, as in the polar arrays in this chapter, AutoCAD is building arcs counterclockwise, consistent with its coordinate system.

⊕ Select an endpoint to complete the arc.

We now draw one more arc, using the start, center, angle method, before going on. This method has some peculiarities in the use of the rubber band that are typical of the ARC command and they can be confusing. An example of how the start, center, angle method might look is shown in Figure 5-9.

⊕ Type u to undo the last arc.

⊕ Type a or select the Arc tool.

AutoCAD asks for a center or start point:

```
Specify start point of arc or [Center]:
```

⊕ Pick a start point near the center of the screen.

AutoCAD prompts

```
Specify second point of arc or [Center/End]:
```

⊕ Type c or right-click and select Center from the shortcut menu.

AutoCAD prompts for a center point:

```
Specify center point of arc:
```

⊕ Pick a center point one to three units below the start point.

AutoCAD prompts, as before,

```
Specify end point of arc or [Angle/chord Length]:
```

⊕ Type a or right-click and select Angle from the shortcut menu.

Notice how the shortcut menu changes to show different options available at each step.

You can type an angle specification or show an angle on the screen. Notice that the rubber band now shows an angle only; its length is insignificant. The indicated angle is being measured from the horizontal, but the actual arc begins at the start point and continues counterclockwise, as illustrated in Figure 5-9. The prompt reads

```
Specify included angle:
```

⊕ Type 45 or show an angle of 45 degrees.

Now that you have tried three of the basic methods for constructing an arc, we strongly suggest that you study the chart in Figure 5-9 and then try the other options. The notes in the right-hand column serve as a guide.

The differences in the use of the rubber band from one option to the next are important. You should understand, for instance, that in some cases the linear rubber band is only significant as a distance indicator; its angle is of no importance and is ignored by AutoCAD. In other cases, it is just the reverse: The length of the rubber band is irrelevant, whereas its angle of rotation is important.

Tip: One additional trick you should try as you experiment with arcs is as follows: If you press Enter or the spacebar at the Specify start point

[Center]: prompt, AutoCAD uses the endpoint of the last line or arc you drew as the new starting point and constructs an arc tangent to it. This is the same as the Continue option on the pull-down menu.

This completes the discussion of the ARC command. Constructing arcs can be tricky. Another option that is available and often useful is to draw a complete circle and then use the TRIM or BREAK command to cut out the arc you want. BREAK and TRIM are introduced in the next chapter.

5.3 Using the ROTATE Command

GENERAL PROCEDURE

1. Select Rotate from the Modify menu, or select the Rotate tool from the Modify toolbar.
2. Define the selection set. (Steps 1 and 2 can be reversed if noun/verb selection is enabled.)
3. Pick a base point.
4. Indicate an angle of rotation.

ROTATE is a fairly straightforward command, and it has some uses that might not be immediately apparent. For example, it frequently is easier to draw an object in a horizontal or vertical position and then ROTATE it into position rather than drawing it in a diagonal position.

In addition to the ROTATE command, there is a rotate mode in the grip edit system, which we introduce later in this section.

⊕ In preparation for this exercise, clear your screen and draw a three-point arc using the points (8,4), (11.5,2), and (15,4), as in Figure 5-10.

We begin by rotating the arc to the position shown in Figure 5-11.

⊕ Select the arc.

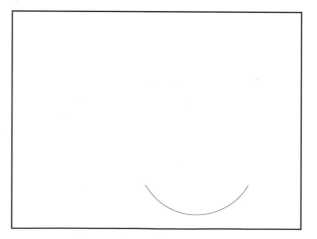

Figure 5-10

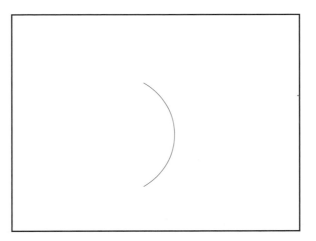

Figure 5-11

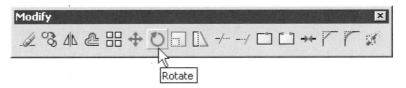

Figure 5-12

⊕   Type Ro, select Rotate from the Modify menu, or select the Rotate tool from the Modify toolbar, as shown in Figure 5-12.

You are prompted for a base point:

                    `Specify base point:`

This is the point around which the object is rotated. The results of the rotation, therefore, are dramatically affected by your choice of base point. Choose a point at the left tip of the arc.

⊕   Point to the left tip of the arc.

The prompt that follows looks like this:

            `Specify rotation angle or [Reference]:`

The default method is used to indicate a rotation angle directly. The object is rotated through the angle specified and the original object is deleted.

Move the cursor in a circle and you will see that you have a copy of the object to drag into place visually. If Ortho is on, turn it off to see the complete range of rotation.

⊕   Type 90 or point to a rotation of 90 degrees.

The results should resemble Figure 5-11.

Notice that when specifying the rotation angle directly like this, the original orientation of the selected object is taken to be 0 degrees. The rotation is figured counterclockwise from there. However, there might be times when you want to

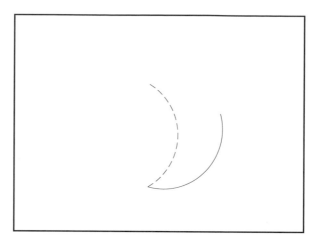

Figure 5-13

refer to the coordinate system in specifying rotation. This is the purpose of the Reference option. To use it, you need to specify the present orientation of the object relative to the coordinate system, and then tell AutoCAD the orientation you want it to have after rotation. Look at Figure 5-13. To rotate the arc as shown, you can either indicate a rotation of –45 degrees or tell AutoCAD that it is currently oriented to 90 degrees and you want it rotated to 45 degrees. Try the following method for practice:

⊕   Repeat the ROTATE command.

⊕   Select the arc.

⊕   Right-click to end selection.

⊕   Choose a base point at the lower tip of the arc.

⊕   Type r or select Reference from the shortcut menu.

⊕   AutoCAD prompts for a reference angle:

> Specify the reference angle <0>:

⊕   Type 90.

AutoCAD prompts

> Specify the new angle:

⊕   Type 45.

Your arc should now resemble the solid arc in Figure 5-13.

Rotating with Grips

Rotating with grips is simple, and there is a useful option for copying, but your choice of object selection methods is limited, as always, to pointing and windowing. Complete the following steps:

⊕   Pick the arc.

The arc is highlighted and grips appear. Notice that these grips are especially designed for arcs.

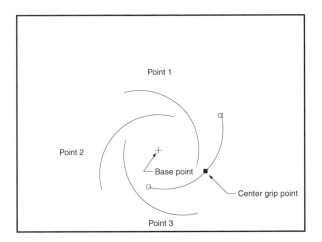

Figure 5-14

⊕ Pick the grip in the middle of the arc.

⊕ Right-click to open the grip shortcut menu.

⊕ Select Rotate.

   Move your cursor in a circle and you will see the arc rotating around the grip at the center of the arc.

⊕ Now type b or right-click again and select Base Point from the menu.

   Base Point allows you to pick a base point other than the selected grip.

⊕ Pick a base point above and to the left of the grip, as shown in Figure 5-14.

   Move your cursor in circles again. You can see the arc rotating around the new base point.

⊕ Type c or open the shortcut menu and select Copy.

   Notice the Command area prompt, which indicates that you are now in a rotate and multiple copy mode.

⊕ Pick a point showing a rotation angle of 90 degrees, as illustrated by the top arc in Figure 5-14.

⊕ Pick a second point showing a rotation angle of 180 degrees, as illustrated by the arc at the left in the figure.

⊕ Pick point 3 at 270 degrees to complete the design shown in Figure 5-14.

⊕ Press Enter or the spacebar to exit the grip mode.

   This capacity to create rotated copies is very useful, as you will find when you do the drawings at the end of this chapter.

5.4 Using Polar Tracking at Any Angle

You might have noticed that using Ortho or Polar Tracking to force or snap to the 90-degree, 180-degree, and 270-degree angles in the last exercise would make the process more efficient. With Polar Tracking, you can extend this concept to

Figure 5-15

include angular increments other than the standard 90-degree orthogonal angles. This feature combined with the Rotate Copy technique facilitates the creation of rotated copies at regular angles. As an example, we use this process to create Figure 5-15.

⊕   To begin this task, Erase or Undo all but one arc on your screen.

⊕   Move the arc to the center of your screen.

We are going to rotate and copy this arc as before, but first we set Polar Tracking to track at 30-degree angles. This is done in the Drafting Settings dialog box.

⊕   Use F9 or the Snap button to turn Snap off.

⊕   Click the Polar button on the status bar so that Polar Tracking is on.

⊕   Right-click the same Polar button.

This opens a small shortcut menu with three options: On, Off, and Settings. On and Off are not very useful because you can turn the Polar button on and off more quickly by clicking the button. However, selecting Settings opens the Drafting Settings dialog box with the Polar Tracking tab selected.

⊕   Select Settings.

You see the Drafting Settings dialog box as shown in Figure 5-16. This is the same dialog box used to specify Snap and Grid settings, but now the Polar Tracking tab is selected. In the next chapter, we use the third tab, Object Snap.

If you are using AutoCAD default settings, the increment angle is 90 degrees. Otherwise, you see whatever increment was set last in your AutoCAD system.

⊕   Open the Increment angle drop-down list.

Notice the standard selections, from 90 at the top to 5 at the bottom. Notice also that you can add custom angles by selecting the Additional angles check box, clicking New, and typing in a new value.

⊕   Select 30 from the list.

30 replaces 90 as the current increment angle. We do not use the other two panels yet. The first panel sets the relationship between Object Snap Tracking

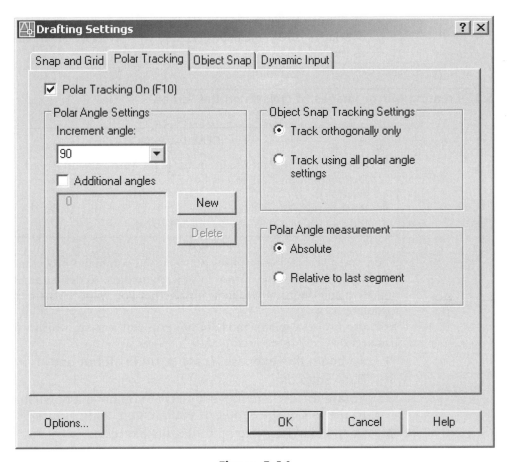

Figure 5-16

Settings and Polar Tracking. This is covered in Chapter 6. The second panel gives you the option of measuring angles from the last line segment drawn instead of measuring from the 0 point of the screen coordinate system (absolute).

⊕ With 30 showing as the current increment angle, click OK.

⊕ Select the arc.

⊕ Click on the grip in the middle of the arc.

⊕ Right-click to open the grip shortcut menu.

⊕ Select Rotate.

⊕ Slowly move the cursor in a wide circle around the selected grip.

   Polar Tracking now tracks and snaps to every 30-degree angular increment.

⊕ Right-click to open the shortcut menu again.

⊕ Select Copy.

⊕ Carefully create a copy at every 30-degree angle until you have created a design similar to Figure 5-15.

If your design is not exactly like ours, in particular if the ends of the arcs overlap or do not meet, it is because you have used an arc that is not the same as the one we used.

5.5 Creating Mirror Images of Objects on the Screen

GENERAL PROCEDURE

1. Select Mirror from the Modify menu, or the Mirror tool from the Modify toolbar.
2. Define a selection set. (Steps 1 and 2 can be reversed if noun/verb selection is enabled.)
3. Point to two ends of a mirror line.
4. Indicate whether to delete the original object.

There are two main differences between the command procedures for MIRROR and ROTATE. First, to mirror an object you have to define a mirror line; second, you have an opportunity to indicate whether you want to retain the original object or delete it.

There is also a mirror mode in the grip edit system, which we explore later in this section.

⊕ To begin this exercise, Erase or Undo all but one arc on your screen.

⊕ Turn Snap on.

⊕ Rotate the arc and move it so that you have a bowl-shaped arc placed to the left of the center of your screen, as in Figure 5-17.

⊕ Keep Polar Tracking on to do this exercise.

⊕ Select the arc.

⊕ Type Mi, select Mirror from the Modify menu, or select the Mirror tool from the Modify toolbar, as shown in Figure 5-18.

Now AutoCAD asks you for the first point of a mirror line:

```
Specify first point of mirror line:
```

Figure 5-17

Figure 5-18

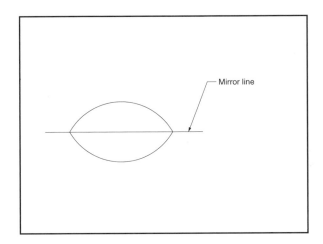

Mirror line

Figure 5-19

A mirror line is just what you would expect; the line serves as the mirror, and all points on your original object are reflected across the line at an equal distance and opposite orientation.

We show a mirror line even with the top of the arc, so that the endpoints of the mirror images are touching.

⊕ Select a point even with the left endpoint of the arc, as in Figure 5-19.

You are prompted to show the other endpoint of the mirror line:

    Specify second point of mirror line:

The length of the mirror line is not important. All that matters is its orientation. Move the cursor slowly in a circle, and you see an inverted copy of the arc moving with you to show the different mirror images that are possible given the first point you have specified.

⊕ Select a point at 0 degrees from the first point, so that the mirror image is directly above the original arc and touching at the endpoints, as in Figure 5-19.

The dragged object disappears until you answer the next prompt, which asks if you want to delete the original object.

    Delete source objects [Yes/No]? <N>:

This time around, do not delete the original.

⊕ Press Enter to retain the old object.

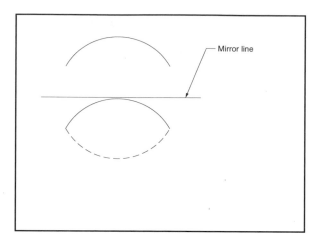

Figure 5-20

Your screen should look like Figure 5-19, without the mirror line in the middle.

Now let's repeat the process, deleting the original this time and using a different mirror line.

⊕ Repeat the MIRROR command.

⊕ Select the original (lower) arc.

⊕ Right-click to end selection.

Create a mirror image above the last one by choosing a mirror line slightly above the two arcs, as in Figure 5-20.

⊕ Select a first point of the mirror line slightly above and to the left of the figure.

⊕ Select a second point directly to the right of the first point.

⊕ Type y or right-click and select Yes from the shortcut menu, indicating that you want the source object, the lower arc, deleted.

Your screen should now resemble Figure 5-21.

Mirroring with Grips

The Mirror grip edit mode works exactly like the Rotate mode, except that the rubber band shows you a mirror line instead of a rotation angle. The option to retain or delete the original is obtained through the Copy option, just as in the Rotate mode. Try the following:

⊕ Select the two arcs on your screen by pointing or using a crossing window.

The arcs are highlighted and grips are showing.

⊕ Pick any of the grips.

⊕ Right-click and then select Mirror from the shortcut menu.

Move the cursor and observe the dragged mirror images of the arcs. Notice that the rubber band operates as a mirror line, just as in the MIRROR command.

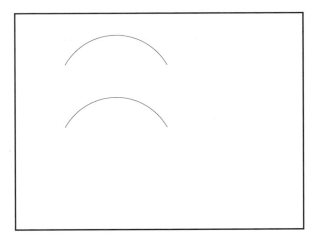

Figure 5-21

⊕   Type b or right-click again and select Base point.

This frees you from the selected grip and allows you to create a mirror line from any point on the screen. Notice the Specify base point: prompt in the command area.

⊕   Pick a base point slightly below the arcs.

⊕   Type c or right-click and select Copy from the shortcut menu.

As in the Rotate mode, this is how you retain the original in a grip edit mirroring sequence.

⊕   Pick a second point to the right of the first.

Your screen should resemble Figure 5-22.

⊕   Press Enter or the spacebar to exit Grip edit mode.

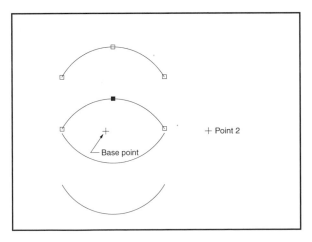

Figure 5-22

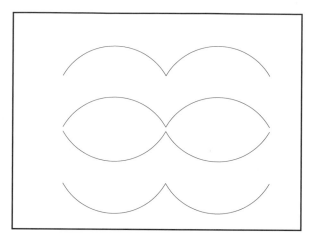

Figure 5-23

We suggest that you complete this exercise by using the Mirror grip edit mode with the copy option to create Figure 5-23.

5.6   Creating Page Setups

GENERAL PROCEDURE

1. Select the Plot tool from the Standard toolbar.
2. Make changes in Plot settings.
3. Click Add to open the Add Page Setup dialog box.
4. Enter a name for the page setup.
5. Click OK.

In this chapter and the next, you move to another level in your exploration of AutoCAD plotting. So far, we have confined ourselves to plot configurations tied directly to objects visible in your model space drawing area. In this chapter, we continue to plot from model space, but introduce the concept and technique of page setups. With page setups, you can name and save different plot configurations so that one drawing can produce several different page setups. We define two simple page setups. You do not need to learn any new options, but you do learn to save settings of the options we have covered so far so that they can be reused as part of a page setup.

⊞   To begin this task, you should be in an AutoCAD drawing using the 1B template.

Any drawing will do. We will continue using the objects drawn in Task 5.5.

The Page Setup Dialog Box

A page setup is nothing more than a group of plot settings, like the ones you have been specifying since Chapter 2. The only difference is that you give the configuration a name and save it on a list of setups. Once named, the plot settings can be restored by selecting the name and they can even be exported to other drawings.

You can define a page setup from the Plot dialog box or from the Page Setup dialog box, accessible through the Page Setup Manager on the File menu. There is little difference between the two dialog boxes. Here we continue to use the Plot dialog box.

⊞   Select the Plot tool from the Standard toolbar.

You should now be in the familiar Plot dialog box. We make a few changes in parameters and then give this page setup a name.

We create a portrait setup and a landscape setup. Besides the difference in orientation, the only difference in settings between the two is that the portrait setup is centered, whereas the landscape setup is plotted from the origin.

Note: Remember that you must have a plotter or a printer selected to do a preview.

⊞   Make sure you have a plotter selected in the Printer/plotter list.

⊞   Open the Paper size list and select an A-size 8.50 × 11.00 sheet.

⊞   Select Limits in the Plot area panel.

⊞   Select Center the Plot in the Plot offset panel.

⊞   Select the Portrait radio button in the Drawing orientation panel.

Notice how the preview image changes. Pause a minute to make sure you understand why the preview looks this way. Assuming you are using the objects drawn in this chapter, or another drawing using the 1B template, you have model space limits set to 18 × 12. You are plotting to an 8.5 × 11 sheet of paper. The 18 × 12 limits have been positioned in portrait orientation, placed across the effective area of the drawing sheet, scaled to fit, and centered on the paper.

Now you name this page setup.

⊞   Click the Add button at the upper right of the dialog box next to the Page setup name box.

This opens the Add Page Setup dialog box shown in Figure 5-24.

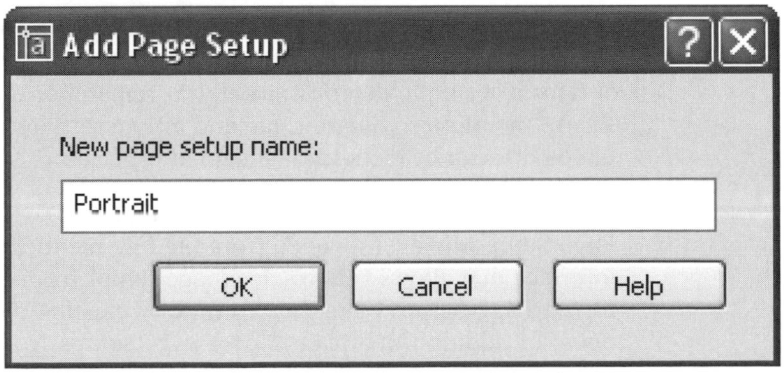

Figure 5-24

✛   Type Portrait as the page setup name.

✛   Click OK.

This brings you back to the Plot dialog box. Portrait is now entered in the Page setup name box. That's all there is to it. The portrait page setup information is now part of the current drawing.

Next, we define a landscape page setup and put it on the list as well. The only difference in this setup is that it is in landscape orientation and plotted from the origin rather than centered.

✛   Select the Landscape radio button in the Drawing Orientation panel.

Notice that Portrait is no longer in the Page setup edit box now that you have changed a parameter.

✛   Clear the check mark on Center the plot.

Notice that the preview image of the page stays in the portrait position even though the plot will be a landscape plot. This is because the sheet size is 8.5×11. If you wanted to rotate this image to the horizontal, you would need to select an 11×8.5 sheet. So now you have the 18×12 limits aligned with the left edge of the page, positioned at the origin of the effective area, and scaled to fit. Let's give this setup a name.

✛   Click Add again.

✛   Type Landscape in the User Defined Page Setups box.

✛   Click OK.

Back in the Plot dialog box, you see that Landscape setup has been entered as the current page setup. You should now restore the portrait settings.

✛   Open the Page setup name drop-down list and select Portrait.

Your portrait settings, including the Portrait radio button and Center the plot, are restored.

✛   Click Preview.

You should see a preview similar to Figure 5-25.

✛   Press Esc to return to the dialog box.

✛   Open the Page setup name drop-down list again and select Landscape.

Your landscape settings are restored.

✛   Click Preview.

You should see a preview similar to Figure 5-26. Notice that AutoCAD turns the paper image to landscape orientation in the full preview.

This is a simple demonstration, but remember that everything from sheet size to the plotter you are using and all the settings in the Plot Configuration dialog box can be included in a named page setup.

Note: Once you have defined page setups you can access them through the Page Setup Manager, opened from the File menu. This dialog box is a simple interface that allows you to select page setups from a list. It will then take you to the Page Setup dialog box to modify existing page setups or create new ones. In addition, you can import page setups from other drawings, as described next.

Figure 5-25

Figure 5-26

Importing Page Setups

A powerful feature of page setups is that they can be exchanged among drawings using the PSETUPIN command. This allows you to import page setups from a known drawing into the current drawing. The procedure is as follows:

1. From a drawing into which you would like to import a page setup, type psetupin at the command line or open the Page Setup Manager and click Import.
2. In the Select Page Setup From File dialog box, enter the name and path of the drawing file from which you would like to import a page setup, or open the folder containing the file and select it.
3. In the Import Page Setups box, select the name of the page setup you want to import.
4. Enter the Plot or Page Setup dialog box and open the Page setup name list. The imported page setup should be there.

> **Note:** Page setups are defined in either model space or paper space as part of a layout. If you create a page setup in model space and then go into a paper space layout, you will not see it on your list. Also, if you define a page setup as part of a paper space layout, you will not see it if you begin a plot from model space.

5.7 Review Material

Questions

1. What factors define a polar array? How many are needed to define an array?
2. What factors define an arc? How many are needed for any single method?
3. How would you use Polar Tracking instead of Polar Array to create Figure 5-6?
4. What is the difference between the three points option in the CIRCLE command and the three points option in the ARC command?
5. Explain the significance of the rubber band in the Start, Center, Angle and the Start, End, Direction methods.
6. How would you use the reference option to rotate a line from 60 degrees to 90 degrees? How would you accomplish the same rotation without using a reference?
7. What is the purpose of the base point option in the grip edit Rotate mode?
8. Why does MIRROR require a mirror line whereas ROTATE requires only a single point?
9. How do you create a landscape plot if your printer prints in portrait orientation?
10. What would happen if a drawing created with our 1B template were printing with a 1-to-1 scale on an A-size printer? What feature of the Plot Configuration dialog box would you use to find out if you weren't sure?

Drawing Problems

1. Draw an arc starting at (10,6) and passing through (12,6.5) and (14,6).
2. Create a mirrored copy of the arc across the horizontal line passing through (10,6).

3. Rotate the pair of arcs from Step 2 45 degrees around the point (9,6).
4. Create a mirrored copy of the pair of arcs mirrored across a vertical line passing through (9,6).
5. Create mirrored copies of both pairs of arcs mirrored across a horizontal line passing through (9,6).
6. Erase any three of the four pairs of arcs on your screen and re-create them using a polar array.

5.8   WWW Exercise 5 (Optional)

In addition to the self-scoring test, Chapter 5 of our companion website gives you another challenge to draw an object using a limited number of objects and edit commands. We also give you links to two new CAD-related websites. When you are ready, complete the following:

⊕ Make sure that you are connected to your Internet service provider.

⊕ Type browser or open the Web toolbar and select the Browse Web tool.

⊕ If necessary, navigate to our companion website at www.prenhall. com/dixriley.

Bon voyage!

5.9 Drawing 5-1: Flanged Bushing

This drawing makes use of a polar array to draw eight screw holes in a circle. It also reviews the use of layers and linetypes. Please save this drawing, as noted subsequently.

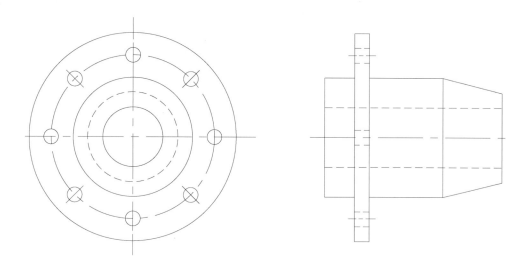

Drawing Suggestions

GRID = 0.25
SNAP = 0.125
LTSCALE = 0.50
LIMITS = (0,0)(12,9)

- Draw the concentric circles first, using dimensions from both views. Remember to change layers as needed.
- Once you have drawn the 2.75-diameter bolt circle, use it to locate one of the bolt holes. Any of the circles at a quadrant point (0 degrees, 90 degrees, 180 degrees, or 270 degrees) will do.
- Draw a center line across the bolt hole, and then ARRAY the hole and the center line 360 degrees. Be sure to rotate the objects as they are copied; otherwise, you will get strange results from your center lines.

Save This Drawing

This drawing is used in Chapter 6 to demonstrate AutoCAD drawing layouts, paper space, and the use of multiple viewports. It is important that you save the drawing so that you can use it to learn these important plotting techniques.

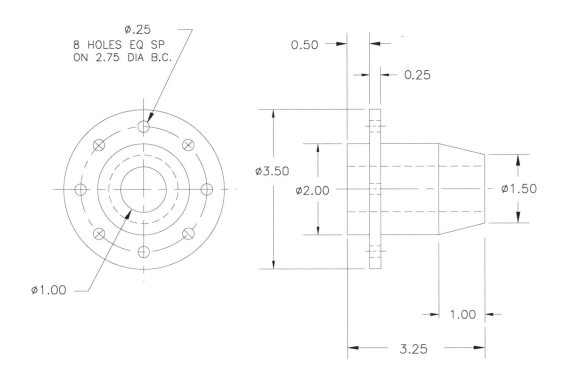

Ø.25
8 HOLES EQ SP
ON 2.75 DIA B.C.

Ø1.00

0.50

0.25

Ø3.50

Ø2.00

Ø1.50

1.00

3.25

FLANGED BUSHING

Drawing 5—1

5.10 Drawing 5-2: Guide

There are six arcs in this drawing, and although some of them could be drawn as fillets, we suggest that you use the ARC command for practice. By drawing arcs, you also avoid a common problem with fillets. Because fillets are designed to round intersections at corners, creating a fillet in the middle of a line erases part of that line unless you turn Trim mode off. This would affect the center line on the left side of the front view of this drawing, for example.

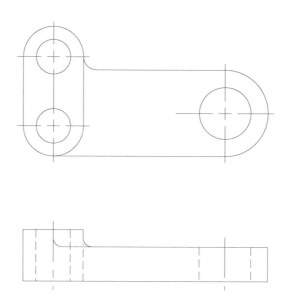

Drawing Suggestions

GRID = 0.25
SNAP = 0.125
LTSCALE = 0.50
LIMITS = (0,0)(12,9)

- The three large arcs in the top view all can be drawn easily using Start, Center, End.
- The smaller 0.375 arc in the top view could be drawn by filleting the top arc with the horizontal line to its right. However, we suggest you try an arc giving Start, Center, End or Start, Center, Angle. Note that you can easily locate the center by moving 0.375 to the right of the endpoint of the upper arc.
- The same method works to draw the 0.25 arc in the front view. Begin by dropping a line down 0.25 from the horizontal line. Start your arc at the end of this line and move 0.25 to the right to locate its center. Then the end is simply 0.25 down from the center (or you could specify an angle of 90 degrees).
- Similarly, the arc at the center line can be drawn from a start point 0.25 up from the horizontal. It has a radius of 0.25 and makes an angle of 90 degrees.

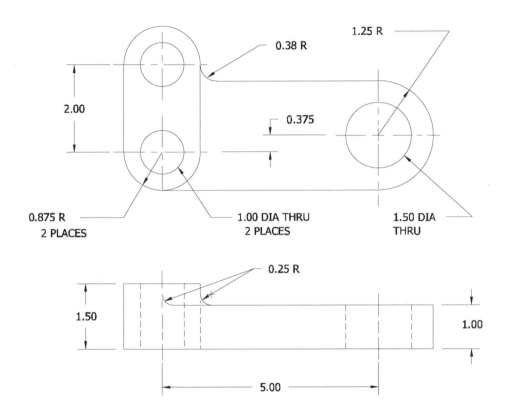

GUIDE
Drawing 5-2

5.11   Drawing 5-3: Dials

This is a relatively simple drawing that gives you some good practice with polar arrays and the ROTATE and COPY commands.

Notice that the needle drawn at the top of the next page is only for reference; the actual drawing includes only the plate and the three dials with their needles.

Drawing Suggestions

GRID = 0.25
SNAP = 0.125
LTSCALE = 0.50
LIMITS = (0,0)(18,12)

- After drawing the outer rectangle and screw holes, draw the leftmost dial, including the needle. Draw a 0.50 vertical line at the top and array it to the left (counterclockwise—a positive angle) and to the right (negative) to create the 11 larger lines on the dial. How many lines in each of these left and right arrays do you need to end up with 11?

- Draw a 0.25 line on top of the 0.50 line at the top of the dial. Then use right and left arrays with a Last selection to create the 40 small markings. How many lines are in each of these two arrays?

- Complete the first dial and then use a multiple copy to produce two more dials at the center and right of your screen. Be sure to use a window to select the entire dial.

- Finally, use the ROTATE command to rotate the needles as indicated on the new dials.

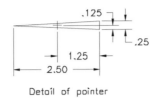

Detail of pointer

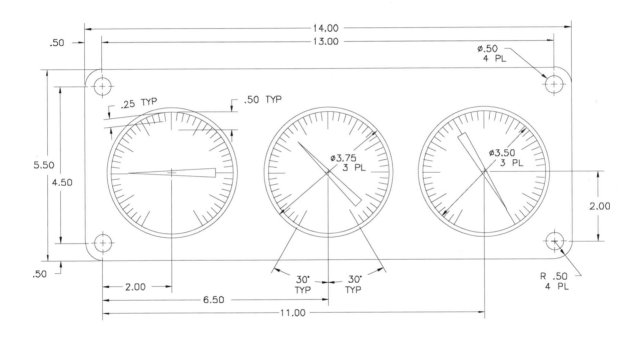

DIALS

Drawing 5–3

5.12   Drawing 5-4: Alignment Wheel

This drawing shows a typical use of the MIRROR command. Carefully mirroring sides of the symmetrical front view saves you from duplicating some of your drawing efforts. Notice that you need a small snap setting to draw the vertical lines at the chamfer.

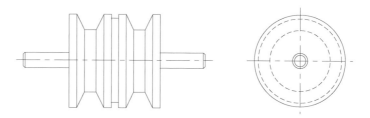

Drawing Suggestions

GRID = 0.25
SNAP = 0.0625
LTSCALE = 0.50
LIMITS = (0,0)(12,9)

- There are numerous ways to use MIRROR in drawing the front view. As the reference shows, there is top–bottom symmetry as well as left–right symmetry. The exercise for you is to choose an efficient mirroring sequence.
- Whatever sequence you use, consider the importance of creating the chamfer and the vertical line at the chamfer before this part of the object is mirrored.
- Once the front view is drawn, the right side view is easy. Remember to change layers for center and hidden lines and to line up the small inner circle with the chamfer.

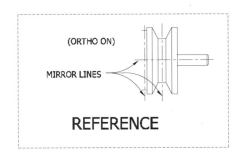

REFERENCE

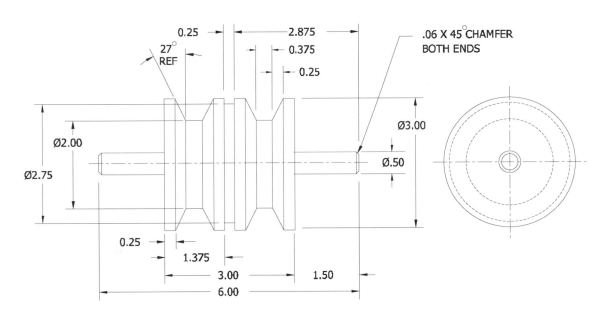

ALIGNMENT WHEEL

Drawing 5-4

5.13 Drawing 5-5: Hearth

Once you have completed this architectural drawing as it is shown, you might want to experiment with filling in a pattern of firebrick in the center of the hearth. The drawing itself is not complicated, but little errors become very noticeable when you try to make the row of 4 × 8 bricks across the bottom fit with the arc of bricks across the top, so work carefully.

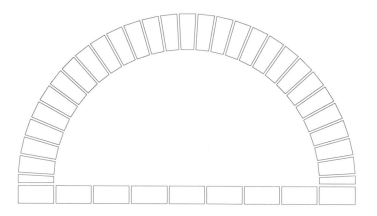

Drawing Suggestions

UNITS = Arcitectural
       Precision = 0′ − 01/8″
LIMITS = (0,0)(12′,9′)
GRID = 1′
SNAP = 1/8″

- Zoom in to draw the wedge-shaped brick indicated by the arrow on the right of the dimensioned drawing. Draw half of the brick only and mirror it across the center line as shown. (Notice that the center line is for reference only.) It is very important that you use MIRROR so that you can erase half of the brick later.
- Array the brick in a 29-item, 180-degree polar array.
- Erase the bottom halves of the end bricks at each end.
- Draw a new horizontal bottom line on each of the two end bricks.
- Draw a 4 × 8 brick directly below the half brick at the left end.
- Array the 4 × 8 brick in a one-row, nine-column array, with 8.5″ between columns.

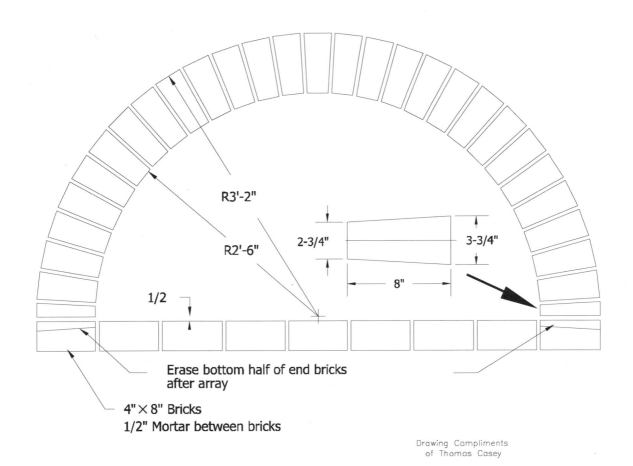

R3'-2"

R2'-6"

2-3/4"   3-3/4"

8"

1/2

Erase bottom half of end bricks
after array

4" × 8" Bricks
1/2" Mortar between bricks

Drawing Compliments
of Thomas Casey

HEARTH

Drawing 5-5

5.14   Drawing 5-6: Slotted Flange

This drawing includes a typical application of polar arrays and arcs. The finished drawing should consist of the 2-D top view and front view, not the 3-D view shown on the drawing page. The center lines and outline of the large circle in the top view are shown in the reference drawing. Use the three-dimensional view as a reference to draw the two-dimensional top and front views.

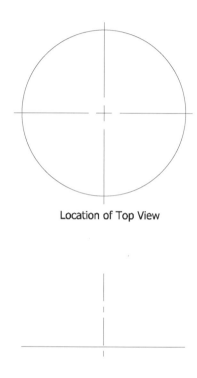

Location of Top View

Location of Front View

Drawing Suggestions

- Begin by drawing the circles in the top view. Use the circles to line up the vertical lines in the front view.
- The small arcs in the slots can be drawn on a center line and rotated and copied into place using grips.

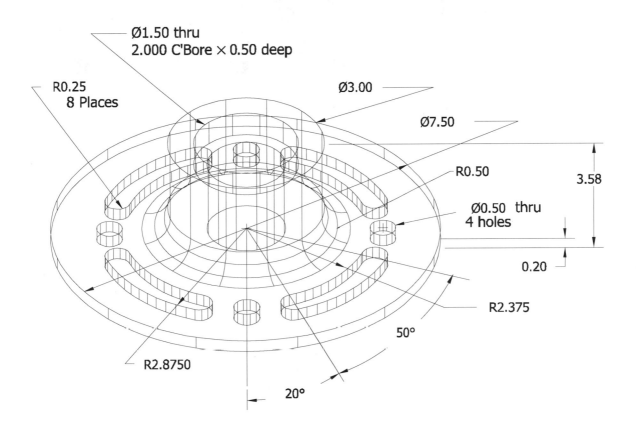

Ø1.50 thru
2.000 C'Bore × 0.50 deep

R0.25
8 Places

Ø3.00

Ø7.50

R0.50

Ø0.50 thru
4 holes

3.58

0.20

R2.375

50°

R2.8750

20°

SLOTTED FLANGE
Drawing 5-6

6 | Object Snap

COMMANDS

BREAK	OFFSET	STRETCH
EXTEND	OSNAP	TRIM
LENGTHEN		

OVERVIEW

This chapter completes the introduction to basic 2-D drafting and editing techniques and brings you to a very significant plateau in your developing AutoCAD technique. The techniques you have learned in Part I form the basis for everything you do in more complex two- and three-dimensional drawings.

In this chapter, you begin to use AutoCAD's very powerful Object Snap and Object Tracking features. These take you to a new level of accuracy and efficiency as a CAD operator. You also learn to BREAK entities on the screen into pieces so that they can be manipulated or erased separately, to shorten objects at intersections with other objects using the TRIM command, or to lengthen them with the EXTEND and LENGTHEN commands. Finally, you move into the world of paper space as you begin to use AutoCAD's layout and multiple viewport system.

TASKS

6.1 Selecting Points with Object Snap (Single-Point Override)

6.2 Selecting Points with OSNAP (Running Mode)

6.3 Object Snap Tracking

6.4 Using the OFFSET Command (Creating Parallel Objects with OFFSET)

6.5 BREAKing Previously Drawn Objects

6.6 Shortening Objects with the TRIM Command

6.7 Extending Objects with the EXTEND Command

6.8 Using STRETCH to Alter Objects Connected to Other Objects

6.9 Changing Lengths with the LENGTHEN Command

6.10 Creating Plot Layouts

6.11 Review Material

6.12 WWW Exercise 6 (Optional)

6.13 Drawing 6-1: Bike Tire

6.1   Selecting Points with Object Snap (Single-Point Override)

GENERAL PROCEDURE

1. Enter a drawing command, such as LINE, CIRCLE, or ARC.
2. Right-click while holding down the Ctrl key.
3. Select an object snap mode from the shortcut menu.
4. Point to a previously drawn object.

or

1. Enter a drawing command, such as LINE, CIRCLE, or ARC.
2. Select an object snap mode from the Object Snap toolbar.
3. Point to a previously drawn object.

Some of the drawings in the last two chapters have pushed the limits of what you can accomplish accurately on a CAD system with incremental snap alone. Object snap is a related tool that works in a very different manner. Instead of snapping to points defined by the coordinate system, it snaps to geometrically specifiable points on objects that you have already drawn. There are 13 varieties of object snap, and each can be used as a one-time option for selecting a point (single-point override) or turned on to affect all point selection (running object snap). In this task, we introduce the single-point method and then move on to the running mode in the next task.

Let's say you want to begin a new line at the endpoint of one that is already on the screen. If you are lucky, the endpoint might be on a snap point, but it is just as likely not to be. Turning snap off and moving the cursor to the apparent endpoint might appear to work, but when you zoom in you probably will find that you have missed the point. Using object snap is the only precise way, and it is as precise as you could want. Let's try it.

⊕   To prepare for this exercise, begin a new drawing using the 1B template.

⊕   Draw a 6 × 6 square with a circle inside, as in Figure 6-1.

To keep the circle centered, draw the square with the RECTANGLE command with corners at (6, 3) and (12, 9). Then the circle can be centered at (9, 6).

⊕   The Polar, Osnap, and Snap buttons should be off for the rest of this exercise. Dyn may be on or off.

⊕   Enter the LINE command (type L or select the Line tool).

We are going to draw a line from the lower left corner of the square to a point on a line tangent to the circle, as shown in Figure 6-2. This task would be extremely difficult without object snap. The corner is easy to locate, because you probably have drawn it on snap, but the tangent might not be.

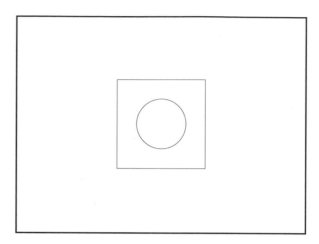

Figure 6-1

We use an endpoint object snap to locate the corner and a tangent object snap to locate the tangent point. When AutoCAD asks for a point, you can select an object snap mode from the object snap shortcut menu.

⊕   At the Specify first point: prompt, instead of specifying a point, hold down the Shift or Ctrl key and right-click.

This opens the shortcut menu illustrated in Figure 6-3.

⊕   Select Endpoint.

This tells AutoCAD that you are going to select the start point of the line by using an endpoint object snap rather than by direct pointing or by entering coordinates.

Now that AutoCAD knows that we want to begin at the endpoint of a previously drawn entity, it needs to know which one.

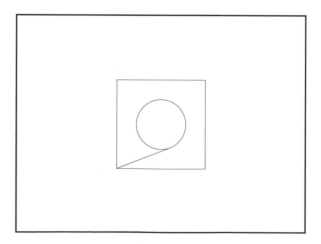

Figure 6-2

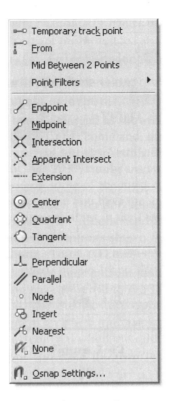

Figure 6-3

⊕ Move the cursor near the lower left corner of the square.

When you are close to the corner, AutoCAD recognizes the endpoint of the lines there and indicates this with an orange box surrounding the endpoint. This object snap symbol is called a marker. There are different-shaped markers for each type of object snap. If you let the cursor rest here for a moment, a label appears, naming the type of object that has been recognized, as shown in Figure 6-4. This label is called a *snap-tip*. Also notice that if the crosshairs are inside the marker, they lock onto the endpoint. This action can be turned on or off and is called the *magnet setting*. You do not have to be locked on to the endpoint, however. As long as the endpoint marker is showing, the endpoint is selected.

⊕ With the endpoint object snap marker showing, press the pick button.

The orange endpoint box and the snap-tip disappear, and there is a rubber band stretching from the lower left corner of the square to the cursor position. In the command area, you see the Specify next point: prompt.

We use a tangent object snap to select the second point.

⊕ At the Specify next point or [Undo]: prompt, open the shortcut menu by pressing Shift + right-click and then select Tangent.

⊕ Move the cursor to the right and position the crosshairs so that they are near the lower right side of the circle.

When you approach the tangent area, you see the yellow tangent marker, as shown in Figure 6-5. Here again, if you let the cursor rest you see a snap-tip.

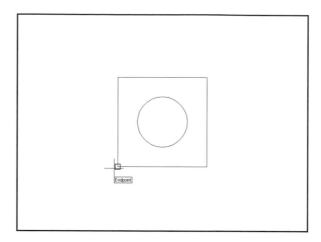

Figure 6-4

⊕ With the tangent marker showing, press the pick button.

AutoCAD locates the tangent point and draws the line. Notice the power of being able to precisely locate the tangent point in this way.

⊕ Press Enter to exit the LINE command.

Your screen should now resemble Figure 6-2.

We repeat the process now, but start from the midpoint of the bottom side of the square instead of its endpoint. Also, this time we use the Object Snap toolbar instead of the shortcut menu. Object snap is such an important feature that you might find yourself leaving this toolbar open frequently.

⊕ Move the cursor over any toolbar on your screen and right-click to open the toolbar shortcut menu.

⊕ Select Object snap.

This opens the Object Snap toolbar shown in Figure 6-6.

⊕ Move the toolbar anywhere out of the way, or dock it along one side.

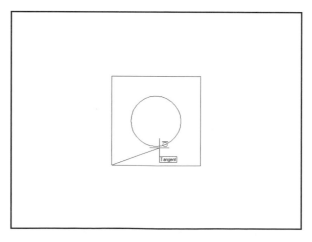

Figure 6-5

Figure 6-6

⊕ Enter the LINE command.

⊕ At the prompt for a point, select the Snap to Midpoint tool from the toolbar.

All of the Osnap modes have fairly obvious icons. Snap to Midpoint is the second tool in the second panel.

⊕ Position the aperture anywhere along the bottom side of the square so that an orange triangle, the snap to midpoint marker, appears at the midpoint of the line.

⊕ Press the pick button.

⊕ At the prompt for a second point, select the Snap to Tangent tool from the toolbar.

Snap to Tangent is the last tool on the right in the third panel.

⊕ Position the aperture along the right side of the circle so that the tangent symbol appears and then press the pick button.

⊕ Press Enter or the spacebar to exit the LINE command.

At this point your screen should resemble Figure 6-7.

That's all there is to it. Remember these steps: (1) Enter a command; (2) when AutoCAD asks for a point, specify an object snap mode; (3) position the crosshairs near an object to which the mode can be applied and let AutoCAD find the point.

Note: Both the shortcut menu and the toolbar are efficient methods of specifying a single-point object snap. However, you can also type the name of any object snap method when AutoCAD asks for a point. All modes have aliases that are the first three letters of the mode: end for endpoint, tan for tangent, and so on.

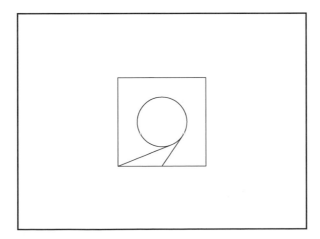

Figure 6-7

6.2 Selecting Points with OSNAP (Running Mode)

GENERAL PROCEDURE

1. Select object snap modes from the Drafting Settings dialog box.
2. Click the Osnap button on the status bar so that it is on.
3. Enter drawing commands.
4. If there is more than one object snap choice in the area, cycle through using the Tab key.

So far we have been using object snap one point at a time. Because object snap is not constantly in use for most applications, this single-point method is common. Often, however, you will find that you are going to be using one or a number of object snap types repeatedly and do not need to select many points without them. In this case, you can keep object snap modes on so that they affect all point selection. This is called *running object snap*. We use this method to complete the drawing shown in Figure 6-8. Notice how each line is drawn from a midpoint or corner to a tangent point on the circle. This is easily done with running object snaps.

⊕ Click the Osnap button on the status bar so that it is on.

When the Osnap button is on, you are in running object snap mode. The modes that are in effect depend on the AutoCAD default settings, or whatever settings were last selected. To change settings or see what settings are on, we open the Drafting Settings dialog box. You used this dialog box in Chapter 2.

⊕ Right-click on the status bar Osnap button.

This opens a small shortcut menu with three options: On, Off, and Settings. On and off are redundant because you can turn Osnap on and off more easily by left-clicking as usual. However, Settings is very useful.

⊕ Select Settings.

⊕ This opens the Drafting Settings dialog box with the Object Snap tab on top, as shown in Figure 6-9.

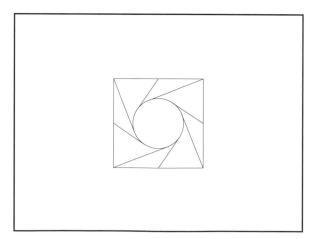

Figure 6-8

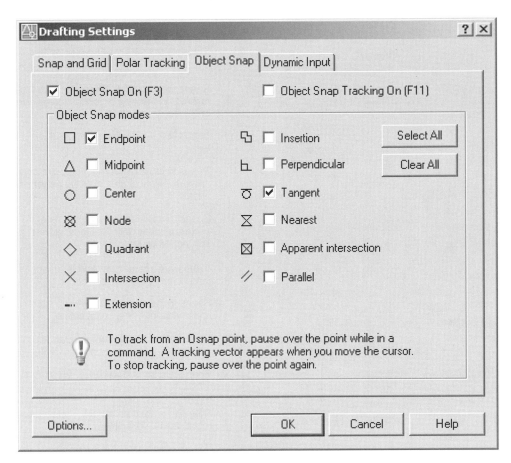

Figure 6-9

You can find a description of all of the object snap modes on the chart in Figure 6-10, but for now we use three: Midpoint, Intersection, and Tangent. Midpoint and Tangent you already know. Intersection snaps to the point where two entities meet or cross. We use an intersect instead of an endpoint to select the remaining three corners of the square, even though an endpoint could be used instead.

⊕ Select the Clear All button.

This will clear any previous object snap selections that may have been made on your system.

⊕ Select Midpoint, Intersection, and Tangent.

When you are finished, your dialog box should resemble Figure 6-9. Notice that Object Snap On (F3) is checked at the top of the box, and Object Snap Tracking On (F11) is not checked. We save Object Snap Tracking for Task 6.3.

⊕ Click OK.

⊕ Enter the LINE command.

⊕ Position the aperture so that the lower right corner is within the box.

An orange X, the intersection marker, appears.

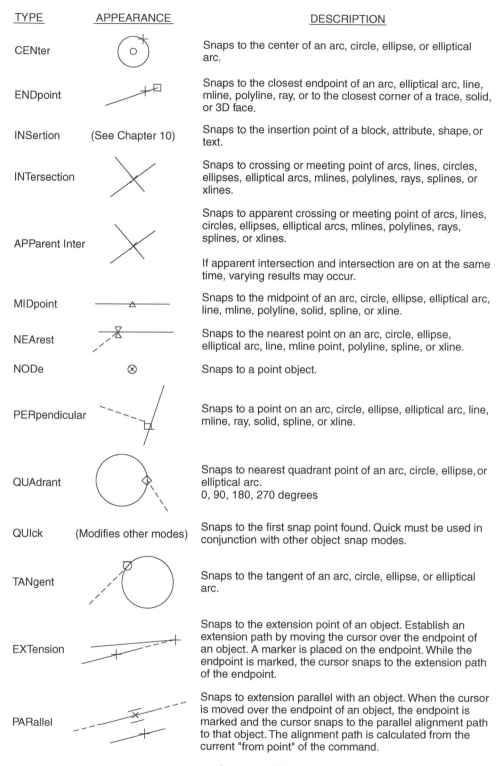

TYPE	APPEARANCE	DESCRIPTION
CENter		Snaps to the center of an arc, circle, ellipse, or elliptical arc.
ENDpoint		Snaps to the closest endpoint of an arc, elliptical arc, line, mline, polyline, ray, or to the closest corner of a trace, solid, or 3D face.
INSertion	(See Chapter 10)	Snaps to the insertion point of a block, attribute, shape, or text.
INTersection		Snaps to crossing or meeting point of arcs, lines, circles, ellipses, elliptical arcs, mlines, polylines, rays, splines, or xlines.
APParent Inter		Snaps to apparent crossing or meeting point of arcs, lines, circles, ellipses, elliptical arcs, mlines, polylines, rays, splines, or xlines. If apparent intersection and intersection are on at the same time, varying results may occur.
MIDpoint		Snaps to the midpoint of an arc, circle, ellipse, elliptical arc, line, mline, polyline, solid, spline, or xline.
NEArest		Snaps to the nearest point on an arc, circle, ellipse, elliptical arc, line, mline point, polyline, spline, or xline.
NODe		Snaps to a point object.
PERpendicular		Snaps to a point on an arc, circle, ellipse, elliptical arc, line, mline, ray, solid, spline, or xline.
QUAdrant		Snaps to nearest quadrant point of an arc, circle, ellipse, or elliptical arc. 0, 90, 180, 270 degrees
QUIck	(Modifies other modes)	Snaps to the first snap point found. Quick must be used in conjunction with other object snap modes.
TANgent		Snaps to the tangent of an arc, circle, ellipse, or elliptical arc.
EXTension		Snaps to the extension point of an object. Establish an extension path by moving the cursor over the endpoint of an object. A marker is placed on the endpoint. While the endpoint is marked, the cursor snaps to the extension path of the endpoint.
PARallel		Snaps to extension parallel with an object. When the cursor is moved over the endpoint of an object, the endpoint is marked and the cursor snaps to the parallel alignment path to that object. The alignment path is calculated from the current "from point" of the command.

Figure 6-10

⊕   With the intersection marker showing, press the pick button.

AutoCAD selects the intersection of the bottom and the right sides and gives you the rubber band and the prompt for the next point.

⊕   Move the crosshairs up and along the right side of the circle until the tangent marker appears.

⊕   With the tangent marker showing, press the pick button.

AutoCAD constructs a new tangent from the lower right corner to the circle.

⊕   Press the spacebar to complete the LINE command sequence.

⊕   Press the spacebar again to repeat LINE so you can begin with a new start point.

We continue to move counterclockwise around the circle. This should begin to be easy now.

⊕   Position the aperture along the right side of the square so that the midpoint triangle marker appears.

⊕   With the midpoint marker showing, press the pick button.

AutoCAD snaps to the midpoint of the side.

⊕   Move up along the upper right side of the circle so that the tangent marker appears.

⊕   With the tangent marker showing, press the pick button.

⊕   Press the spacebar to exit LINE.

⊕   Press the spacebar again to repeat LINE and continue around the circle drawing tangents like this: upper right corner to top of circle, top side midpoint to top left of circle, upper left corner to left side, and left side midpoint to lower left side.

Remember that running Osnap modes should give you both speed and accuracy, so push yourself a little to see how quickly you can complete the figure.

Your screen should now resemble Figure 6-8. Before going on, you should study the object snap chart, Figure 6-10. Before you can effectively analyze situations and look for opportunities to use object snap and object snap tracking, you need to have a good acquaintance with all of the object snap modes.

Tip: Occasionally, you might encounter a situation where there are several possible object snap points in a tight area. If AutoCAD does not recognize the one you want, you can cycle through all the choices by pressing the Tab key repeatedly.

6.3   Object Snap Tracking

GENERAL PROCEDURE

1. Select Object Snap modes from the Drafting Settings dialog box.
2. Click the Otrack button on the status bar so that it is on.
3. Enter drawing commands.
4. To acquire a point for tracking, position the cursor so that the Osnap marker appears, but do not click.
5. Use the temporary construction lines that AutoCAD draws from this acquired point.

Object snap tracking creates temporary construction lines from designated object snap points. Once you are in a Draw command, such as LINE, any object snap point that can be identified in an active object snap mode can be acquired. An acquired point is highlighted with a yellow cross. Once a point is acquired, object snap tracking automatically throws out temporary construction lines from this point. Construction lines are dotted lines like those used by polar tracking. They extend to the edge of the display and are drawn along the horizontal and vertical from the acquired point, or along polar tracking angles. Try the following:

⊕ To begin this task, the Osnap button should be on with the Endpoint mode in effect; all other modes from the last exercise should be turned off.

Remember the following steps:

1. Right-click the Osnap button.
2. Select Settings.
3. Click Clear All in the dialog box.
4. Check Endpoint.
5. Click OK.

⊕ Click the Dyn button to turn dynamic input off.

This is technically not necessary, but you will be able to see other things happening on your screen more easily without the dynamic input display.

⊕ Click the Otrack button on the status bar so that it is in the on position.

⊕ Enter the LINE command.

⊕ Select a first point to the left of the square and circle, as shown by Point 1 in Figure 6-11.

Point Acquisition

To take the next step, you need to learn a new technique called *point acquisition.* Before a point can be used for object snap tracking, it must be acquired, which is a form of selection. To acquire a point, move the cursor over it so that the object

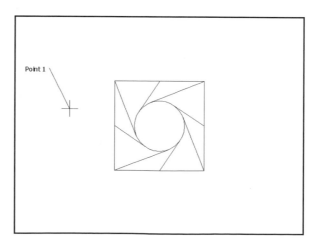

Figure 6-11

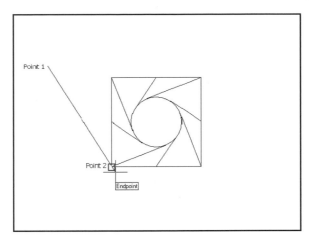

Figure 6-12

snap marker shows and pause for about a second without clicking. Try it with the following steps:

⊕ Move the cursor over the lower left corner of the square, Point 2 in Figure 6-12, so that the endpoint marker appears.

⊕ Pause.

⊕ Now move the cursor away from the corner.

   If you have done this correctly, a small orange cross appears at the corner intersection, as shown in Figure 6-13, indicating that this point has been acquired for object snap tracking. (Repeating this procedure over the same point removes the cross.)

⊕ Move the cursor to a position left of Point 2 and even with the horizontal lower side of the square, as shown in Figure 6-14.

   You see a construction line and a tracking tip like those shown in Figure 6-14.

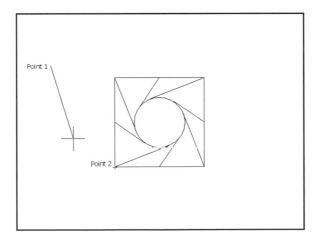

Figure 6-13

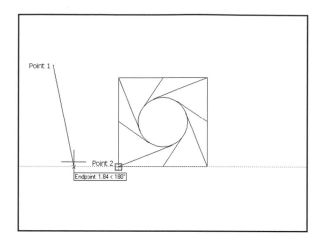

Figure 6-14

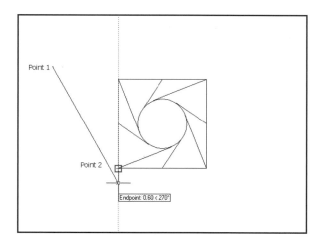

Figure 6-15

⊕   Move the cursor over and down to a position even with and below the vertical left side of the square, as shown in Figure 6-15.

You see a different construction line and tracking tip, like those shown in Figure 6-15.

These construction lines are interesting, but they do not accomplish a great deal because your square is probably constructed on grid snap points anyway. Let's try something more difficult and a lot more interesting. Here we use two acquired points to locate a point that currently is not specifiable either in object snap or incremental snap.

⊕   Move the cursor up and acquire Point 3, as shown in Figure 6-16.

Point 3 is the endpoint of the line drawn from the midpoint of the top side of the square to a point tangent to the circle. You should now have two acquired points, with two orange crosses showing, one at Point 2 and one at Point 3.

⊕   Move the cursor slowly along the left side of the square.

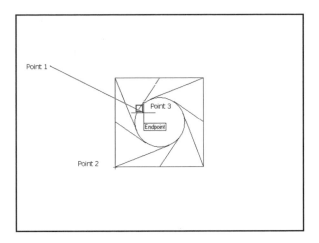

Figure 6-16

You are looking for Point 4, the point where the vertical tracking line from Point 2 intersects the horizontal tracking line from Point 3. When you near it, your screen should resemble Figure 6-17. Notice the double tracking tip Endpoint: <90, Endpoint: <180.

⊕ With the double tracking tip and the two tracking lines showing, press the pick button.

A line is drawn from Point 1 to Point 4.

⊕ Press Enter or the spacebar to exit the LINE command.

Before going on, we need to turn off the running Osnap to Endpoint mode.

⊕ Click the Osnap button or press F3 to turn off running Osnap modes.

If you have followed this exercise closely, you have already greatly increased the power of your understanding of CAD technique. You will find many opportunities to use object snap and object snap tracking from now on.

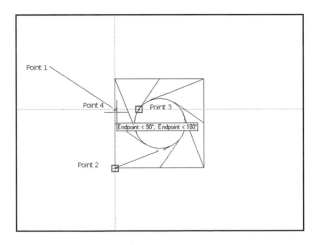

Figure 6-17

Next we move on to a very powerful editing command called OFFSET. Before leaving object snap, be sure that you have studied the chart in Figure 6-10, which shows examples of all the object snap modes.

6.4   Using the OFFSET Command (Creating Parallel Objects with OFFSET)

GENERAL PROCEDURE

1.   Select the Offset tool from the Modify toolbar.
2.   Type or show an offset distance.
3.   Select object to offset.
4.   Show which side to offset.

OFFSET is one of the most powerful editing commands in AutoCAD. With the combination of object snap and the OFFSET command, you can become completely free of incremental snap and grid points. Any point in the drawing space can be precisely located. Essentially, OFFSET creates parallel copies of lines, circles, arcs, or polylines. You can find a number of typical applications in the drawings at the end of this chapter. In this brief exercise, we perform an offset operation to draw some lines through points that would be very difficult to locate without OFFSET.

⊕   Select Offset from the Modify menu, or the Offset tool from the Modify toolbar, as shown in Figure 6-18.

AutoCAD prompts

```
Specify offset distance or [Through]<Through>
```

There are three methods. You can type a distance, show a distance with two points, or pick a point that you want the new copy to run through (the through option). We type a distance.

⊕   Type .257.

We have chosen this rather odd number to make the point that this command can help you locate positions that would be difficult to find otherwise. AutoCAD prompts for an object:

```
Select object to offset or <exit>:
```

⊕   Select the diagonal line drawn in the last exercise.

AutoCAD now needs to know whether to create the offset image above or below the line:

```
Specify point on side to offset:
```

Figure 6-18

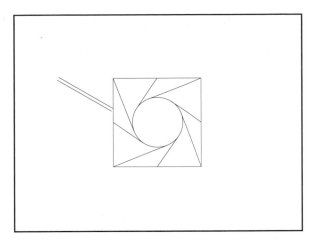

Figure 6-19

⊕   Pick a point anywhere below the line.

   Your screen should now resemble Figure 6-19. AutoCAD continues to prompt for objects to offset using the same offset distance. You can continue to create offset objects at the same offset distance by pointing and clicking.

⊕   Pick the line just created.

⊕   Pick any point below the line.

   A second offset line is added, as shown in Figure 6-20. As long as you stay within the OFFSET command, you can select any object to offset using the same offset distance.

⊕   Pick the circle in the square.

⊕   Pick any point inside the circle.

   An offset circle is added, as shown in Figure 6-20.

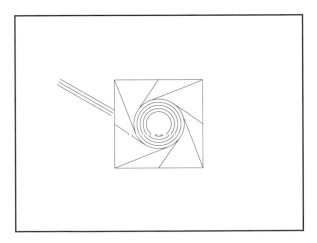

Figure 6-20

⊕ Continue pointing and clicking to create additional offset circles, as shown in Figure 6-20.

⊕ Press Enter to exit the OFFSET command.

When you exit OFFSET, the offset distance is retained as the default, so you can return to the command and continue using the same distance.

Next we turn to five useful commands that allow you to shorten and lengthen objects.

6.5 BREAKing Previously Drawn Objects

GENERAL PROCEDURE

1. Type Br, select Break from the Modify menu, or select the Break tool from the Modify toolbar.
2. Select an object to be broken.
3. Show the first point of the break.
4. Show the second point of the break.

The BREAK command allows you to break an object on the screen into two entities, or to cut a segment out of the middle or off the end. The command sequence is similar for all options. The action taken depends on the points you select for breaking. BREAK works on lines, circles, arcs, and polylines. (Polylines are discussed in Chapter 9.)

⊕ In preparation for this section, clear your screen of objects left from previous tasks and draw a 10.00 horizontal line across the middle of your screen, as in Figure 6-21.

Exact lengths and coordinates are not important. Also, be sure to turn off object snap.

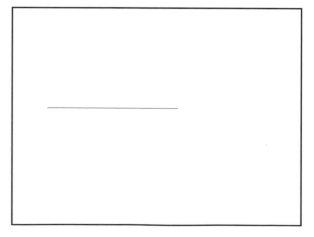

Figure 6-21

Figure 6-22

AutoCAD allows for four different ways to break an object, depending on whether the point you use to select the object is also to be considered a break point. You can break an object at one point or at two points, and you have the choice of using your object selection point as a break point.

We begin by breaking the line you have just drawn into two independent lines using a single break point, which is also the point used to select the line.

⊕   Select the Break at Point tool from the Modify toolbar, as shown in Figure 6-22.

Notice that there is a Break tool that is not the same as the Break at Point tool. Also, be aware that the noun/verb or pick first sequence does not work with BREAK.

AutoCAD prompts you to select an object to break:

Select object:

You can select an object in any of the usual ways, but notice that you can only break one object at a time. If you try to select more—with a window, for example—AutoCAD highlights only one. Because of this, it is best to indicate the object you want to break by pointing to it.

Tip: Object snap modes work well in edit commands such as BREAK. If you wish to break a line at its midpoint, for example, you can use the Midpoint object snap mode to select the line and the break point.

⊕   Select the line by picking any point near its middle. (The exact point is not critical for this exercise; if it were, we might use a midpoint object snap.)

The line has now been selected for breaking, and because there can be only one object, you do not have to press Enter to end the selection process, as you often do in other editing commands. AutoCAD prompts as follows:

Specify second break point or [First point]:_f

When you are using the Break at Point tool, AutoCAD does not take the point you use for selection as the first point of the break. In the command area, notice that the "_f" for the first point option is entered automatically. This means that now you have the opportunity to select the same point or a different point as the point at which to break this line.

⊕   Point to the same point that you just used to select the line, or type @.

The @ symbol is shorthand for the last point entered. In this sequence, AutoCAD automatically enters @ for the second break point. This means that there is only one break point. The line will be broken, but nothing will be erased.

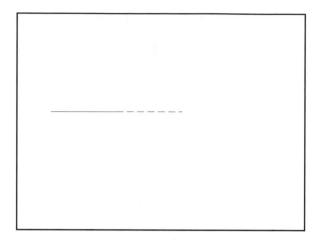

Figure 6-23

The break is complete. To demonstrate that the line is really two lines now, we select the right half of it for our next break.

⊕ Press Enter or the spacebar to repeat the BREAK command, or select the Break tool from the Modify toolbar.

The Break tool is just below the Break at Point tool on the toolbar, or next to it if your toolbar is horizontal.

⊕ Point to the line on the right side of the last break.

The right side of the line should be highlighted, as in Figure 6-23. Clearly, the original line is now being treated as two separate entities.

We shorten the end of this dotted section of the line. Assume that the point you just used to select the object is the point where you want it to end; now all you need to do is to select a second point anywhere beyond the right end of the line.

⊕ Select a second point beyond the right end of the line.

Your line should now be shortened, as in Figure 6-24.

Next we cut a piece out of the middle of the left side.

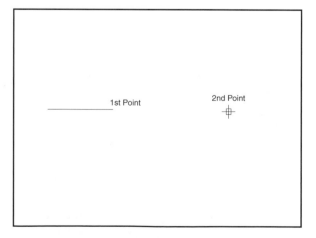

Figure 6-24

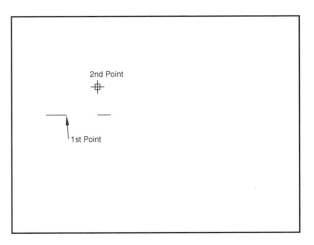

Figure 6-25

⊕   Press Enter or the spacebar to repeat BREAK.

⊕   Select the left side of the original line with a point toward the left end.

    We want to cut a piece out of the middle of the left side, so the next point needs to be to the right of the first point, but still toward the middle of the left-hand line.

Note: It is not necessary that the second point be on the line at all. It could be above or below it, as in Figure 6-25. AutoCAD breaks the line along a perpendicular between the point we choose and the line we are breaking. The same system would apply if we were breaking a polyline. An arc or a circle would be broken along a line between the selected point and the center of the arc or circle.

⊕   Select a second point on or off the line, somewhat to the right of the first point.

    Your line should now have a piece cut out, as in Figure 6-25. Notice that there are now three lines on the screen, one to the left and two shorter lines to the right of the last break.

    BREAK is a useful command, but there are times when it is cumbersome to shorten objects one at a time. The TRIM command has some limitations that BREAK does not have, but it is much more efficient in situations in which you want to shorten objects at intersections.

6.6   Shortening Objects with the TRIM Command

GENERAL PROCEDURE
1.   Type Tr or select Trim from the Modify menu or the Trim tool from the Modify toolbar.
2.   Select a cutting edge or edges.
3.   Right-click to end the cutting-edge selection process.
4.   Select an object to trim.
5.   Select other objects to trim.
6.   Press Enter to return to the command prompt.

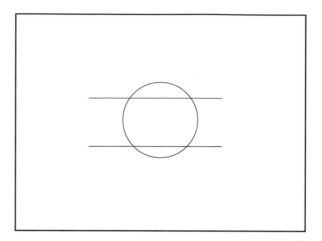

Figure 6-26

The TRIM command works wonders in many situations where you want to shorten objects at their intersections with other objects. It works with lines, circles, arcs, and polylines (see Chapter 9). The only limitations are that you must have at least two objects and they must cross or meet. If you are not trimming to an intersection, use BREAK.

⊕ In preparation for exploring TRIM, clear your screen and then draw two horizontal lines crossing a circle, as in Figure 6-26. Exact locations and sizes are not important.

First, we use the TRIM command to go from Figure 6-26 to Figure 6-27.

⊕ Type Tr or select Trim from the Modify menu or the Trim tool from the Modify toolbar, as shown in Figure 6-28.

The first thing AutoCAD wants you to specify is at least one cutting edge. A cutting edge is an entity you want to use to trim another entity. That is, you want the trimmed entity to end at its intersection with the cutting edge.

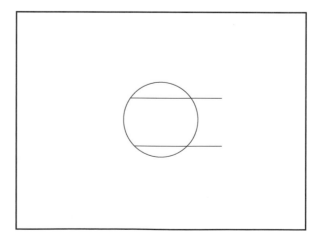

Figure 6-27

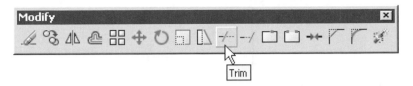

Figure 6-28

```
Current settings: Projection = UCS, Edge = None
Select cutting edges...
Select objects or <Select All>:
```

The current settings are relevant to 3-D drawing and need not concern you at this point. (For your information, Projection and Edge refer to system variables that determine the way AutoCAD interprets boundaries and intersections in 3-D space.) The second line reminds you that you are selecting edges first—the objects you want to trim are selected later. The third line prompts you to select objects to use as cutting edges, or press Enter for the Select All option. The option of selecting all objects is a useful one, as we demonstrate shortly.

For now, select the circle as an edge and use it to trim the upper line.

⊕ **Point to the circle.**

The circle becomes dotted and remains so until you leave the TRIM command. AutoCAD prompts for more objects until you indicate that you are finished selecting edges.

⊕ **Right-click to end the selection of cutting edges.**

You are prompted for an object to trim:

```
Select object to trim or shift-select to extend or
[Fence/Crossing/Project/Edge/eRase/Undo]:
```

This prompt allows you to shift over to the EXTEND command by holding down the Shift key. Then select an object, specify fence or crossing selections, or shift into a mode where objects are erased before you proceed to select objects to trim. We follow a simple procedure to trim off the segment of the upper line that lies outside the circle on the left. The important thing is to point to the part of the object you want to remove, as shown in Figure 6-27.

⊕ **Point to the upper line to the left of where it crosses the circle.**

The line is trimmed immediately, but the circle is still dotted, and AutoCAD continues to prompt for more objects to trim. Note how this differs from the BREAK command, with which you could only break one object at a time.

Also notice that you have an undo option, so that if the trim does not turn out the way you wanted, you can back up without having to leave the command and start over.

⊕ **Point to the lower line to the left of where it crosses the circle.**

Now you have trimmed both lines.

⊕ **Press Enter or the spacebar to end the TRIM operation.**

Your screen should resemble Figure 6-27.

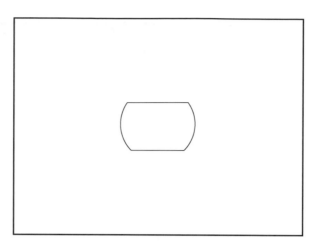

Figure 6-29

More complex trimming is also easy. The key is that you can select all visible objects or as many edges as you like. An entity can be selected as both an edge and an object to trim, as we demonstrate.

⊕ Repeat the TRIM command.

⊕ Press Enter to select all objects.

In this case, AutoCAD will not highlight all objects, but will proceed as if all objects had been selected. There is no need to complete object selection because everything is already selected.

⊕ Point to each of the remaining two-line segments that lie outside the circle on the right and to the top and bottom arcs of the circle to produce the bandage-shaped object in Figure 6-29.

⊕ Press Enter to exit the TRIM command.

6.7   Extending Objects with the EXTEND Command

GENERAL PROCEDURE

1. Type Ex or select Extend from the Modify menu or the Extend tool from the Modify toolbar.
2. Select a boundary or boundaries.
3. Press Enter to end the boundary selection process.
4. Select the object to extend.
5. Select other objects to extend.
6. Press Enter to return to the command prompt.

If you compare the procedures of the EXTEND command and the TRIM command, you notice a remarkable similarity. Just substitute the word "boundary" for "cutting edge" and the word "extend" for "trim" and you've got it. These two commands are conceptually related and are so efficient that it is sometimes good practice to draw a temporary cutting edge or boundary on your screen and erase it after trimming or extending.

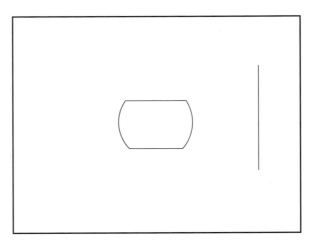

Figure 6-30

⊕   Leave Figure 6-29, the bandage, on your screen and draw a vertical line to the right of it, as in Figure 6-30.

We use this line as a boundary to which to extend the two horizontal lines, as in Figure 6-31.

⊕   Type Ex or select Extend from the Modify menu or the Extend tool from the Modify toolbar, as shown in Figure 6-32.

You are prompted for objects to serve as boundaries:

```
Current settings: Projection=UCS, Edge=None
Select boundary edges...
Select objects or <Select All>:
```

Look familiar? As with the TRIM command, any of the usual selection methods work and there is an option for selecting all objects. For our purposes, simply point to the vertical line.

⊕   Point to the vertical line on the right.

You are prompted for more boundary objects until you exit object selection.

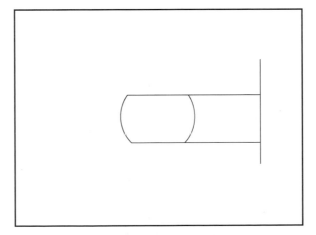

Figure 6-31

Figure 6-32

⊕ Right-click or press the spacebar to end the selection of boundaries.

AutoCAD now asks for objects to extend:

    Select object to extend or shift-select to trim
    or [Fence/Crossing/Project/Edge/eRase/Undo]:

⊕ Point to the right half of one of the two horizontal lines.

You have to point to the line on the side closer to the selected boundary. Otherwise, AutoCAD looks to the left instead of the right and gives you the following message:

    Object does not intersect an Edge

Also, you can select objects to extend only by pointing. Windowing, crossing, or last selections do not work. Arcs and polylines can be extended in the same manner as lines.

⊕ Point to the right half of the other horizontal line. Both lines should be extended to the vertical line.

Your screen should resemble Figure 6-31.

⊕ Press the spacebar to exit the EXTEND command.

6.8 Using STRETCH to Alter Objects Connected to Other Objects

---

GENERAL PROCEDURE

1. Type S or select the Stretch tool from the Modify toolbar or select Stretch from the Modify menu.
2. Select objects to stretch, using at least one window or crossing selection.
3. Press Enter to end selection.
4. Show the first point of stretch displacement.
5. Show the second point of stretch displacement.

The STRETCH command is a phenomenal timesaver in special circumstances in which you want to move objects without disrupting their connections to other objects. Often STRETCH can take the place of a whole series of moves, trims, breaks, and extends. It is commonly used in such applications as moving doors or windows within walls without having to redraw the walls.

The term *stretch* must be understood to have a special meaning in AutoCAD. When a typical stretch is performed, some objects are lengthened, others are shortened, and others are simply moved.

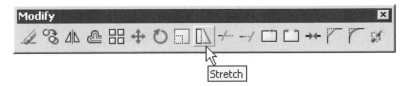

Figure 6-33

There is also a Stretch mode in the grip edit system, as we have seen previously. We take a look at it later in this section.

First, we do a simple stretch on the objects you have already drawn on your screen. This gives you a good basic understanding of the STRETCH command. Further experimentation on your own is recommended.

⊕ Type S, select Stretch from the Modify menu, or select the Stretch tool from the Modify toolbar, illustrated in Figure 6-33.

AutoCAD prompts for objects to stretch in the following manner:

```
Select objects to stretch by crossing-window
or crossing-polygon...
```

This prompt reminds you of a unique quality of the STRETCH command procedure. You must include at least one crossing-window or crossing-polygon selection in your selection set. Beyond that you can also include other selection types. This ensures that you include all the objects in an intersection in the stretch procedure. If this is not your intent, you probably should be using a different modifying command.

⊕ Point to the first corner of a crossing box, as shown by Point 1 (P1) in Figure 6-34.

AutoCAD prompts for a second corner:

```
Specify opposite corner:
```

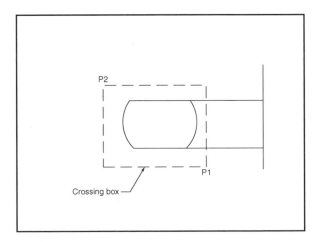

Figure 6-34

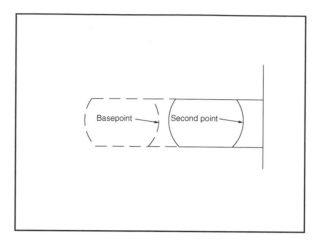

Figure 6-35

✦ Point to a second corner, as shown by Point 2 (P2) in Figure 6-34.

AutoCAD continues to prompt for objects, so we need to show that we are through selecting.

✦ Right-click or press the spacebar to end the selection process.

Now you need to show the degree and direction of stretch you want. In effect, you show AutoCAD how far to move the objects that are completely within the box. Objects that cross the box are extended or shrunk so that they remain connected to the objects that move.

The prompt sequence for this action is the same as the sequence for a move:

```
Specify base point or [Displacement] <Displacement>:
```

✦ Pick any point near the middle of the screen, leaving room to indicate a horizontal displacement to the right, as illustrated in Figure 6-35.

AutoCAD prompts:

```
Specify second point of displacement <or use first point as
                      displacement>:
```

✦ Pick a second point to the right of the first, as shown in Figure 6-35.

Having Ortho on ensures a horizontal move (press F8).

The arcs are moved to the right and the horizontal lines are shrunk as shown. Notice that nothing here is literally being stretched. The arcs are being moved and the lines are being compressed. This is one of the ways STRETCH can be used.

✦ Try performing another stretch like the one illustrated in Figures 6-36 and 6-37.

Here the lines are being lengthened, while one arc moves and the other stays put, so that the original bandage is indeed stretched.

Stretching with Grips

Stretching with grips is a simple operation best reserved for simple stretches. Stretches like the ones you have just performed with the STRETCH command are

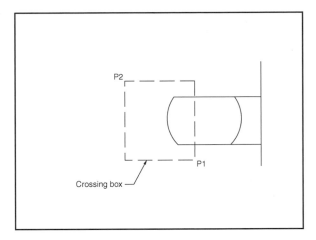

Figure 6-36

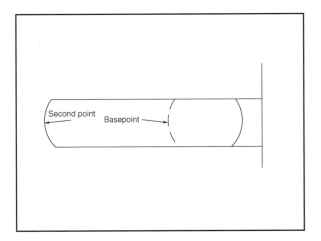

Figure 6-37

possible in grip editing, but they require careful selection of multiple grips. The results are not always what you expect, and it takes more time to complete the process. The type of stretch that works best with grips is illustrated in the following exercise:

⊕   Pick the lower horizontal line.

The line is highlighted and grips appear.

⊕   Pick the vertical line.

Now both lines should appear with grips, as in Figure 6-38. We use one grip on the horizontal line and one on the vertical line to create Figure 6-39.

⊕   Pick the grip at the right end of the horizontal line.

As soon as you press the pick button, the autoedit system puts you into STRETCH mode and the grip changes color.

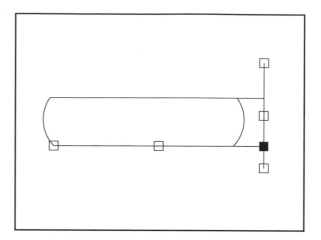

Figure 6-38

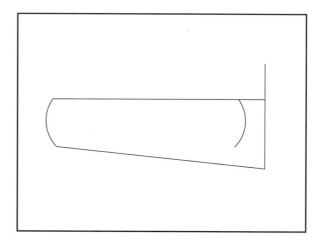

Figure 6-39

In the command area, you see the following:

STRETCH

Specify stretch point or [Base point/Copy/Undo/eXit]:

We stretch the line to end at the lower endpoint of the vertical line.

⊕ Move the crosshairs slowly downward and observe the screen.

If Ortho is off, you see two rubber bands. One represents the line you are stretching, and the other connects the crosshairs to the grip you are manipulating.

⊕ Pick the grip at the bottom of the vertical line.

Your screen should resemble Figure 6-39. Notice how the grip on the vertical line works like an object snap point.

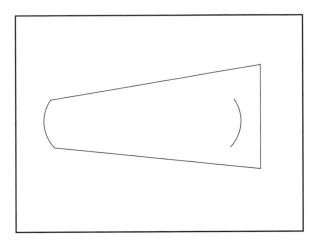

Figure 6-40

⊕   Try one more grip stretch to create Figure 6-40. Stretch the endpoint of the upper line just as you did the lower.

In the next task, you learn the LENGTHEN command—one more edit command for changing the lengths of lines and arcs.

6.9 Changing Lengths with the LENGTHEN Command

> **GENERAL PROCEDURE**
>
> 1. Select Lengthen from the Modify menu.
> 2. Type initials to specify a length option.
> 3. If necessary, type a value.
> 4. Select an object to lengthen.
> 5. Select another object or press Enter to exit the command.

The LENGTHEN command can be used to lengthen or shorten lines, polylines, and arcs using four different methods. In this exercise, we use two methods to further manipulate the objects in Figure 6-40. We begin by lengthening and then shortening the vertical line at the right of the figure.

⊕   Type len or select Lengthen from the Modify menu.

The prompt that follows shows the different lengthening methods:

    Select an object or [DElta/Percent/Total/DYnamic]:

DElta lengthens an object by a specified amount and Percent lengthens it by a percentage of the current length. Total changes the current length to a specified value, and DYnamic allows you to change length by cursor movement.

If you select an object at this prompt, its current length is reported in the command area. We work with DElta and DYnamic.

⊕ Type de for the Delta option or right-click and select Delta from the shortcut menu.

AutoCAD prompts:

```
Enter Delta length or [Angle]<0.00>:
```

Angle allows you to lengthen an arc by a specified angle. To change a linear length, type in a value. A positive value causes objects to be lengthened, and a negative value causes shortening.

⊕ Type 1.

AutoCAD prompts you to select an object:

```
Select an object to change or [Undo]:
```

⊕ Pick a selection point on the upper half of the vertical line.

The object is lengthened by one unit upward, as shown in Figure 6-41. AutoCAD continues to prompt for objects. You can select any line, arc, or polyline. Also, you can pick the same line again to add another one-unit length. Try it.

⊕ Pick another point on the upper half of the vertical line.

The object is lengthened again.

Now try lengthening the arc in the middle of the figure.

⊕ Pick a point on the upper half of the arc.

The arc is lengthened by one unit along a circular path, as shown in Figure 6-42. Now try the Dynamic option.

⊕ Press Enter or the spacebar to exit LENGTHEN.

⊕ Press Enter or the spacebar again to repeat the command.

⊕ Type dy for the Dynamic option or right-click and select Dynamic from the shortcut menu.

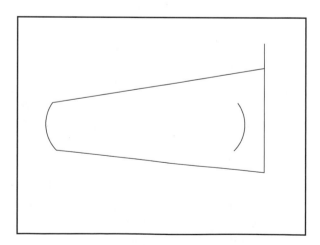

Figure 6-41

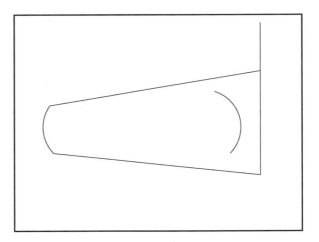

Figure 6-42

You are prompted to select objects.

⊕ Select the angled line at the top of the drawing, choosing a point on the right half of the line.

AutoCAD shows a rubber band and lengthens or shortens the selected line dynamically as you move the cursor.

⊕ Move the cursor back and forth on the screen to get a feel for how the rubber band and crosshairs work in this command option.

The rubber band connects to the old endpoint and the line is lengthened or trimmed by an imaginary line running from the crosshairs perpendicular to the line.

⊕ Select any point and observe the resulting change.

⊕ Type u to undo the change.

You might wish to continue experimenting with LENGTHEN. We encourage you to try the Percent and Total options, to use positive and negative values, and to select arcs and lines to observe the results.

⊕ Press Enter to exit the LENGTHEN command.

In the next task, you take a giant leap in plotting technique as you begin to use paper space, multiple layouts, and multiple viewports within layouts.

6.10 Creating Plot Layouts

GENERAL PROCEDURE

1. Right-click a layout tab and select New layout.
2. Define plot settings.
3. Create paper space viewports.
4. Switch to model space to position or edit objects in the drawing.
5. Switch to paper space to plot.
6. Type or select Plot.
7. Preview plot, change parameters, and execute plotting as usual.

Up until now, we have plotted everything directly from model space. Plotting from model space has its uses, particularly in the early stages of a design process. However, when your focus shifts from modeling issues to presentation issues, paper space layouts have much more to offer. The separation of model space and paper space in AutoCAD allows you to focus entirely on modeling and real-world dimensions when you are drawing, and then shift your focus to paper output issues when you plot. On the drafting board, all drawings are committed to paper from the start. People doing manual drafting are inevitably conscious of scale, paper size, and rotation from start to finish. When draftspeople first begin using CAD systems, they still tend to think in terms of the final hard copy their plotter will produce even as they are creating lines on the screen. The AutoCAD plotting system takes full advantage of the powers of a CAD system, allowing us to ignore scale and other drawing paper issues entirely, if we wish, until it is time to plot.

In addition, the paper space world allows us to create multiple views of the same objects without copying or redrawing them, and to plot these viewports simultaneously. In this task, we create two layouts of Drawing 5-1, the flanged bushing from the last chapter. The first contains only one viewport. The second is used to demonstrate some basic principles of working with multiple viewports.

Opening Layout1

⊞ To begin this exercise, you should open Drawing 5-1, illustrated in Figure 6-43.

If you do not have Drawing 5-1 available, you can approximate it by doing the following:

1. Erase all objects from your screen.
2. Set Limits to (0,0) and (12,9). This is critical. If you use different limits, the exercise is difficult to follow.
3. Draw a circle with diameter 3.50 centered at (3.00,4.00).

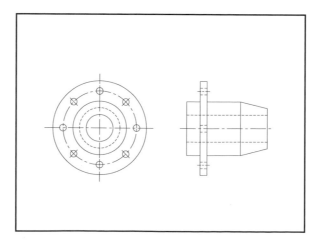

Figure 6-43

4. Draw a second circle with diameter 2.50 centered at the same point.
5. Draw a rectangle with first corner at (6.50,2.75) and second corner at (10.00,5.25).

With Drawing 5-1 on your screen, or an approximation, you are ready to begin.

⊕ **Before leaving model space, turn off the grid (press F7).**

Layouts have their own grid, so if you leave the model space grid on you see overlapping grids that are very confusing.

⊕ **Click the Layout1 tab at the bottom of the drawing area.**

This might automatically call up the Page Setup Manager discussed in Chapter 4. If so, you can ignore it for now. We return to it for the next layout.

⊕ **If necessary, close the Page Setup Manager.**

Once the dialog box is closed, you should see an image similar to the one in Figure 6-44. This is a simple one-viewport layout. AutoCAD has automatically created a single viewport determined by the extents of your drawing. Paper space viewports are sometimes called floating viewports because they can be moved and reshaped. They are somewhat like windows from paper space into model space. Try the remaining steps:

⊕ **Select the viewport border, just as you would select any AutoCAD object.**

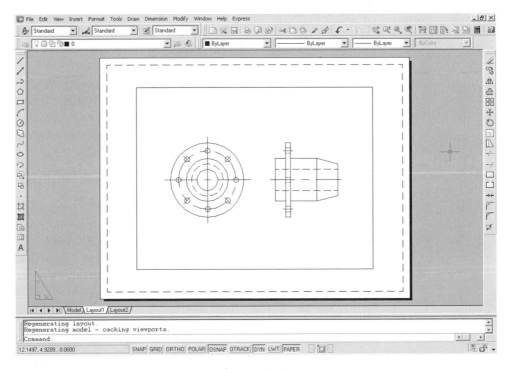

Figure 6-44

Floating viewports are, in fact, AutoCAD objects and are treated and stored as such. You can move them, stretch them, copy them, and erase them. Editing the viewport does not affect the model space objects within the viewport. When a viewport is selected, the border is highlighted and grips are shown at each corner.

⊕ **Type e or select the Erase tool from the Modify toolbar.**

This eliminates the viewport and leaves you with the image of a blank sheet of paper. Without a viewport, you have no view of model space.

⊕ **Undo the Erase to bring the viewport back.**

⊕ **Now try to select any of the objects within the viewport.**

You cannot. As long as you are in paper space, model space objects are not accessible. To gain access to model space objects while in a layout view, you must work in model space inside a selected viewport. This is easily done by double-clicking inside a viewport.

⊕ **Double-click anywhere within the viewport.**

Two things happen. The border of the viewport takes on a bold outline and the Paper button on the status bar switches to Model, indicating that you are now in model space. You also notice that the MSPACE command has been entered at the command prompt. Notice the difference between working within a viewport in a layout and switching into model space by clicking the Model tab. If you click the Model tab, the layout disappears and you are back in the familiar model space drawing area.

⊕ **Try selecting objects in your viewport again.**

Model space objects are now available for editing or positioning within the viewport. While in the model space of a viewport, you cannot select any objects drawn in paper space, including the viewport border.

⊕ **Try selecting the viewport border.**

You do not have access to this paper space object. When you point outside the viewport border you see the selection arrow rather than the crosshairs and selection box.

⊕ **Double-click anywhere outside the viewport border.**

This returns you to paper space.

Next we create a more complex layout.

Creating a New Layout

Layouts are saved automatically and assigned to tabs. You can create new layouts and layout tabs, and you can delete any layout tab. You cannot delete the model tab. There are several ways to create a new layout. The simplest is to use the layout shortcut menu. You probably already have Layout1 and Layout2 tabs, so we create a Layout3 tab and rename it.

⊕ **Right-click the Layout1 or Layout2 tab.**

This opens the shortcut menu illustrated in Figure 6-45. You see the following options: New layout, which creates a new tab; From template, which creates a new layout from a layout template; Delete, which deletes the currently

Figure 6-45

selected layout; Rename, to rename the selected layout tab; Move or Copy, which can be used to copy a layout or change the order of tabs; and Select All Layouts, which allows all layouts to be sent to the plotter at once. The bottom panel of the menu gives convenient access to the Page Setup Manager and Plot dialog boxes.

⊕ Select New layout from the shortcut menu.

A Layout3 tab is added. (If you have no Layout2, then Layout2 is added instead.)

⊕ Right-click the Layout3 tab to open the shortcut menu again.

⊕ Select Rename.

A simple Rename Layout dialog box appears, as shown in Figure 6-46.

⊕ Type 3view and click OK.

The name on the Layout3 tab changes to 3view. We enter this layout, change some plot settings, and create three floating viewports.

⊕ Select the 3view tab.

Plot settings can be applied directly to a layout or taken from a previously defined page setup. Since we are starting from scratch in defining this layout, we go directly to the Plot dialog box and define our settings there. The layout shortcut menu provides easy access to the Plot dialog box.

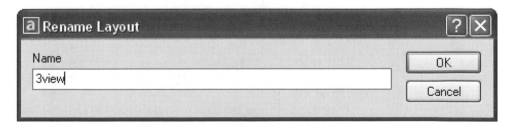

Figure 6-46

⊕   Right-click on the 3view layout tab to open the shortcut menu.

⊕   Select Plot from the shortcut menu.

 In this exercise, we use a D-size drawing sheet for our layout. If you do not have a D-size plotter, we recommend that you use AutoCAD's DWG6 ePlot driver, which is designed to create electronic plots that can be sent out over the Internet or a local network. If you prefer to use a different-size paper, you have to make adjustments as you go along. Using A-size, for example, most specifications can be divided by four. We will include A-size specifications at critical points in case you don't have access to a D-size plotter or want to use a printer.

⊕   In the Printer/plotter panel, select a plotting device that has a D-size sheet option.

⊕   In the Paper size panel, select an ANSI D (34 × 22) paper size.

 Notice that Layout is now the default selection in the What to plot list. We have not encountered this selection because it is not present when you plot from model space.

⊕   If necessary, check Landscape in the Drawing orientation panel.

⊕   Click the Apply to Layout button at the bottom of the dialog box. This is important. The plot settings we have defined will not be applied to the current layout unless we click this button.

 We are now ready to exit the Plot dialog box and work directly on our layout. Since we have applied our settings to the layout, they will be retained if we close the Plot dialog, but not if we click cancel.

⊕   Click the close button in the upper right corner of the dialog box.

 AutoCAD will adjust the layout image to show the currently defined floating viewport on a D-size drawing sheet. Whatever size viewport AutoCAD shows is okay, because we will erase it anyway.

⊕   Select the floating viewport and type e or select the Erase tool.

 You are now looking at a blank sheet of paper in paper space once again. Take a moment to explore the limits of this drawing sheet.

⊕   Turn on the paper space grid (press F7 or click the Grid button on the status bar).

⊕   Turn on incremental snap (press F9 or click the Snap button on the status bar).

⊕   Move the cursor over the lower left corner of the paper grid and locate (0,0).

 This is the origin of the plot, indicated by the corner of the dashed border that shows the effective drawing area.

⊕   Move the cursor to the upper right corner of the effective drawing area.

 This is less than the limits of the grid. The exact point depends on your plotter. With the AutoCAD DWF6 ePlot driver and D-size paper, it is (33.50,20.50).

 Your screen is now truly representative of a drawing sheet. The plot is made 1-to-1, with 1 paper space screen unit equaling 1 inch on the drawing sheet.

There is little reason to do it any other way, because the whole point of paper space is to emulate the paper on the screen.

Now it is time to create viewports.

⊕ Type mv or open the View menu, select Viewports, and then 1 Viewport.

Either of these methods enters the VPORTS command. AutoCAD prompts:

Specify corner of viewport or
[ON/OFF/Fit/Hideplot/Lock/Object/Polygonal/Restore/2/3/4]<Fit>:

We deal only with the Specify corner option in this exercise. With this option, you create a viewport just as you would a selection window.

⊕ Pick point (1.00,1.00) at the lower left of your screen, as shown in Figure 6-47.

If you are not using D-size paper, you can do fine by making your viewports resemble ours in size, shape, and location.

⊕ Pick an opposite corner, as shown in Figure 6-47. This is (20,13) on a D-size sheet.

Your screen is redrawn with the drawing extents at maximum scale centered within the viewport.

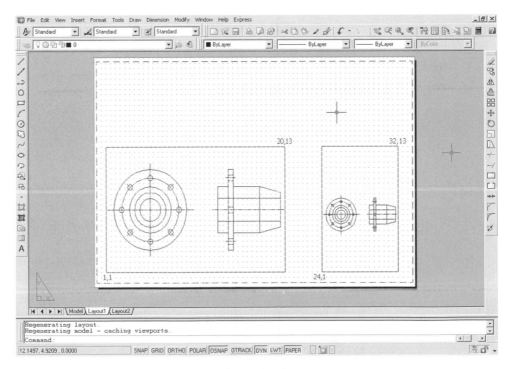

Figure 6-47

Now we create a second viewport to the right of the first.

⊕ Repeat VPORTS.

⊕ Pick point (24.00,1.00), as shown in Figure 6-47.

⊕ Pick point (32.00,13.00), as shown.

You have now created a second viewport. Notice that the images in the two viewports are drawn at different scales. Each is drawn to fit within its viewport. This can create problems later when you add dimension and text. You want to maintain control over the scale of objects within viewports and have a clear knowledge of the relationships among scales in different viewports. For this, we use the ZOOM scale feature of the ZOOM command. We create different zoom magnifications inside the two viewports.

⊕ Double-click inside the left viewport.

This takes you into model space within the left viewport. We are going to zoom so that the two-view drawing is in a precise and known scale relation to paper space.

⊕ Type z to enter the ZOOM command.

Notice the ZOOM command prompt:

```
Specify corner of window, enter a scale factor (nX or
nXP), or [All/Center/Dynamic/Extents/Previous/Scale/
Window] <real time>:
```

In this task, we use two new options, the paper space scale factor option (nXP) and the Center option.

⊕ Type 2xp (on A-size paper divide these factors by four, so you will use .5xp).

This creates only a slight change in the left viewport. XP means times paper. It allows you to zoom relative to paper space units. If you zoom 1xp, then a model space unit takes on the size of a current paper space unit, which in turn equals 1 inch of drawing paper. We zoomed 2xp. This means that one unit in the viewport equals two paper space units, or 2 inches on paper. We now have a precise relationship between model space and paper space in this viewport. The change in presentation size is trivial, but the change in terms of understanding and control is great.

Now we set an XP zoom factor in the right viewport so that we control not only the model space/paper space scale relations, but the scale relations among viewports as well.

⊕ Click inside the right viewport to make it active.

You are already in model space, so double-clicking is unnecessary.

⊕ Reenter the ZOOM command.

In the right viewport, we are going to show a close-up image of the right side view. To accomplish this, we need a larger zoom factor and we need to be centered on the right side view.

⊕ Type c for the Center option.

AutoCAD asks you to specify a center point.

⊕ Pick a point on the center line near the center of the flange.

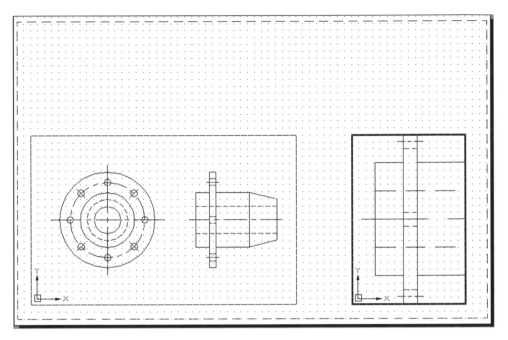

Figure 6-48

Look at Figure 6-48. The point you select becomes the center point of the right viewport when AutoCAD zooms in.

AutoCAD prompts:

> Enter magnification or height<3.00>:

Accepting the default would simply center the image in the viewport. We specify an XP value here.

⊕ Type 4xp.

Your right viewport is dynamically magnified to resemble the one in Figure 6-48. In this enlarged image, one model space unit equals 4 inches in the drawing sheet (1 – 1 on A size).

Tip: You might wish to pan slightly to the left or right to position the image in the viewport. Notice that you can use the scroll bars to pan inside the active viewport without losing horizontal or vertical alignment.

Now that you have the technique, we create one more enlargement, focusing on one of the circle of holes in the flange.

⊕ Double-click anywhere outside the two viewports to return to paper space.

⊕ Enter the MVIEW command.

⊕ Pick point (1.00,14.00).

⊕ Pick point (9.00,20.00).

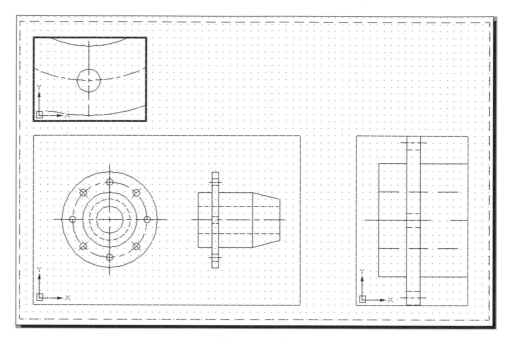

Figure 6-49

⊕ Enter model space in the new viewport and zoom in, centering on the hole at the bottom of the flange in the front view, at six times paper in the new viewport.

This is tricky and might require the use of a Center or Quadrant object snap. Remember that you can access a single-point object snap by holding down Shift, right-clicking, and then selecting from the Osnap shortcut menu.

Your screen should resemble Figure 6-49.

⊕ Before proceeding to plot, try a print preview to ensure that you are ready.

⊕ Select the Plot preview tool from the Standard toolbar.

This full preview should look very much like the layout image. This is the beauty of the AutoCAD plotting system. You have a great deal of control and the ability to assess exactly what your paper output will be before you actually plot the drawing.

⊕ Press esc to exit the preview.

Maximize Viewport Button

Before going on, we introduce the maximize viewport button on the right of the status bar. This button will not only allow you to switch into model space in any viewport, but will maximize that viewport to fit the display. Once you have maximized a viewport, you can cycle through other viewports and maximize them one at a time. Try this:

Figure 6-50

⊕ Click the Maximize Viewport button on the status bar, illustrated in Figure 6-50.

If you entered the model space of a viewport before clicking the button, AutoCAD would maximize that viewport. Otherwise, it will maximize the first viewport you defined. The maximized image will show you whatever is in the viewport, along with whatever portion of the drawing will fit the display at the magnification defined for that viewport.

⊕ Click the small arrow to the right or left of the button.

The arrows cycle you through other viewports in the order they were defined.

⊕ Click the arrows to continue cycling through your three viewports.

⊕ When you are done, click the Maximize button again.

This will minimize the viewport and return you to the paper space layout image. (If you pause with the selection arrow on the button, you will notice that it is now labeled as the Minimize button.)

Plotting the Multiple-View Drawing

Now we are ready to plot. Plotting a multiple-viewport drawing is no different from plotting from a single view. However, now that you have two or three different layouts as well as model space, you need to make sure the layout or layouts you want to plot are selected before you enter the Plot dialog box.

Tip: The selection controls for layout tabs are the same as those for files in Microsoft Office and other Windows applications. To select two or more adjacent tabs, use Shift + Left click. To select individual layout tabs that are separated by other layout tabs, use Ctrl + Left click.

⊕ With the 3view tab selected, select the Plot tool from the Standard toolbar, or right-click on the 3view layout tab and select Plot from the shortcut menu.

At this point you should have no need to adjust settings within the Plot dialog box because you have already made adjustments to the page setup and the plotting device. Notice that Layout is the default for Plot area.

⊕ Prepare your plotter. (Make sure you use the right size paper.)

⊕ Click OK.

Note: If you have done this exercise using the DWG6 ePlot driver, you will note that AutoCAD sends your plot to a file rather than to a plotter. Any drawing can be saved to a file to be plotted later, but anytime you use the ePlot utility your plot will first be saved to a file so that it can be sent over the Internet.

Important: Be sure to save this drawing with its multiple-viewport 3view layout before leaving this chapter, because we return to it in Chapter 8 to explore scaling dimensions between model space and paper space.

6.11   Review Material

Questions

1. Why is it important to keep object snap turned off when you are not using it? What are two simple ways to turn running Osnap on and off?
2. At what point in a command procedure would you use an object snap single-point override? How would you signal the AutoCAD program that you want to use an object snap?
3. How do you access the Object snap shortcut menu?
4. What is an acquired point? How do you acquire a point? How do you eliminate an acquired point?
5. How do you use BREAK to shorten a line at one end? When would you use this procedure instead of the TRIM command? How would you accomplish the same thing with LENGTHEN?
6. You have selected a line to extend and a boundary to extend it to, but AutoCAD gives you the message "Object does not intersect an edge." What happened?
7. What selection method is always required when you use the STRETCH command?
8. Why is it usual practice to plot 1-to-1 in paper space?
9. Why do we use the Zoom XP option when zooming in floating model space viewports?
10. How is CAD different from manual drafting with regard to issues of scaling and paper size?

Drawing Problems

1. Draw a line from (6,2) to (11,6). Draw a second line perpendicular to the first starting at (6,6).
2. Break the first line at its intersection with the second.
3. There are now three lines on the screen. Draw a circle centered at their intersection and passing through the midpoint of the line going up and to the right of the intersection.
4. Trim all the lines to the circumference of the circle.
5. Erase what is left of the line to the right of the intersection and trim the portion of the circle to the left, between the two remaining lines.

6.12 WWW Exercise 6 (Optional)

You conclude Part I of your exploration of online CAD with two more websites that serve as launching pads with links to many other AutoCAD and CAD-related websites. In addition, we offer a challenge to create a design using object snap and a limited number of commands.

⊕   Connect to your Internet service provider.

⊕   Type browser or open the Web toolbar and select the Browser tool.

⊕   If necessary, navigate to our companion website at www.prenhall. com/dixriley.

Enjoy your visit.

6.13   Drawing 6-1: Bike Tire

This drawing can be done very quickly with the tools you now have. It makes use of one object snap, three trims, and a polar array. Be sure to set the limits large, as suggested.

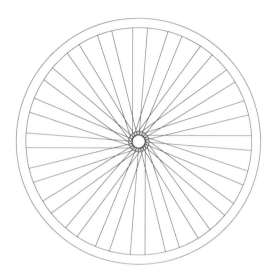

Drawing Suggestions

GRID = 1.00
SNAP = 0.125
LIMITS = (0,0)(48,36)

- Begin by drawing the 1.25, 2.50, 24.00, and 26.00 diameter circles centered on the same point near the middle of your display.
- Draw line (a) using a quadrant object snap to find the first point on the inside circle. The second point can be anywhere outside the 24 circle at 0 degrees from the first point. The exact length of the line is insignificant because you will trim it back to the circle.
- Draw line (b) from the center of the circles to a second point anywhere outside the 24 circle at an angle of 14 degrees. Use the coordinate display or polar tracking to construct this angle. This line also will be trimmed.
- Trim lines (a) and (b) using the 24 circle as a cutting edge.
- Trim the other end of line (b) using the 1.25 circle as a cutting edge.
- Construct a polar array, selecting lines (a) and (b). There are 20 items in the array, and they are rotated as they are copied.

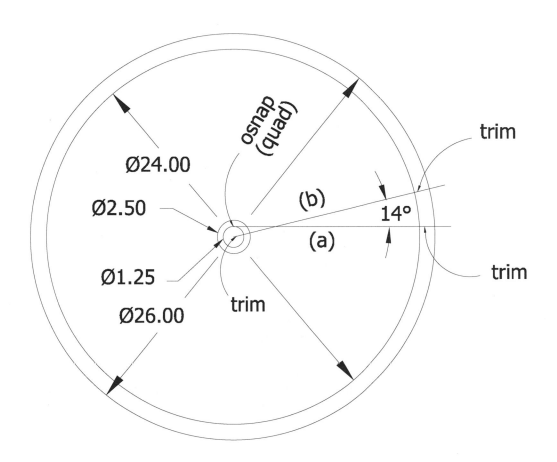

BIKE TIRE

Drawing 6-1

6.14   Drawing 6-2: Archimedes Spiral

This drawing and the next go together as an exercise you should find interesting and enjoyable. These are not technical drawings, but they give you valuable experience with important CAD commands. You create a spiral using a radial grid of circles and lines as a guide. Once the spiral is done, you use it to create the designs in Drawing 6-3.

Drawing Suggestions

GRID = 0.5   SNAP = 0.25
LIMITS = (0,0)(18,12)   LTSCALE = 0.5

- The alternating continuous and hidden lines work as a drawing aid. If you use different colors and layers, they are more helpful. Because all circles are offset 0.50, you can draw one continuous and one hidden circle, then use the OFFSET command to create all the others.
- Begin by drawing one of the continuous circles on Layer 0, centered near the middle of your display, then offset all the other continuous circles.
- Draw the continuous horizontal line across the middle of your six circles and then array it in a three-item polar array.
- Set to Layer 2, draw one of the hidden circles, then offset the other hidden circles.
- Draw a vertical hidden line and array it as you did the horizontal continuous line.
- Set to Layer 1 for the spiral itself.
- Turn on a running object snap to Intersection mode and construct a series of three-point arcs. Be sure to turn off any other modes that might get in your way. Start points and endpoints will be on continuous line intersections; second points always will fall on hidden line intersections.
- When the spiral is complete, turn off Layers 0 and 2. There should be nothing left on your screen, but the spiral itself. Save it or go on to Drawing 6-3.

Grouping Objects

Here is a good opportunity to use the GROUP command. GROUP is discussed more fully in Chapter 10, but you will find it useful here. GROUP defines a collection of objects as a single entity so that they can be selected and modified as a unit. The spiral you have just drawn is used in the next drawing, and it is easier to manipulate if you GROUP it. For more information, see Chapter 10.

1. Type g.
2. In the Object Grouping dialog box, type Spiral for a group name.
3. Click New.
4. Select the six arcs with a window.
5. Right-click to end selection.
6. Click OK.

The spiral can now be selected, moved, rotated, and copied as a single entity.

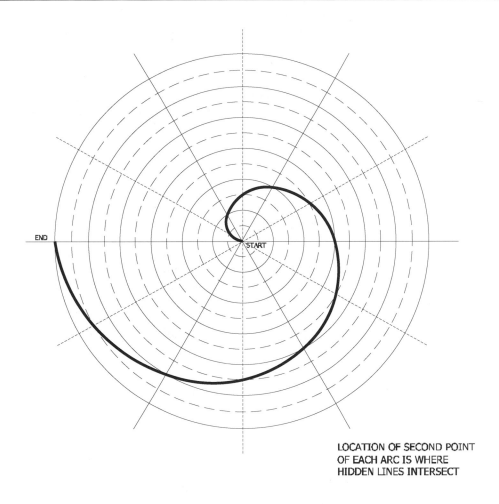

LOCATION OF SECOND POINT
OF EACH ARC IS WHERE
HIDDEN LINES INTERSECT

SOLID CIRCLE RADII	HIDDEN CIRCLE RADII
0.50	0.25
1.00	0.75
1.50	1.25
2.00	1.75
2.50	2.25
3.00	2.75

NOTE: THIS DRAWING IS USED
    ON DRAWING 6-3

SAVE THIS DRAWING!

ARCHIMEDES SPIRAL

Drawing 6-2

6.15   Drawing 6-3: Spiral Designs

These designs are different from other drawings in this book. There are no dimensions, and you use only edit commands now that the spiral is drawn. Below the designs is a list of the edit commands you need. Don't be too concerned with precision. Some of your designs might come out slightly different from ours. When this happens, try to analyze the differences.

Drawing Suggestions

$$\text{LIMITS} = (0,0)(34,24)$$

These large limits are necessary if you wish to draw all of these designs on the screen at once.

In some of the designs and in Drawing 6-4, you need to rotate a copy of the spiral and keep the original in place. You can accomplish this by using the grip edit rotate procedure with the copy option. Setting up Polar snap to track at various angles might also be useful.

How to Rotate an Object and Retain the Original Using Grip Edit

1. Select the spiral.
2. Pick the grip around which you want to rotate, or any of the grips if you are not going to use the grip as a base point for rotation.
3. Right-click and select Rotate from the shortcut menu.
4. Right-click and type b or select Base point from the shortcut menu, if the design needs a base point not on a grip. In this exercise, the base point you choose for rotation depends on the design you are trying to create.
5. Right-click and type c or select Copy from the shortcut menu.
6. Show the rotation angle(s).
7. Press the spacebar to exit the grip edit system.

SPIRAL DESIGNS

(Make from Drawing 6-2)

Drawing 6-3

6.16   Drawing 6-4: Grooved Hub

This drawing includes a typical application of the rotation technique just discussed. The hidden lines in the front view must be rotated 120 degrees and a copy retained in the original position. There are also good opportunities to use MIRROR, object snap, object snap tracking, and TRIM.

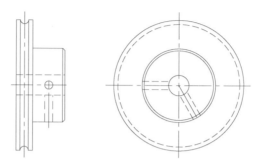

Drawing Suggestions

GRID = 0.5   SNAP = 0.0625
LIMITS = (0,0)(12,9)   LTSCALE = 1

- Draw the circles in the front view and use these to line up the horizontal lines in the left side view. This is a good opportunity to use object snap tracking. By acquiring the quadrant of a circle in the front view, you can track along the horizontal construction lines to the left side view.

- There are several different planes of symmetry in the left side view, which suggests the use of mirroring. We leave it up to you to choose an efficient sequence.

- A quick method for drawing the horizontal hidden lines in the left side view is to acquire the upper and lower quadrant points of the 0.625-diameter circle in the front view to track horizontal construction lines. Draw the lines in the left side view longer than actual length and then use TRIM to erase the excess on both sides of the left side view.

- The same method can be used to draw the two horizontal hidden lines in the front view. A slightly different method that does not use object tracking is to snap lines directly to the top and bottom quadrants of the 0.25-diameter circle in the left side view as a guide and draw them all the way through the front view. Then trim to the 2.25-diameter circle and the 0.62-diameter circle.

- Once these hidden lines are drawn, rotate them, retaining a copy in the original position.

Creating the Multiple-View Layout

Use this drawing to create the multiple-view layout shown below the dimensioned drawing. This three-view layout is very similar to the one created in Task 6.10. Exact dimensions of the viewports are not given. You should create them depending on the paper size you wish to use. What should remain consistent is the scale relationships among the three viewports. On an A sheet, for example, if the largest viewport is zoomed 0.5xp, then the left close-up is 1.0xp and the top close-up is 1.5xp. These ratios have to be adjusted for other sheet sizes.

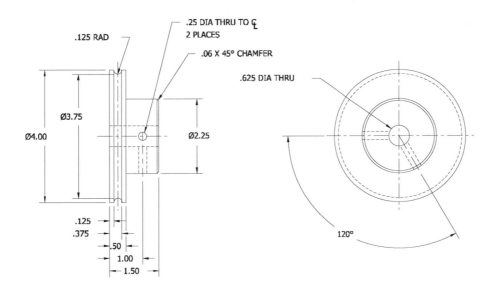

.125 RAD

.25 DIA THRU TO ℄
2 PLACES

.06 X 45° CHAMFER

.625 DIA THRU

Ø3.75

Ø4.00

Ø2.25

.125
.375

.50
1.00
1.50

120°

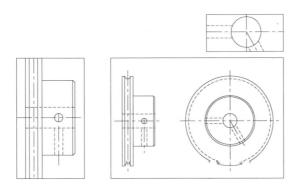

GROOVED HUB
Drawing 6-4

6.17   Drawing 6-5: Cap Iron

This drawing is of a type of blade used in a wood plane. When wood is planed, the cap iron causes it to curl up out of the plane so that it does not jam. There are several good applications for the TRIM command here.

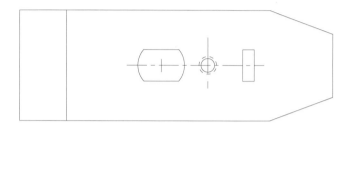

Drawing Suggestions

GRID = 1.00
SNAP = 0.125
LIMITS = (0,0)(18,12)
LTSCALE = 0.25

- The circle with a hidden line outside a continuous line represents a tapped hole. The dimension is given to the hidden line; the continuous inner line is drawn with a slightly smaller radius that is not specified.

- The figure near the center of the top view that has two arcs with 0.38 radii can be drawn exactly the same way as the bandage discussed earlier in this chapter. Draw a circle and two horizontal lines and then trim it all down.

- The small 0.54 and 0.58 arcs in the front view can be drawn using Start, End, Radius.

- The small vertical hidden lines in the front view can be drawn using techniques introduced in the last drawing. Draw lines down from snap points on the figures in the top view and then trim them, or use object snap tracking to create lines with excess length and then trim them. For the tapped hole and the arced opening in the middle, use the right and left quadrant points of the arcs and circle as acquired points or snap points.

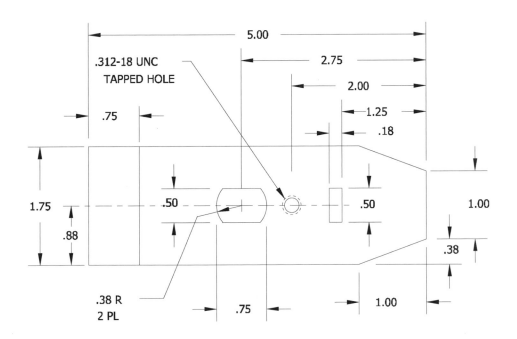

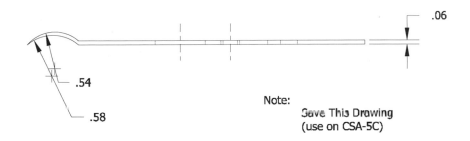

CAP IRON

Drawing 6-5

6.18   Drawing 6-6: Deck Framing

This architectural drawing might take some time, although there is nothing in it you have not done before. Notice that some of the settings are quite different from our 1B template, so be sure to adjust them before beginning.

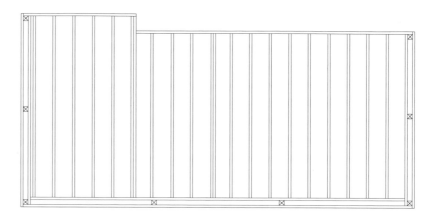

Drawing Suggestions

UNITS = Architectural
PRECISION = 0'-0"
LIMITS = (0',0')(48',36')
GRID = 1'
SNAP = 2"

- Whatever order you choose for doing this drawing, we suggest that you make ample use of COPY, ARRAY, OFFSET, and TRIM.
- Keep Ortho on, except to draw the lines across the middle of the squares, representing upright posts.
- With snap set at 2", it is easy to copy lines 2" apart, as you have to do frequently to draw the 2 × 80 studs.
- You might need to turn Snap off when you are selecting lines to copy, but be sure to turn it on again to specify displacements.
- Notice that you can use ARRAY effectively, but there are three separate arrays. They are all 16" on center, but the double boards in several places make it inadvisable to do a single array of studs all the way across the deck. What you can do, however, is draw, copy, and array all the "vertical" studs at the maximum length first and then go back and trim them to their various actual lengths using the "horizontal" boards as cutting edges.

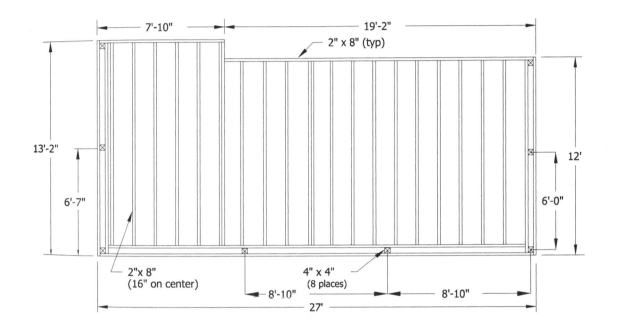

DECK FRAMING

Drawing 6-6

6.19   Drawing 6-7: Tool Block

In this drawing, you need to take information from a three-dimensional drawing and develop it into a 3view drawing. The finished drawing should be composed of the Top View, Front View, and Side View. The reference drawing shows a portion of each view to be developed. You are to complete these views.

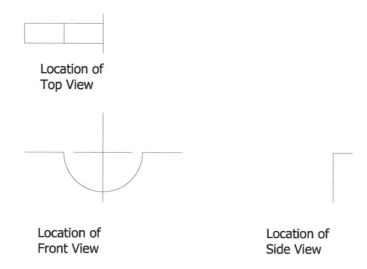

Location of
Top View

Location of
Front View

Location of
Side View

Drawing Suggestions

- Begin by drawing the top view. Use the top view to line up the front view and side view.
- The slot with the angular lines must be drawn in the front view before the other views. These lines can then be lined up with the top and side view and used as guides to draw the hidden lines.
- Be sure to include all the necessary hidden lines and center lines in each view.

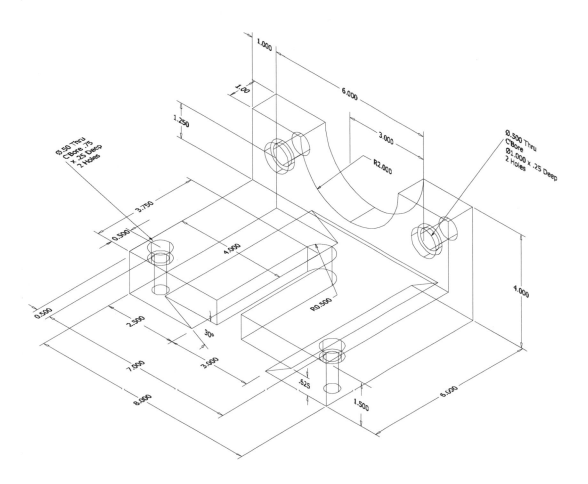

TOOL BLOCK

Drawing 6—7

PART II
TEXT, DIMENSIONS, AND OTHER COMPLEX ENTITIES

7 Text

COMMANDS

CHANGE	DDEDIT	DTEXT	SCALE	TEXT
CHPROP	DDEMODES	MATCHPROP	SPELL	
DDCHPROP	DDMODIFY	MTEXT	STYLE	

OVERVIEW

This chapter begins Part II of the book. Part I focused on basic 2-D entities such as lines, circles, and arcs. In the next four chapters, you learn to draw a number of AutoCAD entities that are constructed as groups of lines, circles, and arcs. Text, dimensions, polylines, and blocks are all entities made up of basic 2-D entities, but you do not have to treat them line by line, arc by arc. In addition, you learn how whole drawings can be inserted in other drawings and how this capability is used to create symbols libraries that can be shared by many users. Also in Part II, you continue to learn AutoCAD editing and plotting features and features that aid in collaborative design projects.

Now it's time to add text to your drawings. In this chapter, you learn to find your way around AutoCAD's DTEXT and MTEXT commands. In addition, you learn many new editing commands that are often used with text, but are equally important for editing other objects.

TASKS

7.1 Entering Left-Justified Text Using DTEXT

GENERAL PROCEDURE

1. Type dt or open the Draw menu, highlight Text, and select Single-Line Text.
2. Pick a start point.
3. Answer prompts regarding height and rotation.
4. Enter text on one line and press Enter.
5. Enter text on other lines or press Enter to exit the command.

AutoCAD provides two commands for entering text in a drawing. DTEXT (also called TEXT) allows you to enter single lines of text and displays them as you type. You can backspace through lines to make corrections if you do not exit the command. MTEXT allows you to type multiple lines of text in a special text editor and then positions them in a windowed area in your drawing. Both commands provide numerous options for placing text and a variety of fonts to use and styles that can be created from them. In the first three tasks, we focus on the basic placement features of the DTEXT command, sticking with the standard style and font.

> **Note:** An older command called TEXT has been eliminated. If you type Text at the command prompt, you get the DTEXT command; if you type the alias t, you get the MTEXT command.

⊕ To prepare for this exercise, open a new drawing using the 1B template and draw a 4.00 horizontal line beginning at (1,1). Then create five copies of the line 2.00 apart, as shown in Figure 7-1.

These lines are for orientation in this exercise only; they are not essential for drawing text.

⊕ Type dt or open the Draw menu, highlight Text, and then select Single Line text, as shown in Figure 7-2.

There is a Text tool on the Draw toolbar, but it enters the MTEXT command.

Either of these methods enters the DTEXT command, and you see a prompt with three options in the command area:

```
Current text style: ™STANDARD⌠ Text height: 0.20
Specify start point of text or [Justify/Style]:
```

Style will be explored in Task 7.8. In this task, we look at different options for placing text in a drawing. These are all considered text justification

Figure 7-1

Figure 7-2

methods and they are listed if you choose the Justify option at the command prompt.

First we use the default method by picking a start point. This gives us left-justified text, inserted left to right from the point we pick.

⊕ **Pick a start point at the left end of the upper line.**

Study the prompt that follows and be sure that you do not attempt to enter text yet:

```
Specify height <0.20>:
```

This gives you the opportunity to set the text height. The number you type specifies the height of uppercase letters in the units you have specified for the current drawing. For now, accept the default height.

⊕ **Press Enter to accept the default height (0.20).**

The prompt that follows allows you to place text in a rotated position:

```
Specify rotation angle of text <0>:
```

The default of 0 degrees orients text in the usual horizontal manner. Other angles can be specified by typing a degree number relative to the polar coordinate system or by showing a point. If you show a point, it is taken as the second point of a baseline along which the text string will be placed. For now, we stick to horizontal text.

⊕ **Press Enter to accept the default angle (0).**

Now, at last, it is time to enter the text itself. In AutoCAD 2006 there is no prompt for text at the Command line. Text is entered directly on the screen at the selected start point.

Notice that a blinking cursor has appeared at the start point on your screen. This shows where the first letter you type will be placed. For our text, type the word Left, identifying this as an example of left-justified text. Watch the screen as you type and you can see dynamic text at work.

⊕ **Type Left and press Enter.**

Remember, you cannot use the spacebar in place of the Enter key when entering text. Notice that the text cursor jumps below the line when you press Enter. Also notice that you are given a second Enter text: prompt in the command area.

⊕ **Type Justified and press Enter.**

The text cursor jumps down again and another Enter text: prompt appears. This is how DTEXT allows for easy entry of multiple lines of text directly on the screen in a drawing. To exit the command, you need to press Enter at the prompt.

⊕ **Press Enter to exit DTEXT.**

This completes the process and returns you to the command prompt.

Figure 7-3 shows the left-justified text you have just drawn.

Before proceeding with other text justification options, we demonstrate two additional features of DTEXT.

⊕ **Press Enter to repeat the DTEXT command.**

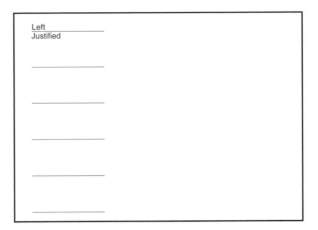

Figure 7-3

If you press Enter again at this point instead of showing a new start point or selecting a justification option, you go right back to the Enter text: prompt as if you had never left the command. Try it.

⊕ **Press Enter.**

You see the Enter text: prompt in the command area and the text cursor reappears on the screen just below the word Justified.

⊕ **Type Text and press Enter.**

⊕ **Press Enter to exit the command.**

Once you have left DTEXT, there are other ways to edit text, which we explore in Tasks 7.5 and 7.6.

7.2 Using Other Text Justification Options

GENERAL PROCEDURE

1. Type dt or open the Draw menu, highlight Text, and select Single Line Text.
2. Choose a justification option.
3. Pick a start point.
4. Answer prompts regarding height and rotation.
5. Enter text.

We now proceed to some of the other text placement options, beginning with right-justified text. The options demonstrated in this exercise are all illustrated in Figure 7-4. For the text in this demonstration we also specify a change in height.

Right-Justified Text

Right-justified text is constructed from an endpoint backing up, right to left.

⊕ **Repeat the DTEXT command.**

You see the same prompt as before.

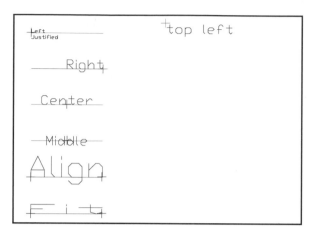

Figure 7-4

⊕ Type r for right-justified text.

Now AutoCAD prompts for an endpoint instead of a start point:

Specify right endpoint of text baseline:

Choose the right end of the second line.

⊕ Point to the right end of the second line.

AutoCAD prompts you to specify a text height. Change the height to 0.50. Notice that AutoCAD gives you a rubber band from the endpoint. It can be used to specify height and rotation angle by pointing, if you like.

⊕ Type .5 or show a height of 0.50 by pointing.

⊕ Press Enter to retain 0 degrees of rotation.

You are now prompted to enter text. Notice the larger text cursor at the right end of the second line.

⊕ Type Right and press Enter.

At this point you should have the word Right showing to the right of the second line. Watch what happens when you press Enter a second time to exit the command.

⊕ Press Enter to exit the command.

Your screen should now include the second line of text in right-justified position, as shown in Figure 7-4.

Centered Text

Centered text is justified from the bottom center of the text.

⊕ Repeat the DTEXT command.

⊕ Type c.

AutoCAD prompts

Specify center point of text:

⊕ Point to the midpoint of the third line.

⊕   Press Enter to retain the current height, which is now set to 0.50.

⊕   Press Enter to retain 0 degrees of rotation.

⊕   Type Center and press Enter.

   Notice again how the letters are displayed on the screen in the usual left-to-right manner, starting at the midpoint of the line.

⊕   Press Enter again to complete the command.

   The word Center should now be centered, as shown in Figure 7-4.

Middle Text

Middle text is justified from the middle of the text both horizontally and vertically, rather than from the bottom center.

⊕   Repeat DTEXT.

⊕   Type m.

   AutoCAD prompts

```
            Specify middle point of text:
```

⊕   Point to the midpoint of the fourth line.

⊕   Press Enter to retain the current height of 0.50.

⊕   Press Enter to retain 0 degrees of rotation.

⊕   Type Middle and press Enter.

⊕   Press Enter again to complete the command.

   Notice the difference between center and middle. Center refers to the midpoint of the baseline below the text. Middle refers to the middle of the text itself, so that the line now runs through the text.

Aligned Text

Aligned text is placed between two specified points. The height of the text is calculated proportional to the distance between the two points, and the text is drawn along the line between the two points.

⊕   Repeat DTEXT.

⊕   Type a.

   AutoCAD prompts

```
        Specify first endpoint of text baseline:
```

⊕   Point to the left end of the fifth line.

   AutoCAD prompts for another point:

```
        Specify second endpoint of text baseline:
```

⊕   Point to the right end of the fifth line.

   Notice that there is no prompt for height. AutoCAD calculates a height based on the space between the points you chose. There is also no prompt for an angle, because the angle between your two points (in this case 0) is used. You could position text at an angle using this option.

⊕ Type Align and press Enter.

As you type, the text size will be adjusted with the addition of each letter.

⊕ Press Enter again to complete the command.

Notice that the text is sized to fill the space between the two points you selected.

Text Drawn to Fit between Two Points

The Fit option is similar to the Align option, except that the specified text height is retained.

⊕ Repeat DTEXT.

⊕ Type f.

You are prompted for two points, as in the Align option.

⊕ Point to the left end of the sixth line.

⊕ Point to the right end of the sixth line.

⊕ Press Enter to retain the current height.

As with the Align option, there is no prompt for an angle of rotation.

⊕ Type Fit and press Enter.

Once again, text size is adjusted as you type, but this time only the width changes.

⊕ Press Enter again to complete the command.

This time the text is stretched horizontally to fill the line without a change in height. This is the difference between fit and align. In the Align option, text height is determined by the width you show. With Fit, the specified height is retained and the text is stretched or compressed to fill the given space.

Other Justification Options

Before proceeding to the next task, take a moment to look at the complete list of justification options. The options are listed on the command line if you enter DTEXT and type J. They are also listed on a drop-down list on your screen if dynamic input is on. The command line prompt looks like this:

```
[Align/Fit/Center/Middle/Right/TL/TC/TR/ML/MC/MR/BL/BC/BR]:
```

The letter options are spelled out in the chart shown in Figure 7-5. We have already explored the first five and the default Left option. For the others, study the figure. As shown on the chart, T is for top, M is for middle, and B is for bottom. L, C, and R stand for left, center, and right, respectively. Notice that it is not necessary to type J and view the list before entering the option. Just enter DTEXT and then the one or two letters of the option. Let's try one:

⊕ Repeat DTEXT and then type tl for the Top Left option or select TL from the dynamic input list.

AutoCAD asks you to Specify top-left point of text. As shown on the chart in Figure 7-5, top left refers to the highest potential text point at the left of the word.

⊕ Pick a top left point, as shown in Figure 7-4 above the words top left.

⊕ Press Enter twice to accept the height and rotation angle settings and arrive at the Text: prompt.

TEXT JUSTIFICATION	
START POINT TYPE ABBREVIATION	TEXT POSITION +INDICATES START POINT OR PICK POINT
A	ALIGN
F	FIT
C	CENTER
M	MIDDLE
R	RIGHT
TL	TOP LEFT
TC	TOP CENTER
TR	TOP RIGHT
ML	MIDDLE LEFT
MC	MIDDLE CENTER
MR	MIDDLE RIGHT
BL	BOTTOM LEFT
BC	BOTTOM CENTER
BR	BOTTOM RIGHT

Figure 7-5

⊕   Type top left and press Enter.

The text is entered from the top left position.

⊕   Press Enter again to complete the command.

Your screen should now resemble Figure 7-4.

7.3   Entering Text on an Angle and Text Using Character Codes

GENERAL PROCEDURE

1.   Enter the DTEXT command.
2.   Specify justification option, start point, and text height.
3.   Specify a rotation angle.
4.   Enter text, including character codes as needed.

We have already seen how you can use DTEXT to enter multiple lines of text. In this task, we explore this further by entering several lines on an angle, adding special character symbols along the way. We create three lines of left-justified text, one below the other and all rotated 45 degrees, as shown in Figure 7-6.

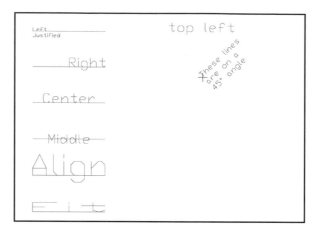

Figure 7-6

⊕ Repeat the DTEXT command.

You see the familiar prompt:

```
Specify start point of text or [Justify/Style]:
```

⊕ Pick a starting point near (12.00,8.00), as shown by the mark next to the word These in Figure 7-6.

⊕ Type .3 to specify a smaller text size.

⊕ Type 45 or show an angle of 45 degrees.

Notice that the text cursor is shown at the specified angle.

⊕ Type These lines and press Enter.

The text is drawn on the screen at a 45-degree angle, and the cursor moves down to the next line. Notice that the text box on the screen is still at the specified angle.

⊕ Type are on a and press Enter.

The Degree Symbol and Other Special Characters

The next line contains a degree symbol. Because you do not have this character on your keyboard, AutoCAD provides a special method for drawing it. Type the text with the %% signs just as shown in the following and then study Figure 7-7, which lists other special characters that can be drawn in the same way.

Control Codes and Special Characters	
Type at Text Prompt	Text on Drawing
%%O OVERSCORE %%U UNDERSCORE 180%%D 2.00 %%P.01 %%C4.00	OVERSCORE UNDERSCORE 180° 2.00 ±.01 ⌀4.00

Figure 7-7

⊕   Type 45% %d.

     DTEXT initially types the percent symbols directly to the screen, just as you have typed them. When you type the d, the character code is translated and redrawn as a degree symbol. Watch.

⊕   Type angle and press Enter.

⊕   Press Enter again to complete the command sequence.

     Your screen should now resemble Figure 7-6.

7.4 Entering Multiline Text Using MTEXT

GENERAL PROCEDURE

1. Type t, select the Multiline Text tool from the Draw toolbar, or open the Draw menu, highlight Text, and select Multiline Text.
2. Specify the first corner.
3. Specify the opposite corner.
4. Type text in the text editor.
5. Click OK.

The MTEXT command allows you to create multiple lines of text in a text editor and position them within a defined window in your drawing. Like DTEXT, MTEXT has nine options for text justification and its own set of character codes.

     We begin by creating a simple left-justified block of text.

⊕   Type t or select the Multiline Text tool from the Draw toolbar, as shown in Figure 7-8.

     You see the following prompt in the command area:

```
-mtext Current text style: STANDARD Text height: 0.30
                    Specify first corner:
```

Also, notice that a multiline text symbol, "abc," has been added to the crosshair.

     Fundamentally, MTEXT lets you define the width of a group of text lines that you create in a special text editor. When the text is entered using MTEXT, Auto-CAD formats it to conform to the specified width and justification method and draws the text on your screen. The width can be defined in several ways. The default method for specifying a width is to draw a window on the screen, but this can be misleading. MTEXT does not attempt to place the complete text inside the window, but only within its width. The first point of the window becomes the insertion

Figure 7-8

point of the text. How AutoCAD uses this insertion point depends on the justification option. The second window point defines the width and the text flow direction (i.e., whether the text lines should be drawn above or below, to the left or right of the insertion point). Exactly how this is interpreted is also dependent on the justification option.

⊕ Pick an insertion point near the middle of your drawing area, in the neighborhood of (12.00,5.00).

AutoCAD begins a window at the selected point and gives you a new prompt:

```
Specify opposite corner or [Height/Justify/Line
spacing/Rotation/Style/Width]:
```

We continue with the default options by picking a second corner. For purposes of demonstration, we suggest a window 3.00 wide, drawn down and to the right.

⊕ Pick a second point 3.00 to the right and about 1.00 below the first point.

As soon as you pick the opposite corner, AutoCAD opens the Multiline Text Editor and associated Text Formatting toolbar illustrated in Figure 7-9. The toolbar gives you the capacity to change text styles and fonts (see Task 7.8) and text height, along with some standard text features like bolding and underlining. Below the toolbar is the text editing window. When you enter text in this window, the text wraps around as it will be displayed in your drawing, according to the width you have specified. This width is represented by the small ruler at the top of the text window. Using the two small triangles at the left end of the ruler, you can also set first line indent and hanging indent tabs for paragraph formatting.

The window is placed at the actual text location and the text is shown in the window at the same size as it will appear in the drawing, unless this would make it either too large or too small for convenient editing. In such cases, the text size is adjusted to a reasonable size for editing and the actual size is only shown when the command is completed.

⊕ Type MTEXT creates lines of text using a text editor.

Text appears in the window as illustrated in Figure 7-9.

Figure 7-9

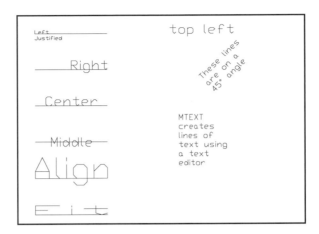

Figure 7-10

⊞ Click the OK button at the right end of the toolbar to leave the editor and complete the command.

You are returned to the drawing window and the new text is added, as shown in Figure 7-10. Notice that the text you typed has been wrapped around to fit within the 3.00 width window; the 0.30 height of the text has been retained; and the 1.00 height of the text window you defined has been ignored.

In a moment, we explore other MTEXT justification options as an editing procedure using DDMODIFY. First, however, we do some simple text editing with DDEDIT.

7.5 Editing Text in Place with DDEDIT and MTEDIT

GENERAL PROCEDURE

1. Select the text you want to edit.
2. Right-click to open the shortcut menu.
3. Select Text Edit from the shortcut menu.
4. Edit text in the Edit Text dialog box.
5. Click OK.

There are several ways to modify text that already exists in your drawing. You can change wording and spelling as well as properties such as layer, style, and justification. For simple changes in the wording of text, use the DDEDIT command, accessed from the Modify menu; for property changes, use the Properties Manager, discussed in Task 7.6.

In this task, we do some simple DDEDIT text editing. Then we use the MTEDIT command to show different justification options of MTEXT paragraphs. In both cases, it is most efficient to select the text first and then use the shortcut menu to enter commands and select options. Start by selecting the first line of the angled text.

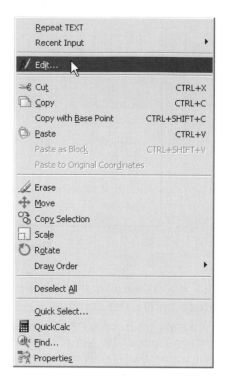

Figure 7-11

⊕ Select the words These lines by clicking on any of the letters.

The words "These lines" are highlighted and a grip appears at the start point of the line, indicating that this single line of text has been selected.

⊕ Right-click to open the shortcut menu shown in Figure 7-11.

⊕ Select Edit from the shortcut menu, as shown.

When you make this selection, the shortcut menu disappears and you see the selected text line highlighted and colored as shown in Figure 7-12. This is the way DDEDIT functions for text created with DTEXT. If you had selected text created with MTEXT, the shortcut menu would have had an Edit Mtext option that would put you in the Multiline Text Editor instead.

We add the word three to the middle of the selected line, as follows.

⊕ Move the screen cursor to the center of the text, between These and lines, and press the pick button.

A flashing cursor should now be present, indicating where text will be added if you begin typing.

Figure 7-12

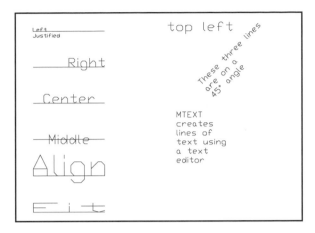

Figure 7-13

⊞   Type the word three and add a space so that the line reads These three lines, as shown in Figure 7-13.

⊞   Press Enter. The cursor disappears, but you are still in the DDEDIT command.

Now let's try it with the text you created in MTEXT. The first difference you notice is that because MTEXT creates multiple lines of text as a group, you cannot select a single line of text. When you click, the whole set of lines is selected.

DDEDIT repeats automatically, so you should have the following prompt in the command area before proceeding:

```
Select an annotation object or [Undo]:
```

If not, repeat DDEDIT.

⊞   Select the text beginning with MTEXT creates.

DDEDIT recognizes that you have chosen text created with MTEXT and opens the Multiline Text Editor, with the text window around the chosen paragraph and the Text Formatting toolbar above.

⊞   Point and click just to the left of the word lines in the text editor.

You should see a white cursor blinking at the beginning of the line.

⊞   Type multiple, so the text reads MTEXT creates multiple lines of text using a text editor.

When you exit the command, the text is redrawn as shown in Figure 7-14. Before leaving the Multiline Text Editor, take a look at the available shortcut menu.

⊞   Move the cursor anywhere within the text edit window and right click.

You see the shortcut menu illustrated in Figure 7-15. Of particular interest are the justification options, which we explore in the next task, the Find and Replace option, and the Symbol option. If you highlight the Symbol option, a submenu with a list of symbols appears, including the degree symbol, the plus or minus symbol, the diameter symbol and others. Selecting from this list saves you from typing the %% characters. If you select Other from the submenu, a

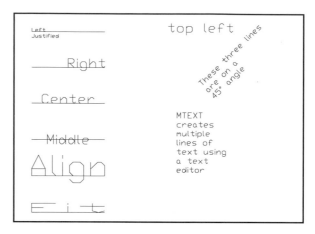

Figure 7-14

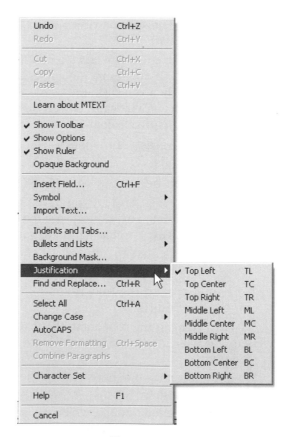

Figure 7-15

Character Mapping dialog box appears with a large selection of fonts to choose from, each having its own standard set of symbols. These options are also available on the toolbars of the Multiline Text Editor.

⊕ Move the cursor anywhere outside the text editor and press the pick button.

The shortcut menu closes but you are still in the DDEDIT command.

⊕ Press Enter or the spacebar to exit the command.

You return to the Drawing Window, with the new text added as shown in Figure 7-14. That's it for DDEDIT. Next we explore PROPERTIES along with more MTEXT justification options.

7.6　Modifying Text with PROPERTIES

GENERAL PROCEDURE

1. Select Properties from the Modify menu.
2. Select text to modify. (Steps 1 and 2 can be reversed if noun/verb editing is enabled in your drawing.)
3. Use the Properties dialog box to specify property changes.
4. Click OK.

PROPERTIES is one of several commands that can be used to change properties of objects in a drawing. It is used with many kinds of objects other than text. Properties include color, layer, linetype, and lineweight, among others. In this exercise, you learn how to use PROPERTIES to change Mtext justification options. We begin this task with a look at the Properties modeless dialog box.

⊕ Draw a 3.00 line just above the Mtext paragraph, as shown in Figure 7-16.

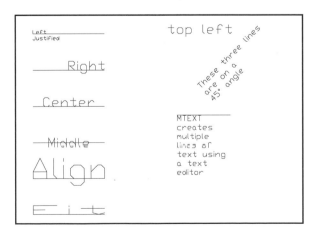

Figure 7-16

This line is only for reference to make the placement of different justification options clearer. It should begin at the same snap point that was used as the insertion point for the text. The left end of the line shows the insertion point, and the length shows the width of the paragraph. We have used the point (9.00,6.00) and the 3.00 width.

⊞ Select the paragraph beginning with MTEXT creates.

⊞ Right-click to open the shortcut menu.

Notice that this is not the same menu you entered when the DDEDIT command had already been entered.

⊞ Select Properties from the bottom of the shortcut menu.

Modeless Dialog Boxes and Palettes

The Properties dialog box illustrated in Figure 7-17 is different from other dialog boxes we have seen. This is our first encounter with a modeless dialog box. Modeless dialog boxes combine some features of toolbars with some features of regular modal dialog boxes, and they have some unique features as well. Like toolbars, you can have more than one open at a time, they can be floating or docked, and they can be left open while other commands are executed. Whereas toolbars are simple sets of tool icons, however, modeless dialog boxes can contain the more

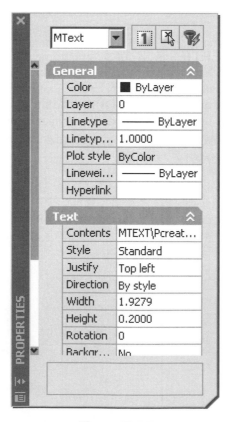

Figure 7-17

complex interfaces of modal dialog boxes, including multiple tabs, panels, scroll bars, drop-down lists, and edit boxes. In AutoCAD many modeless dialog boxes are also referred to as *palettes*.

Take a look at the general format of the Properties palette. On the left is the blue title bar, with a close button (X) at the top and Properties in the middle. Below that are two symbols we explore later in this task. As usual, the dialog box can be moved on the screen by clicking and dragging on the blue title bar.

To the right of the title bar is an area with a small scroll bar, a General list and a Text list, and some buttons at the top. Looking closely at the palette you can see that many items are truncated, with missing text indicated by ellipses (...). To get a better look at these, we resize the palette. This is accomplished by grabbing the right edge of the palette and dragging it out to the right.

⊕ Move your cursor slowly over the right edge of the Properties palette and look for a two-way arrow to appear in place of the crosshairs.

This is a standard cursor symbol used in many Windows-based programs. It is used to stretch borders by dragging.

⊕ With the two-way arrow showing, hold down the pick button and pull the palette border slowly out to the right far enough to show most of the text, but not so far as to cover the Mtext in your drawing.

Your screen should now resemble Figure 7-18.

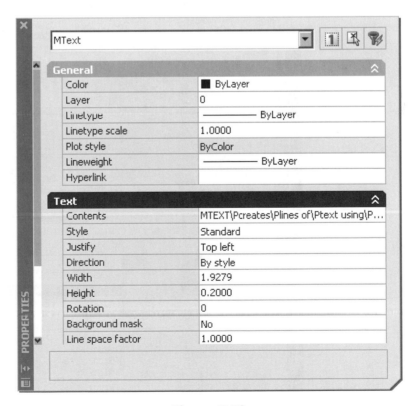

Figure 7-18

In the top list box, you see MText. This indicates the type of object you have selected. If you had chosen multiple objects you could select from a drop-down list opening from this box.

Below the edit box are lists of all the properties that can be modified for the object you have chosen. The first list is the General list, including properties such as layer and color that apply to all objects. In this case the second list is the Text list, showing properties that only apply to text. There is a third list, called Geometry, that contains coordinates of the placement of the object within the drawing. To see the Geometry list, use the scroll bar to the left of the lists. There you find the coordinates of the start point of the MText.

We are going to make a change in text justification, but notice that there are also options here to change text content and text style (Task 7.8). To change MText content select Contents from the Text list. An ellipsis button appears in the right column. Clicking this would open the Multiline Text Editor with the selected text. In this exercise, however, we do not change the text itself, but only the justification.

⊕ Select Justify from the Text list.

When Justify is selected, a drop-down list arrow appears in the right column, next to Top left.

⊕ Click the arrow.

This opens a list box with a list of nine justification options, as shown in Figure 7-19. The list should look familiar to you because it includes some of the same choices as the text justification options introduced previously for

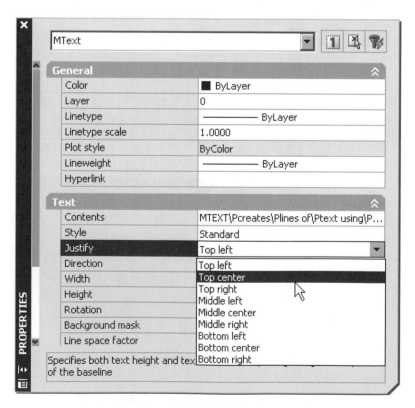

Figure 7-19

DTEXT. The difference is that here you place and justify multiple lines of text as a group.

Notice that the current justification is Top left. We change it to Top center, the second option on the list.

⊕ Click Top center.

The list box closes, and Top center should now be shown in the Justify edit box. You can also see that the change is immediately reflected in your drawing even while the dialog box is still open.

Auto-hide

Before leaving the Properties dialog box, we demonstrate one additional important feature of AutoCAD's modeless dialog boxes and palettes. Just below the word Properties on the title bar, you see a symbol with a small bar on the left and two arrowheads or triangles pointing in opposite directions on the right. If you let your cursor rest on this icon you see a tooltip that says Auto-hide.

⊕ Click the Auto-hide button on the title bar.

The palette closes, but the title bar remains, as shown in Figure 7-20. Also note that the two arrowheads have been replaced by a single arrowhead. This indicates that Auto-hide is on for this dialog box.

⊕ Move your cursor over the title bar and let it rest a moment.

The palette opens automatically. It is not necessary to click to open it.

Figure 7-20

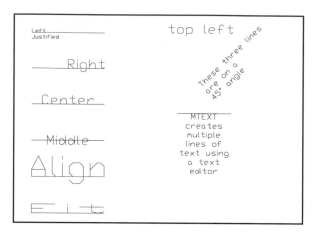

Figure 7-21

✦ Move your cursor back into the drawing area and let it rest there without clicking.

   The palette closes again, but the title bar stays open.

This is the Auto-hide feature. It allows your modeless dialog box or palette to remain accessible while taking up very little space in your drawing area. This is a very handy feature. You can reverse the setting simply by clicking the Auto-hide icon again.

> **Note:** At the very bottom of the title bar there is a square-shaped icon. The tooltip for this icon says Properties. This refers to the properties of the dialog box window itself and has nothing to do with the PROPERTIES command we are exploring in this task. Dialog box properties for this dialog box include Auto-hide, docking, moving, and resizing. If you click on the Properties icon you see a shortcut menu, but most of these options are available without opening the menu.

Finally, close the Properties dialog box before moving on.

✦ Click the Close button at the top of the Properties dialog box title bar to exit the dialog box.

✦ Press Esc to clear grips.

   Your text is redrawn as shown in Figure 7-21. The paragraph is now in centered format, centered in the original insertion window. You might wish to continue with other justification options. Also, study Figure 7-22, which illustrates Mtext justification options.

7.7   Using the SPELL Command

GENERAL PROCEDURE
1.   Select Spelling from the Tools menu.
2.   Select objects.
3.   Press Enter to end selection.
4.   Use the dialog box to ignore, change, or add words the spell checker does not recognize.

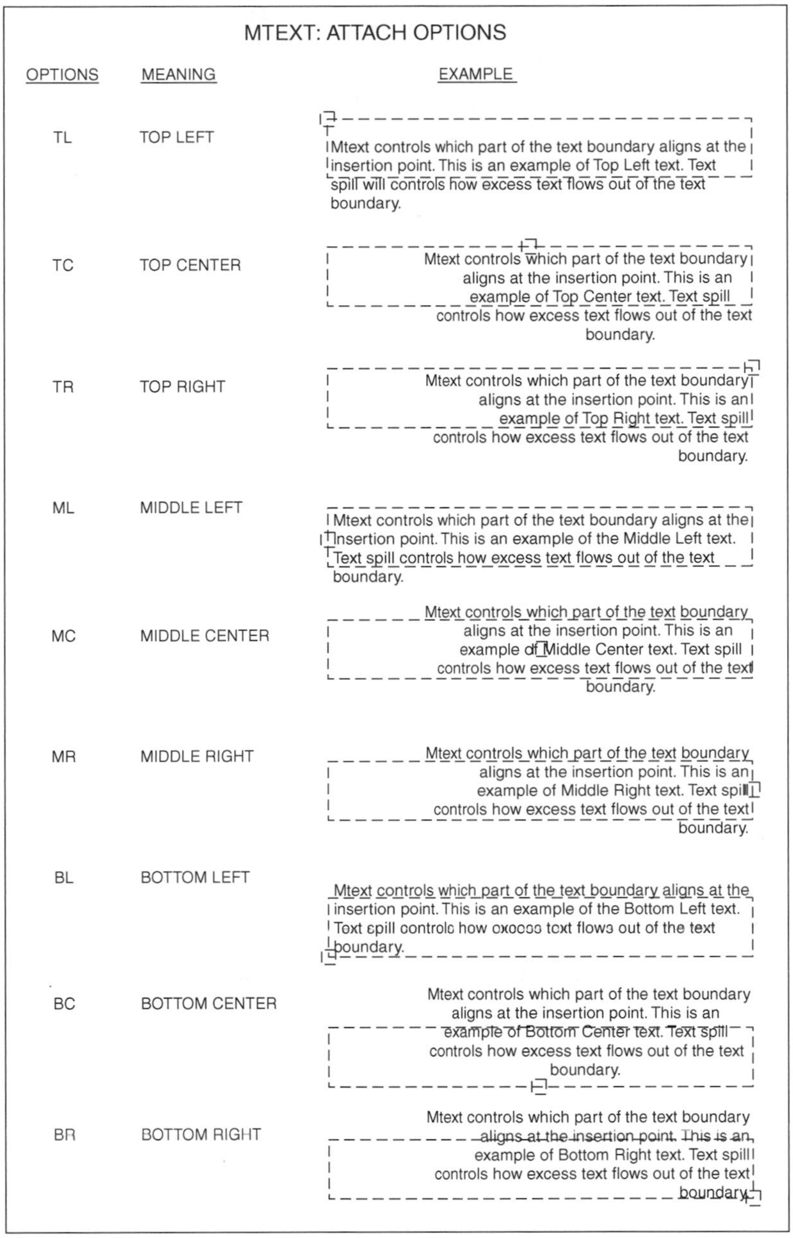

MTEXT: ATTACH OPTIONS

OPTIONS	MEANING	EXAMPLE
TL	TOP LEFT	Mtext controls which part of the text boundary aligns at the insertion point. This is an example of Top Left text. Text spill will controls how excess text flows out of the text boundary.
TC	TOP CENTER	Mtext controls which part of the text boundary aligns at the insertion point. This is an example of Top Center text. Text spill controls how excess text flows out of the text boundary.
TR	TOP RIGHT	Mtext controls which part of the text boundary aligns at the insertion point. This is an example of Top Right text. Text spill controls how excess text flows out of the text boundary.
ML	MIDDLE LEFT	Mtext controls which part of the text boundary aligns at the Insertion point. This is an example of the Middle Left text. Text spill controls how excess text flows out of the text boundary.
MC	MIDDLE CENTER	Mtext controls which part of the text boundary aligns at the insertion point. This is an example of Middle Center text. Text spill controls how excess text flows out of the text boundary.
MR	MIDDLE RIGHT	Mtext controls which part of the text boundary aligns at the insertion point. This is an example of Middle Right text. Text spill controls how excess text flows out of the text boundary.
BL	BOTTOM LEFT	Mtext controls which part of the text boundary aligns at the insertion point. This is an example of the Bottom Left text. Text spill controls how excess text flows out of the text boundary.
BC	BOTTOM CENTER	Mtext controls which part of the text boundary aligns at the insertion point. This is an example of Bottom Center text. Text spill controls how excess text flows out of the text boundary.
BR	BOTTOM RIGHT	Mtext controls which part of the text boundary aligns at the insertion point. This is an example of Bottom Right text. Text spill controls how excess text flows out of the text boundary.

Figure 7-22

AutoCAD's SPELL command is simple to use and very familiar to anyone who has used spell checkers in word processing programs. We use SPELL to check the spelling of all the text we have drawn so far.

⊞   Type sp or select Spelling from the Tools menu.

You see a Select objects: prompt on the command line. At this point, you could point to individual objects. Any object can be selected, although no checking is done if you select a line, for example.

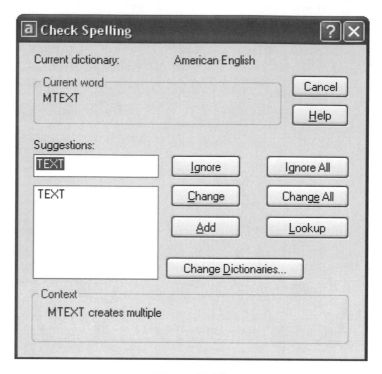

Figure 7-23

For our purposes we use an All option to check all the spelling in the drawing.

⊕ Type all.

AutoCAD continues to prompt for object selection until you press Enter.

⊕ Press Enter to end object selection.

This brings you to the Check Spelling dialog box shown in Figure 7-23. If you have followed the exercise so far and not misspelled any words along the way, you see MTEXT in the Current word box and TEXT as a suggested correction. Ignore this change, but before you leave SPELL, look at what is available: You can ignore a word the checker does not recognize or change it. You can change a single instance of a word or all instances in the currently selected text. You can add a word to a customized dictionary or you can change to another dictionary.

⊕ Click Ignore.

If your drawing does not contain other spelling irregularities, you should now see an AutoCAD message that reads

                Spelling check complete.

⊕ Click OK to end the spell check.

If you have made any corrections in spelling, they are incorporated into your drawing at this point.

7.8 Changing Fonts and Styles

GENERAL PROCEDURE

1. Select Text Style from the Format menu.
2. Click New.
3. Type in a name for the new style.
4. Click OK.
5. Change settings in the Text Style dialog box. Specify height, width, and font.
6. Click Close.

By default, the current text style in any AutoCAD drawing is called STANDARD. It is a specific form of a font called txt that comes with the software. All the text you have entered so far has been drawn with the standard style of the txt font.

Changing fonts is a simple matter. However, there is room for confusion in the use of the words style and font. *Fonts* are the basic patterns of character and symbol shapes that can be used with the DTEXT and MTEXT commands. *Styles* are variations in the size, orientation, and spacing of the characters in those fonts. It is possible to create your own fonts, but for most of us this is an esoteric activity. In contrast, creating your own styles is easy and practical.

We begin by creating a variation of the STANDARD style you have been using:

⊕ Type st or select Text Style from the Format menu.

Either method opens the Text Style dialog box shown in Figure 7-24. You probably see STANDARD listed in the Style Name box. However, it is possible

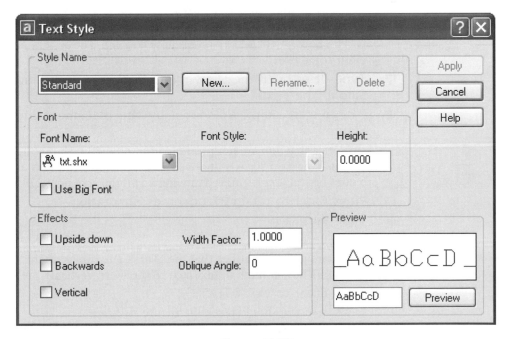

Figure 7-24

that other styles are listed. In this case, you should open the list with the arrow on the right and select STANDARD, the AutoCAD default style. We will create our own variation of the STANDARD style and call it VERTICAL. It uses the same txt character font, but is drawn down the display instead of across.

⊕ Click New.

AutoCAD opens a smaller dialog box that asks for a name for the new text style.

⊕ Type vertical.

⊕ Click OK.

This returns you to the Text Style dialog box, with the new style listed in the Style Name area. We use the vertical text effect to make this style different.

⊕ Click the Vertical check box in the Effects area at the lower left of the dialog box.

Notice the change to vertically oriented text in the Preview panel at the lower right of the dialog box.

We also give this style a fixed height and a width factor. Notice that the current height is 0.00. This does not mean that your characters will be drawn 0.00 units high. It means that there will be no fixed height, so you can specify a height whenever you use this style. STANDARD currently has no fixed height, so VERTICAL has inherited this setting. Try giving our new VERTICAL style a fixed height.

⊕ Double-click in the Height edit box and then type .5.

⊕ Double-click in the Width Factor box and type 2.

⊕ Click Close to exit the Text Style dialog box.

⊕ You see a message that says "The current style has been modified. Do you want to save your changes?" Click Yes.

The new VERTICAL style is now current. To see it in action you need to enter some text.

⊕ Type dt or open the Draw menu, highlight Text, and then highlight Single Line Text.

⊕ Pick a start point, as shown by the placement of the letter V in Figure 7-25.

Notice that you are not prompted for a height because the current style has height fixed at 0.50. Also notice that the default rotation angle is set at 270. Your vertical text is entered moving down the screen at 270 degrees.

⊕ Press Enter to retain 270 degrees of rotation.

⊕ Type Vertical.

⊕ Press Enter to end the line.

Before going on, notice that the DTEXT text placement box has moved up to begin a new column of text next to the word vertical.

⊕ Press Enter to exit DTEXT.

Your screen should resemble Figure 7-25.

There are now two text styles in the current drawing, both of which use the txt font. Next we create a third style using a different font and some of the other style

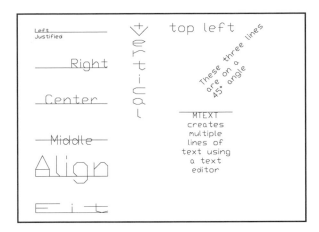

Figure 7-25

options. Pay attention to the Preview panel in the dialog box, which updates automatically to show your changes.

⊕   Type st or select Text Style from the Format menu.

⊕   Click New to give the style a name.

⊕   In the New Text Style dialog box, give the style the name Slanted.

⊕   Click OK to close the New Text Style box.

⊕   Open the Font Name list by clicking the arrow.

   A lengthy list of fonts is available.

⊕   Scroll to romand.shx and stop.

   Romand stands for Roman Duplex, an AutoCAD font.

⊕   Click romand.shx to place it in the Font Name box.

⊕   Clear the Vertical check box.

⊕   Set the text Height to 0.00.

⊕   Set the Width Factor to 1.

⊕   Set Oblique Angle to 45.

   This causes your text to be slanted 45 degrees to the right. For a left slant, you would type a negative number.

⊕   Click Close to exit the Text Style dialog box.

   Now enter some text to see how this slanted Roman Duplex style looks.

⊕   Click Yes to confirm that you want to save changes to the current style.

⊕   Enter the DTEXT command and answer the prompts to draw the words Roman Duplex with a 0.50 height, as shown in Figure 7-26.

Switching the Current Style

All new text is created in the current style. The style of previously drawn text can be changed, as we see later. Once you have a number of styles defined in a drawing, you can switch from one to another by using the Style option of the DTEXT and MTEXT commands or by selecting a text style from the Text Style dialog box.

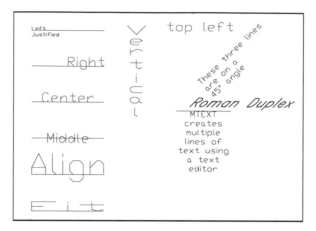

Figure 7-26

Note: If you change the definition of a text style, all text previously drawn in that style will be regenerated with the new style specifications.

7.9 Changing Properties with MATCHPROP

GENERAL PROCEDURE

1. Select the Match Properties tool from the Standard toolbar, or Match Properties from the Modify menu.
2. Select a source object with properties you wish to transfer to another object.
3. If necessary, specify properties you wish to match.
4. Select destination objects.
5. Press Enter to end object selection.

MATCHPROP is a very efficient command, that lets you match all or some of the properties of an object to those of another object. Properties that can be transferred from one object to another, or to many others, include layer, linetype, color, and linetype scale. These settings are common to all AutoCAD entities. Other properties that only relate to specific types of entities are thickness, text style, dimension style, and hatch style. In all cases, the procedure is the same.

Here we use MATCHPROP to change some previously drawn text to the new Slanted style.

⊕ Select the Match Properties tool from the Standard toolbar, as shown in Figure 7-27.

You can also type ma or select Match Properties from the Modify menu. AutoCAD prompts:

Select source object:

You can have many destination objects, but only one source object.

Figure 7-27

⊕ Select the text Roman Duplex, drawn in the last task in the Slanted style.

AutoCAD switches to the Match Properties cursor, shown in Figure 7-28, displays a list of active settings, and prompts

```
Current active settings: Color Layer Ltype Ltscale
   Lineweight Thickness
PlotStyle Text Dim Hatch
Select destination object(s) or [Settings]:
```

At this point, you can limit the settings you want to match by typing s for settings, or you can select destination objects, in which case all properties are matched.

⊕ Type s.

This opens the Property Settings dialog box, shown in Figure 7-29. The Basic Properties panel shows properties that can be changed and the settings that will be used based on the source object you have selected.

At the bottom, you see Dimension, Text, and Hatch in the Special Properties panel. These refer to dimension, text, and hatch styles that have been defined in your drawing. If any one of these is not selected, Match Properties ignores style definitions and only matches the basic properties selected.

⊕ Click OK to exit the dialog box.

AutoCAD returns to the screen with the same prompt as before.

⊕ Select the words Align and Vertical.

These two words are redrawn in the Slanted style, as shown in Figure 7-30. AutoCAD returns the Select destination objects prompt so that you can continue to select objects.

⊕ Press Enter to exit the command.

The CHANGE Command

The CHANGE command is an older AutoCAD command that has largely been replaced by other editing commands. CHANGE works at the command line and allows you to modify all of the basic text properties, including insertion point, style, height, rotation angle, and text content. You can select as many objects as you like and CHANGE cycles through them. In addition, CHANGE can be used to alter

Figure 7-28

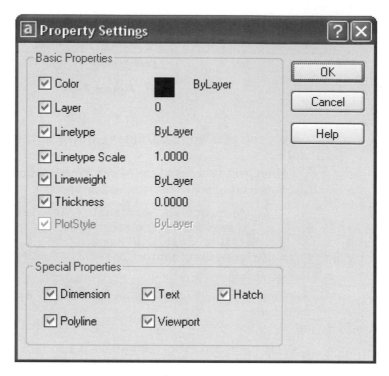

Figure 7-29

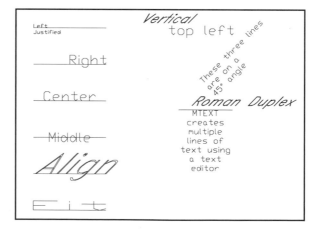

Figure 7-30

the endpoints of lines and the size of circles. With lines, CHANGE performs a function similar to the EXTEND command, but without the necessity of defining an extension boundary. CHANGE causes circles to be redrawn so that they pass through a designated change point. The effects of change points on lines and circles are shown in Figure 7-31.

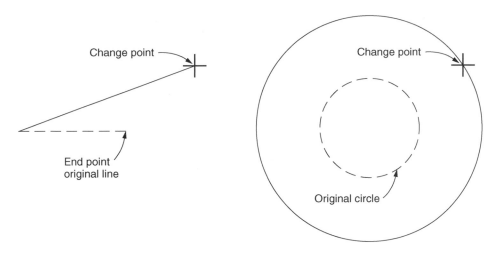

Change point

End point
original line

Change point

Original circle

Figure 7-31

7.10   Scaling Previously Drawn Entities

GENERAL PROCEDURE

1. Select the Scale tool from Modify toolbar.
2. Select objects.
3. Pick a base point.
4. Enter a scale factor.

Any object or group of objects can be scaled up or down using the SCALE command or the Grip edit scale mode. In this exercise, we practice scaling some of the text and lines that you have drawn on your screen. Remember, however, that there is no special relationship between SCALE and text and that other types of entities can be scaled just as easily.

⊕   Select the Scale tool from Modify toolbar, as shown in Figure 7-32.

You can also type sc or select Scale from the Modify menu.
AutoCAD prompts you to select objects.

⊕   Use a crossing box (right to left) to select the set of six lines and text drawn in Task 7.1.

⊕   Press Enter or right-click to end selection.

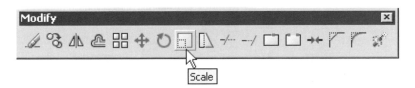

Figure 7-32

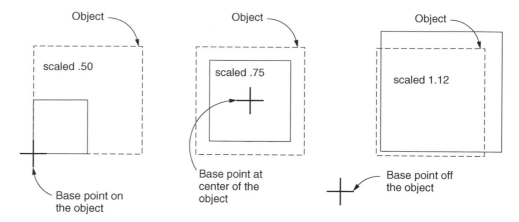

Figure 7-33

You are prompted to pick a base point:

                    Specify base point:

The concept of a base point in scaling is critical. Imagine for a moment that you are looking at a square and you want to shrink it using a scale-down procedure. All the sides will be shrunk the same amount, but how do you want this to happen? Should the lower left corner stay in place and the whole square shrink toward it? Or should everything shrink toward the center? Or toward some other point on or off the square? (See Figure 7-33.) This is what you tell AutoCAD when you pick a base point.

⊕ Pick a base point at the left end of the bottom line of the selected set (shown as Base point in Figure 7-34).

AutoCAD now needs to know how much to shrink or enlarge the objects you have selected:

            Specify scale factor or [Reference]:

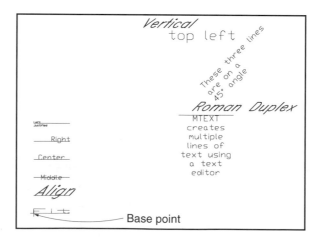

Figure 7-34

We get to the reference method in a moment. When you enter a scale factor, all lengths, heights, and diameters in your set are multiplied by that factor and redrawn accordingly. Scale factors are based on a unit of 1. If you enter .5, objects are reduced to half their original size. If you enter 2, objects become twice as large.

⊞   Type .5 and press Enter.

Your screen should now resemble Figure 7-34.

Scaling by Reference

This option can save you from doing the arithmetic to figure out scale factors. It is useful when you have a given length and you know how large you want that length to become after the scaling is done. For example, we know that the lines we just scaled are now 2.00. Let's say that we want to scale them again to become 2.33 long—a scale factor of 1.165. But who wants to stop and figure that out? This could be done using the following procedure:

1. Enter the SCALE command.
2. Select the lines.
3. Pick a base point.
4. Type r or select Reference.
5. Type 2 for the reference length.
6. Type 2.33 for the new length.

Note: You can also perform reference scaling by pointing. In the foregoing procedure, you could point to the ends of the 2.00 line for the reference length and then show a 2.33 line for the new length.

Scaling with Grips

Scaling with grips is very similar to scaling with the SCALE command. To illustrate this, try using grips to return the text you just scaled back to its original size.

⊞   Use a window or crossing box to select the six lines and the text drawn in Task 7.1 again.

There are several grips on the screen: three on each line and two on most of the text entities. Some of these overlap or duplicate each other.

⊞   Pick the grip at the lower left corner of the word Fit, the same point used as a base point in the last scaling procedure.

⊞   Right-click to open the shortcut menu and then select Scale.

⊞   Move the cursor slowly and observe the dragged image.

AutoCAD uses the selected grip point as the base point for scaling unless you specify that you want to pick a different base point.

Notice that you also have a reference option as in the SCALE command. Unlike the SCALE command, you also have an option to make copies of your objects at different scales.

As in SCALE, the default method is to specify a scale factor by pointing or typing.

⊕ Type 2 or show a length of 2.00. (We reduced the objects by a factor of .5, so we need to enlarge them by a factor of 2 to return to the original size.)

Your text returns to its original size, and your screen should resemble Figure 7-30 again.

⊕ Press Esc to clear grips.

Note: Grips can be used to edit text in the usual grip edit modes of moving, copying, rotating, mirroring, and scaling. The stretch mode works the same as moving. Grips cannot be used to reword, respell, or change text properties.

7.11 Creating Tables and Fields

AutoCAD has features for creating tables similar to those available in most word processing programs. Standard tables consist of a title, a row of column headers, and any number of data rows. In this exercise we will create a simple table with two columns and three rows of data. We will also take the opportunity to demonstrate the use of fields, which are text objects that can be inserted and easily updated when the information they hold changes.

⊕ To begin this drawing you can be in any AutoCAD drawing.

We will continue to use the text demonstration drawing created in this chapter, but will zoom into the area where we insert our table.

⊕ Zoom into an empty window of space in your drawing approximately 4.00 by 4.00.

⊕ Select Table from the Draw menu or the Table button from the Draw toolbar, as shown in Figure 7-35.

Either method will open the Insert Table dialog box, shown in Figure 7-36. Look at the Table Style Settings panel on the left. This panel shows that the current table style is called Standard and that the text height for the table is 0.18. It also shows a preview image of the style, with a Title, a row of headers, and data rows. The number of rows and columns is not part of the style definition. These can be changed in the panel on the right. If you click the ellipsis button next to the Table Style name box you will see a Table Style definition dialog box that will allow you to create and modify new table styles. The characteristics of text and borders in the Title, Column Head, and Data sections of the table can all be modified and saved as a style. For this exercise we use the standard table style.

Figure 7-35

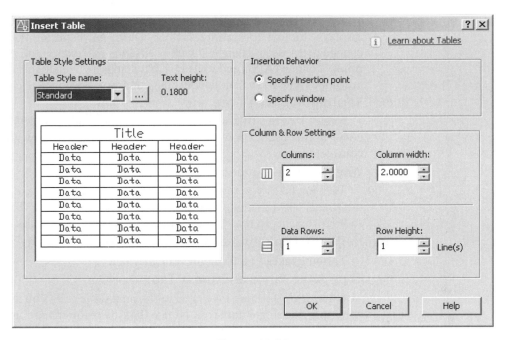

Figure 7-36

Note: The text styles in a table definition are independent of text style in the drawing. Text styles for each component of the table can be selected from the available styles and are not affected by the current style in the drawing. The default text style is Standard text.

Now look at the Column & Row Settings panel on the right. We begin by specifying a table with two columns and one row. Later we add two more rows.

✛ Click the up or down arrow in the Columns box to set the number of columns to 2.

✛ Double-click in the Column width box and type 2.00.

✛ Click the arrows in the Data Rows to set the number of rows to 1.

✛ Click the arrows under Row Height to set the row height to 1 line.

You are now ready to insert this table into your drawing. Tables are inserted in one of two ways, indicated by the two buttons in the panel at the top right labeled Insertion Behavior. You can use an insertion point or show a placement by specifying a window. We use the simpler insertion point method.

✛ Check to make sure that the Specify insertion point button is selected.

✛ Click OK to exit the dialog box.

The dialog box disappears and you return to the drawing with a preview image of your table to drag into place.

✛ Select an insertion point, leaving enough space for the addition of two rows at the bottom of the table.

As soon as you pick an insertion point, AutoCAD highlights the title row and displays the text formatting toolbar. Here you have another opportunity to change text style and height as well as entering the text. AutoCAD also adds temporary column (A, B) and row (1) markers in gray outside the actual table. These are guides only and will not appear in your drawing when you leave the command.

⊕ For the title, type Date and Time Formats.

Notice that this title wraps around within the table cell. The text appears to cover up the header row, but this row will be "pushed down" when the title is completed.

⊕ When you have typed the title, press Tab.

Tabbing takes you to the next cell of the table. In this case it also moves the table cells down to make room for the two lines of the title. The text formatting toolbar remains so that you can enter and format text for the column headers.

⊕ In the first column header cell, type Format and then press Tab.

Tabbing takes you to the next header cell.

⊕ Type Appearance and press Tab.

Once again, tabbing takes you to the next table cell. You are now in the first column of the single data row. Notice that the column headings are centered in their cells, as shown in Figure 7-37. This middle center justification is specified in the Standard table style definition and can be changed by opening the Table Style dialog box.

Tip: When entering data in table cells, you can move sequentially through cells using the Tab key. To reverse directions and move backward, hold down Shift while pressing Tab.

We will be entering time and date format symbols in the Format column and actual date and time fields in the Appearance column. The text in the Appearance column will be inserted as fields that can be updated automatically. We use dates and times because they demonstrate updating very readily.

⊕ In the first data row, first column, as shown in Figure 7-37, type HH:mm, and press Tab.

This is the common symbol for time in an hours and minutes format. This is 24-hour time (2:00 P.M. will appear as 14:00). Tabbing takes you to the second column, which we will leave blank for the moment. Tabbing again will create a new row.

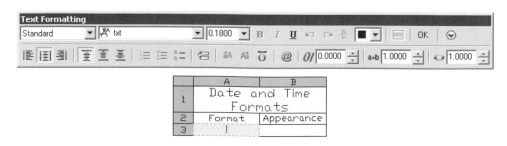

Figure 7-37

✧ Press Tab again to create a second data row.

The Text Formatting toolbar is still open and you are ready to enter text into the second data row, first column.

✧ Type h:mm:ss tt.

This symbolizes time in hours, minutes, and seconds. The tt stands for A.M. or P.M.

Note: The use of the two uppercase H's for the hour minute format and a single lowercase h for the hour minute second format seems inconsistent, but we adhere to this convention because that is the way it appears in the Field dialog box.

✧ Press Tab to complete the cell and move to the second column.

✧ Press Tab again to leave this cell blank and create a third data row.

✧ In the third data row, first column, type M/dd/yyyy and press Tab once.

This is a date in month, day, year format, with a four-place number for the year.

Inserting Fields

You are now in the last row, last column of the table and instead of typing text here, we will insert a date field, in month, day, year format. Then we will return to the other rows in this column and enter time fields.

✧ From the Multiline Text Editor, select the Insert Field tool, shown in Figure 7-38.

This will open the Field dialog box, shown in Figure 7-39. There are many types of predefined fields shown in the Field names box on the left. What appears in the Format list on the right depends on the type of field selected.

✧ Select Date in the Field names list.

With Date selected, you see the Example formats for dates and times. There are many options and you will have to scroll to see them all. Notice that the Date format symbols for the selected format are displayed in the Date format box above the examples.

✧ Select the example at top of the list, which will be the current date in M/dd/yyyy format.

✧ With this format selected, click OK.

The date will be entered in the cell as shown in Figure 7-40. It will be displayed in gray, indicating that this is not ordinary text, but a field. If this drawing were to be plotted, the gray would not appear in the plot.

Figure 7-38

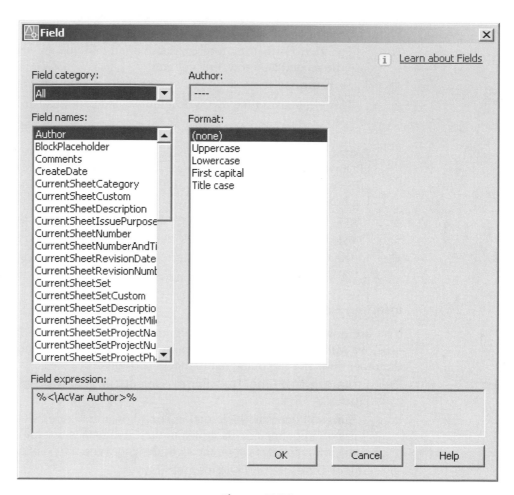

Figure 7-39

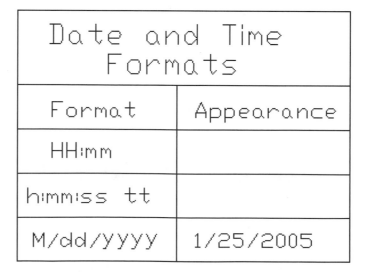

Figure 7-40

Note: Fields can be inserted anywhere in a drawing. To insert a field without a table, select Field from the Insert menu. This will call the Field dialog box and the rest of the process will be the same.

At this point we will exit the table and return to the drawing.

⊞ To return to the drawing, click OK on the Text Formatting toolbar.

Your table should now resemble Figure 7-40.

We could have filled out all the table cells without leaving the table, but it is important to know how to enter data after a table has already been created. Different selection sequences will select cells in different ways. For example, if you pick a cell border, you will select the entire table. If you pick within a cell, you will select the cell, but will not have access to text entry and formatting. Double-clicking within a cell will open the text formatting toolbar.

⊞ Double-click inside the first data row, second column, below the Appearance header.

The cell is highlighted and the Text Formatting toolbar is displayed again.

⊞ Select the Insert Field tool from the toolbar.

The Field dialog box opens. We select the HH:mm example to match the format we have indicated in the Format column. You will find this selection seventh up from the bottom of the examples list. It will have hours and minutes with no A.M. or P.M.

⊞ Highlight the HH:mm date format example.

When it is highlighted, HH:mm will appear in the Date Format box.

⊞ Click OK.

A time field will be entered into your table.

Now proceed to the remaining cell.

⊞ Press Tab twice to move to the empty cell.

⊞ Select the Insert Field tool.

⊞ Select the h:mm:ss tt example.

This will be eighth from the bottom, just above your last selection.

⊞ Click OK.

⊞ Click OK on the Text Formatting toolbar to return to the drawing.

Your table should now resemble Figure 7-41 with three fields in the three right-hand data cells.

Updating Fields

Fields may be updated manually or automatically, individually or in groups. To update an individual field, double-click in the cell to open the Text Formatting toolbar and right-click to open the shortcut menu. Select Update field from the shortcut menu. This also works with individual fields that are not in a table. Double clicking on the field object will open the Text Formatting toolbar just as it does in a table.

For our demonstration we will update all the fields in our table at once, using the Tools menu.

⊞ Select any border of the table.

This will select the entire table.

⊞ With the entire table selected, open the Tools menu and select Update Fields, at the bottom of the first section of the menu.

Date and Time Formats	
Format	Appearance
HH:mm	17:31
h:mm:ss tt	5:31:32
M/dd/yyyy	1/25/2005

Figure 7-41

Notice how the two time fields are updated, while the date field remains the same.

Fields also update automatically when certain things occur, as controlled by settings in the User Preferences dialog box. To reach these settings, select Options from the Tools menu. Select the User Preferences tab and then the Field Update Settings button in the Fields panel. Fields may be automatically updated when a file is opened, saved, plotted, regenerated, or transmitted over the Internet. Any combination of these may be selected. By default, all are selected.

Note: There may be times when you wish to convert a field to regular text. This could happen if you were working on a project for some time and wished to set the date permanently upon completion, for example. To convert a field to text, double-click the field to open the Text Formatting toolbar, right-click to open the shortcut menu, and select Convert Field to Text.

7.12   Using AutoCAD Templates, Borders, and Title Blocks

Now that you have learned how to create text in this chapter and how to use paper space layouts in the last chapter, you can take full advantage of the AutoCAD templates with predrawn borders and title blocks. In this exercise we create a new drawing using an AutoCAD B-size template, add some simple geometry, and add some text to the title block. The work you do here can be saved and used as a start to completing Drawing 7-2, the gauges at the end of the chapter.

⊕   To begin, type new, select New from the File menu, or select the QNew tool from the Standard toolbar.

⊕   In the familiar Select template dialog box, double-click ANSI B – Color Dependent Plot Styles.

⊕   With ANSI B–Color Dependent Plot Styles showing in the File name box, click Open.

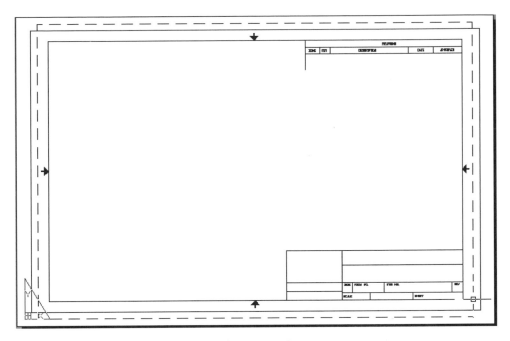

Figure 7-42

This opens a new drawing in a paper space layout with a predrawn border and title block, as illustrated in Figure 7-42. Notice the paper space icon at the lower left of the screen. Next we switch to model space.

⊕ Click the Model tab at the bottom of the drawing area.

In model space you see a blank screen. Turning on the grid gives you a better sense of the drawing space.

⊕ Press F7 to turn on the grid.

The grid appears at the left side of the drawing area.

⊕ Zoom All or use the horizontal scroll bar to center the grid.

By moving the cursor to the upper right corner of the grid, you notice that the model space limits for this drawing are set at (12,9). Note that these limits apply to model space limits only. The paper space limits are different, and are set up to print to a B-size drawing sheet. As we have seen, model space and paper space limits are usually completely unrelated. The current 12×9 model space limits are fine for our purposes. We are going to take the first step in creating the geometry of Drawing 7-2 by drawing a 5.00 circle.

⊕ Type c or select the Circle tool from the Draw toolbar to execute the CIRCLE command.

⊕ Create a 2.50 radius circle with center point at (3.00,5.00), as shown in Figure 7-43.

As you do this, notice also that having started this drawing with a different template, none of the layers or other settings you have previously created in your 1B template are defined in this drawing.

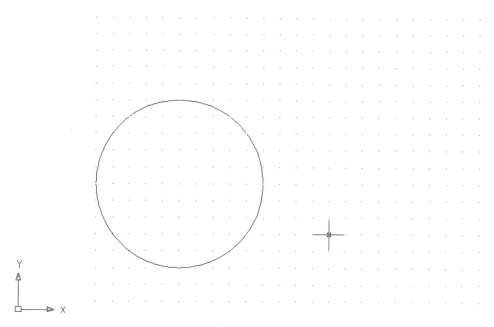

Figure 7-43

Now we return to the paper space layout. Notice that this layout is labeled on a tab at the bottom of the drawing area.

⊕ Click the ANSI B Title Block tab.

You return to paper space with the circle added as shown in Figure 7-44. Take a minute to explore the layout. The bordered area where the circle is drawn is actually a viewport.

⊕ Double-click inside the border.

The border is highlighted by bolding, indicating that the viewport is active. The paper space icon disappears, indicating that you are in the viewport and do not currently have access to paper space objects.

⊕ Select the circle.

The circle is shown with highlighting and grips, indicating that you have access to the model space objects within the viewport.

⊕ Double-click outside the border.

The paper space icon returns, the viewport border is no longer bold, and the highlighting and grips disappear from the circle. You are now back in paper space. Next we add two items of text to the title block. To facilitate this we make some changes to the paper space grid and snap.

⊕ Press F7 or click the Grid button to turn on the paper space grid.

Notice that the paper space grid in this template is set to .50. If you move your cursor to the upper right corner of the "paper," you also notice that this layout emulates a 16.50 × 10.50 drawing sheet. We are going to create text in two of the areas of the title block, as shown in Figure 7-45. Notice, however, that the current grid and snap make this difficult.

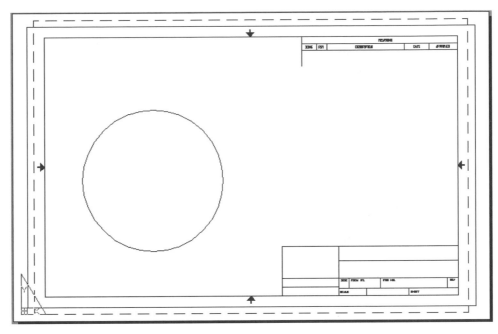

Figure 7-44

⊕   Type grid and change the grid setting to .25.

⊕   Type snap and change the snap setting to .125.

⊕   Zoom into a window around the title block, as shown in Figure 7-45.
     You are now ready to add text.

⊕   Type dt to enter the DTEXT command and pick a start point near
     (12.25,1.75), as shown.

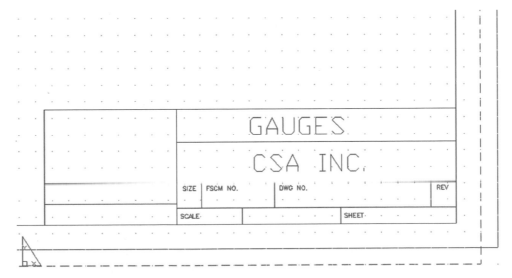

Figure 7-45

⊕   Specify a text height of .25 and a rotation angle of 0.
⊕   Type Gauges.
⊕   Press Enter twice to exit DTEXT.
⊕   Repeat DTEXT and type CSA INC. at (12.25,1.25), as shown in Figure 7-45.
⊕   Press Enter twice to exit DTEXT.
⊕   Zoom All to view the complete layout.

There you go. You are well on your way to completing Drawing 7-2, complete with title block.

7.13   Review Material

Questions

1. What is the main difference between DTEXT and MTEXT?
2. You have drawn two lines of text using DTEXT and have left the command to do some editing. You discover that a third line of text should have been entered with the first two lines. What procedure allows you to add the third line of text efficiently so that it is spaced and aligned with the first two, as if you had never left DTEXT?
3. What is the difference between center-justified text and middle-justified text?
4. What is the purpose of %% in text entry?
5. In the MTEXT command, what information does AutoCAD take from the two corners of the rectangle you specify before entering text? What else is needed to predict how AutoCAD interprets these point selections?
6. What aspect of text can be changed with DDEDIT? What aspects of text can be changed with PROPERTIES? What is the purpose of MATCHPROP?
7. How do you check all the spelling in your drawing at once?
8. What is the difference between a font and a style?
9. What can happen if you choose the wrong base point when using the SCALE command?
10. How would you use SCALE to change a 3.00 line to 2.75? How could you use LENGTHEN (Chapter 6) to do the same thing?
11. You have completed the outline of a table in your drawing, but have left the TABLE command. How would you reenter an individual cell of the table and insert a field in that cell?
12. You wish to use an AutoCAD-provided border and title block for your drawing. Where would you find the one you wish to use?

Drawing Problems

1. Draw a 6 × 6 square. Draw the word Top on top of the square, 0.4 unit high, centered on the midpoint of the top side of the square.
2. Draw the word Left 0.4 unit high, centered on the left side of the square.
3. Draw the word Right 0.4 unit high, centered on the right side of the square.

4. Draw the word Bottom 0.4 unit high, below the square so that the top of the text is centered on the midpoint of the bottom side of the square.
5. Draw the words This is the middle inside the square, 0.4 unit high, so that the complete text wraps around within a 2-unit width and is centered on the center point of the square.

7.14 WWW Exercise 7 (Optional)

In Chapter 7 of our companion website, we ask you to explore the Web and bring back information on an important innovator in the field of architecture. We define your task and give you two links to get you started. We also give you another design challenge and, as always, the self-scoring test for this chapter. So, when you are ready, complete the following:

⊞ Make sure that you are connected to your Internet service provider.

⊞ Type browser, open the Web toolbar, and select the Browse the Web tool, or open your system browser from the Windows taskbar.

⊞ If necessary, navigate to our companion website at www.prenhall.com/dixriley.

Happy hunting!

7.15   Drawing 7-1: Title Block

This title block gives you practice in using a variety of text styles and sizes. You might want to save it and use it as a title block for future drawings. In Chapter 10, we show you how to insert one drawing into another, so you can incorporate this title block into any drawing.

QTY REQ'D	D E S C R I P T I O N		P A R T N O.	ITEM NO.
	BILL OF MATERIALS			
UNLESS OTHERWISE SPECIFIED DIMENSIONS ARE IN INCHES	DRAWN BY: *Your Name*	DATE		
REMOVE ALL BURRS & BREAK SHARP EDGES	APPROVED BY:		*CSA INC.*	
TOLERANCES FRACTIONS ± 1/64 DECIMALS ANGLES ± 0°–15' XX ± .01 XXX ± .005	ISSUED:		DRAWING TITLE:	
MATERIAL:	FINISH:	SIZE C	CODE IDENT NO. 38178	DRAWING NO.	REV.
		SCALE:	DATE:	SHEET	OF

Drawing Suggestions

$$GRID = 1$$
$$SNAP = 0.0625$$

- Make ample use of TRIM as you draw the line patterns of the title block. Take your time and make sure that at least the major divisions are in place before you start entering text into the boxes.
- Set to the text layer before entering text.
- Use DTEXT with all the STANDARD, 0.09, left-justified text.
- Remember that once you have defined a style, you can make it current in the DTEXT command. This saves you from restyling more than necessary.
- Use %%D for the degree symbol and %%P for the plus or minus symbol.

ALL TEXT UNLESS OTHERWISE NOTED IS:
Font (SIMPLEX)
Height (0.09)
Left justified

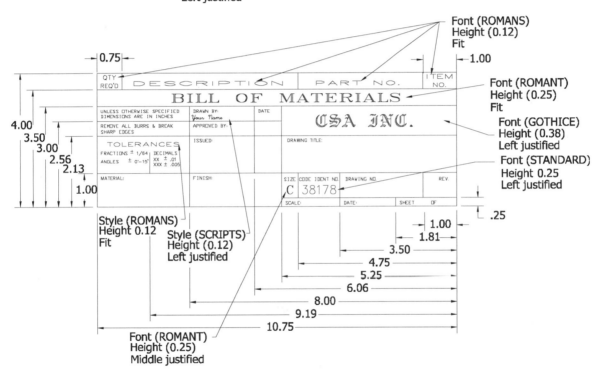

Font (ROMANS)
Height (0.12)
Fit

Font (ROMANT)
Height (0.25)
Fit

Font (GOTHICE)
Height (0.38)
Left justified

Font (STANDARD)
Height 0.25
Left justified

Style (ROMANS)
Height 0.12
Fit

Style (SCRIPTS)
Height (0.12)
Left justified

Font (ROMANT)
Height (0.25)
Middle justified

TITLE BLOCK

Drawing 7-1

7.16   Drawing 7-2: Gauges

This drawing teaches you some typical uses of the SCALE and DDEDIT commands. Some of the techniques used are not obvious, so read the suggestions carefully.

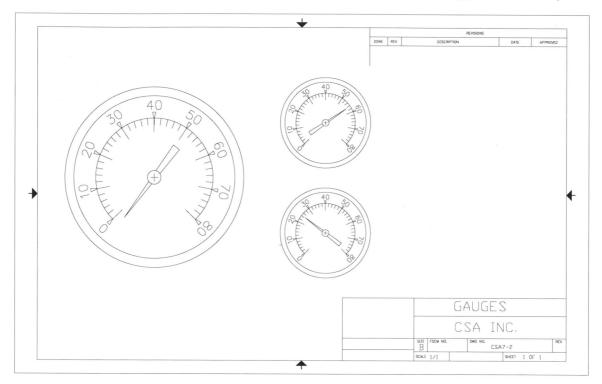

Drawing Suggestions

GRID = 0.5
SNAP = 0.125

- Draw three concentric circles at diameters of 5.0, 4.5, and 3.0. The bottom of the 3.0 circle can be trimmed later.
- Zoom in to draw the arrow-shaped tick at the top of the 3.0 circle. Then draw the 0.50 vertical line directly below it and the number 40 (middle-justified text) above it.
- These three objects can be arrayed to the left and right around the perimeter of the 3.0 circle using angles of +135 and −135 as shown.
- Use DDEDIT to change the arrayed numbers into 0, 10, 20, 30, and so on. You can do all of these without leaving the command.
- Draw the 0.25 vertical tick directly on top of the 0.50 mark at the top center and array it left and right. There should be 20 marks each way.
- Draw the needle horizontally across the middle of the dial.
- Make two copies of the dial; use SCALE to scale them down as shown. Then move them into their correct positions.
- Rotate the three needles into positions as shown.

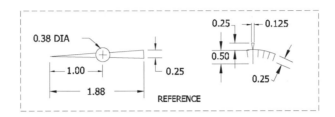

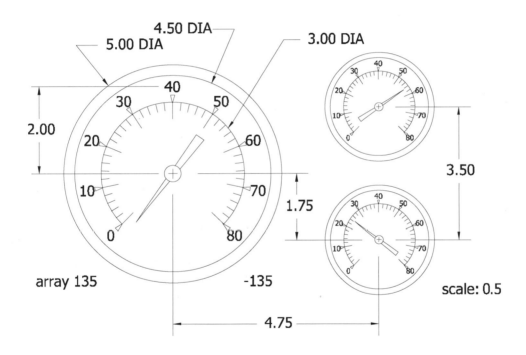

GAUGES
Drawing 7-2

7.17   Drawing 7-3: Stamping

This drawing is trickier than it appears. There are many ways that it can be done. The way we have chosen not only works well, but makes use of a number of the commands and techniques you have learned in the last two chapters. Notice that a change in limits is needed to take advantage of some of the suggestions.

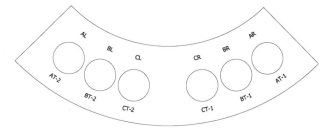

Drawing Suggestions

GRID = 0.50
SNAP = 0.25
LIMITS = (0,0)(24,18)

- Draw two circles, of radius 10.25 and 6.50, centered at about (13,15). These are trimmed later.
- Draw a vertical line down from the center point to the outer circle. We copy and rotate this line to form the ends of the stamping.
- Use the Rotate copy mode of the grip edit system to create copies of the line rotated 45 degrees and −45 degrees. (The coordinate display shows 315 degrees.)
- Trim the lines and the circles to form the outline of the stamping.
- Draw a 1.50-diameter circle in the center of the stamping, 8.50 down from (13,15). Draw middle-justified text, AR, 7.25 down, and AT-1 down 9.75 from (13,15).
- Follow the procedure given in the next subsection to create offset copies of the circle and text; then use DDEDIT to modfiy all text to agree with the drawing.

Grip Copy Modes with Offset Snap Locations

Here is a good opportunity to try another grip edit feature. If you hold down the Shift key while picking multiple copy points, AutoCAD is constrained to place copies only at points offset from each other the same distance as your first two points. For example, try the following steps:

1. Select the circle and the text.
2. Select any grip to initiate grip editing.
3. Select Rotate from the shortcut menu.
4. Type b or select Base point from the shortcut menu.
5. Pick the center of the stamping (13,15) as the base point.
6. Type c or select Copy from the shortcut menu.
7. Hold down the Shift key and move the cursor to rotate a copy 11 degrees from the original.
8. Keep holding down the Shift key as you move the cursor to create other copies. All copies are offset 11 degrees.

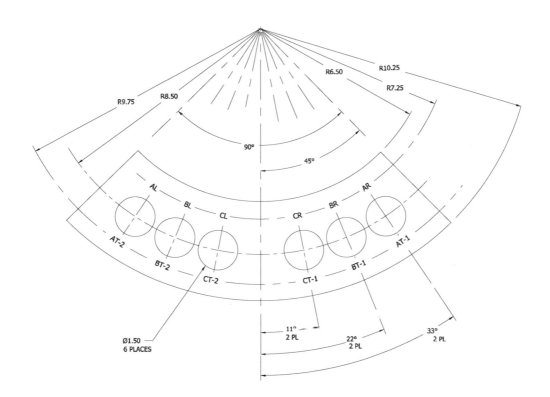

STAMPING
Drawing 7-3

7.18   Drawing 7-4: Control Panel

Done correctly, this drawing gives you a good feel for the power of the commands you now have available to you. Be sure to take advantage of combinations of ARRAY and DDEDIT as described. Also, read the suggestion on moving the origin before you begin. Moving the origin in this drawing makes it easier to read the dimensions, which are given in ordinate form measured from the (0,0) point at the lower left corner of the object.

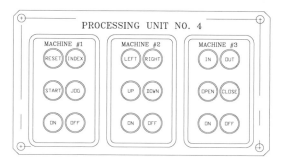

Drawing Suggestions

$$GRID = 0.50$$
$$SNAP = 0.0625$$

- After drawing the chamferred outer rectangle, draw the double outline of the left button box, and fillet the corners. Notice the different fillet radii.
- Draw the On button with its text at the bottom left of the box. Then array it 2 × 3 for the other buttons in the box.
- Use DDEDIT to change the lower right button text to Off and draw the MACHINE # text at the top of the box.
- ARRAY the box 1 × 3 to create the other boxes.
- Use DDEDIT to change text for other buttons and machine numbers as shown.

Moving the Origin with the UCS Command

The dimensions of this drawing are shown in ordinate form, measured from a single point of origin in the lower left-hand corner. In effect, this establishes a new coordinate origin. If we move our origin to match this point, then we can read dimension values directly from the coordinate display. This could be done by setting the lower left-hand limits to (−1,−1). However, it can be completed more efficiently using the UCS command to establish a user coordinate system with the origin at a point you specify. User coordinate systems are discussed in depth in Chapter 12. For now, here is a simple procedure:

1. Type ucs.
2. Type o for the Origin option.
3. Point to the new origin.

That's all there is to it. Move your cursor to the new origin and watch the coordinate display. It should show 0.00,0.00,0.00, and all values are measured from there.

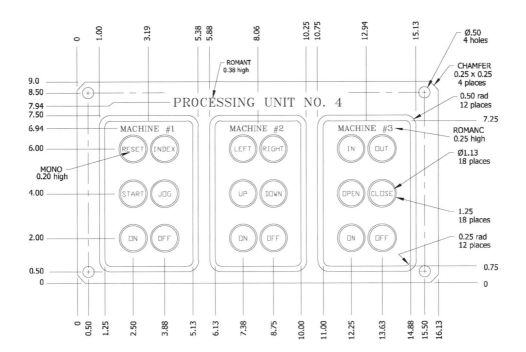

CONTROL PANEL
Drawing 7-4

7.19   Drawing 7-5: Tower

This architectural drawing takes some time, and you utilize many commands that you have learned in this and previous chapters. Notice that the settings are quite different from our standard template, so be sure to change them before beginning.

Drawing Suggestions

UNITS = Architectural Smallest fraction = 1
GRID = 10′
SNAP = 1′

- This drawing can be transfered, using the proper scale, from the book to your AutoCAD. You can use the scale provided on the drawing or use an architectural scale with the setting of 1/32″ = 1′. Either transfer method produces similar results.
- Whatever order you choose for doing this drawing, we suggest that you make ample use of COPY, ARRAY, TRIM, and OFFSET.
- Keep Ortho on, except to draw lines at an angle.
- With Snap set at 1/16, it is easy to copy and array lines and shapes, as you do frequently to reproduce the many rectangular shapes.
- You might need to turn Snap off when you are selecting lines to copy, but be sure to turn it on again to specify displacements.
- Notice that you can use polar ARRAY effectively to draw the text in a circle and then use DDEDIT to change the text. Choose a text font that is similar to that shown. (We used Dutch 801 Rm BT.)

TOWER

Drawing 7-5

Scale

This drawing courtesy of Matt Rose

7.20   Drawing 7-6: Koch Snowflake

The Koch Snowflake design can be done in numerous ways, all involving similar techniques of reference scaling, rotating, and polar arraying. We give you a few suggestions and hints, but you are largely on your own in solving this visual design puzzle.

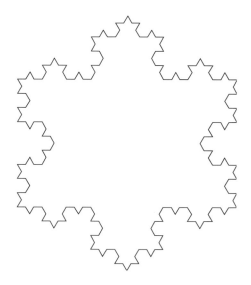

Drawing Suggestions

- Begin by creating an equilateral triangle. Because it is important to know the center point of this triangle, construct it from a circle, as shown. The radial lines are drawn by arraying a single line from the center point three times in a 360-degree polar array.

- After drawing the initial equilateral triangle you make frequent use of reference scaling.

- The number 3 is important throughout this design. Consider how you will use the number 3 in the reference scaling option.

- You will have frequent use for center, intersection, and midpoint object snaps.

- Do not move the original triangle so that you can always locate its center point. There are at least two ways to find the center point of other triangles you create. One involves constructing a 3P circle and another involves three construction lines.

- A lot of trimming and erasing is required to create the final design.

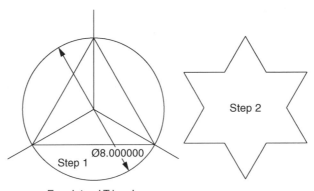

Step 1   Ø8.000000

Step 2

Equalateral Triangle

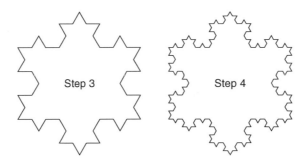

Step 3

Step 4

KOCH SNOWFLAKE
Drawing 7-6

8 | Dimensions

COMMANDS

BHATCH	DIMANGULAR	DIMLINEAR	PROPERTIES
BPOLY	DIMBASELINE	DIMOVERRIDE	QDIM
DDIM	DIMCONTINUE	DIMSTYLE	QLEADER
DIMALIGNED	DIMEDIT	DIMTEDIT	

OVERVIEW

The ability to dimension your drawings and add crosshatch patterns greatly enhances the professional appearance and utility of your work. AutoCAD's dimensioning features form a complex system of commands, subcommands, and variables that automatically measure objects and draw dimension text and extension lines. With AutoCAD's dimensioning tools and variables, you can create dimensions in a wide variety of formats, and these formats can be saved as styles. The time saved by not drawing each dimension object line by line is among the most significant advantages of CAD.

TASKS

8.1 Creating and Saving a Dimension Style

> **GENERAL PROCEDURE**
>
> 1. Type d, select Style from the Dimension menu, or select the Dimension Style tool from the Dimension toolbar.
> 2. Click New.
> 3. Give your new dimension style a name.
> 4. Click OK to exit the Create New Dimension Style dialog box.
> 5. Select settings for Lines, Symbols and Arrows, Text, Fit, Primary Units, Alternate Units, and Tolerances.
> 6. Click OK to exit.

Dimensioning in AutoCAD is highly automated and very easy compared to manual dimensioning. To achieve a high degree of automation while still allowing for the broad range of flexibility required to cover all dimension styles, the AutoCAD dimensioning system is necessarily complex. In the exercises that follow, we guide you through the system, show you some of the options available, and give you a solid foundation for understanding how to get what you want out of AutoCAD dimensioning. We create a basic dimension style and use it to draw standard dimensions and tolerances. We leave it to you to explore the many possible variations.

In AutoCAD, it is best to begin by naming and defining a dimension style. A *dimension style* is a set of dimension variable settings that control the text and geometry of all types of AutoCAD dimensions. We recommend that you create the new dimension style in your template drawing and save it. Then you do not have to make these changes again when you start new drawings.

⊕ To begin this exercise, open the 1B template drawing.

This is the first time that we have modified our template since Chapter 3. To modify it you must open it like any drawing. Remember to look for this file in the Template folder; it has a .dwt file extension. Use the OPEN command to access the Select File dialog box. Select Drawing Template File (*.dwt) from the File of type drop-down list. This automatically opens the Template folder. Select lb.dwt from the list or thumbnail gallery.

We make changes in dimension style settings in the template drawing so that all dimensions showing distances are presented with two decimal places and angular dimensions have no decimals. This becomes the default dimension setting in any drawing created using the 1B template. 1B already uses 2 decimal places for drawing units, but this setting does not carry over to dimensioning.

⊕ Type d, select Dimension Style from the Format menu, select Style from the Dimension menu, or open the Dimension toolbar and select the Dimension Style tool (see Figure 8-1).

Figure 8-1

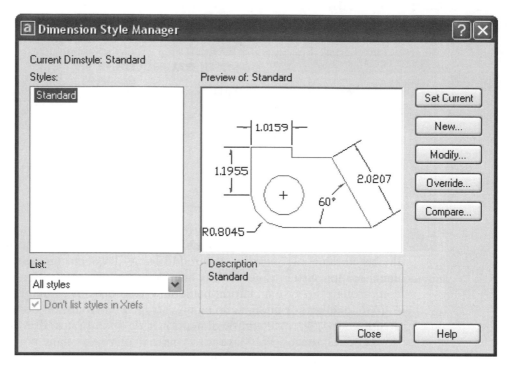

Figure 8-2

Tip: Dimensioning is a good example of a case in which you might want to open a toolbar and leave it open for a while. Because dimensioning is often saved for last in a drawing and can be done all at once, bringing up the toolbar and keeping it on your screen while you dimension might be most efficient. We suggest that you open the Dimension toolbar now and leave it open for this exercise. Remember, you can open a toolbar by right-clicking on any open toolbar and then selecting a toolbar name from the shortcut menu that appears.

Any of the preceding methods open the Dimension Style Manager shown in Figure 8-2. The current dimension style is called Standard. Among other things, the AutoCAD Standard dimension style uses four-place decimals in all dimensions, including angular dimensions. If you see something other than four-place decimals, it simply means that someone has changed this setting on your system.

To the right of the Styles box is a preview image that shows you many of the Standard settings. The preview image is updated immediately any time you make a change in a dimension setting.

To the right of the preview is a set of five buttons, the second of which is New.

⊕   Click New.

> This opens the small Create New Dimension Style dialog box shown in Figure 8-3.

⊕   If necessary, double-click in the New Style Name edit box to highlight the words Copy of Standard.

> Note that the new style is based on the current Standard style. It starts with all of the Standard settings. Anything we don't change is the same as in the Standard style.

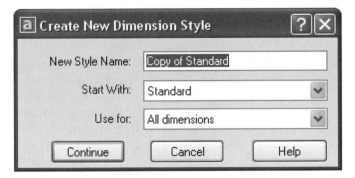

Figure 8-3

⊕   Type 1B.

   Any name will do. We chose this one to go with the template file name.

⊕   Click Continue.

   This creates the new dimension style and takes us into the New Dimension Style dialog box, shown in Figure 8-4. Here there are seven tabs that allow us

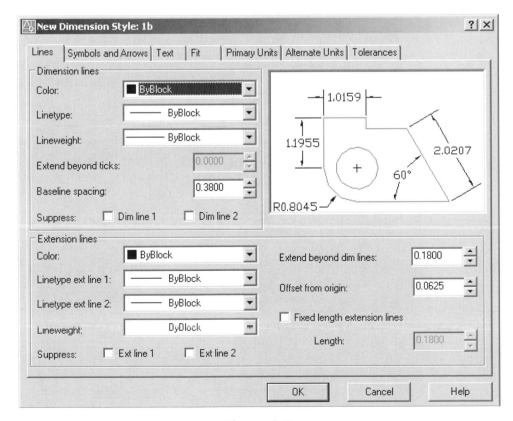

Figure 8-4

to make many changes in Dimension Lines, Symbols and Arrows, Text, Fit, Primary Units, Alternate Units, and Tolerances.

⊕ Click the Primary Units tab.

This brings up the Primary Units window, shown in Figure 8-5. There are adjustments available for linear and angular units. The lists under units and angles are similar to the lists used in the Drawing Units dialog box. In the Linear dimensions panel, Unit format should show Decimal. In the Angular dimensions panel, Units format should show Decimal Degrees. If for any reason these are not showing in your box, you should make these changes now. For our purposes, all we need to change is the number of decimal places showing in the Precision box. By default, it is 0.0000. We change it to 0.00.

⊕ Click the arrow to the right of the Precision box in the Linear dimensions panel.

This opens a list of precision settings ranging from 0 to 0.00000000.

⊕ Click 0.00.

This closes the list box and shows 0.00 as the selected precision. Notice the change in the preview image, which now shows two-place decimals. At this point, we are ready to complete this part of the procedure by returning to the Dimension Style Manager.

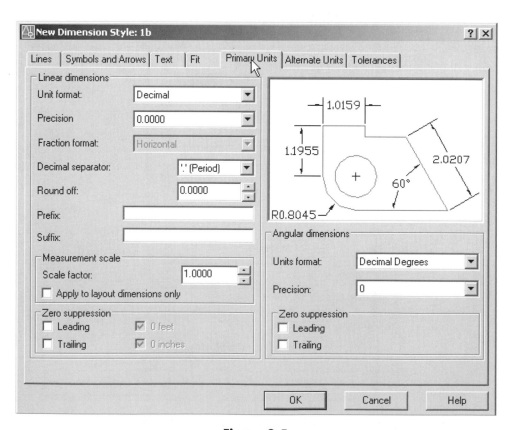

Figure 8-5

Before leaving the New Dimension Style dialog box, you should open the other tabs and take a look at the large variety of dimension features that can be adjusted. Each of the many options changes a dimension variable setting. Dimension variables have names and can be changed at the command line by typing in the name and entering a new value, but the dialog box makes the process much easier and the preview images give you immediate visual feedback.

In the Lines tab and Symbols and Arrows tab you find options for changing the size and positioning of dimension geometry. In Text, you are able to adjust the look and placement of dimension text. This tab includes the option of selecting different text styles previously defined in the drawing. In Fit, you can tell AutoCAD how to manage situations where there is a tight fit, creating some ambiguity about how dimension geometry and text should be arranged. Primary Units, as you know, lets you specify the units in which dimensions are displayed. Alternate Units offers the capacity to include a secondary unit specification along with the primary dimension unit. A common use for this feature would be to give dimensions in both inches and centimeters, for example. Tolerances are added to dimension specifications to give the range of acceptable values in, for example, a machining process. The Tolerances tab gives several options for how tolerances are displayed.

⊕ Click OK to exit the New Dimension Style dialog box.

Back in the Dimension Style Manager dialog box you can see that 1B has been added to the list of styles. At this point, you should have at least the Standard and 1B dimension styles defined in your drawing. 1B should be selected. The preview image shows the selected style.

Note: When a dimension style is selected in the Dimension Style Manager, it is not necessarily the current style in the drawing. To make a style current, you also need to click Set Current. You can tell which style is current by looking at the Override button. It is accessible when the current style is selected and unavailable otherwise. This also indicates that you can temporarily override settings in the current style only.

⊕ Click Set Current to set 1B as the current dimension style.

⊕ Click Close to exit the Dimension Style dialog box.

⊕ Save and close template drawing 1B.

⊕ Select New and open a new drawing using the 1B template.

If the new drawing is opened with the 1B template, the 1B dimension style is current for the next task. If the dimension toolbar is open, 1B shows as the current dimension style in the list box on the right side of the toolbar.

8.2 Drawing Linear Dimensions

GENERAL PROCEDURE

1. Select Linear from the Dimension menu, or select the Linear tool from the Dimension toolbar.
2. Select an object or show two extension line origins.
3. Show the dimension line location.

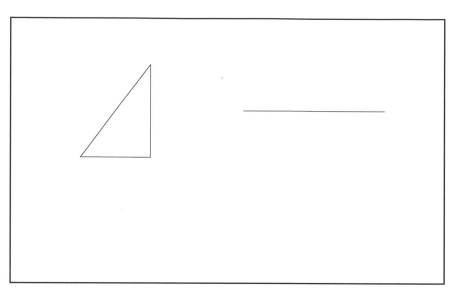

Figure 8-6

AutoCAD has many commands and features that aid in the drawing of dimensions, as evidenced by the fact that there is an entire pull-down menu for dimensioning only. In this exercise, you create some basic linear dimensions in the now-current 1B style.

⊕ To prepare for this exercise, draw a triangle (ours is 3.00,4.00,5.00) and a line (6.00) above the middle of the display, as shown in Figure 8-6.

> Exact sizes and locations are not critical. We begin by adding dimensions to the triangle.

⊕ After creating these objects, open the Layer drop-down list and make the Dim layer current.

> The dimensioning commands are streamlined and efficient. Their full names, however, are all rather long. They all begin with dim and are followed by the name of a type of dimension (e.g., DIMLINEAR, DIMALIGNED, and DIMANGULAR). Use the Dimension menu or the Dimension toolbar to avoid typing these names.
>
> We begin by placing a linear dimension below the base of the triangle.

⊕ Select Linear from the Dimension menu, or select the Linear tool from the Dimension toolbar, as shown in Figure 8-7.

> This initiates the DIMLINEAR command, with the following prompt appearing in the command area:

Figure 8-7

> Specify first extension line origin or <select object>:

There are two ways to proceed at this point. One is to show where the extension lines should begin, and the other is to select the object you want to dimension and let AutoCAD position the extension lines. In most simple applications, the latter method is faster.

⊕ Press Enter to indicate that you will select an object.

AutoCAD replaces the crosshairs with a pick box and prompts for your selection:

> Select object to dimension:

⊕ Select the horizontal line at the bottom of the triangle, as shown by Point 1 in Figure 8-8.

AutoCAD immediately creates a dimension, including extension lines, dimension line, and text, that you can drag away from the selected line. AutoCAD places the dimension line and text where you indicate, but keeps the text centered between the extension lines. The prompt is as follows:

> Specify dimension line location or
> [MText/Text/Angle/Horizontal/Vertical/Rotated]:

In the default sequence, you simply show the location of the dimension. If you wish to alter the text content, you can do so using the Mtext or Text options, or you can change it later with a command called DIMEDIT. Angle, Horizontal, and Vertical allow you to specify the orientation of the text. Horizontal text is the default for linear dimensions. Rotated allows you to rotate the complete dimension so that the extension lines move out at an angle from the object being dimensioned. (Text remains horizontal.)

Note: If the dimension variable dimsho is set to 0 (off), you are not given an image of the dimension to drag into place. The default setting is 1 (on), so this

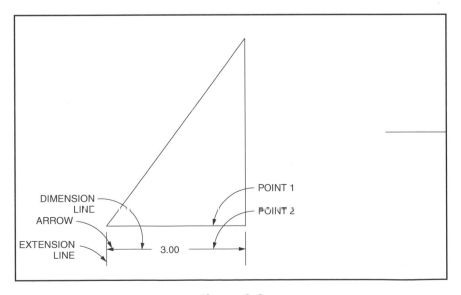

Figure 8-8

should not be a problem. If, however, it has been changed in your drawing, type dimsho and then 1 to turn it on again.

⊕ Pick a location about 0.50 below the triangle, as shown by Point 2 in Figure 8-8.

Bravo! You have completed your first dimension. (Notice that our figure and others in this chapter are shown zoomed in on the relevant object for the sake of clarity. You can zoom or not, as you like.)

At this point, take a good look at the dimension you have just drawn to see what it consists of. As in Figure 8-8, you should see the following components: two extension lines, two arrows, a dimension line on each side of the text, and the text itself.

Notice also that AutoCAD has automatically placed the extension line origins a short distance away from the triangle base. (You might need to zoom in to see this.) This distance is controlled by a dimension variable called dimexo, which can be changed in the Modify Dimension Style dialog box, Lines tab and Symbols and Arrows tab in the Extension lines panel. The setting is called Offset from origin.

Next, we place a vertical dimension on the right side of the triangle. You can see that DIMLINEAR handles both horizontal and vertical dimensions.

⊕ Repeat the DIMLINEAR command.

You are prompted for extension line origins as before:

```
Specify first extension line origin or <select object:
```

This time we show the extension line origins manually.

⊕ Pick the right-angle corner at the lower right of the triangle, Point 1 in Figure 8-9.

AutoCAD prompts for a second point:

```
Specify second extension line origin:
```

Even though you are manually specifying extension line origins, it is not necessary to show the exact point where you want the line to start. AutoCAD

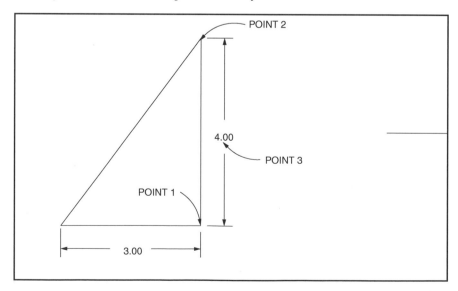

Figure 8-9

Figure 8-10

automatically sets the dimension lines slightly away from the line as before, according to the setting of the dimexo dimension variable.

⊕ Pick the top intersection of the triangle, Point 2 in Figure 8-9.

From here on, the procedure is the same as before. You should have a dimension to drag into place, and the following prompt:

```
Specify dimension line location or
[Mtext/Text/Angle/Horizontal/Vertical/Rotated]:
```

⊕ Pick a point 0.50 to the right of the triangle, Point 3 in Figure 8-9.

Your screen should now include the vertical dimension, as shown in Figure 8-9.

Now let's place a dimension on the diagonal side of the triangle. For this, we need the DIMALIGNED command.

⊕ Select Aligned from the Dimension menu, or the Aligned tool from the Dimension toolbar, as shown in Figure 8-10.

⊕ Press Enter, indicating that you will select an object.

AutoCAD gives you the pick box and prompts you to select an object to dimension.

⊕ Select the hypotenuse of the triangle.

⊕ Pick a point approximately 0.50 above and to the left of the line.

Your screen should resemble Figure 8-11. Notice that AutoCAD retains horizontal text in aligned and vertical dimensions as the default.

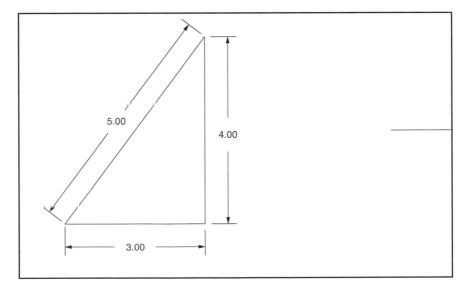

Figure 8-11

8.3   Drawing Multiple Linear Dimensions: QDIM

> **GENERAL PROCEDURE**
>
> 1. Select Quick Dimension from the Dimension menu or the Quick Dimension tool from the Dimension toolbar.
> 2. Select objects to dimension. (Steps 1 and 2 can be reversed if noun/verb editing is enabled.)
> 3. Specify a multiple dimension type.
> 4. Show dimension line location.

QDIM is a miracle-working command that automates the creation of certain types of multiple dimension formats. With this command, you can create a whole series of related dimensions with a few mouse clicks. To introduce QDIM, we create a continuous dimension series dimensioning the bottom of the triangle, the space between the triangle and the line, and the length of the line itself. Then we edit the series to show several points along the line. Finally, we change the dimensions on the line from a continuous series to a baseline series. In later tasks, we return to QDIM to create other types of multiple dimension sets.

⊕ Select the bottom of the triangle and the 6.00 line to the right of the triangle.

Noun/verb editing allows you to select objects before entering QDIM. Your selected lines are highlighted and have grips showing.

⊕ Select Quick Dimension from the Dimension menu or the Quick Dimension tool from the Dimension toolbar, as shown in Figure 8-12.

AutoCAD prompts

```
Specify dimension line position, or
[Continuous/Staggered/Baseline/Ordinate/Radius/Diameter/
datumPoint/Edit/seTtings] <Continuous>:
```

The options here are various forms of multiple dimensions. Continuous, Staggered, Baseline, and Ordinate are all linear styles. Radius and Diameter are for dimensioning circles and arcs. Datum Point is used to change the point from which a set of linear dimensions is measured, Edit has several functions we explore in a moment, and Settings allows a choice of how associated dimensions created with QDIM work.

Continuous dimensions are the AutoCAD default, but this might have changed if someone else has used QDIM on your system, because the last option used is retained as the default.

Figure 8-12

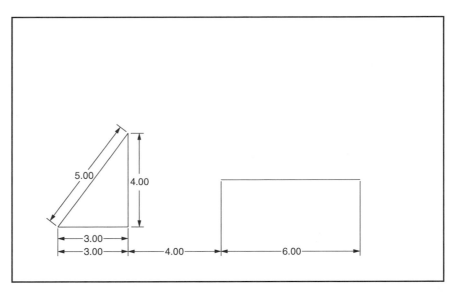

Figure 8-13

⊕   If necessary, type c for the Continuous option.

Continuous dimensions are positioned end to end, as shown in Figure 8-13. AutoCAD creates three linear dimensions at once and positions them end to end.

⊕   Select a point about 1.5 units below the triangle, as shown in Figure 8-13.

Next we edit the dimension on the right, so that the line length is measured to several different lengths.

⊕   Repeat QDIM.

⊕   Select the dimension at the right, below the 6.00 line.

Notice that this dimension can be selected independently. The three continuous dimensions just created are separate objects, even though they were created simultaneously.

Note: The objects selected for the QDIM command can be dimensions or objects to be dimensioned. If you select objects, QDIM creates new dimensions for these objects; if you select dimensions, QDIM edits or re-creates these dimensions depending on the options you select.

⊕   Right-click to end object selection.

AutoCAD gives you a single dimension to drag into place. If you pick a point now, the selected 6.00 dimension is re-created at the point you choose. We do something more interesting.

⊕   Type e for the Edit option.

QDIM prompts

Indicate dimension point to remove, or [Add/eXit] <eXit>:

We add dimension points.

⊕   Type a for the Add option.

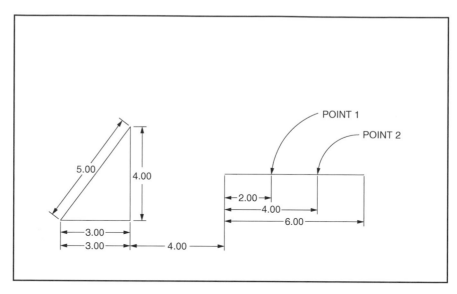

Figure 8-14

Small white Xs are added at the endpoints of the line. These indicate the current dimension points. The prompt changes slightly as follows:

    Indicate dimension point to add, or [Remove/eXit] <eXit>:

⊕ Pick Point 1, as shown in Figure 8-14.

This point is two units from the left endpoint of the line. QDIM continues to prompt for points.

⊕ Pick Point 2, as shown in Figure 8-14.

This point is two units from the right endpoint of the line.

⊕ Press Enter or the spacebar to end point selection.

QDIM now divides the single 6.00 dimension into a series of three continuous 2.00 dimensions. We are not done yet. We choose to draw these three dimensions in Baseline format.

⊕ Type b for the Baseline option.

QDIM immediately switches the three dragged dimensions to a baseline form.

⊕ Pick a point so that the top, shortest dimension of the three is positioned about 1.00 below the line.

Your screen is redrawn with three baseline dimensions as shown in Figure 8-14. We have more to say about this powerful command as we go along. In the next task, we use it to create ordinate dimensions.

DIMBASELINE and DIMCONTINUE

Baseline and Continuous format dimensions can also be created one at a time using individual commands. The following general procedure is used with these commands:

1. Draw an initial linear dimension.
2. Select Baseline or Continue from the Dimension menu or the Baseline dimension or Continue dimension tool from the Dimension toolbar.

3. Pick a second extension line origin.
4. Pick another second extension line origin.
5. Press Enter to exit the command.

8.4 Drawing Ordinate Dimensions

GENERAL PROCEDURE

1. Define a coordinate system with the origin at the corner of the object to be dimensioned.
2. Select Ordinate from the Dimension menu or the Ordinate tool from the Dimension toolbar.
3. Select a location to be dimensioned.
4. Pick a leader endpoint.
5. Press Enter or change dimension text.

Ordinate dimensions are another way to specify linear dimensions. They are used to show multiple horizontal and vertical distances from a single point or the corner of an object. Because these fall readily into a coordinate system, it is efficient to show these dimensions as the x and y displacements from a single point of origin. There are two ways to create ordinate dimensions. AutoCAD ordinarily specifies points based on the point (0,0) on your screen. Using QDIM, you can specify a new Datum Point that serves as the origin for a set of ordinate dimensions. Using DIMORDINATE, it is necessary to temporarily move the origin of the coordinate system to the point from which you want dimensions to be specified. In this task, we demonstrate both.

QDIM and the Datum Point Option

⊕ To prepare for this exercise, switch to Layer 1 and add a 4.00 vertical line up from the left endpoint of the 6.00 horizontal line, as shown in Figure 8-15.

We use ordinate dimensions to specify a series of horizontal and vertical distances from the intersection of the two lines. First, we use QDIM to add ordinate dimensions along the new vertical line. Then we use DIMORDINATE to add ordinate dimensions to the horizontal line.

⊕ Select Dim as the current layer again.

⊕ Enter the QDIM command.

⊕ Select the new vertical line.

⊕ Right-click to end object selection.

⊕ Type o for the Ordinate option.

⊕ Select a point about 1.00 unit to the left of the line, as shown in Figure 8-16.

The two dimensions you see are at the ends of the line and show the y value of each endpoint. Whether in QDIM or in DIMORDINATE, AutoCAD automatically chooses the x or y value depending on the object you choose and the

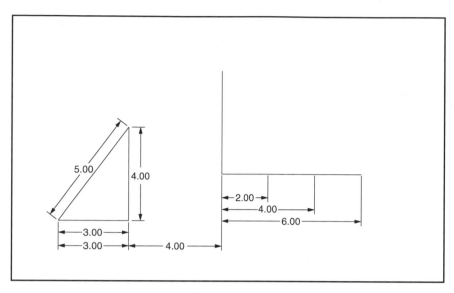

Figure 8-15

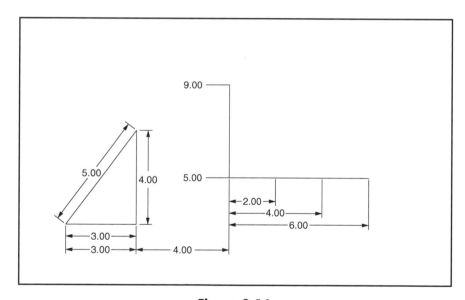

Figure 8-16

position of the leaders relative to the dimensioned points. Because the values you see are measured from the origin at the lower left corner of the grid, they are not particularly useful. A more common use would be to measure points from the intersection of the two lines. This method was used to dimension Drawing 7-4, the Control Panel, in the last chapter, for example. To complete this set of dimensions, we go back into QDIM, select a new datum point, and add and remove dimension points as shown in Figure 8-17.

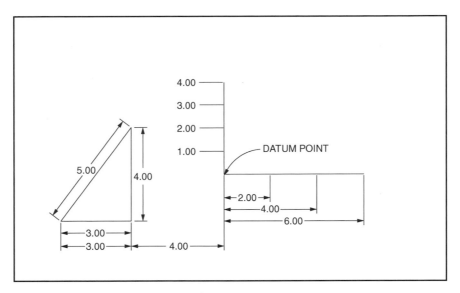

Figure 8-17

⊕　Repeat QDIM.

⊕　Select the bottom ordinate dimension (5.00 in our illustration).

⊕　Select the top ordinate dimension (9.00 in our illustration).

　　Notice that these need to be selected separately.

⊕　Right-click to end geometry selection.

⊕　Type p for the Datum Point option.

　　Notice the uppercase P in the option; if you type d you get the Diameter option instead. QDIM prompts

　　　　　　　　　Select new datum point:

⊕　Select the intersection of the two lines, as shown in Figure 8-17.

　　The new datum point is now established. We add three new dimension points and remove one before leaving QDIM.

⊕　Type e for the Edit option.

　　Even though Remove might be the default edit option, you cannot have fewer than two dimension points in QDIM, so you need to add first.

⊕　Type a to add points.

⊕　Add points 1.00, 2.00, and 3.00 up from the bottom of the line.

　　As you add points, they are marked by Xs.

⊕　Type r to remove points.

⊕　Remove the point at the intersection of the two lines.

⊕　Press Enter or the spacebar to endpoint selection.

⊕　Pick a point about 1.00 unit to the left of the vertical line, as before.

　　Your screen should resemble Figure 8-17. Next we dimension the horizontal line using the DIMORDINATE command.

DIMORDINATE and the UCS Command

We use DIMORDINATE to create a series of ordinate dimensions above the horizontal 6.00 line. This method requires you to create a new origin for the coordinate system using the UCS command. User coordinate systems are crucial in 3-D drawing and are explored in depth in Chapter 12. Although DIMORDINATE only creates one dimension at a time, it does have some advantages over the QDIM system. To begin with, you do not have to go back and edit the dimension to add and remove points. Additionally, you can automatically create a variety of leader shapes.

⊕ Open the Tools menu and select Move UCS.

This selection executes the UCS command and automates the entry of the Move option. Specifying a new coordinate system by moving the point of origin is the simplest of many options in the UCS command. AutoCAD prompts

```
Specify new origin point or [Zdepth] <0,0,0>:
```

⊕ Pick the intersection of the two lines.

If you move your cursor to the intersection and watch the coordinate display, you can see that this point is now read as (0.00,0.00,0.00). If your user coordinate system icon is on and set to move to the origin, it moves to the new point.

⊕ Select Ordinate from the Dimension menu, or select the Ordinate tool from the Dimension toolbar, as shown in Figure 8-18.

AutoCAD prompts

```
Specify feature location:
```

In actuality, all you do is show AutoCAD a point and then an endpoint for a leader. Depending on where the endpoint is located relative to the first point, AutoCAD shows dimension text for either an *x* or a *y* displacement from the origin of the current coordinate system.

⊕ Pick a point along the 6.00 line, 1.00 to the right of the intersection, as shown in Figure 8-19.

AutoCAD prompts

```
Non-associative dimension created
Specify leader end point or [Xdatum/Ydatum/Mtext/Text]:
```

The first line tells you that ordinate dimensions created in this fashion are nonassociative. Associativity is discussed in Task 8.10. The second line prompts you to specify a leader endpoint. You can manually indicate whether you want the dimension text to show the *x* or *y* coordinate by typing x or y. However, if you choose the endpoint correctly, AutoCAD picks the right coordinate automatically. You can also provide your own text, but that would defeat the purpose of setting up a coordinate system that automatically gives you the distances from the intersection of the two lines.

Figure 8-18

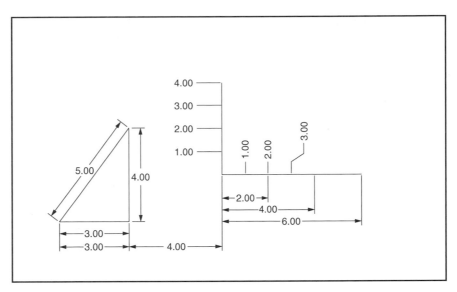

Figure 8-19

⊕ Pick an endpoint 0.5 directly above the line, as shown in Figure 8-19.

Your screen should now include the 1.00 ordinate dimension shown in Figure 8-19.

⊕ Repeat DIMORDINATE and add the second ordinate dimension at a point 2.00 from the origin.

⊕ Repeat DIMORDINATE once more.

⊕ Pick a point on the line 3.00 from the origin.

⊕ Move your cursor left and right to see some of the leader shapes that DIMORDINATE creates depending on the endpoint of the leader.

⊕ Pick an endpoint slightly to the right of the dimensioned point to create a broken leader similar to the one in Figure 8-19.

When you are done, you should return to the world coordinate system. This is the default coordinate system and the one we have been using all along.

⊕ Type ucs, or open the Tools menu and highlight New UCS.

⊕ Type w, or select World from the New UCS submenu.

This returns the origin to its original position at the lower left of your screen.

8.5   Drawing Angular Dimensions

GENERAL PROCEDURE

1. Select Angular from the Dimension menu or the Angular tool from the Dimension toolbar.
2. Select two lines that form an angle.
3. Pick a dimension location.

Figure 8-20

Angular dimensioning works much like linear dimensioning, except that you are prompted to select objects that form an angle. AutoCAD computes an angle based on the geometry that you select (two lines, an arc, part of a circle, or a vertex and two points) and constructs extension lines, a dimension arc, and text specifying the angle. There is no angular option in the QDIM command.

For this exercise, we return to the triangle and add angular dimensions to two of the angles, as shown in Figure 8-21.

⊕ Select Angular from the Dimension menu or the Angular tool from the Dimension toolbar, as shown in Figure 8-20.

The first prompt is

`Select arc, circle, line, or specify vertex>:`

The prompt shows that you can use DIMANGULAR to dimension angles formed by arcs and portions of circles as well as angles formed by lines. If you press Enter, you can specify an angle manually by picking its vertex and a point on each side of the angle. We begin by picking lines, the most common procedure in angular dimensioning.

⊕ Select the base of the triangle.

You are prompted for another line:

`Select second line:`

⊕ Select the hypotenuse.

As in linear dimensioning, AutoCAD now shows you the dimension lines and lets you drag them into place. The prompt asks for a dimension arc location and also allows you the option of changing the text or the text angle:

`Specify dimension arc line location or [Mtext/Text/Angle]:`

⊕ Move the cursor around to see how the dimension can be placed and then pick a point between the two selected lines, as shown in Figure 8-21.

The lower left angle of your triangle should now be dimensioned, as in Figure 8-21. Notice that the degree symbol is added by default in angular dimension text.

We dimension the upper angle by specifying its vertex.

⊕ Repeat DIMANGULAR.

⊕ Press Enter.

AutoCAD prompts for an angle vertex.

⊕ Point to the vertex of the angle at the top of the triangle.

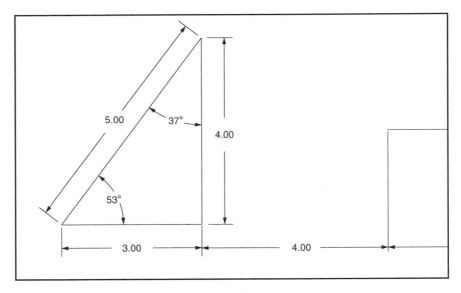

Figure 8-21

AutoCAD prompts

     `Specify first angle endpoint:`

⊕ Pick a point along the hypotenuse.

  To be precise, this should be a snap point. The most dependable one is the lower left corner of the triangle. AutoCAD prompts

     `Specify second angle endpoint:`

⊕ Pick any point along the vertical side of the triangle.

  There should be many snap points on the vertical line, so you should have no problem.

⊕ Move the cursor slowly up and down within the triangle.

  Notice how AutoCAD places the arrows outside the angle when you approach the vertex and things get crowded. Also notice that if you move outside the angle, AutoCAD switches to the outer angle.

⊕ Pick a location for the dimension arc, as shown in Figure 8-21.

Angular Dimensions on Arcs and Circles

You can also place angular dimensions on arcs and circles. In both cases, AutoCAD constructs extension lines and a dimension arc. When you dimension an arc with an angular dimension, the center of the arc becomes the vertex of the dimension angle, and the endpoints of the arc become the start points of the extension lines. In a circle, the same format is used, but the dimension line origins are determined by the point used to select the circle and a second point, which AutoCAD prompts you to select. These options are illustrated in Figure 8-22.

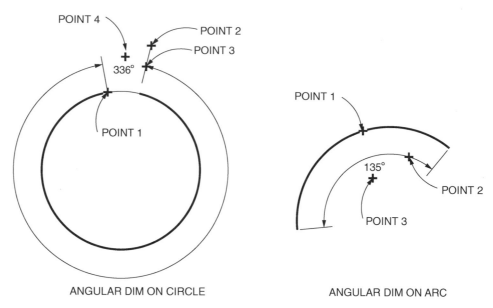

ANGULAR DIM ON CIRCLE   ANGULAR DIM ON ARC

Figure 8-22

8.6   Dimensioning Arcs and Circles

GENERAL PROCEDURE
1. Select Radius or Diameter from the Dimension menu, or select the Radius or Diameter tool from the Dimension toolbar. 2. Pick an arc or circle. 3. Type text or press Enter. 4. Pick a leader line endpoint location.

The basic process for dimensioning circles and arcs is as simple as those we have already covered. It can get tricky, however, when AutoCAD does not place the dimension where you want it. Text placement can be controlled by adjusting dimension variables. In this exercise, we create a center mark and some diameter and radius dimensions. Then we return to the QDIM command to see how multiple circles can be dimensioned at once.

⊕   To prepare for this exercise, switch to Layer 1 and draw two circles at the bottom of your screen, as shown in Figure 8-23.

   The circles we use have radii of 2.00 and 1.50.

⊕   Return to the Dim layer.

⊕   Select Center Mark from the Dimension menu or the Center Mark tool from the Dimension toolbar, as shown in Figure 8-24.

   Center marks are the simplest of all dimension features to create and they are created automatically as part of some radius and diameter dimensions. AutoCAD prompts

       Select arc or circle:

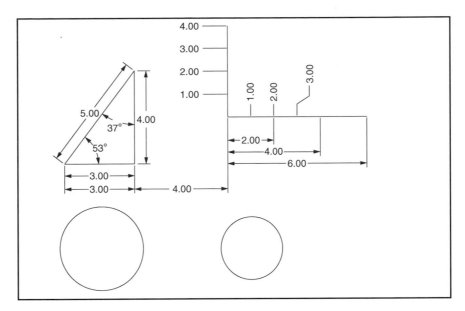

Figure 8-23

Figure 8-24

⊕ Select the smaller circle.

A center mark is drawn in the 1.50 circle, as shown in Figure 8-25. The standard center mark is a small cross. The size of the cross can be changed in a small panel at the bottom right of the Lines tab and Symbols and Arrows tab of the Modify Dimension Style dialog box. Here you also have a choice of standard continuous lines or broken center lines to form the mark.

⊕ Now we add the diameter dimension shown on the larger circle in Figure 8-25.

⊕ Select Diameter from the Dimension menu or the Diameter tool from the Dimension toolbar.

AutoCAD prompts

```
Select arc or circle:
```

⊕ Select the larger circle.

AutoCAD shows a diameter dimension and asks for a dimension line location with the following prompt:

```
Specify dimension line location or [Mtext/Text/Angle]:
```

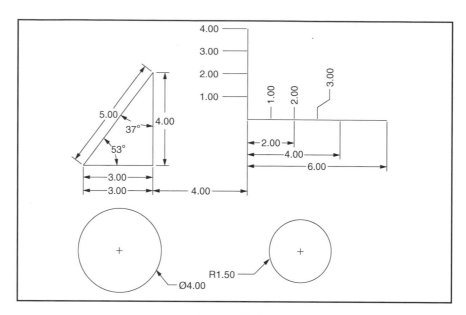

Figure 8-25

The Text and Angle options allow you to change the dimension text or put it at an angle. If you move your cursor around, you see that you can position the dimension line anywhere around or inside the circle.

⊕ Pick a dimension position so that your screen resembles Figure 8-25.

Notice that the diameter symbol prefix and the center mark are added automatically by default.

Radius Dimensions

The procedures for radius dimensioning are exactly the same as those for diameter dimensions and the results look the same. The only differences are the radius value of the text and the use of R for radius in place of the diameter symbol.

We draw a radius dimension on the smaller circle.

⊕ Select Radius from the Dimension menu or the Radius tool from the Dimension toolbar.

⊕ Select the 1.50 (smaller) circle.

⊕ Move the cursor around the circle, inside and outside.

⊕ Pick a point to complete the dimension, as shown in Figure 8-25.

The R for radius and the center mark are added automatically.

Dimensioning Circles and Arcs with QDIM

Multiple radius or diameter dimensions can be created with QDIM. When this technique is used, all leaders are created at the same angle. Try the following:

⊕ Select Quick Dimension from the Dimension menu, or the Quick Dimension tool from the Dimension toolbar.

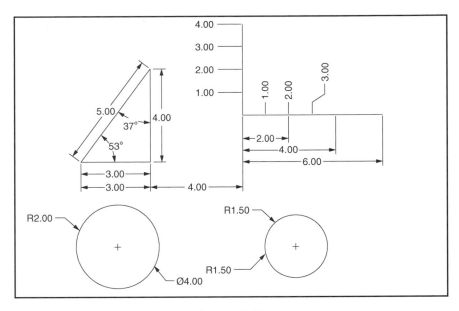

Figure 8-26

✦ Select both circles.

✦ Right-click to end object selection.

✦ Type r for the Radius option.

A rubber band is shown from the center point of the first circle selected to a dimension line point. This rubber band does not resemble the dimensions that will be drawn. QDIM prompts

```
Specify dimension line position, or
[Continuous/Staggered/Baseline/Ordinate/Radius/Diameter/
datumPoint/Edit] <Radius>:
```

✦ Specify a line position by picking a point, as shown in Figure 8-26.

Radius dimensions are added to both circles as shown in Figure 8-26. The Diameter option works in exactly the same way.

8.7 Dimensioning with Leaders

GENERAL PROCEDURE

1. Select Leader from the Dimension menu or the Leader tool from Dimension toolbar.
2. Select a start point.
3. Select an endpoint.
4. Select another endpoint.
5. Type dimension text.

Radius and diameter dimensions, along with ordinate dimensions, make use of leaders to connect dimension text to the object being dimensioned. Leaders can

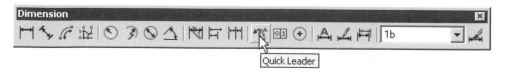

Figure 8-27

also be created independently to attach annotation to all kinds of objects. They can be used to dimension objects in crowded areas of a drawing. Unlike other dimension formats, in which you select an object or show a length, a leader is simply a line or series of lines with an arrow at the end to visually connect an object to its annotation. Because of this, when you create a dimension with a leader, AutoCAD does not recognize and measure any selected object or distance. You need to know the dimension text you want to use before you begin.

The QLEADER command organizes leader options into a single tabbed dialog box. In this exercise, we use QLEADER to create two leaders with associated text. One is as simple as we can make it and the other is more complex.

⊕ Select Leader from the Dimension menu, or select the Quick Leader tool from the Dimension toolbar, as shown in Figure 8-27.

AutoCAD prompts you for a point:

```
Specify first leader point, or [Settings]<Settings>:
```

Usually you want the leader arrow to start on the object, not offset, as an extension line would be. Often this requires the use of an object snap.

⊕ Hold down Shift and right-click your mouse to open the object snap shortcut menu.

⊕ Select Nearest from the fourth panel of the menu.

The Nearest object snap mode specifies that you want to snap to the nearest point on whatever object you select. If you have not used this object snap mode before, take a moment to get familiar with it. As you move around the screen, you see the Nearest snaptool whenever the crosshairs approach an object. If you allow the crosshairs to rest on a point, the Nearest tooltip label appears as well.

⊕ Position the crosshairs so that the upper right side of the 1.50-radius circle crosses the aperture, and press the pick button.

The leader is snapped to the circle and a rubber band appears, extending to the crosshairs. AutoCAD prompts for a second point:

```
Specify next point:
```

⊕ Pick a second point for the leader, up and to the right of the first point, as shown on the smaller circle in Figure 8-28.

QLEADER prompts for another point. This allows you to create broken leaders made up of a series of line segments.

⊕ Press Enter to indicate that you are ready to create the annotation.

Leader text is created as Mtext. AutoCAD prompts

```
Specify text width <0.00>:
```

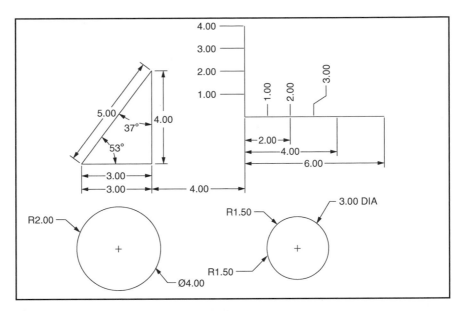

Figure 8-28

You are being asked to specify text width as in the MTEXT command. The width is the width of the complete annotation, not the character size. With text width set at 0, the width is not limited.

⊕ Press Enter or the spacebar to accept the default text width.

You are prompted to enter text:

```
Enter first line of annotation text <Mtext>:
```

⊕ Type 3.00 DIA and press Enter.

QLEADER prompts for additional lines of text:

```
Enter next line of annotation text:
```

If you continue entering text, it is added beneath the first line in MTEXT paragraph form.

Tip: Because text created in the QLEADER command is created as Mtext, it can be edited using all the tools available for Mtext, including the PROPERTIES command, MTEDIT, and the Mtext Text Editor.

⊕ Press Enter (not the spacebar, because you are entering text) to complete the command.

The annotated leader illustrated on the smaller circle in Figure 8-28 should be added to your drawing. If you look closely, you notice that a short horizontal line segment is added automatically to "connect" the text to the leader.

Next we use the Leader Settings dialog box to create a more complex spline (curved leader) attached to three lines of Mtext.

⊕ Repeat QLEADER.

⊕ Press Enter or the spacebar to open the Leader Settings dialog box, shown in Figure 8-29.

There are three tabs in this dialog box. Annotation allows you to switch from Mtext to other types of annotation, which we do not explore at this point. The Leader Line & Arrow tab gives you options for changing the look and style of the leader and arrow. Attachment gives you options for attaching the leader to different points on the annotation text. These options are similar to the Mtext justification options.

⊕ Select the Leader Line & Arrow tab, as shown in Figure 8-29.

⊕ Select Spline in the Leader Line panel.

⊕ Open the Arrowhead options list and select Open 30.

⊕ Click the Attachment tab.

⊕ In the list of radio buttons under Text on right side select Middle of multi-line text.

⊕ Click OK.

You should now be out of the dialog box and back to the prompt

```
Specify first leader point, or [Settings]<settings>:
```

⊕ Hold down Shift and right-click to open the object snap shortcut menu and select Nearest from the shortcut menu again.

⊕ Pick a leader start point on the upper right side of the larger, 2.00-radius circle.

⊕ Pick a second point for the leader about 45 degrees and 1.00 unit up and to the right of the first point.

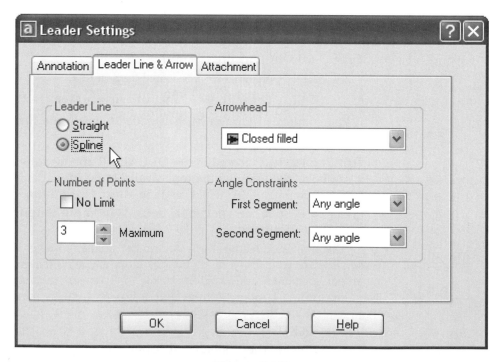

Figure 8-29

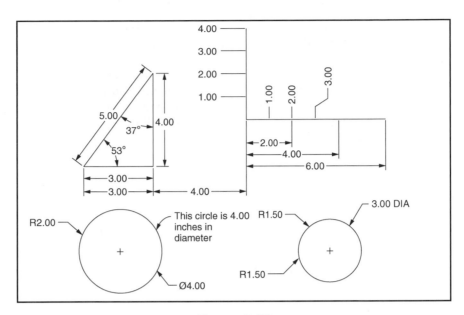

Figure 8-30

⊕ Move the cursor slowly around the second point. If Snap is on, turn it off (press F9).

　　The line now bends and curves to the new point you are about to select.

⊕ Pick the third point slightly above and to the right of the second to create a curved leader similar to the one in Figure 8-30.

　　QLEADER now prompts for an annotation text width as before.

⊕ Type 2 and press Enter.

　　QLEADER prompts for text.

⊕ Type This circle is 4.00 inches in diameter and press Enter.

⊕ Press Enter to complete the command.

　　Your screen should now resemble Figure 8-30. Because you have specified a width of 2, the text wraps around automatically.

8.8 Changing and Overriding Dimension Variables

GENERAL PROCEDURE

1. Select Override from the Dimension menu.
2. Type a dimension variable name.
3. Type a new value.
4. Select dimensions to alter.

As you know from Task 8.1, you can save and restore dimension styles using the Dimension Style dialog box. When a new style is created and becomes current, all subsequent dimensions are drawn using the new style. Sometimes, however, you might not want to create a whole new style to draw one or two dimensions that are slightly different from the others in your drawing. Or you might want to create a new style and apply it to some previously drawn dimensions. The first case is handled using a dimension override, the DIMOVERRIDE command. The second is done by changing dimension variables and then using the Apply option in the DIMSTYLE command. We demonstrate both, beginning with an override, and then look at a complete listing of all the dimension variables and their current settings.

⊕ Select Override from the Dimension menu.

AutoCAD prompts

```
Enter dimension variable name to override or
[Clear overrides]:
```

We can create some easily visible changes by altering the scale of a dimension using the dimscale variable.

⊕ Type dimscale.

AutoCAD prompts for a new value and gives you the current value:

```
Enter new value for dimension variable <1.00>:
```

⊕ Type 2.

AutoCAD continues to prompt for variables to override so that we can change more than one at a time.

⊕ Press Enter or the spacebar.

Now that we have provided a new temporary dimension scale, we need to select dimensions that we want to show this scale. You see the Select Objects prompt. We can use all of our usual selection methods here, including windowing and the All option. In this case, we change one dimension only.

⊕ Select the 3.00 linear dimension at the base of the triangle.

⊕ Press Enter to end object selection.

The 3.00 dimension text is redrawn twice as large, as shown in Figure 8-31. This alteration in dimension style is a one-time-only override. The change in dimscale has not been retained in memory, and any new dimensions drawn would have dimscale of 1.00. To make a more permanent change in style, we could go to the Dimension Style dialog box as before. Changes made in this way, however, are applied to all dimensions previously drawn in the current dimension style. By changing a dimension variable at the command line, we can gain the option of applying the change to selected dimensions only.

To change a variable at the command line, just type its name and then enter the new value.

⊕ Type dimscale.

AutoCAD prompts

```
Enter new value for DIMSCALE <1.00>:
```

⊕ Type 2.

This brings you back to the command prompt. The variable has been changed in the current dimension style, as you would see by opening the

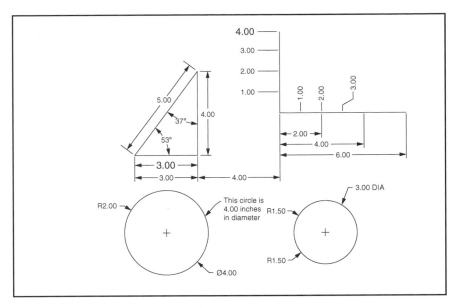

Figure 8-31

Dimension Style dialog box or by creating a new dimension. Now you need to update selected dimensions with the changed variable.

⊕ Select Update from the Dimension menu or the Dimension Update tool from the Dimension toolbar, as shown in Figure 8-32.

These selections actually enter the DIMSTYLE command. The minus sign in front of the command specifies that it is the command-line version, not the dialog box. In the command area, you see a list of variables that have been changed and then a prompt with options for other types of changes:

```
Current dimension overrides:
DIMSCALE 2.00
Enter a dimension style option
[Save/Restore/STatus/Variables/Apply/?] <Restore>:
```

Do not be confused by the use of the word override here. There is a difference between one-time overrides like the one we did using the DIMOVERRIDE command, and running overrides like this one, which are retained in the current style until the style is restored to its original configuration.

We use the Apply option to apply the change in dimscale to one of our previously drawn dimensions. If you have selected Update from the Dimension menu,

Figure 8-32

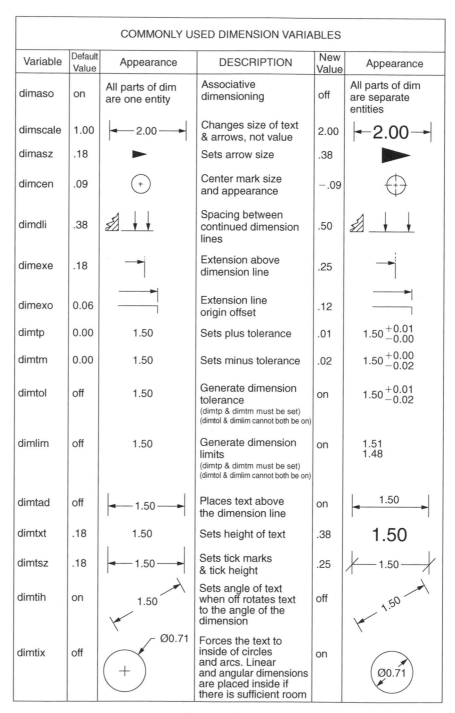

COMMONLY USED DIMENSION VARIABLES					
Variable	Default Value	Appearance	DESCRIPTION	New Value	Appearance
dimaso	on	All parts of dim are one entity	Associative dimensioning	off	All parts of dim are separate entities
dimscale	1.00	⊢—2.00—⊣	Changes size of text & arrows, not value	2.00	⊢—2.00—⊣
dimasz	.18	▶	Sets arrow size	.38	◣
dimcen	.09	⊕	Center mark size and appearance	−.09	⊕
dimdli	.38		Spacing between continued dimension lines	.50	
dimexe	.18		Extension above dimension line	.25	
dimexo	0.06		Extension line origin offset	.12	
dimtp	0.00	1.50	Sets plus tolerance	.01	$1.50\,^{+0.01}_{-0.00}$
dimtm	0.00	1.50	Sets minus tolerance	.02	$1.50\,^{+0.00}_{-0.02}$
dimtol	off	1.50	Generate dimension tolerance (dimtp & dimtm must be set) (dimtol & dimlim cannot both be on)	on	$1.50\,^{+0.01}_{-0.02}$
dimlim	off	1.50	Generate dimension limits (dimtp & dimtm must be set) (dimtol & dimlim cannot both be on)	on	1.51 1.48
dimtad	off	⊢—1.50—⊣	Places text above the dimension line	on	⊢— 1.50 —⊣
dimtxt	.18	1.50	Sets height of text	.38	1.50
dimtsz	.18	⊢—1.50—⊣	Sets tick marks & tick height	.25	⟋—1.50—⟋
dimtih	on	1.50	Sets angle of text when off rotates text to the angle of the dimension	off	1.50
dimtix	off	Ø0.71 ⊕	Forces the text to inside of circles and arcs. Linear and angular dimensions are placed inside if there is sufficient room	on	Ø0.71

Figure 8-33

Apply is entered automatically. AutoCAD needs to know which dimensions we want to apply the change to:

                    Select objects:

⊕   Select the 4.00 top ordinate dimension.

⊕   Press Enter to end object selection.

      The 4.00 dimension text is enlarged as shown in Figure 8-31.

While we are using the –DIMSTYLE command, use it to look at a list of all the dimension variables and their current settings. Setting dimension variables is easy, but the sheer number (67 in AutoCAD 2006) can be overwhelming. The dimension variable chart (Figure 8-33) shows you some of the most commonly used variables. You don't need to know all of them because you have the great convenience of being able to see previews of most dimension variables in the Dimension Style dialog boxes.

⊕   Repeat –DIMSTYLE.

⊕   Type st.

You see 67 variables listed with their current settings and a phrase describing the effect of each setting. You have to scroll to see the whole list.

Finally, before moving on, use the Restore option to remove the change in dimscale.

⊕   Repeat –DIMSTYLE.

⊕   Type r, or press Enter, because Restore is the default option.

      AutoCAD prompts

          Enter a dimension style name, [?] or <select dimension>:

⊕   Type 1b or the name of your current dimension style.

This restores the original values of the 1B dimension style. To return altered dimensions to these original style settings, use Update from the Dimension menu or the Dimension Update tool from the toolbar again.

8.9 Changing Dimension Text

Dimensions can be edited in many of the same ways that other objects are edited. They can be moved, copied, stretched, rotated, trimmed, extended, and so on. There are numerous ways to change dimension text and placement. Try the following quick demonstrations.

The DIMEDIT Command

⊕   Type dimedit or select the Dimension Edit tool from the Dimension toolbar, as shown in Figure 8-34.

Figure 8-34

AutoCAD prompts with options:

```
Enter type of dimension editing [Home/New/Rotate/Oblique]
<Home>:
```

Home, Rotate, and Oblique are placement and orientation options; New refers to new text content.

⊕ Type n or select New from the dynamic input list.

AutoCAD opens the Multiline Text Editor and waits for you to enter text. You see the two toolbars and a small edit box for text, with 0.00 highlighted in the edit box. In this edit box you can completely change the dimension text or you can add to the existing text. If you leave the 0.00 highlighted and type to the right or left of the text, whatever you type will be added to the existing dimension text. If you type over the highlighted 0.00, whatever you type will replace other dimension text.

We change the 5.00 aligned dimension to read 5.00 mm.

⊕ Click on the right side of the 0.00, so that the flashing cursor moves to the right and the text remains highlighted.

This can be tricky. The edit box is small and it is easy to remove the highlighting accidentally.

⊕ Type a space and then mm.

The text appears in the edit box.

⊕ Click OK to close the editor and return to the drawing.

AutoCAD prompts for objects to receive the new text:

```
                          Select Objects:
```

⊕ Select the 5.00 aligned dimension on the hypotenuse of the triangle.
⊕ Press Enter or right-click to end object selection.

The text is redrawn, as shown in Figure 8-35. This command is very convenient when you want to add or change text in a dimension without re-creating the dimension.

The Dimension Edit Shortcut Menu

Selecting a previously drawn object and right-clicking will open a shortcut menu with numerous options for changing the selected object. The exact options shown depend on the objects selected. If you choose only dimension objects, you have options to change dimension text position, dimension unit precision, dimension style, and arrow position. You will also be able to access other standard edit commands such as Erase, Move, Copy, Scale, and Rotate.

⊕ Select the 6.00 dimension below the horizontal line.
⊕ Right-click to open the shortcut menu shown in Figure 8-36.

In the second section from the top of the menu, you see Dim Text position, Precision, Dim Style, and Flip Arrow.

⊕ Let the cursor rest on Dim Text position, and then Move with leader, as shown.

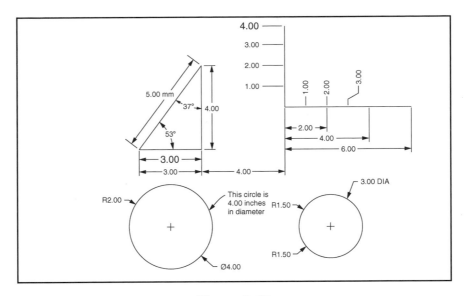

Figure 8-35

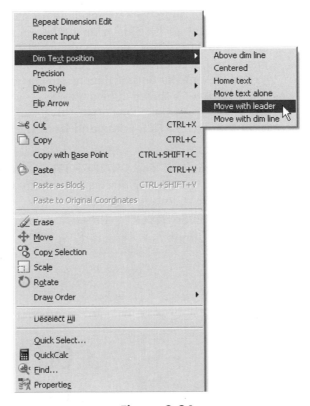

Figure 8-36

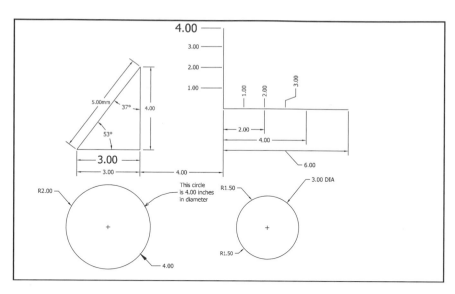

Figure 8-37

With this option, AutoCAD frees up the selected dimension text and lets you drag it into a new position, adding a leader from the text to the dimension line.

⊕ Pick a new location for the dimension text, as shown in Figure 8-37.

Notice the other options available for moving dimension text. Also notice the other options for dimension editing on the shortcut menu. In addition to changing text position, you can change the precision of dimension measurements or the dimension style of selected dimensions. You can also flip arrows so that they appear outside dimension lines instead of between. An example of flipped arrows is shown in Figure 8-38.

Accessing the PROPERTIES Command from the Shortcut Menu

The PROPERTIES command gives you direct access to many dimension variables, including text content. The PROPERTIES command can be opened from the Modify menu, or by selecting objects first and then right-clicking to open the shortcut menu. Try the following:

⊕ Pick the lower baseline dimension on the 6.00 line again.

⊕ With this dimension selected, right-click your mouse.

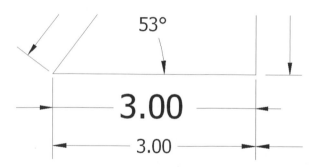

Figure 8-38

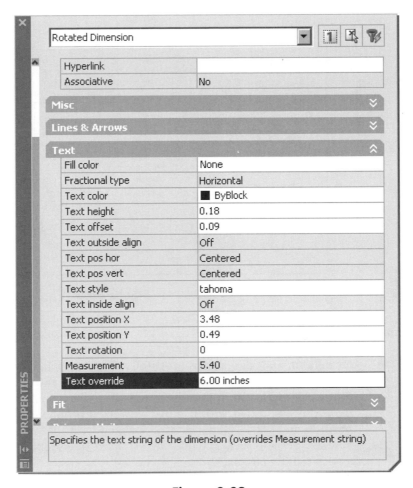

Figure 8-39

⊕ From the bottom of the menu, select Properties.

This opens the Properties palette, as shown in Figure 8-39. We encountered this palette in Chapter 7. The palette is responsive to the type of object selected, however, so it appears with different lists. You need to scroll down to see all the lists. The number of lists is another indication of the complexity of dimension options. They include the General list, Miscellaneous, Lines and Arrows, Text, Fit, Primary Units, Alternate Units, and Tolerances. These tabs provide yet another way to modify dimension variables.

⊕ Scroll down the Text list to Text override, which is at the bottom of the list.

⊕ Click Text override.

⊕ Type 6.00 inches in the edit box and press Enter.

⊕ Close the Properties dialog box.

⊕ Press Esc to clear grips.

Your screen is redrawn with the dimension text shown in Figure 8-40.

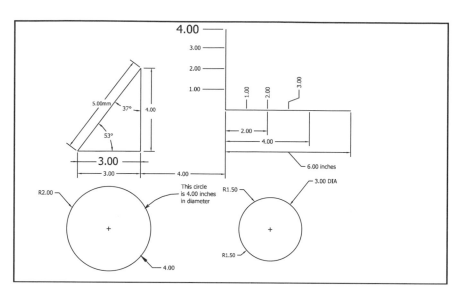

Figure 8-40

8.10 Using Associative Dimensions

By default, most dimensions in AutoCAD are associative with the geometry of the objects they dimension. This means that changes in the dimensioned objects are automatically reflected in the dimensions. If a dimensioned object is moved, the dimensions associated with it move as well. If a dimensioned object is scaled, the position and text of dimensions associated with that object change to reflect the new size of the object. The following simple exercise illustrates several points about associated dimensions.

⊞ Select the 2.00 circle.

⊞ Click on any of the grips, move the circle about 2.00 units to the left, and click again to complete the move.

Your screen should resemble Figure 8-41. Notice that the 4.00 diameter dimension and the 2.00 radius dimension move with the circle, that the leader from the Mtext dimension text stretches to maintain connection with the circle, but that the text does not move. We explain this in a moment, but first try the following steps:

⊞ Select any of the grips again.

⊞ Right-click to open the grip shortcut menu.

⊞ Select Scale.

⊞ Type .5 for a scale factor.

Your screen is redrawn to resemble Figure 8-42. Notice now that the scale factor is reflected in the diameter dimension (4.00 has changed to 2.00), but not in the leadered text. The diameter dimension is a true associative dimension; it moves and updates to reflect changes in the circle. The connection point of the leadered dimension is associated with the circle, but the text is not. Therefore, the leader stretches to stay connected to the circle, but the text does

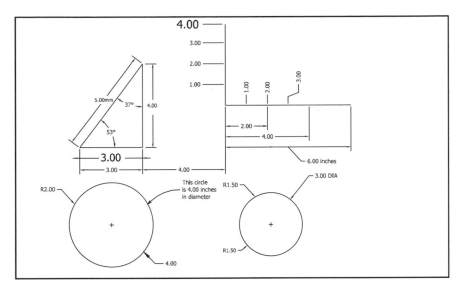

Figure 8-41

not move or change with the circle. This is the rule for dimensions created with QLEADER.

Changing Associativity of Dimensions

Nonassociative dimensions can be made associative using the DIMREASSOCI-ATE command. Associated dimensions can be disassociated with the DIMDISAS-SOCIATE command. In each case the procedure is a simple matter of entering the

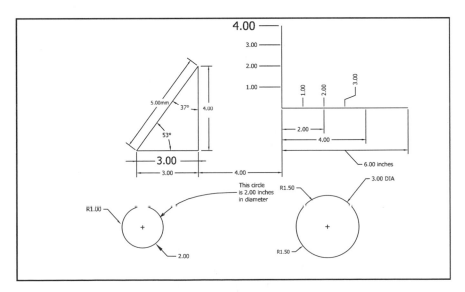

Figure 8-42

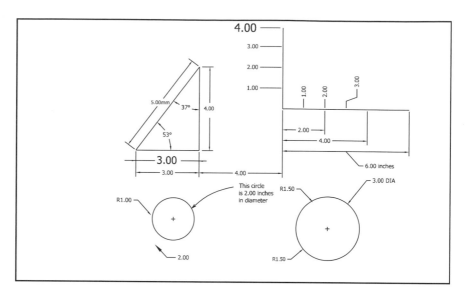

Figure 8-43

command and selecting dimensions to associate or disassociate. For example, try the following:

⊕   Type dimdisassociate.

   AutoCAD prompts

```
Select dimensions to disassociate...
Select objects:
```

⊕   Select the 2.00 diameter dimension.

⊕   Right-click or press Enter to end object selection.

   Now try moving the circle again to observe the changes.

⊕   Select the circle again, select a grip, and move the circle back to the right again.

   This time the 2.00 diameter does not move with the circle, as shown in Figure 8-43. The leadered dimension and the radius dimension adjust as before to stay attached to the circle. The diameter dimension is currently not associated to the circle. To reassociate it, use the DIMREASSOCIATE command, as follows:

⊕   Type dimreassociate.

⊕   Select the 2.00 diameter dimension.

⊕   Right-click to end object selection.

   AutoCAD recognizes that this is a diameter dimension and prompts for a circle or arc to attach it to. Notice that this means you could associate the dimension to any arc or circle, not just the one to which it was previously attached.

⊕   Select the circle on the left again.

   The diameter dimension moves and attaches to the 2.00 radius circle again, as shown in Figure 8-44.

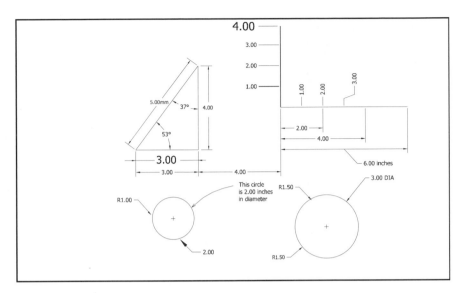

Figure 8-44

8.11 Using the HATCH Command

GENERAL PROCEDURE

1. Select Hatch from the Draw menu or the Hatch tool from the Draw toolbar.
2. Select a pattern.
3. Define style parameters.
4. Define boundaries of object to be hatched.

Automated hatching is another immense time saver. AutoCAD has two basic methods of hatching, both accessible through the HATCH command, which calls the Hatch and Gradient dialog box. In one method, you select a point within an area to be hatched and AutoCAD searches for the nearest boundary surrounding the point. In the other method, you specify the boundaries themselves by selecting objects. By default, AutoCAD creates associated hatch patterns. Associated hatching changes when the boundaries around change. Nonassociated hatching is completely independent of the geometry that contains it.

⊞   To prepare for this exercise, clear your screen of all previously drawn objects and then draw three rectangles, one inside the other, with the word TEXT with a height of 1.00 at the center, as shown in Figure 8-45.

⊞   Select Hatch from the Draw menu, or the Hatch tool on the Draw toolbar, as shown in Figure 8-46.

Both of these methods initiate the HATCH command, which calls the Hatch and Gradient dialog box shown in Figure 8-47. The Hatch tab gives you access to AutoCAD's library of more than 50 standard hatch patterns. Gradient creates solid fills with a wide range of gradient color schemes.

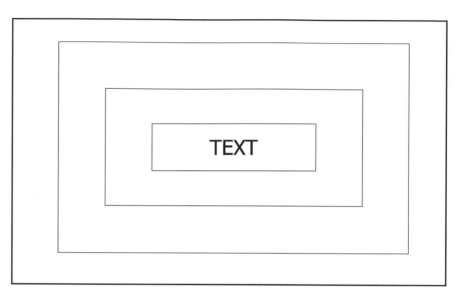

Figure 8-45

Figure 8-46

We explore the Hatch tab first.

⊕ If necessary, click the Hatch tab.

At the top of the Hatch tab window, you see the Type box. Before we can hatch anything, we need to specify a hatch pattern. Later we show AutoCAD what we wish to hatch using the Add: Pick points button on the right.

The Pattern type currently shown in the image box is a predefined pattern. Before we look at predefined patterns we create a simple user-defined pattern of straight lines on a 45-degree angle.

⊕ Click on the arrow to the right of Predefined.

This opens a list including Predefined, User-defined, and Custom patterns.

⊕ Select User-defined.

When you select a user-defined pattern, the swatch box, which shows an example of the pattern, changes to show a set of horizontal lines. To create our user-defined pattern, we specify an angle and a spacing.

⊕ Double-click in the Angle edit box, and then type 45, or open the list and select 45.

⊕ Double-click in the Spacing edit box, and then type .5.

Next we need to show AutoCAD where to place the hatching. To the right in the dialog box is a set of buttons with icons. The first two options are Add: Pick

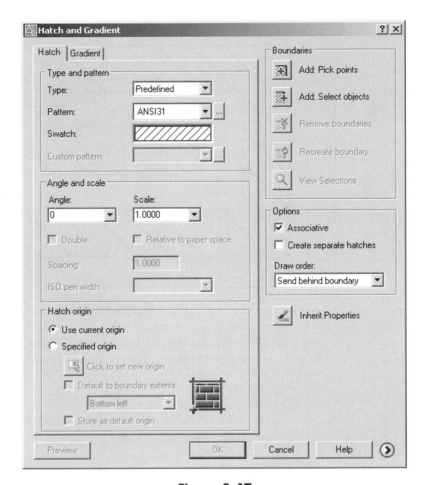

Figure 8-47

points and Add: Select objects. Using the Add: Pick points option, you can have AutoCAD locate a boundary when you point to the area inside it. The Add: Select objects option can be used to create boundaries by selecting entities that lie along the borders of the area you wish to hatch.

⊕ Click Add: Pick points.

The dialog box disappears temporarily and you are prompted as follows:

```
Select internal point:
```

⊕ Pick a point inside the largest, outer rectangle, but outside the smaller rectangles.

AutoCAD displays the following messages, although you might have to press F2 to see them:

```
Selecting everything...
Selecting everything visible...
Analyzing the selected data...
Analyzing internal islands...
```

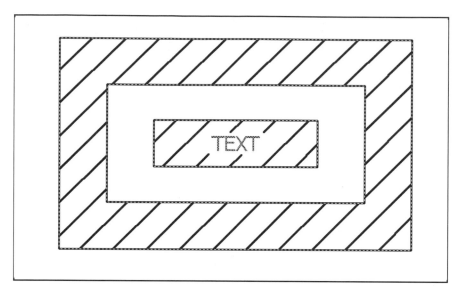

Figure 8-48

In a large drawing, this process can be time consuming because the program searches all visible entities to locate the appropriate boundary. When the process is complete, all of the rectangles and the text are highlighted. It happens very quickly in this case.

AutoCAD continues to prompt for internal points so that you can define multiple boundaries. Let's return to the dialog box and see what we've done so far.

⊕   **Press Enter to end internal point selection.**

The dialog box reappears. Several of the options that were unavailable before are now accessible. We make use of the Preview button at the bottom left of the dialog box. Preview allows us to see what has been specified without leaving the command, so that we can continue to adjust the hatching until we are satisfied.

⊕   **Click Preview.**

Your screen should resemble Figure 8-48. Notice the way the command has recognized and treated internal boundaries. Boundaries are hatched or left clear in alternating fashion, beginning with the outermost boundary and working inward. This demonstrates the "normal" style of hatching. Other styles can be achieved by clicking the Remove boundaries button and selecting internal boundaries to be removed. When a boundary has been removed, AutoCAD will ignore it and hatch across it to the next boundary.

⊕   **Press Esc to return to the Hatch and Gradient dialog box.**

Notice that right-clicking or pressing Enter takes you out of the command and applies the hatching to your drawing.

⊕   **When you are done experimenting, select Normal style hatching again and return to the Hatch tab.**

Now let's take a look at some of the fancier stored hatch patterns that AutoCAD provides.

⊕   **Click the arrow to the right of User-Defined and select Predefined.**

⊕   **Now click either the ellipsis button or the Swatch.**

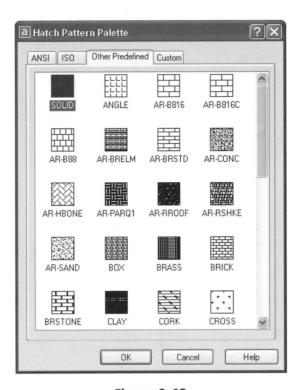

Figure 8-49

This opens the Hatch Pattern Palette, as shown in Figure 8-49. This dialog box contains AutoCAD's library of predefined hatch patterns. They are shown in tabbed dialog box fashion with four tabs. The first three contain images of patterns. The Custom tab is empty unless you have created and saved your own custom patterns. To produce the hatched image in Figure 8-50, we chose the Escher pattern.

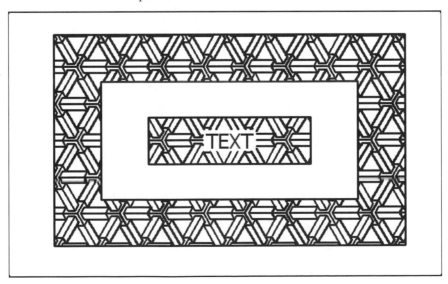

Figure 8-50

⊕ Click the Other Predefined tab.

⊕ Scroll down the list until you come to Escher.

⊕ Select Escher.

⊕ Click OK to exit the Pattern Palette.

To produce the figure, we also used a larger scale in this hatching.

⊕ Click the arrow in the Scale list box to open the list of scale factors and select 1.50.

⊕ Click the arrow in the Angle list box and select 0.

⊕ Click Preview.

Your screen should resemble Figure 8-50, but remember this is still just the preview.

⊕ Press Enter to accept the hatch.

Gradient Fill

AutoCAD has an option to create gradient fill color schemes as an additional presentation feature. We add a gradient fill to the area between the two inner rectangles that our hatch pattern has left clear.

⊕ Reenter the HATCH command.

⊕ Click the Gradient tab.

This opens the Gradient fill window, illustrated in Figure 8-51. Your screen shows gradations of blue and white that we cannot show here. If you select the Two-color radio button, you see yellow instead of white. By selecting the ellipsis button on either of the two color bars you open the Select Color dialog box we explored in Chapter 3. This gives you access to the full range of AutoCAD index colors, true colors, and color books. Here we apply a simple one-color gradient fill from the nine choices in the dialog box.

⊕ Select the first box in the second row, as shown in Figure 8-51.

When you select the box it is highlighted with a dashed border. Next we need to define an area to fill. This is done in the same way as defining an area for hatching.

⊕ Click Add: Pick points.

Pick a point in the unhatched area between the two inner rectangles.

⊕ Press Enter to return to the dialog box.

⊕ Click Preview.

Your screen should resemble Figure 8-52.

Finally, we leave the HATCH command and return to the drawing.

⊕ Press Enter or right-click to exit the HATCH command and apply the hatch pattern and fill to your drawing.

Note: When using the Boundary Creation dialog box (BOUNDARY command), the same procedures that are used to create polyline hatch boundaries can be used to create boundaries independent of any hatching operation. Select Boundary from the Draw menu to access this dialog box.

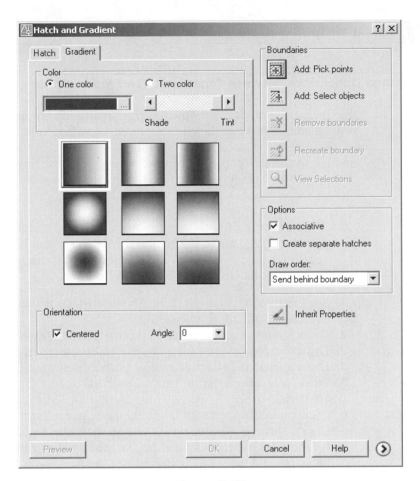

Figure 8-51

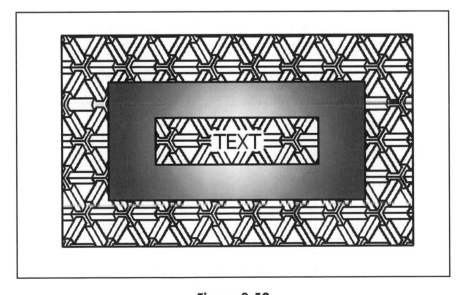

Figure 8-52

8.12 Scaling Dimensions between Paper Space and Model Space

In Chapter 6, you learned how to create multiple-viewport layouts. Now that you will be adding text and dimensions to your drawings, questions arise about the relationship between objects and annotations, particularly when you move between model space and paper space. To begin, we show how the Zoom XP feature introduced in Chapter 6 allows you to create precise scale relationships between model space images and paper space units.

> ***Important:*** This task begins with the 3view multiple-viewport layout of Drawing 5-1 created in Chapter 6. With luck, you have saved this layout and can open it now. If so, you can skip this note. If not, you can create an approximation of the drawing and layout as follows:

1. Set Limits to (0,0) and (12,9). This is critical. If you use different limits, the exercise is difficult to follow.
2. Draw a circle with diameter 3.50 centered at (3.00,4.00).
3. Draw a second circle with diameter 2.50 centered at the same point.
4. Draw a small 0.25-diameter circle at the lower quadrant of the 2.50 circle.
5. Draw a rectangle with first corner at (6.50,2.75) and second corner at (10.00,5.25).
6. Create a new layout with D-size limits in paper space.
7. Create three viewports, positioned as shown in Figure 8-53. The zoom factor for the large viewport should be 2xp. The smaller viewport to the right should be at 4xp and the smallest viewport at the top should be at 6xp. See Chapter 6, Task 6.10 for further details, if necessary.

⊹   To begin this task, open Drawing 5-1 and click the 3view layout tab.

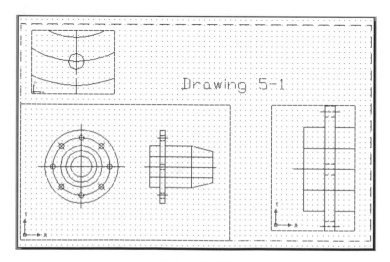

Figure 8-53

Drawing Text in Paper Space

As a general rule, text should be created in paper space. To see why, try entering some text in paper space and model space as follows:

⊕ Double-click anywhere outside the viewports to ensure that you are in paper space.

⊕ Type dt or select Text and then Single Line text from the Draw menu.

⊕ Pick a start point outside any of the viewports.

> Our text begins about three units over the right side of the left viewport, as shown in Figure 8-53.

⊕ Type 1 for a text height of one unit.

This assumes that you are using the D-size paper space limits from Chapter 6. If not, you have to adjust for your own settings. On A-size paper the text height is about 0.25.

⊕ Press Enter for 0 rotation.

⊕ Type Drawing 5-1.

⊕ Press Enter twice.

> Your screen should have text added, as shown in Figure 8-53.

⊕ Double-click in the lower left, largest viewport to enter model space in this viewport.

⊕ Type dt or select Text and then Single Line text from the Draw menu.

⊕ Pick a start point below the left view in the viewport, as shown in Figure 8-54.

⊕ Press Enter to retain a height of 1.00 units.

⊕ Press Enter for 0 rotation.

⊕ Type Bushing and Press Enter twice.

> Your screen should resemble Figure 8-54.

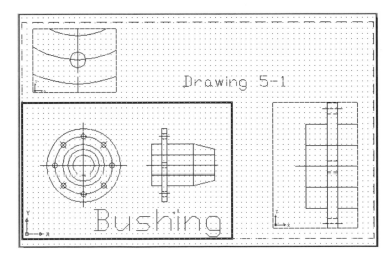

Figure 8-54

What has happened here? Why is Bushing drawn twice as big as Drawing 5-1? Do you remember the Zoom XP scale factor we used in this viewport? This viewport is enlarged by two times paper space, so any text you draw inside it is enlarged by a factor of two as well. If you want, try drawing text in either of the other two viewports. You find that text in the right viewport is magnified four times the paper space size and text in the uppermost viewport is magnified six times.

You could compensate for these enlargements by dividing text height by factors of 2, 4, and 6, but that would be cumbersome. Furthermore, if you decide to change the zoom factor at a later date, you would have to re-create any text drawn within the altered viewport. Otherwise, your text sizes in the overall drawing would become inconsistent. For this reason, it is recommended that text be drawn in paper space and kept consistent with paper space units.

Dimensioning in Paper Space with Association to Model Space Objects

In AutoCAD, dimensions can also be drawn in paper space, as a rule. Dimensions drawn in paper space maintain their associativity to model space objects. They move and update to reflect changes in the model space geometry. By keeping dimensions in paper space, you avoid dimension text scaling issues similar to those demonstrated in the previous section. You also avoid the problem of dimensions that are created at one scale in one viewport showing up in another scale in another viewport. In this exercise, we create a simple dimension in paper space and show how it maintains associativity to its model space objects.

⊕ Make the dim layer current.

⊕ Make sure you are in paper space.

⊕ Select Diameter from the Dimension menu.

⊕ Pick the bottom bolt hole circle on the bushing in the lower left viewport, as shown by the dimension in Figure 8-55.

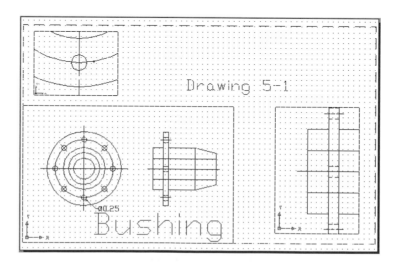

Figure 8-55

Notice that you have no trouble selecting the circle even though it is in model space and you are currently in paper space. Remember that you cannot ordinarily select model space objects when you are in paper space, or vice versa. This exception is an AutoCAD feature that allows you to associate paper space dimensions with model space objects.

⊕ Pick a dimension location below and to the right of the circle, as shown.

⊕ Press Enter to accept the dimension text (.25).

The dimension is drawn, but the text size is smaller than that shown. The text is being drawn using the dimension text default size, which is .18. This was adequate when we were in model space, but now that we are in paper space on a different scale, we want to increase the text scale. This can be done in the Dimension Style dialog box, using the Text tab, or at the command line, as we demonstrate here.

⊕ Type dimtxt.

This is the dimtxt dimension variable. AutoCAD prompts

```
Enter new value for DIMTXT <.18>:
```

⊕ Type .5.

⊕ Open the Dimension menu and select Update.

⊕ Select the .25 diameter dimension.

Your screen is redrawn to resemble Figure 8-55. We perform one edit in model space to demonstrate that this paper space dimension is associated with its model space geometry.

⊕ Double-click in the lower left viewport.

⊕ Try selecting the 0.25 diameter dimension.

You cannot select this paper space object while in model space.

⊕ Double-click in the upper left viewport to make it active.

⊕ Select the 0.25 diameter circle in this viewport.

⊕ Select any of the grips on the circle.

⊕ Right-click to open the grip edit shortcut menu.

⊕ Select Scale from the shortcut menu.

⊕ Type in a scale value of 2.

⊕ Press Esc to remove grips.

Your screen should resemble Figure 8-56. Notice that the dimension is updated to reflect the change. Notice also that the dimension is only drawn in connection with the lower viewport, but that it is updated along with the geometry when it is changed in the upper viewport.

Turning Viewport Borders Off

We have used the borders of our viewports as part of our plotted drawings in this drawing layout. Frequently, you want to turn them off. In a typical three-view drawing, for example, you do not draw borders around the three views.

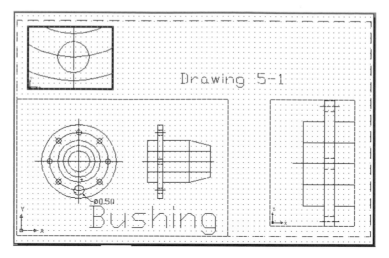

Figure 8-56

In multiple-viewport paper space drawings, the visibility of viewport borders is easily controlled by putting the viewports on a separate layer and then turning the layer off before plotting. You can make a "border" layer, for example, and make it current while you create viewports. You could also use PROPERTIES to move viewports to the border layer later.

8.13 Review Material

Questions

1. You are working in a drawing with units set to architectural, but when you begin dimensioning, AutoCAD provides four-place decimal units. What is the problem? What do you need to do so that your dimensioning units match your drawing units?
2. Describe at least one way to change the size of the arrowheads in the dimensions of a drawing.
3. What changes can be made with the Edit option of the QDIM command?
4. What types of changes to dimension objects can be made with the Edit shortcut menu?
5. What is a "nearest" object snap, and why is it important when dimensioning with leaders?
6. Why is it useful to move the origin of the coordinate system to make good use of ordinate dimensioning? What option to this is available in the QDIM command?
7. You have created a number of dimensions in a drawing and wish to change some of them to a new dimension style. Assuming you have already created the new dimension style, what procedure allows you to update some of your previously drawn dimensions? What item on the Dimension menu executes this command?
8. What is the difference between hatching by selecting internal points and by selecting objects?

9. What is associative dimensioning? What command makes a nonassociative dimension associative?
10. Name two reasons for dimensioning in paper space.

Drawing Problems

1. Create a new dimension style called Dim-2. Dim-2 uses architectural units with 1/2″ precision for all units except angles, which use two-place decimals. Text in Dim-2 is 0.5 unit high.
2. Draw an isosceles triangle with vertexes at (4,3), (14,3), and (9,11). Draw a 2″ circle centered at the center of the triangle.
3. Dimension the base and one side of the triangle using the Dim-2 dimension style.
4. Add a diameter dimension to the circle and change a dimension variable so that the circle is dimensioned with a diameter line drawn inside the circle.
5. Add an angle dimension to one of the base angles of the triangle. Make sure that the dimension is placed outside of the triangle.
6. Hatch the area inside the triangle and outside the circle using a predefined crosshatch pattern.

8.14　WWW Exercise 8 (Optional)

In Chapter 8 of our companion website, we challenge you to find information on a great innovator in the fields of graphic arts whose name has come up in this chapter. We give you links to get you started and then send you on your way. We also offer you another design challenge and, as always, the self-scoring test for this chapter. So, when you are ready, complete the following:

⊕　Make sure that you are connected to your Internet service provider.

⊕　Type browser, open the Web toolbar, and select the Browse the Web tool, or open your system browser from the Windows taskbar.

⊕　If necessary, navigate to our companion website at www.prenhall. com/dixriley.

Happy hunting!

8.15   Drawing 8-1: Tool Block

In this drawing, the dimensions should work well without editing. The hatch is a simple user-defined pattern used to indicate that the front and right views are sectioned views.

Drawing Suggestions

> GRID = 1.0
> SNAP = 0.125
> HATCH line spacing = 0.125

- As a general rule, complete the drawing first, including all crosshatching, and then add dimensions and text at the end.
- Place all hatching on the hatch layer. When hatching is complete, set to the dim layer and turn the hatch layer off so that hatch lines do not interfere when you select lines for dimensioning.
- The section lines in this drawing can be easily drawn as leaders. Set the dimension arrow size to 0.38 first. Check to see that Ortho is on; then begin the leader at the tip of the arrow and make a right angle as shown. After picking the other endpoint of the leader, press Enter to bring up the First line of annotation prompt. Type a space and press Enter so you have no text. Press Enter again to exit.
- You need to set the dimtix variable (Dimension outside align in the Properties dialog box) to on to place the 3.25-diameter dimension at the center of the circle in the top view and off to create the leader style diameter dimension in the front section.
- Remember, multiple lines of text can be drawn with the QLEADER command and can be specified to be centered on the leader.

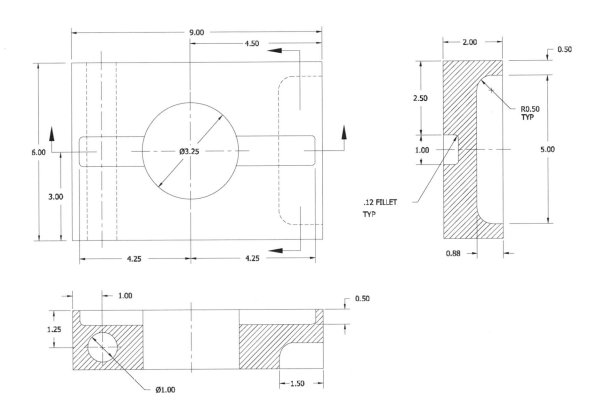

TOOL BLOCK

Drawing 8-1

8.16   Drawing 8-2: Flanged Wheel

Most of the objects in this drawing are straightforward. The keyway is easily done using the TRIM command. If necessary, use the Edit shortcut menu or grips to move the diameter dimension, as shown in the reference.

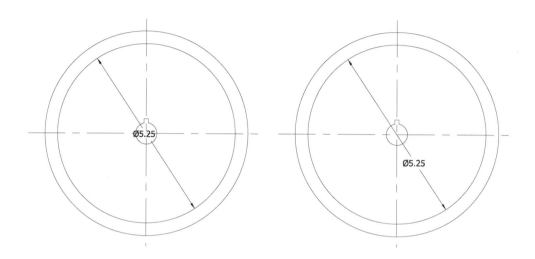

Drawing Suggestions

GRID = 0.25
SNAP = 0.0625
HATCH line spacing = 0.50

- You need a 0.0625 snap to draw the keyway. Draw a 0.125 × 0.125 square at the top of the 0.63-diameter circle. Drop the vertical lines down into the circle so they can be used to TRIM the circle. TRIM the circle and the vertical lines, using a window to select both as cutting edges.

- Remember to set to layer hatch before hatching, layer text before adding text, and layer dim before dimensioning.

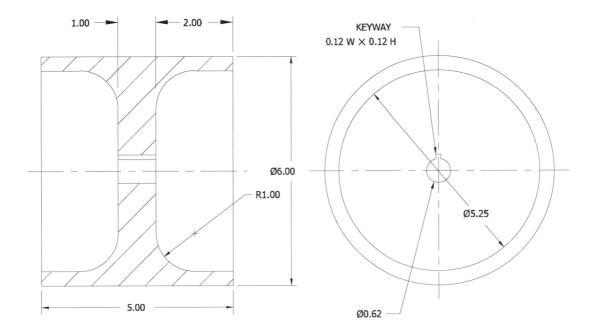

FLANGED WHEEL

Drawing 8-2

8.17   Drawing 8-3: Shower Head

This drawing makes use of the procedures for hatching and dimensioning you learned in the last two drawings. In addition, it uses an angular dimension, baseline dimensions, leaders, and %%c for the diameter symbol.

Drawing Suggestions

GRID = 0.25
SNAP = 0.125
HATCH line spacing = 0.25

- You can save some time on this drawing by using MIRROR to create half of the right side view. Notice, however, that you cannot hatch before mirroring, because the MIRROR command reverses the angle of the hatch lines.

- To achieve the angular dimension at the bottom of the right side view, you need to draw the vertical line coming down on the right. Select this line and the angular line at the right end of the shower head, and the angular extension is drawn automatically. Add the text 2 PL using the DIMEDIT command.

- Notice that the diameter symbols in the vertical dimensions at each end of the right side view are not automatic. Use %%c to add the diameter symbol to the text.

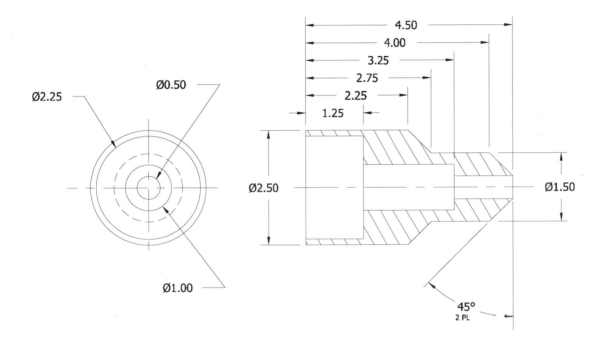

SHOWER HEAD

Drawing 8-3

8.18   Drawing 8-4: Nose Adapter

Make ample use of ZOOM to work on the details of this drawing. Notice that the limits are set larger than usual, and the snap is rather fine by comparison.

Drawing Suggestions

> LIMITS = (0,0) (36,24)
> GRID = 0.25
> SNAP = 0.125
> HATCH line spacing = 0.25

- You need a 0.125 snap to draw the thread representation shown in the reference. Understand that this is nothing more than a standard representation for screw threads; it does not show actual dimensions. Zoom in close to draw it, and you should have no trouble.

- This drawing includes two examples of simplified drafting practice. The thread representation is one, and the other is the way in which the counterbores are drawn in the front view. A precise rendering of these holes would show an ellipse, because the slant of the object dictates that they break through on an angle. However, to show these ellipses in the front view would make the drawing more confusing and less useful. Simplified representation is preferable in such cases.

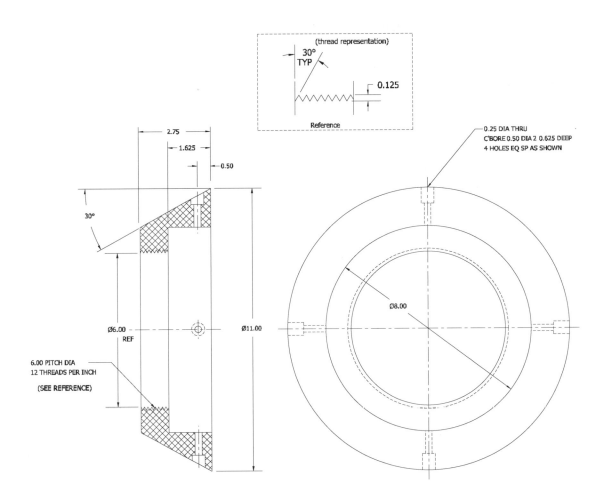

NOSE ADAPTER
Drawing 8-4

8.19 Drawing 8-5: Plot Plan

This architectural drawing makes use of three hatch patterns and several dimension variable changes. Be sure to make these settings as shown.

Drawing Suggestions

GRID = 10′
SNAP = 1′
LIMITS = 180′, 120′
LTSCALE = 2′

- The "trees" shown here are symbols for oaks, willows, and evergreens.
- HATCH opens a space around text inside a defined boundary; however, sometimes you want more white space than HATCH leaves. A simple solution is to draw a rectangle around the text area as an inner boundary. Later you can erase the box, leaving an island of white space around the text.

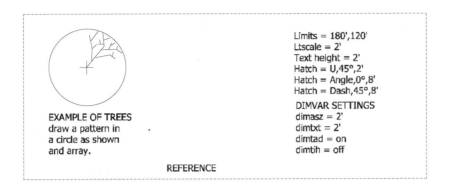

Limits = 180',120'
Ltscale = 2'
Text height = 2'
Hatch = U,45°,2'
Hatch = Angle,0°,8'
Hatch = Dash,45°,8'

DIMVAR SETTINGS
dimasz = 2'
dimtxt = 2'
dimtad = on
dimtih = off

EXAMPLE OF TREES
draw a pattern in
a circle as shown
and array.

REFERENCE

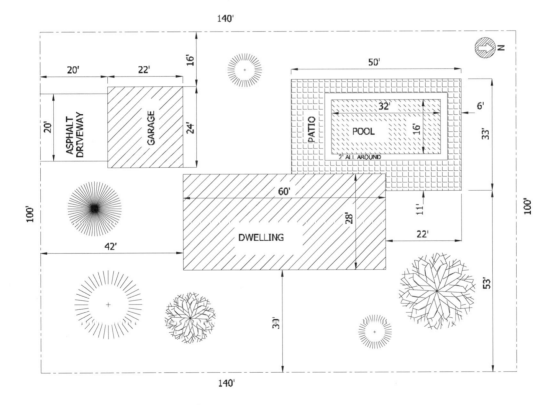

PLOT PLAN

Drawing 8-5

8.20 Drawing 8-6: Panel

This drawing is primarily an exercise in using ordinate dimensions. Both the drawing of the objects and the adding of dimensions are facilitated dramatically by this powerful feature.

Drawing Suggestions

> GRID = 0.50
> SNAP = 0.125
> UNITS = three-place decimal

- After setting grid, snap, and units, create a new user coordinate system with the origin moved in and up about one unit each way. This technique was introduced in Task 8.6. For reference, here is the procedure:

1. Select Move UCS from the Tools menu.
2. Pick a new origin point.

- From here on all of the objects in the drawing can be easily placed using the x and y displacements exactly as they are shown in the drawing.
- When objects have been placed, switch to the dim layer and begin dimensioning using the ordinate dimension feature. You should be able to move along quickly, but be careful to keep dimensions on each side of the panel lined up. That is, the leader endpoints should end along the same vertical or horizontal line.

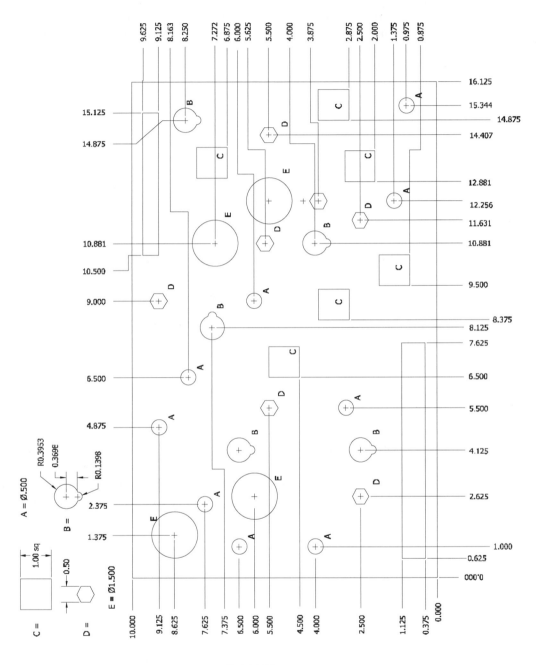

PANEL
DRAWING 8-6

8.21 Drawing 8-7: Angle Support

In this drawing, you are expected to use the 3-D view to create three orthographic views. Draw a front view, top view, and side view. The front and top views are drawn showing all necessary hidden lines, and the right side view is drawn in full section. The finished multiview drawing should be fully dimensioned.

TOP VIEW

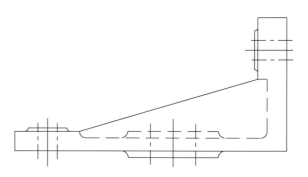

FRONT VIEW   RIGHT SIDE VIEW

Drawing Suggestions

- Start this drawing by laying out the top view. Use the top view to line up the front view and side view.
- Use the illustration of the right side view when planning out the full section. Convert the hidden lines to solid lines and use HATCH to create crosshatching.
- Complete the right-side view in full section, using the ANSI31 hatch pattern.
- Be sure to include all the necessary hidden lines and center lines in each view.

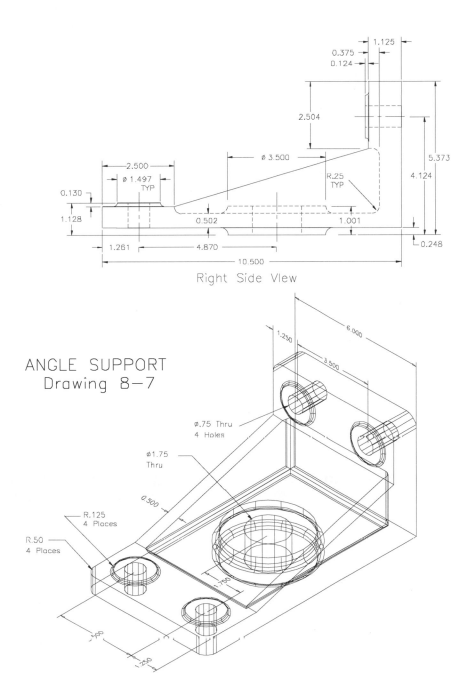

1.125
0.375
0.124
2.504
5.373
4.124
2.500
Ø 1.497
TYP
Ø 3.500
R.25
TYP
0.130
1.128
0.502
1.001
1.261
4.870
0.248
10.500

Right Side View

ANGLE SUPPORT
Drawing 8–7

6.000
1.250
3.500

Ø.75 Thru
4 Holes

Ø1.75
Thru

0.500

R.125
4 Places

R.50
4 Places

.750

.500
.250

8.22   Drawing 8-8: Mirror Mounting Plate

This drawing introduces AutoCAD's geometric tolerancing capability, an additional feature of the dimension system. Geometric tolerancing symbols and values are added using a simple dialog box interface. For example, to add the tolerance values and symbols below the leadered dimension text on the .128 diameter hole at the top middle of the drawing, follow these steps. All other tolerances in the drawing are created in the same manner.

* After creating the objects in the drawing, create the leadered dimension text beginning with .128 DIA THRU . . . as shown.
* Select Tolerance from the Dimension menu, or the Tolerance tool from the Dimension toolbar, as illustrated in Figure 8-57.
* Fill in the values and symbols as shown in Figure 8-58. To fill in the first black symbol box, click the box and select a symbol. To fill in the diameter symbol, click the second black box and the symbol is filled in automatically. To fill in any of the Material Condition boxes, click the box and select a symbol.
* Click OK.
* Drag the tolerance boxes into place below the dimension text as shown in the drawing.

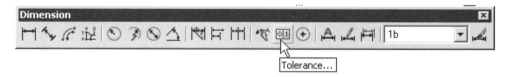

Figure 8-57

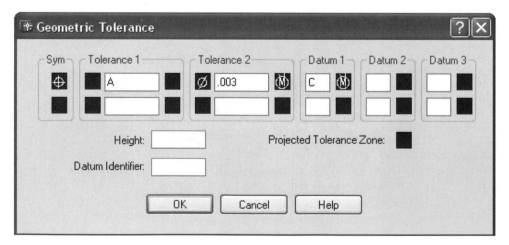

Figure 8-58

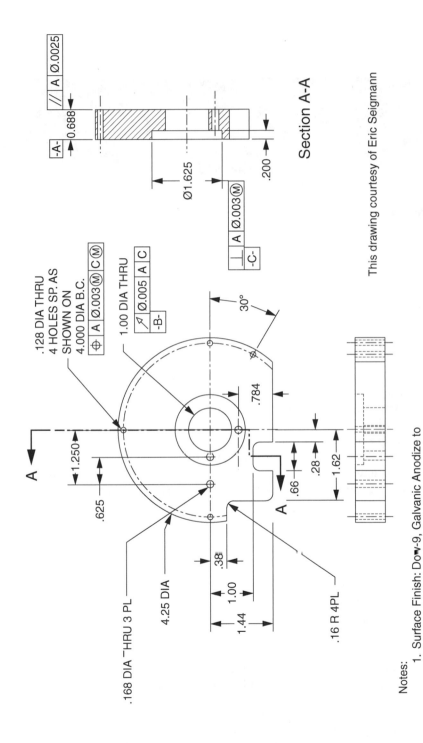

Section A-A

This drawing courtesy of Eric Seigmann

MIRROR MOUNTING PLATE
Drawing 8-8

Notes:

1. Surface Finish: Dow-9, Galvanic Anodize to
Black - To MIL-S-3 71C, Type 4

9

Polylines

COMMANDS

DONUT	MLINE	PLINE	REVCLOUD	SPLINE
FILL	MLSTYLE	POINT	SKETCH	
MLEDIT	PEDIT	POLYGON	SOLID	

OVERVIEW

This chapter should be fun. As you can see by the preceding list, you will be learning a large number of new commands. You can see new things happening on your screen with each command. The commands in this chapter are used to create special entities, some of which cannot be drawn any other way. All of them are complex objects made up of lines, circles, and arcs (like the text, dimensions, and hatch patterns discussed in the previous two chapters), but they are stored and treated as singular entities. Some of them, such as polygons and donuts, are familiar geometric figures, whereas others, like polylines, are peculiar to CAD.

TASKS

9.1 Drawing POLYGONs

GENERAL PROCEDURE

1. Select Polygon from the Draw menu or select the Polygon tool from the Draw toolbar.
2. Type the number of sides.
3. Pick a center point.
4. Indicate Inscribed or Circumscribed.
5. Show the radius of the circle.

Among the most interesting and flexible of the entities you can create in AutoCAD is the polyline. In this chapter, we begin with two regularly shaped polyline entities, polygons and donuts. These entities have their own special commands, separate from the general PLINE command (Tasks 9.4 and 9.5), but are created as polylines and can be edited just as any other polyline would be.

Polygons with any number of sides can be drawn using the POLYGON command. (Rectangles can be drawn by showing two corners using the RECTANG command, which draws polyline rectangles.) In the default sequence, AutoCAD constructs a polygon based on the number of sides, the center point, and a radius. Optionally, the edge method allows you to specify the number of sides and the length and position of one side (see Figure 9-1).

⊕ To begin, open a new drawing using the 1B template.

⊕ Select Polygon from the Draw menu, or select the Polygon tool from the Draw toolbar, as shown in Figure 9-2.

AutoCAD's first prompt is for the number of sides:

```
Enter number of sides <4>:
```

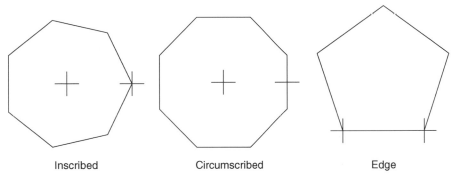

| Inscribed | Circumscribed | Edge |

Figure 9-1

Figure 9-2

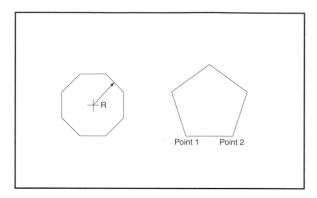

Figure 9-3

⊕ Type 8.

Now you are prompted to show either a center point or the first point of one edge:

        Specify center of polygon or [Edge]:

⊕ Pick a center point, as shown by the center mark on the left in Figure 9-3.

From here the size of the polygon can be specified in one of two ways, as shown in Figure 9-1. The radius of a circle is given and the polygon drawn either inside or outside the imaginary circle. Notice that in the case of the inscribed polygon, the radius is measured from the center to a vertex, whereas in the circumscribed polygon it is measured from the center to the midpoint of a side. You can tell AutoCAD which you want by typing i or c:

    Enter an option [Inscribed in circle/Circumscribed about
                    circle] <I>:

Inscribed is the default. We use the circumscribed method instead.

⊕ Type c or right-click and select Circumscribed about circle from the shortcut menu.

Now you are prompted to show a radius of this imaginary circle (i.e., a line from the center to a midpoint of a side):

            Specify radius of circle:

⊕ Show a radius similar to the one in Figure 9-3.

We leave it to you to try the inscribed option. We draw one more polygon, using the edge method.

⊕ Press Enter or the spacebar to repeat the POLYGON command.
⊕ Type 5 for the number of sides.
⊕ Type e or right-click and select Edge from the shortcut menu.

AutoCAD issues a different series of prompts:

            Specify first endpoint of edge:

⊕ Pick Point 1, as shown on the right in Figure 9-3.

AutoCAD prompts

> Specify second endpoint of edge:

⊕ Pick a second point as shown.

Your screen should resemble Figure 9-3.

9.2 Drawing DONUTs

GENERAL PROCEDURE

1. Select Donut from the Draw menu.
2. Type or show an inside diameter.
3. Type or show an outside diameter.
4. Pick a center point.
5. Pick another center point.
6. Press Enter to exit the command.

The DONUT command is logical and easy to use. You show inside and outside diameters and then draw as many donut-shaped objects of the specified size as you like.

⊕ Clear your display of polygons before continuing.

⊕ Select Donut from the Draw menu.

AutoCAD prompts

> Specify inside diameter of donut <0.50>:

We change the inside diameter to 1.00.

⊕ Type 1.

AutoCAD prompts

> Specify outside diameter of donut <1.00>:

We change the outside diameter to 2.00.

⊕ Type 2.

AutoCAD gives you a donut to drag into place and prompts

> Specify center of donut or [exit]:

⊕ Pick any point.

A donut is drawn around the point you chose, as shown by the "fat" donuts in Figure 9-4. (If your donut is not filled, see Task 9.3.)

AutoCAD stays in the DONUT command, allowing you to continue drawing donuts.

⊕ Pick a second center point.

⊕ Pick a third center point.

You should now have three "fat" donuts on your screen as shown.

⊕ Press Enter or the spacebar or right-click to exit the DONUT command.

Now draw the "thin" donuts in the figure.

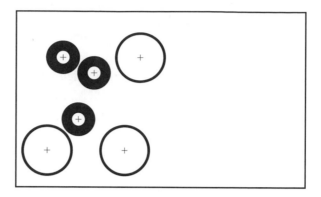

Figure 9-4

⊞ Repeat DONUT.

⊞ Change the inside diameter to 3.00 and the outer diameter to 3.25.

⊞ Draw three or four "thin" donuts, as shown in Figure 9-4.

When you are done, leave the donuts on the screen so that you can see how they are affected by the FILL command.

9.3   Using the FILL Command

GENERAL PROCEDURE
1.   Type Fill.
2.   Type on or off.
3.   Type or select Regen.

Donuts, wide polylines (Tasks 9.4 and 9.5), and 2-D solids (Task 9.7) are all affected by FILL. With FILL on, these entities are displayed and plotted as solid filled objects. With FILL off, only the outer boundaries are displayed. (Donuts are shown with radial lines between the inner and outer circles.) Because filled objects are slower to regenerate than outlined ones, you might want to turn FILL off as you are working on a drawing and turn it on when you are ready to print or plot.

⊞ For this exercise, you should have at least one donut on your screen from Task 9.2.

⊞ Type fill.

AutoCAD prompts

                    Enter Mode [ON/OFF] <ON>:

⊞ Type off or select off from the dynamic input display.

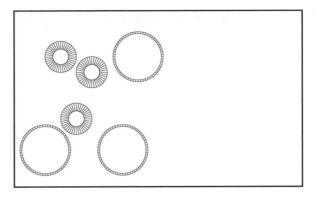

Figure 9-5

You do not see any immediate change in your display when you do this. To see the effect, you have to regenerate your drawing.

⊕ Type re or select Regen from the View menu.

Your screen is regenerated with FILL off and should resemble Figure 9-5. Many of the special entities that we discuss in the remainder of this chapter can be filled, so we encourage you to continue to experiment with FILL as you go along.

9.4 Drawing Straight Polyline Segments

GENERAL PROCEDURE

1. Select Polyline from the Draw menu, or select the Polyline tool from the Draw toolbar.
2. Pick a start point.
3. Type or select Width, Halfwidth, or other options.
4. Pick other points.

In the last two chapters, you saw how text, dimensions, and hatch patterns are all created as complex entities that can be selected and treated as single objects. In the next chapter, you see how to create groups and blocks from separate entities. In this chapter, we are focusing on the polyline. You have already drawn several polylines without going through the PLINE command. Donuts and polygons both are drawn as polylines and therefore can be edited using the same edit commands that work on other polylines. You can, for instance, fillet all the corners of a polygon at once, using the Pline option in the FILLET command. Using the PLINE command itself, you can draw anything from a simple line to a series of lines and arcs with varying widths. Most important, polylines can be edited using many of the ordinary edit commands as well as a set of specialized editing procedures found in the PEDIT command.

We begin by creating a simple polyline rectangle. The process is much like drawing a rectangular outline with the LINE command, but the result is a single object rather than four distinct line segments.

Figure 9-6

⊕ Clear your display of donuts before continuing.

⊕ Select Polyline from the Draw menu or the Polyline tool from the Draw toolbar, as shown in Figure 9-6.

AutoCAD begins with a prompt for a starting point, as in the LINE command:

Specify start point:

⊕ Pick a start point, similar to P1 in Figure 9-7.

From here the PLINE prompt sequence becomes more complicated:

Current line width is 0.00
Specify next point or [Arc/Halfwidth/Length/Undo/Width]:

The prompt begins by giving you the current line width, left from any previous use of the PLINE command.

Then the prompt offers options in the usual format. Arc leads you into another set of options that deals with drawing polyline arcs. We save polyline arcs for Task 9.5. We get to the other options momentarily.

This time around we draw a series of 0-width segments, just as we would in the LINE command.

⊕ Pick an endpoint, similar to P2 in Figure 9-7.

AutoCAD draws the segment and repeats the prompt. Notice that after you have picked two points, AutoCAD adds a Close option to the command prompt.

⊕ Pick another endpoint, P3 in Figure 9-7.

⊕ Pick another endpoint, P4 in Figure 9-7.

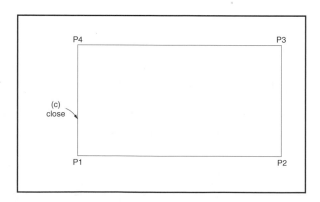

Figure 9-7

⊕ Type c or right-click and select Close from the shortcut menu to complete the rectangle, as shown in Figure 9-7.

Note: The Close option is very important in drawing closed polylines. AutoCAD recognizes the polyline as a closed object only if you use the Close option.

⊕ Now select the rectangle by pointing to any of its sides.

You can see that the entire rectangle is selected, rather than just the side you pointed to. This means, for example, that you can fillet or chamfer all four corners of the rectangle at once. Try it if you like, using the following procedure:

1. Select the Fillet tool from the Modify toolbar.
2. Type r.
3. Specify a radius.
4. Type p to indicate that you want to fillet an entire polyline.
5. Select the rectangle.

Note: If a corner is left without a fillet, it is probably because you did not use the Close option when you completed the rectangle.

Now let's create a rectangle with wider lines.

⊕ Press Esc to remove grips.

⊕ Enter the PLINE command.

⊕ Pick a starting point, as shown by P1 in Figure 9-8.

AutoCAD prompts

Specify next point or [Arc/Close/Halfwidth/Length/Undo/Width]:

This time we need to make use of the Width option.

⊕ Type w or right-click and select Width from the shortcut menu.

AutoCAD responds with

Specify starting width <0.00>:

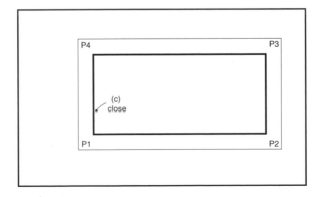

Figure 9-8

You are prompted for two widths, a starting width and an ending width. This makes it possible to draw tapered lines. For this exercise, our lines have the same starting and ending width.

Note: The Halfwidth option differs from Width only in that the width of the line to be drawn is measured from the center out. With either option, you can specify by showing a width rather than typing a value.

⊕ Type .25.

AutoCAD prompts

Specify ending width <0.25>:

Notice that the starting width has become the default for the ending width. To draw a polyline of uniform width, we accept this default.

⊕ Press Enter or the spacebar to keep the starting width and ending width the same.

AutoCAD returns to the previous prompt:

Specify next point or [Arc/Halfwidth/Length/Undo/Width]:

⊕ Pick an endpoint, as shown by P2 in Figure 9-8.

⊕ Continue picking Points P3 and P4 to draw a second rectangle, as shown in Figure 9-8.

⊕ Use the Close option to draw the last side.

When the object is complete, AutoCAD creates joined corners. If you do not close the last side, the lower left corner overlaps rather than joins. Notice also that once a polyline has been given a width, it is affected by the FILL setting.

The only options we have not discussed in this exercise are Length and Undo. Length allows you to type or show a value and then draws a segment of that length starting from the endpoint of the previous segment and continuing in the same direction. (If the last segment was an arc, the length is drawn tangent to the arc.) Undo undoes the last segment, just as in LINE.

In the next task, we draw some polyline arc segments.

9.5 Drawing Polyline Arc Segments

GENERAL PROCEDURE

1. Enter the PLINE command.
2. Pick a start point.
3. Specify a width.
4. Type a or select arc.
5. Type or select options or pick an endpoint.

A word of caution: Because of the flexibility and power of the PLINE command, it is tempting to think of polylines as always having weird shapes, tapered lines, and strange sequences of lines and arcs. Books tend to perpetuate this by consistently giving peculiar examples to show the range of what you can do with polylines. This

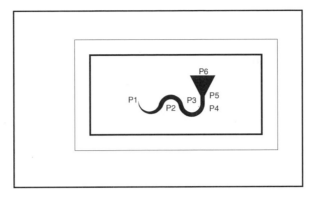

Figure 9-9

is useful, but misleading. Remember, polylines are practical entities even for relatively simple applications such as the rectangles drawn in Task 9.4.

Having said that, we proceed to add our own bit of strangeness to the lore of the polyline. We draw a polyline with three arc segments and one tapered straight line segment, as shown in Figure 9-9. We call this thing a goosenecked funnel. You might have seen something like it at your local garage.

⊕   Select Polyline from the Draw menu or select the Polyline tool from the Draw toolbar.

⊕   Pick a new start point, as shown by P1 in Figure 9-9.

⊕   Type w or right-click and select Width to set new widths.

⊕   Type 0 for the starting width.

⊕   Type .5 for the ending width.

⊕   Type a or right-click and select Arc.

This opens the arc prompt, which looks like this:

```
Specify endpoint of arc or
[Angle/CEnter/Direction/Halfwidth/Line/Radius/Second
pt/Undo/Width]:
```

Let's look at this prompt for a moment. To begin with, there are four options that are familiar from the previous prompt. Halfwidth, Undo, and Width all function exactly as they would in drawing straight polyline segments. The Line option returns you to the previous prompt so that you can continue drawing straight line segments after drawing arc segments.

The other options, Angle, CEnter, Direction, Radius, Second pt, and Endpoint of arc, allow you to specify arcs in ways similar to the ARC command. One difference is that AutoCAD assumes that the arc you want will be tangent to the last polyline segment entered. This is often not the case. The Center and Direction options let you override this assumption where necessary, or you can begin with a short line segment to establish direction before entering the arc prompt.

⊕   Pick an endpoint to the right, as shown by P2 in Figure 9-9, to complete the first arc segment.

Tip: If you did not follow the order shown in the figures and drew your previous rectangle clockwise, or if you have drawn other polylines in the meantime, you might find that the arc does not curve downward, as shown in Figure 9-9. This is because AutoCAD starts arcs tangent to the last polyline segment drawn. Fix this by using the Direction option. Type d and then pick a point straight down. Now you can pick an endpoint to the right as shown.

AutoCAD prompts again:

```
Specify endpoint of arc or
[Angle/CEnter/CLose/Direction/Halfwidth/Line/Radius/Second
pt/Undo/Width]:
```

For the remaining two arc segments, retain a uniform width of 0.50.

⊕ Enter Points P3 and P4 to draw the remaining two arc segments as shown.

> Now we draw two straight line segments to complete the polyline.

⊕ Type l or right-click and select Line from the shortcut menu. (This takes you back to the original prompt.)

⊕ Pick P5 straight up about 1.00 as shown.

⊕ Type w or right-click and select Width from the shortcut menu.

⊕ Press Enter to retain 0.50 as the starting width.

⊕ Type 3 for the ending width.

⊕ Pick an endpoint up about 2.00 as shown by P6.

⊕ Press Enter or the spacebar to exit the command.

> Your screen should resemble Figure 9-9.

9.6 Editing Polylines with PEDIT

GENERAL PROCEDURE

1. Type pe or open the Modify menu, highlight Object, and select Polyline.
2. Select a polyline.
3. Type or select a PEDIT option.
4. Follow the prompts.

The PEDIT command provides a subsystem of special editing capabilities that work only on polylines. We do not attempt to have you use all of them; you might never need some of them. Most important is that you be aware of the possibilities so that when you find yourself in a situation calling for a PEDIT procedure you know what to look for. After executing the following task, study Figure 9-12, the PEDIT chart.

We perform two edits on the polylines already drawn.

⊕ Type pe or open the Modify menu, highlight Object, and select Polyline.

This executes the PEDIT command. There is also an Edit Polyline tool on the Modify II toolbar. You are prompted to select a polyline:

Select polyline or [Multiple]:

⊕ Select the outer 0-width polyline rectangle drawn in Task 9.4.

Notice that PEDIT works on only one object at a time. If you want to edit more than one polyline with the same PEDIT option, type m for the Multiple option. You are prompted as follows:

Enter an option [Open/Join/Width/Edit
vertex/Fit/Spline/Decurve/Ltype gen/Undo]:

These same options are displayed in a drop-down list on the dynamic input display. Open is replaced by Close if your polyline has not been closed. Undo and eXit are self-explanatory. Other options are illustrated in Figure 9-12. Edit vertex brings up the subset of options shown on the right side of the chart. When you do vertex editing, AutoCAD marks one vertex at a time with an X. You can move the X to other vertices by pressing Enter or typing n.

Now we edit the selected polyline by changing its width.

⊕ Type w or select Width from the dynamic input display menu.

This option allows you to set a new uniform width for an entire polyline. All tapering and variation is removed when this edit is performed.

AutoCAD prompts

Specify new width for all segments:

⊕ Type .25.

Your screen is redrawn to resemble Figure 9-10.

The prompt is returned and the polyline is still selected so that you can continue shaping it with other PEDIT options.

⊕ Press Enter or the spacebar to exit PEDIT.

⊕ Press Enter or the spacebar to repeat PEDIT.

This exiting and reentering is necessary to select another polyline to edit, using a different type of edit.

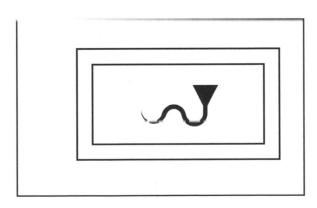

Figure 9-10

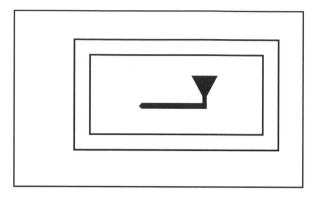

Figure 9-11

⊕ Select the gooseneck funnel polyline.

    This time we try the Decurve option. Decurve straightens all curves within the selected polyline.

⊕ Type d or select Decurve from the dynamic input display menu.

⊕ Press Enter or the spacebar to exit PEDIT.

    Your screen should resemble Figure 9-11.

To complete this exercise, we suggest that you try some of the other editing options. In particular, you can get interesting results from Fit and Spline. Be sure to study the PEDIT chart (Figure 9-12) before going on to the next task.

9.7 Drawing 2-D SOLIDs

GENERAL PROCEDURE

1. Type so or open the Draw toolbar, highlight Surfaces, and select 2-D Solid.
2. Pick a first point.
3. Pick a second point.
4. Pick a third point.
5. Pick a fourth point or press Enter to draw a triangular section.
6. Pick another third point or press Enter to exit the command.

SOLID allows you to draw rectangular and triangular solid-filled shapes in two dimensions by specifying points that become corners or vertices. There is no relation between the 2-D solid command and 3-D solid modeling, which is the subject of Chapter 14.

    There is a trick to using SOLID for rectangular sections involving the order in which you enter points. If you enter them in the wrong order, you will get the bowtie effect shown in Figure 9-13. It is natural to enter points in a rectangle by moving around the perimeter. However, AutoCAD solids are drawn with edges

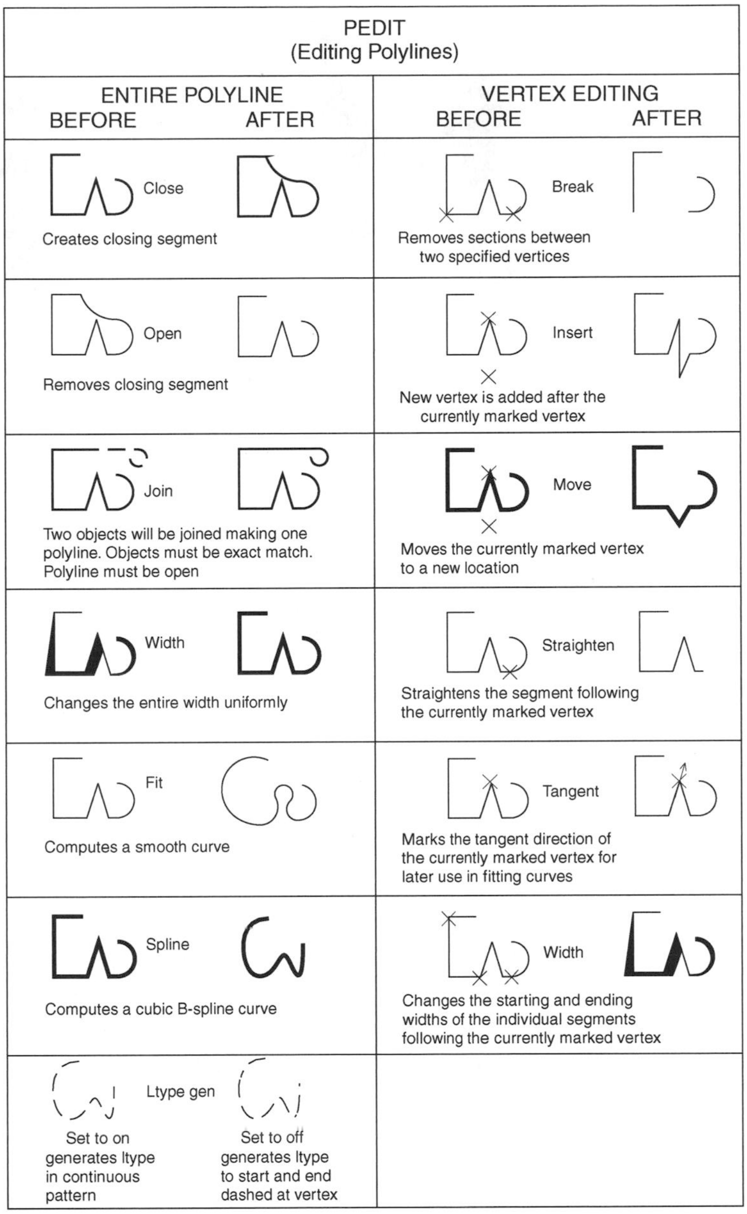

PEDIT (Editing Polylines)			
ENTIRE POLYLINE		**VERTEX EDITING**	
BEFORE AFTER		BEFORE AFTER	

ENTIRE POLYLINE

Close — Creates closing segment

Open — Removes closing segment

Join — Two objects will be joined making one polyline. Objects must be exact match. Polyline must be open

Width — Changes the entire width uniformly

Fit — Computes a smooth curve

Spline — Computes a cubic B-spline curve

Ltype gen — Set to on generates ltype in continuous pattern / Set to off generates ltype to start and end dashed at vertex

VERTEX EDITING

Break — Removes sections between two specified vertices

Insert — New vertex is added after the currently marked vertex

Move — Moves the currently marked vertex to a new location

Straighten — Straightens the segment following the currently marked vertex

Tangent — Marks the tangent direction of the currently marked vertex for later use in fitting curves

Width — Changes the starting and ending widths of the individual segments following the currently marked vertex

Figure 9-12

between Point 1 and Point 3 and between Point 2 and Point 4, so you need to be careful about the order in which you pick points.

⊕   To begin this task, clear the screen of polylines left over from Task 9.6.

⊕   FILL should be on for this exercise. We begin with a rectangular solid.

⊕   Type so or open the Draw menu, highlight Surfaces, and select 2-D Solid.

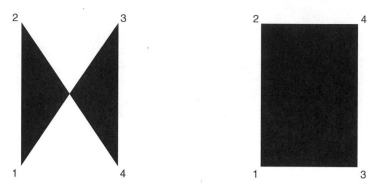

Figure 9-13

There is also a 2-D Solid tool on the Surfaces toolbar.
AutoCAD prompts for a series of points, beginning with this:

Specify first point:

⊕   Pick a point similar to P1 (5,3) in Figure 9-14.

The SOLID command uses no rubber band or other visual feedback, so you
might wish to use our coordinates to stay on track. You simply see the next
prompt:

Specify second point:

⊕   Pick a point similar to P2 (5,10).

These first two points become the endpoints of one side of a rectangular
solid. AutoCAD prompts

Specify third point:

⊕   Pick a point similar to P3 (10,3).

Remember that an edge is drawn between Point 1 and Point 3. AutoCAD
prompts

Specify fourth point:

⊕   Pick a point similar to P4 (10,10) in Figure 9-14.

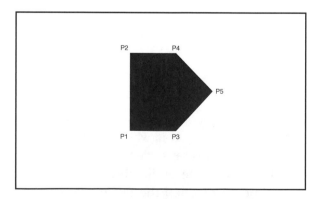

Figure 9-14

When the fourth point is entered, AutoCAD draws a solid rectangle and continues to prompt for points.

Specify third point:

If you continue entering points, the previous Points 3 and 4 become Points 1 and 2 of the new section. You can draw a triangular section by picking a third point and then pressing Enter in response to the prompt for a fourth point. This also means that you need to press Enter twice when you want to exit SOLID. We draw a triangular solid before exiting.

⊕ Pick a point similar to P5 (14,6.5) in Figure 9-14.

⊕ Press Enter in response to the Fourth point: prompt.

> Your screen should resemble Figure 9-14.

⊕ Press Enter again to exit the command.

9.8 Drawing and Editing Multilines

GENERAL PROCEDURE

1. Type ml or select Multiline from the Draw menu.
2. Pick a start point.
3. Pick a next point.
4. Pick another point, or press Enter to exit the command.

Multilines are groups of parallel lines with various forms of intersections and end caps. Each individual line is called an element, and you can have up to 16 elements in a single multiline style. Drawing multilines is about as simple as drawing lines. The complexity comes in defining multiline styles and in editing intersections. In this task, we draw standard multilines, create a new style, and edit the intersection of two multilines.

⊕ To begin this exercise, clear the screen of solids or other objects left from previous exercises.

> First, we draw some standard multilines.

⊕ Type ml or select Multiline from the Draw menu.

> AutoCAD issues the following prompt:

> > Current settings: Justification = Top, Scale = 1.00, Style = STANDARD
> > Specify start point or [Justification/Scale/Style]:

If you stick with the default option, you can see that the MLINE sequence is exactly like drawing a line. Justification refers to the way elements are positioned in relation to the points you pick on the screen. The default justification is Top. This means that the top element of the multiline is positioned at the crosshairs when you pick points. Try it. We discuss the other options later.

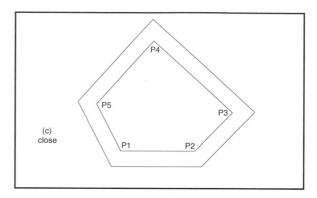

Figure 9-15

⊞ Pick a start point similar to P1 in Figure 9-15.

AutoCAD gives you a standard, two-element multiline to drag and prompts for another point:

Specify next point:

Move the cursor and notice how the crosshairs continue to connect with the top element. The other two options for justification are Zero and Bottom. Zero lines up in the middle of the elements, at the zero point or origin. You will understand this better after we create a new style. Bottom lines up on the bottom element.

⊞ Pick a second point similar to P2 in Figure 9-15.

Exact lengths and angles are not important. Move the cursor around and notice how AutoCAD adjusts the corner to maintain parallel line elements.

AutoCAD has added an Undo option now that you have one multiline segment complete:

Specify next point or [Undo]:

⊞ Pick P3, as in Figure 9-15.

Once you have two complete multiline segments, AutoCAD adds a close option:

Specify next point or [Close/Undo]:

⊞ Pick P4, as in Figure 9-15.
⊞ Pick P5, as in Figure 9-15.
⊞ Type c or right-click and select Close to close and complete the figure.

Creating Multiline Styles

The real power of multilines comes when you learn to create your own multiline style. This is done through the Multiline Style dialog box, called by the MLSTYLE command.

⊞ Select Multiline Style from the Format menu.

This opens the dialog box shown in Figure 9-16. Standard is the name of the current multiline style, which, as we have seen, includes two continuous line

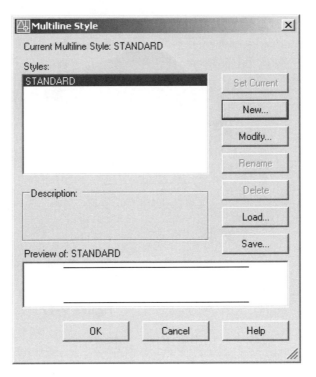

Figure 9-16

elements. We begin by adding a new style to the list of multiline styles and then adding a third element to the new style.

⊞   **Click the New button.**

    This opens a small Create New Multiline Style dialog box.

⊞   **Type new in the New style name box.**

⊞   **Click Continue.**

    This brings you to the New Multiline Style box shown in Figure 9-17. The panel on the left is labeled Caps. Here you can control the way joints and ends of multilines are treated. The variety of options is shown in Figure 9-18. For our purposes, it is not necessary to add joints or end caps at this point.

    Now look at the Elements panel on the right. It shows that there are now only two elements: One is offset 0.5 above the origin point of the multiline (0.0) and the other is offset −0.5, or 0.5 below the origin. Standard multilines have a zero point between the two lines, but because the default justification is top, the crosshairs line up on the top element. With zero justification they would line up at 0.0. With bottom justification they would line up on the −0.5 element.

⊞   **Click Add.**

    This is how we begin to add a new element. As soon as you click Add, a third element is added to the box. Notice that it is offset 0.0. In other words, it is right on the zero line between the two offset lines. For this style, leave it there. If we needed to offset it, we would type a new offset number in the Offset box.

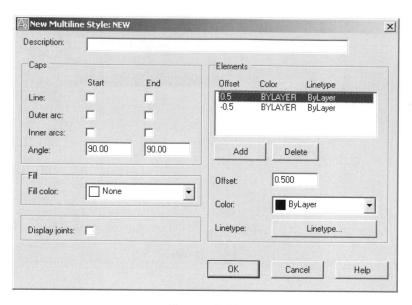

Figure 9-17

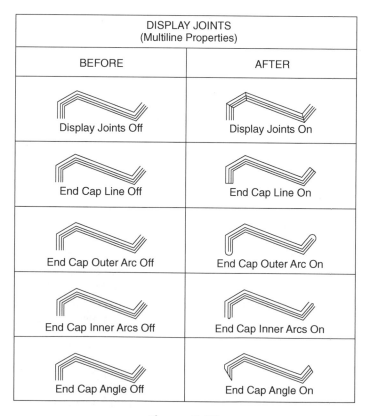

Figure 9-18

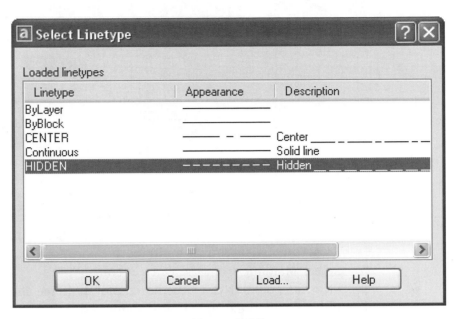

Figure 9-19

Next, notice that all three elements are listed as having BYLAYER color and linetype. This means that the color and linetype are determined by whatever layer the multiline is drawn on. We change the linetype of our newly added middle element. This element should be highlighted. If it is not, click on it to highlight it before proceeding.

⊕ Click Linetype.

This opens the Select Linetype dialog box shown in Figure 9-19. This box contains all the loaded linetypes in your drawing. From past exercises, you should at least have the hidden and center linetypes loaded, so we use one of these. (If for any reason your template drawing does not have the hidden linetype, or if you want to use a linetype that is not loaded, select Load in this dialog box and load it now.)

⊕ Scroll down the list until you see HIDDEN.

⊕ Select HIDDEN.

⊕ Click OK.

Notice that the element at 0.0 now has the hidden linetype style.

⊕ Click OK again.

When you return to the Multiline Style dialog box, you should see that the middle element has been added to the Preview box but is shown as a continuous line. The Preview box shows elements by position, but does not show color or linetype. Also, you see that the New style has been added to the list of styles.

⊕ Click the Set Current button to set New as the current Multiline style.

Now you are ready to leave the box and draw some new multilines.

⊕ Click OK to exit the dialog box.

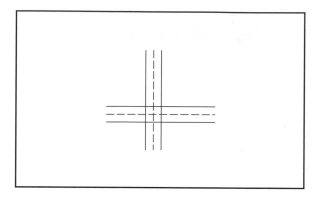

Figure 9-20

⊕ Erase previously drawn multilines.

⊕ Select Multiline from the Draw menu.

⊕ Pick two points to draw the horizontal multiline shown in Figure 9-20.

⊕ Press Enter to exit the MLINE command.

⊕ Repeat MLINE and pick two more points to draw the vertical multiline shown in Figure 9-20.

Editing Multiline Intersections

Multilines can be modified using many of the same edit commands that are used with other entities. In addition, there is a special MLEDIT command for editing the intersection of two multilines. The possibilities are easy to see because the dialog box illustrates the options using a figure similar to the one you have just drawn.

⊕ Select Object and then Multiline from the Modify menu.

There is also a Multiline Edit tool on the Modify II toolbar. These selections open the Multiline Edit Tools dialog box shown in Figure 9-21. When

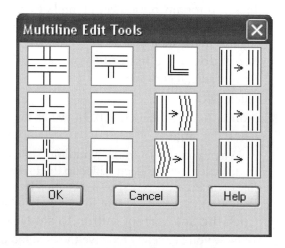

Figure 9-21

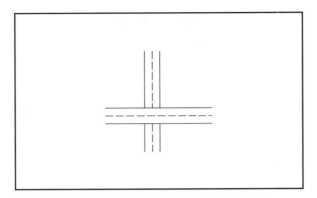

Figure 9-22

you select any of the 12 images in the box, the name of that type of edit is shown at the lower left corner of the box. Because the figure on your screen is similar to the one used in these image boxes, what you see is pretty much what you get when you perform any of these edits.

⊕ Click on the top left image box.

Now you need to select the two multilines to edit.

⊕ Pick the vertical multiline.

The order in which you pick is clearly significant with this and many of the other multiline edits. In this case, the second multiline selected does not change and appears to cross over the first.

⊕ Pick the horizontal multiline.

Your screen should resemble Figure 9-22.

⊕ Press Enter to exit the command.

With up to 16 elements, all of the AutoCAD color options, 58 standard linetypes, and the different end-cap forms and types of intersection edits, the possibilities for creating multiline styles are substantial. We encourage you to experiment before going on.

9.9 Drawing SPLINES

GENERAL PROCEDURE
1. Select the Spline tool from the Draw toolbar.
2. Pick points.
3. Close or specify start and end tangent directions.

A spline is a smooth curve passing through a specified set of points. In AutoCAD, splines are created in a precise mathematical form called nonuniform rational B-spline (NURBS). Splines can be drawn with varying degrees of tolerance, meaning the degree to which the curve is constrained by the defined points. With zero tolerance, the

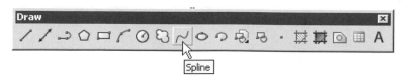

Figure 9-23

curve passes through all points. With higher degrees of tolerance, the curve tends toward, but does not necessarily pass through, each point. In addition to tolerance and the set of points needed to define a spline, tangent directions are needed for the starting and ending portions of the curve. From Chapter 8, recall that dimension leaders can be drawn as splines. Polylines can be converted to spline curves. Splines can be used to create any smooth curve that can be defined by a set of control points. In this task, we use SPLINE to draw a curve surrounding the multilines drawn in Task 9.8.

⊕ Select the Spline tool from the Draw toolbar, as shown in Figure 9-23.

AutoCAD prompts

```
Specify first point or [Object]:
```

⊕ Pick a point roughly 1.00 unit to the left of the top element of the horizontal multiline, P1 as shown in Figure 9-24.

AutoCAD prompts for a next point and continues to prompt for points until you press Enter.

⊕ Pick a second point about 1.00 unit above the left side of the horizontal multiline, P2 as shown in Figure 9-24.

As soon as you have two points, AutoCAD shows a spline that drags with your cursor as you select a third point. The prompt also changes to add two options:

```
Specify next point or [Close/Fit tolerance] <start tangent>:
```

The Fit tolerance option determines the degree to which the curve is constrained by the selected points, as discussed previously. Close works as in other

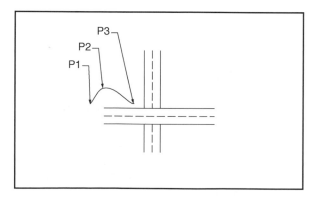

Figure 9-24

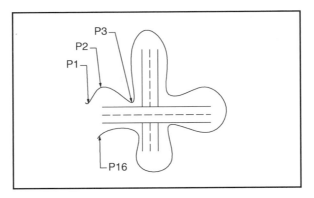

Figure 9-25

commands to create a closed object. If the object is closed, there is no need for tangent specifications. Otherwise, the start and end directions need to be specified when point selection is complete.

⊕ Pick a third point, P3 as shown in Figure 9-25.

From here on, you are on your own as you continue entering points to surround the multilines. We have made no attempt to specify precise points. We used 16 points to go all the way around without crossing the multilines, as shown in Figure 9-25. The exact number of points you choose is not important for this task.

⊕ Continue selecting points to surround the multilines without touching them.

⊕ After you reach and pick a point similar to P16 in Figure 9-25, press Enter or the spacebar.

This indicates that you are finished specifying points. We left the spline open to demonstrate the tangent specifications. When you press Enter, the cursor is attached to the start point, P1 again, and the prompt is this:

```
Specify start tangent:
```

⊕ Pick a point above P1.

The cursor is now attached to P16 again and the prompt is this:

```
Specify end tangent:
```

⊕ Pick a point below P16.

Your screen resembles Figure 9-25.

Editing Splines

Splines can be edited in the usual ways, but they also have their own edit command, SPLINEDIT. Because splines are defined by sets of points, one useful option is to use grips to move grip points. The SPLINEDIT command gives you additional options, including the option to change the tolerance, to add fit points for greater definition, or to delete unnecessary points. An open spline can be closed, or the start and end tangent directions can be changed. To access SPLINEDIT, select Object and then Spline from the Modify menu.

9.10 Drawing Revision Clouds

GENERAL PROCEDURE

1. Select the Revcloud tool from the Draw toolbar.
2. Pick a start point and draw a rough circle around the desired area.
3. Bring the cloud outline back to the start point and let AutoCAD close the cloud automatically.

Revision clouds are a simple graphic means of highlighting areas in a drawing that have been edited. They are primarily used in large projects where a number of people are working on a drawing or a set of drawings. Revision clouds can be very quickly created to highlight an error or a place where changes have been made. They have a shape that is very unlikely to be confused with any actual geometry in your drawing. Try this:

⊕ Pick the Revcloud tool from the Draw toolbar, as shown in Figure 9-26.

AutoCAD prompts

```
Minimum arc length: 0.50 Maximum arc length: 0.50
Specify start point or [Arc length/Object] <Object>:
```

Drawing a revision cloud is a simple matter of moving the crosshairs in a circle around an area, as if you were circling it with a pencil in a paper drawing. We draw a cloud around the open end of the spline curve.

⊕ Pick any point about 1.00 away from the left end of the spline curves, as shown in Figure 9-27.

AutoCAD prompts

```
Guide crosshairs along cloud path...
```

Figure 9-26

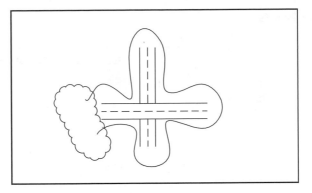

Figure 9-27

⊕ Move the cursor in a rough circle around the open ends of the curve to create a cloud similar to the one shown in Figure 9-27.

When you come near the starting point, the cloud closes automatically. Revclouds can also be created from circles, rectangles, or other closed objects. These can be drawn in the usual manner and then converted to clouds using the Object option. The Arc length option allows you to change the size of the individual arcs that make up the cloud. As you might expect, a completed revision cloud is a polyline. Good practice will likely require that you create revision clouds on a special layer.

The SKETCH Command

The SKETCH command allows you to draw freehand lines. It is rarely used in drafting applications, but it is important to know that it is available. SKETCH creates an irregular line or curve made up of many very short line segments. You control the coarseness of the sketch by specifying the length of the individual segment. Sketched lines take up a large amount of memory, so they should be used sparingly. The key to SKETCH is becoming familiar with its pen-up, pen-down action. Type sketch to enter the command, set the coarseness of line segments, then press and release the pick button to draw (pen down) and press it again to stop (pen up). Also, get used to the idea that sketched lines are not part of the drawing until you record them or exit the SKETCH command.

Note: Sketched lines can be created as independent line segments or as polylines. This is controlled by the variable SKPOLY. With SKPOLY set to 1, SKETCH creates polylines. With SKPOLY set to 0 (the default), SKETCH creates individual line segments.

9.11 Drawing Points

GENERAL PROCEDURE

1. Select the Point tool from the Draw toolbar.
2. Pick a point.

On the surface, this is the simplest DRAW command in AutoCAD. However, if you look at Figure 9-28, you can see figures that were drawn with the POINT command that do not look like ordinary points. This capability adds a bit of power and complexity to the otherwise simple POINT command.

⊞ Erase objects from previous exercises.

⊞ Turn off the grid (press F7).

⊞ Select the Point tool from the Draw toolbar, as shown in Figure 9-29.

You can also type po or select Point from the Draw menu.

⊞ Pick a point anywhere on the screen.

AutoCAD places a point at the specified location and prompts for more points. Look closely and you can see the point you have drawn. Besides those odd instances in which you might need to draw tiny dots like this, points can also serve as object snap nodes. See the OSNAP chart (Figure 6-10) in Chapter 6.

What about those circles and crosses in Figure 9-28? AutoCAD has 18 other simple forms that can be drawn as points. Before we change the point form, we need to see our options.

⊞ Select Point Style from the Format menu.

AutoCAD displays a Point Style dialog box with an icon menu, as shown in Figure 9-30. It shows you graphic images of your choices. You can pick any of the point styles shown by pointing. You can also change the size of points using the Point Size edit box.

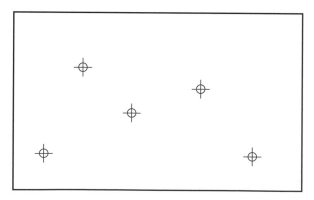

Figure 9-28

Figure 9-29

⊞ Pick the style in the middle of the second row.

⊞ Click OK to exit the dialog box.

When you complete the dialog box, any points previously drawn are updated to the new point style. Notice that this means you can have only one point style in your drawing at a time. New points are also drawn with this style.

⊞ Select the Point tool from the Draw toolbar.

⊞ Pick a point anywhere on your screen.

AutoCAD draws a point in the chosen style, as shown in Figure 9-30.

If you have selected the POINT command from the toolbar, AutoCAD continues to draw points wherever you pick them until you press Esc to exit the command.

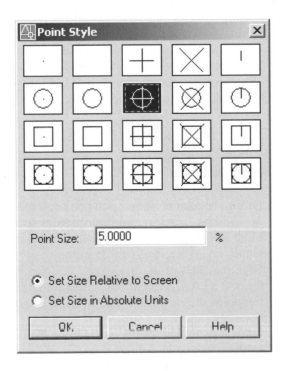

Figure 9-30

If you have entered POINT from the command line or selected Single Point from the Draw menu, you have to repeat it to draw more points.

⊞   Repeat POINT, if necessary, and pick another point.

   Draw a few more points, or return to the dialog box to try another style.

⊞   If necessary, press Esc to exit the POINT command.

9.12   Review Material

Questions

1. If you wanted to draw a polygon around the outside of a circle so that its sides were tangent to the circle, what option of the POLYGON command would you use?
2. Explain this statement: Halfwidth is to width as radius is to diameter.
3. Why does PLINE prompt for two different widths?
4. Why is it important to use the Close option when drawing closed polygons using the PLINE command?
5. How does AutoCAD decide in which direction to draw a polyline arc?
6. You are drawing a rectangular 2-D solid 2 units high by 4 units wide. Your first point is at (2,2) and your second point is at (2,4). Assuming you want to move to the right, where should Points 3 and 4 be? List them in order.
7. Where is the zero point in a standard AutoCAD multiline?
8. What properties make up a multiline style definition?
9. When is it necessary to use the MLEDIT command?
10. What is the difference between a spline curve constructed with a 0 tolerance and one with a 0.5 tolerance?
11. For what reason is it advisable to use the SKETCH command sparingly?

Drawing Problems

1. Draw a regular six-sided polygon centered at (9,6) with a circumscribed radius of 3.0 units. The top and bottom sides should be horizontal.
2. Fillet all corners of the hexagon with a single execution of the FILLET command, giving a radius of 0.25 unit.
3. Give the sides of the hexagon a uniform width of 0.25 unit.
4. Draw a STANDARD two-element multiline justified to its zero point from the midpoint of one angled side of the hexagon to the midpoint of the diagonally opposite side.
5. Draw a second multiline in the same manner, using the other two angled sides so that the two multilines cross.
6. Edit the intersection of the two multilines to create an open cross intersection.

9.13   WWW Exercise 9 (Optional)

In Chapter 9 of our companion website, we challenge you to find information on one of the 20th century's greatest architects. We give you two links to get you started and then you are on your own. We also offer you another design challenge and the self-scoring test for this chapter. When you are ready, complete the following:

⊕   Make sure that you are connected to your Internet service provider.

⊕   Type browser, open the Web toolbar, and select the Browse the Web tool, or open your system browser from the Windows taskbar.

⊕   If necessary, navigate to our companion website at www.prenhall. com/dixriley.

9.14   Drawing 9-1: Backgammon Board

This drawing should go very quickly. It is a good warm-up that gives you practice with MLINE, PLINE, and SOLID. Remember that the dimensions are always part of your drawing now, unless otherwise indicated.

Drawing Suggestions

GRID = 1.00
SNAP = 0.125

- First create the multiline line style for the frame with three elements 0.25, 0.00, and −0.50 and joints on as shown. Then draw the 15.50 × 17.50 multiline frame.
- Draw a 0-width 15.50 × 13.50 polyline rectangle and then OFFSET it 0.125 to the inside. The inner polyline is actually 0.25 wide, but it is drawn on center, so the offset must be half the width.
- Enter the PEDIT command and change the width of the inner polyline to 0.25. This gives you your wide filled border.
- Draw the four triangles at the left of the board and then array them across. The filled triangles are drawn with the SOLID command; the others are just outlines drawn with LINE or PLINE. (Notice that you cannot draw some solids filled and others not filled.)
- The dimensions in this drawing are straightforward and should give you no trouble. Remember to set to layer dim before dimensioning.

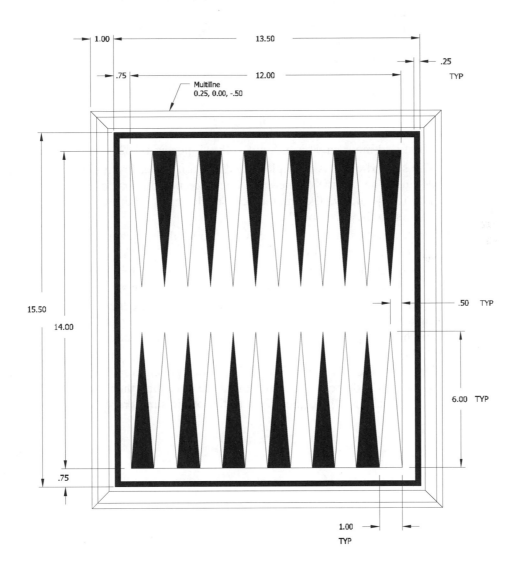

1.00   13.50   .25   TYP

.75   12.00

Multiline
0.25, 0.00, -.50

15.50   14.00   .50   TYP

6.00   TYP

.75

1.00   TYP

BACKGAMMON BOARD

Drawing 9-1

9.15 Drawing 9-2: Dart Board

Although this drawing might seem to resemble the previous one, it is quite a bit more complex and is drawn in an entirely different way. Using SOLID to create the filled areas here would be impractical because of the arc-shaped edges. We suggest you use donuts and TRIM them along the radial lines.

Drawing Suggestions

$$LIMITS = (0,0) \ (24,18)$$
$$GRID = 1.00$$
$$SNAP = 0.125$$

- The filled inner circle is a donut with 0 inner and 0.62 outer diameters.
- The second circle is a simple 1.50-diameter circle. From here, draw a series of donuts. The outside diameter of one becomes the inside diameter of the next. The 13.00- and 17.00-diameter outer circles must be drawn as circles rather than donuts so they are not filled.
- Draw a radius line from the center to one of the quadrants of the outer circle and array it around the circle.
- You might find it easier and quicker to turn fill off before trimming the donuts. Also, use layers to keep the donuts separated visually by color.
- To trim the donuts, select the radial lines as cutting edges. This is easily done using a very small crossing box around the center point of the board. Otherwise, you have to pick each line individually in the area between the 13.00 and 17.00 circles.
- Draw the number 5 at the top of the board using a middle text position and a rotation of 2 degrees. Array it around the circle and then use the DDEDIT command to change the copied fives to the other numbers shown.

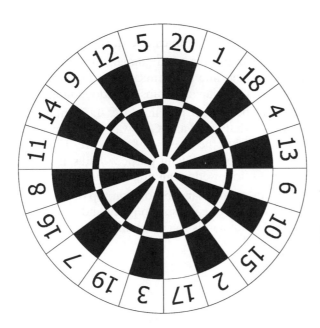

DIAMETERS
Ø.62
Ø1.50
Ø7.50
Ø8.25
Ø13.00
Ø17.00

DART BOARD
Drawing 9-2

9.16   Drawing 9-3: Printed Circuit Board

This drawing uses donuts, solids, and polylines. Also notice the ordinate dimensions.

Drawing Suggestions

UNITS = 4-place decimal
LIMITS = (0,0) (18,12)
GRID = 0.5000
SNAP = 0.1250

- Because this drawing uses ordinate dimensions, moving the 0 point of the grid using the UCS command makes the placement of figures very easy.
- The 26 rectangular tabs at the bottom can be drawn as polylines or solids.
- After placing the donuts according to the dimensions, draw the connections to them using polyline arcs and line segments. These are simple polylines of uniform 0.03125 halfwidth. The triangular tabs are added later.
- Remember, AutoCAD begins all polyline arcs tangent to the last segment drawn. Often this is not what you want. One way to correct this is to begin with a line segment that establishes the direction for the arc. The line segment can be extremely short and still accomplish your purpose. Thus, many of these polylines consist of a line segment, followed by an arc, followed by another line segment.
- There are two sizes of the triangular tabs, one on top of the rectangular tabs and one at each donut. Draw one of each size in place and then use multiple COPY, MOVE, and ROTATE commands to create all the others.

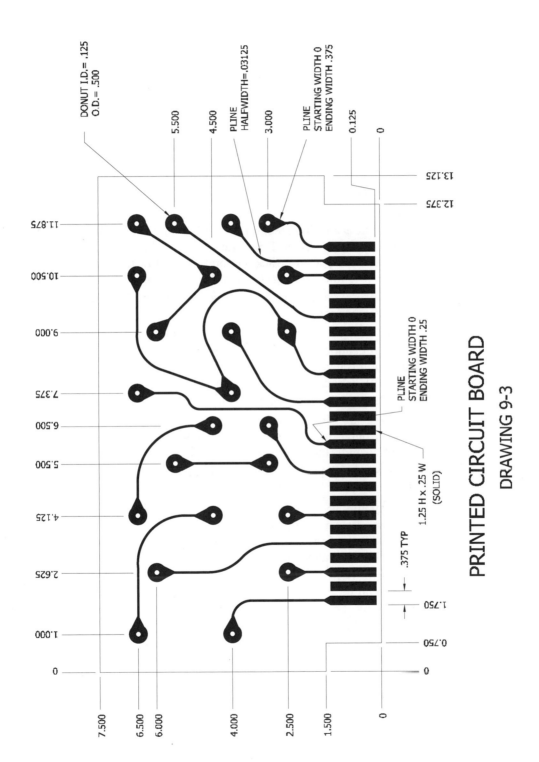

PRINTED CIRCUIT BOARD
DRAWING 9-3

419

9.17   Drawing 9-4: Carbide Tip Saw Blade

This is a nice drawing that requires the creation of an odd shape combining a donut and a 2-D solid that can be filled to form the carbide tips. There is also an opportunity to use temporary tracking points.

Drawing Suggestions

GRID = 1.00
SNAP = 0.125

- After drawing the 7.25-diameter circle, draw a vertical line 1.50 over from the center line. This line becomes the left side of the detailed cut.
- Enter the LINE command and then use object snap and object snap tracking to acquire a point at the intersection of the line and the circle. Still in the LINE command, type tt or select Temporary track point from the Osnap shortcut menu and pick a temporary tracking point 0.58 below the intersection. Draw the horizontal center line running through the track point and out to the right.
- Offset the vertical center line 0.16 to the right of the 0.58 line, then change its layer to Layer 3 to make it a center line.
- Use the center lines to draw the 0.16-radius semicircular arc.
- From the right endpoint of the arc, draw a line extending upward at 80 degrees. The dimension is given as 10 degrees from the vertical, but the coordinate display shows 80 degrees from the horizontal.
- Offset this line 0.06 to the right and left to create the lines for the left and right sides of the carbide tip.
- Draw a horizontal line 0.12 up from the center line. You can use a temporary track point again to locate this point.
- Trim the line with the sides of the carbide tip and create 0.06-radius fillets right and left.
- Draw the 3.68-radius circle to locate the outside of the tip.
- To fill the tip, draw a donut with 0 inside diameter and 0.12 outside diameter in the lower section of the tip and a quadilateral 2-D solid to fill the rest of the tip. (The solid will have four straight edges and, technically, will only approximate the outer edge.) FILL should be on.
- Break and trim the three 80-degree lines, leaving three extension lines for use in dimensioning. Then copy the whole area up to the right for the detail. When you start working on the detail, scale it up 2.00.
- In the original view, erase the extension lines and then array the cut and carbide tip around the circle. Trim the 7.25 circle out of the new cuts and tips.
- Be sure to type in your own values as you dimension the detail because it has been scaled.

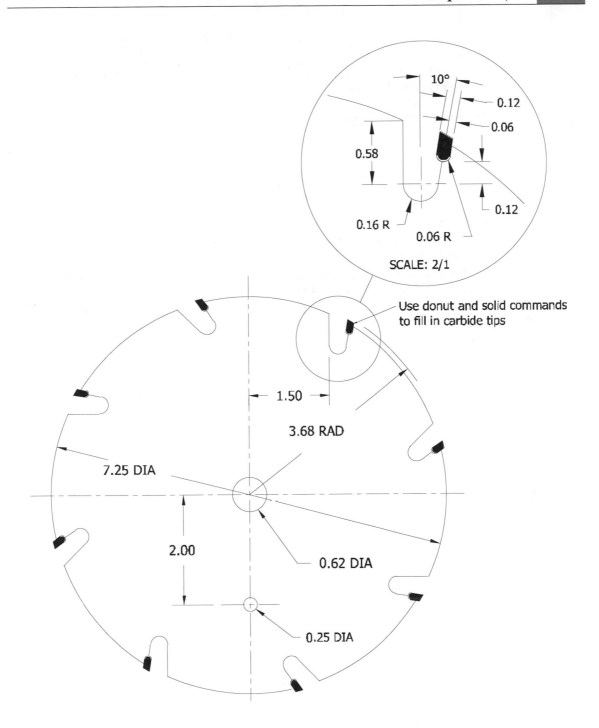

10°

0.12

0.06

0.58

0.12

0.16 R

0.06 R

SCALE: 2/1

Use donut and solid commands
to fill in carbide tips

1.50

3.68 RAD

7.25 DIA

0.62 DIA

2.00

0.25 DIA

CARBIDE TIP SAW BLADE

Drawing 9-4

9.18 Drawing 9-5: Gazebo

This architectural drawing makes extensive use of both the POLYGON command and the OFFSET command.

Drawing Suggestions

UNITSC = Architectural
GRID = 1'
SNAP = 2"
LIMITS = (0',0')(48',36')

- All radii except the 6" polygon are given from the center point to the midpoint of a side. In other words, the 6" polygon is inscribed, whereas all the others are circumscribed.
- Notice that all polygon radii dimensions are given to the outside of the 2" × 4". Offset to the inside to create the parallel polygon for the inside of the board.
- Create radial studs by drawing a line from the midpoint of one side of a polygon to the midpoint of the side of another, or the midpoint of one to the vertex of another as shown; then offset 1" each side and erase the original. Array around the center point.
- Trim lines and polygons at vertices.
- You can make effective use of MIRROR in the elevation.

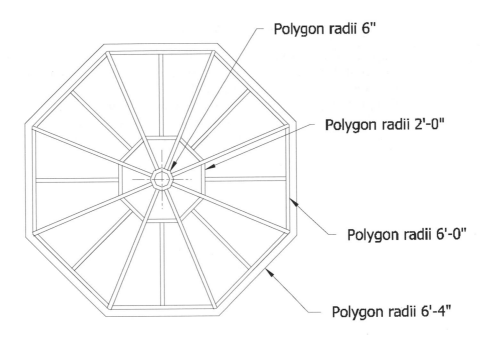

Polygon radii 6"

Polygon radii 2'-0"

Polygon radii 6'-0"

Polygon radii 6'-4"

ROOF FRAMING

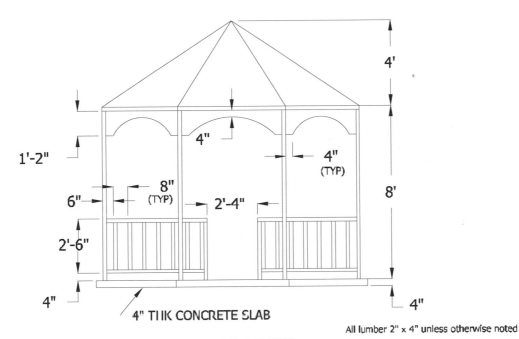

4'

1'-2"

4"

4"
(TYP)

8"
(TYP)

6"

2'-4"

8'

2'-6"

4"

4"

4" THIK CONCRETE SLAB

All lumber 2" x 4" unless otherwise noted

FRONT ELEVATION

GAZEBO
Drawing 9-5

9.19   Drawing 9-6: Frame

This drawing gives you practice using the MLINE command. The object is to draw the front, left side, and top views. Position the views as indicated in the reference drawing. Although at first glance this drawing appears to be easy, it is somewhat complex, so proceed with caution. There are numerous ways in which the drawing can be done, but we suggest you take advantage of the MLINE command to draw each view. The drawing should be fully dimensioned, and all hidden lines are shown.

Top

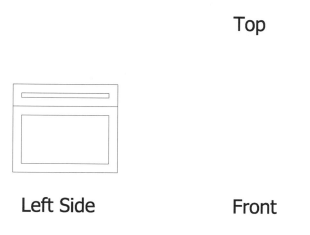

Left Side   Front

Drawing Suggestions

- Begin by setting the MLINE command to a spacing of 1/2″.
- Draw the left side view first using the MLINE command and use the c to close the lines. Notice that the hidden lines are not shown in the reference drawing. You are to provide all hidden lines.
- Use the left side view to line up the front view, making sure you use the MLINE command.
- Finally, draw the top view using the front view for alignment.

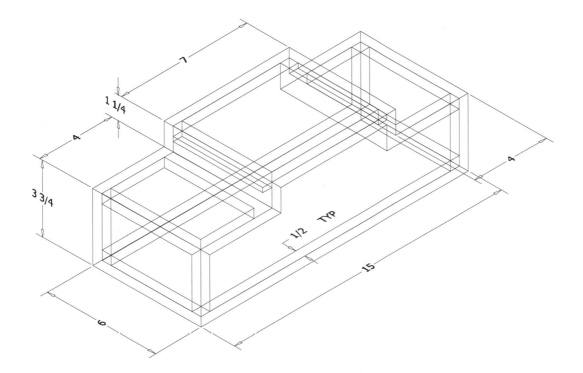

FRAME

Drawing 9-6

9.20　Drawing 9-7: Clock Face

This drawing gives you practice using different filled polyline forms. All procedures for creating the clock face, ticks, hands, and numbers should be familiar from this chapter and from previous drawings in other chapters.

Drawing Suggestions

- Notice the architectural units used in the drawing. Observe the dimensions and select appropriate Limits, Grid, and Snap settings.
- All three hands can be drawn as filled polylines.
- Clock ticks are also filled polylines.
- The font is Impact.

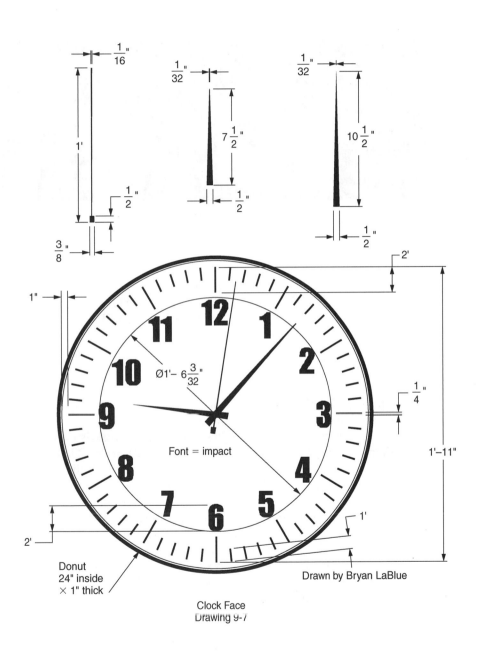

$\frac{1}{16}$"

1'

$\frac{1}{2}$"

$\frac{3}{8}$"

$\frac{1}{32}$"

$7\frac{1}{2}$"

$\frac{1}{2}$"

$\frac{1}{32}$"

$10\frac{1}{2}$"

$\frac{1}{2}$"

2'

1"

Ø1'– $6\frac{3}{32}$"

Font = impact

$\frac{1}{4}$"

1'–11"

1'

2'

Donut
24" inside
× 1" thick

Drawn by Bryan LaBlue

Clock Face
Drawing 9-7

10 Blocks, Attributes, and External References

COMMANDS

ADCENTER	ATTEXT	EXPLODE	XATTACH
ATTDEF	BEDIT	GROUP	XCLIP
ATTDISP	BLOCK	INSERT	XOPEN
ATTEDIT	COPYCLIP	WBLOCK	XREF

OVERVIEW

The primary goal of this book is to teach you how to be an efficient AutoCAD user. To work effectively in a professional design environment, however, requires more than proficiency in drafting techniques. Most design work is done in collaboration with other designers, engineers, managers, and customers. This chapter begins to introduce you to some of the techniques and features that allow you to communicate and share the powers of AutoCAD with others.

To begin, you learn to create groups and blocks. A *group* is simply a set of objects that can be selected, named, and manipulated collectively. A *block* is a set of objects defined as a single entity and saved so that it can be scaled and inserted repeatedly and potentially passed on to other drawings. Blocks become part of the content of a drawing that can be browsed, viewed, and manipulated within and between drawings using the AutoCAD DesignCenter. The DesignCenter and other functions, including the Windows clipboard and externally referenced drawings (Xrefs), allow AutoCAD objects and drawings to be shared with other drawings and applications and with CAD operators at other workstations on a local network or on the Internet. In this chapter, we also introduce you to block attributes. An *attribute* is an item of information attached to a block, such as a part number or price, that is stored along with the block definition. All the information stored in attributes can be extracted from a drawing into a spreadsheet or database program and used to produce itemized reports.

The procedures introduced in this chapter are among the most complex in this book. Particularly in the exercises where you are working with more than one drawing, it is very important to follow the text and instructions closely and to save your work if you do not complete the exercise in one session.

TASKS

10.1   Creating Groups

GENERAL PROCEDURE

1.   Type G or select Object Group from the Tools menu.
2.   Type a name.
3.   Click New.
4.   Select objects to be included in the group definition.
5.   Press Enter to end object selection.
6.   Click OK to exit the dialog box.

The simplest way to create a complex entity from previously drawn entities is to group them into a unit with the GROUP command. Groups are given names and can be selected for all editing processes if they are defined as selectable.

In this exercise, we form groups from objects that also are used later to define blocks. In this way, you get a feel for the different functions of these two methods of creating collections of objects. You begin by creating simple symbols for a computer, monitor, digitizer, and keyboard. Take your time getting these right because once created, they can also be inserted when you complete Drawing 10-1 at the end of the chapter.

⊕   First, start a drawing using the 1B template and make the following changes in the drawing setup:

   1. Set to Layer 0 (the reason for doing this is discussed in the note following this list).

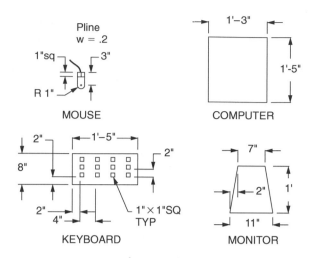

Figure 10-1

2. Change to architectural units, with precision $= 0' - 0''$.
3. Set GRID $= 1'$.
4. Set SNAP $= 1''$.
5. Set LIMITS $= (0',0')$ $(12',9')$. Be sure to include the feet symbol.
6. Zoom All.

Note: Blocks created on Layer 0 are inserted on the current layer. Blocks created on any other layer stay on the layer on which they are created. Inserting blocks is discussed in Task 10.3.

⊕ **Draw the four objects shown in Figure 10-1.**

Draw the geometry only; the text and dimensions in the figure are for your reference only and should not be on your screen. Notice that the computer is a simple rectangular representation of an old-style computer cpu that sits horizontally under the monitor. Later we will modify the definition of this block so that it has the flexibility to also represent a typical tower-style computer.

We define the keyboard as a group.

⊕ **Save this drawing as A.**

We will be working with two drawings later in this chapter and call them A and B for clarity. A has $12' \times 9'$, A-size limits and B is based on our standard 1B template. For now you continue working in Drawing A and do not need to create B until later on.

⊕ **Type g.**

This opens the Object Grouping dialog box shown in Figure 10-2. At the top of the box is the Group Name list box. It is empty now because there are no groups defined in this drawing. Below that is the Group Identification area, with edit boxes for entering a group name and a group description. The flashing cursor bar should be in the Group Name box so that you can enter a name. Our first group is the set of rectangles you have drawn as a symbol for a keyboard.

Figure 10-2

⊕ Type keyboard in the Group Name edit box.

Now look at the Create Group panel. The three boxes here are New, Selectable, and Unnamed. To create a group, you must indicate that it is a new group. First, however, you need to be sure that the group is defined as selectable, if that is your intention, as it most often will be. Unnamed groups are usually groups that have been created by copying named groups. In these cases, AutoCAD assigns names beginning with *A and followed by a number.

⊕ Be sure that Selectable is checked.

⊕ Click New in the Create Group panel.

At this point the dialog box disappears to give you access to objects in your drawing. You see a Select Objects: prompt at the command line.

⊕ Select the keyboard outer rectangles and small rectangles using a window.

⊕ Press Enter to end object selection.

This brings back the dialog box. KEYBOARD should now be in the list box, with a Yes to the right of it indicating that it is a selectable group.

⊕ Click OK to exit the dialog box.

The keyboard is now defined in the drawing as a selectable group. To see that this is so, try selecting it.

⊕ Position the pick box anywhere on the Keyboard and press the pick button.

You see from the highlights and blue grip boxes that the complete group is selected. That is all you need to do with groups at this point. Groups are useful for copying and manipulating groups of objects that tend to stay together.

⊕ Press Esc to remove grips.

The following notes help you go further with groups if you wish:

1. If you click Find Name and then select any object that is part of a group, AutoCAD shows you the name (or names) of the group (or groups) that the object belongs to.
2. Unnamed groups are only included in the Group Name list if Include Unnamed is selected.
3. In editing commands you can select a group by pointing or by typing g at the Select Objects prompt and then typing the name of the group.
4. If the PICKSTYLE variable is set to 0 (default value is 1), you can select groups only by typing their names, not by pointing.

Concerning the Change Group area of the dialog box, the following apply:

1. Remove and Add allow you to remove and add individual objects of a previously defined group.
2. The objects in a group have a defined order, which can be changed using the Group Order dialog box. Select Re-Order in the Object Grouping dialog box.
3. You can change the description of a previously defined group by highlighting the name on the group list, typing or editing the description, and then clicking Description.
4. You can delete a group definition by highlighting its name on the group list and then clicking Explode. The individual objects remain in the drawing.
5. To switch the selectability status of a defined group between Yes and No, use the Selectable box at the bottom right of the dialog box.

10.2 Creating Blocks

GENERAL PROCEDURE

1. Type b, select the Make Block tool from the Draw toolbar, or open the Draw menu, highlight Block, and then select Make.
2. Type a name.
3. Pick an insertion point.
4. Select objects to be included in the block definition.

Blocks have more features than groups. Blocks can be stored as part of an individual drawing or as separate drawings. They can be inserted into the drawing in which they were created, or into other drawings, and can be scaled as they are inserted. In AutoCAD 2006, blocks can also be defined as dynamic, meaning that they are flexible and can be altered in specific ways to represent variations of the

Figure 10-3

block. In general, the most useful blocks are those that can be used repeatedly in many drawings and therefore can become part of a library of predrawn objects used by you and others. In mechanical drawing, for instance, you might want a set of screws drawn to standard sizes that can be used at any time. If you are doing architectural drawing, you might find a library of doors and windows useful. You will see examples of predefined symbol libraries later in this chapter when you explore the AutoCAD DesignCenter and tool palettes.

In this chapter, we are creating a set of simple symbols for some of the tools we know you will use no matter what kind of CAD you are doing—namely, computers, monitors, keyboards, digitizers, plotters, and printers. We define them as blocks, insert them, and assemble them into a workstation. Later we define the complete workstation as a block and insert workstations into an architectural drawing called CAD Room.

⊕ Type b; select the Make Block tool from the Draw toolbar, as shown in Figure 10-3; or open the Draw menu, highlight Block, and then select Make.

These methods execute the BLOCK command and open the Block Definition dialog box shown in Figure 10-4.

⊕ Type computer in the Block name box.

Next, you choose an object to define the block.

⊕ Click Select objects.

The dialog box disappears, giving you access to objects in the drawing.

Note: Be sure to use the Select objects button, not the Quick Select button. Quick Select executes the QSELECT command and opens the Quick Select dialog box. The purpose of this dialog box is to establish filtering criteria so that defined types of objects can be selected more quickly in a complex drawing, filtering out objects that do not meet the selection criteria.

⊕ Select the computer rectangle.

AutoCAD continues to prompt for object selection.

⊕ Right-click to end object selection.

This brings you back to the dialog box.

Blocks are intended to be inserted into drawings, so any block definition needs to include an insertion base point. Insertion points and insertion base points are critical in using blocks. The insertion base point is the point on the block that is at the intersection of the crosshairs when you insert the block. Therefore, when defining a block, try to anticipate the point on the block you would most likely use to position the block on the screen. If you do not define

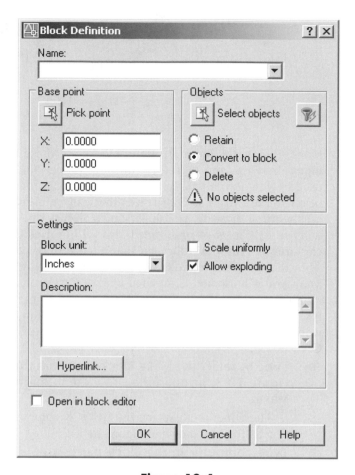

Figure 10-4

an insertion base point, AutoCAD uses the origin of the coordinate system, which might be quite inconvenient.

⊕ Click on the Pick point icon.

⊕ Press Shift and right-click to open the object snap shortcut menu.

⊕ Use a midpoint object snap to pick the middle of the bottom line of the computer as the insertion point, as shown in Figure 10-5.

When creating blocks, you have three choices regarding what happens to objects included in the block definition, shown by the three radio buttons in the Objects panel. Objects can be retained in the drawing separate from the block definition, converted to an instance of the new block, or deleted from the screen. In all instances, the object data are retained in the drawing database as the block definition.

A common practice is to create a number of blocks, one after the other, and then assemble them at the end. To facilitate this method, select the Delete radio button. With this setting, newly defined blocks are erased from the screen automatically. They can be retrieved using OOPS if necessary (but not

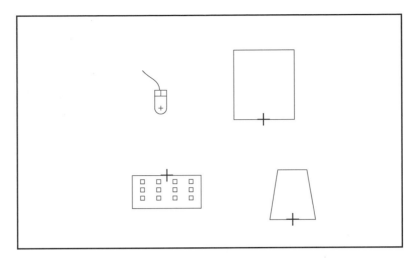

Figure 10-5

U, as this would undo the block definition). In our case, deleting blocks as we define them also helps make a clearer distinction between block references and block definitions.

⊕ Select the Delete radio button.

The block definition is complete.

⊕ Click OK to exit the dialog box.

You have created a "computer" block definition. The computer has vanished from your screen, but can be inserted using the INSERT command, which we turn to momentarily. Now repeat the BLOCK process to make a keyboard block.

⊕ Repeat BLOCK.

⊕ Type keyboard in the Block name box.

⊕ Click Select objects.

⊕ Select the keyboard.

Because you have already defined the keyboard as a selectable group, one pick selects the whole thing. In the command area, AutoCAD shows how many individual objects are in the selection set, and also that there is one group in the set. The group definition of the keyboard now becomes part of the block definition.

⊕ Press Enter to end selection.

⊕ Click the Pick point button.

⊕ Pick the midpoint of the top line of the keyboard as the insertion base point.

⊕ Click OK.

⊕ Repeat the blocking process two more times to create monitor and mouse blocks, with insertion base points as shown in Figure 10-5.

When you are finished, your screen should be blank. At this point, your four block definitions are stored in your drawing base. In the next task, we insert them into your current drawing to create a computer workstation assembly. Before going on, take a look at these other commands that are useful in working with blocks. Many of them are used in the tasks that follow.

Command	Usage
BASE	Allows you to specify a base insertion point for an entire drawing. The base point is used when the drawing is inserted in other drawings.
DBLIST	Displays information for all entities in the current drawing database. Information includes type of entity and layer. Additional information depends on the type of entity. For blocks, it includes insertion point, x scale, y scale, rotation, and attribute values.
EXPLODE	Reverses an instance of a block so that objects that have been combined in the block definition are redrawn as individual objects. Exploding a block reference has no effect on the block definition.
LIST	Lists information about a single block or entity. Information listed is the same as that in DBLIST, but for the selected entity only.
MINSERT	Multiple insert. Allows you to insert arrays of blocks. MINSERT arrays take up less memory than arrays of inserted blocks.
PURGE	Deletes unused blocks, layers, linetypes, shapes, or text styles from a drawing.
WBLOCK	Saves a block to a separate file so that it can be inserted in other drawings. Does not save unused blocks or layers and therefore can be used to reduce drawing file size.

10.3 Inserting Blocks into the Current Drawing

GENERAL PROCEDURE

1. Type i, select Block from the Insert menu, or select the Insert Block tool from the Draw toolbar.
2. Type or select a block name.
3. Pick an insertion point.
4. Answer prompts for horizontal and vertical scale and for rotation angle.

The INSERT command is used to position block references in a drawing. Here you begin to distinguish between block definitions, which are not visible and reside in the database of a drawing, and block references, which are instances of a block inserted into a drawing. The four block definitions you created in Task 10.2 are now part of the drawing database and can be inserted in this drawing anywhere you like. In this task, we focus on inserting into the current drawing. In the next task, we explore sharing blocks between drawings.

Among other things, these procedures are useful in creating assembly drawings. Assembling blocks can be done efficiently using appropriate object snap modes to place objects in precise relation to one another. Assembly drawing is the focus of the drawing tasks at the end of this chapter.

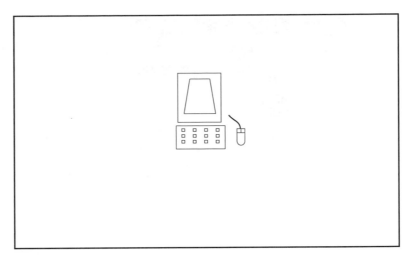

Figure 10-6

In this task, we insert the computer, monitor, keyboard, and mouse back into the drawing to create the workstation assembly shown in Figure 10-6. We also discuss other options for drawing file management, including the use of complete drawings as blocks or as external references.

⊕ If you are still on Layer 0, switch to Layer 1.

⊕ Type i, select Block from the Insert menu, or select the Insert Block tool from the Draw toolbar, as shown in Figure 10-7.

This opens the Insert dialog box shown in Figure 10-8. In addition to the Block Name list box at the top of the dialog box, there are several scaling options that allow you to scale and rotate the block as you insert it. This vastly increases the flexibility and power of the blocking system. The issue of scaling becomes particularly important when you move between drawings. What would happen if you inserted a 20-foot object into a drawing that has $12' \times 9'$ limits? We shall see in Task 10.4.

Unlike the SCALE command, which automatically scales both horizontally and vertically, blocks can be stretched or shrunk in either direction independently as you insert them. You can type an x scale factor or specify both an x and a y factor at once by showing two corners of a window using the Corner option. Use of z is reserved for 3-D applications. The Uniform option scales x, y, and z uniformly.

Figure 10-7

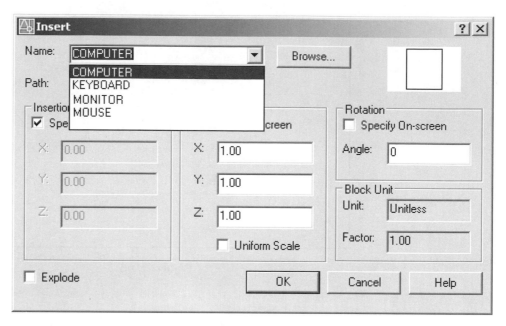

Figure 10-8

Now is a good time to see that your block definitions are still in your database, even though they are no longer on the screen.

⊕ Click the arrow in the Name list box.

You should see a list like this:

COMPUTER
KEYBOARD
MONITOR
MOUSE

⊕ Select COMPUTER from the list.

⊕ Click OK to exit the dialog box and begin inserting the block.

From here on, you follow prompts from the command line. AutoCAD now needs to know where to insert the computer, and you see this prompt:

Specify insertion point or
[Scale/X/Y/Z/Rotate/PScale/PX/PY/PZ/PRotate]:

Notice that AutoCAD gives you a block to drag into place and that it is positioned with the block's insertion base point at the intersection of the crosshairs. The options provide the same scaling functions as the dialog box. The P options are for previewing as you insert.

⊕ Pick a point near the middle of the screen, as shown in Figure 10-6.

Notice that the block is inserted on Layer 1 even though it was created on Layer 0. Remember that this only works with blocks drawn on Layer 0. Blocks drawn on other layers stay on the layer on which they were drawn when they are inserted.

Now let's add a monitor.

⊕ Repeat the INSERT command.

Notice that the last block inserted becomes the default block name in the Block Name box. This facilitates procedures in which you insert the same block in several different places in a drawing.

⊕ Select MONITOR from the Name list.

⊕ Click OK.

⊕ Pick an insertion point two or three inches above the insertion point of the computer, as shown in Figure 10-6.

You should have the monitor sitting on top of the computer and be back at the command prompt. We next insert the keyboard, as shown in Figure 10-6.

⊕ Repeat INSERT.

⊕ Select KEYBOARD from the Name list.

⊕ Click OK.

⊕ Pick an insertion point one or two inches below the computer, as shown in Figure 10-6.

You should now have the keyboard in place.

⊕ Repeat INSERT once more and place a mouse block reference to the right of the other block references as shown in Figure 10-6.

Congratulations! You have completed your first assembly. Next we modify the definition of the computer block so that it may represent a different style of computer.

10.4 Adding Parameters and Actions in the Block Editor

GENERAL PROCEDURE

1. Select Block Editor from the Tools menu or the Block Editor tool from the Standard toolbar.
2. Select a block. (Steps 1 and 2 can be reversed.)
3. From the Block Authoring Palettes, select a Parameter.
4. Specify the parameter location.
5. From the Block Authoring Palettes, select an Action.
6. Specify the action location.

The Block Editor is an AutoCAD 2006 feature with vast potential. It is a whole subsystem of screens, symbols, and commands that allows you to add dynamic parameters to newly defined or previously defined blocks. In this context, a parameter is an aspect of the geometry of a block definition that may be designated as variable. Parameters are always associated with Actions. When a dynamic block is inserted, it takes the standard form of its original definition. Unlike other blocks, however, once a dynamic block is inserted it can be selected and altered in specific ways. The ways in which a dynamic block can be altered depend on the parameters and actions that have been added to the definition.

Figure 10-9

In this exercise we will demonstrate dynamic capabilities by adding a linear parameter and a stretch action to the computer block. This will allow us to adjust the shape of the computer so that it may represent a tower style computer as well as one placed horizontally under the monitor.

⊕ To begin this task, you should be in Drawing A with the four blocks inserted in the last section, shown in Figure 10-6.

⊕ Select the computer block.

⊕ Open the Tools menu and select Block Editor, or select the Block Editor tool from the Standard toolbar, as shown in Figure 10-9.

This executes the BEDIT command and opens the Edit Block Definition dialog box shown in Figure 10-10. Because you selected the computer block before entering the dialog, the computer block should be selected in the block list and an image of the block should be displayed in the Preview box. Once inside the Block Editor, you have access to a set of commands and procedures that cannot be accessed anywhere else. All of these commands begin with the letter B and work on blocks that have been selected for editing.

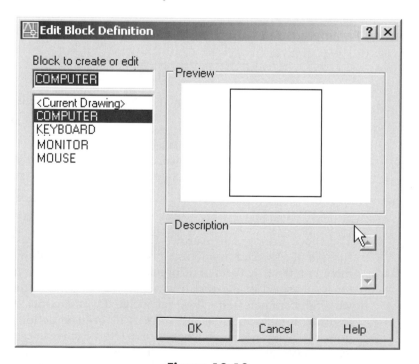

Figure 10-10

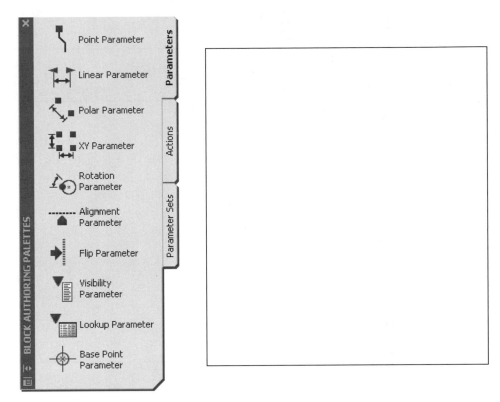

Figure 10-11

⊕ Click OK.

This brings you to the Block Authoring Palettes window shown in Figure 10-11. On the right is the block itself in a special editing window where you can work directly on the block geometry. The Block Authoring Palettes has three tabs. The first is for defining parameters, the second for actions, and the third is for sets of parameters and actions that are frequently paired. Here we add a linear parameter so that the width of the block can be altered, then we add a stretch action to show how the parameter will be edited after it is inserted.

⊕ From the palettes select Linear Parameter.

This executes the BPARAMETER command with the Linear option. Other options are shown on the palette. AutoCAD prompts:

```
Specify start point or [Name/Label/Chain/Description/
              Base/Palette/Value set]:
```

We specify a parameter indicating that the width of the computer may be altered.

⊕ Pick a start point on one of the vertical sides of the computer block.

If the sides do not fall on snap points, you can use a Nearest object snap to locate the line precisely.

AutoCAD displays a Distance label, a line, and two arrows.

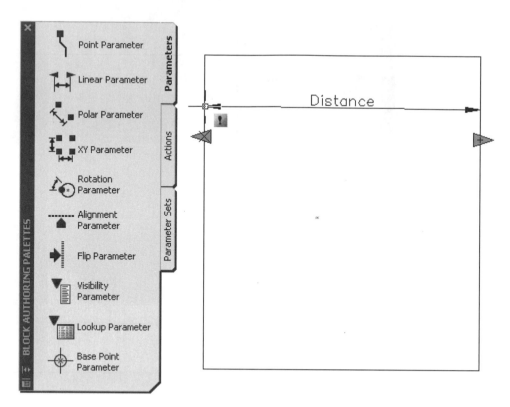

Figure 10-12

⊕ Pick a point directly across the width of the computer, as shown in Figure 10-12.

The length of the parameter is now established. AutoCAD prompts you to specify a label location.

⊕ Pick a location point for the parameter label as shown in Figure 10-12.

The parameter is now defined, but it is incomplete because there is no action defined for altering the parameter. The yellow box with the exclamation point is an alert to remind you of this. If you let your cursor rest on the yellow alert, you will see a message that says "No actions associated with the parameter."

⊕ Click the Actions tab on the Block Authoring Palettes.

The Actions tab is shown in Figure 10-13.

⊕ Select Stretch Action from the palettes.

This executes the BACTION command with the Stretch option. AutoCAD prompts

                    Select Parameter:

⊕ Select any part of the parameter or its label.

AutoCAD prompts

    Specify parameter point to associate with action or enter
            [sTart point/Second point] <Start>:

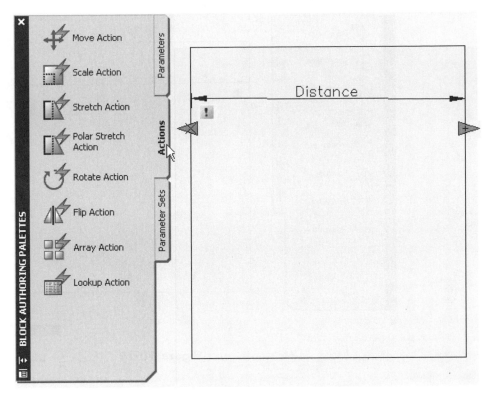

Figure 10-13

The points you can select are the two triangles on the sides of the block. These are the start point and the end point of the linear parameter. The behavior of the geometry is dependent on the point you select.

⊕ **Pick the right end point.**

With this point selected we will be able to alter the width of the rectangle from the right side. AutoCAD now asks you to specify a stretch frame, just as you would do in the STRETCH command.

```
Specify first corner of stretch frame or [CPolygon]:
```

This window will frame the portion of the rectangle to be stretched.

⊕ **Pick two points to define a stretch frame around the right side of the rectangle, as shown in Figure 10-14.**

AutoCAD now asks you to select objects. For our purposes you can basically repeat the two points just selected to frame the right side again. Keep in mind, however, that in a more complex block you might not want all objects to be affected by the stretch. This prompt allows you to select objects to include in the stretch.

⊕ **Pick two points again.**

⊕ **Right click or press ENTER to end object selection.**

Finally, AutoCAD asks you to specify a location for the action symbol. This is merely a visual key as to the purpose of the parameter and action. The action

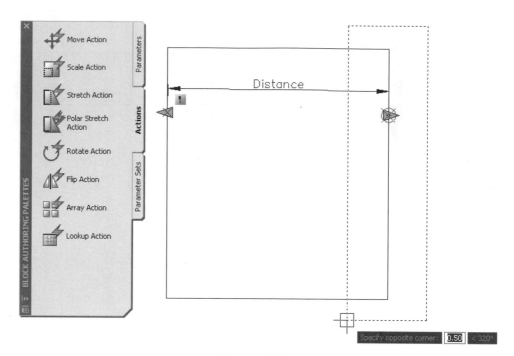

Figure 10-14

location will not appear when the block is inserted and will not affect how the action works. Two good possibilities for this action would be along the right side of the block or on the right side of the parameter location itself, as shown in Figure 10-15.

✛ Pick a location for the Stretch Action symbol, as shown in Figure 10-15.

✛ Click on Close Block Editor to exit the block editing system.

This selection is located in the center of the Block Editor toolbar, illustrated in Figure 10-16. When you select it, AutoCAD will display a message that tells you that changes in block definitions may update existing block references.

✛ Click Yes to save the new block definition and update block references.

This brings us back to the drawing editor. The four block references are assembled there as before. The computer block has been updated, but there is no visible change until we select it. To complete this exercise we select the computer and implement the stretch action.

✛ Select the computer.

The computer is highlighted, but new dynamic block grips have been added to indicate the linear parameter as shown in Figure 10-17.

✛ Select the dynamic block grip on the right side of the computer block. This is the point selected previously in defining the linear parameter.

✛ Move your cursor back and forth so that you can see how the block is stretched.

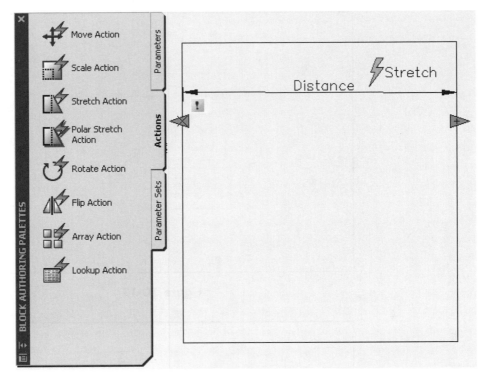

Figure 10-15

⊕ Move your cursor to the left to shrink the computer block to a 6″ width.

We now have a narrowed version of the computer block, which can represent a tower-style computer. All we need to do is to move it over to the left.

⊕ Using the square grip, move the computer 6″ to the left, as shown in Figure 10-18.

⊕ Press Esc to remove grips.

Your screen should resemble Figure 10-18.

This has been a brief introduction to the capabilities of the Block Editor. We provide another brief demonstation later to show how one aspect of a dynamic block may be moved in relation to others.

In the next two tasks, we explore moving blocks between drawings and moving drawn objects between applications using the Windows clipboard.

Figure 10-16

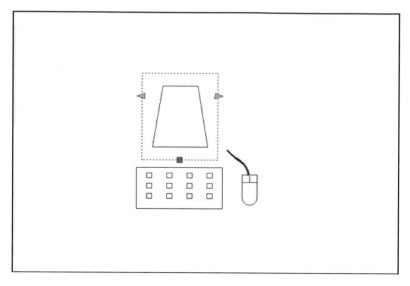

Figure 10-17

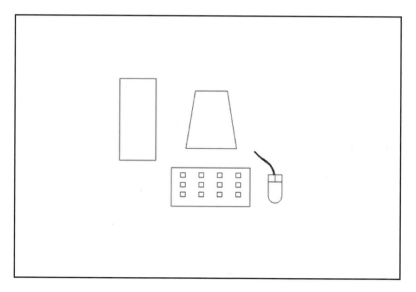

Figure 10-18

10.5　Using the Windows Clipboard

GENERAL PROCEDURE

1. Select the Cut or Copy tool from the Standard toolbar.
2. Select objects. (Steps 1 and 2 can be reversed.)
3. Open another drawing or a different Windows application.
4. Type Ctrl + V or select Paste in that drawing or application.

Figure 10-19

The Windows clipboard makes it very easy to copy objects from one AutoCAD drawing to another or into other Windows applications. You use the Copy and Cut tools from the Standard toolbar, which activate the COPYCLIP and CUTCLIP commands. Cutting removes the selected objects from your AutoCAD drawing, whereas copying leaves them in place. When you send blocks to an AutoCAD drawing via the clipboard, they are defined as blocks in the new drawing as well. Block names and definitions are maintained, but there is no option to scale as there is when you INSERT blocks.

In this task, we create a new drawing called B and copy the assembled workstation into it. The steps would be the same to copy the objects into another Windows application. The procedure is very simple and works with any Windows application that supports Windows Object Linking and Embedding (OLE).

⊕   To begin this task you should be in Drawing A with the assembled blocks on your screen, resembling Figure 10-18.

⊕   Select the Copy tool from the Standard toolbar, as shown in Figure 10-19.

AutoCAD prompts for object selection.

⊕   Using a window selection, select all the objects in the computer workstation assembled in Task 10.3.

⊕   Press Enter to end object selection.

AutoCAD saves the selected objects to the clipboard. Nothing happens on your screen, but the selected objects are stored and could be pasted back into this drawing, another AutoCAD drawing, or another Windows application. Next we open a new drawing.

⊕   Select the New tool from the Standard toolbar and open a new drawing using the 1B template.

We call this Drawing B and create it using our standard 1B template. You can have multiple drawings open in a single AutoCAD session.

⊕   Save the new drawing, giving it the name B.

Drawing B should now be open in the drawing area with Drawing A also open in the background. You will not see A while you are in B.

⊕   In Drawing B, select the Paste tool from the Standard toolbar. This tool is just to the right of the Copy tool.

AutoCAD prompts for an insertion point and gives you an image to drag into place. You see a very large image of the keyboard, as shown in Figure 10-20. Actually, the whole workstation is there, but the computer, monitor, and mouse are off the screen. They are so large because the scale of this drawing is very different from the one the objects were drawn in. The original drawing has been set up with architectural units and limits so that its block definitions

Figure 10-20

can be used in Drawing 10-1, the CAD Room, at the end of the chapter. In the new drawing, based on the 1B template, the 18 × 12 units are being interpreted as inches, so the keyboard is coming in at 17″, covering most of the screen. Without the scaling capacity of the INSERT command, you have no control over this interpretation.

⊹ Pick an insertion point at the lower left of your screen, as shown in Figure 10-20.

That's all there is to it. It is equally simple to paste text and images from other compatible Windows applications into AutoCAD. Just reverse the process, cutting or copying from the other application and pasting into AutoCAD.

We will undo this paste procedure in a moment, but first take a moment to try out the DBLIST command and see how these objects appear in the database of the new drawing.

⊹ Type dblist, press Enter, and then press F2.

In the text window, you see a series of four entity listings like this:

```
        BLOCK REFERENCE      Layer: "1"
                    Space: Model space
         Handle = D2
         "monitor"
     at point, X = 9.00 Y = 5.00 Z = 0.00
            X scale factor 1.00
            Y scale factor 1.00
   rotation angle          0
            Z scale factor 1.00
```

You have to press Enter to see the whole list. The four pasted blocks are the only entities in the new drawing. If there were other objects, they would be listed here as well.

⊹ Press F2 to return to the Drawing Window.

⊹ Press U until everything has been undone in Drawing B.

The issue of scaling is handled differently when you paste AutoCAD objects into other applications. In those cases, objects are automatically scaled to fit in the document that receives them. Most applications have their own editing feature, which allows you to adjust the size of the objects after they have been pasted.

10.6 Inserting Blocks and External References into Other Drawings

---

GENERAL PROCEDURE

1. Prepare a drawing to be inserted into other drawings.
2. Open a second drawing.
3. Enter the INSERT or XATTACH command.
4. Enter the name and path of the drawing to be inserted or referenced, or browse to find the file.
5. Answer prompts for scale and rotation.

Any drawing can be inserted as a block or external reference into another drawing. The process is much like inserting a block within a drawing, but you need to specify the drawing location. In this task, we attach Drawing A as an external reference in Drawing B. The process for inserting blocks into other drawings is identical to attaching an external reference.

External References

Externally referencing a drawing is a powerful alternative to inserting it as a block. The principal difference between inserted drawings and externally referenced drawings is that inserted drawings are actually merged with the current drawing database, whereas externally referenced drawings are only linked. If the referenced drawing is changed, the changes are reflected in the current drawing the next time it is loaded or when the Reload option of the XREF Manager is selected. This allows designers at remote locations to work on different aspects of a single master drawing, which can be updated as changes are made in the various referenced drawings.

Because attaching a reference only loads enough information to point to the externally referenced drawing, it does not increase the size of the current drawing file as significantly as INSERT does.

⊕ **You should be in Drawing B to begin this task, with everything undone.**

To switch back to Drawing A, use the open drawing list at the bottom of the Window menu, as follows.

⊕ **Open the Window menu and select Drawing A, as shown in Figure 10-21.**

This brings you back into your original drawing with the computer workstation objects displayed as shown previously in Figure 10-18. You could use this drawing as a block or external reference without further adjustment, but using the BASE command to add an insertion base point for the drawing is convenient. BASE works for either blocking or referencing.

⊕ **Type base.**

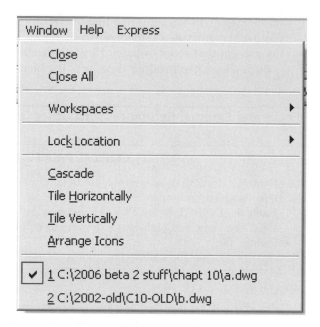

Figure 10-21

AutoCAD prompts

        `Enter base point, <0'-0", 0'-0", 0'-0">:`

This indicates that the current base point is at the origin of the grid. We move it to the lower left corner of the keyboard.

⊞   **Pick the lower left corner of the keyboard.**

The new base point is registered, but there is no change in the drawing.

⊞   **Type Ctrl + S, click the Save tool, or select Save from the File menu to save Drawing A.**

If you don't save the drawing after changing the base point, the base point is not used when the drawing is referenced.

Note: Be sure to pay attention to where you are saving Drawing A so that you can easily find it again.

⊞   **Open the File menu and select Close to close Drawing A.**

This returns you to Drawing B. There should be no objects in this drawing.

⊞   **Open the Insert menu and select External Reference.**

This executes the XATTACH command and opens the Select Reference File dialog box, shown in Figure 10-22. This is basically the same dialog box you see when you enter any command in which you select a file.

⊞   **If necessary, double-click the folder that contains Drawing A, or use the Up One Level button to locate the folder you need.**

⊞   **Select Drawing A from the list of files or from the thumbnail gallery, depending on your operating system.**

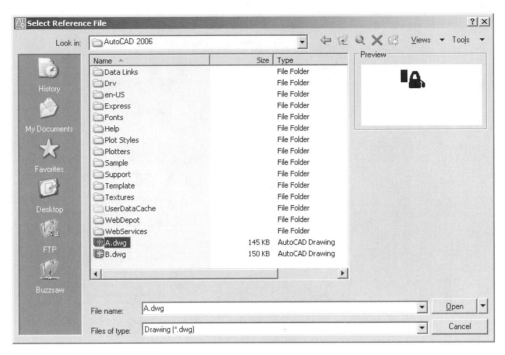

Figure 10-22

✛ Click Open.

This opens the External Reference dialog box, shown in Figure 10-23. Note that this box is nearly identical to the Insert dialog box shown previously in Figure 10-8. A should be entered in the name box, and its path identified below the name.

✛ Click OK to exit the dialog box.

You are now back to the Drawing B Drawing Window. As in the last task, you have a very large image of the keyboard, but this time there is a prompt for scale factors in the command area.

✛ Type s for the Scale option.

This option takes a uniform scale factor for the complete inserted drawing.

✛ Type 1/8.

You could also type .125, but it is worth noting that the INSERT and XATTACH commands take fractions or scale ratios at the scale factor prompt.

✛ Pick an insertion point near the middle of the screen.

At this scale, the workstation appears on your screen much as it does in Drawing A. Before going on, try using the LIST command to see how the newly inserted external reference is specified in the database of Drawing B.

✛ Select the workstation.

It only takes one pick, as this is now a single entity.

✛ Type list.

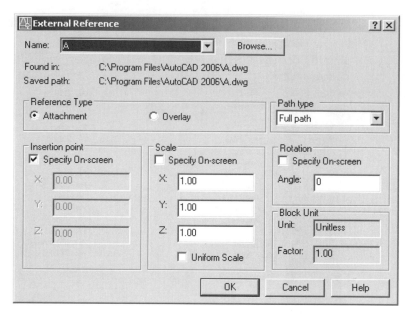

Figure 10-23

In the text window, you see a listing similar to this:

```
BLOCK REFERENCE Layer: "0"
                   Space: Model space
         Handle = D3
     "A"
       External reference
at point, X = 9.00 Y = 5.00 Z = 0.00
           X scale factor 0.13
           Y scale factor 0.13
     rotation angle       0
           Z scale factor 0.13
```

Notice that the drawing name has become the block definition name, that the block is identified as an external reference, and that the *x*, *y*, and *z* scale factors have been rounded off to .13 (from .125 = 1/8).

⊞ Press F2 to return to the drawing window.

Stop for a moment to consider your two drawings. Drawing A is closed but has been attached to Drawing B as an external reference. Drawing A has the architectural units and limits established at the beginning of the chapter. It has four separate blocks currently assembled into a workstation. Drawing B has our standard 1B units and limits and has one instance of Drawing A attached as an external reference. In the tasks that follow, we continue to make changes to these drawings. Later, you will see that changes in Drawing A are reflected in Drawing B. In the next task, we introduce an exciting tool for managing drawing data, the AutoCAD DesignCenter.

Before leaving this section, here is a final note.

Raster Images

A *raster image* is an image such as a picture or photograph that has been encoded as a matrix of dots or pixels. Any ordinary computer graphic image is an example. Such images can be brought into an AutoCAD drawing much as an external reference would be. Raster images are attached and linked to AutoCAD drawings, but they do not actually become part of the drawing database so they do not take up large amounts of memory. Once attached, raster images can be inserted repeatedly in the same drawing just like blocks. Raster images can be scaled as they are inserted. To insert a raster image, select Raster Image from the Insert menu.

10.7 Using the AutoCAD DesignCenter

The AutoCAD DesignCenter enables you to manipulate drawing content similar to the way Windows Explorer handles files and folders. The interface is familiar, with a tree view on the left and a list of contents on the right. The difference is the types of data you see. With the DesignCenter you can look into the contents of open or closed drawing files and easily copy or insert content into other open drawings. Blocks, external references, layers, linetypes, dimension styles, text styles, table styles, and page layouts are all examples of content defined in a drawing that can be copied into another drawing to reduce duplicated effort.

In this task, we begin by opening the DesignCenter and examining some of the available content. Leave Drawing B open and Drawing A closed.

⊕ To begin this task you should have Drawing B open on your screen.

⊕ Click on the DesignCenter tool on the Standard toolbar, as shown in Figure 10-24.

This executes the ADCENTER command and opens the DesignCenter palette shown in Figure 10-25. If anyone has used DesignCenter on your computer, you are likely to see something slightly different from our illustration, because the DesignCenter stores changes and resizing adjustments. In particular, if you do not see the tree view on the left as shown, you have to use the Tree View button to restore the tree view to your palette before going on.

⊕ If necessary, click the Tree View Toggle button, as shown in Figure 10-26.

Your DesignCenter should now have a tree view on the left and a content area on the right. Like the Properties Manager, the DesignCenter is a modeless dialog box. It has features similar to the Properties Manager, including the convenient auto-hide option, accessed by right-clicking the title bar and selecting from the shortcut menu (see Chapter 7, Task 7.6).

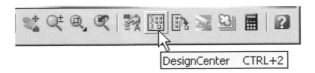

Figure 10-24

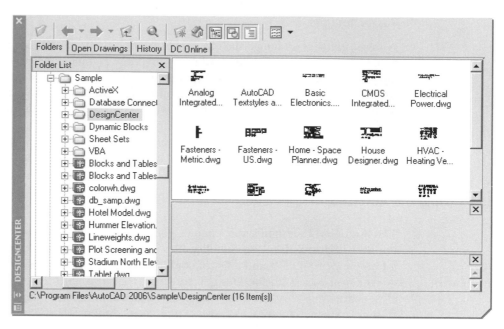

Figure 10-25

The DesignCenter is a complex palette that gives you access to a vast array of resources. There is a toolbar-like set of buttons at the top of the palette, including the Tree View Toggle button. Below these are four tabs and below these is the main work area of the palette, with a tree view on the left and a content area on the right. The tree view area shows a hierarchically arranged list of files, folders, and locations. The content area shows icons representing drawings and drawing contents of the folders or files currently selected in the tree view. What appears in the tree view depends on which tab is selected. The Folders tab shows the complete desktop hierarchy of your computer. The Open Drawings tab lists only open AutoCAD drawings. History shows a history of drawing files that have been specifically opened in the DesignCenter. If you are connected to the Internet, DC Online takes you to a comprehensive online library of standard parts and symbols for various design industries. With the DC Online tab selected, you also see a different set of buttons at the top of the palette.

We begin by selecting the Open Drawings tab and seeing what the DesignCenter shows us regarding our current drawing.

⊕ Click the Open Drawings tab.

Now you have a very simple window with the open drawing and content types in the tree view and the content area, as shown in Figure 10-27.

Figure 10-26

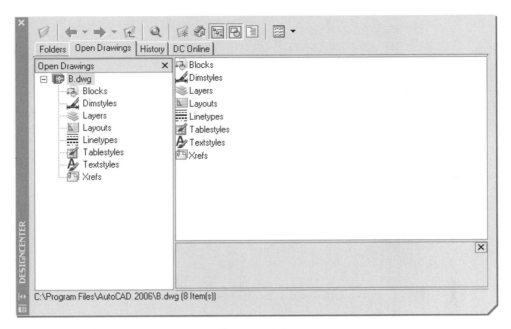

Figure 10-27

You see icons representing standard content types: Blocks, Dimstyles, Layers, Layouts, Linetypes, Tablestyles, Textstyles, and Xrefs. All drawings show the same list, although not all drawings have content defined in each category. Content in any of the categories can be copied into other drawings.

In the tree view, the list of types is as far as you can go. In the palette, however, there is another level.

⊕ **Click Xrefs in the tree view at the end of the list.**

You see an icon representing the attached Drawing A in the content area, as shown in Figure 10-28. If you like, check out the other contents. In Dimstyles you find the Standard style and the 1B style defined in Chapter 8. In Layers you find all the layers defined in the 1B template. In Layouts you find Layouts 1 and 2, which are there by default. In Linetypes you find the Acad.lin, assuming you have loaded them into your template. In Textstyles you see the Standard style.

Now try looking into Drawing A. It is closed, but its contents are still accessible in the DesignCenter.

⊕ **Click the Folders tab.**

This opens the folder hierarchy for your computer's hard drive as shown previously in Figure 10-25. You need to use the scroll bars in the tree view window to find where you have saved Drawing A.

⊕ **Scroll to the folder containing Drawing A.**

⊕ **Open the folder and select Drawing A.**

It is not necessary to open the list of contents under Drawing A in the tree view. As long as Drawing A is selected, you can open contents in the content area.

⊕ **With Drawing A selected in the tree view, double-click the Blocks icon in the content area.**

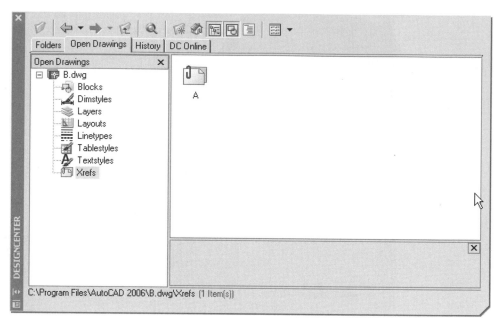

Figure 10-28

You see the familiar set of four blocks shown in Figure 10-29. At this point you could easily drag any of these blocks right off the palette into Drawing B. Instead, we insert a symbol from the DesignCenter's predrawn sample blocks. These are easily located using the Favorites button.

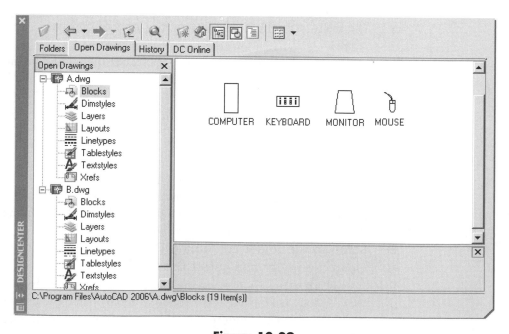

Figure 10-29

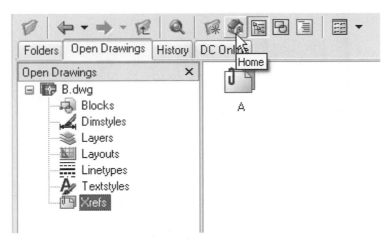

Figure 10-30

⊕ Click the Home button at the top of the DesignCenter palette, as shown in Figure 10-30.

This takes you directly to the DesignCenter folder, which contains sample drawings and blocks, as illustrated in Figure 10-31. In the content area, you see a set of sample drawing thumbnails.

⊕ Scroll down and select Home-Space Planner.dwg.

As soon as you select this drawing, you again see the familiar set of icons for standard drawing content.

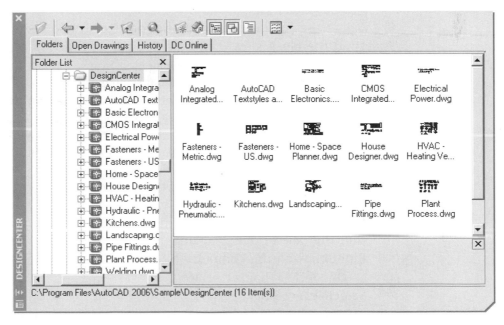

Figure 10-31

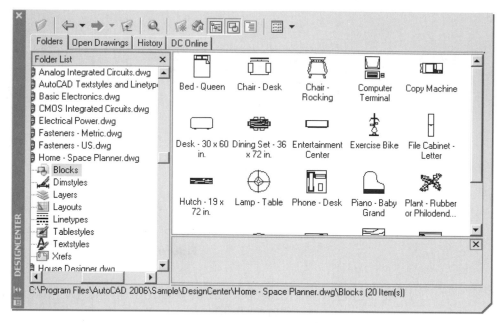

Figure 10-32

⊕ Double-click the Blocks icon in the content area.

Now you see a set of blocks representing household furniture, as shown in Figure 10-32. Look for the computer terminal. We insert this symbol, which is similar to our own workstation symbol, into Drawing B.

Blocks can be inserted from the DesignCenter by dragging, but there are some limitations, as you will see.

⊕ Select the computer block in the palette.

⊕ Drag the block slowly into the Drawing B drawing area.

As soon as you are in the drawing area, you see a very large image of the computer block. This is a now familiar scaling problem.

⊕ Return your cursor to the palette without releasing the block.

We now explore a more precise and dependable method for inserting blocks from the DesignCenter. This second method allows you to scale the block as you insert it. First, however, it is convenient to put the DesignCenter palette in Auto-hide mode.

⊕ Right-click the DesignCenter palette's title bar.

⊕ Select Auto-hide.

⊕ If the palette is hidden, move the cursor over the palette title bar so that the palette opens again.

⊕ Right-click on the computer block.

This opens a shortcut menu.

⊕ Select Insert Block.

You see the Insert dialog box with Computer Terminal in the Name edit box. From here on, the procedure is just like inserting a block within its original drawing.

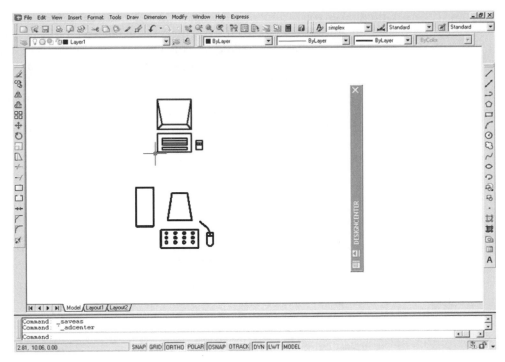

Figure 10-33

⊕ Select the Uniform Scale check box.

⊕ Enter 1/8 or .125 in the X Scale box.

⊕ Click OK.

As the dialog box closes, the auto-hide feature activates and the DesignCenter collapses so that only the title bar remains. This makes it easy to pick an insertion point in the drawing area.

⊕ Select an insertion point anywhere above the workstation Xref, as shown in Figure 10-33.

⊕ Move the cursor back into the DesignCenter title bar.

The palette opens again.

⊕ Click the Open Drawings tab.

⊕ Double-click the Blocks icon in the palette.

The ComputerTerminal block definition from the Home-Space Planner drawing is now in the database of Drawing B.

Other Features of the DesignCenter

Before leaving the DesignCenter, here are a few more features, controlled by the buttons at the top. Looking across the toolbar, the Load button opens a standard file selection dialog box where you can load any folder or drawing file into the DesignCenter. The Back and Forward buttons take you to previous tree view and content area displays. The Up button takes you up one level in whatever folder hierarchy you are exploring. The Search button opens a Search dialog box, allowing you to search for files, folders, and text in a variety of ways familiar in Windows applications. The Favorites button takes you to a set of defined favorite locations. By default, this includes the DesignCenter folder and the AutoCAD predefined hatch pattern sets. The Home button, as we have seen, takes you directly to the DesignCenter folder. The Tree View Toggle button opens and closes the tree view panel. With the panel closed there is more room to view contents. The Preview button opens and closes a panel below the content area that shows preview images of selected contents. The Description button opens and closes a panel below the Preview panel that displays text describing a selected block. Finally, the Views button allows choice over the style in which content is displayed in the content area. Before moving on, close the DesignCenter.

⊕ Click the close symbol (X) at the top of the DesignCenter title bar.

10.8 Defining Attributes

GENERAL PROCEDURE

1. Select Block and then Define Attributes from the Draw menu.
2. Specify attribute modes.
3. Type an attribute tag.
4. Type an attribute prompt.
5. If desired, type a default attribute value.
6. Include the attribute in a block definition.

We have introduced many new concepts in this chapter. We have gone from simply grouping objects together to sharing drawing content between drawings. Now we add additional information to block definitions using AutoCAD's attribute feature. When you add attributes to a block definition, you create the ability to pass drawing data between drawings and nongraphic applications, typically database and spreadsheet programs. Attributes hold information about blocks in a drawing in a form that can be read out to other programs and organized into reports or bills of materials. Attributes can be confusing, and you should not spend too much time worrying about their details unless you are currently involved in an application that requires their use. On the other hand, they are a powerful tool, and if you have a basic understanding of what they can do, you could be the one in your work setting to recognize when to use them.

One of the difficulties of learning about attributes is that you have to define them before you see them in action. It is therefore a little hard to comprehend what your definitions mean the first time around. Bear with us and follow instructions closely; it is worth your effort.

In this task, we define attributes that hold information about our CAD workstations. The attributes are defined in a flexible manner so that the workstation block can represent any number of hardware configurations. One instance of the workstation block could represent a Compaq computer with a Pentium III processor and an Acer monitor, for example, whereas another instance of the same block could represent an IBM computer with a Pentium 4 processor and an NEC monitor.

When we have defined our attributes, we create a block called ws that includes the whole computer workstation assembly and its attributes. To accomplish this, we return to Drawing A and add attributes to our workstation assembly there. Because Drawing A is now attached to Drawing B as an external reference, this also gives us the opportunity to learn more about working with Xrefs and to observe the effects of editing an Xref.

Assuming you are still in Drawing B from the previous section, we begin this task by demonstrating AutoCAD's XOPEN command, which allows you to quickly open an Xref from within a drawing without searching through a file hierarchy to locate the referenced drawing.

⊕ Select the computer workstation in Drawing B that was inserted as an external reference to Drawing A.

The workstation is highlighted and a grip is placed at the previously defined insertion base point.

⊕ With the external reference highlighted, right-click.

This opens the lengthy shortcut menu shown in Figure 10-34.

⊕ Select Open Xref.

Drawing A opens in the drawing area. You should see the original workstation assembly on Layer 1 in this drawing, just as you created it in Task 10.3. Drawing A is open just as if you had opened it using the OPEN command. You now have the two drawings open again. Drawing A is current, with Drawing B open in the background.

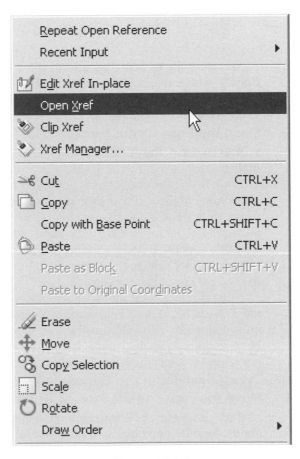

Figure 10-34

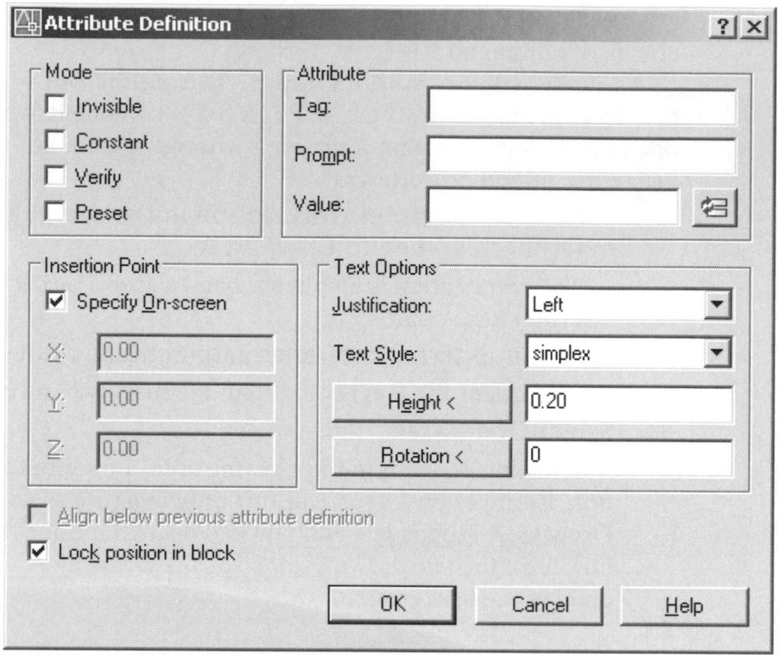

Figure 10-35

We are going to add attributes to these blocks in Drawing A and then define the whole assembly and its attributes as a single block called ws. First, we define an attribute that allows us to specify the type of computer in any individual reference to the ws block.

⊕ Open the Draw menu, highlight Block, and select Define Attributes.

This executes the ATTDEF command and opens the Attribute Definition dialog box shown in Figure 10-35.

Look first at the check boxes at the top left in the Mode panel. For our purposes none of these boxes should be checked. These are the default settings, which we will use in this first attribute definition. When our workstation block is inserted, the computer attribute value will be visible in the drawing (because Invisible is not selected), variable with each insertion of the block (because Constant is not selected), not verified (Verify is not selected), and not preset to a value (Preset is not selected).

Next, look at the Attribute panel to the right. The cursor should be blinking in the Tag edit box. Like a field name in a database file, a tag identifies the kind of information this particular attribute is meant to hold. The tag appears in the block definition as a field name. In occurrences of the block in a drawing, the tag is replaced by a specific value. Computer, for example, could be replaced by IBM.

⊕ Type Computer in the Tag edit box.

⊕ Move the cursor to the Prompt edit box.

As with the tag, the key to understanding the attribute prompt is to be clear about the difference between block definitions in the drawing database and block references in a drawing. Right now, we are defining an attribute. The attribute definition becomes part of the definition of the ws block and is used whenever ws is inserted. With the definition we are creating, there is a prompt whenever we insert a ws block that asks us to enter information about the computer in a given configuration.

⊕ Type Enter computer type.

We also have the opportunity to specify a default attribute value, if we wish, by typing in the Value edit box. Here, we leave this field blank, specifying no default value in our attribute definition.

Note: Notice that we could also insert a field in the value box, so that the value could be updated automatically.

The panel labeled Text options allows you to specify text parameters as you would in DTEXT. Visible attributes appear as text on the screen. Therefore, the appearance of the text needs to be specified. The only change we make is to specify a height.

⊕ Double-click in the edit box to the right of Height and then type 4″.

If you click the Height button itself, the dialog box disappears so that you can indicate a height by pointing.

Finally, AutoCAD needs to know where to place the visible attribute information in the drawing. You can type in *x*, *y*, and *z* coordinate values, but you are much more likely to show a point.

⊕ Check to see that Specify On-screen is checked in the Insertion Point panel.

⊕ Click OK.

The dialog box disappears to allow access to the screen. You also see a Start point: prompt in the command area.

We place our attributes 8 inches below the keyboard.

⊕ Pick a start point 8 inches below the left side of the keyboard (see Figure 10-36).

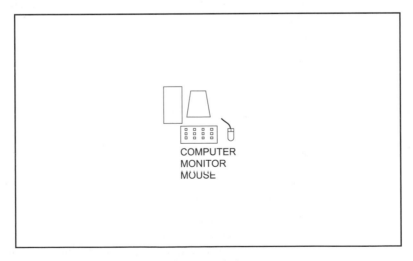

Figure 10-36

The dialog box disappears and the attribute tag Computer is drawn as shown. Remember, this is an attribute definition, not an occurrence of the attribute. Computer is our attribute tag. After we define the workstation as a block and the block is inserted, answer the Enter computer type: prompt with the name of a computer type, and the name itself is shown in the drawing rather than this tag.

Now we proceed to define three more attributes using some different options.

⊕ Repeat ATTDEF by pressing Enter or by right-clicking and selecting Repeat Define Attributes from the shortcut menu.

We use all the default modes again, but we provide a default monitor value in this attribute definition.

⊕ Type Monitor for the attribute tag.

⊕ Type Enter monitor type for the attribute prompt.

⊕ Type 20″ CRT for the default attribute value.

Now when AutoCAD shows the prompt for a monitor type, it also shows 20″ CRT as the default, as you will see.

Note: The button to the right of the Attribute Value edit box allows you to insert a field as the attribute value. This would mean that the value of the attribute could be a field that would automatically update when the field data changed.

You can align a series of attributes by selecting the Align below previous attribute definition check box at the lower left of the dialog box.

⊕ Select the Align below previous attribute definition check box.

⊕ Click OK to complete the dialog box.

The attribute tag Monitor should be added to the workstation below the Computer tag, as shown in Figure 10-36.

Next, we add an invisible, preset attribute for the mouse. Invisible means that the attribute text is not visible when the block is inserted, although the information is in the database and can be extracted. Preset means that the attribute has a default value and does not issue a prompt to change it. However, unlike constant attributes, you can change preset attributes using the Attribute Manager, which we explore in Task 10.10.

⊕ Repeat ATTDEF.

⊕ Select the Invisible check box.

⊕ Select the Preset check box.

⊕ Type Mouse for the attribute tag.

You do not need a prompt, because the preset attribute is automatically set to the default value.

⊕ Type MS Mouse for the default attribute value.

⊕ Select the Align below previous attribute definition check box to position the attribute below Monitor in the drawing.

⊕ Click OK to complete the dialog.

The Mouse attribute tag should be added to your screen, as shown in Figure 10-36. When a workstation block is inserted, the attribute value MS Mouse is written into the database, but nothing appears on the screen because the attribute is defined as invisible.

Finally comes the most important step of all: We must define the workstation as a block that includes all our attribute definitions.

⊕   Type b or select the Make Block tool from the Draw toolbar.

⊕   Type ws for the block name.

⊕   Click Select Objects.

⊕   Window the workstation assembly and all three attribute tags.

⊕   Press Enter to end object selection.

⊕   Click Pick Point.

⊕   Pick an insertion point at the midpoint of the bottom of the keyboard.

⊕   Select the Delete radio button.

⊕   Click OK to close the dialog box.

The newly defined block disappears from the screen.

The ws block with its three attribute definitions is now present in the Drawing A database. Before moving on, we insert three instances of the block and provide some notes on editing attributes and attribute values.

Inserting Blocks with Attributes

Inserting blocks with attributes is no different from inserting any block, except that you will be prompted for attribute values.

⊕   To complete this task, insert three workstations, using the following procedure (note the attribute prompts):

1. Type I or select the Insert Block tool from the Draw toolbar.
2. Type or select ws for the block name.
3. Click OK to exit the dialog box.
4. Pick an insertion point.
5. Answer the attribute prompts for monitors and computers.

We specified two different configurations for this exercise, using processor types to designate the computers, as shown in Figure 10-37. The first two are

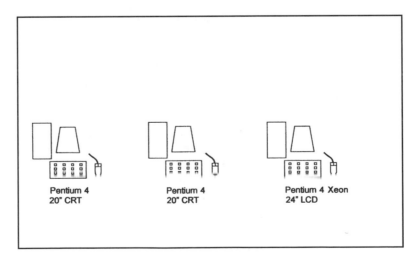

Pentium 4
20" CRT

Pentium 4
20" CRT

Pentium 4 Xeon
24" LCD

Figure 10-37

Pentium 4 computers with the default 20″ CRT monitor. The third is a Pentium 4 Xeon computer with a 24″ LCD (flatscreen) monitor. This exercise will be easier to follow if you use the same attribute values. Notice that you are not prompted for mouse specifications because that attribute is preset.

When you are done, your screen should resemble Figure 10-37.

Editing Attribute Values and Definitions

Once you begin to work with defined Attributes you may have occasion to edit them. The first thing to consider whenever you edit attributes is whether you wish to edit attribute values in a block reference or whether you want to edit the actual attribute definition. There are four major commands used to edit attributes. ATTDISP, ATTEDIT, and EATTEDIT work on attribute values in inserted blocks and BATTMAN works directly on Attribute definitions. The chart following explains their uses.

Command	Usage
ATTDISP	Allows control of the visibility of all attribute values in inserted blocks, regardless of their defined visibility mode. There are three options. Normal means that visible attributes are visible and invisible attributes are invisible. On makes all attributes visible. Off makes all attributes invisible.
EATTEDIT	Opens the Enhanced Attribute Edit dialog box for editing individual attribute values in inserted blocks. It allows you to change individual attribute values, text position, height, angle, style, layer, and color of attribute values.
ATTEDIT	Allows single or global editing of attrubute values from the command line. Global editing allows editing text strings in all attribute values that fit criteria you define.
BATTMAN	Opens the Block Attribute Manager and allows editing of attribute definitions. In this dialog box you can edit tags, prompts, default values, and modes for all blocks defined in a drawing. Changes are made directly to the block definition and reflected in blocks subsequently inserted.

10.9 Working with Parameters in Block References

Having three references to the ws block on the screen in Drawing A provides an opportunity to learn more about how parameters and actions work within dynamic blocks. WS is a nested block made up of four component blocks, the computer, the monitor, the mouse, and the keyboard. In the last task we defined attributes for three of these components. Going back to Task 10.4, recall that we added a linear parameter and a stretch action to the original computer block so that we could reshape it to represent a tower-style computer. Notice that all of our ws blocks now contain this representation. So, what has become of our original shape and the parameter and action associated with it? In this task we offer a brief exploration of the behavior of parameters and nested blocks.

⊕ To begin, you should be in Drawing A with the three ws block references shown previously in Figure 10-37.

⊕ Select any of the three block references.

The entire block will be highlighted and there will be one grip at the base point, which is the midpoint of the top of the keyboard. Notice the parameter and action that were added to the computer block back in Task 10.4 are not accessible. Using the grip, the entire block reference can be moved, mirrored, rotated, scaled, or stetched (the same as move in this case), but no component can be manipulated independently.

⊕ With a block reference highlighted, select the Block Editor tool from the Standard toolbar.

You see all the component blocks in the Block to Create or Edit list, with ws highlighted on the list and previewed on the right.

⊕ With ws highlighted, click OK.

This brings you to the Block Editor window. The ws block is shown in the window, with the Block Authoring Palettes open on the left.

⊕ In the block editing window, select the computer rectangle.

You see the parameter grips previously defined in Task 10.4, as shown in Figure 10-38. What this means is that here in the Block Editor you can move and reshape the computer just as you have done previously. Notice the difference, though. Here you would be changing the shape of the computer within the block definition so that when you closed the Block Editor, all three block references would be updated with the new shape. The computer block is a dynamic block nested within the ws block, which is not a dynamic block. In order to add

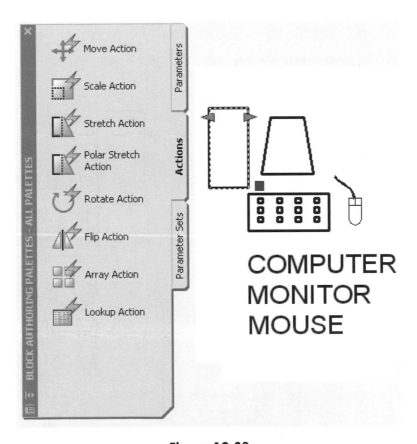

Figure 10-38

dynamic capabilities to the ws block definition, we need to add them at this level. We could repeat the adding of a linear parameter and a stretch action to the computer block, but instead we add a simple move point and action to the monitor. This will allow us to move the monitor independently in each block reference, and will also give you an introduction to the use of parameter sets. A parameter set is simply a combination of a parameter and an action paired together.

⊕ Press Esc to remove grips from the computer.

⊕ Select the monitor.

The monitor will be highlighted with a single grip at its base point.

⊕ Select the Parameter Sets tab at the bottom right on the Block Authoring Palettes.

Notice that all the selections on this tab are combinations of parameters and actions.

⊕ From the top of the list, select Point Move.

AutoCAD prompts:

```
Specify parameter location or [Name/Label/Chain/
                    Description/Palette]:
```

⊕ Right-click and select midpoint from the object snap shortcut menu.

AutoCAD prompts for a label location.

⊕ Pick a label location similar to that shown in Figure 10-39.

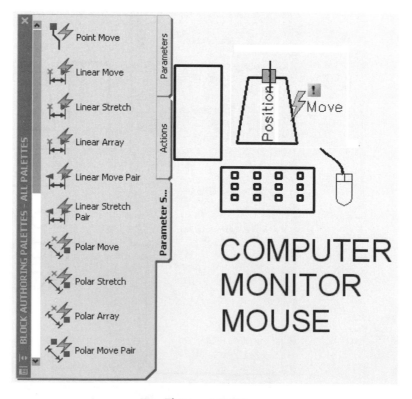

Figure 10-39

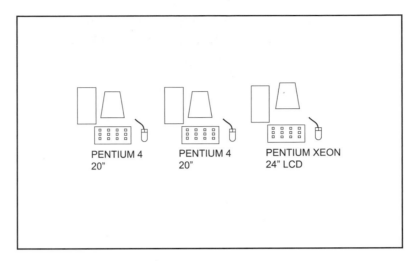

Figure 10-40

The point parameter and the move action have both been added to the block definition, but the move action must still be associated with a set of objects, as indicated by the yellow alert.

⊕ Double-click the yellow alert symbol (exclamation point).

This must be a double-click to execute the BACTIONSET command and allow you to select objects. You should have a Select Objects prompt on the dynamic display and the command line.

⊕ Select the monitor.

⊕ Press Enter to complete object selection.

This returns you to the command prompt, but you are still in the Block Editor.

⊕ Click the Close Block Editor button on the Block Editor toolbar.

AutoCAD intervenes with a box asking if you want to save changes to the ws block.

⊕ Click Yes.

You return to the drawing with the three block references.

⊕ Select the block reference on the right.

The block reference is highlighted as before, but you now have an additional grip at the midpoint of the back of the monitor. This will allow you to move the monitor in any block reference without affecting other references.

⊕ Select the grip at the back (top) of the monitor in the selected reference.

⊕ Move the monitor back a few inches, as shown in Figure 10-40.

⊕ Press Esc to remove grips.

10.10 Working with External References

You have made numerous changes to Drawing A. Attributes have been added, a ws block created, three references to the new block have been inserted into the drawing, and one monitor has been moved. This provides us a good opportunity

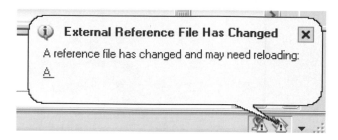

Figure 10-41

to turn our attention back to Drawing B and look at the Drawing A external reference there to see how Xrefs work in action.

⊕ Before leaving Drawing A, click the Save tool on the Standard toolbar to save your changes.

This is not just to safeguard changes. It is necessary to save changes to an Xref before the changes can be read into another drawing.

⊕ Open the Window menu and select Drawing B, or use the OPEN command if Drawing B has been closed.

You should be back in Drawing B with a workstation Xref and a computer terminal block on your screen, as shown previously in Figure 10-33. You should also see a balloon notification in the lower right corner of your screen, as shown in Figure 10-41, indicating that an externally referenced drawing has been changed and giving you the name of the Xref. To clearly understand the use of this notification, imagine for a moment that you are working with a team of designers. The focus of the project is a master drawing that contains references to several external drawings and these drawings are being created or edited by designers at various locations connected by a network or the Internet. The external reference update notification instantly informs anyone looking at the master drawing that one or more of the external references have changed and should be reloaded to keep things up to date. Be aware that this notification would not appear if the changes made to Drawing A had not been saved.

The first thing we need to do is reload the Drawing A Xref to bring our changes into Drawing B.

⊕ Click the blue underlined link to Drawing A in the notification balloon.

This executes the Reload XREF command and automatically updates the external reference to Drawing A, which now includes all three references to the ws block. Drawing B is updated to reflect the changes in Drawing A, as shown in Figure 10-42. Following are a few notes on working with external references.

Editing External References in Place

External references can be edited within the current drawing and even used to update the original referenced drawing. This should be done sparingly and for simple edits only; otherwise the current drawing will expand to take up more memory and the point of using an external reference instead of a block reference is lost.

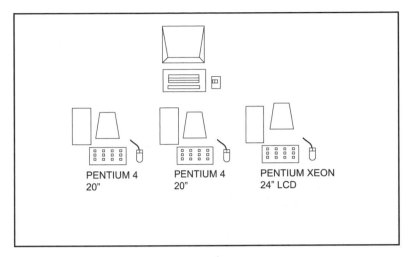

Figure 10-42

To edit a block or external reference in place, open the Modify menu, highlight Xref and Block Editing, and select Edit Reference In-Place from the submenu.

Clipping External References

External references can also be clipped so that only a portion of the referenced drawing is actually displayed in the current drawing. This would allow different users on the same network to share portions of their drawings without altering the original drawings to eliminate aspects that would not be useful in a master drawing. Clipping boundaries can be defined by a rectangular window, a polygon window, or an existing polyline. Clipping is performed with the XCLIP command and can be used on block references as well as external references. You can type the command, or select a reference, right-click to open a shortcut menu, and select Xref Clip from the Modify menu.

For example, you could clip the attributes in Drawing B so that only the workstations remained visible. The process would be:

1. In Drawing B, select the three workstation reference to Drawing A.
2. Right-click to open the shortcut menu.
3. Select Clip Xref.
4. Press enter to accept the default, rectangular boundary.
5. Pick two points to define a window around the workstations, but not around the attributes.

Clipping an instance of an Xref does not alter the Xref definition; it only suppresses the display of the objects outside the clipping boundary.

Parameters in External References

If you select any of the three workstations in Drawing B, all three will be highlighted. There will be only one grip at the base point defined when you inserted Drawing A as an external reference in B. The parameters defined for the computer and the monitor will not be accessible. Unlike in Drawing A, these parameters will not be accessible in the Block Editor. In fact, the ws block itself is not visible in the Block Editor, nor is the external reference to Drawing A, because it is an external reference, not a block.

In the next section, we return to our attribute information.

10.11   Extracting Attribute Information from Drawings

Attribute extraction is a powerful and complex feature that allows attribute information to be extracted from a drawing and transferred to spreadsheet or database programs for use in the preparation of parts lists, bills of material, and other documentation. For example, with a well-managed system of parts and attributes you can do a drawing of a construction project and get a complete price breakdown and supply list directly from the drawing database, all processed by computer. To accomplish this, you need carefully defined attributes and a program such as Microsoft Excel that is capable of receiving the extracted information and formatting it into a useful report. This attribute information file receives the information from the AutoCAD drawing that is then read by a database or spreadsheet application.

In this demonstration, you extract attribute information from blocks in Drawing A to an AutoCAD table, which you can then insert in the drawing. The steps are the same as if you were exporting the information to a spreadsheet or database program, but can be completed successfully without leaving AutoCAD. If you are in Drawing B from the previous task, you should start by switching back to Drawing A.

⊞   To begin, you should be in Drawing A with three ws blocks and their attribute values on your screen.

⊞   Open the Tools menu and select Attribute Extraction.

You see the Attribute Extraction Wizard, as shown in Figure 10-43. This wizard takes you through the steps of selecting attributes to extract and creating a table that can be exported or inserted.

The first step in this wizard is to select a template file or to create a file from scratch. Typically the template is a database or spreadsheet laid out to receive the information from your attributes and perhaps to manipulate that information to produce a report. In this demonstration, we can proceed without a predefined template.

⊞   If necessary, select the Create table or external file from scratch button.

⊞   Click Next.

This brings you to the box shown in Figure 10-44, where you can select a data source from which to be extracted. The source can be the current drawing, blocks within the drawing, or other drawings you select.

⊞   Check to see that the Current drawing radio button is selected and then click Next to move on to the Select Attributes screen, shown in Figure 10-45.

The Select Attributes screen asks you to determine whether to include blocks without attributes and general block properties in attribute extraction. Drawing A has nested blocks without attributes. As you recall, the ws workstation is made up of the computer, keyboard, monitor, and mouse blocks. Extraction is simpler if these are not included.

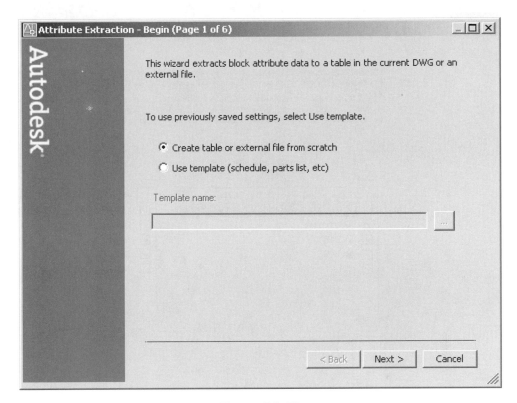

Figure 10-43

Figure 10-44

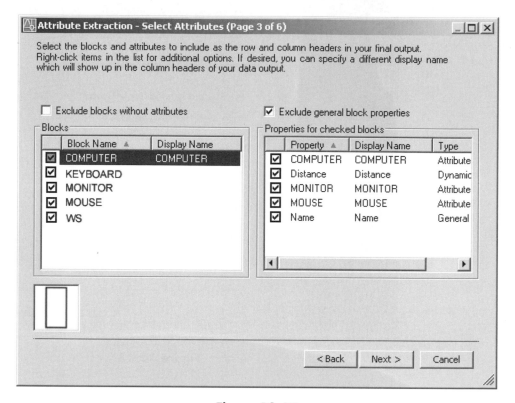

Figure 10-45

⊕ Check the Exclude blocks without attributes box. The Exclude general block properties box should also be checked by default.

⊕ If any other blocks remain on the list, uncheck them, so that only the ws blocks are extracted.

The Properties for checked blocks list on the right also contains some information that we do not include in our table, so these must be de-selected.

⊕ Check the boxes for Position X and Position Y so that these are de-selected.

⊕ Click Next to move on to the Finalize Output screen, illustrated in Figure 10-46.

This screen gives you a good idea of what the output of your extraction will look like. Notice that the attribute extraction program has broken down the output into two types of workstations based on the attribute information. There are two workstations with CRT monitors and one with an LCD monitor. Notice again that the count information that is extracted could be an important factor used in pricing this configuration of workstations.

At the bottom left of the screen there is an important panel where you can choose whether to extract data to an AutoCAD table or an external file. In our case we will choose to stay with an AutoCAD table. To extract to a file we could simply check the External file box and then specify a location and file type for the file.

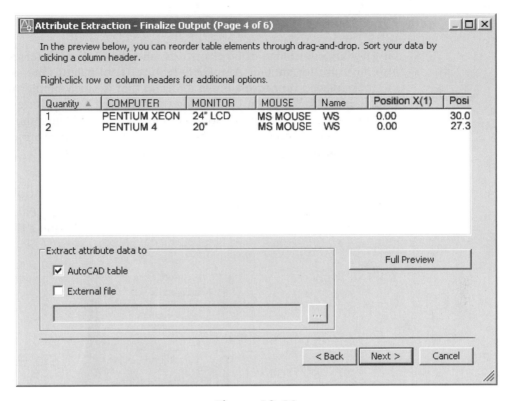

Figure 10-46

⊕   Click Next to move on to the Table style screen.

    The table style screen allows access to the table style dialog box introduced in Chapter 7. We will stick with the standard table style and add a title to our output.

⊕   Double-click in the title edit box and type Workstations.

⊕   Click Next to proceed.

⊕   Click Finish.

    You have completed the attribute extraction process; all that remains is to insert the table into your drawing. You see a small table connected to the crosshairs.

⊕   Pick a point on your screen below the middle block reference.

⊕   Zoom into a window around the inserted table.

    Your screen should resemble Figure 10-47.

WORKSTATION				
Quantity	COMPUTER	MONITOR	MOUSE	Name
1	PENTIUM XEON	24" LCD	MS MOUSE	WS
2	PENTIUM 4	20"	MS MOUSE	WS

Figure 10-47

10.12   Creating Tool Palettes

Given your knowledge of blocks, Xrefs, and the DesignCenter, at this point you also have use for another AutoCAD feature. Tool palettes are simply collections of blocks placed very accessibly in a format that is much simpler than the Design-Center palette. We begin by opening the standard Tool Palettes window, which contains a variety of annotation symbols. After exploring the features of the palette, we create a new tab on the palette and add some of our own blocks.

⊕   To begin this task, you should be in Drawing A.

We begin by opening the Tool Palettes window.

⊕   Open the Tools menu and select Tool Palettes window.

Your screen should resemble Figure 10-48. The Tool Palettes window is a simple modeless dialog box with at least seven tabs and a title bar. Each tab

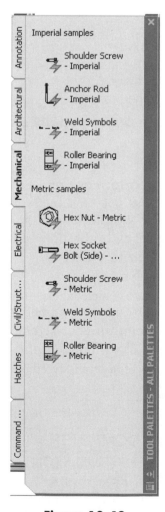

Figure 10-48

has a set of annotation symbols and objects for use in various AutoCAD applications. You can drag these symbols into your drawing or right-click and change properties, such as scale, as you insert them.

Creating Tool Palettes

The real power of tool palettes comes from the ease with which you can populate them with your own content. Try this:

⊕ Open the DesignCenter by clicking on the DesignCenter tool, or by selecting DesignCenter from the Tools menu.

⊕ Click the Open Drawings tab.

⊕ Double-click the Blocks icon.

You can see the set of blocks in Drawing A, including ws, the computer, keyboard, monitor, and mouse blocks.

⊕ Right-click the keyboard block.

⊕ From the shortcut menu, select Create Tool Palette.

Watch the Tool Palettes window. Two things happen: A new tab is created and the keyboard block is added to it. It's that simple. You now have your own tool palette to work with. Let's add another block, so you can see how to add a block without creating another new tab.

⊕ In the DesignCenter right-click the mouse block.

⊕ Select Copy from the shortcut menu.

⊕ Move your cursor over to the Tool Palettes window.

⊕ Right-click to open the shortcut menu again.

⊕ Select Paste.

The mouse block is added to your new tool palette, as shown in Figure 10-49. It's that simple. Keep in mind that the tools on a tool palette are accessible only as long as the reference is clear. If they originate from an externally referenced drawing, the reference path must be clear and accessible. If the referenced drawing is moved or deleted, the tool will no longer be available.

Tool Palette Transparency

We will cover one more tool palette feature before moving on. Tool palettes can be made transparent so that the drawing area behind them is visible even when the tool palette is open.

⊕ To explore this feature, right-click the Tool Palette title bar and select Transparency.

This opens the Transparency dialog box illustrated in Figure 10-50. The degree of transparency or opaqueness is controlled by the slider in the middle.

⊕ To see transparency at work, move the slider all the way to the right and then click OK to exit the dialog box.

Your Tool Palettes window takes on a "ghostly" appearance, allowing you to see objects behind it. The Tool Palettes window also has the auto-hide feature,

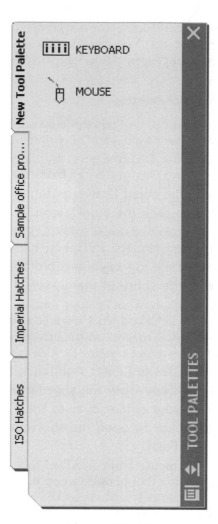

Figure 10-49

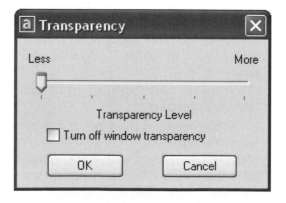

Figure 10-50

which can be combined with transparency to reduce interference with the drawing space.

⊕ Before going on, close the Tool Palettes window and the DesignCenter.

In the next task you learn how to reverse the block definition process.

10.13 Exploding Blocks

GENERAL PROCEDURE

1. Type x, select Explode from the Modify menu, or select the Explode tool from the Modify toolbar.
2. Select objects.
3. Press Enter to carry out the command.

The EXPLODE command undoes the work of the BLOCK or GROUP command. It takes a set of objects that have been defined as a block or group and re-creates them as independent entities. EXPLODE works on dimensions and hatch patterns as well as on blocks created in the BLOCK command or tools inserted from a tool palette. It does not work on externally referenced drawings until they have been attached permanently through the Bind option of the XREF command.

⊕ To begin this task, you should have Drawing A on your screen.

Let's try exploding a workstation.

⊕ Type x, select Explode from the Modify menu, or select the Explode tool from the Modify toolbar, as shown in Figure 10-51.

You are prompted to select objects.

⊕ Select the center workstation.

⊕ Press Enter to end object selection and carry out the command.

You should notice immediately that the attribute values are replaced by attribute tags.

⊕ Try selecting any part of the workstation.

All the component parts of the previously blocked workstation can now be selected separately, including the attribute tags. If you select the computer rectangle, you see that the parameter and action are once again accessible. If you select the monitor you see that the original grip at the front of the block has returned, but that the move parameter point, which was part of the ws block definition, is no longer present. You should also see a balloon notification at

Figure 10-51

the lower right of your screen alerting you that the table of extracted attribute information is now outdated.

Note: Exploding removes only one layer of block definition. If a block is made up of other blocks, these "nested" blocks remain as independent blocks after exploding. Attribute value information is removed by exploding, leaving the attribute tag instead.

Congratulations! This has been a tough chapter with a lot of new information and procedures to learn. You have gained a greater sense of the tools available for using AutoCAD in collaborative work environments. You should now appreciate that although the basic drafting tools available in AutoCAD are impressive themselves, there are powerful features here that go well beyond the one-person, one-workstation arena to include collaboration among individuals, companies, and worksites across the globe. You can find more information on tools for collaboration in Appendix E.

10.14   Review Material

Questions

1. Why is it usually a good idea to create blocks on Layer 0?
2. What is the difference between a group and a block?
3. What is an insertion base point, as used in the BLOCK command? What is an insertion point, as used in the INSERT command?
4. Why are blocks, external references, and raster images all inserted with a scale factor?
5. How could you create a complete drawing using only the INSERT command?
6. What would you have to do to create blocks with geometry that could be edited after they were inserted?
7. What is the purpose of the yellow exclamation point that appears whenever you add a parameter to a block?
8. What is the difference between COPY and COPYCLIP?
9. What is an attribute tag? What is an attribute prompt? What is an attribute value?
10. What are the three settings of ATTDISP?
11. What is the purpose of attribute extraction?
12. What other complex entities can be exploded besides blocks?
13. What happens to attribute values when a block is exploded?
14. What is the main thing you can accomplish with the AutoCAD DesignCenter that cannot be done with INSERT or XATTACH?

Drawing Problems

1. Open a new drawing using the 1B prototype and create a hexagon circumscribed around a circle so that both have a 1.0-unit radius. These objects should be created so that when they are defined as a block, they are inserted on Layer 2 regardless of what layer is current at the time.
2. Define an attribute to go with the hexagon and circle. The tag should identify the two as a hex bolt; the prompt should ask for a hex bolt diameter. The

attribute should be visible in the drawing, center justified 0.5 unit below the block, with text 0.3 unit high.

3. Create a block with the bolt and its attribute. Leave a clear screen when you are done.
4. Draw a rectangle on Layer 1, with lower left corner at (0,4) and upper right corner at (18,8).
5. Insert 0.5-diameter hex bolts at (2,6) and (16,6). Insert a 1.0-unit hex bolt at (9,6). The sizes of each hex bolt should appear beneath the bolt.

10.15   WWW Exercise 10 (Optional)

The new material in this chapter opens the door to several new Internet access procedures. In this task, we show you how to insert hyperlinks into drawings so that anyone using your drawing can jump from an object directly to a specified Internet address. All you have to do is insert a hyperlink and make sure that whoever wants to use that hyperlink is connected to the Internet at the time. Hyperlinks can also be used to connect to other drawing files, views, or layouts. For demonstration, we insert a hyperlink into Drawing A, attached to a workstation block. The hyperlink is defined to link to our companion website. Then we go through the procedure for connecting to the website through the hyperlink. Here we go.

⊕   To begin this task, you should be in Drawing A.

  If for any reason this drawing is not readily available, any drawing will do, but the illustrations will not match.

⊕   If you have not already done so, connect to your Internet service provider.

⊕   Open the Insert menu and select Hyperlink.

  Hyperlinks are connected to objects, so AutoCAD prompts you to select objects. The prompt is plural, indicating that you can select more than one object to connect to the same hyperlink.

⊕   Select the workstation on the left.

⊕   Select the workstation on the right.

⊕   Right-click to end object selection.

  This brings you to the Insert Hyperlink dialog box shown in Figure 10-52.

⊕   Look over the box to see the array of options you have for linking through this feature.

⊕   Type www.prenhall.com/dixriley in the Type the file or Web page name edit box.

⊕   Click OK to exit the dialog box

  The dialog box disappears. The links have been inserted, but nothing happens until you select a hyperlink.

⊕   Move your cursor over either of the selected workstations. (We chose the one on the right.) When you see the hyperlink cursor as shown in Figure 10-53, let the cursor rest.

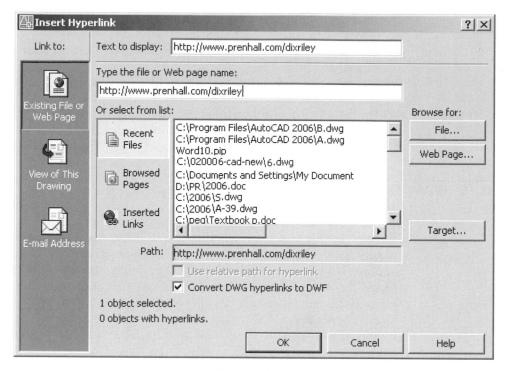

Figure 10-52

You see the hyperlink symbol and below it the hyperlink specification, as shown in Figure 10-52.

⊕ With the hyperlink symbol displayed, press the pick button.

The workstation is selected but nothing else happens.

⊕ Right-click anywhere in the drawing area.

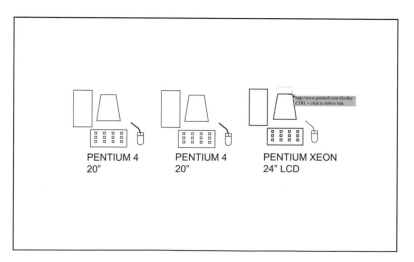

Figure 10-53

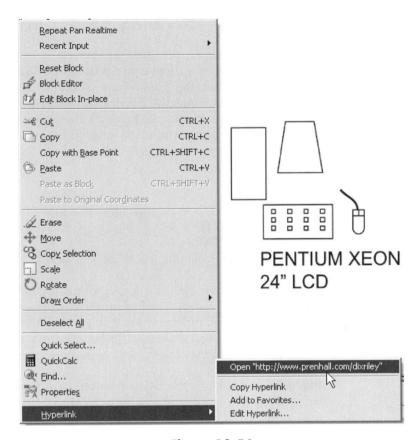

Figure 10-54

A shortcut menu appears with Hyperlink on the bottom.

⊕ **Highlight Hyperlink at the bottom of the shortcut menu.**

This opens a submenu, as shown in Figure 10-54.

⊕ **Select Open www.prenhall.com/dixriley.**

We are sure you can find many uses for this great feature. See you at the website!

10.16   Drawing 10-1: CAD Room

This architectural drawing is primarily an exercise in using blocks and attributes. Use your ws block and its attributes to fill in the workstations and text after you draw the walls and countertop. New blocks should be created for the plotters and printers, as described subsequently. The drawing setup is consistent with Drawing A from the chapter so that blocks can be easily inserted without scaling. When you have completed this drawing, you might want to try extracting the attribute information to a word processor or Excel file.

Drawing Suggestions

$$UNITS = Architectural, precision = 0' - 0''$$
$$GRID = 1'$$
$$SNAP = 1''$$
$$LIMITS = (0',0')(48',36')$$

* The "plotter" block is a 1×3 rectangle, with two visible, variable attributes (all the default attribute modes). The first attribute is for a manufacturer and the second for a model. The "printers" are 2×2.5 with the same type of attributes. Draw the rectangles, define their attributes eight inches below them, create the block definitions, and then insert plotters and printers as shown.

  Note: Do not include the labels "plotter" and "laser printer" in the block, because text in a block is rotated with the block. This would give you inverted text on the front countertop. Insert the blocks and add the text afterward. The attribute text can be handled differently, as described later.

* The "8 pen plotter" was inserted with a y scale factor of 1.25.

The Mirrtext System Variable

The two workstations on the front counter could be inserted with a rotation angle of 180 degrees, but then the attribute text would be inverted also and would have to be turned around using EATTEDIT. Instead, we have reset the mirrtext system variable so that we could mirror blocks without attribute text being inverted:

1. Type mirrtext.
2. Type 0.

Now you can mirror objects on the back counter to create those on the front. With the mirrtext system variable set to 0, text included in a MIRROR procedure is not inverted as it would be with mirrtext set to 1. This applies to attribute text as well as ordinary text. However, it does not apply to ordinary text included in a block definition.

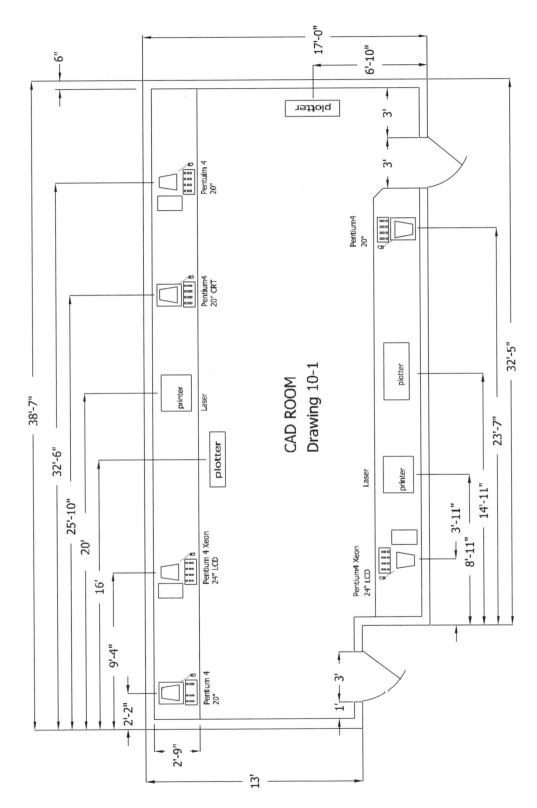

CAD ROOM
Drawing 10-1

Pentium 4
20"

Pentium4
20" CRT

Laser

printer

plotter

Pentium 4 Xeon
24" LCD

Pentium 4
20"

plotter

Pentium4
20"

Laser

plotter

printer

Pentium4 Xeon
24" LCD

17'-0"

6'-10"

6"

38'-7"

32'-6"

25'-10"

20'

16'

9'-4"

2'-2"

2'-9"

13'

3'

3'

3'

32'-5"

23'-7"

14'-11"

8'-11"

3'-11"

1'

3'

10.17 Drawing 10-2: Office Plan

This drawing is primarily an exercise in the use of predrawn blocks and symbols. With a few exceptions, everything in the drawing can be inserted from the AutoCAD DesignCenter.

Drawing Suggestions

- Observe the overall 62′ × 33′ dimensions of the office space and choose appropriate architectural limits, snap settings, and grid settings for the drawing.
- We have not provided dimensions for the interior spaces, so you are free to choose dimensions as you wish.
- All walls can be drawn as 6″ wide filled multilines.
- All doors and furniture can be inserted from the DesignCenter.
- The large meeting room table is not predrawn. Create a simple filleted rectangle with dimensions as shown. It might be defined and saved as a block for future use.

33 ft.

Sink

Toilet

File Cabinet

Lamp

Computer
Desk

Chair

Phone

Copy Machine

Sink

Toilet

Lamp
File Cabinet

Computer
Desk

Chair

Phone

Copy Machine

Sofa

Table

Chair

Copy Machine

Phone
Chair

Computer
Desk

File Cabinet
Lamp

Sofa

Copy Machine

62 ft.

Copy Machine

Lamp
File Cabinet

Computer
Desk

Phone

Chair

Sofa

File Cabinet
Lamp

Computer
Desk

Chair

Phone

Chair

Plant

Chair

Chair

Chair

Desk
10' × 5'

Chair

Chair

Chair

Sofa

Table

Office Area = 2050 sq ft

Office Plan
DRAWING 10-2

487

10.18   Drawing 10-3: Base Assembly

This is a good exercise in assembly drawing procedures. You draw each of the numbered part details and then assemble them into the base assembly.

Drawing Suggestions

We no longer provide you with units, grid, snap, and limit settings. You can determine what you need by looking over the drawing and its dimensions. Remember that you can always change a setting later if necessary.

- You can create your own title block from scratch or develop one from Title Block (Drawing 7-1), if you have saved it. Once created and saved or wblocked, a title block can be inserted and scaled to fit any drawing. AutoCAD also comes with drawing templates that have borders and title blocks.

Using Table to Create a Bill of Materials

1. To create the bill of materials in this drawing, open the Table dialog box and create a new table style with no title and no header row. (Uncheck the boxes that say Include Title row and Include Header row in the Title and Column Header tabs of the New Table Style dialog box.)
2. Modify the new table style row height by adjusting the text style and height in the Modify Table Style dialog box.
3. Select the new style and insert a table with 4 columns and 7 rows.
4. Once the table is inserted you can adjust column width by first selecting the entire table, then pressing Ctrl as you pick a grip at the top of a column. Moving the selected grip while you hold down Ctrl will move the column border without altering the rest of the table.

Managing Parts Blocks for Multiple Use

You draw each of the numbered parts (B101-1, B101-2, etc.) and then assemble them. In an industrial application, the individual part details would be sent to different manufacturers or manufacturing departments, so they must exist as separate, completely dimensioned drawings as well as blocks that can be used in creating the assembly. An efficient method is to create three separate blocks for each part detail: one for dimensions and one for each view in the assembly. The dimensioned part drawings include both views. The blocks of the two views have dimensions, hidden lines, and center lines erased.

Think carefully about the way you name blocks. You might want to adopt a naming system like the following: B101-1D for the dimensioned drawing, B101-1T for a top view without dimensions, and B101-1F for a front view without dimensions. Such a system makes it easy to call out all the top view parts for the top view assembly, for example. A more detailed procedure is outlined for Drawings 10-4 and 10-5.

- Notice that the assembly requires you to do a considerable amount of trimming away of lines from the blocks you insert. This can be easily completed, but you must remember to EXPLODE the inserted blocks first.

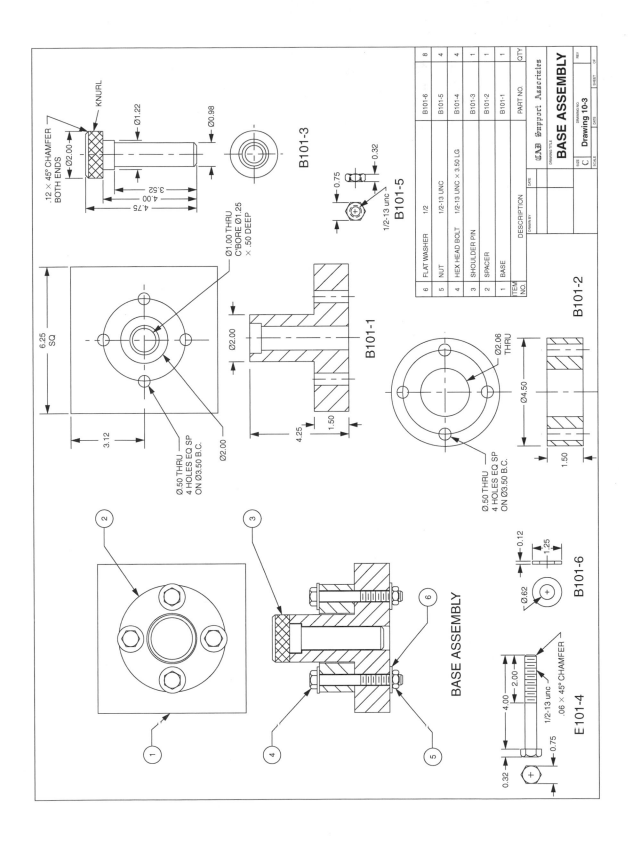

.12 × 45° CHAMFER
BOTH ENDS

KNURL

Ø1.22
Ø2.00
Ø0.98

3.52
4.00
4.75

B101-3

0.32
0.75
1/2-13 unc

B101-5

Ø1.00 THRU
CBORE Ø1.25
× .50 DEEP

6.25
SQ

3.12

Ø2.00

Ø.50 THRU
4 HOLES EQ SP
ON Ø3.50 B.C.

Ø2.00

4.25
1.50

B101-1

Ø2.06
THRU

Ø4.50

1.50

Ø.50 THRU
4 HOLES EQ SP
ON Ø3.50 B.C.

B101-2

ITEM NO.			PART NO.	QTY
6	FLAT WASHER	1/2	B101-6	8
5	NUT	1/2-13 UNC	B101-5	4
4	HEX HEAD BOLT	1/2-13 UNC × 3.50 LG	B101-4	4
3	SHOULDER PIN		B101-3	1
2	SPACER		B101-2	1
1	BASE		B101-1	1
ITEM NO.	DESCRIPTION		PART NO.	QTY

(AB Support Assetities

DRAWING TITLE
BASE ASSEMBLY

DRAWING NO.
Drawing 10-3

SIZE C | SCALE | DATE | SHEET | OF | REV

DRAWN BY | DATE

2

3

BASE ASSEMBLY

1

4

6

5

Ø.62
0.12
1.25

B101-6

4.00
2.00
0.75
0.32

1/2-13 unc
.06 × 45° CHAMFER

E101-4

489

10.19   Drawings 10-4 and 10-5:
Double Bearing Assembly and Scooter Assembly

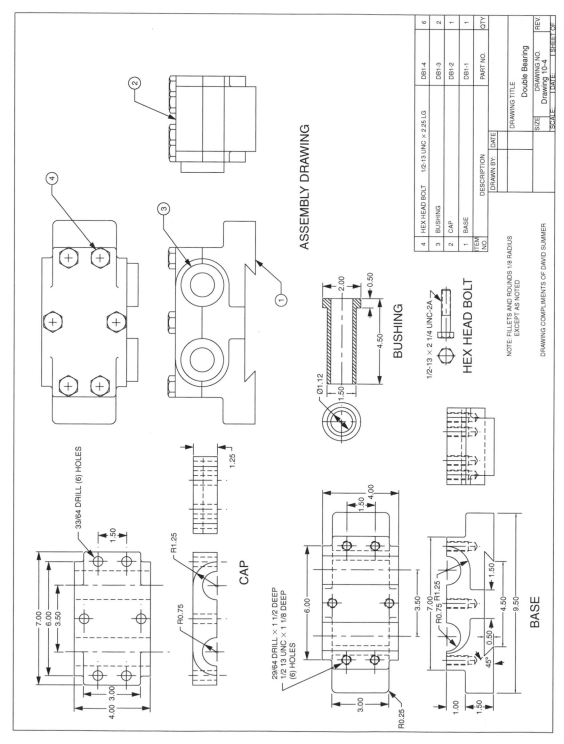

ASSEMBLY DRAWING

BUSHING

HEX HEAD BOLT

1/2-13 × 2 1/4 UNC-2A

CAP

BASE

33/64 DRILL (6) HOLES

29/64 DRILL × 1 1/2 DEEP
1/2 13 UNC × 1 1/8 DEEP
(6) HOLES

NOTE: FILLETS AND ROUNDS 1/8 RADIUS
EXCEPT AS NOTED

DRAWING COMPLIMENTS OF DAVID SUMMER

ITEM NO.	DESCRIPTION		PART NO.	QTY
4	HEX HEAD BOLT	1/2-13 UNC × 2.25 LG	DB1-4	6
3	BUSHING		DB1-3	2
2	CAP		DB1-2	1
1	BASE		DB1-1	1

DRAWN BY: DATE:

DRAWING TITLE   Double Bearing

SIZE   DRAWING NO.   Drawing 10-4   REV.

SCALE: DATE: SHEET OF

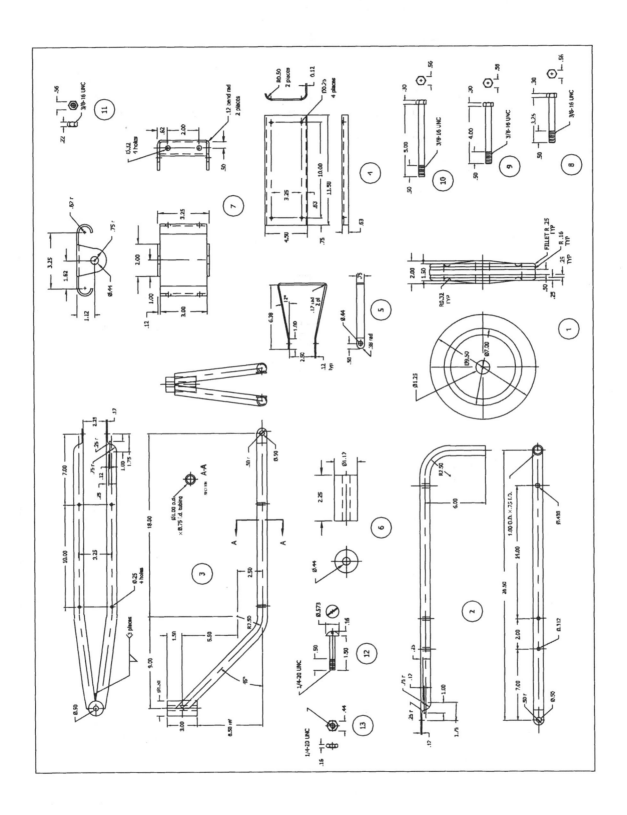

491

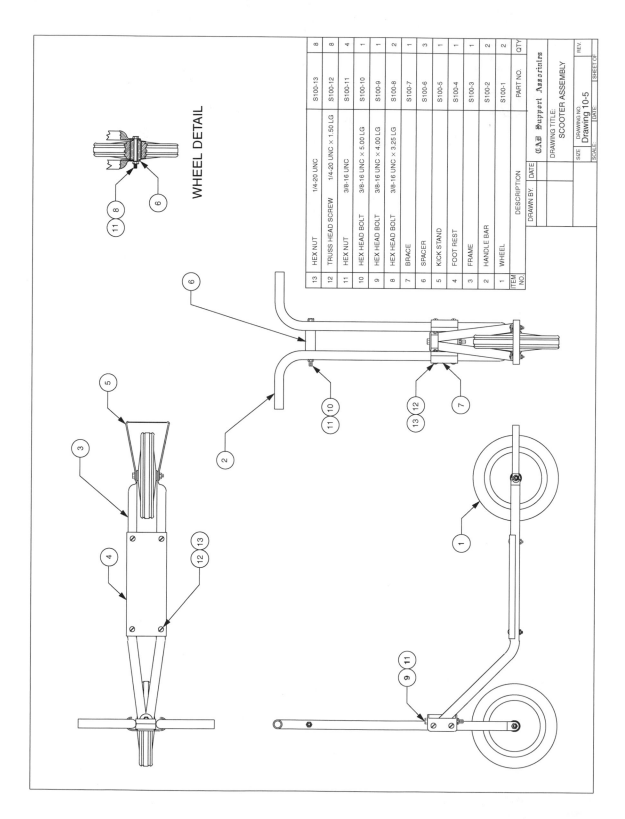

WHEEL DETAIL

ITEM NO.	DESCRIPTION		PART NO.	QTY
13	HEX NUT	1/4-20 UNC	S100-13	8
12	TRUSS HEAD SCREW	1/4-20 UNC × 1.50 LG	S100-12	8
11	HEX NUT	3/8-16 UNC	S100-11	4
10	HEX HEAD BOLT	3/8-16 UNC × 5.00 LG	S100-10	1
9	HEX HEAD BOLT	3/8-16 UNC × 4.00 LG	S100-9	1
8	HEX HEAD BOLT	3/8-16 UNC × 3.25 LG	S100-8	2
7	BRACE		S100-7	1
6	SPACER		S100-6	3
5	KICK STAND		S100-5	1
4	FOOT REST		S100-4	1
3	FRAME		S100-3	1
2	HANDLE BAR		S100-2	2
1	WHEEL		S100-1	2

CAD Support Associates

DRAWN BY | DATE

DRAWING TITLE:
SCOOTER ASSEMBLY

DRAWING NO. Drawing 10-5   REV.

SIZE   SCALE: DATE: SHEET OF

PART III

ISOMETRIC DRAWING AND THREE-DIMENSIONAL MODELING

11 Isometric Drawing

COMMANDS

ELLIPSE   SNAP (ISOMETRIC)   VIEW

OVERVIEW

Part III of this book takes you in a whole new direction. You begin to use the AutoCAD drawing window in new ways to represent isometric and 3-D spaces. Everything you know about two-dimensional drafting translates and possibilities expand as the familiar grid and snap are turned and rotated to define new coordinate systems. We begin with simple two-dimensional isometric drawing and then move on to true three-dimensional modeling.

Learning to use AutoCAD's isometric drawing features should be a pleasure at this point. There are very few new commands to learn, and anything you know about manual isometric drawing is easier on the computer. Once you know how to get into the isometric mode and change from plane to plane, you can rely on previously learned skills and techniques. Many of the commands you have learned will work readily and you will find that using the isometric drawing planes is an excellent warm-up for 3-D wireframe drawing, which is the topic of Chapter 12.

TASKS

11.1 Using Isometric SNAP

GENERAL PROCEDURE

1. Right-click on Snap or Grid on the status bar.
2. Select Settings.
3. In the Drafting Settings dialog box, select the Isometric snap radio button.
4. Click OK.

To begin drawing isometrically, you need to switch to the isometric snap style. You find the grid and crosshairs behaving in ways that might seem odd at first, but you quickly get used to them.

⊕   Begin a new drawing using the 1B template.

⊕   Right-click on the Snap or Grid button on the status bar.

⊕   Select Settings from the shortcut menu.

   You see the Drafting Settings dialog box. Remember, you can also open this dialog by typing ds or selecting Drafting Settings from the Tools menu.

⊕   Click the Isometric snap radio button in the Snap type & style panel at the lower right.

⊕   Click OK.

   At this point, your grid and crosshairs are reoriented so that they resemble Figure 11-1. This is the isometric grid. Grid points are placed at 30-degree, 90-degree, and 150-degree angles from the horizontal. The crosshairs are initially turned to define the top isometric plane. The three isoplanes are discussed in Task 11.2.

Note: Because AutoCAD retains the isoplane setting from the most recent drawing session, it is possible that your crosshairs might be turned to the right or left isoplane instead of the top, as shown. It is not necessary to change the setting in this task.

⊕   To get a feeling for how this snap style works, enter the LINE command and draw some boxes, as shown in Figure 11-2.

   Make sure that Ortho is off and Snap is on, or you will be unable to draw the lines shown.

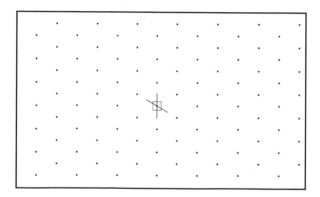

Figure 11-1

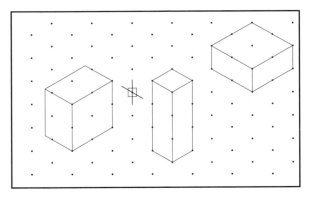

Figure 11-2

11.2 Switching Isometric Planes

> **GENERAL PROCEDURE**
>
> 1. Press F5 once to switch to the "right" isoplane.
> 2. Press F5 again to switch to the "left" isoplane.
> 3. Press F5 again to return to the "top" isoplane.

If you tried to draw the boxes in Task 11.1 with Ortho on, you discovered that it is impossible. Without changing the orientation of the crosshairs, you can draw in only two of the three isometric planes. We need to be able to switch planes so that we can leave Ortho on for accuracy and speed. There are several ways to do this, but the simplest, quickest, and most convenient way is to use the F5 key.

Before beginning, take a look at Figure 11-3. It shows the three planes of a standard isometric drawing. These planes are often referred to as top, front, and right. However, AutoCAD's terminology is top, left, and right. We stick with AutoCAD's labels in this book.

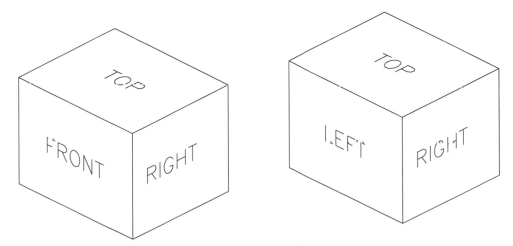

Figure 11-3

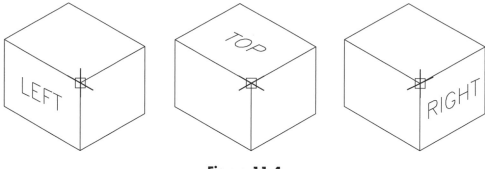

Figure 11-4

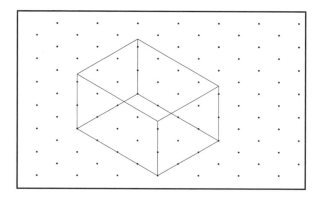

Figure 11-5

Now look at Figure 11-4 and you can see how the isometric crosshairs are oriented to draw in each of the planes.

⊕ Press F5 to switch from top to right.

⊕ Press F5 again to switch from right to left.

⊕ Press F5 once more to switch back to top.

⊕ Now turn Ortho on and draw a box outline like the one in Figure 11-5.

You need to switch planes several times to accomplish this. Notice that you can switch planes using F5 without interrupting the LINE command. If you find that you are in the wrong plane to construct a line, switch planes. Because every plane allows movement in two of the three directions, you can always move in the direction you want with one switch. However, you might not be able to hit the snap point you want. If you cannot, switch planes again.

11.3   Using COPY and Other Edit Commands

Most commands work in the isometric planes just as they do in standard orthographic views. In this exercise, we construct an isometric view of a bracket using the LINE, COPY, and ERASE commands. Then we draw angled corners using CHAMFER. In the next task, we draw a hole in the bracket with ELLIPSE, COPY, and TRIM.

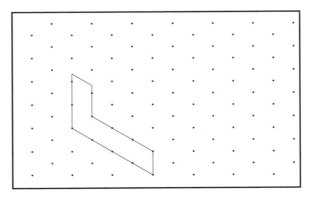

Figure 11-6

⊕   To begin this exercise, clear your screen of boxes and check to see that Ortho is on.

⊕   Switch to the left isoplane.

⊕   Draw the L-shaped object shown in Figure 11-6.

Notice that this is drawn in the left isoplane and that it is 1.00 unit wide.

Next, we copy this object 4.00 units back to the right to create the back surface of the bracket.

⊕   Select the Copy tool from the Modify toolbar.

⊕   Use a window or crossing box to select all the lines in the L.

⊕   Right-click to end object selection.

⊕   Pick a base point at the inside corner of the L.

It is a good exercise to turn Ortho on, switch planes, and move the object around in each plane. You can move in two directions in each isoplane. To move the object back to the right, as shown in Figure 11-7, you must be in either the top or the right isoplane.

⊕   If necessary, switch to the top or right isoplane and pick a second point of displacement four units back to the right, as shown in Figure 11-7.

⊕   Press Enter to exit COPY.

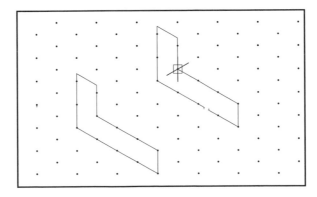

Figure 11-7

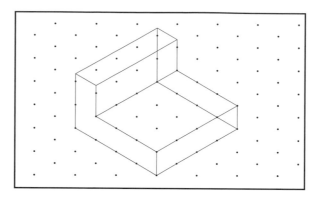

Figure 11-8

⊕ Enter the LINE command and draw the connecting lines in the right plane, as shown in Figure 11-8.

    If you wish, you can draw only one of the lines and use the COPY command to create the others. Be sure to turn Ortho off to do this.

Creating Chamfers in an Isometric View

Keep in mind that angular lines in an isometric view do not show true lengths. Angular lines must be drawn between endpoints located along paths that are vertical or horizontal in one of the three drawing planes. In our exercise, we create angled lines by using the CHAMFER command to cut the corners of the bracket. This is no different from using CHAMFER in orthographic views.

⊕ Select Chamfer from the Modify menu or the Chamfer tool from the Modify toolbar.

⊕ Type d.

    AutoCAD prompts for a first chamfer distance.

⊕ Type 1.

⊕ Press Enter to accept 1.00 as the second chamfer distance.

⊕ Pick two edges of the bracket to create a chamfer, as shown in Figure 11-9.

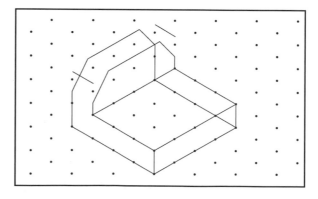

Figure 11-9

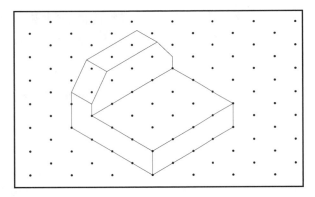

Figure 11-10

⊕ Repeat CHAMFER.

⊕ Chamfer the other three corners so that your drawing resembles Figure 11-9.

⊕ Erase the two small lines left hanging at the previous corners.

⊕ To complete the bracket, enter the LINE command and draw lines between the new chamfer endpoints.

⊕ Finally, erase the two unseen lines on the back surface to produce Figure 11-10.

11.4   Drawing Isometric Circles with ELLIPSE

GENERAL PROCEDURE

1. Locate the center point of the isometric circle.
2. Select the Ellipse tool from the Draw toolbar.
3. Type i.
4. Pick the center point.
5. Type or show the radius or diameter.

The ELLIPSE command can be used to draw true ellipses in orthographic views or ellipses that appear to be circles in isometric views (called *isocircles* in AutoCAD). In this task, we use the latter capability to construct a hole in the bracket.

⊕ To begin this task you should have the bracket shown in Figure 11-10 on your screen.

The first thing you need to draw an isocircle is a center point. Often, it is necessary to locate this point carefully using temporary lines, object snap tracking, or point filters (see Chapter 12). You must be sure that you can locate the center point before entering the ELLIPSE command.

In our case, it is easy because the center point is on a snap point.

⊕ Select Ellipse from the Draw menu, or select the Ellipse tool from the Draw toolbar, as shown in Figure 11-11.

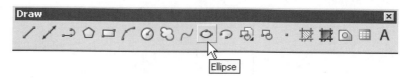

Figure 11-11

AutoCAD prompts

`Specify axis endpoint of ellipse or [Arc/Center/Isocircle]:`

The option we want is Isocircle. Ignore the others for the time being.

⊹ **Type i or right-click and select Isocircle from the shortcut menu.**

AutoCAD prompts

`Specify center of isocircle:`

If you could not locate the center point, you would have to exit the command now and start over.

⊹ **Use the snap and grid to pick the center of the surface, as shown in Figure 11-12.**

AutoCAD gives you an isocircle to drag, as in the CIRCLE command. The isocircle you see depends on the isoplane you are in. To understand this, try switching planes to see how the image changes.

⊹ **Stretch the isocircle image out and then press F5 to switch isoplanes. Observe the isocircle. Try this two or three times.**

⊹ **Switch to the top isoplane before moving on.**

AutoCAD is prompting for a radius or diameter:

`Specify radius of isocircle or [Diameter]:`

A radius specification is the default here, as it is in the CIRCLE command.

⊹ **Type a value or pick a point so that your isocircle resembles the one in Figure 11-12.**

Next, we use the COPY and TRIM commands to create the bottom of the hole.

⊹ **Select the Copy tool from the Modify toolbar.**

⊹ **Select the isocircle by pointing, or type l for last.**

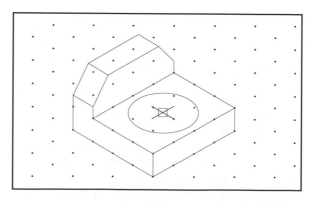

Figure 11-12

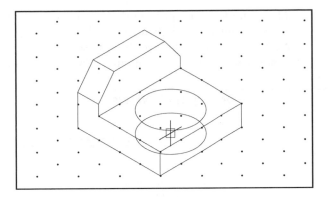

Figure 11-13

⊕ Right-click to end object selection.

⊕ Pick a base point.

Any point could be used as the base point. A good choice would be the top of the front corner. If you do this, then choosing the bottom of the front corner as a second point gives you the exact thickness of the bracket.

⊕ Pick a second point 1.00 unit below the base point. Make sure that you are in an isoplane that allows movement from top to bottom.

Your screen should now resemble Figure 11-13. The last thing we must do is trim the hidden portion of the bottom of the hole.

⊕ Press Enter to exit COPY.

⊕ Select the Trim tool from the Modify toolbar.

⊕ Pick the first isocircle as a cutting edge.

⊕ Press Enter to end cutting edge selection.

⊕ Select the hidden section of the lower isocircle.

⊕ Press Enter to exit TRIM.

The bracket is now complete and your screen should resemble Figure 11-14.

Note: Sometimes you do not get the results you expect when using TRIM in an isometric view. It might be necessary to use BREAK and ERASE as an alternative.

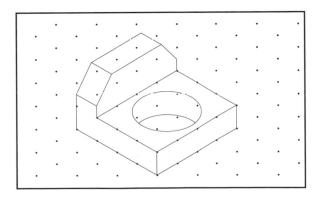

Figure 11-14

This completes the present discussion of isometric drawing. You can find more in the drawing suggestions at the end of this chapter.

Now we go on to explore the nonisometric use of the ELLIPSE command and then show you the VIEW command for saving named views in a drawing.

11.5 Drawing Ellipses in Orthographic Views

GENERAL PROCEDURE

1. Select the Ellipse tool from the Draw toolbar.
2. Pick one endpoint of an axis.
3. Pick the second endpoint.
4. Pick a third point showing the length of the other axis.

The ELLIPSE command is important for drawing isocircles, but also for drawing true ellipses in orthographic views. There is also an option to create elliptical arcs.

An ellipse is determined by a center point and two perpendicular axes of differing lengths. In AutoCAD, these specifications can be shown in two nearly identical ways, each requiring you to show three points (see Figure 11-15). In the default method, you show two endpoints of an axis and then show half the length of the other axis, from the midpoint of the first axis out. (The midpoint of an axis is also the center of the ellipse.) The other method allows you to pick the center point of the ellipse first, then the endpoint of one axis, followed by half the length of the other axis.

⊕ In preparation for this exercise, return to the standard snap mode using the following procedure:

1. Right-click on Snap or Grid and open the Drafting Settings dialog box from the shortcut menu.
2. Click the Rectangular snap radio button.
3. Click OK.

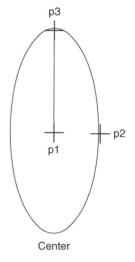

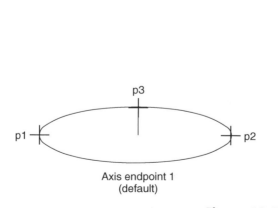

Axis endpoint 1
(default)

Center

Figure 11-15

Your grid is returned to the standard pattern and the crosshairs are horizontal and vertical again. Notice that this does not affect the isometric bracket you have just drawn.

Note: If your grid does not return to its original shape it may be because isometric snap values have been retained in the Snap X and Grid X spacing boxes. To fix this, reenter the Drafting Settings dialog box and manually return Snap X spacing to 0.125 and Grid X spacing to 0.50.

We briefly explore the ELLIPSE command and draw some standard ellipses.

⊕ Select the Ellipse tool from the Draw toolbar or Ellipse from the Draw menu.

AutoCAD prompts

```
Specify axis endpoint of ellipse or [Arc/Center]:
```

⊕ Pick an axis endpoint, as shown by p1 on the ellipse at the lower left in Figure 11-16.

AutoCAD prompts for the other endpoint:

```
Specify other endpoint of axis:
```

⊕ Pick a second endpoint as shown by p2.

AutoCAD gives you an ellipse to drag and a rubber band so that you can show the length of the other axis. Only the length of the rubber band is significant; the angle is already determined to be perpendicular to the first axis. Because of this, the third point only falls on the ellipse if the rubber band happens to be exactly perpendicular to the first axis.

The prompt that follows allows you to show the second axis distance as before, or a rotation around the first axis:

```
Specify distance to other axis or [Rotation]:
```

The rotation option is awkward to use, and we do not explore it here; see the AutoCAD Command Reference for more information.

⊕ Pick p3 as shown.

This point shows half the length of the other axis.

The first ellipse should now be complete. Now we draw one showing the center point first.

⊕ Repeat the ELLIPSE command.

⊕ At the first prompt, type c or right-click and select Center from the shortcut menu.

AutoCAD gives you a prompt for a center point:

```
Specify center of ellipse:
```

⊕ Pick a center point, as shown by p1 at the middle left of Figure 11-16.

Now you have a rubber band stretching from the center to the end of an axis and the following prompt:

```
Specify endpoint of axis:
```

⊕ Pick an endpoint, as shown by p2 in Figure 11-16.

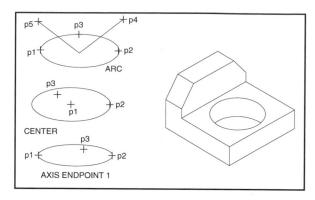

Figure 11-16

The prompt that follows allows you to show the second axis distance as before, or a rotation around the first axis:

        Specify distance to other axis or [Rotation]:

⊕ Pick an axis distance, as shown by p3.

Here again the rubber band is significant for distance only. The point you pick falls on the ellipse only if the rubber band is stretched perpendicular to the first axis. Notice that it is not so in Figure 11-16.

Drawing Elliptical Arcs

Elliptical arcs can be drawn by trimming complete ellipses or by using the Arc option of the ELLIPSE command. Using the Arc option, you first construct an ellipse in one of the two methods shown previously and then show the arc of that ellipse that you want to keep. Determining arcs can be quite complicated because of the many different parameters available. You should remember this from Chapter 5, in which you learned the ARC command. In this exercise, we stick to a simple procedure; you should have no difficulty pursuing the more complex options on your own.

⊕ Enter the ELLIPSE command.

⊕ Type a or right-click and select Arc from the shortcut menu.

If you select the Ellipse Arc tool from the Draw toolbar, this option is entered automatically.

⊕ Pick a first axis endpoint, as shown by p1 at the upper left in Figure 11-16.

⊕ Pick a second endpoint, p2 in the figure.

⊕ Pick p3 to show the second axis distance.

AutoCAD draws an ellipse as you have specified, but the image is only temporary. Now you need to show the arc you want drawn. The two options are Parameter and Start angle. Parameter takes you into more options that allow you to specify your arc in different ways, similar to the options of the ARC command. We stick with the default option.

⊕ Pick p4 to show the angle at which the elliptical arc begins.

Move the cursor slowly now and you can see all the arcs that are possible starting from this angle.

⊕ Pick p5 to indicate the end angle and complete the command.

11.6　Saving and Restoring Displays with VIEW

GENERAL PROCEDURE

1. Select the Named Views tool from the Standard toolbar.
2. Select New to create a new view.
3. Type a view name.
4. Click Define Window.
5. Select points.
6. Click OK.
7. Click OK.

The word view in connection with the VIEW command has a special significance in AutoCAD. It refers to any set of display boundaries that have been named and saved using the VIEW command. It also refers to a defined 3-D viewpoint that has been saved with a name. Views that have been saved can be restored rapidly and by direct reference rather than by redefining the location, size, or viewpoint of the area to be displayed. VIEW can be useful in creating drawing layouts and any time you know that you will be returning frequently to a certain area of a large drawing. It saves you from having to zoom out to look at the complete drawing and then zoom back in again on the area you want. It can also save the time required in creating a 3-D viewpoint. In this chapter, we use 2-D views only. In the next chapter, we introduce 3-D viewpoints.

Imagine that we have to complete some detail work on the area around the hole in the bracket and also on the top corner. We can define each of these as a view and jump back and forth at will.

⊕　To begin this exercise, you should have the bracket on your screen, as shown in Figure 11-17.

⊕　Select Named Views from the View menu, as shown in Figure 11-18.

This opens the View dialog box shown in Figure 11-19. There are two tabs: one for Named Views and one for Orthographic & Isometric Views. Isometric here refers to certain standard 3-D viewpoints, not to the 2-D isometric drawing that we are exploring in this chapter. We introduce these 3-D viewpoints in the next chapter. In this chapter, we use only the Named Views tab.

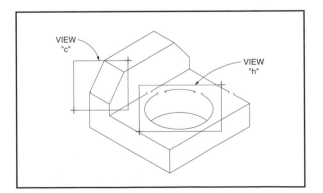

Figure 11-17

Figure 11-18

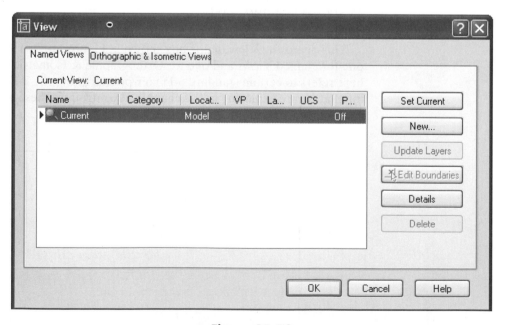

Figure 11-19

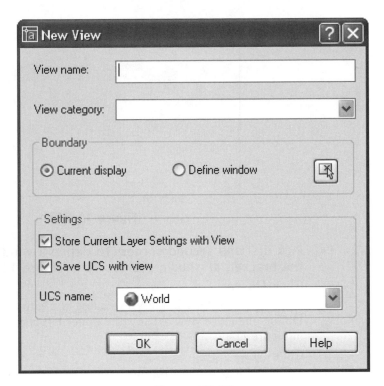

Figure 11-20

⊕ If necessary, click the Named Views tab.

The first thing we need to do is define some views. Then we see how to switch from one view to another. The first view to define is the current view. We give it a new name and save it so that we can return to it quickly.

⊕ Click on New.

This takes you to the New View dialog box shown in Figure 11-20. Notice that the Current display radio button is selected. All we have to do is give the current display a name to save it as a named view.

⊕ Type A in the View name edit box.

Views are designed for speed, so it makes sense to assign them short names, unless you are defining many views and need them clearly identified with longer names.

⊕ Click OK.

The View dialog box reappears, with A showing on the list of defined views. Next we use a window to define a smaller view.

⊕ Click New to return to the New View dialog box.

⊕ Type H in the View name edit box. We are using the name H for hole because this view zooms in on the hole.

⊕ Select the Define window radio button.

The dialog box closes, giving you access to the screen.

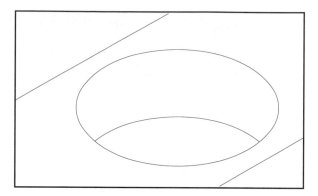

Figure 11-21

⊕ Pick first and second corners to define a window around the hole in the bracket, as shown previously in Figure 11-17.

⊕ Click OK.

You are now back in the View dialog box with A and H on the list of views. Define one more view to show the upper left corner of the bracket, as shown in Figure 11-17.

⊕ Click New.

⊕ Type C for the view name.

⊕ Select the Define window radio button.

⊕ Define a window, as shown in Figure 11-17.

⊕ Click OK.

You have now defined three views. To see the views in action we must set them as current.

⊕ Highlight H in the Named views list.

⊕ Click Set Current.

Notice that the current view is listed above the Named view list.

⊕ Click OK.

Your screen should resemble Figure 11-21.

Now switch to the corner view.

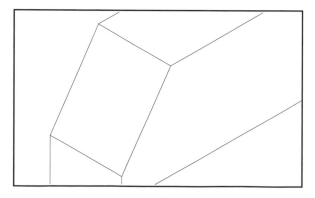

Figure 11-22

⊕   Repeat the VIEW command.
⊕   Highlight C.
⊕   Click Set Current.
⊕   Click OK.

   Your screen should resemble Figure 11-22.

11.7   Review Material

Questions

1. What are the angles of the crosshairs and grid points in an isometric grid?
2. What function key is used to switch from one isometric plane to another?
3. What are the names for the isometric planes in AutoCAD?
4. What is an isocircle? Why are isocircles drawn in the ELLIPSE command?
5. How many different isocircles can you draw that have the same radius and the same center point?
6. How many points does it take to define an ellipse?
7. What do these points define in each of the two basic methods of drawing an orthographic ellipse?
8. What must you do before you can use the VIEW command to restore a view?
9. What are the two basic ways to define a view?
10. How do you enter the VIEW command? What is the name of the dialog box it calls?

Drawing Problems

1. Using the isometric grid, draw a 4-by-4 square in the right isoplane.
2. Copy the square back four units along the left isoplane.
3. Connect the corners of the two squares to form an isometric cube. Erase any lines that would be hidden in this object.
4. Use text rotation and obliquing to draw the word Top in the top plane of the cube so that the text is centered on the face and aligned with its edges. The text should be 0.5 unit high.
5. In a similar manner, draw the word Left at the center of the left side and the word Right at the center of the right side. All text should align with the face that it is on.

11.8   WWW Exercise 11 (Optional)

You are now ready for Chapter 11 of the companion website. Complete the following steps:

⊕   Make sure that you are connected to your Internet service provider.
⊕   Type browser, open the Web toolbar and select the Browse the Web tool, or open your system browser from the Windows taskbar.
⊕   If necessary, navigate to our companion website at www.prenhall .com/dixriley.

   Good luck on the test!

11.9   Drawing 11-1: Mounting Bracket

This drawing is a direct extension of the exercises in the chapter. It gives you practice in basic AutoCAD isometrics and in transferring dimensions from orthographic to isometric views.

Drawing Suggestions

- When the center point of an isocircle is not on snap, as in this drawing, you need to create a specifiable point and snap onto it or use object snap and object snap tracking. For example, acquire the midpoints of the sides and then snap to the intersection of the two tracking lines.

- Often, when you try to select a group of objects to copy, there are many crossing lines that you do not want to include in the copy. This is an ideal time to use the Remove option in object selection. First, window the objects you want along with those nearby that are unavoidable, and then remove the unwanted objects one by one.

- Sometimes, you might get unexpected results when you try to TRIM an object in an isometric view. AutoCAD divides an ellipse into a series of arcs, for example, and only trim a portion. If you do not get the results you want, use the BREAK command to control how the object is broken, and then erase what you do not want.

- There is no Arc option when you use ELLIPSE to draw isocircles, so semicircles like those at the top and bottom of the slots must be constructed by first drawing isocircles and then trimming or erasing unwanted portions.

- Use COPY frequently to avoid duplicating your work. Because it might take a considerable amount of editing to create holes and fillets, do not COPY until edits have been completed on the original.

- The row of small arcs that show the curve in the middle of the bracket are multiple copies of the fillet at the corner.

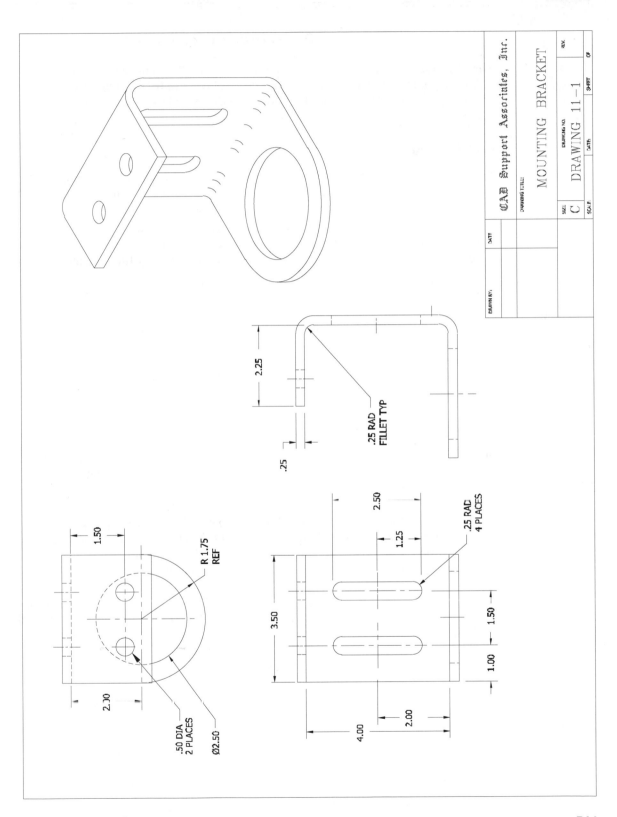

CAB Support Associates, Inc.

DRAWING TITLE:
MOUNTING BRACKET

DRAWING NO.
DRAWING 11-1

SIZE C

REV.

SCALE

SHEET

OF

DRAWN BY:

DATE

DATE:

2.25

.25

.25 RAD
FILLET TYP

1.50

2.30

R 1.75
REF

.50 DIA
2 PLACES

Ø2.50

2.50

1.25

.25 RAD
4 PLACES

3.50

1.50

1.00

4.00

2.00

11.10   Drawing 11-2: Radio

This drawing introduces text and is greatly simplified by the use of the rectangular ARRAY command. Placing objects on different layers so they can be turned on and off during TRIM, BREAK, and ERASE procedures makes things considerably less messy.

Drawing Suggestions

- Use the box method to create this drawing. That is, begin with an isometric box according to the overall outside dimensions of the radio. Then go back and cut away the excess as you form the details of the drawing.
- The horizontal grill can be done with a rectangular array because it runs straight on the vertical. Look carefully at the pattern to see where it repeats. Draw one set and then array it. Later, you can go back and trim away the dial and speaker areas.
- Draw isocircles over the grill and break away the lines over the speaker. When you are ready to hatch the speaker, draw another trimmed isocircle to define the hatch boundary, create the hatch, and then erase the boundary.
- The knobs are isocircles with copies to show thickness. You can use tangent-to-tangent osnaps to draw the front-to-back connecting lines.
- The text is created on two different angles that line up with the left and right isoplanes. We leave it to you to discover the correct angles.

Aligning Text to Isometric Planes

Adding text to isometric drawings has some challenges you have not encountered previously. To create the appearance that text aligns with an isometric plane, it needs to be altered in two ways. First, the whole line of text needs to be rotated to align with one side of the plane. Second, the obliquing angle of individual characters needs to be adjusted to match the tilt of the plane. Rotation angle, you recall, is handled through the command sequence of the DTEXT command. Obliquing angle is set as a text style characteristic using the STYLE command (from the Format menu, select Text Style). In this drawing, you need the following combinations: for text in the right isoplane, specify +30 for both the rotation angle and the obliquing angle; for text in the left isoplane, specify −30 for both angles; and for the text running vertically in the right plane (9V Battery), specify 90 for the rotation angle and −30 for the obliquing angle.

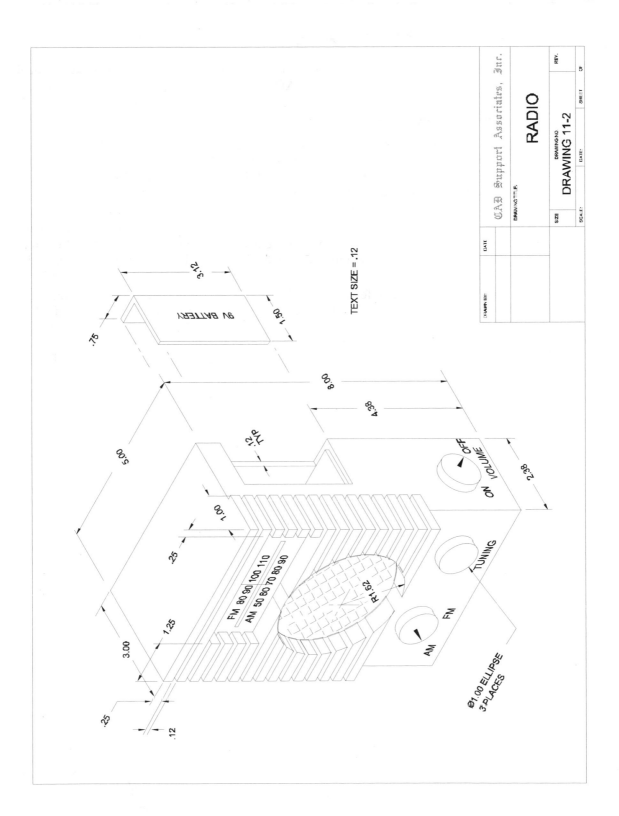

TEXT SIZE = .12

3.12

9V BATTERY

1.50

.75

8.00

4.38

.12
TYP

2.38

5.00

1.00

.25

ON VOLUME OFF

FM 80 90 100 110
AM 50 60 70 80 90

1.00

.25

TUNING

1.25

R1.62

3.00

FM

AM

.25

.12

Ø1.00 ELLIPSE
3 PLACES

CAD Support Associates, Inc.

DATE

DRAWN BY:

DRAWING TITLE:

RADIO

DRAWING NO
DRAWING 11-2

REV.

SIZE

DATE:

SCALE:

SHEET

OF

11.11 Drawing 11-3: Fixture Assembly

This is a difficult drawing. It takes time and patience, but teaches you a great deal about isometric drawing in AutoCAD.

Drawing Suggestions

- This drawing can be completed either by drawing everything in place as you see it or by drawing the parts and moving them into place along the common center line that runs through the middle of all the items. If you use the former method, draw the center line first and use it to locate the center points of isocircles and as base points for other measures.

- As you go, look for pieces of objects that can be copied to form other objects. Avoid duplicating efforts by editing before copying. In particular, where one object covers part of another, be sure to copy it before you trim or erase the covered sections.

- To create the chamfered end of Item 4, begin by drawing the 1.00 diameter cylinder 3.00 long with no chamfer. Then copy the isocircle at the end forward 0.125. The smaller isocircle is 0.875 (7/8), because 0.0625 (1/16) is cut away from the 1.00 circle all around. Draw this smaller isocircle and trim away everything that is hidden. Then draw the slanted chamfer lines using LINE, not CHAMFER. Use the same method for Item 5.

- In both the screw and the nut, you need to create hexes around isocircles. Use the dimensions from a standard bolt chart.

- Use three-point arcs to approximate the curves on the screw bolt and the nut. Your goal is a representation that looks correct. It is impractical and unnecessary to achieve exact measures on these objects in the isometric view.

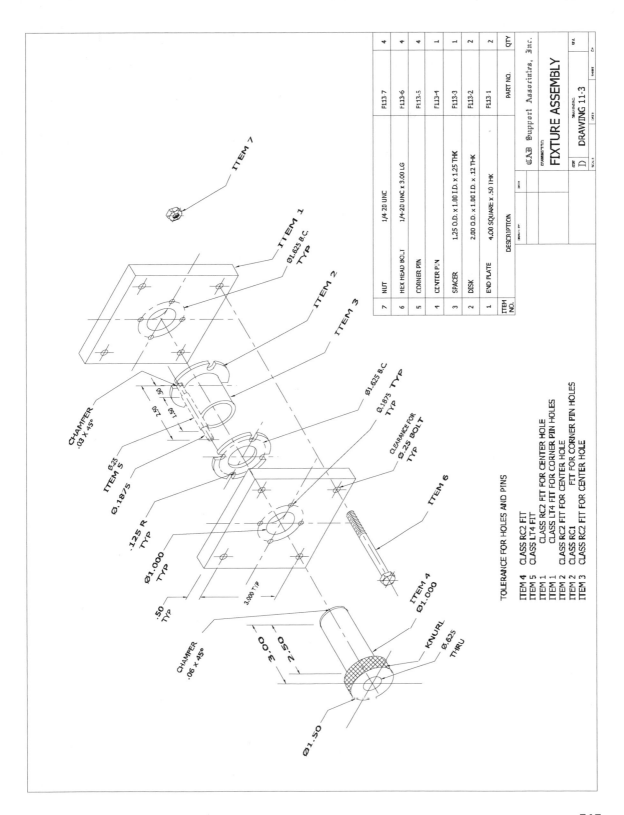

TOLERANCE FOR HOLES AND PINS

ITEM 4   CLASS RC2 FIT
ITEM 5   CLASS LT4 FIT
ITEM 1   CLASS RC2 FIT FOR CENTER HOLE
ITEM 1   CLASS LT4 FIT FOR CORNER PIN HOLES
ITEM 2   CLASS RC2 FIT FOR CENTER HOLE
ITEM 2   CLASS RC1   FIT FOR CORNER PIN HOLES
ITEM 3   CLASS RC2 FIT FOR CENTER HOLE

ITEM NO.	DESCRIPTION		PART NO.	QTY
7	NUT	1/4 20 UNC	F113 7	4
6	HEX HEAD BOLT	1/4-20 UNC x 3.00 LG	F113-6	4
5	CORNER PIN		F113-5	4
4	CENTER PIN		F113-4	1
3	SPACER	1.25 O.D. x 1.00 I.D. x 1.25 THK	F113-3	1
2	DISK	2.00 O.D. x 1.00 I.D. x .12 THK	F113-2	2
1	END PLATE	4.00 SQUARE x .50 THK	F113 1	2

CAB Support Associates, Inc.

FIXTURE ASSEMBLY

DRAWING 11-3

11.12 Drawing 11-4: Flanged Coupling

The isometric view in this three-view drawing must be completed working off the center line.

Drawing Suggestions

- Draw the major center line first. Then draw vertical center lines at every point where an isocircle is to be drawn. Make sure to draw these lines extra long so that they can be used to trim the isocircles in half. By starting at the back of the object and working forward, you can take dimensions directly from the right side view.

- Draw the isocircles at each center line and then trim them to represent semi-circles.

- Use endpoint, intersection, and tangent-to-tangent osnaps to draw horizontal lines.

- Trim away all obstructed lines and parts of isocircles.

- Draw the four slanted lines in the middle as vertical lines first. Then, with Ortho off, change their endpoints, moving them 0.125 closer.

- Remember, MIRROR does not work in the isometric view, although it can be used effectively in the right side view.

- Use BHATCH to create the crosshatching.

- If you have made a mistake in measuring along the major center line, STRETCH can be used to correct it. Make sure that Ortho is on and that you are in an iso-plane that lets you move the way you want.

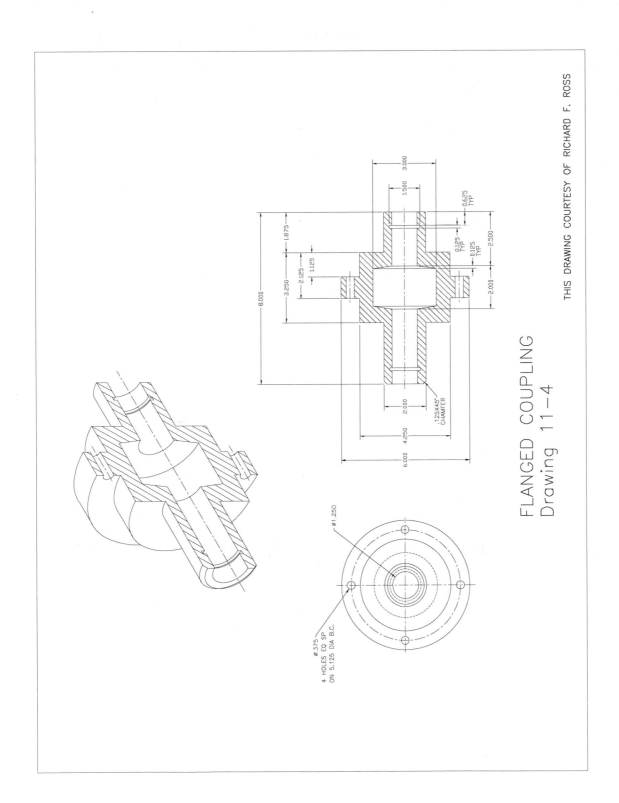

FLANGED COUPLING
Drawing 11–4

3.000
1.500
0.625 TYP
1.875
0.125 TYP
0.125 TYP
2.500
8.000
3.250
2.125
1.125
2.000
.125X45° CHAMFER
2.000
4.250
6.000

THIS DRAWING COURTESY OF RICHARD F. ROSS

Ø1.250

Ø.375
4 HOLES EQ SP
ON 5.125 DIA B.C.

11.13 Drawing 11-5: Garage Framing

This is a fairly complex drawing that takes lots of trimming and careful work. Changing the snapang (snap angle) variable so that you can draw slanted arrays is a method that can be used frequently in isometric drawing.

Drawing Suggestions

- You will find yourself using COPY, ZOOM, and TRIM a great deal. OFFSET also works well.

- You might want to create some new layers with different colors. Keeping different parts of the construction walls, rafters, and joists on different layers allows you to have more control over them and adds a lot of clarity to what you see on the screen. Turning layers on and off can considerably simplify trimming operations.

- You can cut down on repetition in this drawing by using arrays on various angles. For example, if the snapang variable is set to 150 degrees, the 22-foot wall in the left isoplane can be created as a rectangular array of studs with 1 row and 17 columns set 16 inches apart. To do so, follow this procedure:

  1. Type snapang.
  2. Enter a new value so that rectangular arrays are built on isometric angles (30 or 150).
  3. Enter the ARRAY command and create the array. Use negative values where necessary.
  4. Trim the opening for the window.

- One alternative to this array method is to set your snap to 16″ temporarily and use multiple COPY to create the columns of studs, rafters, and joists. Another alternative is to use the grip edit offset snap method beginning with an offset snap of 16″ (i.e., press Shift when you show the first copy displacement and continue to hold down Shift as you make other copies).

- The cutaway in the roof that shows the joists and the back door is drawn using the standard nonisometric ELLIPSE command. Then the rafters are trimmed to the ellipse and the ellipse is erased. Do this procedure before you draw the joists and the back wall. Otherwise, you trim these as well.

- Use CHAMFER to create the chamfered corners on the joists.

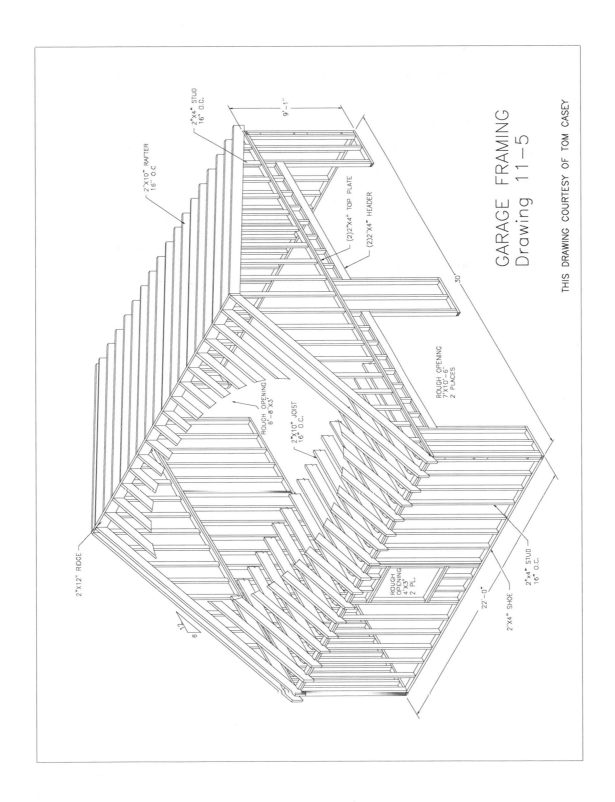

2"x4" STUD
16" O.C.

9'-1"

2"x10" RAFTER
16" O.C

(2)2"x4" TOP PLATE

(2)2"x4" HEADER

30

ROUGH OPENING
7'X10'-6"
2 PLACES

ROUGH OPENING
6'-8"X3'

2"x10" JOIST
16" O.C.

2"x12" RIDGE

12
6

ROUGH
OPENING
4'X3'
2 PL.

2"x4" SHOE

2"x4" STUD
16" O.C.

22'-0"

GARAGE FRAMING
Drawing 11-5

THIS DRAWING COURTESY OF TOM CASEY

11.14   Drawing 11-6: Cast Iron Tee

The objective of this exercise is to complete the isometric view of the tee using dimensions from the three-view drawing. Begin this isometric by working off the center line.

Drawing Suggestions

- Be sure that Ortho is on and that you are in an isoplane that is correct for the lines you want to draw. Take full advantage of object snap as you lay out this drawing.

- Draw the two major center lines as shown in isometric first. Draw them to exact length. Then draw vertical center lines at every point where an isocircle is to be drawn. These center lines should be drawn longer so the isocircles trim more easily. Notice that OFFSET and MIRROR do not work very well in the isometric mode.

- After establishing the centers, draw the isocircles for the three flanges.

- When you have completed the flanges, draw the isocircles for the wall of the tee.

- Draw all horizontal and vertical lines and trim away all nonvisible lines and parts of isocircles. Fillet the required intersections.

- After completing the outline of the tee, use BHATCH to create the crosshatching.

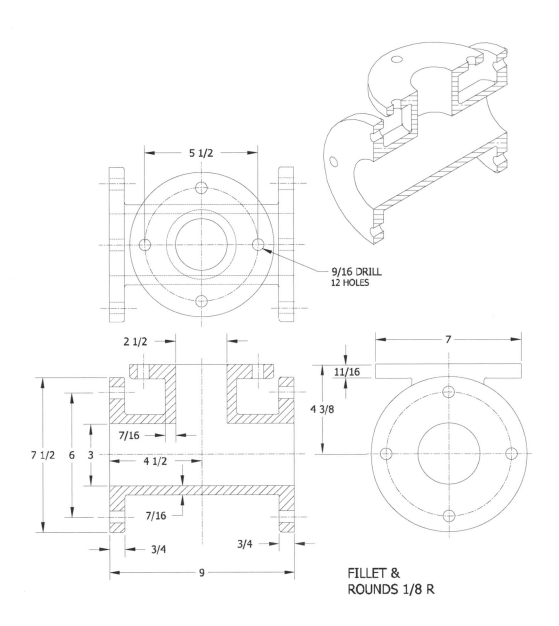

5 1/2

9/16 DRILL
12 HOLES

2 1/2

11/16

4 3/8

7/16

7 1/2   6   3

4 1/2

7/16

3/4   3/4

9

7

FILLET &
ROUNDS 1/8 R

3" CAST IRON TEE
Drawing 11-6

11.15   Drawing 11-7: Valve

For the purposes of this chapter, the isometric view is most important. The three detail views, the title block, and the border can be included or not, as assigned.

Drawing Suggestions

- Use the box method to create the isometric view in this drawing. Begin with an isometric box according to the overall outside dimensions of the valve. Then go back and cut away the excess so the drawing becomes half the valve, exposing the interior details of the object.
- As in all section drawings, no hidden lines are shown.
- In addition to flat surfaces indicated by hatching, the interior is made up of iso-circles of different sizes on different planes.
- Keep all construction lines and center lines until drawing is complete (draw them on a separate layer and you can turn off that layer when you don't need them).
- The tapped holes are drawn with a series of isocircles that can be arrayed. This is only a representation of a screw thread, so it is not drawn to precise dimensions. Draw one thread and copy it to the other side.

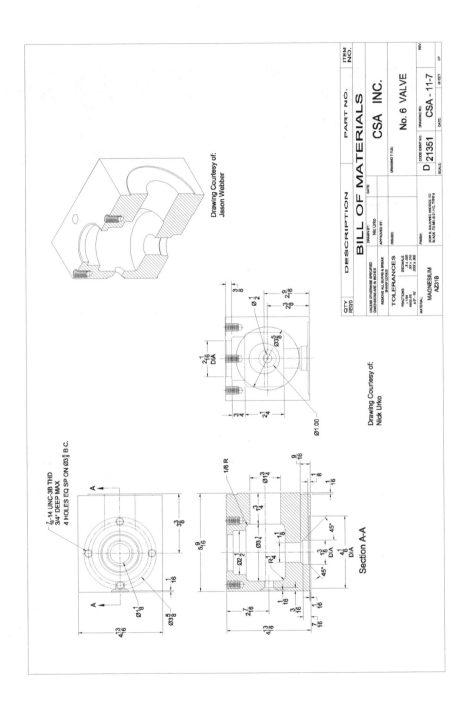

Drawing Courtesy of:
Jason Webber

Drawing Courtesy of:
Nick Urko

Section A-A

7/16-14 UNC-3B THD
3/4" DEEP MAX
4 HOLES EQ SP ON Ø3⅝ B.C.

QTY REQD	DESCRIPTION	PART NO.
	BILL OF MATERIALS	CSA INC.

DRAWING TITLE:

No. 6 VALVE

UNLESS OTHERWISE SPECIFIED
DIMENSIONS ARE IN INCHES

REMOVE ALL BURRS & BREAK
SHARP EDGES

TOLERANCES

FRACTIONS: ± 1/64
ANGLES: ±0° - 15'
DECIMALS: .X ± .030 .XX ± .010 .XXX ± .005

MATERIAL:
MAGNESIUM
AZ31B

DRAWN BY: Nic Urko
APPROVED BY:
ISSUED:

FINISH:
DOW 9, GALVANO ANODIZE, TO
BLACK TO MIL-A-3-11C, TYPE 4

CODE IDENT NO. D
DRAWING NO. 21351
CSA - 11-7

SCALE: DATE:

ITEM NO.

PART NO.

REV

523

12 Wireframe Models

COMMANDS

RULESURF   UCS   UCSICON   VPOINT

OVERVIEW

It is now time to begin thinking in three dimensions. 3-D drawing in AutoCAD is logical and efficient. You can create wireframe models, surface models, or solid models and display them from multiple points of view. In this chapter, we focus on user coordinate systems, 3-D viewpoints, and wireframe modeling. These are the primary tools you need to understand how AutoCAD allows you to work in three dimensions on a two-dimensional screen. Tasks 12.1 through 12.5 take you through a complete 3-D wireframe modeling exercise using four different coordinate systems that we define. As in the last chapter, there are few new commands to learn.

If you have completed Chapter 11, you will find that working on isometric drawings has prepared you well for 3-D drawing. There is a similar process of switching from plane to plane, but there are two key differences. First, you are not restricted to three isometric planes: You can define a user coordinate system aligned with any specifiable plane. Second, and most important, the model you draw has true 3-D characteristics. You can view it, edit it, and plot it from any point in space.

TASKS

12.1   Creating and Viewing a 3-D Wireframe Box

In this task, we create a simple 3-D box that we can edit in later tasks to form a more complex object. If your UCS icon is not visible (see Figure 12-1), follow this procedure to turn it on:

1. Open the View menu, highlight Display, and then UCS Icon, as shown in Figure 12-2.
2. Select On from the submenu.

For now, simply observe the icon as you go through the process of creating the box, and be aware that you are currently working in the same coordinate system that you have always used in AutoCAD. It is called the world coordinate system (WCS), to distinguish it from others you create yourself beginning in Task 12.2.

Currently, the origin of the WCS is at the lower left of your grid. This is the point (0,0,0) when you are thinking 3-D, or simply (0,0) when you are in 2-D. The *x*-coordinates increase to the right horizontally across the screen, and the *y*-coordinates increase vertically up the screen as usual. The *z*-axis, which we have ignored until now, currently extends out of the screen toward you and perpendicular to the *x*- and *y*-axes. This orientation of the three planes is called a plan view. Soon we will switch to a front, right, top, or southeast isometric view.

Let's begin.

⊕   Start a new drawing using the 1B template.

⊕   Draw a 2.00 by 4.00 rectangle near the middle of your screen, as shown in Figure 12-1. Do not use the RECTANG command to draw this figure because we want to select individual line segments later on.

Changing Viewpoints

To move immediately into a 3-D mode of drawing and thinking, our first step is to change our viewpoint on this object. There are three commands that allow you to create 3-D points of view: VPOINT, DVIEW, and 3DORBIT. 3DORBIT and

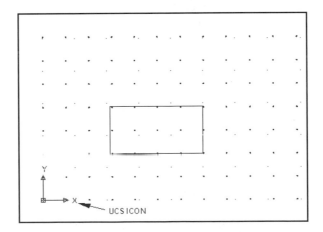

Figure 12-1

Figure 12-2

DVIEW are best suited for creating carefully adjusted presentation images, including perspective views. The VPOINT command is simpler and best used for setting up basic views during the drawing and editing process. A good understanding of all the VPOINT options increases your understanding of AutoCAD's 3-D space. For this reason, we have included at the end of this chapter an optional discussion of the different options available in the VPOINT command. There are three or four different methods, developed over time as Autodesk has simplified the viewpoint definition process.

The simplest and most efficient method is to use the Named Views dialog box introduced in the previous chapter. For now, this is the only method you need.

⊕ Open the View menu and select Named Views.

This opens the View dialog box, which was used in Chapter 11 to create named views. In this chapter, we use the Orthographic & Isometric Views tab.

⊕ Click the Orthographic & Isometric Views tab, as shown in Figure 12-3.

This dialog box uses simple cube images to show 10 standard preset views. Imagine your point of view to be perpendicular to the blue face of the cube in each case. In the six orthographic views, objects are presented from points of view along each of the six axis directions. You see objects in the drawing from directly above (top, positive z) or directly below (bottom, negative z), or by looking in along the positive or negative x-axis (left and right) or the positive or negative y-axis (front and back).

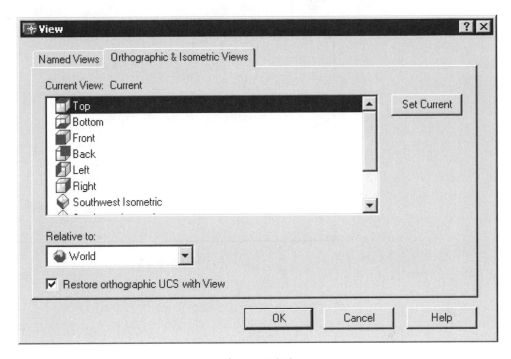

Figure 12-3

The four isometric views present objects at 45-degree angles from the XY-axis and take you up 30 degrees out of the XY plane. We use a southeast isometric view. It is simple if you imagine a compass. The lower right quadrant is the southeast. In a southeast isometric view, you are looking in from this quadrant and down at a 30-degree angle. Try it.

⊕ Select SE Isometric from the list of views.
⊕ Click Set Current.
⊕ Click OK.

The dialog box closes and the screen is redrawn to the view shown in Figure 12-4. Notice how the grid and the coordinate system icon have altered to show our current orientation. These visual aids are extremely helpful in viewing 3-D objects on the flat screen and imagining them as if they were positioned in space.

At this point you might want to experiment with the other views in the View dialog box. You will probably find the isometric views most interesting. Pay attention to the grid and the icon as you switch views. Variations of the icon you might encounter here and later on are shown in Figure 12-5. With some views, you have to think carefully and watch the icon to understand which way the object is being presented.

When you have finished experimenting, be sure to return to the southeast isometric view shown in Figure 12-4. We use this view frequently throughout this chapter and the next.

Whenever you change viewpoints, AutoCAD displays the drawing extents, so that the object fills the screen and is as large as possible. Often, you need to zoom out a bit to get some space to work in. This is easily done using the Scale(X) option of the ZOOM command.

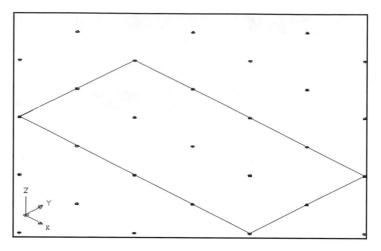

Figure 12-4

If the icon is displayed at the origin of the current UCS, a cross (+) appears in the icon. If the icon is displayed in the lower left corner of the viewport, no cross appears in the icon.

If you have multiple viewports, each viewport displays its own UCS icon.

AutoCAD displays the UCS icon in various ways to help you visualize the orientation of the drawing plane. The following figure shows some of the possible icon displays.

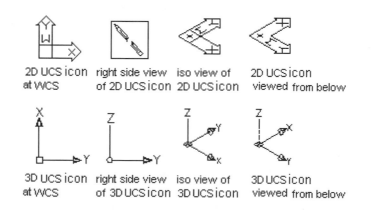

You can use the UCSICON command to switch between the 2D UCS icon and the 3D UCS icon. You can also use the command to change the size, color, arrowhead type, and icon line width of the 3D UCS icon.

Figure 12-5

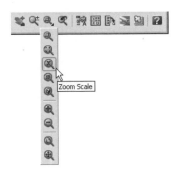

Figure 12-6

⊕ Open the View menu, highlight Zoom, and select Scale, or select the Zoom Scale tool from the Zoom flyout on the Standard toolbar, as shown in Figure 12-6.

⊕ Type .5x.

This tells AutoCAD to adjust and redraw the display so that objects appear half as large as before. Your screen is redrawn with the rectangle at half its previous magnification.

Entering 3-D Coordinates

Next we create a copy of the rectangle placed 1.25 above the original. This brings up a basic 3-D problem: AutoCAD interprets pointer device point selections as being in the XY plane, so how does one indicate a point or a displacement in the Z direction? There are three possibilities: typed 3-D coordinates, X/Y/Z point filters, and object snaps. Object snap requires an object already drawn above or below the XY plane, so it is of no use right now. We use typed coordinates first and then discuss how point filters could be used as an alternative. Later, we use object snap as well.

3-D coordinates can be entered from the keyboard in the same manner as 2-D coordinates. Often, this is an impractical way to enter individual points in a drawing. However, within COPY or MOVE, it provides a simple method for specifying a displacement in the Z direction.

⊕ Select Copy from the Modify menu, or select the Copy tool from the Modify toolbar.

AutoCAD prompts for object selection.

⊕ Select the complete rectangle.

⊕ Press Enter or right-click to end object selection.

AutoCAD now prompts for the base point of a vector or a displacement value:

```
Specify base point or displacement, or [Multiple]:
```

Typically, you would respond to this prompt and the next by showing the two endpoints of a vector. However, we cannot show a displacement in the Z direction by pointing. This is important for understanding AutoCAD coordinate systems. Unless an object snap is used, all points picked on the screen with

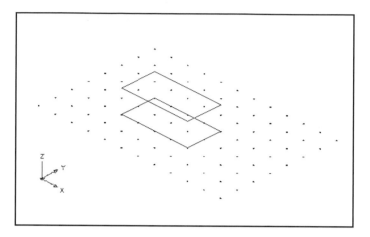

Figure 12-7

the pointing device are interpreted as being in the XY plane of the current UCS. Without an entity outside the XY plane to use in an object snap, there is no way to point to a displacement in the Z direction.

✦ Type 0,0,1.25.

AutoCAD now prompts

> Specify second point of displacement,
> or <use first point as displacement>:

You can type the coordinates of another point, or press Enter to tell AutoCAD to use the first entry as a displacement from (0,0,0). In this case, pressing Enter indicates a displacement of 1.25 in the Z direction and no change in X or Y.

✦ Press Enter or right-click.

AutoCAD creates a copy of the rectangle 1.25 directly above the original. Your screen should resemble Figure 12-7.

X/Y/Z Point Filters (Optional)

Point filters can be very useful in 3-D, although they might seem odd until you get a feel for when to use them. In a point filter, we filter out coordinates from one point and use them to create a new point. Notice that in the displacement we just entered, the only thing that changes is the Z value. Note also that we could specify the same displacement using any point in the XY plane as a base point. For example, (3,6,0) to (3,6,1.25) would show the same displacement as (0,0,0) to (0,0,1.25). In fact, we don't even need to know what X and Y are as long as we know that they don't change.

That is how an .XY point filter works. We borrow, or "filter," the X and Y values from a point, without pausing to find out what the values actually are, and then specify a new Z value. Other types of filters are possible, of course, such as .Z or .YZ.

You can use a point filter, like an object snap, any time AutoCAD asks for a point. After a point filter is specified, AutoCAD always prompts with an of. In our case, you are being asked, "You want the X and Y values of what point?" In response, you pick a point, and then AutoCAD asks you to fill in Z. Notice that point filters can be "chained" so that, for example, you can filter the X value from one point and combine it with the filtered Y value from another point.

To use an .XY filter in the COPY command instead of typing coordinates, for example, you could follow this procedure:

1. Enter the COPY command.
2. Select the rectangle.
3. For the displacement base point, pick any point in the XY plane.
4. At the prompt for a second point, type .xy.
5. At the of prompt, type @ or pick the same point again.
6. At the (need Z): prompt, type 1.25. The result would be Figure 12-7, as before.

> **Note:** There is a Point Filters cascading submenu on the object snap shortcut menu. To access it, hold down the Shift key and right-click anywhere in the drawing area. From the shortcut menu, highlight Point Filters and select a point filter type from the submenu.

Using Object Snap

We now have two rectangles floating in space. Our next job is to connect the corners to form a wireframe box. This is easily managed using Endpoint object snaps and it is a good example of how object snaps allow us to construct entities not in the XY plane of the current coordinate system.

⊕ Right-click the Osnap button on the status bar.

⊕ Select Settings from the cursor menu.

⊕ Click Clear All to clear all object snap check boxes.

⊕ Select the Endpoint check box.

⊕ Select the Object Snap On check box at the top left of the dialog box.

⊕ Click OK.

> The running Endpoint object snap is now on and affects all point selections. Object snaps are very useful in 3-D drawing and the Endpoint mode can be used frequently.

Now we draw some lines:

⊕ Enter the LINE command and connect the upper and lower corners of the two rectangles, as shown in Figure 12-8.

> We have removed the grid for clarity, but you probably want to leave yours on.

Before going on, pause to take note of what you have drawn. The box on your screen is a true wireframe model. Unlike an isometric drawing, it is a 3-D model that can be turned, viewed, and plotted from any point in space. It is not, however, a solid model or a surface model. It is only a set of lines in 3-D space. Removing hidden lines or shading would have no effect on this model because no surfaces are represented. Surfaces and solids are addressed in Chapters 13 and 14.

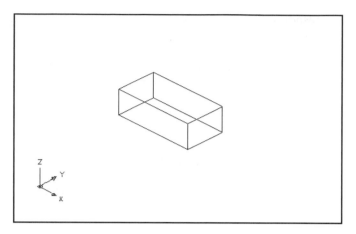

Figure 12-8

In the next task, you begin to define your own coordinate systems that allow you to perform drawing and editing functions in any plane you choose.

12.2   Defining and Saving User Coordinate Systems

GENERAL PROCEDURE
1.   Type ucs or select New UCS from the Tools menu.
2.   Choose an option.
3.   Specify a coordinate system.
4.   Name and save the new coordinate system.

In this task, you begin to develop new vocabulary and techniques for working with objects in 3-D space. The primary tool is the UCS command. You also learn to use the UCSICON command to control the placement of the coordinate system icon.

Until now, we have had only one coordinate system to work with. All coordinates and displacements have been defined relative to a single point of origin. Keep in mind that viewpoint and coordinate system are not the same, although they use similar vocabulary. In Task 12.1, we changed our point of view, but the UCS icon changed along with it, so that the orientations of the x-, y-, and z-axes relative to the object were retained. With the UCS command, you can free the coordinate system from the viewpoint and define new coordinate systems at any point and any angle in space. When you do, you can use the coordinate system icon and the grid to help you visualize the planes you are working in, and all commands and drawing aids function relative to the new system.

The coordinate system we are currently using, WCS, is unique. It is the one we always begin with. The square at the base of the coordinate system icon indicates that we are working in the WCS. A UCS is nothing more than a new point of origin and a new orientation for the x-, y-, and z-axes.

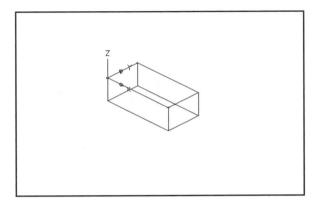

Figure 12-9

Figure 12-10

We begin by defining a UCS in the plane of the top of the box, as shown in Figure 12-9.

⊕ Leave the Endpoint osnap mode on for this exercise.

⊕ Open the Tools menu and highlight New UCS.

There is also a UCS tool on the UCS toolbar shown in Figure 12-10, but you have to open the toolbar before you can access it. If you type ucs or select the tool from the toolbar, you work with prompts at the command line. Here we begin using the pull-down menu options and later use the command line as well.

On the pull-down menu, you see options on a submenu, as illustrated in Figure 12-11. We begin by using Origin to create a UCS that is parallel to the WCS.

⊕ Select Origin from the submenu.

AutoCAD prompts for a new origin:

Specify new origin point <0,0,0>:

This option does not change the orientation of the three axes. It simply shifts their intersection to a different point in space. We use this procedure to define a UCS in the plane of the top of the box.

⊕ Use the Endpoint object snap to select the top left corner of the box, as shown by the location of the icon in Figure 12-9.

Notice that the square is gone from the icon. However, the icon might not have moved. Depending on the setting of the UCSICON command, it might still be at the lower left of the screen. It is visually helpful to place it at the origin of the new UCS, as in the figure.

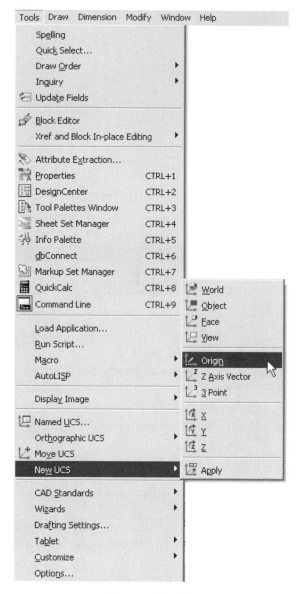

Figure 12-11

⊕ Open the View menu, highlight Display, and then UCS Icon.

⊕ If necessary, select Origin, so that there is a check mark next to it.

The icon moves to the origin of the new current UCS, as in Figure 12-9. With UCSICON set to origin, the icon shifts to the new origin whenever we define a new UCS. The only exception would be if the origin were not on the screen or were too close to an edge for the icon to fit. In these cases, the icon would be displayed in the lower left corner again.

The UCS we have just created makes it easy to draw and edit entities that are in the plane of the top of the box and to perform editing in planes that are parallel to it, such as the bottom. In the next task, we begin drawing and editing using different coordinate systems, and you can see how this works. For now, we spend a little more time on the UCS command itself. We define two more UCSs, but first let's save this one so that we can recall it quickly when we need it later.

⊕   **Open the Tools menu and highlight Named UCS.**

The new UCS is on the list as Unnamed, along with World and Previous.

⊕   **Select Unnamed.**

The word Unnamed should be selected for editing. We name our coordinate system Top. This is the UCS we use to draw and edit in the top plane. This UCS would also make it easy for us to create an orthographic top viewpoint later on.

⊕   **Type Top and press Enter.**

The Top UCS is now saved and can be recalled by opening this dialog box, selecting it in the name list, and clicking Set Current.

Next we define a Left UCS using the 3 point option.

⊕   **Click OK to close the dialog box.**

⊕   **Open the Tools menu, highlight New UCS, and select 3 Point from the submenu.**

AutoCAD prompts

        `Specify new origin point <0,0,0>:`

In this option, you show AutoCAD a new origin point, as before, and then a new orientation for the axes as well. Notice that the default origin is the current one. If we retained this origin, we could define a UCS with the same origin and a different axis orientation.

Instead, we define a new origin at the lower left corner of the left side of the box, as shown in Figure 12-12.

⊕   **With the Endpoint osnap on, pick P1, as shown in Figure 12-12.**

AutoCAD now prompts you to indicate the orientation of the *x*-axis:

        `Specify point on positive portion`
        `of the X axis <1.00,0.00,-1.25>:`

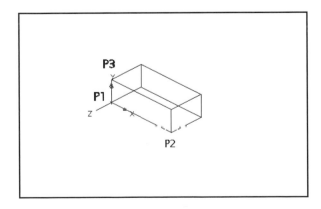

Figure 12-12

⊕ Pick the right front corner of the box, P2, as shown.

The object snap ensures that the new *x*-axis aligns with the left side of the object. AutoCAD prompts for the *y*-axis orientation:

```
Specify point on positive-Y portion
of the UCS XY plane <0.00,1.00,-1.25>:
```

By definition, the *y*-axis is perpendicular to the *x*-axis; therefore, AutoCAD needs only a point that shows the plane of the *y*-axis and its positive direction. Because of this, any point on the positive side of the *y* plane specifies the *y*-axis correctly. We have chosen a point that is on the *y*-axis itself.

⊕ Pick P3, as shown.

When this sequence is complete, notice that the coordinate system icon has rotated along with the grid and moved to the new origin as well. This UCS is convenient for drawing and editing in the left plane of the box, or editing in any plane parallel to the left plane, such as the back plane.

Now save the Left UCS, using the command line this time.

⊕ Press Enter to repeat the UCS command.

If dynamic input is on, you will see a drop-down list of options.

⊕ Type s or select Save from the drop-down list.

⊕ Type Left to name the UCS.

Finally, we use the Origin and Y axis rotation options together to create a right-side UCS.

⊕ Open the Tools menu and highlight New UCS.

⊕ Select Origin from the submenu.

⊕ Pick the lower front right corner of the box for the origin, as shown in Figure 12-13.

The UCS icon moves to the selected point.

⊕ Press Enter or the spacebar to repeat the UCS command.

We rotate the UCS icon around its *y*-axis to align it with the right side of the box.

In using any of the rotation options (X, Y, and Z), the first thing you have to decide is which axis is the axis of rotation. If you look at the current position

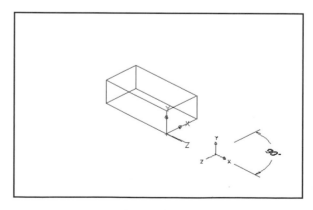

Figure 12-13

of the icon and think about how it will look when it aligns with the right side of the box, you can see that the *y*-axis retains its position and orientation while the *x*- and *z*-axes turn through 90 degrees. In other words, because *x* rotates around *y*, *y* is the axis of rotation.

If dynamic input is on, you will see the drop-down list again. You can ignore it and go straight to entering rotation options.

⊕ **Type y and press Enter.**

Now AutoCAD prompts for a rotation:

        Specify rotation angle around Y axis <90>:

It takes some practice to differentiate positive and negative rotation in 3-D. If you like, you can use AutoCAD's right-hand rule, which can be stated as follows: If you are hitchhiking (pointing your right thumb) in a positive direction along the axis of rotation, your fingers curl in the direction of positive rotation for the other axes. In this case, align your right thumb with the positive *y*-axis, and you see that your fingers curl in the direction in which we want the *x*-axis to rotate. Therefore, the rotation of *x* around *y* is positive.

⊕ **Type 90 or press Enter to accept the default rotation.**

You should now have the UCS icon aligned with the right side of the box, as shown in Figure 12-13. Save this UCS before going on to Task 12.3.

⊕ **Press Enter to repeat the UCS command.**

⊕ **Type s or select Save from the drop-down list.**

⊕ **Type Right.**

12.3   Using Draw and Edit Commands in a UCS

Now the fun begins. Using our three new coordinate systems and one more we define later, we give the box a more interesting "slotted wedge" shape. In this task, we cut away a slanted surface on the right side of the box. Because the planes we are working in are parallel to the left side of the box, we begin by making the left UCS current. All our work in this task is done in this UCS.

⊕ **Open the Tools menu and select Named UCS.**

This opens the Named UCS dialog box again, with three new coordinate systems as shown in Figure 12-14. Now that we have these coordinate systems defined, this dialog box provides a simple way to switch among them.

⊕ **Highlight left in the dialog box.**

⊕ **Click Set Current.**

⊕ **Click OK.**

The UCS icon returns to the left plane.

Look at Figure 12-15. We draw a line down the middle of the left side (Line 1) and use it to trim another line coming in at an angle (Line 2).

⊕ **Type L or select the Line tool from the Draw toolbar.**

⊕ **Hold down Shift and right-click to open the Object Snap Cursor menu.**

⊕ **Select Midpoint.**

This temporarily overrides the Endpoint object snap.

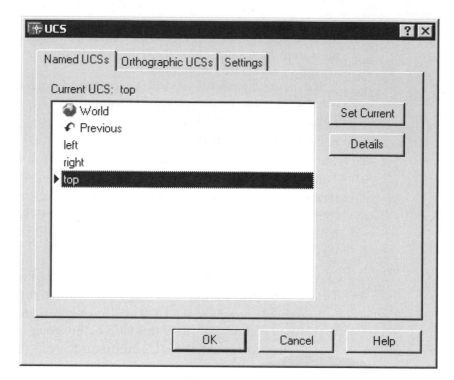

Figure 12-14

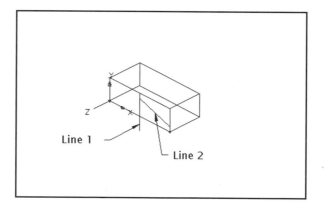

Figure 12-15

⊕ Point to the top edge of the left side of the box.

    AutoCAD snaps to the midpoint of the line.

⊕ Make sure that Ortho is on (press F8 or click the Ortho button).

    Notice how Ortho works as usual, but relative to the current UCS.

⊕ Pick a second point anywhere below the box.

    This line is trimmed later, so the exact length does not matter.

⊕   Exit the LINE command.

Next we draw Line 2 on an angle across the left side. This line becomes one edge of a slanted surface. Your snap setting needs to be at 0.25 or smaller, and Ortho needs to be off. The grid, snap, and coordinate display all work relative to the current UCS, so it is a simple matter to draw in this plane.

⊕   Turn grid snap on (press F9 or click the Snap button) and check your snap setting by observing the coordinate display. Change it to 0.25 if necessary.

⊕   Turn Ortho off.

⊕   Turn Osnap off (press F3 or click the Osnap button).

⊕   Enter the LINE command.

⊕   Use incremental snap to pick a point 0.25 down from the top edge of the box on Line 1, as shown in Figure 12-15.

⊕   Pick a second point 0.25 up along the right front edge of the box, as shown.

⊕   Exit the LINE command.

Now trim Line 1.

⊕   Select the Trim tool from the Modify toolbar.

AutoCAD presents the following message, but you might need to switch to the text window (press F2) to see it:

View is not plan to UCS. Command results may not be obvious.

In the language of AutoCAD 3-D, a view is plan to the current UCS if the XY plane is in the plane of the monitor display and its axes are parallel to the sides of the screen. This is the usual 2-D view, in which the *y*-axis aligns with the left side of the display and the *x*-axis aligns with the bottom of the display. In previous chapters, we always worked in plan view. In this chapter, we have not been in plan view since the beginning of Task 12.1.

With this message, AutoCAD is warning us that boundaries, edges, and intersections might not be obvious as we look at a 3-D view of an object. For example, lines that appear to cross might be in different planes.

Having read the warning, we continue.

⊕   Select Line 2 as a cutting edge.

⊕   Press Enter or right-click to end cutting edge selection.

⊕   Point to the lower end of Line 1.

⊕   Press Enter or the spacebar to exit TRIM.

Your screen should resemble Figure 12-16.

Now we copy our two lines to the back of the box. Because we will be moving out of the left plane, which is also the XY plane in the current UCS, we require the use of Endpoint object snaps to specify the displacement vector.

⊕   Select the Copy tool from the Modify toolbar.

⊕   Pick Lines 1 and 2. (You might need to turn off incremental snap at this point to pick Line 1.)

⊕   Press Enter or right-click to end object selection.

⊕   Click the Osnap button to turn object snap on.

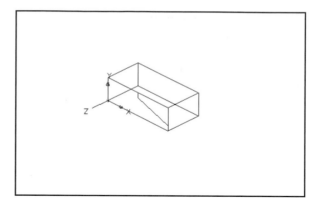

Figure 12-16

⊕ Use the running Endpoint osnap to pick the lower front corner of the box, P1 as shown in Figure 12-17. Be careful to avoid picking the endpoint of Line 2.

⊕ At the prompt for a second point of displacement, use the Endpoint osnap to pick the lower right back corner of the box, P2 as shown.

⊕ Press Enter to exit COPY.

Your screen should now resemble Figure 12-17.

What remains is to connect the edges we have just outlined and then trim away the top of the box. We continue to work in the left UCS and use Endpoint osnaps.

We use a multiple COPY to copy one of the previously drawn edges in three new places.

⊕ Repeat COPY.

⊕ Pick the bottom right edge for copying (the edge between P1 and P2 in Figure 12-17).

⊕ Press Enter to end object selection.

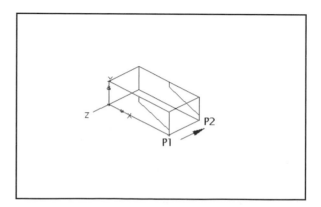

Figure 12-17

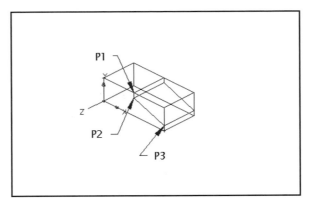

Figure 12-18

⊞ Pick the front endpoint of the selected edge to serve as a base point of displacement.

⊞ Pick the top endpoint of Line 1 (P1 in Figure 12-18).

⊞ Pick the lower endpoint of Line 1 (P2) as another second point.

⊞ Pick the right endpoint of Line 2 (P3) as another second point.

⊞ Press Enter to exit the COPY command.

Finally, we need to do some trimming.

⊞ Select the Trim tool from the Modify toolbar.

For cutting edges, we want to select Lines 1 and 2 and their copies in the back plane (Lines 3 and 4 in Figure 12-19). Because this can be difficult, a quick alternative to selecting these four separate lines is to use a crossing box to select the whole area or press Enter to Select All. As long as your selection includes the four lines, it will be effective.

⊞ Press Enter to select all objects as cutting edges.

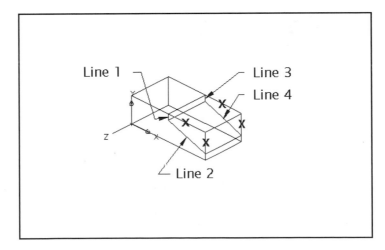

Figure 12-19

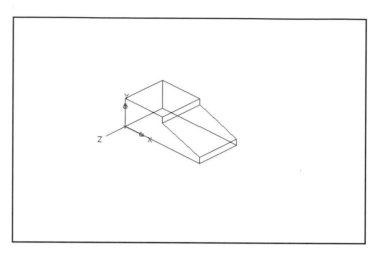

Figure 12-20

With this selection you do not have to press Enter again. Because you've already selected everything, AutoCAD does not ask for further object selection.

Note: Trimming in 3-D can be tricky. Remember where you are. Edges that do not run parallel to the current UCS might not be recognized at all.

⊞ One by one, pick the top left and top back edges to the right of the cut, and the right front and right back edges above the cut, as shown by the Xs in Figure 12-19.

⊞ Press Enter to exit the TRIM command.

⊞ Use the ERASE command to erase the top edge that is left hanging in space.

We use ERASE here because this line does not intersect any edges. Your screen should now resemble Figure 12-20.

12.4   Working on an Angled Surface

In this task, we take our 3-D drawing technique a step further by constructing a slot through the new slanted surface and the bottom of the object. This requires the creation of a new UCS. In completing this task, you also use the OFFSET command and continue to develop a feel for working with multiple coordinate systems.

Begin by defining a UCS along the angled surface.

⊞ Open the Tools menu, highlight New UCS, and select 3 Point.

⊞ Using the Endpoint osnap, pick P1, as shown in Figure 12-21.

⊞ Using an Endpoint osnap, pick P2, as shown.

⊞ Using an Endpoint osnap, pick P3, as shown.

⊞ Repeat the UCS command.

⊞ Type s or select Save.

⊞ Type Angle for the name of the UCS.

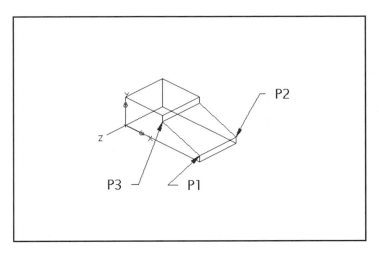

Figure 12-21

Now we are ready to work in the plane of the angled surface.

From here on, we have moved our UCS icon back to the lower left of the screen for the sake of clarity in our illustrations. You can leave it at its origin on your screen, if you like, or move it by opening the View menu, highlighting Display, then UCS Icon, and then clearing Origin.

⊕   Turn Osnap off (press F3 or click the Osnap button).

⊕   If Ortho is off, turn it on (press F8 or click the Ortho button).

   We create Line 1 across the angled surface, as shown in Figure 12-22, by off-setting the top right front edge of the wedge.

⊕   Select the Offset tool from the Modify toolbar.

⊕   Type or show a distance of 1.50.

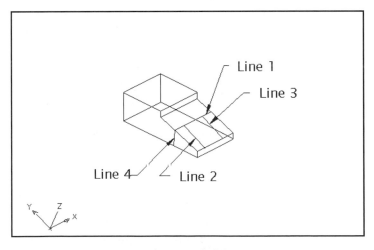

Figure 12-22

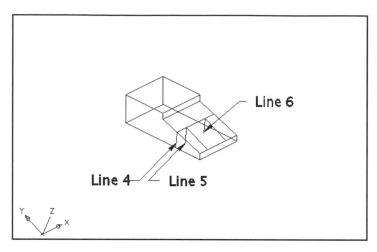

Figure 12-23

⊕ Pick the top right front edge (the top edge at the tapered right end of the wedge).

⊕ Point anywhere above and to the left of the edge.

⊕ Exit OFFSET.

⊕ Turning off osnap and using incremental snap, draw Lines 2 and 3 perpendicular to the first, as shown. They should be over 0.50 and 1.50 from the current *y*-axis.

　Watch the coordinate display and notice how the coordinates work in this UCS as in any other.

⊕ Turn Ortho off.

⊕ Using incremental snap for the top point and a perpendicular object snap for the lower point, drop Line 4 down to the bottom left front edge.

　This is a single-point osnap. Use the osnap shortcut menu. Notice again how object snap modes work for you, especially to locate points that are not in the XY plane of the current UCS.

⊕ Create Lines 5 and 6, as shown in Figure 12-23, by making two copies of Line 4, extending down from the ends of Lines 2 and 3, as shown.

⊕ Erase Line 4 from the left plane.

⊕ Turn osnap on.

⊕ Using Endpoint osnaps, connect Lines 5 and 6 to each other in the plane of the bottom of the object.

⊕ Using Endpoint and Perpendicular osnaps, connect Lines 5 and 6 to the bottom edge of the right side.

⊕ Using Endpoint osnaps, draw two short vertical lines on the right side, connecting to Lines 2 and 3.

⊕ Trim line 1 and the two lines on the right side across the opening of the slot to create Figure 12-24.

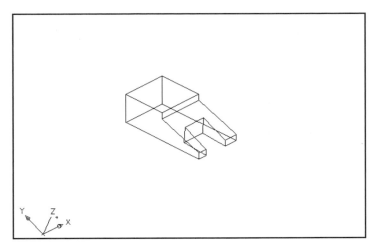

Figure 12-24

12.5   Using RULESURF to Create 3-D Fillets

GENERAL PROCEDURE

1.   Create fillets in two planes.
2.   Open the Draw menu, highlight Surfaces, and select Ruled Surface.
3.   Pick a fillet.
4.   Pick the corresponding side of the fillet in the other plane.

There are two parts to completing this task. First, we fillet the top and bottom corners of the slot drawn in Task 12.4. Then we use the RULESURF command to create filleted surfaces between the top and bottom of the slot. RULESURF is a surface command that we use in the next chapter, but we use it here as the most effective way to create a 3-D fillet in our wireframe model.

⊕   To begin this task you should be in the Angle UCS, as in Task 12.4, and your screen should resemble Figure 12-24.

⊕   Select the Fillet tool from the Modify menu.

AutoCAD prompts as usual:

```
Current settings: Mode = TRIM, Radius = 0.50
Select first object or [Polyline/Radius/Trim]:
```

⊕   Type r.

⊕   Type .25 for the radius value

⊕   Type m for the Multiple option.

⊕   Pick two lines that meet at one of the upper corners of the slot.

Look at Figure 12-25 to see where we are headed.

⊕   Pick two lines that meet at the other upper corner of the slot.

⊕   Pick two lines that meet at one of the lower corners of the slot.

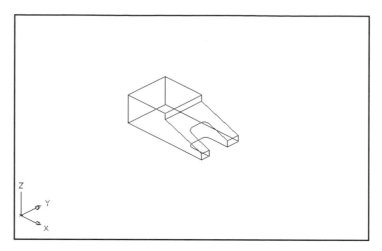

Figure 12-25

⊞ Pick two lines that meet at the other lower corner of the slot.

⊞ Press Enter to exit FILLET.

⊞ Erase the two vertical lines left outside the fillets.

Your screen should resemble Figure 12-25.

Now we use RULESURF to connect the upper and lower fillets with 3-D surfaces. RULESURF is one of several commands that create 3-D surfaces. These commands create entities called *3-D polygon meshes*, which are discussed in detail in Chapter 13. This quick introduction allows you to create 3-D fillets in the drawings at the end of this chapter.

The RULESURF command creates a 3-D surface between two lines or curves in 3-D space. Our two curves are the upper and lower fillets at each of the two corners.

⊞ Open the Draw menu, highlight Surfaces, and select Ruled Surface.

AutoCAD prompts

Select first defining curve:

⊞ Pick one of the top fillets, as shown by Pick fillet 1 in Figure 12-26.

AutoCAD prompts for a second curve:

Select second defining curve:

⊞ Pick the corresponding fillet in the bottom plane, with a pick point on the corresponding side, as shown by Pick fillet 2 in Figure 12-26.

AutoCAD draws a set of faces to represent the surface curving around the fillet radius, as shown in Figure 12-27.

The trick in using RULESURF is to be sure that you show a pick point toward one side of the curve and that you pick the next curve with a point on the corresponding side. Otherwise, you get an hourglass effect, as shown in Figure 12-28.

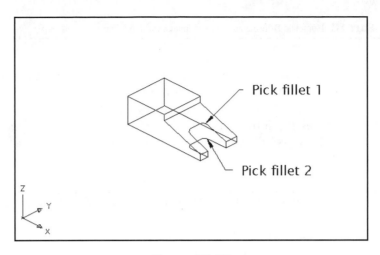

Figure 12-26

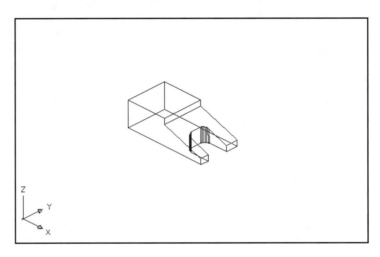

Figure 12-27

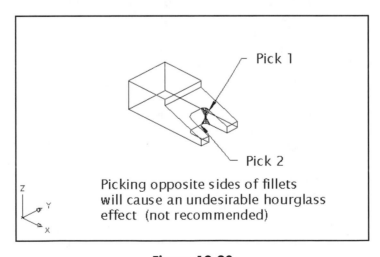

Figure 12-28

⊞ To complete this task, repeat the RULESURF command and draw the fillet at the other corner of the groove.

When you are finished, your screen should resemble Figure 12-27. This completes the introduction to drawing 3-D wireframe models and using UCSs. What follows is an optional discussion of other methods for using the VPOINT command.

12.6 Exploring Other Methods of Using the VPOINT Command

This discussion of other methods of using VPOINT is intended as a reference. The information presented here is not necessary to complete the drawings in this chapter, and no specific exercise is presented. However, if you are interested in gaining a full understanding of the VPOINT command, try creating the views described and outlined in the charts and figures in this section. Of particular importance is the Viewpoint Presets dialog box, opened by the DDVPOINT command. In Chapters 13 and 4 you can also find exercises using the more dynamic 3DORBIT command for fine tuning and creating perspective and cutaway views.

Entering 3-D Coordinates of a Viewpoint (Vector)

If you enter VPOINT by typing the command, you see the following messages and prompts:

```
***Switching to the WCS***
Current view direction: VIEWDIR=1.00,-1.00,1.00
Specify a view point or [Rotate] <display compass and tripod>:
```

From the first line, you learn that all views are defined relative to the WCS, regardless of what UCS is current at the time the command is entered. From the second line, you see the current setting of the variable VIEWDIR, which holds the vector definition of the current viewpoint. Assuming you are in the southeast isometric view, you see (1.00,−1.00,1.00). Reading this section will help you understand how the vector definition relates to the view definition. The third line gives you three options: You can specify a viewpoint by typing vector numbers, typing rotation specifications, or using the compass and tripod images. The latter two options are explained later in this discussion.

The default method is to type in vector specifications. If you enter the VPOINT command from the WCS plan view, the default viewpoint is given as (0,0,1). This means that you are viewing the object from a point somewhere along the positive z-axis. You are at 0 in the x and y directions and at +1 in the z direction. In other words, you are directly above the XY plane looking straight down, a plan view. Think of the x-coordinate as controlling right–left orientation, the y-coordinate as controlling back–front orientation, and the z-coordinate as controlling up–down orientation.

By changing the x-coordinate to 1 (right) and leaving y at 0 (neither front nor back) and z at 1 (above), you can create a viewpoint above and to the right of the object (1,0,1). Similarly, (1,−1,1) would move you to the right ($x = 1$), back you up a bit ($y = −1$) so that you are in front of the object, and raise your point of view ($z = 1$) so that you are above the object looking down. This common

(1,−1,1) viewpoint is the same as the southeast viewpoint used throughout this chapter.

We explore other methods of specifying viewpoints in a moment, but first look at the viewpoint vector chart that follows. It summarizes the effects of the x, y, and z specifications and gives you combinations for some standard views. You should have a good understanding of why each view appears as it does.

We suggest that you try some of these viewpoints and experiment with others not listed. Your goal should be to get a feel for how different combinations move your point of view in relation to objects on the screen. You can use numbers other than 1, but precise distance relationships are difficult to follow in viewpoint definition.

<table>
<tr><td colspan="4" align="center">Vector Chart</td></tr>
<tr><td>X
Right–Left</td><td>Y
Back–Front</td><td>Z
Up–Down</td><td>View
Description</td></tr>
<tr><td>0</td><td>0</td><td>1</td><td>Plan or top</td></tr>
<tr><td>0</td><td>0</td><td>−1</td><td>"Worm's eye" or bottom</td></tr>
<tr><td>1</td><td>0</td><td>0</td><td>Right side</td></tr>
<tr><td>−1</td><td>0</td><td>0</td><td>Left side</td></tr>
<tr><td>0</td><td>1</td><td>0</td><td>Back</td></tr>
<tr><td>0</td><td>−1</td><td>0</td><td>Front</td></tr>
<tr><td>1</td><td>1</td><td>1</td><td>Northeast isometric</td></tr>
<tr><td>1</td><td>−1</td><td>1</td><td>Southeast isometric</td></tr>
</table>

Rotation

A second option shown in the prompt is Rotation. In this method, AutoCAD prompts for two angles. The first is an angle in the XY plane. It is measured from the x-axis, with 0 being straight out to the right, as usual.

The second angle goes up or down from the XY plane, with 0 being ground level. Thus, an angle of 90 degrees from the XY plane would define the plan view.

The following rotation chart gives you the rotation versions of some of the same major views shown in the Named View dialog box and the vector chart.

DDVPOINT

Rotated views are also accessible through the DDVPOINT command, which calls the Viewpoint Presets dialog box (Viewpoint Presets on the 3D Views submenu) shown in Figure 12-29. DDVPOINT can also be initiated by typing vp at the command line. We use this method to create a northeast isometric or back, right, top view.

⊕ Type vp or open the View menu, highlight 3D Views, and click Viewpoint Presets.

This opens the Viewpoint Presets dialog box, as shown in Figure 12-29. Using this method, AutoCAD lets you choose the two angles it needs to create a new viewpoint from the two "dials" on the left and right. The angle from the x-axis can be specified by selecting a point in the circle on the left or by typing a number in the edit box at the bottom. The angle from the XY plane can be typed or shown using the semicircle at the right of the dialog box. As you make

Rotation Chart

From X	From XY	View Description
0	0	Right side
0	90	Plan
90	0	Back side
180	0	Left side
270	0	Front
45	30	Northeast isometric
−45 (or ±315)	30	Southeast isometric
45	−30	Back, right, bottom
etc.	etc.	

selections by pointing in the circle or semicircle, the "needle" moves and the angle value is entered in the edit box.

⊞ Set the angle from the *x*-axis by picking the 45-degree area in the dial on the left, as shown in Figure 12-29.

Notice that selecting this box enters the value 45.0 in the From: X Axis edit box and moves the white pointer to 45. The angle of 45 moves us into the back, right viewpoint area, the northeast quadrant.

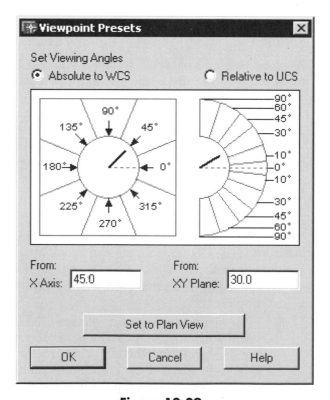

Figure 12-29

The second angle specification (the angle from the XY plane) can be shown in a similar manner by picking a point on the semicircle at the right or by typing a value in the edit box at the bottom. The angle you specify is the *z* dimension viewing position, a viewing height above or below the object. We choose to look down at an angle of 30 degrees.

⊕ Pick the area labeled +30.

   This moves the white pointer and enters the value 30 in the XY Plane edit box.

⊕ When your dialog box shows 45.0 and 30.0 as the two viewing angles, click OK to create the new viewpoint.

   Your screen should be redrawn to show a northeast isometric view.

Using the two angles in the dialog box to set rotation in the XY plane and the viewing height, you can create a large variety of points of view. We encourage you to experiment with these. Try changing the first angle to 225 to create a southwest isometric view. What two angles give you a front view at ground level? What does a view from below the object look like? As you experiment, pay attention to the UCS icon. With some views, you have to think carefully and watch the icon to understand which way the object is being presented.

The Compass and Axes System

If you enter the VPOINT command and then press Enter in response to the prompt, you see a display that resembles Figure 12-30.

The triple axes represent the orientation of the object. When you move your cursor, you can see these rotating. Some users might find this visualization easier to comprehend because it represents the object itself rather than your point of view in relation to the object. However, this effect is much more clearly realized in the 3DORBIT command, discussed in Chapter 13.

The other part of the display is a rather unusual representation of a globe. The horizontal and vertical axes show the X and Y dimensions, as you would expect, and the circles show the Z dimension. This actually shows a globe transformed into a

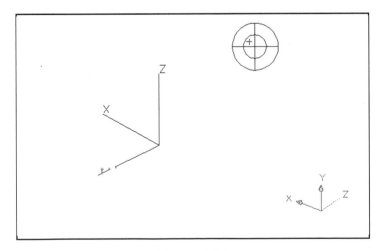

Figure 12-30

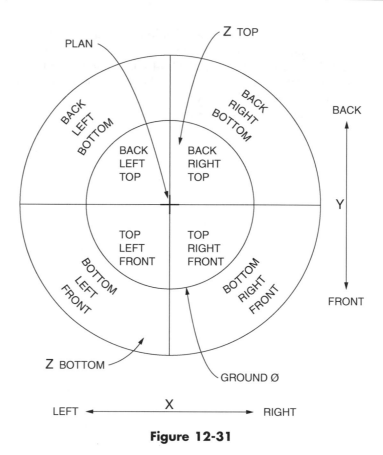

Figure 12-31

cone and then flattened. The north pole of the globe has become a point at the center of the compass, and the south pole has been widened into a circle at the outside of the compass. In between is another circle representing the equator, or ground 0 region.

This simply means that anywhere inside the first circle gives you a top-down view; outside the first circle gives you a bottom-up view. Anywhere on the middle circle gives you a ground-level view.

Notice the small cross that moves as you move your cursor. This represents your point of view in the coordinate system.

Figure 12-31 gives you a summary of the compass points and how they relate to standard views. Try them out if you like.

12.7 Review Material

Questions

1. It is possible to create a 3-D view in which the grid is indistinguishable from an isometric snap grid. How are this grid and objects drawn on it different from the isometric grid and objects drawn on it?

2. What is a wireframe model?
3. What is the significance of the box on the UCS icon?
4. What coordinates indicate a displacement of −5 in the z direction from the point (6,6,6)?
5. Why is it usually necessary to utilize object snap to select a point on an object outside of the XY plane of the current UCS?
6. What information defines a UCS?
7. What is the right-hand rule?
8. What command did you use in this chapter to draw a surface rather than a wire entity?
9. You were apparently able to draw a line from a point in the XY plane to a point above the plane without using object snap because both points appeared to be on grid snap points. What happens when you view this line from another viewpoint?
10. What angle from the XY plane defines a plan view?
11. What angle in the XY plane defines a front view?

Drawing Problems

1. Set up a southeast isometric 3-D viewpoint in the WCS and draw a regular hexagon with a circumscribed radius of 4.0 units.
2. Create a half-sized scaled copy of the hexagon centered at the same center as the original hexagon; then move the smaller hexagon 5.0 units up in the z direction.
3. Connect corresponding corners of the two hexagons to create a tapered hexagonal prism in three dimensions.
4. Create a UCS aligned with any of the faces of the hexagonal prism.
5. Use this UCS to draw the text Lamp Shade, at 0.3 unit high, on the face that aligns with the new UCS.
6. View the object from the world plan view, the plan view of the current UCS, and a northwest isometric view.

12.8 WWW Exercise 12 (Optional)

Whenever you are ready, complete the following:

⊕ Make sure that you are connected to your Internet service provider.

⊕ Type browser, open the Web toolbar, and select the Browse the Web tool, or open your system browser from the Windows taskbar.

⊕ If necessary, navigate to our companion website at www.prenhall. com/dixriley.

12.9   Drawing 12-1: Clamp

This drawing is similar to the one you did earlier in the chapter. Two major differences are that it is drawn from a different viewpoint and it includes dimensions in the 3-D view. This clamp drawing gives you additional practice in defining and using UCSs. Your drawing should include dimensions, border, and title.

Drawing Suggestions

*   We drew the outline of the clamp in a horizontal position and then worked from a northeast isometric point of view.
*   Begin in WCS plan view, drawing the horseshoe-shaped outline of the clamp. This includes fillets on the inside and outside of the clamp. The more you can do in plan view before copying to the top plane, the less duplicate editing you need to do later.
*   When the outline is drawn, switch to a northeast isometric view.
*   Copy the clamp outline up 1.50.
*   Define UCSs as needed, and save them whenever you are ready to switch to another UCS. You need to use these systems in your dimensioning.
*   The angled face, the slots, and the filleted surfaces can be drawn just as in the chapter.

Dimensioning in 3-D

The trick to dimensioning a 3-D object is that you need to restore the appropriate UCS for each set of dimensions. Think about how you want the text to appear. If text is to be aligned with the top of the clamp (e.g., the 5.75 overall length), you need to draw that dimension in a top UCS; if it is to align with the front of the object (the 17-degree angle and the 1.50 height), draw it in a front UCS, and so forth.

*   Define a UCS with the View option to add the border and title. Type UCS, and then v. This creates a UCS aligned with your current viewing angle.
*   Notice that this type of dimensioning can only be done in model space. Paper space is two dimensional by definition, so you cannot align dimensions with 3-D coordinate systems.

Setting Surftab1

Notice that there are eight lines defining the RULESURF fillets in this drawing, compared to six in the chapter. This number of lines is controlled by the setting of the Surftab1 variable, which is discussed in Chapter 13. You can change it by typing Surftab1 and entering 8 for the new value.

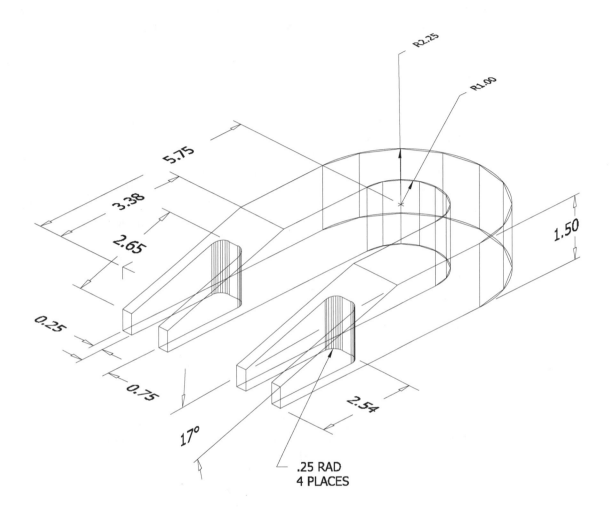

R2.25

R1.00

5.75

3.38

2.65

1.50

0.25

0.75

17°

2.54

.25 RAD
4 PLACES

CLAMP

DRAWING 12-1

12.10   Drawing 12-2: Guide Block

In this drawing, you work from dimensioned views to create a wireframe model. This brings up some new questions: Which view should you start with? How do you translate the views into the 3-D image? A good general rule is this: Draw the top or bottom in the XY plane of the WCS. Otherwise, you have trouble using the VPOINT command.

Drawing Suggestions

- In this drawing, it is tempting to draw the right side in WCS plan view first because that is where most of the detail is. If you do this, however, you have difficulty creating the view as shown. Instead, we suggest that you keep the bottom of the object in the WCS XY plane and work up from there, as has been the practice throughout this chapter. The reason for this is that the VPOINT command works relative to the WCS. Therefore, front–back, left–right, and top–bottom orientations make sense only if the top and bottom are drawn plan to the WCS.
- Draw the 12.50 × 8.00 rectangle shown in the top view and then copy it up 4.38 to form the top of the guide's base.
- Change to the same southeast isometric 3-D viewpoint used in the chapter.
- Connect the four corners to create a block outline of the base of the object.
- Now you can define a new UCS on the right side and do most of your work in that coordinate system, as that is where the detail is. Once you have defined the right-side UCS, you might want to go into its plan view to draw the right-side outline, including the arc and circle of the guide. Then come back to the 3-D view to copy back to the left.

  Tip: You can save some time switching viewpoints by using the VIEW command. When a view is saved, it includes the 3-D orientation along with the zoom factor that was current at the time of the save. Also, ZOOM previous can be used to restore a previous 3-D point of view. It does not, however, restore a UCS.

- Use RULESURF with Surftab1 set to 16 to fill in surfaces between the arcs and circles.

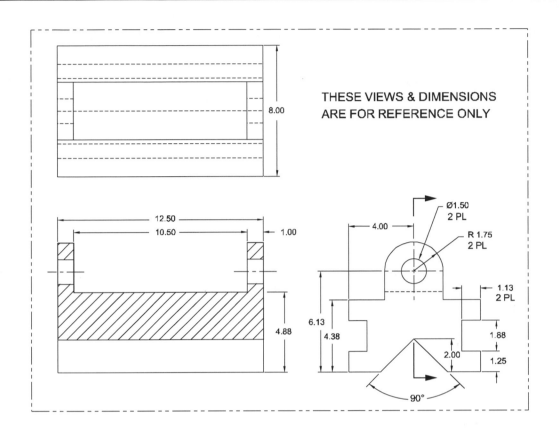

THESE VIEWS & DIMENSIONS
ARE FOR REFERENCE ONLY

8.00

12.50
10.50
1.00
4.88

Ø1.50
2 PL

R 1.75
2 PL

4.00

1.13
2 PL

6.13
4.38

1.88

2.00

1.25

90°

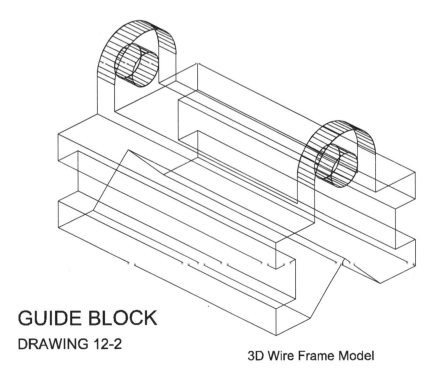

GUIDE BLOCK
DRAWING 12-2

3D Wire Frame Model

12.11   Drawing 12-3: Slide Mount

This drawing continues to use the same views, coordinate systems, and techniques as the previous drawings, but it has more detail and is a bit trickier.

Drawing Suggestions

- Draw the H-shaped outline of the top view in the WCS plan.
- Copy up in the z direction.
- Connect the corners to create a 3-D shape.
- Define a right-side view and create the slot and holes.
- Copy back to the left side, connect the corners, and trim inside the slot.
- Return to WCS (bottom plane).
- Use RULESURF between circles to create mounting holes.
- Draw filleted cutout and countersunk holes. Each countersunk hole requires three circles—two small and one larger.
- Use RULESURF to create inner surfaces of countersunk holes.

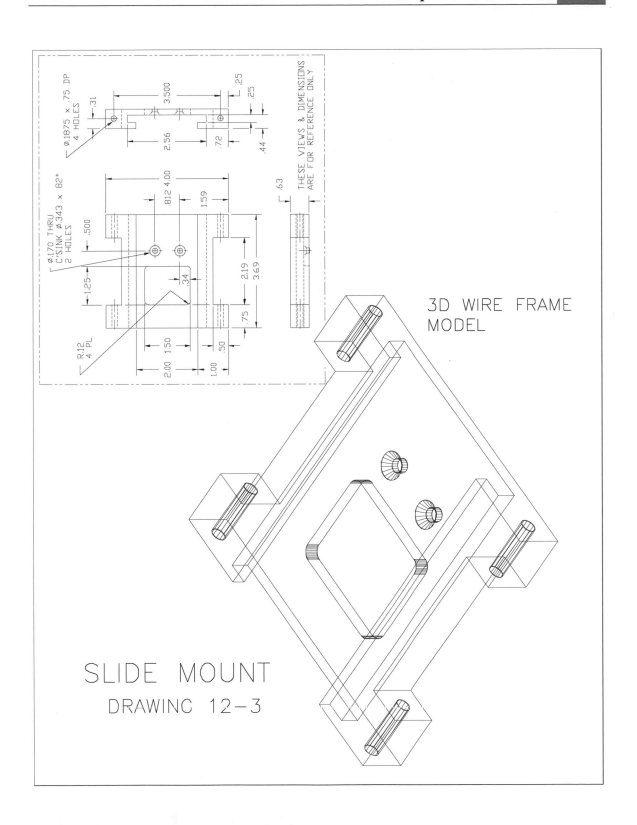

Ø.1875 x .75 DP
4 HOLES

3.500

.25
.25

2.56

.72

.44

.31

THESE VIEWS & DIMENSIONS
ARE FOR REFERENCE ONLY

Ø.170 THRU
C'SINK Ø.343 x 82°
2 HOLES

.812 4.00

1.59

.500

.34

2.19
3.69

1.25

.75

.63

R.12
4 PL

1.50

.50

2.00

1.00

3D WIRE FRAME
MODEL

SLIDE MOUNT
DRAWING 12-3

12.12   Drawing 12-4: Stair Layout

This wireframe architectural detail gives you a chance to use architectural units and limits in 3-D. It requires the use of a variety of edit commands.

Drawing Suggestions

- In the WCS plan view, begin with a 2″ × 12′ rectangle that will become the bottom of a floor joist. This keeps the bottom floor in the plan view, consistent with our practice in this chapter.
- Copy the rectangle up 8″ and connect lines to form the complete joist.
- Array 16″ on center to form the first floor.
- Copy all joists up 9′6″ to form the second floor.
- Create the stairwell opening in the second floor with double headers at each end.
- Add the subfloor to the first floor.
- The outline of the stair stringers can be constructed in a number of ways. One possibility is as follows: Draw a guideline down from the front of the left double header and then another over 10′10″ to locate the end of the run. From the right end of the run, draw one riser and one tread, beginning from the top surface of the subflooring; use a multiple copy and Endpoint osnaps to create the other steps. When you get to the top, you need to trim the top tread slightly to bring it flush with the header.
- We leave it to you to construct the back line of the stringer. It needs to be parallel with the stringer line and down 1′ from the top tread, as shown.

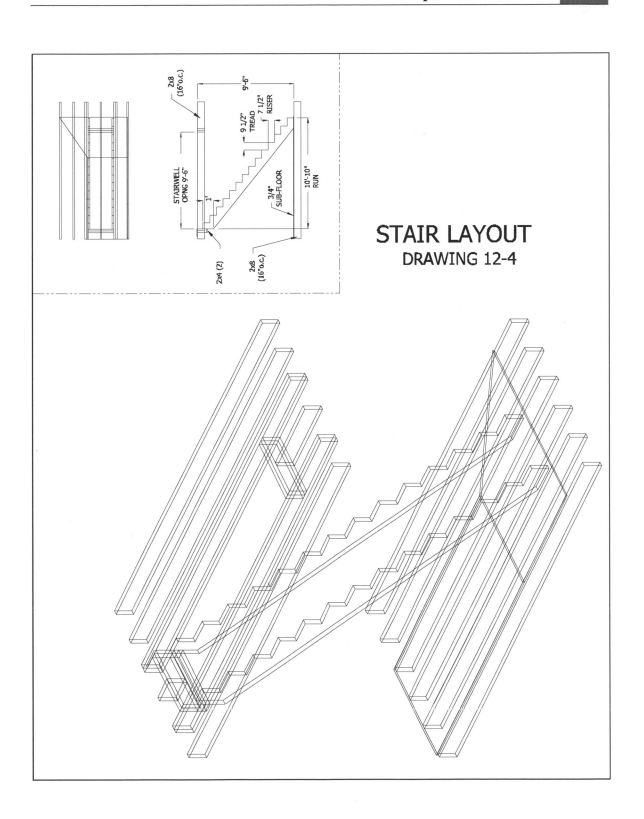

2x8
(16"o.c.)

9'-6"

9 1/2"
TREAD

7 1/2"
RISER

STAIRWELL
OPNG 9'-6"

10'-10"
RUN

3/4"
SUB-FLOOR

1"

2x4 (2)

2x8
(16"o.c.)

STAIR LAYOUT
DRAWING 12-4

12.13   Drawing 12-5: Housing

The objective for this drawing is to create a 3-D wireframe model of the housing. The RULESURF command is used extensively. If you use Section B-B as your front view, you will find it easier to create the 3-D wireframe.

Drawing Suggestions

- Draw the rectangular outline of the top view in the WCS plan.
- Copy up in the z direction to the appropriate levels.
- Change the origin of the UCS in the z direction to the proper height; then create the inner rectangle.
- Fillet all corners and rulesurf as necessary to create a 3-D shape.
- Use RULESURF between circles to create cylindrical pads and semicircular cutouts. Be sure to change the UCS to the appropriate position when adding detail to a particular view.
- Each counterbore hole requires three circles—two small and one larger.
- Use RULESURF to create inner surfaces of counterbore holes.

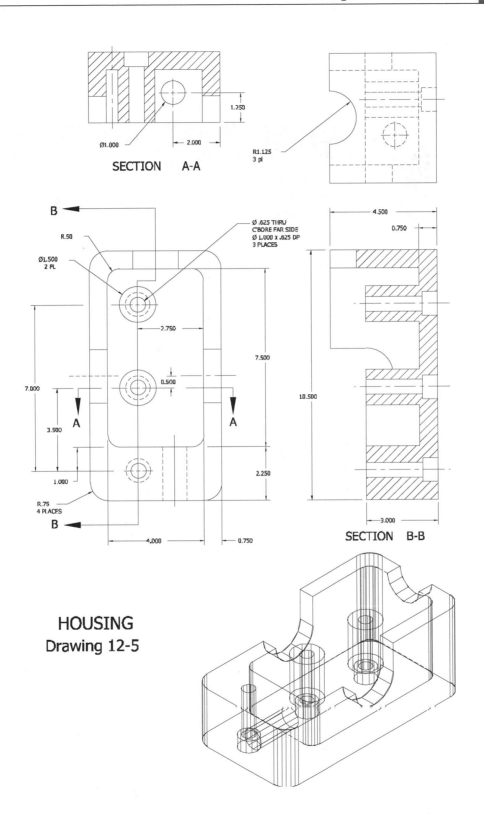

SECTION   A-A

Ø1.000

1.250

2.000

R1.125
3 pl

B

R.50

Ø1.500
2 PL

Ø .625 THRU
C'BORE FAR SIDE
Ø 1.000 X .625 DP
3 PLACES

2.750

0.500

7.500

7.000

3.500

A   A

1.000

R.75
4 PLACES

B

4.000   0.750

2.250

4.500

0.750

10.500

3.000

SECTION   B-B

HOUSING
Drawing 12-5

13 Surface Models

COMMANDS

3DFACE	EDGESURF	REVSURF	VPORTS
3DMESH	HIDE	RULESURF	
3DORBIT	PEDIT	TABSURF	

OVERVIEW

In this chapter, you experience a remarkable expansion of 3-D drawing power as we explore AutoCAD surface modeling. You can quickly see how surface models can be used to create far more realistic images than those that can be produced with wireframe models. Wireframe models create precise mathematical images of the edges and boundaries of objects in space. Surface models fill in the space between the lines with entities that represent the surfaces of objects. In this chapter, we introduce ways to create and present 3-D surfaces. The VPORTS command allows the creation of multiple tiled viewports so that an object can be viewed from several points of view simultaneously for more precise drawing and editing. The 3DFACE command is introduced to draw three- and four-sided surfaces. Polygon meshes are used to represent more complex three-dimensional surfaces. Most impressive of all, you begin to use AutoCAD's 3DORBIT command, which allows you to rotate images in 3-D space in real time as a more dynamic method of adjusting viewpoints.

TASKS

13.1 Using Multiple Tiled Viewports

GENERAL PROCEDURE

1. Highlight Viewports on the View menu.
2. Select New Viewports.
3. Select number and orientation of viewports.
4. Define views in each viewport.

A major feature needed to draw effectively in 3-D is the ability to view an object from several different points of view simultaneously as you work on it. The VPORTS command is easy to use and can save you from jumping back and forth between different views of an object. Viewports can be used in 2-D to place several zoom magnifications on the screen at once. More important, viewports can be used to place several 3-D viewpoints on the screen at once. This is a significant drawing aid. If you do not continually examine an object from different points of view, it is easy to create entities that appear correct in the current view but are clearly incorrect from other points of view.

In this task, we divide your screen in half and define two views so that you can visualize an object in plan view and 3-D isometric view at the same time. As you work, remember that this is only a display command. The viewports we use in this chapter are simple model space "tiled" viewports. Tiled viewports cover the complete drawing area, do not overlap, and cannot be plotted simultaneously. Plotting multiple viewports is accomplished in paper space layouts with floating viewports, as demonstrated previously in Chapter 6.

⊕ To begin, open a new drawing using the 1B template.

⊕ Highlight Viewports on the View menu.

This opens the submenu shown in Figure 13-1.

⊕ In this task, we use the New Viewports option.

⊕ Select New Viewports.

This opens the Viewports dialog box shown in Figure 13-2. The dialog box has two tabs. Because you selected New Viewports from the menu, the New Viewports tab is showing. If you had selected Named Viewports, the other tab would be showing. The two tabs are similar, but New Viewports contains predefined options, whereas the Named Viewports tab contains viewport configurations that have been previously created and saved in your drawing.

Looking at the New Viewports tab, at the top you see an edit box where you can give a name to a viewport configuration when you define it. This is only useful if you create a configuration that is not already on the list. The white panel on the left lists predefined configurations. Active Model Configuration is basically the current configuration in the drawing. Single is the one viewport drawing area we have been working in since the beginning. The others are defined by number and location of viewports.

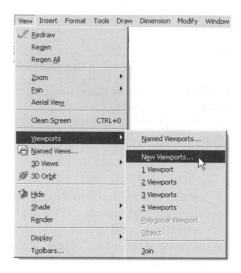

Figure 13-1

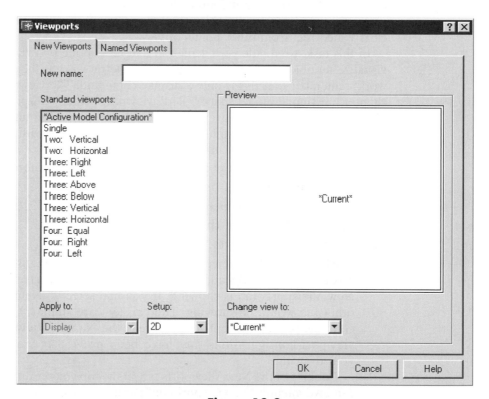

Figure 13-2

⊕   Select Two Vertical:

The preview on the right changes to show two vertical viewports, as illustrated in Figure 13-3. Notice that both viewports contain the current model space display. Look at the three list boxes at the bottom of the dialog box. The Apply

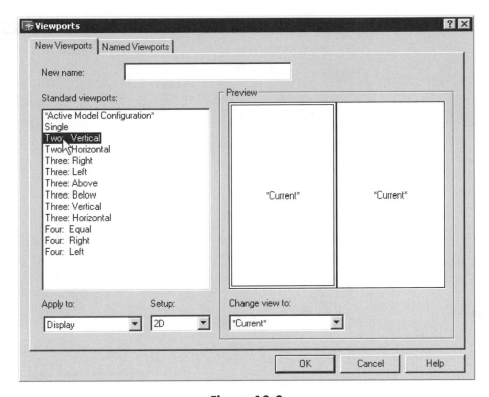

Figure 13-3

to: list gives you the choice of applying configuration changes to the whole display or just to a selected viewport. This means you can create viewports by dividing already defined viewports. For now, Display should be selected in this list.

The Setup list has two options, 2D and 3D. Standard 2-D configurations always start with the current view in each viewport. 3-D configurations add standard top, front, and southeast isometric views. If you look at the third list box, labeled Change view to: you can see that Current is the only choice. Now try the following:

⊕ Open the Setup list and select 3D.

The preview changes to show a top view on the left and a southeast isometric view on the right, as shown in Figure 13-4. Notice that the top viewport is selected with a border in the preview and that *Top* is now showing in the Change view to: list.

⊕ Open the Change view to: list.

In addition to Top, you will see Bottom, Front, Back, Left, and four standard isometric viewpoint options. With this list, you can change the view in any selected viewport to create your own configuration. Then if you add a name in the New name edit box at the top of the dialog box, the named configuration is added to a list on the Named Viewports tab.

⊕ Select the right viewport in the preview by double clicking anywhere inside it.

The right viewport is selected with a border and the Change view list shows Southeast Isometric. If you open the list, you see the same set of eight options.

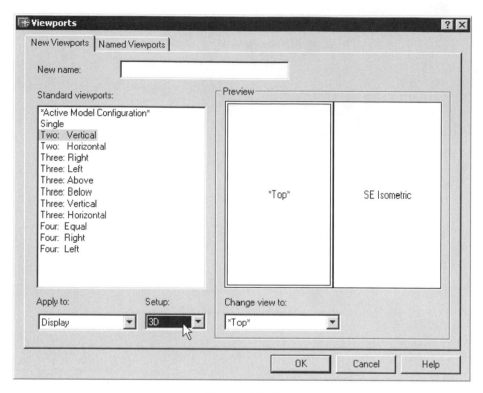

Figure 13-4

The standard Two: Vertical 3D viewport with a top view on the left and a southeast isometric view on the right is the configuration we work with in this chapter, but before leaving the dialog box, look at some other options.

⊕ Select Three: Right.

Your preview now resembles the one in Figure 13-5. This is also a very common configuration.

⊕ Select Four: Equal, and any other configurations you wish to preview.

⊕ Select Two: Vertical again before leaving the dialog box.

⊕ Click OK to exit the dialog box.

Your screen should resemble Figure 13-6, except that the grid is off in the right viewport.

If you move your pointing device back and forth between the windows, you see an arrow when you are on the left and the crosshairs when you are on the right. This indicates that the right window is currently active. Drawing and editing can be performed only in the active window. To work in another window, you need to make it current by picking it with your pointing device. Often this can be done while a command is in progress.

⊕ Move the cursor into the left window and press the pick button on your pointing device.

Now the crosshairs appear in the left viewport, and you see the arrow when you move into the right viewport.

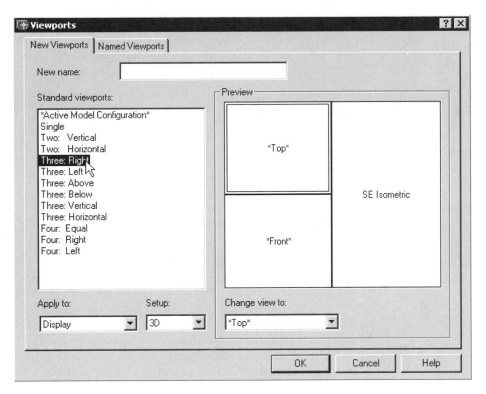

Figure 13-5

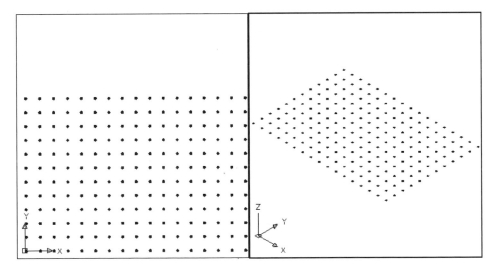

Figure 13-6

⊕ Move the cursor back to the right and press the pick button again.
    This makes the right window active again.

⊕ If the grid is off in your right viewport, turn it on (press F7).

We are now ready to begin drawing in this viewport configuration. Once you have defined viewports, any drawing or editing in the active viewport appears in all the viewports. As you draw, watch what happens in both viewports.

13.2   Creating Surfaces with 3DFACE

GENERAL PROCEDURE

1. Open the Draw menu, highlight Surfaces, and select 3D Face, or select the 3D Face tool from the Surfaces toolbar.
2. Pick three or four points going around the face.
3. Continue defining edges or press Enter to exit the command.

3DFACE creates triangular and quadrilateral surfaces. 3-D faces are built by entering points in groups of three or four to define the outlines of triangles or quadrilaterals, similar to objects formed by the 2D SOLID command. The surface of a 3-D face is not shown on the screen, but it is recognized by the HIDE command and by the RENDER command and other rendering programs, such as 3D Studio.

Layering is critical in surface modeling. Surfaces quickly complicate a drawing so that object selection and object snap become difficult or impossible. Also, you might want to be able to turn layers off or freeze them to achieve the results you want from the HIDE command. You might eventually want a number of layers specifically defined for faces and surfaces, but this is not necessary for the current exercise.

⊕   **Open the Draw menu and highlight Surfaces.**

This calls the submenu shown in Figure 13-7. There is also a Surfaces toolbar with a 3D Face tool, as shown in Figure 13-8.

⊕   **Select 3D Face.**

AutoCAD prompts

      `Specify first point or [Invisible]:`

You can define points in either of the two viewports. In fact, you can even switch viewports in the middle of the command.

⊕   **Pick a point similar to P1, as shown in Figure 13-9.**

AutoCAD prompts

      `Specify second point or [Invisible]:`

⊕   **Pick a second point, moving around the perimeter of the face, as shown.**

Be aware that the correct order for defining 3-D faces is different from the 2-D SOLID command (see Chapter 9). It is important to pick points in order around the face; otherwise, you get a bowtie or hourglass effect.

AutoCAD prompts

      `Specify third point or [Invisible]<exit>:`

Figure 13-7

Figure 13-8

⊕ Pick a third point, as shown.

AutoCAD prompts

Specify fourth point or [Invisible]<create three-sided face>:

Note: If you pressed Enter now, AutoCAD would draw the outline of a triangular face, using the three points already given.

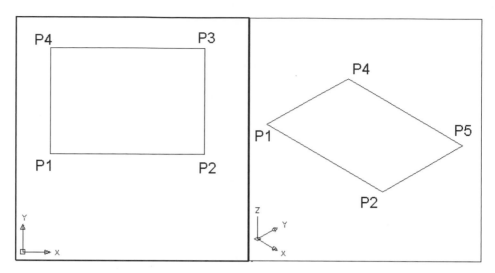

Figure 13-9

⊕   Pick the fourth point of the face.

AutoCAD draws the fourth edge of the face automatically when four points have been given, so it is not necessary to complete or close the rectangle.

AutoCAD continues to prompt for third and fourth points so that you can draw a series of surfaces to cover an area with more than four edges. Keep in mind, however, that drawing faces in series is only a convenience. The result is a collection of independent three- and four-sided faces.

⊕   Press Enter or the spacebar to exit the 3DFACE command.

In the next task, we copy this face to demonstrate the HIDE command. But first, a word about invisible edges.

Invisible Edges in 3-D Faces

The edges of a 3-D face can be visible or invisible as desired. To define an invisible edge, type i before entering the first point of the edge. You can even define phantom 3-D faces in which no edges are visible. There is also an EDGE command that allows you to change the visibility of edges after they have been drawn.

Take a look at Figure 13-10. This figure illustrates the need for invisible edges in 3-D faces. Because 3DFACE only draws triangles or quadrilaterals, objects with more than four edges must be drawn as combinations of three- and four-sided shapes. An octagon, for example, can be drawn as two trapezoids and a rectangle, as shown. However, you would not want the two horizontal edges across the middle showing, so the command allows you to make them invisible by typing i before picking the point that begins the invisible edge. This takes forethought and planning. You must remember that the endpoint of a visible edge also might be the starting point of the next invisible edge.

It might be easier to draw edges visible and then go back and make some invisible using the EDGE command. You can access EDGE by opening the Draw

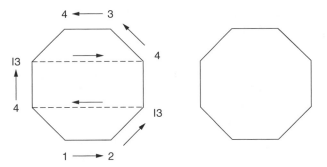

Figure 13-10

menu, highlighting surfaces, and selecting Edge. The command asks you to select edges and then reverses the visibility of any edge you select. It includes a Display option, which displays all edges so that they can be selected.

Note: Invisible edges are hidden if the Splframe system variable is set to 0, the default setting. If the variable is set to 1, invisible edges are displayed. To change this setting, type splframe and then 1.

13.3 Removing Hidden Lines with HIDE

GENERAL PROCEDURE
1. Type hi, or open the View menu and select Hide.
2. Wait.

The HIDE command is easy to execute. However, execution can be slow in large drawings, and careful work might be required to create a drawing that hides the way you want it to. This is an important objective in surface modeling. When you have everything right, HIDE temporarily removes all lines and objects that would be obstructed in the current view, resulting in a more realistic representation of the object in space. A correctly surfaced model can also be used to create a shaded rendering. Hiding has no effect on wireframe drawings, because there are no surfaces to obstruct lines behind them.

⊕ To begin this exercise, you should have the 3-D face from the previous task on your screen.

⊕ Copy the face up two units in the z direction, using the following procedure:

1. Select the Copy tool from the Modify menu.
2. Select the face.
3. Right-click to end object selection.

4. Type and enter 0,0,2.
5. Press Enter or the spacebar at the prompt for a second point.

You now have two 3-D faces in your drawing. Because the second is directly over the first, you cannot see both in the top view. From the southeast isometric viewpoint in the right viewport, however, the second face only partially covers the first. Because these are surfaces rather than wireframes, the top face should hide part of the lower face.

✛ Make the right viewport active.

✛ Type hi, or open the View menu and select Hide.

Your screen should be regenerated to resemble Figure 13-11. In this case, the hiding and regeneration happen very quickly. In a larger drawing, you have to wait.

The following are some important points about hidden line removal that you should read before continuing:

1. Hidden line removal can be performed from the Plot Configuration dialog box. However, due to the time involved and the difficulty of getting a hidden view just right, it is usually better to experiment on the screen first and then plot with hidden lines removed when you know you will get the image you want.

2. The image created through hidden line removal is not retained in blocking, wblocking, grouping, or saving views.

3. Layer control is important in hidden line removal. Layers that are frozen are ignored by the HIDE command, but layers that are off are treated like visible layers. This can, for example, create peculiar blank spaces in your display if you have left surfaces or solids on a layer that is off at the time of hidden line removal.

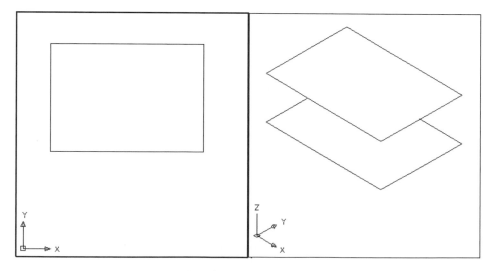

Figure 13-11

13.4   Using 3-D Polygon Mesh Commands

GENERAL PROCEDURE

1. Create geometry to be used in defining the surface.
2. If necessary, set Surftab1 and Surftab2.
3. Enter a 3-D polygon mesh command.
4. Use existing geometry to define the surface.

3DFACE can be used to create simple surfaces. However, most surface models require large numbers of faces to approximate the surfaces of real objects. Consider the number of faces in Figure 13-12, the globe you create when you do Drawing 13-3. Obviously, you would not want to draw such an image one face at a time.

AutoCAD includes a number of commands that make the creation of some types of surfaces very easy. These powerful commands create 3-D polygon meshes. Polygon meshes are made up of 3-D faces and are defined by a matrix of vertices. They can be treated as single entities and edited with the PEDIT command or exploded into individual 3-D faces.

⊕   To begin this task, erase the two faces from the last task and draw an arc and a line below it, as shown in Figure 13-13. Exact sizes and locations are not important.

The entities can be drawn in either viewport.

Now we define some 3-D surfaces using the arc and line you have just drawn.

Figure 13-12

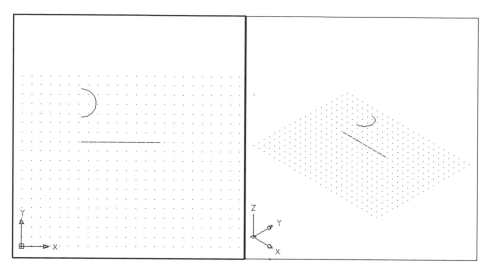

Figure 13-13

TABSURF

The first surface we draw is called a *tabulated surface*. To use the TABSURF command, you need a line or curve to define the shape of the surface and a vector to show its size and direction. The result is a surface generated by repeating the shape of the original curve at every point along the path specified by the vector.

⊞ Open the Draw menu, highlight Surfaces, and select Tabulated Surface.

There is also a Tabulated Surface tool on the Surfaces toolbar, shown previously in Figure 13-8. AutoCAD prompts

        Select object for path curve:

The path curve is the line or curve that determines the shape of the surface. In our case, it is the arc.

⊞ Pick the arc.

AutoCAD prompts for a vector:

        Select object for direction vector:

We use the line. Notice that the vector does not need to be connected to the path curve. Its location is not significant, only its direction and length.

There is an oddity here to watch for as you pick the vector. If you pick a point near the left end of the line, AutoCAD interprets the vector as extending from left to right. Accordingly, the surface is drawn to the right. By the same token, if your point is near the right end of the line, the surface is drawn to the left. Most of the time you can avoid confusion by picking a point on the side of the vector nearest the curve itself.

⊞ Pick a point on the left side of the line.

Your screen is redrawn to resemble Figure 13-14. Notice that this is a flat surface even though it might look 3-D in the left viewport. Tabulated surfaces can be fully 3-D, depending on the path and vector chosen to define them. In

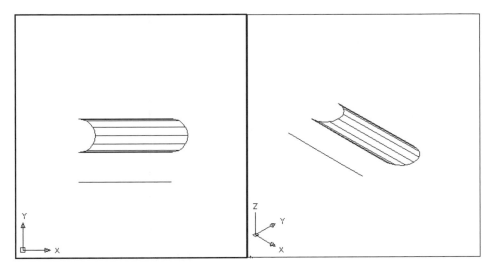

Figure 13-14

this case we have an arc and a vector that are both entirely in the XY plane, so the resulting surface is also in that plane.

Surftab1

Notice that the surface is defined by long, narrow faces that run parallel to the vector. If you zoom up on either end of the surface, you see that the arc is only approximated by the shorter edges of these six faces. Unlike the polygons or broken curves AutoCAD sometimes uses to display arcs and circles, to speed regeneration time, this mesh of quadrilateral faces is the actual current definition of this surface. To achieve a more accurate approximation, we can increase the number of faces. This is done by changing the setting of the Surftab1 variable and drawing the object again.

Let's undo the tabulated surface so that we can draw it again with a new Surftab1 setting.

⊕ Type u or select the Undo tool from the Standard toolbar.

⊕ Type surftab1.

AutoCAD prompts

        Enter new value for SURFTAB1 <6>:

The default value shows why we see six lines in the tabulated surface. When we change the setting, we get a different number of lines and degree of accuracy.

⊕ Type 12.

⊕ Open the Draw menu, highlight Surfaces, and select Tabulated Surface.

⊕ Pick the arc for the path curve.

⊕ Pick the line for the direction vector.

Your screen should now resemble Figure 13-15.

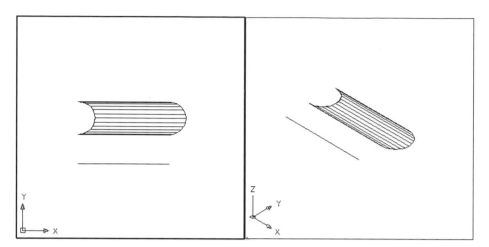

Figure 13-15

RULESURF

TABSURF is useful in defining surfaces that are the same on both ends, assuming you have one end and a vector. Often, however, you have no vector, or you need to draw a surface between two different paths. In these cases, you need the RULESURF command.

For example, what if we need to define a surface between the line and the arc? Let's try it.

⊕ Type u to undo the last tabulated surface.

⊕ Open the Draw menu, highlight Surfaces, and select Ruled Surface.

You are familiar with this command sequence from Chapter 12. The first prompt is

```
Select first defining curve:
```

⊕ Pick the arc, using a point near the bottom.

Remember that you must pick points on corresponding sides of the two defining curves to avoid an hourglass effect. AutoCAD prompts

```
Select second defining curve:
```

⊕ Pick the line, using a point near the left end.

Your screen should resemble Figure 13-16. Again, notice that this surface is within the XY plane even though it might look 3-D. Ruled surfaces can be drawn just as easily between curves that are not coplanar.

If you look closely, you notice that this ruled surface is drawn with 12 faces, the result of our Surftab1 setting.

Some other typical examples of ruled surfaces are shown in the chart in Figure 13-22 at the end of this task.

EDGESURF

TABSURF creates surfaces that are the same at both ends and move along a straight-line vector. RULESURF draws surfaces between any two boundaries.

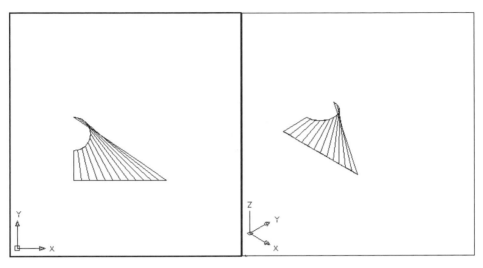

Figure 13-16

EDGESURF draws surfaces that are bounded by four curves. Edge-defined surfaces have a lot of geometric flexibility. The only restriction is that they must be bounded on all four sides. That is, they must have four edges that touch.

To create an EDGESURF, we need to undo our last ruled surface and add two more edges.

⊕ Type u.

⊕ Add a line and an arc to your screen, as shown in Figure 13-17.

  Remember, you can draw in either viewport.

⊕ Open the Draw menu, highlight Surfaces, and select Edge Surface.

  AutoCAD prompts for the four edges of the surface, one at a time:

    Select object 1 for surface edge:

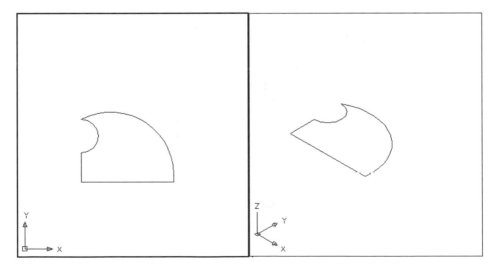

Figure 13-17

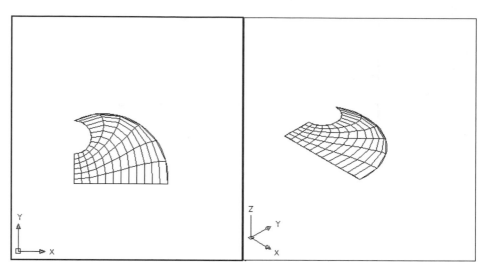

Figure 13-18

⊞ Pick the smaller arc.

  AutoCAD prompts

    Select object 2 for surface edge:

⊞ Pick the larger arc.

  AutoCAD prompts

    Select object 3 for surface edge:

⊞ Pick the longer line.

  AutoCAD prompts

    Select object 4 for surface edge:

⊞ Pick the shorter line.

  Your screen should now resemble Figure 13-18.

Surftab2

There is something new to be aware of here. With TABSURF and RULESURF, surfaces were defined by edges moving in only one direction. With EDGESURF, you have a matrix of faces and edges going two ways. Notice that there are 12 edges going one way and 6 going the other, as shown in Figure 13-18. This brings us to the variable Surftab2. If we change its setting to 12 also, we see 12 edges in each direction.

  Try it.

⊞ Type u to undo the EDGESURF command.

⊞ Type surftab2.

⊞ Type 12.

⊞ Enter the EDGESURF command and select the four edges again.

  The result should resemble Figure 13-19.

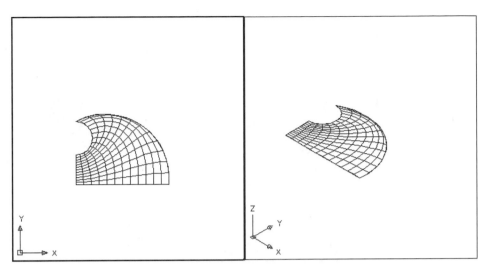

Figure 13-19

REVSURF

We have one more 3-D polygon mesh command to explore, and this one is probably the most impressive of all. REVSURF creates surfaces by spinning a curve through a given angle around an axis of revolution. Just as tabulated surfaces are spread along a linear path, surfaces of revolution follow a circular or arc-shaped path. As a result, surfaces of revolution are always fully 3-D, even if their defining geometry is in a single plane, as it is here.

⊕ In preparation for this exercise, undo the EDGESURF, so that your screen resembles Figure 13-17 again.

We create two surfaces of revolution. The first is a complete 360-degree surface using the smaller arc and the smaller line for definition. The second is a 270-degree surface using the larger arc and the larger line.

⊕ Open the Draw menu, highlight Surfaces, and select Revolved Surface.

AutoCAD needs an object to revolve and an axis of revolution to define the surface. The first prompt is

         Select object to revolve:

⊕ Pick the smaller arc.

AutoCAD prompts

         Select object that defines the axis of revolution:

⊕ Pick the smaller line.

AutoCAD now needs to know whether you want the surface to begin at the object itself or somewhere else around the circle of revolution:

         Specify start angle <0>:

The default is to start at the object.

⊕ Press Enter or the spacebar.

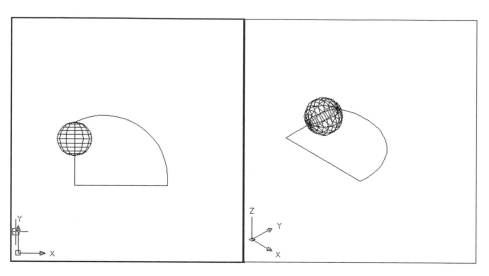

Figure 13-20

AutoCAD prompts

```
Specify included angle (+=ccw, -=cw) <360>:
```

Entering a positive or negative degree measure causes the surface to be drawn around an arc rather than a full circle. The default gives us a complete circle.

⊕ Press Enter or the spacebar.

Your screen should be drawn to resemble Figure 13-20. If you look closely, you can see that this globe has 12 edges in each direction. REVSURF, like EDGESURF, uses both Surftab1 and Surftab2. Also notice that this command gives us a way to create spheres. If the path curve is a true semicircle and the axis is along the diameter of the semicircle, then the result is a sphere. However, there is another way to create a sphere, which we discuss in Task 13.5.

Now we create a larger surface that does not start at 0 degrees and does not include a full circle.

⊕ Press the spacebar to repeat the REVSURF command.

⊕ Pick the larger arc as the object to revolve.

⊕ Pick the left end of the longer line for the axis of revolution.

If you pick the right end, the positive and negative angles are reversed in the two steps following.

⊕ Type 90 for the start angle.

This causes the surface to begin 90 degrees up from the XY plane.

⊕ Type −270 for the included angle.

This causes the surface to revolve 270 degrees clockwise around the axis. The result should resemble Figure 13-21. You might have to use PAN or the scroll bars in one or both viewports to position the objects on the screen as we have shown them.

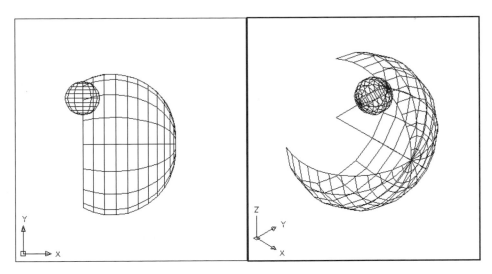

Figure 13-21

Leave this set of surfaces on your screen for the next task, where we use them to demonstrate the 3DORBIT command. Take a look at the polygon mesh examples in Figure 13-22 before proceeding.

13.5 Adjusting Viewpoints with 3DORBIT

GENERAL PROCEDURE

1. Center objects within the viewport.
2. Select objects for viewing.
3. Select 3D Orbit from the View menu.
4. Dynamically adjust viewpoint and shading.

The 3DORBIT command is a dramatic method for adjusting 3-D viewpoints and images. You can quickly see how much more powerful this command is than the VPOINT command and preset views we have introduced so far. This power can lead you into confusing places, however, and should be seen as a tool with its own uses that are distinct from the uses of the simpler preset views with which you are familiar. Using standard views like top, front, and isometric views is generally all you need for the creation and editing of objects, and sticking with these views keeps you well grounded and clear about your position in relation to objects on the screen. However, when you move from drawing and editing into presentation, you find 3DORBIT vastly more satisfying and freeing than the static viewpoint options.

You have on your screen an odd set of surfaces in which a large half-opened globe appears to be swallowing a smaller sphere. Because this is a fully three-dimensional surface model and no two sides of this image are the same, it is ideal for demonstrating 3DORBIT in action.

⊕   Begin by making the right viewport active.

3DORBIT makes use of a tool called an arcball, as shown in Figure 13-23. The first thing you need to do to get a feel for how the arcball works is to have your objects

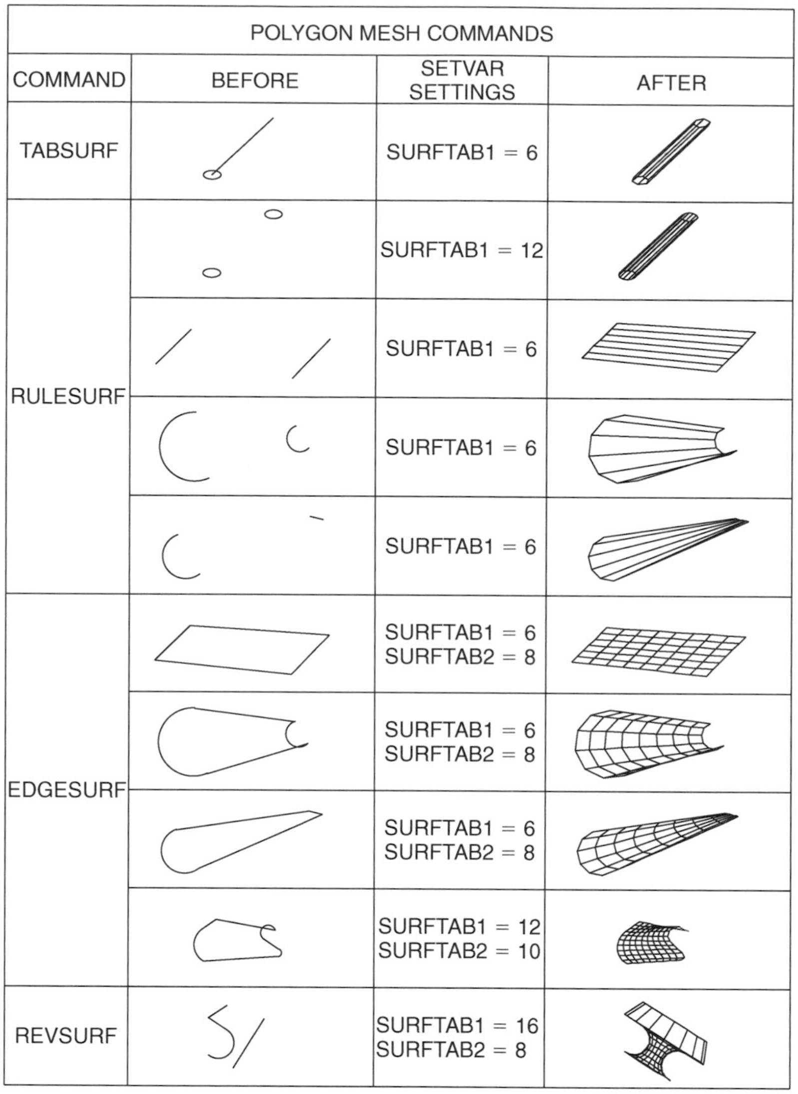

POLYGON MESH COMMANDS			
COMMAND	BEFORE	SETVAR SETTINGS	AFTER
TABSURF		SURFTAB1 = 6	
RULESURF		SURFTAB1 = 12	
		SURFTAB1 = 6	
		SURFTAB1 = 6	
		SURFTAB1 = 6	
EDGESURF		SURFTAB1 = 6 SURFTAB2 = 8	
		SURFTAB1 = 6 SURFTAB2 = 8	
		SURFTAB1 = 6 SURFTAB2 = 8	
		SURFTAB1 = 12 SURFTAB2 = 10	
REVSURF		SURFTAB1 = 16 SURFTAB2 = 8	

Figure 13-22

roughly centered within the arcball circle. You can do this precisely using Zoom Center or you can be less precise using the drawing area scroll bars. It is simple if you understand one thing: The center of the arcball is the center of the current viewport. Therefore, to place your objects near the center of the arcball, you must place them near the center of the viewport, or, more precisely, you must place the center point of the objects at the center of the display. We will be switching back to a single viewport configuration, but it might be easier to center objects in the current setup, so we do that first.

⊕ Using Zoom Center or the horizontal and vertical scroll bars, adjust objects in the right viewport so that they are roughly centered on the center of the viewport.

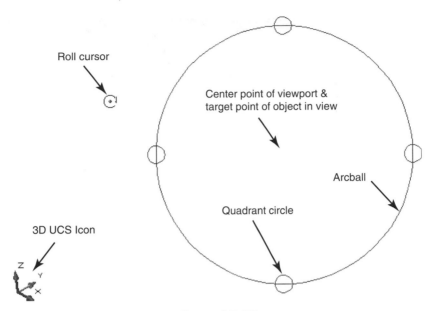

Roll cursor

Center point of viewport &
target point of object in view

Arcball

Quadrant circle

3D UCS Icon

Figure 13-23

Now we switch to a single viewport.

⊕ Turn off the Grid in the right viewport (F7).

⊕ With the right viewport active, open the View menu, highlight Viewports, and select 1Viewport.

Your screen should resemble Figure 13-24. Before entering 3DORBIT you can select viewing objects. 3DORBIT performance is improved by limiting the number of objects used in viewing. Whatever adjustments are made to the viewpoint on the selected objects are applied to the viewpoint on the entire drawing when the command is exited. In our case, we have a fairly simple image to view, so we can use the whole drawing.

Figure 13-24

Figure 13-25

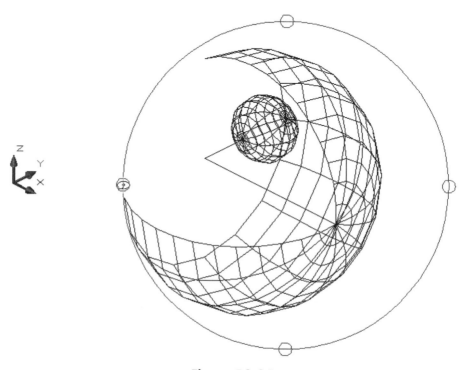

Figure 13-26

⊞ Open the View menu and select 3D Orbit.

There is also a 3D Orbit toolbar with a 3D Orbit tool, as shown in Figure 13-25. Your screen is redrawn with the arcball surrounding your surface model, as shown in Figure 13-26. Notice also the 3D UCS icon with the *x*-axis in red, the *y*-axis in green, and the *z*-axis in blue.

The Arcball and Rotation Cursors

The arcball is a somewhat complex image, but it is very easy to use once you get the hang of it. We already know that the center of the arcball is the center of the viewport, or the center of the drawing area in this case because we are working in a single viewport. AutoCAD uses a camera–target analogy to explain viewpoint adjustment. Your viewpoint on the drawing is called the *camera position*. The point at which the camera is aimed is called the *target*. In 3DORBIT, the target point is fixed at the center of the arcball. As you change viewpoints, you are moving yourself around in relation to this fixed target point.

There are four modes of adjustment, which we take up one at a time. Each mode has its own cursor image, and the mode you are in depends on where you start in relation to the arcball. Try the following steps:

⊕ Carefully move the cursor into the small circle at the left quadrant of the arcball, as shown in Figure 13-26.

When the cursor is placed within either the right or the left quadrant circle, the horizontal rotation cursor appears. This cursor consists of a horizontal elliptical arrow surrounding a small sphere, with a vertical axis running through the sphere. Using this cursor creates horizontal motion around the vertical axis of the arcball. This cursor and the others are shown in Figure 13-27.

3D ORBIT CURSOR	
CURSOR	DESCRIPTION
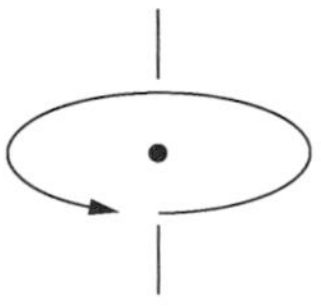 HORIZONTAL	Horizontal cursor icon displays when you move the cursor over one of the small circles on the left or right of the arcball. Clicking and dragging from either of these points rotates the view around the vertical axis that extends through the center of the arcball. The vertical axis is located on the cursor by a vertical line.
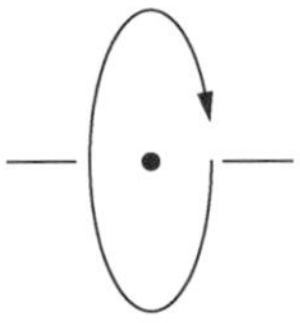 VERTICAL	Vertical cursor icon displays when you move the cursor over one of the small circles on the top or bottom of the arcball. Clicking and dragging from either of these points rotates the view around the horizontal axis that extends through the center of the arcball. The horizontal axis is located on the cursor by a horizontal line.
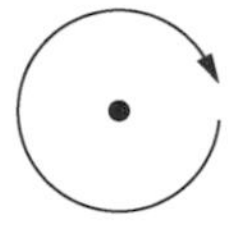 ROLL	Roll cursor icon displays when you move the cursor outside the arcball. Clicking outside the arcball and dragging the cursor around the arcball moves the view around an axis that extends through the center of the arcball, perpendicular to the screen. This is called a roll.
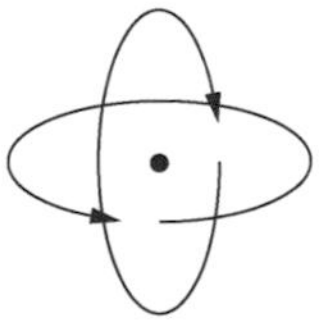 FREE ROTATION	Free rotation cursor icon displays when you move the cursor inside the arcball. Clicking inside the arcball and dragging the cursor around manipulates the view freely. It works as if your cursor were grabbing a sphere surrounding the objects and dragging the sphere around the target point. You can drag horizontally, vertically, and diagonally.
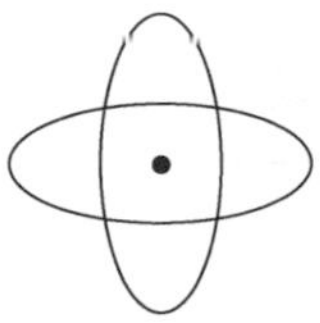 3DCORBIT	Continuous orbit cursor displays when you select it from the shortcut menu under (more). Click in the drawing area and drag the cursor in any direction to get the objects moving in the direction that you specify. The speed of the cursor movement determines the speed at which the objects spin.

Figure 13-27

⊕ With the cursor in the left quadrant circle and the horizontal cursor displayed, press the pick button and hold it down.

Adjustments in 3DORBIT are made by pressing the pick button, holding it down, and dragging it across the screen.

⊕ Slowly drag the cursor from the left quadrant circle to the right quadrant circle, observing the surface model and the 3D UCS icon as you go.

As long as you keep the pick button depressed, the horizontal cursor is displayed.

⊕ With the cursor in the right quadrant circle, release the pick button.

You have created a 180-degree rotation. Your screen should resemble Figure 13-28.

⊕ With the cursor in the right quadrant circle and the horizontal cursor displayed, press the pick button again and then move the cursor slowly back to the left quadrant circle.

If you move very slowly and watch closely, you notice that there is some ambiguity in what you are seeing. Are the objects continuing a 360-degree rotation, or reversing the previous 180 degrees? Try it again without releasing the pick button.

⊕ Place the cursor in the left quadrant circle, press the pick button, drag to the right, and then move back to the left.

Observe carefully. If foreground and background suddenly shift for you, that's good. That is the ambiguity we are talking about. We resolve this confusion in Task 13.6, but first try the vertical rotation cursor.

⊕ Carefully move the cursor into the small circle at the top of the arcball.

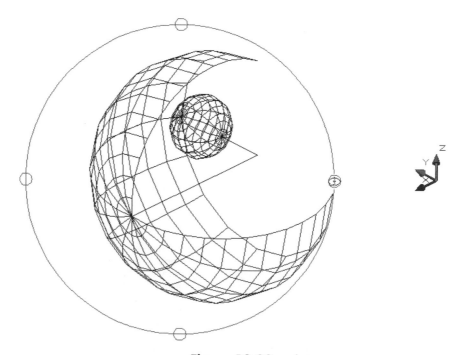

Figure 13-28

The vertical rotation cursor appears. When this cursor is visible, rotation is around the horizontal axis, as shown in the chart in Figure 13-27.

⊕ With the vertical rotation cursor displayed, press the pick button and drag down toward the circle at the lower quadrant.

⊕ This time, do not release the pick button, but continue moving down to the bottom of the screen.

The viewpoint continues to adjust and the vertical cursor is displayed as long as you hold down the pick button. Notice that 3D Orbit uses the entire screen, not just the drawing area. You can drag all the way down through the command line, the status bar, and the Windows taskbar.

⊕ Spend some time experimenting with vertical and horizontal rotation. We know you want to.

Note that you always have to start in a quadrant to achieve horizontal or vertical rotation. What happens when you move horizontally with the vertical cursor displayed or vice versa? How much rotation can you achieve in one pick-and-drag sequence vertically? What about horizontally? Are they the same amount? Why is there a difference?

⊕ When you have finished experimenting, try to rotate the image back to its original position, shown previously in Figure 13-26.

If you are unable to get back to this position, don't worry. We show you how to do this easily in Task 13.6. Now let's try the other two modes.

⊕ Move the cursor anywhere outside the arcball.

With the cursor outside the arcball you can see the roll icon, the third icon in the chart in Figure 13-27. Rolling creates rotation around an imaginary axis pointing directly toward you out of the center of the arcball.

⊕ With the roll icon displayed, press the pick button and drag the cursor in a wide circle well outside the circumference of the arcball.

Notice again that you can use the entire screen, outside of the arcball.

⊕ Try rolling both counterclockwise and clockwise.

⊕ Release the pick button and then start again.

Note that you must be in the drawing area with the roll icon displayed to initiate a roll and that you must stay outside the arcball.

Finally, try the free rotation cursor. This is the most powerful, and therefore the trickiest form of rotation. The free cursor appears when you start inside the arcball or when you cross into the arcball while rolling. It allows rotation horizontally, vertically, and diagonally, depending on the movement of your pointing device.

⊕ Move the cursor inside the arcball and watch for the free rotation icon.

⊕ With the free rotation icon displayed, press the pick button and drag the cursor within the arcball.

Make small movements vertically, horizontally, and diagonally. What happens if you move outside the arcball?

There is less room to work with the free icon, but it gives you a less restricted type of rotation. Making small adjustments seems to work best. Imagine that you are grabbing the objects and turning them a little at a time. Release the pick button and grab again. You might need to do this several times to reach a desired position.

⊕ Try returning the image to approximate the southeast isometric view before proceeding.

You have now explored all of the rotation modes of the 3DORBIT command. In the next task, we move on to some other options readily available in this powerful command. Leave everything as is on your screen. It is best to continue without leaving the 3DORBIT command.

13.6 Hiding, Shading, and Continuous Orbit

3DORBIT is more than an enhanced viewpoint command. It has powerful options for creating shaded views, perspective views, and clipped views and can even be used to create a continuous motion effect. We explore some of these options now and leave the rest for Chapter 14.

⊕ To begin this task you should have objects centered within your display as shown previously in Figure 13-24. If you are not in 3DORBIT from Task 13.5, select 3D Orbit from the View menu.

3DORBIT options are accessed through the shortcut menu shown in Figure 13-29. We explore these from the bottom up, looking at the lower two panels and one option from the second panel and leaving other options for Chapter 14.

⊕ Right-click anywhere in the drawing area to open the shortcut menu.

Preset and Reset Views

At the bottom of the bottom panel, there is a Preset Views option that provides convenient access to the standard 10 orthographic and isometric viewpoints we have encountered in this chapter and the last. Above this is a Reset View option.

Figure 13-29

This option quickly returns you to the view that was current before you entered 3DORBIT. This is a great convenience, because you can get pretty far out of adjustment and have a difficult time finding your way back.

⊕   Select Reset View from the shortcut menu.

Regardless of where you have been within the 3DORBIT command, your viewpoint is immediately returned to the southeast isometric view shown in Figure 13-26. If you have left 3DORBIT, the view is reset to whatever view was current before you reentered the command. If you have attempted to return to this view manually using the cursors, you can see that there is still a slight adjustment to return your viewpoint to the precise isometric view.

Visual Aids

⊕   Right-click to open the shortcut menu again.

Moving up to the bottom of the third panel, you can see a Visual Aids selection. Highlighting this line opens a submenu with three options: Compass, Grid, and UCS icon. We demonstrate the grid, but do not recommend either the grid or the compass because they add confusion to the image on your screen. The compass adds an adjustable gyroscope-style image to the arcball. There are three rings of dashed ellipses showing the planes of the x-, y-, and z-axes of the current UCS. Try this if you like. We do not find it particularly helpful.

The Grid option adds a 3-D version of the grid with gridlines instead of dots, as shown in Figure 13-30. Try it.

⊕   Select Grid from the submenu.

The 3-D grid is added as shown in Figure 13-30.

⊕   Try adjusting viewpoints with any of the cursors and see how the grid moves with the objects.

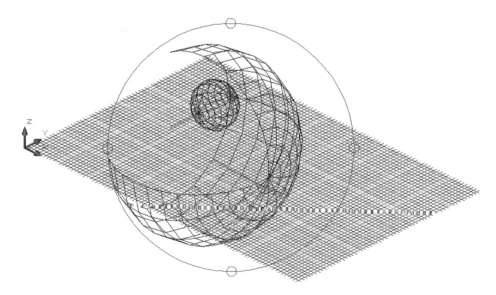

Figure 13-30

⊕ When you are satisfied, right-click to open the shortcut menu and select Reset View.

⊕ To turn off the grid, open the shortcut menu, highlight Visual Aids, and select Grid.

The third option on the submenu turns the 3D UCS icon on and off.

Shading Modes

Shading is a very powerful feature that brings you to the essence of what surface modeling is all about. We explore shading and rendering further in Chapter 14, but adding shading to surface objects is a simple process and there is no reason not to do it now. Shaded objects are not ambiguous in the way that wireframe images can be, so it is sometimes helpful to be able to add shading while you are adjusting viewpoints. Shading added within the 3DORBIT command is retained when you exit the command.

⊕ Right-click to open the shortcut menu.

⊕ Highlight Shading Modes.

This opens a submenu with six choices. Wireframe is the current mode. Hidden creates an image with hidden lines removed. Try it.

⊕ Select Hidden from the submenu.

Your screen is redrawn with an image like the one in Figure 13-31. This is like the image we created earlier in the chapter with the HIDE command,

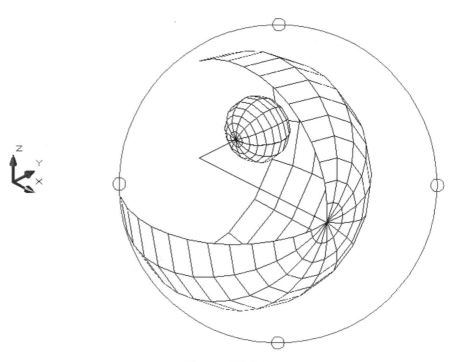

Figure 13-31

except that now you see that the image can be turned without losing the effect of removing hidden lines.

⊕ Rotate the image using any of the cursors.

Observe how the hidden line effect is retained as the point of view changes.

⊕ Rotate the image through 360 degrees vertically or horizontally.

Notice that there is no longer any ambiguity about the direction of rotation.

Hidden images might be the most useful for basic view definition, but shaded views take you to a new level of dramatic and realistic presentation. Here and in Chapter 14 when we explore rendering, you can see that our black and gray illustrations cannot do justice to the images on your screen.

⊕ Open the shortcut menu, highlight Shading Modes, and select Flat Shaded.

Your screen should resemble Figure 13-32. We chose this option only because it would reproduce most clearly in a grayscale illustration.

⊕ Try the other three options as well.

As you try the other options, look at the lighting effects. You can see that flat shading adds a lighting effect in a flat, face-by-face format. The reflected light from each face is distinct from faces in adjoining regions and consistent across each face. Gouraud shading produces a smooth, faceless image in which reflected light changes gradually across the object without regard to face boundaries. Both flat and Gouraud shading can be created with or without face edges displayed.

⊕ When you are done experimenting, leave objects in whatever shading and point of view you have developed.

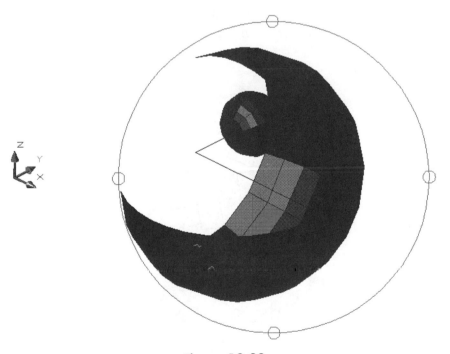

Figure 13-32

Continuous Orbit

Continuous orbit might or might not be the most useful feature of AutoCAD, but it is certainly the most dramatic and the most fun. With continuous orbit you can set objects in motion that continues when you release the pick button.

⊕ Right-click to open the shortcut menu.

⊕ Highlight More at the bottom of the second panel.

This opens a submenu with eight options. We explore only one in this chapter. Continuous orbit can also be initiated from the command line. The command is 3DCORBIT.

⊕ Select Continuous Orbit from the submenu.

The arcball disappears and the continuous orbit icon is displayed, consisting of a sphere surrounded by two ellipses as shown in Figure 13-33. The concept is simple: Dragging the cursor creates a motion vector. The direction and speed of the vector is applied to the model to set it in rotated motion around the target point. Motion continues until you press the pick button again.

⊕ With the continuous orbit cursor displayed, press and hold the pick button, then drag the cursor at a moderate speed in any direction.

We cannot illustrate the effect, but if you have done this correctly, your model should now be in continuous rotation. Try it again.

⊕ Press and hold the pick button at any time to stop rotation.

⊕ Press and hold the pick button again and drag the cursor in a different direction, at a different speed.

⊕ Press and hold the pick button to stop rotation.

⊕ Press the pick button, drag, and release again.

Now try changing directions without stopping.

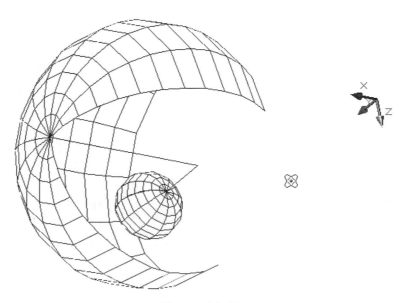

Figure 13-33

⊕ While the model is spinning, press and hold the pick button and drag in another direction.

Have a ball. Experiment. Play. There's no way we can stop you anyway. Try to create gentle, controlled motions in different directions. Try to create fast spins in different directions. Try to create diagonal, horizontal, and vertical spins.

Tip: The best way to achieve control over continuous orbit is to pick a point actually on the model and imagine that you are grabbing it and spinning it. It is much easier to communicate the desired speed and direction in this way. Note the similarity between the action of continuous orbit and the free rotation icon. The grabbing and turning is the same, but continuous orbit keeps moving when you release the pick button, whereas free rotation stops. Also notice that however complex your dragging motion is, continuous orbit only registers one vector, the speed and direction of your last motion before releasing the pick button.

One more trick before we leave:

⊕ Set your model into a moderate spin in any direction.

⊕ With your model spinning, right-click to open the shortcut menu.

You might have a momentary hesitation, but the model keeps spinning. Many of the shortcut menu options can be accessed without disrupting continuous orbit.

⊕ Select Reset View from the shortcut menu.

The model makes an immediate adjustment to the original view and continues to spin without interruption.

⊕ Open the shortcut menu again.

⊕ Highlight Shading Modes and select the shading mode of your choice.

Shading is added and the model keeps spinning.

⊕ Open the shortcut menu again and add the grid.

⊕ Open the shortcut menu again and add the compass.

Pretty impressive.

⊕ When you are done playing, remove the grid and compass, and then press Enter, Esc, or the spacebar to exit 3DORBIT.

You return to the command prompt, but any changes you have made in point of view and shading are retained. The 3D UCS icon can also be left on, but it can be turned off by opening the View menu, highlighting Display, UCS Icon, and selecting Off.

Before going on you might want to try editing or drawing with your shaded surface model in view. For example, try moving the model using the MOVE command. You should find that drawing and editing commands continue to work and do not disrupt the shading of the model.

Next, we demonstrate the use of the 3D Objects dialog box, which contains commands to create nine more basic surface models. As you create these objects, you might want to return to 3DORBIT to see how it looks with other objects in view.

13.7 Creating Surface Models Using the 3D Objects AutoLISP Routines

---

GENERAL PROCEDURE

1. Type 3D or open the Draw menu, highlight Surfaces, and select 3D Surfaces.
2. Choose an object and follow the prompts.

AutoCAD provides nine AutoLISP routines that create three-dimensional surface models of basic shapes. AutoLISP routines act just like commands, but only work if AutoLISP is loaded with appropriate memory allocation.

Like the 3-D meshes explored in Task 13.4, the 3-D surface models created this way can be treated as single entities or exploded and edited as collections of 3-D faces. Each of the objects has its own set of prompts, depending on its geometry. We demonstrate one object in this task and leave the rest for you to explore on your own.

⊕ To begin this task, clear your screen of objects left from Task 13.6.

⊕ Open the View menu, highlight 3D Views, and select SE Isometric.

Your screen should show a single viewport with a southeast isometric view.

⊕ If necessary, turn on the Grid (press F7).

Note: 3DORBIT graphics are typically not retained after the command is exited. If you wish to use the 3-D grid outside of the 3DORBIT command, open the View menu, highlight Shade, and select 3D Wireframe. To return the standard 2-D grid, select 2D Wireframe from the same menu.

⊕ Open the Draw menu, highlight Surfaces, and select 3D Surfaces.

This opens the 3D Objects dialog box shown in Figure 13-34. You can also select Object tools from the Surfaces toolbar, shown previously in Figure 13-8.

Note: To create 3-D surface models, you must use the 3-D command, the Surfaces toolbar, or the 3D Objects dialog box. Typing sphere, cone, torus, and so on directly at the command line creates solid models instead of surface models. We use these commands in Chapter 14.

⊕ Select the torus, as shown, by clicking on the torus image or the word Torus on the list.

⊕ Click OK.

This brings you to the first Torus prompt:

> Specify center point of torus:

⊕ Pick a center point as shown by P1 in Figure 13-35.

AutoCAD prompts

> Specify radius of torus or [Diameter]:

The next point we pick shows the overall radius of the torus.

⊕ Show a radius distance of about 6.00 units, as shown by P2 in Figure 13-35.

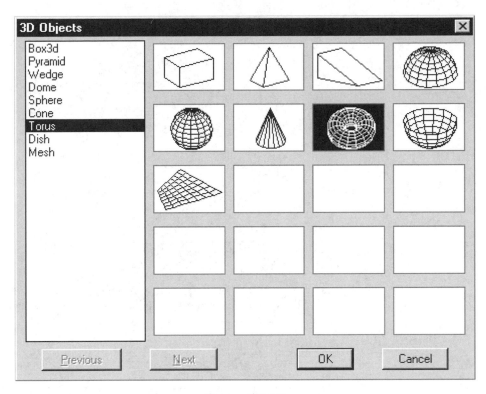

Figure 13-34

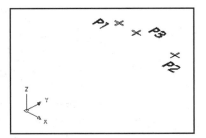

Figure 13-35

AutoCAD prompts

Specify radius of tube or [Diameter]:

This is the diameter or radius of the torus tube. If you specify the tube size by pointing, remember that the distance is being shown from the center point of the torus, at P1, to P3, although the tube actually is constructed from its own center line at P2.

⊕ Show a radius of about 2.00 units, as shown by P3 in Figure 13-35.

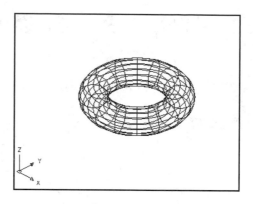

Figure 13-36

AutoCAD prompts

`Enter number of segments around tube circumference <16>:`

You are prompted for segment numbers around the tube and around the torus. These specify mesh density just like Surftab1 and Surftab2.

⊞ Press Enter to accept the default of 16 segments.

AutoCAD prompts

`Enter number of segments around torus circumference <16>:`

⊞ Press Enter to accept the default of 16 segments.

Your screen should resemble Figure 13-36. As in the case of the 3-D polygon mesh commands, notice how much surface modeling this AutoLISP routine accomplishes through a few simple prompts.

13.8 Creating Approximated Surfaces Using PEDIT

GENERAL PROCEDURE

1. Draw a 3DMESH in three dimensions.
2. Select Polyline from the Modify menu (the PEDIT command).
3. Select the mesh.
4. Enter an option.
5. Exit PEDIT.

Within the PEDIT command, there are some very impressive 3-D design features that we introduce in this task. These techniques are not needed in the drawings that follow, but your knowledge of AutoCAD and surface modeling would not be complete without them.

The techniques of curve and surface approximation are most useful when you have a curved object in mind but have not derived exact specifications for it, or when an irregular curved object passes through many different planes and would be very hard to draw face by face. You might be able to draw an outline and specify some key points, but beyond that what you conceive might be simply a smooth curve that follows the basic shape of your outline. AutoCAD provides mathematical algorithms that can translate outlines into smooth curves. This can be accomplished with 2-D and 3-D polylines and with 3-D meshes.

3-D meshes can be curved according to three different formulas, controlled by the variable Surftype (not to be confused with Surftab1 and Surftab2). Surftype can be set to 5 for a quadratic approximation, 6 for cubic approximation, and 8 for Bezier.

In this exercise, we create a simple rectangular 3-D mesh in one plane, move two of its vertices to make it three-dimensional, and then use the Smooth option of the PEDIT command to create approximated surfaces.

⊕   To begin this task, clear your screen of all objects left from the last task.

You should be in a single viewport with a southeast isometric view showing. If you have not already done so, you should return to the 2-D grid for this exercise.

3DMESH

The 3DMESH command allows you to create 3-D polygon meshes manually, vertex by vertex. Because of the time involved, the complete command is best used as a programmer's tool. However, there is an AutoLISP program that provides a very simple version of the 3DMESH command, which we demonstrate here. Those interested in the full command sequence should see the AutoCAD Command Reference.

⊕   Zoom in so that the grid covers most of the screen.

⊕   Open the Draw menu, highlight Surfaces, and select 3D Surfaces from the submenu.

This opens the 3D Objects dialog box used in the last task.

⊕   Select Mesh from the list on the left, or the Mesh icon in the third row.

⊕   Click OK.

AutoCAD prompts

Specify first corner point of mesh:

We are prompted for four corners to define the outer boundaries of the mesh, and then for two numbers to specify the number of vertices.

⊕   Pick a corner, as shown by P1 in Figure 13-37.

AutoCAD prompts for another corner:

Specify second corner point of mesh:

⊡   Pick a second corner, P2, 4.00 to the right of P1.

⊕   Pick a third corner, P3, 3.00 in the y direction from P2.

⊕   Pick a fourth corner, P4 as shown.

When you have picked four corners, your mesh should be outlined and one side highlighted. AutoCAD is asking for the number of vertices to be defined in the M direction. The letters M and N are used to designate the number of

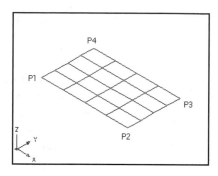

Figure 13-37

vertices in the two directions in which the mesh is defined. The M size is equivalent to the Surftab1 setting:

```
Enter mesh size in the M direction:
```

⊞   Type 5.

AutoCAD highlights a side perpendicular to the first and prompts

```
Enter mesh size in the N direction:
```

Like Surftab2, the N specification determines the number of vertices in this direction.

⊞   Type 5 again.

Your screen should resemble Figure 13-37.

The mesh is drawn with five vertices in each direction. Later, we copy it twice so that we can produce three different types of smooth surfaces, but first we need to move some vertices up and down in the z direction to give it three-dimensionality. This can be done using XY filters and the grip edit stretch mode.

⊞   Select the mesh.

The mesh is highlighted and grips appear at each vertex.

⊞   Pick the grip at the far right corner of the mesh (P3).

The stretch mode works the same as in previous chapters, except that now we move vertices up and down out of the XY plane. If you have not previously used point filters, here is an opportunity to become familiar with this useful 3-D tool.

⊞   Type .xy or open the shortcut menu (Shift+right-click), select Point Filters, and then select .XY.

AutoCAD prompts

```
                              .xy of
```

We are going to move the vertex straight up into the z dimension, so we want the same x- and y-coordinates with a new z. The XY filter takes the x and y values from whatever point we specify and combines them with a new z value. We can pick the same vertex again to show x and y, or we can type @, indicating

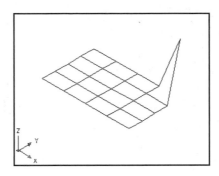

Figure 13-38

the last point entered. The *z* value needs to be typed because there are no objects outside of the XY plane to snap onto.

⊕   Type @ or pick the highlighted vertex grip again.

AutoCAD responds

(need Z):

⊕   Type 3.

This moves the corner vertex up 3.00, as shown in Figure 13-38.

Now we move the opposite corner down −4.00.

⊕   Pick the grip at the far left corner (P1), opposite from the corner you just edited.

⊕   Type .xy or open the shortcut menu, select Point filters, and select .XY.

⊕   Type @ or pick the same grip again.

⊕   Type −4.

⊕   We are now ready to create a cubic-style smoothed surface from our 3-D mesh.

⊕   Open the Modify menu, highlight Object, and select Polyline.

This executes the PEDIT command. AutoCAD prompts for a polyline, but 3-D polygon meshes can also be selected.

⊕   Pick any point on the mesh.

The mesh is not highlighted when you pick it, but you see the following command prompt:

Enter an option
[EditVertex/Smoothsurface/Desmooth/Mclose/Nclose/Undo]:

If dynamic input is on you see these options on a drop-down list. The option we use is Smooth surface.

⊕   Type s or select Save from the drop-down list.

Your screen is redrawn to resemble Figure 13-39.

Note: If the variable Splframe is set to 1, your screen shows no change. Splframe shows the frame or outline used in defining an approximated curve. Because of the complexity of meshes, AutoCAD does not show a curved surface

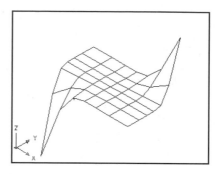

Figure 13-39

and its frame at the same time. With Splframe set to the default of 0, you see the smoothed version with no frame. With a setting of 1, you see the original frame without the approximation.

Next we make copies of the mesh and smooth the copies with the variable Surftype set to create quadratic and Bezier surfaces.

⊞ Press the spacebar to exit the PEDIT command.

⊞ Make two copies of the mesh, to the left and right of the original.

⊞ If necessary, zoom out to display complete copies.

⊞ Type surftype.

⊞ Type 5.

Surftype is 6 for cubic (the default), 5 for quadratic, and 8 for Bezier.

⊞ Open the Modify menu, highlight Object, and select Polyline.

⊞ Select the first copy of the mesh.

⊞ Type s or select Smooth surface from the drop-down list.

Watch carefully. The differences between cubic and quadratic surfaces in this object are slight. We have indicated them with arrows in Figure 13-40 for your convenience. To show a more dramatic difference, you would need to create a more dramatic 3-D figure by moving more vertices up or down. If you have the time, be our guest. Also consider changing the density of surface approximation through the variables Surfu and Surfv. For more information, see the AutoCAD Command Reference.

⊞ Press Enter to exit the PEDIT command.

⊞ Type surftype.

⊞ Type 8 for a Bezier surface.

⊞ Open the Modify menu, select Object, and then Polyline.

⊞ Select the remaining copy of the mesh.

⊞ Type s to smooth the mesh.

Your meshes resemble those in Figure 13-40.

Now that you know how to create smoothed surfaces, creating two-dimensional curve approximations should be easy. We include the following discussion as a reference.

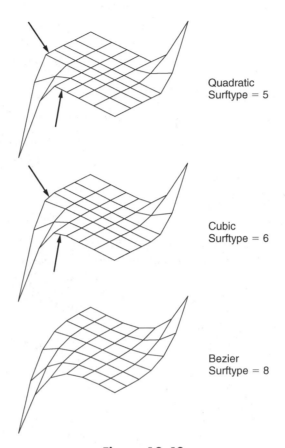

Quadratic
Surftype = 5

Cubic
Surftype = 6

Bezier
Surftype = 8

Figure 13-40

Curve Approximation

Creating approximated curves in two dimensions is analogous to smoothing surfaces in three dimensions. The process is the same, with a few changes in variable names. Instead of beginning with a 3-D mesh, you begin with a polyline. Polyline frames can be curved through the Fit or Spline option of the PEDIT command. Fit replaces all straight segments of a polyline with pairs of arc segments. The resulting curve passes through all existing vertices, and new vertices are created to join the arcs. Spline curves follow the shape of their frames, but they do not necessarily pass through all vertices. Instead, they pass through the first and last points and tend toward the ones between according to either the quadratic or cubic formula. (There is no Bezier option for spline curves.)

If the Splineframe variable is set to 1 instead of the default 0, AutoCAD displays the defining frame along with the curve. Also, the degree of accuracy of curve approximation can be varied by changing the setting of the Splinesegs variable. This variable controls the number of segments a polyline is considered to have in the calculations of the spline formulas.

Examples of fit and spline curves are shown in Figure 13-41.

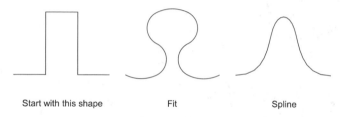

Start with this shape   Fit   Spline

Figure 13-41

13.9 Review Material

Questions

1. Why is it important to keep two or more different views of an object on the screen as you are drawing and editing it?
2. What two basic geometric shapes can be drawn as a 3-D face?
3. How does the HIDE command treat objects on layers that are turned off?
4. What geometry is needed to define a tabulated surface? A ruled surface? An edge surface? A revolved surface?
5. What one basic surface entity makes up all AutoCAD surfaces?
6. Where is the center of the 3DORBIT arcball in relation to the screen, the drawing area, and the current viewport? What else is centered at the center of the arcball?
7. What action is produced by each of the four rotation cursors in 3DORBIT?
8. Explain the camera and target metaphor used by the 3DORBIT command. How is it used to define views?
9. What is the difference between a flat shaded model and a Gouraud shaded model?
10. What system variable do you need to change to switch between the 2-D grid and the 3-D grid?
11. What is curve approximation? What command and what option are used to create curves from straight polylines and 3-D meshes?

Drawing Problems

1. Beginning with a blank drawing using the 1B template, create a three-tiled viewport screen configuration with two viewports on the left and one viewport on the right.
2. Create a world plan view in the top left viewport, a front view in the bottom left viewport, and a southeast isometric view in the large right viewport.
3. Draw a line from (9,9,0) to (11,9,0). Draw a polyline from (9,9,0) to (a) (7,9,0); (b) (7,7,0); (c) (6,5,0); and (d) (4,4,0).
4. Modify the polyline so that it takes the shape of a spline curve.
5. Create a 360-degree surface of revolution by revolving the spline curve around the original 2.00 unit line.
6. Make the right viewport active, enter 3DORBIT, and create a Gouraud shaded image.

13.10   WWW Exercise 13 (Optional)

Whenever you are ready, complete the following:

⊕   Make sure that you are connected to your Internet service provider.

⊕   Type browser, open the Web toolbar, and select the Browse the Web tool, or open your system browser from the Windows taskbar.

⊕   If necessary, navigate to our companion website at www.prenhall .com/ dixriley.

13.11   Drawing 13-1: REVSURF Designs

The REVSURF command is fascinating and powerful. As you get familiar with it, you might find yourself identifying objects in the world that can be conceived as surfaces of revolution. To encourage this process, we have provided this page of 12 REVSURF objects and designs.

To complete the exercise, you need only the PLINE and REVSURF commands. In the first six designs, we have shown the path curves and axes of rotation used to create the design. In the other six, you are on your own.

Exact shapes and dimensions are not important in this exercise, but imagination is. When you have completed our designs, we encourage you to invent your own. Also, consider adding shading to any of your designs and viewing them from different viewpoints using 3DORBIT.

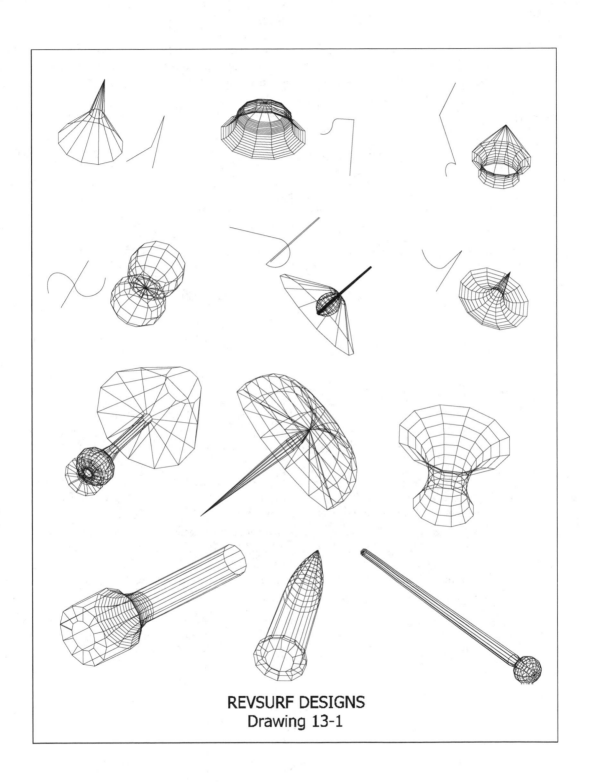

REVSURF DESIGNS
Drawing 13-1

13.12   Drawing 13-2: Picnic Table

This is a tricky drawing that must be done carefully. It requires efficient use of the UCS command along with a number of edit commands. To create an image that hides as shown in the reference, you must cover all surfaces with 3-D faces.

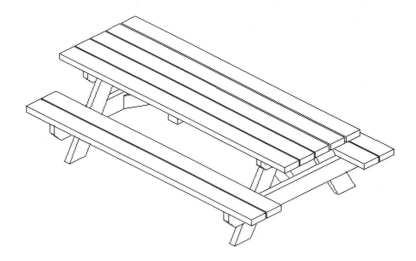

Drawing Suggestions

- Use a three-viewport configuration, with top (plan) and front views on the left and a 3-D view on the right. Be sure to keep an eye on all viewports as you go, because it is quite likely that you will create some lines that look correct in one view, but not in others.
- Use a separate layer for 3-D faces and add the faces as you go. This saves you from retracing your steps. Notice that the faces on the chamfered braces are drawn with one invisible line across the middle.
- We recommend that you start with the top of the table and work down. Placing the legs directly behind the chamfered braces can be tricky. One way to do this is to draw the legs even with the side of the table first (in a UCS with its XY plane flush with a side of the table) and then move them back.
- Save the angled braces for last. Once the leg braces are drawn, you can locate the angled braces by drawing a line from the midpoint of the small brace in the middle of the table top to the midpoint of the bottom of a leg brace. Then offset this line 1″ each way to create the two lower edges of one angled brace.

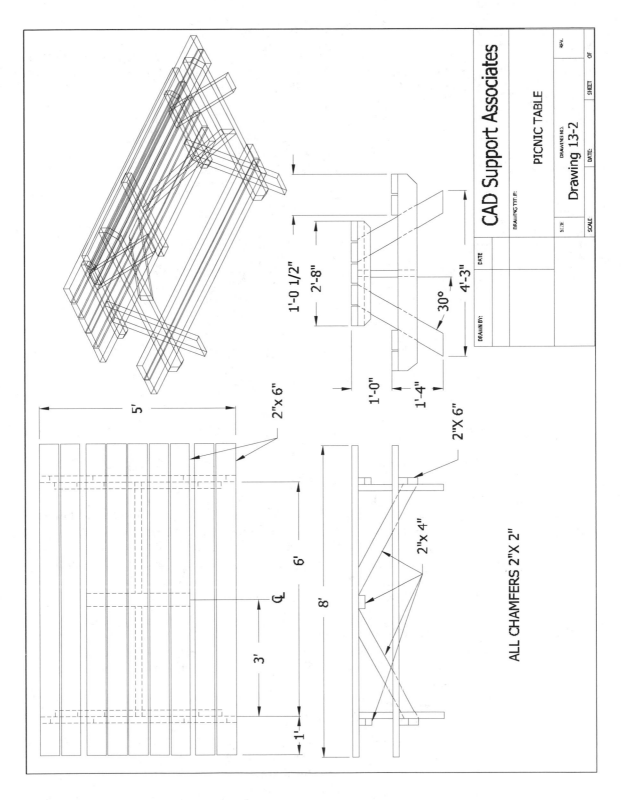

ALL CHAMFERS 2"X 2"

2"x 6"

2"x 6"

2"X 6"

2"x 4"

5'

6'

3'

1'

8'

1'-0 1/2"

2'-8"

4'-3"

30°

1'-0"

1'-4"

CAD Support Associates

DRAWING TITLE:

PICNIC TABLE

DRAWING NO.

Drawing 13-2

SIZE

SCALE

DATE:

SHEET   OF

REV.

DRAWN BY:

DATE

13.13   Drawing 13-3: Globe

This drawing uses several of the 3-D mesh commands. Some of the 3-D construction is a little tricky, but you might be pleasantly surprised. Follow the suggestions and you will find that this one is easier than it looks.

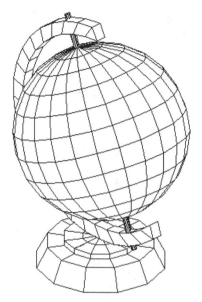

Drawing Suggestions

- Use a three-viewport configuration with top and front views on the left and an isometric 3-D view on the right.
- Begin with the base circles, drawing in the plan (top) view, and then move the circles into place along the z-axis.
- Move the small inner circle up 12.25 to locate the top of the shaft. Draw the center line from the center of this circle to the top center of the base. Then copy this line on itself and rotate the line and circle 23.5 degrees around the midpoint of the line to position the center of the shaft.
- Offset the shaft center line 0.125. Later, you will trim a 4.00-diameter circle to this line. Then using the center line of the shaft as the axis of rotation for a REVSURF leaves a hole in the middle of the globe for the shaft.
- Draw the 4.00, 4.75, and 5.38 circles and trim them to the vertical, 23.5-degree, and 46-degree lines as shown.
- With your UCS parallel to the front view, copy the 4.75 and 5.38 circles 1.25 and 2.25 in the z direction to form the two sides of the globe support. Erase the original circles.
- Tabsurf the shaft.
- Rulesurf the base circles. There are three ruled surfaces to complete the base.
- Revsurf the top of the base, using a single line from a quadrant to the center for a path curve and the vertical centerline for the axis.
- Rulesurf the globe support. This requires four ruled surfaces.
- Revsurf the globe.
- Freeze all nonsurface lines before hiding.

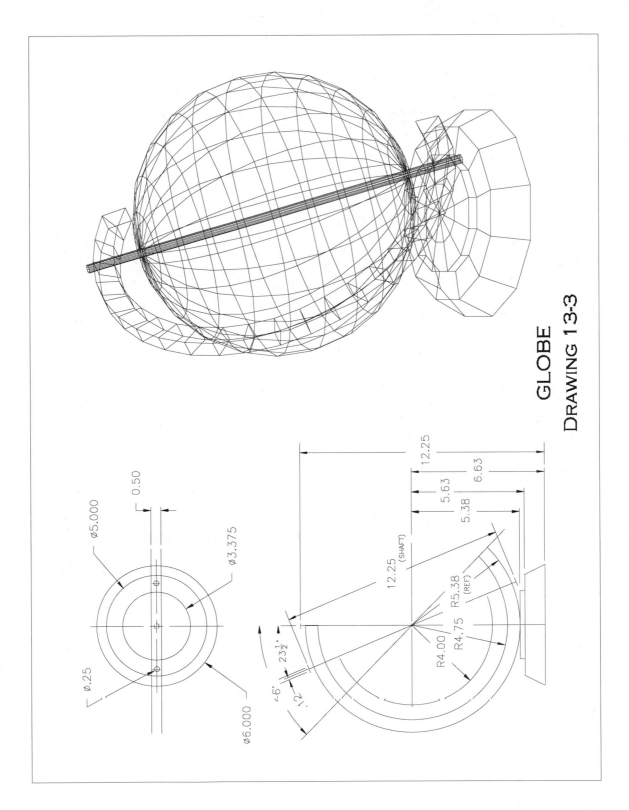

GLOBE
DRAWING 13-3

Ø5.000
0.50
Ø3.375
Ø.25
Ø6.000

12.25
5.63
6.63
5.38
12.25
(SHAFT)
R4.00
R4.75
R5.38
(REF)
6°
23½°

611

13.14   Drawing 13-4: Nozzle

This is a tough drawing that gives you a real 3-D workout. You need to define numerous UCSs as you go. Your goal should be to create the two views, A and B. Dimensioning is not part of the exercise. The dimensioned figure is not a complete wireframe, but a guide to show you the abstract relationships necessary to complete the surface model.

Drawing Suggestions

- We began in a front, right, top view. This puts the main center line of the nozzle in the XY plane of the WCS, and the circles that show the outlines of the nozzle would be perpendicular to it. When we were done, we rotated the point of view on the objects slightly to show them more clearly.
- Make ample use of COPY and OFFSET in drawing the circles and center lines of the nozzle, the hexes and circles of the knob, and the polyline curve path of the nozzle.
- The circle and center line at the right end of the 45-degree angle can be constructed using a COPY and ROTATE of the circle and center line just in front of the angle. This must be done in a UCS parallel to the WCS.
- The curve in the nozzle is a −45-degree REVSURF around the center line 1.00 to the right of the turn.
- The two darkened lines show the path curves used with REVSURF to draw the nozzle and the knob. Construct lines first and then go over them with PLINE or 3DPOLY. 3DPOLY is similar to PLINE, but it uses 3-D points instead of 2-D points and has no option to draw arcs. In general, 3-D polylines are more flexible and can be drawn at times when the current UCS would not allow the construction of a 2-D polyline.
- The center line through the knob (along the arrow) runs perpendicular to the polyline outline of the nozzle. Use a perpendicular osnap to construct the center line and then define UCSs in relation to the center line to construct the knob.
- When this one is complete, you should take it into 3DORBIT, shade it, and view it from different angles.

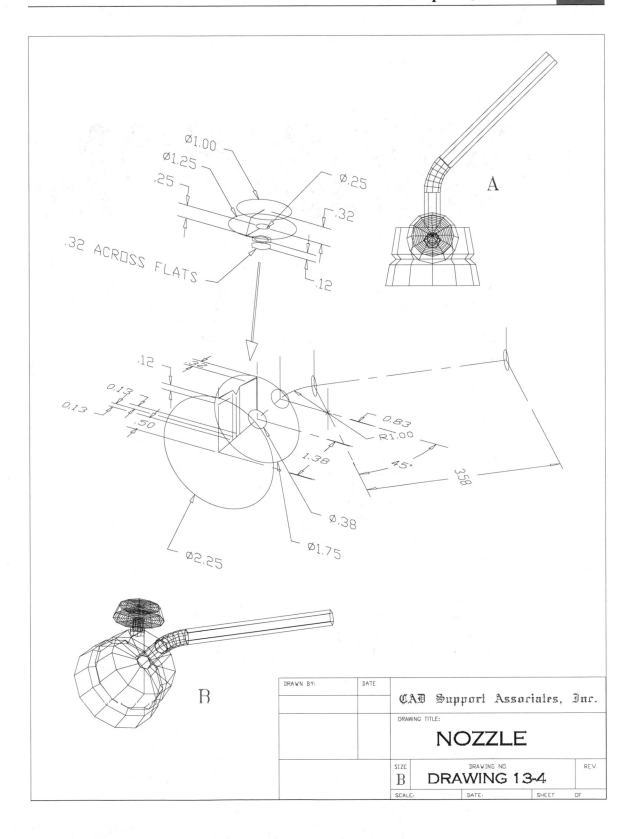

Ø1.00
Ø1.25
.25
Ø.25
.32
.32 ACROSS FLATS
.12

A

.12
0.13
0.13
.50
0.83
R1.00
1.38
45°
3.58
Ø.38
Ø1.75
Ø2.25

B

DRAWN BY:	DATE	CAD Support Associates, Inc.		
		DRAWING TITLE: **NOZZLE**		
		SIZE **B**	DRAWING NO. **DRAWING 13-4**	REV.
		SCALE:	DATE:	SHEET OF

14 Solid Models

COMMANDS

BOX	MATLIB	SECTION	SUBTRACT
CYLINDER	RENDER	SHADE	UNION
EXTRUDE	REVOLVE	SLICE	WEDGE
INTERSECT	RMAT	SOLIDEDIT	3DORBIT
LIGHT	SCENE	SPHERE	

OVERVIEW

Solid modeling is in many ways easier than either wireframe or surface modeling. In solid modeling, you can draw a complete solid object by picking a few points in a fraction of the time it would take to draw line by line, surface by surface. Furthermore, once the object is drawn, it contains far more information than a wireframe or surface model. In this chapter, you draw a simple solid model using several solid drawing and editing commands. Then you create sectioned, rendered, and perspective views of the model.

TASKS

14.1 Creating Solid BOXes and WEDGEs

GENERAL PROCEDURE

1. Enter BOX or WEDGE.
2. Specify corner point and distances in the XY plane of the current UCS (or define a base plane first and then specify points).
3. Specify a height.

Solid modeling requires a somewhat different type of thinking from any of the drawings you have completed so far. Instead of focusing on lines and arcs, edges and surfaces, you need to imagine how 3-D objects might be pieced together by combining or subtracting basic solid shapes. This building block process is called constructive solid geometry and includes joining, subtracting, and intersecting operations. A simple washer, for example, could be made by cutting a small cylinder out of the middle of a larger cylinder. In AutoCAD solid modeling, you can begin with a flat outer cylinder, then draw an inner cylinder with a smaller radius centered at the same point, and then subtract the inner cylinder from the outer, as illustrated in Figure 14-1.

This operation, which uses the SUBTRACT command, is the equivalent of cutting a hole and is one of three Boolean operations (after the mathematician George Boole) used to create composite solids. UNION joins two solids to make a new solid, and INTERSECT creates a composite solid in the space where two solids overlap (see Figure 14-1).

In this chapter, you create a composite solid from the union and subtraction of several solid primitives. Primitives are 3-D solid building blocks—boxes, cones, cylinders, spheres, wedges, and torus. They all are regularly shaped and can be defined by specifying a few points and distances.

⊕ To begin this task, start a new drawing and go into a top, right, front view (315 degrees from the *x*-axis and 45 degrees from the XY plane).

Notice that this is a slightly higher viewing angle than the southeast isometric view we used in the previous two chapters. If you are unfamiliar with the use of the Viewpoint Preset dialog box, use the following procedure:

1. Type vpoint.
2. Type r for Rotate.
3. Type 315 for the angle in the XY plane from the *x*-axis.
4. Type 45 for the angle from the XY plane.

⊕ Type box or open the Draw menu, highlight Solids, and select Box.

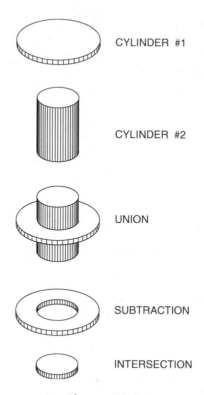

CYLINDER #1

CYLINDER #2

UNION

SUBTRACTION

INTERSECTION

Figure 14-1

Box

Figure 14-2

There is also a Solids toolbar with a Box tool, as illustrated in Figure 14-2. In the command area you see the following prompt:

    Specify corner of box or [CEnter] <0,0,0>:

CEnter allows you to begin defining a box by specifying its center point. Here we will use the Corner of box option to begin drawing a box in the base-plane of the current UCS. We draw a box with a length of 4, width of 3, and height of 1.5.

⊕ Pick a corner point similar to P1 in Figure 14-3.

    AutoCAD prompts

    Specify corner or [Cube/Length]:

With the Cube option, you can draw a box with equal length, width, and height by specifying one distance. The Length option allows you to specify length, width, and height separately. With the default option you can show the

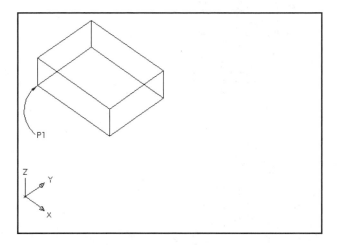

Figure 14-3

length and width at the same time by picking the other corner of the base of the box (the default method). We use the Length option first. It is the most reliable and easy to use.

⊕   **Type L or right-click and select Length from the shortcut menu.**

AutoCAD prompts for a length. Notice that length is measured along the *x*-axis and width is measured along the *y*-axis, as shown in Figure 14-3.

⊕   **Type 4 or show a length of 4 by picking two points.**

AutoCAD prompts for a width.

⊕   **Type 3 or pick two points 3 units apart.**

Now AutoCAD prompts for a height. Height is measured along the *z*-axis. As usual, you cannot pick points in the *z* direction unless you have objects to snap to. Instead, you can type a value or show a value by picking two points in the XY plane.

⊕   **Type 1.5 or pick two points 1.5 units apart.**

Your screen should resemble Figure 14-3. Zoom in if you like.

Next we create a solid wedge. The process is exactly the same, but there is no Cube option and we use the default option of showing a length and width by picking two corner points.

⊕   **Type we or open the Draw menu, highlight Solids, and select Wedge.**

AutoCAD prompts

```
Specify first corner of wedge or [CEnter] <0,0,0>:
```

⊕   **Pick the front corner point of the box, P1 in Figure 14-4.**

As in the BOX command, AutoCAD prompts for a cube, length, or the other corner:

```
Specify corner or [Cube/Length]:
```

This time we specify the other corner.

⊕   **Pick a point 4.00 over in the *x* direction and 3.00 back in the *y* direction, as shown by P2 in Figure 14-4.**

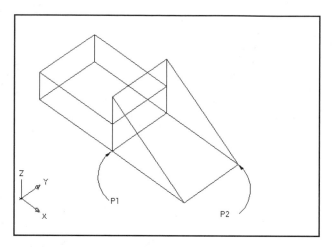

Figure 14-4

This point should be easy to find because the back corner lines up with the back of the box already drawn.

After you pick the second corner, the rubber band disappears and AutoCAD prompts for a height.

⊕ Type 3 or show a distance of 3 units.

AutoCAD draws the wedge you have specified. Notice that a wedge is simply half a box, cut along a diagonal plane.

Your screen should resemble Figure 14-4. Although the box and the wedge appear as wireframe objects, they are really quite different, as you will find. In Task 14.2, we join the box and the wedge to form a new composite solid.

14.2   Creating the UNION of Two Solids

GENERAL PROCEDURE

1. Open the Modify menu, highlight Solids Editing, and select Union.
2. Select solid objects to join. (Steps 1 and 2 can be reversed if noun/verb selection is enabled.)

Unions are simple to create and usually easy to visualize. The union of two objects is an object that includes all points that are on either of the objects. Unions can be performed just as easily on more than two objects. The union of objects can be created even if the objects have no points in common (i.e., they do not touch or overlap).

Right now we have two distinct solids on the screen; with UNION we can join them.

⊕ Open the Modify menu, highlight Solids Editing, and select Union.

There is also a Union tool on the Solids Editing toolbar, as shown in Figure 14-5. AutoCAD prompts you to select objects.

Figure 14-5

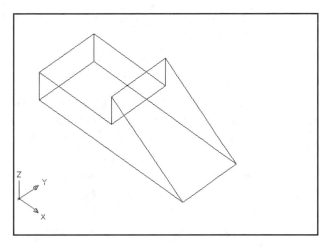

Figure 14-6

⊕ Point or use a crossing box to select both objects.
⊕ Press Enter to end object selection.
    Your screen should resemble Figure 14-6.

14.3 Working above the XY Plane Using Elevation

GENERAL PROCEDURE

1. Type elev.
2. Enter elevation and thickness values.

In this task, we draw two more solid boxes while demonstrating the use of elevation to position objects above the XY plane of the current UCS. Changing elevations simply adds a single z value to all new objects as they are drawn and can be used as an alternative to creating a new UCS. With an elevation of 1.00, for example, new objects would be drawn 1.00 above the XY plane of the current UCS. In the ELEV command, you can also specify a thickness setting to create 3-D objects, but these are created as surface models, not solids.

⊕ To begin this task you should have the union of a wedge and a box on your screen, as shown in Figure 14-6.

We begin by drawing a second box positioned on top of the first box. Later, we move it, copy it, and subtract it to form a slot in the composite object.

⊞ Type elev.

AutoCAD prompts

Specify new default elevation <0.00>:

The elevation is always set at 0 unless you specify otherwise.

⊞ Type 1.5.

This brings the elevation up 1.5 out of the XY plane, putting it even with the top of the first box you drew.

AutoCAD now prompts for a new thickness. Thickness does not apply to solid objects because they have their own thickness.

⊞ Press Enter or the spacebar to retain 0.00 thickness.

This brings us back to the command prompt. If you watch closely you can see that the grid has moved up into the new plane of elevation.

⊞ Type box or open the Draw menu, highlight Solids, and select Box.

⊞ Pick the far upper left corner of the box, Point 1 in Figure 14-7.

⊞ Type L or right-click and select Length from the shortcut menu.

⊞ Type 4 or pick two points (Points 1 and 2 in Figure 14-7) to show a length of 4 units.

⊞ Type .5 or pick two points (Points 1 and 3) to show a width of 0.5 units.

⊞ Type 2 or pick two points to show a height of 2 units.

Your screen should resemble Figure 14-7. Notice how you were able to pick points on top of the box because of the change in elevation just as if we had changed coordinate systems. Before going on, return to 0.00 elevation.

⊞ Type elev.

⊞ Type 0.

⊞ Press Enter to retain 0.00 thickness.

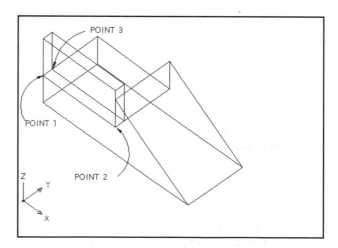

Figure 14-7

14.4 Creating Composite Solids with SUBTRACT

GENERAL PROCEDURE

1. Create solid objects to subtract and objects to be subtracted from.
2. Position objects relative to each other.
3. Type su or open the Modify menu, highlight Solids Editing, and select Subtract.
4. Select objects to be subtracted from.
5. Select objects to subtract.

SUBTRACT is the logical opposite of UNION. In a union operation, all the points contained in one solid are added to the points contained in other solids to form a new composite solid. In a subtraction, all points in the solids to be subtracted are removed from the source solid. A new composite solid is defined by what is left.

In this exercise, we use the objects already on your screen to create a slotted wedge. First, we need to move the thin upper box into place, then we copy it to create a longer slot, and finally we subtract it from the union of the box and wedge.

⊕ To begin this task, you should have the composite box and wedge solid and the thin box on your screen, as shown in Figure 14-7.

Before subtracting, we move the box to the position shown in Figure 14-8.

⊕ Type m or select the Move tool from the Modify toolbar.

⊕ Select the narrow box drawn in the last task.

⊕ Right-click to end object selection.

⊕ At the Specify base point or displacement prompt use a midpoint object snap to pick the midpoint of the top right edge of the narrow box.

⊕ At the Specify second point of displacement prompt use another midpoint object snap to pick the top edge of the wedge, as shown in Figure 14-8.

This moves the narrow box over and down. If you were to perform the subtraction now, you would create a slot, but it would only run through the box,

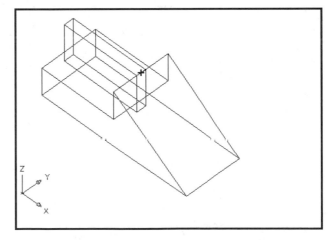

Figure 14-8

not the wedge. We can create a longer slot by copying the narrow box over to the right using grips.

⊕ Select the narrow box.

⊕ Pick any of the eight grips.

⊕ If Ortho is off, turn it on.

Now if you move the cursor in the *x* direction, you see a copy of the box moving with you. Solids cannot be stretched, so we must make a copy to lengthen the slot.

⊕ Type c or right-click and select Copy from the shortcut menu.

⊕ Move the cursor between 3.00 and 4.00 units to the right and press the pick button.

If you don't go far enough, the slot will be too short. If you go past 4.00, the slot will be interrupted by the space between the box and the copy.

⊕ Press Enter to leave the grip edit mode.

⊕ Press Esc to remove grips.

Your screen should resemble Figure 14-9.

⊕ Type su or open the Modify menu, highlight Solids Editing, and select Subtract.

There is also a Subtract tool on the Solids Editing toolbar, shown previously in Figure 14-5.

AutoCAD asks you to select objects to subtract from first:

```
Select solids and regions to subtract from ...
Select objects:
```

⊕ Pick the composite of the box and the wedge.

⊕ Right-click to end selection of source objects.

AutoCAD prompts for objects to be subtracted:

```
Select solids and regions to subtract ...
Select objects:
```

⊕ Pick the two narrow boxes.

⊕ Right-click to end selection.

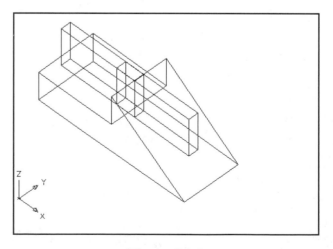

Figure 14-9

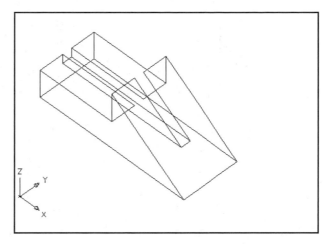

Figure 14-10

Your screen should resemble Figure 14-10.

Next, we draw a solid cylinder, move it into place, and subtract it to form a hole at the right end of the slot.

⊞ **Open the Draw menu, highlight Solids, and select Cylinder.**

There is also a Cylinder tool on the Solids toolbar, shown previously in Figure 14-2.

AutoCAD prompts

```
Current wire frame density: ISOLINES = 4
Specify center point for base of cylinder or
[Elliptical]<0,0,0>:
```

We demonstrate the significance of the isolines setting in a moment.

⊞ **Pick any convenient center point away from the composite solid.**

It does not matter where the cylinder is drawn because we are going to move it to the end of the slot using a midpoint object snap.

To create a hole the same width as the slot, we need a diameter of 0.5 or a radius of 0.25.

⊞ **Type .25 for the radius value.**

The cylinder must be made high enough to reach through the slot. Any height over 1.00 will do.

⊞ **Type 1 for the height.**

The cylinder is drawn as shown in Figure 14-11 except that your cylinder probably has only four vertical lines. (They actually look like two lines, because they hide each other.) The density of lines displayed by AutoCAD to represent curved solid surfaces is controlled by the Isolines system variable. We change ours to show eight lines.

⊞ **Type isolines.**

AutoCAD prompts

```
Enter new value for ISOLINES <4>:
```

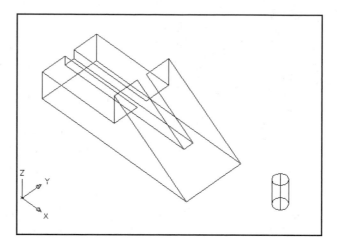

Figure 14-11

⊕   Type 8.

⊕   Type Regen or open the View menu and select Regen.

    Next, we move the cylinder to the end of the slot using a grip edit and a midpoint object snap.

⊕   Select the cylinder.

    There is a grip at the top and bottom centers of the cylinder. We want to move the top center to the midpoint of the end of the wedge. Zoom in if you need to.

⊕   Select the top center grip on the cylinder.

⊕   Use a midpoint object snap to move the cylinder to the end of the slot, as shown in Figure 14-12.

    Now it's time to subtract.

⊕   Type su or open the Modify menu, highlight Solids Editing, and select Subtract.

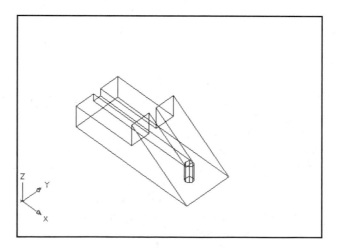

Figure 14-12

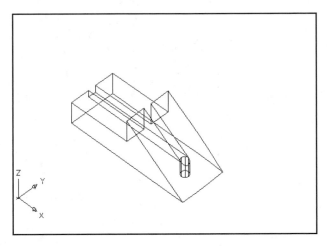

Figure 14-13

⊕ Select the composite object.
⊕ Right-click to end object selection.
⊕ Select the cylinder.
⊕ Right-click to end object selection.

Your screen should resemble Figure 14-13.

14.5 Creating Chamfers and Fillets on Solid Objects

GENERAL PROCEDURE

1. Type cha, select Chamfer from the Modify menu, or select the Chamfer tool from the Modify toolbar.
2. Pick a base surface.
3. Press Enter or type n to select the next surface.
4. Enter chamfer distances.
5. Pick edges to be chamfered.
6. Press Enter to end object selection.

Constructing chamfers and fillets on solids is simple, but the language of the prompts can cause confusion due to some ambiguity in the designation of edges and surfaces to be modified. We begin by putting a chamfer on the back left edge of the model.

⊕ To begin this task, you should have the solid model shown in Figure 14-13 on your screen.

⊕ Type cha, select Chamfer from the Modify menu, or select the Chamfer tool from the Modify toolbar.

The first chamfer prompt is the same as always:

```
(TRIM mode) Current chamfer Dist1 = 0.00, Dist2 = 0.00
Select first line or [Polyline/Distance/Angel/Trim/Method]:
```

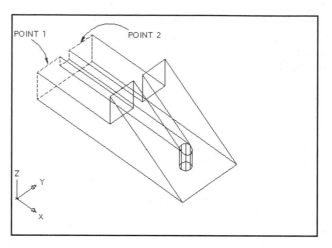

Figure 14-14

⊕ Select Point 1, as shown in Figure 14-14.

The selection preview will highlight the whole solid, but when you pick point 1, AutoCAD highlights the back left surface and prompts

```
Base surface selection...
Enter surface selection option [Next/OK (current)]
<OK>:
```

We are constructing a chamfer on the left surface of the object. However, chamfers and fillets happen along edges that are common to two surfaces. What is a base surface in relation to a chamfered edge? Actually, it refers to either of the two faces that meet at the edge where the chamfer will be. As long as you pick this edge, you are bound to select one of these two surfaces, and either will do. Which of the two surfaces is the base surface and which is the adjacent surface does not matter until you enter the chamfer distances, and then only if the distances are unequal. However, AutoCAD allows you to switch to the other surface that shares this edge, by typing n for the Next option.

⊕ Press Enter.

AutoCAD prompts

```
Specify base surface chamfer distance <0.00>:
```

⊕ Type .5 for the base surface distance.

Now AutoCAD prompts

```
Specify other surface chamfer distance <0.50>:
```

Now you can see the significance of base surface. The chamfer is created with the first distance on the base surface side and the second distance on the other surface side. If the chamfer is symmetrical, it does not matter which is which.

⊕ Type .25 for the other base surface distance.

This constructs a chamfer that cuts 0.5 down into the left side and 0.25 back along the top side.

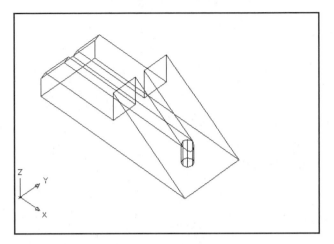

Figure 14-15

Now AutoCAD prompts for the edge or edges to be chamfered:

Select an edge or [Loop]:

Loop constructs chamfers on all edges of the chosen base surface. Selecting edges allows you to place them only on the selected edges. You have no difficulty selecting edges if you pick the edge you wish to chamfer again. The only difference is that you need to pick twice, once on each side of the slot.

⊕   Pick the top back left edge of the model, to one side of the slot (Point 1 in Figure 14-14 again).

    Once again, the entire solid is previewed, but only the back left edge is selected.

⊕   Pick the same edge again, but on the other side of the slot (Point 2 in Figure 14-14).

⊕   Press Enter to end edge selection (right-clicking opens a shortcut menu).

    Your screen should resemble Figure 14-15.

Creating Fillets

The procedure for creating solid fillets is simpler. There is one less step because there is no need to differentiate between base and other surfaces in a fillet.

⊕   Select Fillet from the Modify menu or the Fillet tool from the Modify toolbar.

    AutoCAD gives you current settings and prompts

    Select first object or [Polyline/Radius/Trim/mUltiple]:

⊕   Pick the edge where the box and the wedge meet, Point 1 in Figure 14-16.

    AutoCAD prompts

            Enter fillet radius <0.50>:

⊕   Press Enter or type .5.

    The next prompt looks like this:

            Select an edge or [Chain/Radius]:

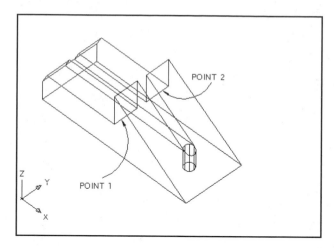

Figure 14-16

Chain allows you to fillet around all the edges of one side of a solid object at once. For our purposes, we do not want a chain. Instead, we want to select the two edges on either side of the slot.

⊕ Pick the same edge on the other side of the slot, Point 2 in Figure 14-16.

You see this prompt again:

$$Select\ an\ edge\ or\ [Chain/Radius]:$$

The prompt repeats to allow you to select more edges to fillet.

⊕ Press Enter to end selection of edges.

Your screen should resemble Figure 14-17.

Important: Before proceeding, save the composite wedge as a block so that you can insert it later when we use it to explore shading and rendering.

⊕ Type b or select the Make Block tool from the Draw toolbar.

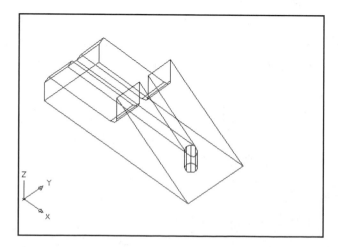

Figure 14-17

⊕ Type w for the block name.

⊕ Click Select Objects.

⊕ Select the composite wedge.

⊕ Right-click to end object selection.

⊕ Click Pick Point.

⊕ Select an insertion base point; any corner will do.

⊕ Click the Delete radio button.

⊕ Click OK.

When the block definition is complete, the wedge disappears from the screen. We insert this block later and use it to explore lighting and rendering techniques. First, however, there are some other solid modeling commands to demonstrate.

14.6 Creating Solid Objects with EXTRUDE

GENERAL PROCEDURE

1. Create a polyline, circle, or region shape in two dimensions.
2. Open the Draw menu, highlight Solids, and select Extrude.
3. Select objects.
4. Specify an extrusion height.
5. Specify an extrusion taper angle.

AutoCAD includes two additional ways to create solid objects. First, using the EXTRUDE command, simple 2-D polylines and regions can be built up or repeated along a linear path stretching up or down from the plane in which they are drawn. Second, using REVOLVE, 2-D polylines and regions can be revolved around an axis along a circular or semicircular path. The REVOLVE command is very similar to REVSURF, but it creates a solid rather than a surface model.

In this task, we draw a simple polyline shape and extrude it to create a solid. In Task 14.8, we begin working with regions.

⊕ To begin this task, your screen should be clear of all objects left from the previous task.

⊕ Draw a 2.00 by 4.00 polyline rectangle, as shown in Figure 14-18.

Be sure to use PLINE or RECTANG to create this 2-D polyline. 3DPOLY, which draws 3-D polylines, does not work with EXTRUDE.

⊕ Open the Draw menu, highlight Solids, and select Extrude.

There is also an Extrude tool on the Solids toolbar, shown previously in Figure 14-2. AutoCAD prompts you to select objects. Only regions, polylines, and circles can be extruded.

⊕ Select the rectangle.

⊕ Press Enter to end object selection.

AutoCAD prompts

```
Specify height of extrusion or <Path>:
```

The Path option is a powerful feature that allows you to create an extrusion along any pathway in the *z* direction. As in the TABSURF command, you

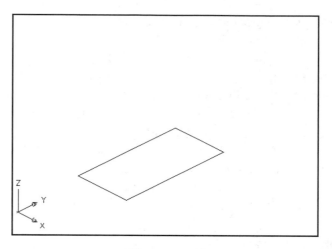

Figure 14-18

need a line or polyline to serve as a pathway. A solid can then be created by essentially repeating the 2-D object(s) at every point along the selected path.

If you use the default Height of extrusion option, the extrusion is measured straight up into the z direction (or down if you enter a negative number).

⊕ Type 3 or show a distance of 3.00 units. (Distance can be shown in the XY plane.)

AutoCAD prompts

```
Specify angle of taper for extrusion <0>:
```

This prompt gives you the opportunity to create a tapered extrusion by specifying an angle between the z-axis and the edge of the extruded object.

⊕ Type 10.

Your screen should resemble Figure 14-19. Be aware that if your taper angle is too large, edges might meet before the specified height is reached. In the

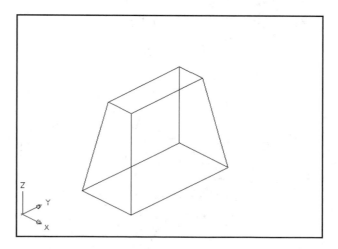

Figure 14-19

case of an extrusion with a rectangular base, this would result in a prism, with a ridge at the top rather than a smaller rectangle.

The extruded solid you have just created functions exactly like the solid objects created earlier. It can be used in union, subtraction, and intersection with other solids to create complex solid objects. It can also be modified face by face using a set of options in the SOLIDEDIT command, as we see in the next task.

14.7 Editing 3-D Solid Faces with SOLIDEDIT

GENERAL PROCEDURE

1. Draw 3-D solid shapes.
2. Open the Modify menu and highlight Solids Editing.
3. Select a face editing option.
4. Select faces of a solid object.
5. Follow the prompts.

AutoCAD has features for editing the faces of previously drawn solids. This adds an extraordinary amount of flexibility and power to the whole solid modeling process. Instead of having to draw, redraw, and combine 3-D primitives to create the desired model, you can move, copy, rotate, offset, extrude, taper, and even color the faces of solids in your drawing. Faces include not only the obvious exterior surfaces, but also interior surfaces, such as the cylindrical hole at the center of a nut.

The options for editing faces are extensive. We introduce three and offer a chart, Figure 14-27, that shows what to expect from the other possibilities. We begin by extruding a face on the solid created in the last task.

⊕ To begin this task, you should be in a single view with the extruded and tapered rectangle shown in Figure 14-19.

⊕ Open the Modify menu and highlight Solids Editing, or open the Solids Editing toolbar, as shown in Figure 14-20.

 The submenu lists the same options as those available on the toolbar, and in the same order.

⊕ Select Extrude Faces, or the Extrude Faces tool from the toolbar, as shown.

 Either selection enters the SOLIDEDIT command and automatically enters the Extrude Faces option. AutoCAD prompts for faces:

 Select faces or [Undo/Remove]:

Figure 14-20

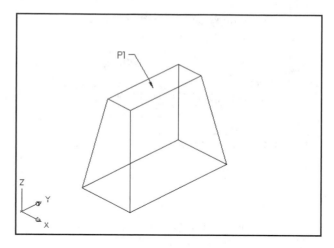

Figure 14-21

You can select faces by pointing within the boundary of the face, or by using a crossing window, crossing polygon, or fence. Pointing is the default; for the other methods enter c, cp, or f. In this case, all windows are crossing windows so they can be shown right to left or left to right. If you point, be aware that many point selections are ambiguous. That is, the point could be in one of several different faces. This is the reason for the Undo and Remove options.

We extrude the face on the top of the object.

⊕   Select a point similar to P1 in Figure 14-21.

If your point selection causes two or more faces to be selected, type u and select again, or type r and then select faces to remove from the selection set.

⊕   Press Enter to end face selection.

AutoCAD prompts

        Specify height of extrusion or [Path]:

⊕   Type 1.

We extrude the top face upward at a taper angle equal and opposite to the previous extrusion so that the object funnels out at the top, as shown in Figure 14-22. AutoCAD prompts

        Specify angle of taper for extrusion <0>:

What would the default taper angle look like? For our purpose we use –10 because we used 10 for the previous extrusion.

⊕   Type "–10."

Your screen should resemble Figure 14-22. Be aware that extrusion is directed normal (perpendicular) to the extruded face, unless otherwise specified. Extrusion is quite flexible and can be performed along paths and curves as well as normals.

Next, we move the right side faces out to widen the object. Notice that you are still in the SOLIDEDIT command.

⊕   Type m or select the Move Faces tool from the Solids Editing toolbar or right-click and select Move Faces from the shortcut menu. If dynamic input is on you can also select Move from the drop-down list.

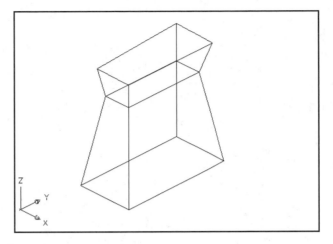

Figure 14-22

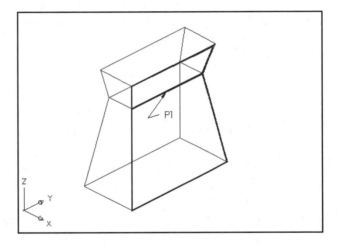

Figure 14-23

⊞ Pick a point on the middle edge of the right side, similar to P1 in Figure 14-23.

Picking this edge, which is common to the two right side faces, selects both faces, as shown.

⊞ Press Enter to end object selection.

Now AutoCAD prompts for a displacement just as in the MOVE command.

⊞ Enter two points to show a displacement of 0.50 unit in the *x* direction of the current UCS.

Your screen should resemble Figure 14-24.

We perform one more edit and then leave you with the chart, Figure 14-27. In this one, we rotate the two faces on the left around the lower edge. The lower edge stays in place and the upper and middle edges rotate out to the left. The object is stretched by the rotation.

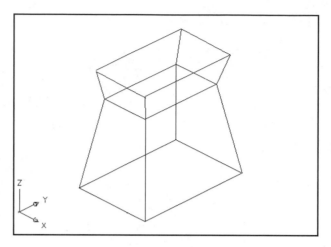

Figure 14-24

⊕ Type r or select Rotate from the dynamic input drop-down list.

⊕ Pick a point on the middle edge of the left side, as shown by P1 in Figure 14-25.

⊕ Press Enter to end face selection.

AutoCAD highlights the two left faces and prompts

```
Specify an axis point or
[Axis by object/View/Xaxis/Yaxis/Zaxis]
<2points>:
```

This is one of the more complex SOLIDEDIT prompts. It is asking you to define an axis of rotation by picking two points on a line, or by specifying an object or UCS axis to serve as the axis of rotation.

⊕ Pick the far corner of the lower left side, P2 in Figure 14-25.

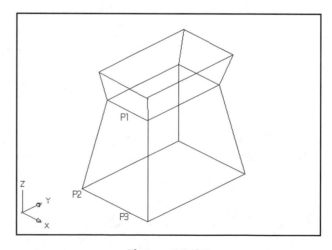

Figure 14-25

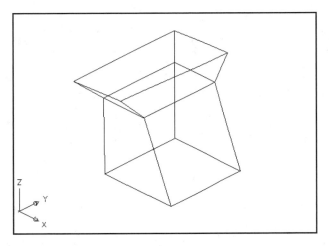

Figure 14-26

⊕ Pick any other point along the lower edge of the left face, P3 in Figure 14-25.

Now AutoCAD prompts for an angle of rotation, as in the ROTATE command:

Specify a rotation angle or [Reference]:

By rotating the faces back through 20 degrees, we can turn the lower face 10 degrees out from the base (because it is now tapered 10 degrees in), and stretch the top face out so that it flares even further. The rule for rotation direction is the standard AutoCAD right-hand rule. Point your right thumb parallel to the axis of rotation you just defined and you can see that this outward turning of the faces is a positive angle.

⊕ Type 20.

Your screen should resemble Figure 14-26.

Take the time to study the SOLIDEDIT options shown in Figure 14-27. This is a very powerful command that gives you great control of solid modeling procedures.

14.8   Creating 2-D Region Entities

> **GENERAL PROCEDURE**
>
> 1. Draw 2-D polyline shapes.
> 2. Type region or select the Region tool from the Draw toolbar.
> 3. Select Objects.

Regions are the 2-D equivalent of 3-D solids. They can be combined through union, subtraction, and intersection using the same commands utilized with solids. Regions are similar to faces in that they cover 2-D spaces. Like polylines, they can be extruded to form 3-D solids.

SOLIDEDIT FACE		
Options	**Description**	
Extrude	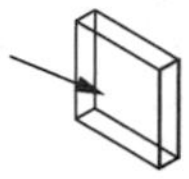 Select Face P2—P1 Select Points	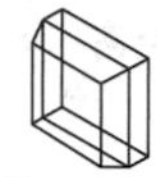 Face Extruded Angle 20°
Move	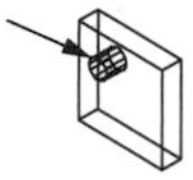 Select Face P1 P2 Select Points	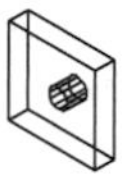 Face Moved
Offset	 Select Face P1 P2 Select Points	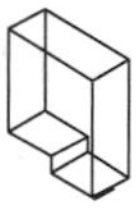 Face Offset Angle 12°
Delete	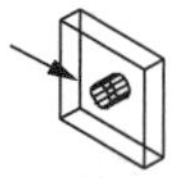 Select Face	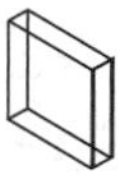 Face Deleted
Rotate	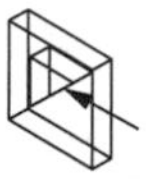 Select Face P1—P2 Select Axis	 Face Rotated
Tapered	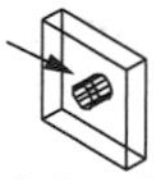 Select Face P2—P1 Select Points	 Face Tapered
Copy	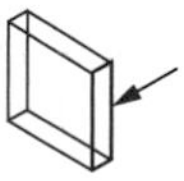 Select Face P1—P2 Select Points	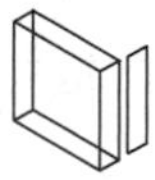 Face Copied

Figure 14-27

In this task, we create a simple composite region from two polyline rectangles. Individual regions are created using the REGION command on previously drawn polylines, or by copying the faces of previously drawn 3-D solids.

⊕ To begin this task, erase the solid from the last task and draw a rectangle again, or copy the bottom face and erase the rest to create a 2.00 × 4.00 polyline rectangle as shown previously in Figure 14-18.

If you wish to use the Copy Faces option of SOLIDEDIT as an exercise, the procedure is as follows:

1. Open the Modify menu, highlight Solids Editing, and select Copy Faces.
2. Type c for a crossing window selection.
3. Select the bottom face with a window that crosses a single bottom edge.
4. Type r and remove the adjacent face that will be highlighted.
5. Press Enter to end face selection.
6. Enter two points of a displacement for the copy.
7. Press Enter to exit SOLIDEDIT.
8. Erase the solid.

⊕ Draw a second complete polyline rectangle, 1.00 × 2.00, centered on the midpoint of the edge of the first, as shown in Figure 14-28.

Note: If you use the PLINE command, you must draw all four sides of this rectangle, even though you cannot see the side that lies along the left side of the larger rectangle. Regions can only be constructed from closed polyline figures.

Next, we convert the two rectangles into 2-D regions. If you used the SOLIDEDIT Copy Faces procedure, the copied face is already a region, but the steps that follow are the same.

⊕ Select Region from the Draw menu or the Region tool from the Draw toolbar.

AutoCAD prompts you to select objects.

⊕ Pick both rectangles with a window or crossing window.

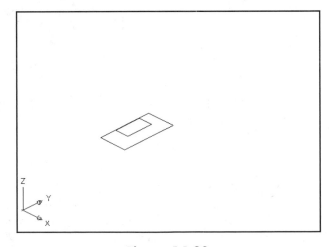

Figure 14-28

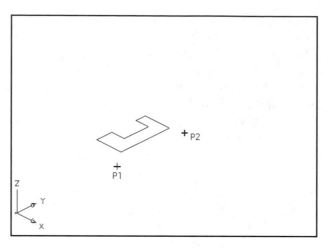

Figure 14-29

⊕ Press Enter to end object selection.

You see no change, although there is a message in the command area that says that two regions have been created. If the face is already a region, it says one region has been created instead.

Now if you subtract the smaller rectangle from the larger, you can see that these regions behave just like 3-D solids.

⊕ Open the Modify menu, highlight Solids Editing, and select Subtract.

⊕ Select the larger rectangle as the region to subtract from.

⊕ Press Enter or right-click to end object selection.

⊕ Select the smaller rectangle as the region to subtract.

⊕ Press Enter or right-click to end object selection.

Your screen should resemble Figure 14-29.

14.9 Creating Solids by Revolving 2-D Entities Using REVOLVE

GENERAL PROCEDURE

1. Draw regions or 2-D polyline shapes.
2. Open the Draw menu, highlight Solids, and select Revolve.
3. Select objects.
4. Specify an axis of revolution.
5. Specify an angle of revolution.

REVOLVE is a powerful solid modeling command that creates solid objects by revolving 2-D polyline shapes and regions around an axis. It functions in ways very similar to the REVSURF surface modeling command.

In this task, we create a spool-shaped 3-D solid by revolving the composite region from the last task around an axis in the XY plane to the right of the region.

⊕ To begin this task, you should have the composite region as shown in Figure 14-29 on your screen.

⊕ Open the Draw menu, highlight Solids, and select Revolve.

There is also a Revolve tool on the Solids Editing toolbar, shown previously in Figure 14-5.

⊕ Select the composite region.

⊕ Right-click to end selection.

AutoCAD prompts

```
Specify start point for axis of revolution or
define axis by [Object/X (axis)/Y (axis)]:
```

Object allows you to select a line or a one-segment polyline as the axis of revolution. X and Y allow you to specify one of the axes of the current UCS. We specify an axis by pointing.

⊕ Pick a start point 1.00 unit to the right of the region, as shown by P1 in Figure 14-29.

AutoCAD prompts for an endpoint of the axis.

⊕ Pick an endpoint like P2 in Figure 14-29.

AutoCAD prompts

```
Specify angle of revolution <360>:
```

Like REVSURF, REVOLVE gives you the option of creating only a portion of the circle of revolution. Unlike REVSURF, there is no option to begin the object somewhere other than in the plane of the region itself.

⊕ Press Enter to create the full circle.

Your screen should resemble Figure 14-30.

In the next two tasks, we continue to demonstrate methods for manipulating solids by creating a cutaway view and a section.

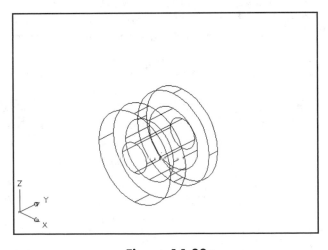

Figure 14-30

14.10 Creating Solid Cutaway Views with SLICE

GENERAL PROCEDURE

1. Open the Draw menu, highlight Solids, and select Slice, or select the Slice tool from the Solids toolbar.
2. Select objects.
3. Specify a cutting plane.
4. Specify a point on the plane.
5. Pick a side to retain.

A single solid or composite solid can be sliced along its intersection with a specifiable plane. The plane is specified in terms common to several solid commands.

In this task, we cut the object created in the last task along a plane parallel to the current z- and y-axes and retain the left portion so that we can view the inside of the spool.

⊕ **Open the Draw menu, highlight Solids, and select Slice.**

There is also a Slice tool on the Solids Editing toolbar, shown previously in Figure 14-5. AutoCAD prompts you to select objects.

⊕ **Select the spool.**

⊕ **Right-click to end object selection.**

AutoCAD now prompts for plane specification:

```
Specify first point on slicing plane by
[Object/Zaxis/View/XY/YZ/ZX/3points] <3points>:
```

A similar prompt is used in the SECTION command, which we explore next. The slicing plane requested here can be determined by an object, by a point on the z-axis, by one of the current UCS planes, or by showing three points. In this task, we use a YZ plane.

Take a look at Figure 14-31. It should help you visualize the XY, YZ, and ZX planes. The actual slicing plane is parallel to a plane of origin in the current UCS. In other words, it does not have to have the same origin. Once you have determined which plane you want to use, the next step is to specify a point on the plane.

⊕ **Type yz or right-click and select YZ from the shortcut menu.**

AutoCAD prompts for a point on the YZ plane. The default point is (0,0,0), which specifies the YZ plane of the current UCS. Any other point specifies a plane parallel to the current YZ plane.

⊕ **Pick a point similar to P1 in Figure 14-32, so that the y-axis of the crosshairs runs through the center of the spool.**

This causes the spool to be cut along its center line. AutoCAD prompts

```
Specify a point on the desired side of the plane or
[keep Both sides]:
```

⊕ **Pick a point similar to P2 in Figure 14-32, to the left of the previous point (i.e., left in the x direction).**

This shows that you want to retain the portion of the spool that lies along the left side of the cutting plane. Your screen should resemble Figure 14-32.

Next, we create a cross section of the remaining half.

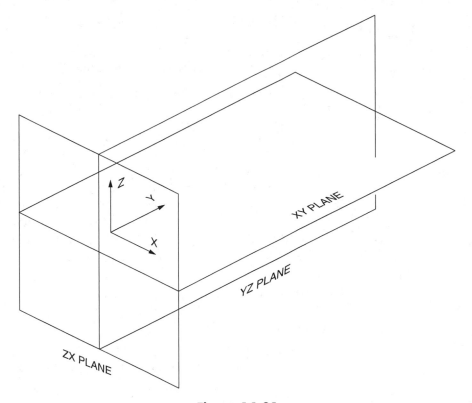

Figure 14-31

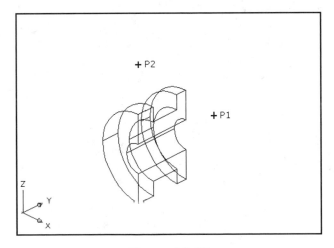

Figure 14-32

14.11 Creating Sections with SECTION

GENERAL PROCEDURE

1. Open the Draw menu, highlight Solids, and select Section.
2. Select objects.
3. Specify a sectioning plane.

Sectioning works just like slicing, but the outcome is a 2-D region taken from the solid along the specified plane. In this task, we create a region section of the spool by sectioning it along the XY plane. The result is a U-shaped block. It looks exactly like the region we used to create the revolved solid in the first place.

⊕ Open the Draw menu, highlight Solids, and select Section.

There is also a Section tool on the Solids Editing toolbar, shown previously in Figure 14-5.

⊕ Select the cut spool.

⊕ Right-click to end object selection.

AutoCAD prompts

```
Specify first point on Section plane by
[Object/Zaxis/View/XY/YZ/ZX/3points] <3points>:
```

This is nearly the same prompt as the slicing plane prompt. This time we cut along the current XY plane.

⊕ Type xy or right-click and select XY from the shortcut menu.

AutoCAD prompts for a point on the XY plane. Any point will do.

⊕ Press Enter for the point (0,0,0) or pick any point.

AutoCAD creates the section. To see it well, you need to move it or move the spool.

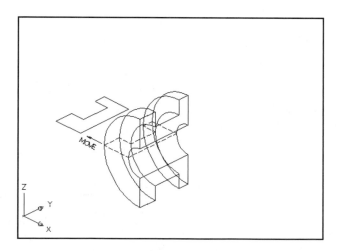

Figure 14-33

⊕ Enter the Move command, type L for last, end object selection, and then show a displacement to move the section away from the spool.

When you are finished, your screen should resemble Figure 14-33.

14.12 SHADING Solid Models

GENERAL PROCEDURE
1. Adjust layers, colors, and variables to create desired effects.
2. Type shade or select the Shade tool from the Render toolbar.

Shaded images are simple to create, as you know from using the 3DORBIT command. There are relatively few variables to manipulate. For more dramatic and realistic images you need to delve into the realm of rendering, introduced in the next task. Unlike shading, rendering involves a large number of variables and requires a great deal of practice before you become proficient.

In working with shaded images, your only options concern the color of objects in the image, the manner in which edges are shown, the color of edges, and the relative amounts of diffuse and ambient light. In this exercise, we create a shaded image of the composite wedge from earlier in the chapter. In the next task, we use the same object for rendering. We begin by inserting the wedge.

⊕ Erase all objects from your screen.

⊕ Type i or select the Insert Block tool from the Draw toolbar.

⊕ Select the Wedge block from the block list.

⊕ Click OK.

⊕ Insert the wedge near the middle of your grid.

Because this book does not contain color illustrations, we have moved our wedge to Layer 0 so that the image is shaded in gray and white. If you do the same, your screen images will more closely match our illustrations. The following procedure is provided if you wish to work with gray and white rather than color images:

1. Make Layer 0 current by opening the Layer list on the Standard toolbar and clicking Layer 0.
2. Explode the Wedge block.
3. Draw a line anywhere on Layer 0.
4. Use the Match Properties tool from the Standard toolbar to move the wedge to Layer 0.
5. Erase the line.

⊕ Turn off the grid.

You do not want the grid in your shaded or rendered images.

⊕ Open the View menu and highlight Shade.

This opens the submenu shown in Figure 14-34. There are seven options. The first three are wireframe and hidden images. The next four correspond

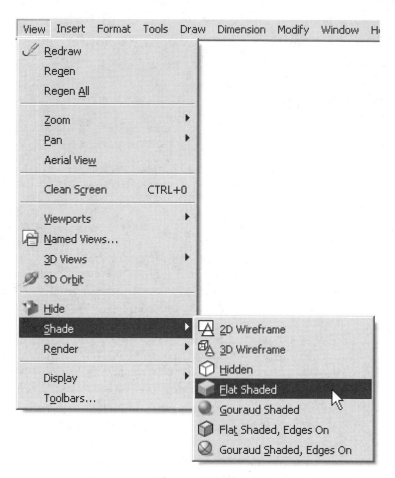

Figure 14-34

to the four settings of the Shadedge variable. Shadedge determines whether edges of shaded objects are outlined and the complexity of color values used.

⊕ Select Flat Shaded.

This produces a shaded image similar to Figure 14-35. We suggest that you try the other three settings to see how they appear on your screen before going on to the next task. The differences are not dramatic and might not be noticeable at all with the current light settings. At this point, you should also take advantage of the 3DORBIT command to get a good look at the shaded object.

⊕ Enter the 3DORBIT command and view the shaded image from different angles.

Notice how the lighting effects on faces change as your viewpoint changes.

⊕ Reset the view before leaving 3DORBIT.

Reminder: When AutoCAD shades or renders objects, it automatically changes the Shademode variable to 3D. As discussed previously in Chapter 13, to remove shading or rendering, it is necessary to change Shademode back to 2D. (Type shademode and then 2, or open the View menu, highlight Shade, and select 2D Wireframe.)

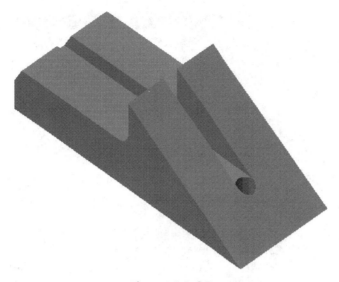

Figure 14-35

14.13 RENDERing Solid Models

GENERAL PROCEDURE

1. Position lights.
2. Attach materials.
3. Adjust light intensity.
4. Render.
5. Save scene.

Rendering goes far beyond shading by creating the effect of light falling on the various surfaces of a solid or surface model. Rendering is a complex craft and mastery of it requires many hours of experimentation. Most of the techniques involved concern the placement and setting of lights. There are four types of lights, and each light has its own set of variables and settings that dramatically affects the end result. Knowing the various lights, how to position them, and how to understand their respective settings is a good place to begin. However, this knowledge alone will not take you very far. You need to accumulate hours of experience to know what you want and how to achieve it.

In this task, we show you how to position lights and how to use some of the most critical settings. We continue to use the wedge shaded in the last task and to work on Layer 0.

⊕   To begin this task, you should have the wedge on your screen in a southeast viewpoint, as in the last task.

Ambient Light

First, we simply render the object as is without any change in lighting. What you see is entirely dependent on the default ambient light setting. Ambient light is

Figure 14-36

background light that fills space and is the same everywhere. It has no direction and can only be varied as to color and intensity.

⊞ Open the View menu, highlight Render, and select Render.

There is also a Render tool on the Render toolbar, shown in Figure 14-36. AutoCAD displays the Render dialog box shown in Figure 14-37. Ignore the options in the dialog box for now.

⊞ Click Render at the bottom.

After a few moments you see an image similar to the one in Figure 14-38. As you can see, this image is not much of an advancement over the shaded images in the last task. To enhance the lighting, we need the LIGHT command.

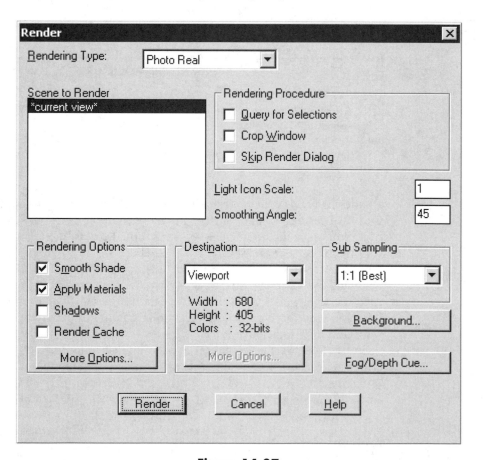

Figure 14-37

Figure 14-38

The Lights Dialog Box

Lights are created, placed, and modified using the Lights dialog box.

⊕   Open the View menu, highlight Render, and select Light.

There is also a Lights tool on the Render toolbar, shown in Figure 14-36. The LIGHT command opens the Lights dialog box, shown in Figure 14-39. Look at the Ambient Light panel on the right. Ambient light has only color and intensity

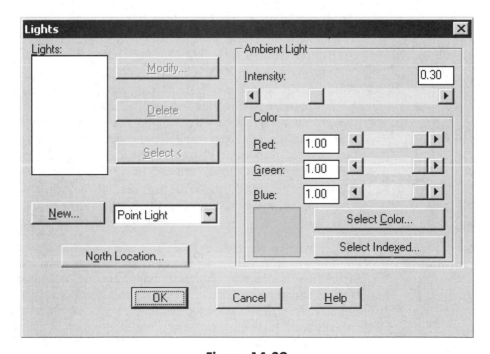

Figure 14-39

settings. With the scroll bar at the top, you can vary the intensity from 0 to 1.00. The default setting is 0.30. Try changing the intensity using the following procedure:

1. Using the scroll bar, select greater ambient light intensity. Increase it to 1.00 to see the effect clearly.
2. Click OK.
3. Open the View menu, highlight Render, and select Render.
4. Click Render in the Render dialog box.

In the Ambient Light panel, are three scroll bars for mixing the amounts of red, green, and blue light. All types of lights have these scroll bars so that you can vary the color quality of the light coming from individual light sources as well as ambient light color. Feel free to experiment with color settings at this time. The effect of the color mix is especially clear on a gray-and-white object like ours. The following steps change the color of ambient light in your rendering. Along the way, we also show you how to simplify the rendering procedure for repeated renderings.

⊕ Open the Lights dialog box and return the ambient light intensity to .30.

⊕ Set the green and blue scroll bars to 0 and leave the red at 1.00.

⊕ Click OK.

When you are adjusting rendering schemes you want to perform the rendering operation frequently to see how your changes look. To make this procedure more efficient, you can choose to bypass the Render dialog box, as follows:

⊕ Open the View menu, highlight Render, and select Render.

⊕ In the Render dialog box, look for the Rendering Procedure panel in the upper right. Click Skip Render Dialog.

This changes the default behavior of the RENDER command. From now on AutoCAD renders the current view immediately without intervening dialog boxes when you type render or select Render from the View menu. To reverse the procedure and access the Render dialog box again, type rpref or select Preferences from the Render submenu, and then clear the Skip Render Dialog button in the Rendering Procedure panel.

The new rendered image appears pink on your screen.

⊕ When you are ready to move on, return the color scroll bars to 1.00 and the intensity to about 0.00 to better match our grayscale illustrations.

Changing the Background Color

You might find that certain rendered images are too dark against the AutoCAD background screen color. You can remedy this by changing to a different background color through the Preferences dialog box. Or, you can add a background to your rendering through the Background dialog box, which is part of the rendering system. The difference is that the rendered background becomes part of the rendering, whereas the AutoCAD window background does not. In this task we add a true background. For reference, the procedure for changing the AutoCAD window color is as follows:

1. Open the Tools menu and select Options from the bottom of the menu.
2. Click the Display tab.
3. Click Colors.
4. Select a color from the color list.
5. Click Apply & Close.
6. Click OK.

To introduce true rendering backgrounds we add a gradient background. Because of the colors involved, we cannot illustrate the results.

⊕   Open the View menu, highlight Render, and select Background.

This opens the Background dialog box illustrated in Figure 14-40. There are many possibilities available that we do not explore here. Typically when you first open the dialog box the Solid radio button is selected and so is the AutoCAD background check box. With these two settings, many options are inaccessible, and the AutoCAD window color is used for the rendering background color.

⊕   Select the Gradient radio button.

The AutoCAD background check box becomes inaccessible automatically, because it is solid and incompatible with a gradient color scheme. The color adjustment area and the horizon, height, and rotation area are now accessible. To see what the current gradient looks like, use the Preview box.

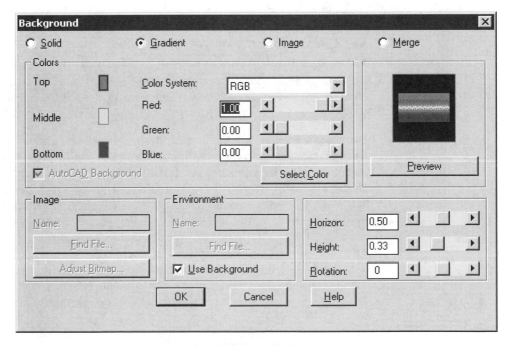

Figure 14-40

⊕   Click Preview.

> The preview image appears, showing a background that grades from red to green to blue. Notice that these are the colors shown on the left next to top, middle, and bottom. One of these three is highlighted with a dark border. The selected color can be adjusted with the three color scroll bars in the middle. These scrolls can be used like a palette to mix the amounts of red, green, and blue in the top, middle, and bottom colors. Finally, the horizon, height, and rotation scroll bars can be used to vary the proportions and orientation of color lines in the gradient.
>
> You should experiment with these settings to get a feel for how they work.

⊕   When you have finished experimenting, click OK to retain the background you have created.

⊕   Type render or open the View menu, highlight Render, and select Render.

> You should see your ambient light rendering with a color gradient background. Even a simple gradient background produces a dramatic effect. Next we add some more focused lighting.

We explore three types of light placement. To define light position, it is helpful to create a three-viewport configuration so that you can see what is happening from different viewpoints.

⊕   Open the View menu, highlight Viewports, and select New Viewports.

⊕   Select Three: Right.

⊕   Select 3D from the Setup list.

⊕   Click OK.

> Your screen is redrawn with a three-viewport configuration: top and front views on the left, southeast isometric view on the right.

⊕   Click in the top left viewport and zoom .5x.

⊕   Click in the bottom left viewport and zoom .5x.

> Your screen should now resemble Figure 14-41, except that you have shaded objects. Except where we are showing a specific rendering, we continue to show wireframe images for simplicity and clarity.

> **Note:** In AutoCAD, UCSs are defined per viewport. You can have a different UCS in each viewport if you like. The standard viewport configurations you can select from the Viewports dialog box use a convention of matching the UCS to the view in orthographic views. You can find a front UCS in a front view, a top UCS in a top view, and so on. The isometric view keeps the active coordinate system, in this case, the WCS, which we have previously viewed in 2-D plan or top view. This means that the top and southeast isometric views are on the same grid and working with the same UCS, whereas the front view has its own UCS. The front UCS is derived through simple rotation of the xyz-axis around the WCS origin and therefore has no specified relation to the objects in the drawing. In other words, the objects in the front view are not on the grid at all.

Spotlight

We are going to add a spotlight on the right side of the object, aimed in along the slot. Light placement is probably the most important consideration in rendering. If

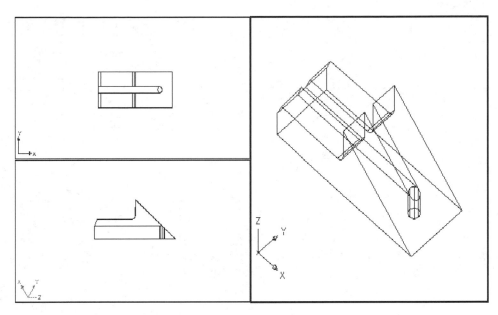

Figure 14-41

you have used point filters previously, then you have already learned all you need to know to position lights. Keep in mind that lights are usually positioned above the XY plane and are probably alone in space. Point filters can be very helpful in this situation because there is nothing to snap them on to.

Before we can add a light, we must designate the light type, specify that it is new, and give it a name.

⊕ Click in the upper left viewport to make the top view active.

It is extremely important that you work in either the top view or the southeast isometric view. The front view currently has a different UCS and produces very different results. You must enter the correct viewport and therefore the desired UCS before entering the LIGHTS command.

⊕ Open the View menu, highlight Render, and select Light.

⊕ Click the arrow next to Point Light at the left of the Lights dialog box.

The options shown are Point Light, Distant Light, and Spotlight. We begin with a spotlight because its focus and directionality make it easy to understand.

⊕ Click Spotlight.

⊕ Click New.

This opens the New Spotlight dialog box shown in Figure 14-42. Notice first that there is a place for a name, a scroll bar for intensity, and three scroll bars for color, just as in the Ambient Light panel. There are also panels for position, hotspot and falloff, and attenuation. We discuss these in a moment, but first let's give the light a name and a position.

⊕ Type Spot in the Light Name edit box.

⊕ Type 5 in the Intensity edit box, or move the scroll bar to an intensity of about 5.00.

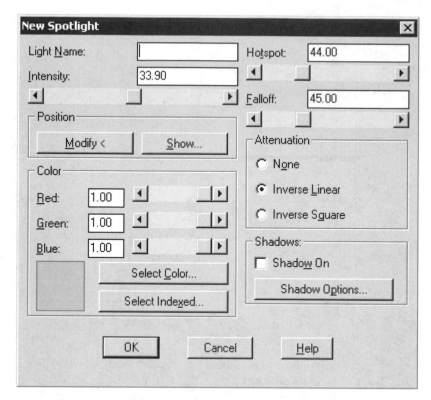

Figure 14-42

⊕ Click Modify in the Position panel.

This closes the dialog box temporarily and gives you access to your drawing. On the command line, you see the following prompt:

Enter light target <current>:

Spotlights have a target and a source position. As is the case with real spotlights, AutoCAD rendering spotlights are carefully placed and aimed at a particular point in the drawing. The light falls in a cone shape and diminishes from the center of the cone. You can vary the size of the focal beam using the Hotspot scroll bar and the size of the surrounding falloff area using the Falloff scroll bar.

For this exercise, we place a light above and to the right of the wedge, aimed directly into the slot. We use point selection and XY filters to place the target and the light source where we want them.

⊕ At the prompt for a light target, type .xy or hold down Shift and right-click to open the object snap shortcut menu, highlight Point Filters, and select .XY.

AutoCAD prompts .xy of and waits for you to choose a point in the XY plane.

Moving the cursor within the viewport, you should notice that AutoCAD has created a default target placement, which you can ignore.

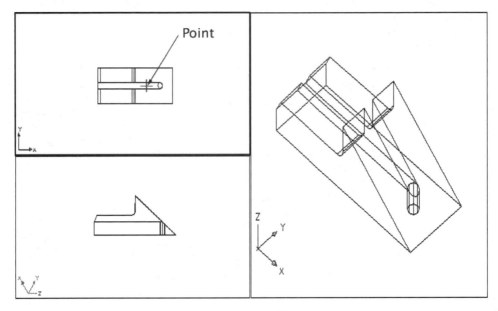

Figure 14-43

⊕ Pick a point about 1.0 unit to the left of the cylindrical hole, as shown in Figure 14-43.

AutoCAD now prompts for a *z* value:

(need Z):

To place the target point right in the slot, we need to have a *z* value of 1.00. (The bottom of the slot is 1.00 above the XY plane.)

⊕ Type 1.

The target point has been specified. Now AutoCAD prompts for the spotlight location:

Enter light location <current>:

We use an .xy filter to place the light source to the right and above the wedge.

⊕ Type .xy or open the shortcut menu, highlight Point Filter, and select .XY.

⊕ In response to the of prompt, select a point about 2.00 units to the right of the wedge, as shown in Figure 14-44.

⊕ In response to the need Z prompt, type 5 to position the spotlight 5.00 above the XY plane.

This brings back the New Spotlight dialog box.

⊕ Click OK to exit the New Spotlight dialog box.

⊕ Click OK to exit the Lights dialog box.

You now see a spotlight icon in your drawing. The three-view configuration shows clearly how it is positioned and directed. Let's render the scene again to see the spotlight in action.

⊕ Click the right viewport to make it active.

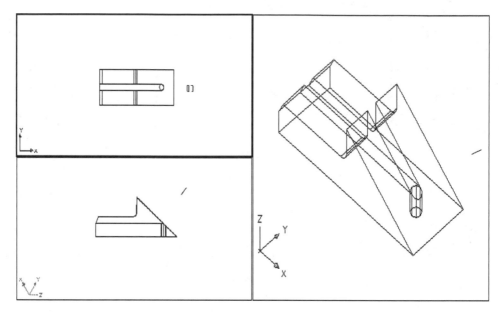

Figure 14-44

⊕ Type render or open the View menu, highlight Render, and select Render.

You see a rendered image similar to the one in Figure 14-45. In this image, you can clearly see how the spotlight hits the wedge just behind the hole and falls off in waves along the back of the object.

To achieve a more precise light cone, you can change from a Gouraud style rendering to a Phong rendering. To do this, we need to access the Render dialog box again. We can do this without changing the current procedure that bypasses the dialog box.

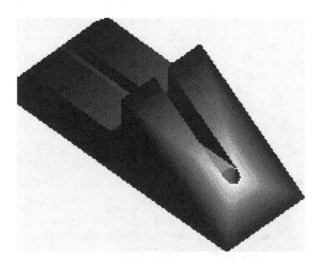

Figure 14-45

⊕ Type rpref or open the View menu, highlight Render, and select Preferences.

This opens the Rendering Preferences dialog box, which is exactly the same as the Render dialog box, except that there is an OK instead of a Render button at the bottom. You cannot render directly from the Render Preferences dialog box.

⊕ From the Render Preferences dialog box, first check to see that Render is selected in the Rendering Type list at the top of the dialog box and then click the More Options button in the Rendering Options panel.

⊕ Select the Phong radio button in the Render Quality panel.

⊕ Click OK.

⊕ Click OK to exit the Rendering Preferences dialog box.

⊕ Type render or open the View menu, highlight Render, and select Render.

Your new rendered image should resemble Figure 14-46.

Next we add a point light. Before going on, you might want to experiment with some of the other features of spotlighting (available in the New Spotlight or Modify Spotlight subdialog of the Lights dialog box). Try varying the hotspot and falloff. Notice that the hotspot must always be smaller than the falloff. You also see significant differences when you vary the attenuation. Attenuation is the rate at which light intensity diminishes relative to distance from the light source. In the default Inverse Linear setting, light two units away from its source appears half as bright. If you switch to Inverse Square attenuation, light at two units is only one fourth as bright as it is at the source. Switching to Inverse Square thus causes the light from a spotlight to diminish more quickly over a shorter distance.

When you have finished experimenting, we suggest that you return to our settings so that your images continue to resemble ours. These include the following: Ambient light is at 0.00 intensity and all colors are at 1.00. The spotlight is at about

Figure 14-46

5.00 intensity, all colors are at 1.00, hotspot is at 44 degrees with falloff at 45 degrees, and attenuation is inverse linear.

Point Light

Point light works like a light bulb with no shade. It radiates outward equally in all directions. Like spotlighting, the light from a point light attenuates over distance.

In this exercise, we place a point light right inside the slot of the wedge. This clearly shows the light bulb effect of a small point of light radiating outward.

⊕ Make the upper left viewport active.

⊕ Open the View menu, highlight Render, and select Light.

⊕ Click the arrow to the right of Spotlight and switch to Point Light.

⊕ Click New.

⊕ Type point in the Light Name edit box.

⊕ Click Modify.

For a point light, you only need to specify a location, because point light has no direction other than outward from the source. The prompt is

Enter light location <current>:

We use the same point-filtering system to locate this light.

⊕ At the prompt, type .xy or open the cursor menu, highlight Point Filters, and select .XY.

⊕ At the of prompt, pick a point in the top view at the center of the slot and about 1.00 unit behind the plane where the box and the wedge join, as shown in Figure 14-47.

⊕ Type 1.25 for a z value.

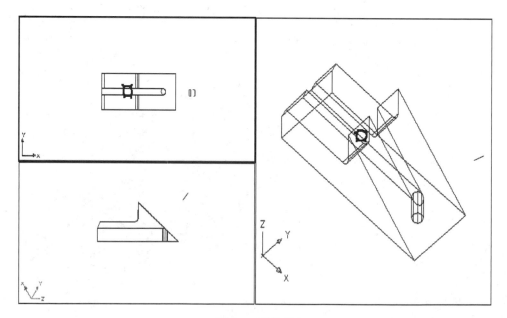

Figure 14-47

Figure 14-48

Because the slot is at 1.00 from the XY plane, this puts the point light just above the bottom of the slot.

⊕ Click OK.

⊕ Click OK again to exit the Lights dialog box.

⊕ Click the right viewport to make it active.

⊕ Type render or open the View menu, highlight Render, and select Render.

Your rendered object should resemble Figure 14-48. In this image, you can clearly see the effect of the point light within the slot along with the spotlight falling on the right side of the object.

Distant Light

The last type of light is called distant light. It is often used to achieve the effect of direct sunlight. In AutoCAD rendering, a distant light source emits beams of light that are parallel and travel in one direction only. Distant light does not attenuate. It is the same at any distance from the source. Distant light placement is defined by a directional vector; the command-line prompt asks for a "to" point and a "from" point. You can define this vector precisely using point filters, as we have done previously. The to point will probably be on an object or in the XY plane. The from point will be above the XY plane. Most important is the angle and direction between the two points. You can define these points using point filters, as we have done previously, or you can use the sunlight-oriented Azimuth and Altitude dials shown in the Distant Light dialog box. Because you have already used point filters, we introduce the dial system here for variety.

⊕ Open the View menu, highlight Render, and select Light.

⊕ Click the arrow to the right of Point Light and switch to Distant Light.

⊕ Click New.

This opens the New Distant Light dialog box shown in Figure 14-49. You should see scroll bars for intensity and color on the left. On the right, you can

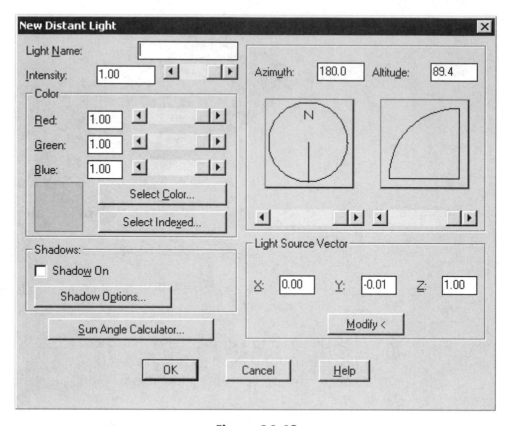

Figure 14-49

see the Azimuth and Altitude dials and scroll bars above a Light Source Vector modification panel. By clicking Modify, you could proceed to place the distant light source with to and from points using point selection and point filters. The Azimuth and Altitude system might help you to think more specifically in terms of sunlight. The Azimuth setting determines the position of sunlight relative to the east–west horizon. In other words, it simulates the variations of sunlight depending on your position on the planet and the time of year. The Altitude setting simulates time-of-day variations. In the northern hemisphere in late morning, for example, the sun is coming from the south (180 degrees, opposite north on the Azimuth dial) from an altitude of, let's say, 65 degrees. You can use the scroll bars, points on the dials, or typing in the edit boxes to achieve these settings. You can also use the Sun Angle Calculator to find appropriate settings for different times and places.

⊕ Type distant in the Light Name edit box.

⊕ Using the scroll bar, move the Azimuth setting all the way to the right so that the edit box reads 180 degrees.

⊕ Using the scroll bar, move the Altitude setting partway to the right so that the edit box shows 65 degrees.

   Changes in these settings also cause changes in the Light Source Vector panel and the dials above the scroll bars.

Figure 14-50

⊕ Using the Intensity scroll bar at the upper left of the dialog box, reduce the light intensity to about .60.

⊕ Click OK.

⊕ Click OK in the Lights dialog box.

⊕ Type render or open the View menu, highlight Render, and select Render.

Your image should resemble the rendering in Figure 14-50. By comparing this image with the one in Figure 14-48, you can see the effect of adding distant "sunlight" to this rendering.

The Render Window

To get a full view of a rendered image, it is often desirable to send the rendering to the Render Window rather than to view the rendering within a single viewport. Renderings sent to the Render Window are also saved during the current drawing session so you can quickly compare results. To use the Render Window, you have to make one change in the Rendering Preferences or Render dialog box.

⊕ Type rpref or open the View menu, highlight Render, and select Preferences.

⊕ In the dialog box, look for the Destination panel in the middle. Click the arrow to the right of the box that says Viewport.

Clicking the arrow opens a list that shows Viewport, Render Window, and File as Destination options. Rendering to a viewport you have already done; rendering to a file sends the rendering information directly to a file without displaying the image on your screen. Render files can be created in TGA, TIFF, GIF, PostScript, X11, PBM, PGM, PPM, BMP, PCX, SUN FITS, FAX G III, and IFF formats and can then be displayed in other graphics systems.

⊕ Click Render Window.

The list closes and Render Window is shown in the Destination box.

⊕ Click OK.

⊕ Type render or open the View menu, highlight Render, and select Render.

The rendered wedge is shown in the Render Window. This window has standard Windows features and can be moved, maximized, or minimized. Once it is opened, there is a label for it on the Windows taskbar. It appears when you click the already opened AutoCAD button. You can switch between the Drawing Window and the Render Window using the two options shown. The Render Window also has its own set of options for changing the resolution and the size of the window. These are accessed from the File menu of the Render Window.

⊕ Click the maximize button to see a full-screen rendered image.

⊕ Click the AutoCAD drawing name label on the Windows taskbar to return to the Drawing Window.

Scenes

A rendered scene is made up of a view and a set of lights. Once you have positioned lights, you might want to present the image from different points of view and use different configurations of lights. Defined scenes can be saved so that you can re-create them easily and even switch from one to another. For example, let's create a scene without the spotlight to see the effect of the distant light and the point light together.

⊕ Open the View menu, highlight Render, and select Scene.

There is also a Scene tool on the Render toolbar, shown previously in Figure 14-36. This opens the Scenes dialog box shown in Figure 14-51.

⊕ Select New.

⊕ Type nospot for a scene name. (Spaces are not allowed in names.)

⊕ Highlight Point and Dist in the Lights area. (Hold down the Shift key to highlight both names.)

Make sure that Spot is not highlighted.

⊕ Click OK.

⊕ In the Scenes dialog box, make sure that NOSPOT is highlighted and then click OK.

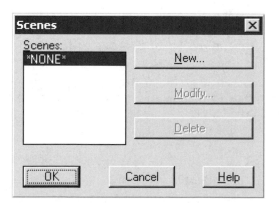

Figure 14-51

Figure 14-52

Now that the new scene is defined, you can create a new rendering.

⊕ **Open the View menu, highlight Render, and select Render.**

Your Nospot scene should resemble Figure 14-52 and is rendered to the Render Window.

⊕ **Click on the AutoCAD drawing name label on the Windows taskbar to return to the Drawing Window.**

Notice that the image in the viewport is not the new rendering, but the previous image with the spotlight included. The rendered image in the Render Window does not affect the image in the viewport.

Attaching Materials

Materials can be created or selected from AutoCAD's materials library. Each material definition has its own characteristic color, ambient light color, reflection color, and roughness value. Materials can also be created or modified. Changing an object's material dramatically affects the way it is rendered, so it usually makes sense to attach materials before adjusting light intensity and color. In this exercise, we simply take you through the procedure of loading materials from the AutoCAD library and attaching them to an object. When you experiment on your own, you see color effects that we cannot show in this book.

⊕ **Open the View menu, highlight Render, and select Materials.**

There is also a Materials tool on the Render toolbar, as shown in Figure 14-53.

Notice that there is a Materials Library option as well as a Materials option. These two options refer to the MATLIB and RMAT commands. MATLIB

Figure 14-53

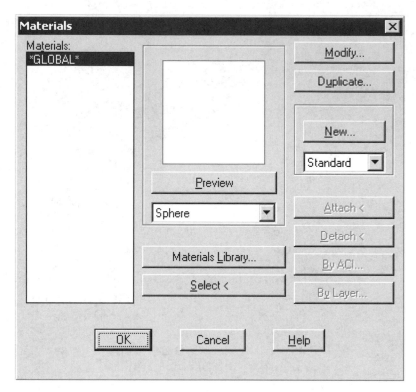

Figure 14-54

opens the Materials Library dialog box and RMAT opens the Materials dialog box. Materials Library is used to load Materials into a drawing, whereas Materials is used to attach, modify, and create materials. Because you can access the Materials Library through the Materials dialog box, it might be more efficient to go this way. RMAT opens the Materials dialog box shown in Figure 14-54. Before we can attach a material, we must load at least one from the Materials Library. To use this box, select a material or materials on the right and then select Import to bring them into your drawing.

⊕ Click Materials Library.

This opens the Materials Library dialog box shown in Figure 14-55. To load materials, they must be selected on the right and then imported.

⊕ Select Beige Matte.

⊕ While Beige Matte is highlighted, click Import.

The Beige Matte material definition is loaded and you can see it on the Materials list at the left.

⊕ Click OK.

Now you must attach the material to the object you are rendering. When there is more than one object, you can attach different materials to different objects.

⊕ Click Attach.

The dialog box disappears and you see this prompt:

        Select objects to attach BEIGE MATTE to:

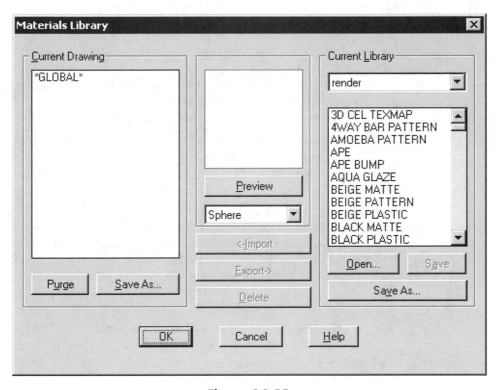

Figure 14-55

⊕ Select the wedge.

⊕ Right-click to end object selection.

⊕ Click OK.

You are now ready to render.

⊕ Type render or open the View menu, highlight Render, and select Render.

Your rendered image is similar to the last image, but it appears in beige tones.

14.14 Creating Perspective and Clipped Views with 3DORBIT

GENERAL PROCEDURE

1. Create objects.
2. Enter 3DORBIT.
3. Adjust viewpoint.
4. Open shortcut menu.
5. Highlight Projection.
6. Select Perspective.
7. Exit 3DORBIT.

We have a few more presentation tricks to show you before we are done. In this task, you learn how to use the 3DORBIT command to create simple perspective views. In perspective projections, all parallel lines converge at one horizon point. In the usual parallel projection, parallel lines are presented as parallel on the screen. Perspective projection replicates the way the eye sees objects as they recede into the distance.

⊕ To begin this task you should have the 3-D solid wedge model on your screen from the last task.

⊕ If necessary, click in the right viewport to make it active.

⊕ Open the View menu, highlight Viewports, and select 1 Viewport.

You should have the model in a southeast isometric view in a single viewport. Whatever shading or rendering you have is fine for this task.

⊕ Using the scroll bars, center the model within the drawing area.

The next step is to adjust the viewpoint on the object to create a "long, flat" view. This type of view shows the effect of perspective projection more dramatically than the views we have been using. This can be done by adjusting the viewpoint in the 3DORBIT command, but we provide a method using the VPOINT command, which allows a more precise adjustment to match our illustrations.

⊕ Open the View menu, highlight 3D Views, and select Viewpoint Presets.

⊕ In the Viewpoint Presets dialog box, enter 345 for the angle from the *x*-axis and 15 for the angle from the XY plane.

⊕ Click OK to exit the dialog box.

Your screen should resemble Figure 14-56.

⊕ Open the View menu and select 3DORBIT.

You see the familiar arcball, which you do not need because your viewpoint is already adjusted.

⊕ Right-click to open the shortcut menu.

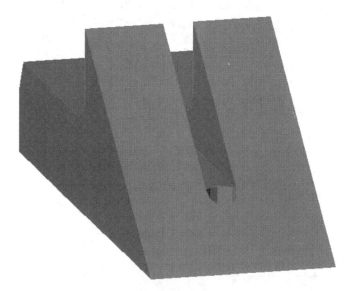

Figure 14-56

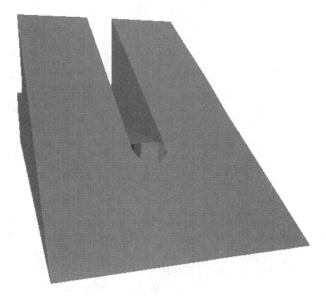

Figure 14-57

⊕ Highlight Projection, and select Perspective.

The menu disappears and the wedge is presented in perspective projection, as shown in Figure 14-57. Compare this with the previous parallel projection image. If you want a little more dramatic demonstration, add the grid and then switch back and forth between perspective and parallel projections.

Note: Whatever projection you are in when you leave 3DORBIT is maintained in your drawing. By leaving objects in perspective, you can create perspective renderings. However, you cannot edit, pick points, zoom, or pan in your drawing while in a perspective view.

3DORBIT Zoom, Pan, and Camera Adjustments

While you are in 3DORBIT and in a perspective projection, it is a good time to explore the 3DORBIT Zoom, Pan, and Camera adjustment options. The difference between camera adjustment and zooming, for example, is more evident in a perspective projection.

⊕ Stay in 3DORBIT and right-click to open the shortcut menu.

⊕ If you have not already done so, turn on the 3DORBIT grid.

⊕ Open the shortcut menu again and select Pan.

The Zoom and Pan options work just like the Realtime ZOOM and PAN options you are used to. You should see the Pan hand cursor icon.

⊕ Use the cursor to pan left and right, up and down.

Notice that in perspective projection, panning actually turns the model. Try panning in parallel projection to see the difference.

⊕ Open the shortcut menu and switch to parallel perspective.

You are still in panning mode when the menu closes.

⊕   Pan left and right again.

Observe how everything shifts together in a completely parallel manner. Now try zooming in parallel.

⊕   Open the shortcut menu and select Zoom.

You see the Realtime ZOOM cursor.

⊕   Click and drag the cursor up and down the screen to zoom in and out.

Notice that zoom takes you in and out of the center point of the display, so that you move directly into the grid or a point on the object. Now stay in zooming mode and switch to a perspective projection.

⊕   Open the shortcut menu, highlight Projection, and select Perspective again.

You are still in zoom mode when the menu closes.

⊕   Click and drag the cursor up and down the screen to zoom in and out.

Notice how zooming in perspective is the same as zooming in parallel because you are moving straight in and out on a single line directed at the target point at the center. Now try adjusting the camera distance.

⊕   Open the cursor menu, highlight More, and select Adjust Distance.

You see the camera adjustment cursor, which works like the Realtime ZOOM cursor but produces a different effect.

⊕   Click and drag the cursor up and down the screen slowly to adjust camera distance in and out.

Observe how adjusting the camera distance produces a long, flat motion that brings you down into the wedge and beyond to where there is no object visible. Now switch back to a parallel projection.

⊕   Open the shortcut menu, highlight Projection, and select Parallel.

⊕   Click and drag the cursor up and down the screen to adjust camera distance in and out.

In parallel projection, you observe no difference between zooming and adjusting camera distance.

Before going on to the clipping plane options that complete this task, you should also try the Swivel Camera option. This option moves your point of view around the target point at the center of the display and adjusts your view of objects accordingly. It is probably easier to comprehend this action in the current parallel projection, but you are encouraged to experiment in perspective as well.

Adjusting Clipping Planes in 3DORBIT

The last feature of the 3DORBIT command that we demonstrate is the Clipping plane option. With this feature, you can add an invisible plane in front of or behind objects. With a front clipping plane, for example, any part of the object that would be in front of the plane is not displayed. In this way, you can show a view of the inside of an object without actually sectioning it.

⊕   Open the shortcut menu and select Reset View to return to the 345 degrees from X, 15 degrees from XY view with which we began this exercise (Figure 14-56 or 14-57, depending on which projection you are in).

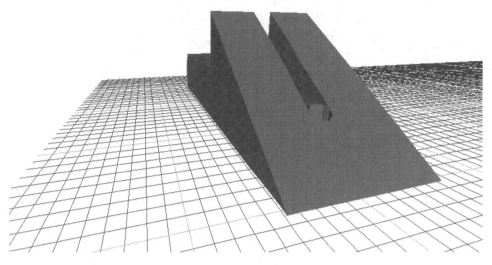

Figure 14-58

⊕ If necessary, open the shortcut menu and switch to a perspective projection, as shown previously in Figure 14-57.

⊕ Open the shortcut menu again and pan and zoom so that your grid and wedge are positioned similar to Figure 14-58.

This makes it easier for you to see the clipping planes in action.

⊕ Open the shortcut menu, highlight More, and select Adjust Clipping Planes.

This opens an Adjust Clipping Planes window, as shown in Figure 14-59. In this window, the grid and wedge have been rotated 90 degrees, so that you can adjust clipping planes from above. The green and white lines across the middle of the window represent the clipping plane, and the icons on the toolbar above let you control which plane you are adjusting, and also to turn clipping planes on and off. In the current default setting, the front clipping plane has been turned on and its adjustment tool is in the on position. Looking at the image in the drawing area, you can clearly see that the front part of the wedge has been clipped away. Clicking and dragging the plane in the Adjust Clipping Planes window brings it back into view.

⊕ Open the shortcut menu again and select Front Clipping on.

⊕ Click and drag the cursor up and down in the Adjust Clipping Planes window.

Observe the model as you move the plane. Notice that you don't have to be on the line of the plane to drag it. Clicking and dragging vertically anywhere in the window causes the plane to move. When the two planes come together, the back plane moves also, as if it were being pushed.

⊕ Move the front plane to create an image similar to Figure 14-60, showing the inside of the hole in the wedge.

There you have it. You have come a long way since drawing your first line in Chapter 1. You will find many drawings in this chapter and in Appendix A on which to practice your skills. Good luck!

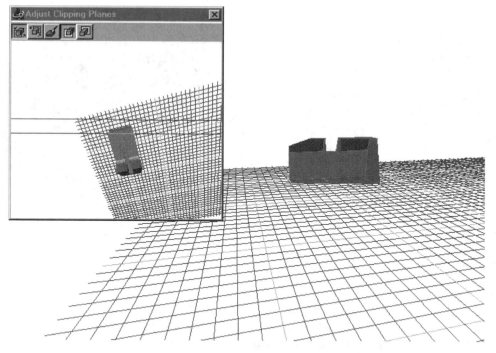

Figure 14-59

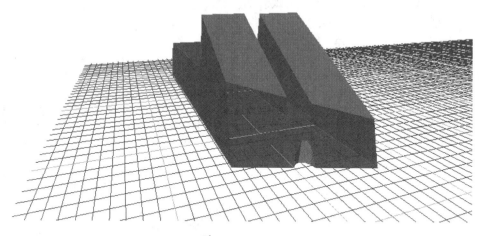

Figure 14-60

14.15   Review Material

Questions

1. What 3-D solid objects and commands would you use to create a square nut with a bolt hole in the middle?
2. What command allows you to draw outside the XY plane of the current UCS without the use of typed coordinates, object snap, or point filters?

3. Why is there a prompt for a base surface in CHAMFER, but not in FILLET?

4. What are names of three ways to select faces for editing in the SOLIDEDIT command?

5. What is the difference between a REGION and a 2D SOLID? What is the difference between a REGION and a 3DFACE?

6. What options are available for the creation of different effects in shaded images?

7. What is the major additional effect available in rendered images that is not available in shaded images?

8. How would you use a point filter to place a spotlight 5.0 units above the point (3,5,0)?

9. What is ambient light?

10. What are the shapes and qualities of spotlights, point lights, and distant lights? What is attenuation, and how does it affect each type of lighting?

11. What four qualities make up a material definition?

12. What are some limitations on the capacity to manipulate perspective projection views in the Drawing Window?

13. Why are objects rotated 90 degrees in the Adjust Clipping Planes window?

Drawing Problems

1. Open a new drawing with the 1B prototype, switch to a southeast isometric view, and draw a solid cylinder, centered at (9,6,0), with a radius of 3.0 units and a height of 5.0 units.

2. On Layer 1, draw a solid box 2.0 × 2.0 units at the base, with a height of 5.0 units, centered at (9,6,0).

3. Subtract the box from the cylinder.

4. Create a section view of the composite object cut along the diagonal of the rectangular hole.

5. Create a rendered image with a solid blue background, a spotlight with target at (9,6,3) and source at (14,8,6), and a distant light at the default position.

14.16   WWW Exercise 14 (Optional)

Now, one last time, complete the following:

⊕ Make sure that you are connected to your Internet service provider.

⊕ Type browser, open the Web toolbar and select the Browse the Web tool, or open your system browser from the Windows taskbar.

⊕ If necessary, navigate to our companion website at www.prenhall.com/dixriley.

See you there.

14.17   Drawings 14-1 through 14-5: Bushing Mount, Link Mount, 3-D Assembly, Tapered Bushing, Pivot Mount

We offer the following drawing suggestions for Drawing 14-1. The principles demonstrated here carry over into Drawings 14-2 through 14-5, and you should be capable of handling them on your own at this point. In all cases, you are encouraged to experiment with renderings when the model is complete.

Use an efficient sequence in the construction of composite solids. In general, this means saving union, subtraction, and intersection operations until most of the solid objects have been drawn and positioned. This approach allows you to continue to use the geometry of the parts for snap points as you position other parts.

Drawing Suggestions

- Use at least two views, one plan and one 3-D, as you work.
- Begin with the bottom of the mount in the XY plane. This means drawing a $6.00 \times 4.00 \times 0.50$ solid box sitting on the XY plane.
- Draw a second box, $1.50 \times 4.00 \times 3.50$, in the XY plane. This becomes the upright section at the middle of the mount. Move it so that its own midpoint is at the midpoint of the base.
- Draw a third box, $1.75 \times 0.75 \times 0.50$, in the XY plane. This is copied and becomes one of the two slots in the base. Move it so that the midpoint of its long side is at the midpoint of the short side of the base. Then, move it 1.125 along the x-axis.
- Add a 0.375-radius cylinder with 0.50 height at each end of the slot.
- Copy the box and cylinders 3.75 to the other side of the base to form the other slot.
- Create a new UCS 2.00 up in the z direction. You can use the origin option and give (0,0,2) as the new origin. This puts the XY plane of the UCS directly at the middle of the upright block, where you can easily draw the bushing.
- Move out to the right of the mount and draw the polyline outline of the bushing, as shown in the drawing. Use REVOLVE to create the solid bushing.
- Create a cylinder in the center of the mount, where it can be subtracted to create the hole in the mount upright.
- Union the first and second boxes.
- Subtract the boxes and cylinders to form the slots in the base and the bushing-sized cylinder to form the hole in the mount.

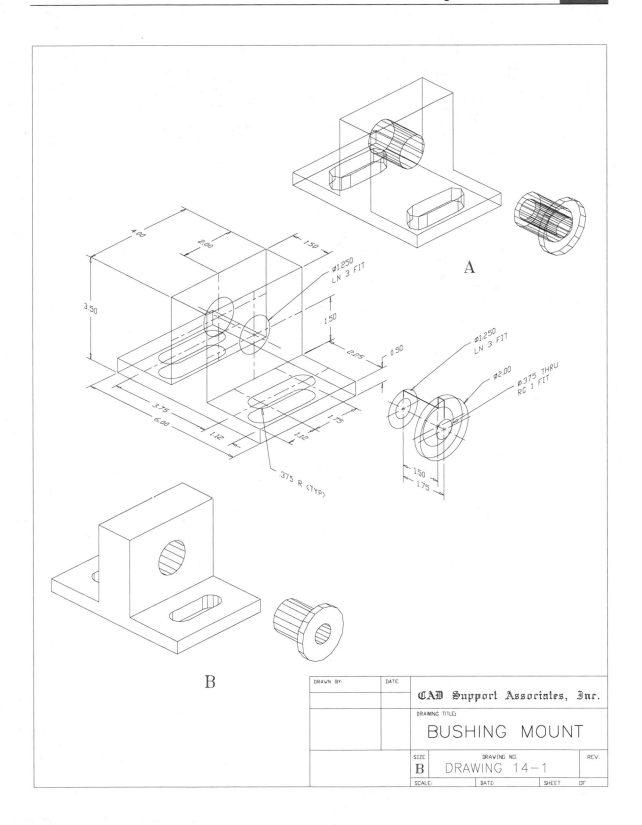

A

B

Ø1.250
LN 3 FIT

Ø1.250
LN 3 FIT

Ø2.00

Ø.375 THRU
RC 1 FIT

4.00

2.00

1.50

3.50

1.50

2.25

0.50

3.75

6.00

1.12

1.12

1.75

1.50

1.75

.375 R (TYP)

DRAWN BY:	DATE		
		CAD Support Associates, Inc.	
		DRAWING TITLE: **BUSHING MOUNT**	
		SIZE **B**	DRAWING NO. DRAWING 14–1	REV.
		SCALE:	DATE: SHEET OF

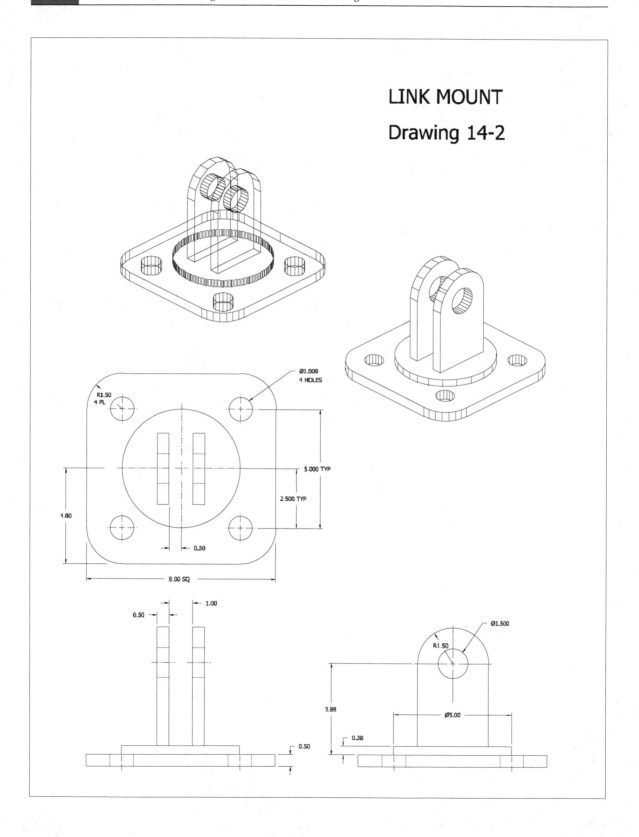

LINK MOUNT

Drawing 14-2

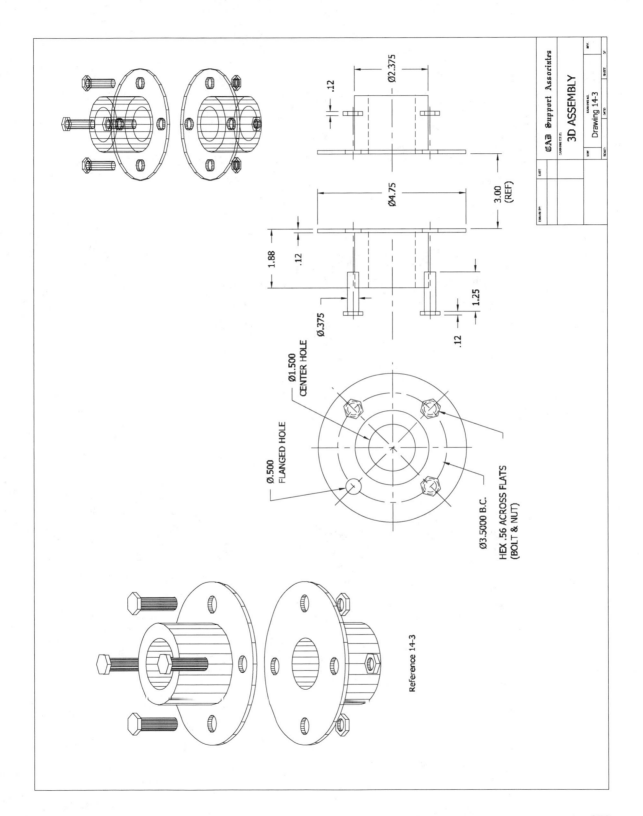

Ø2.375

.12

Ø4.75

3.00 (REF)

1.88

.12

Ø.375

1.25

.12

Ø1.500
CENTER HOLE

FLANGED HOLE
Ø.500

Ø3.5000 B.C.

HEX .56 ACROSS FLATS
(BOLT & NUT)

Reference 14-3

CAD Support Associates

3D ASSEMBLY

Drawing 14-3

673

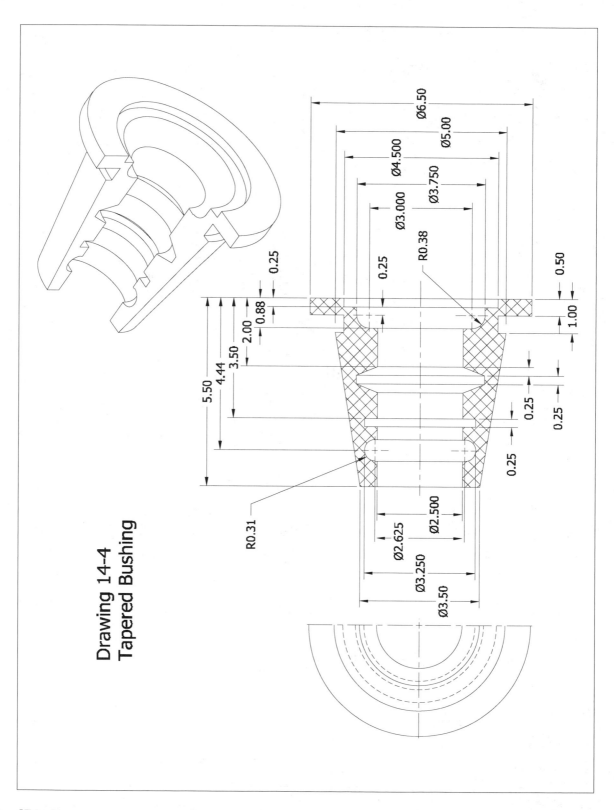

Drawing 14-4
Tapered Bushing

Drawing 14-5
Pivot Mount

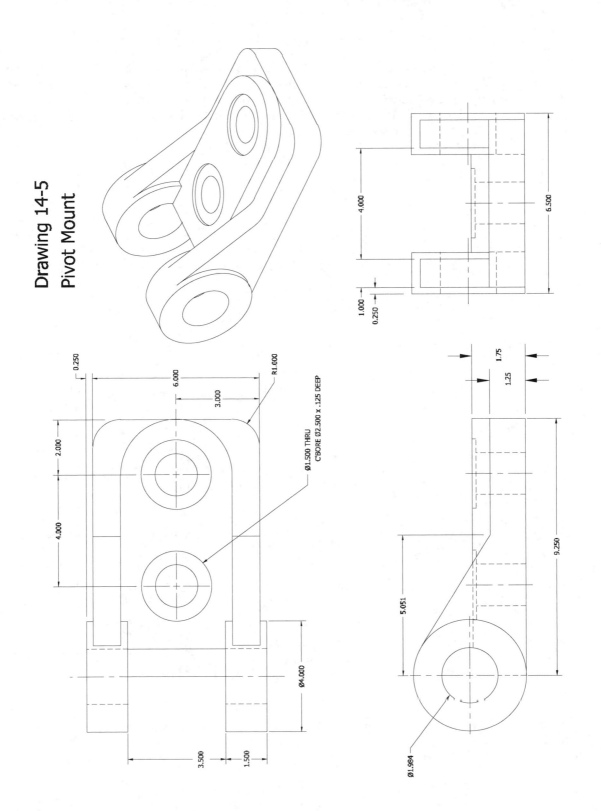

0.250

6.000

3.000

R1.000

2.000

4.000

Ø1.500 THRU
C'BORE Ø2.500 x .125 DEEP

Ø4.000

3.500

1.500

4.000

6.500

1.000

0.250

1.75

1.25

9.250

5.051

Ø1.984

14.18   Drawings 14-6A, B, C, D, E, and F

The drawings that follow, shown six to a page and labeled 14-6A, B, C, D, E, and F, are 3-D solid models derived from drawings done earlier in the book. You can start from scratch or begin with the 2-D drawing and use some of the geometry as a guide to your 3-D model. Either way, the dimensions for these drawings are those shown in preceding chapters.

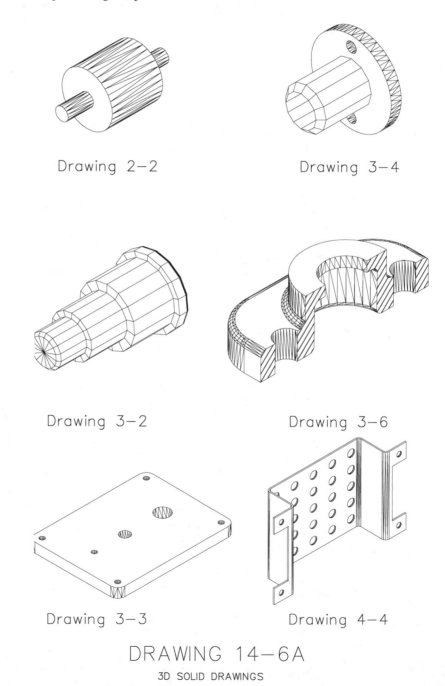

Drawing 2–2   Drawing 3–4

Drawing 3–2   Drawing 3–6

Drawing 3–3   Drawing 4–4

DRAWING 14–6A

3D SOLID DRAWINGS

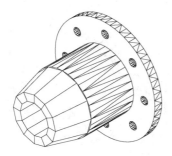

Drawing 5–1

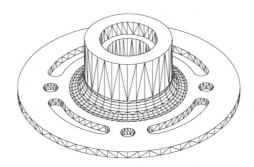

Drawing 5–6

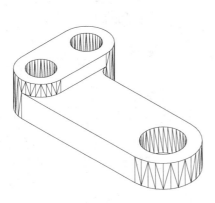

Drawing 5–2

Drawing 6–4

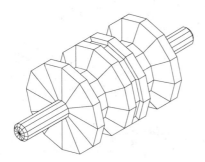

Drawing 5–4

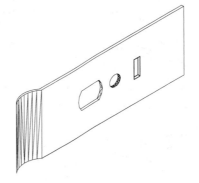

Drawing 6–5

DRAWING 14–6B

3D SOLID DRAWINGS

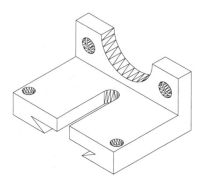

Drawing 6—7

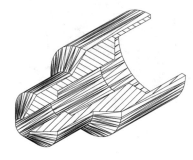

Drawing 8—3

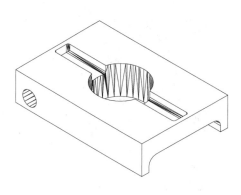

Drawing 8—1

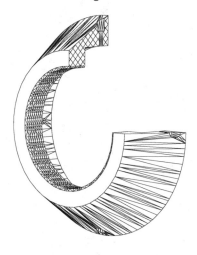

Drawing 8—4

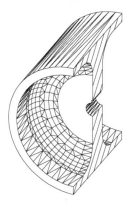

Drawing 8—2

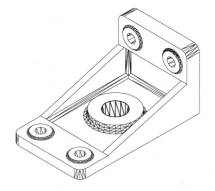

Drawing 8—7

DRAWING 14—6C

3D SOLID DRAWINGS

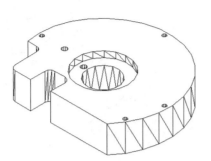

Drawing 8-8

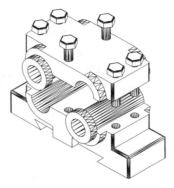

Drawing 10-3

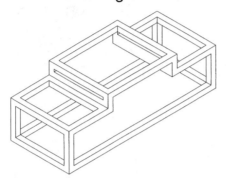

Drawing 9-6

Drawing 11-1

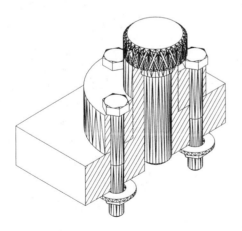

Drawing 10-2

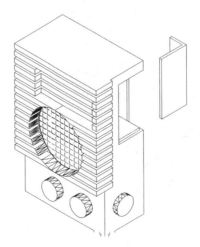

Drawing 11-2

DRAWING 14-6D
3D SOLID DRAWINGS

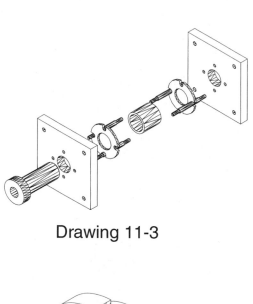

Drawing 11-3

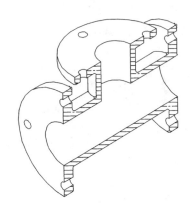

Drawing 11-6

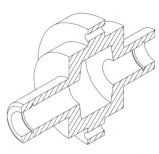

Drawing 11-4

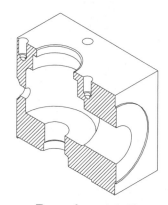
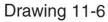

Drawing 11-7

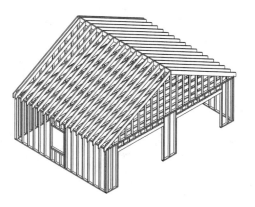

Drawing 11-5

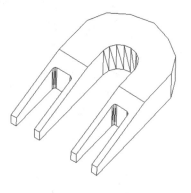

Drawing 12-1

DRAWING 14-6E
3D SOLID DRAWINGS

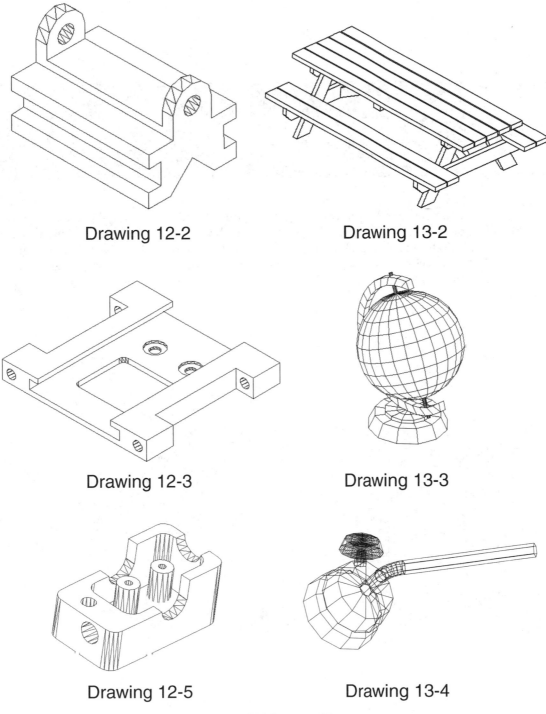

Drawing 12-2

Drawing 13-2

Drawing 12-3

Drawing 13-3

Drawing 12-5

Drawing 13-4

DRAWING 14-6F
3D SOLID DRAWINGS

Drawing Projects

The drawings on the following pages are offered as additional challenges and are presented without suggestions. They may be drawn in two or three dimensions and may be presented as multiple view drawings, hidden line drawings, or rendered drawings. In short, you are on your own to explore and master everything you have learned in this book.

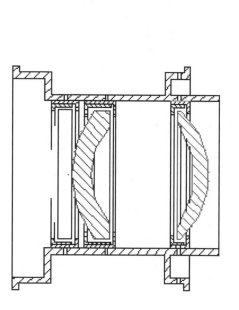

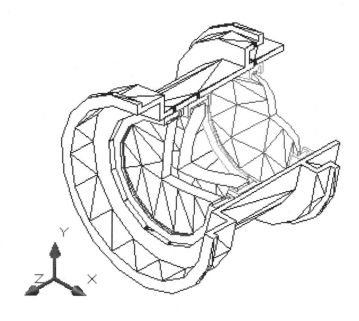

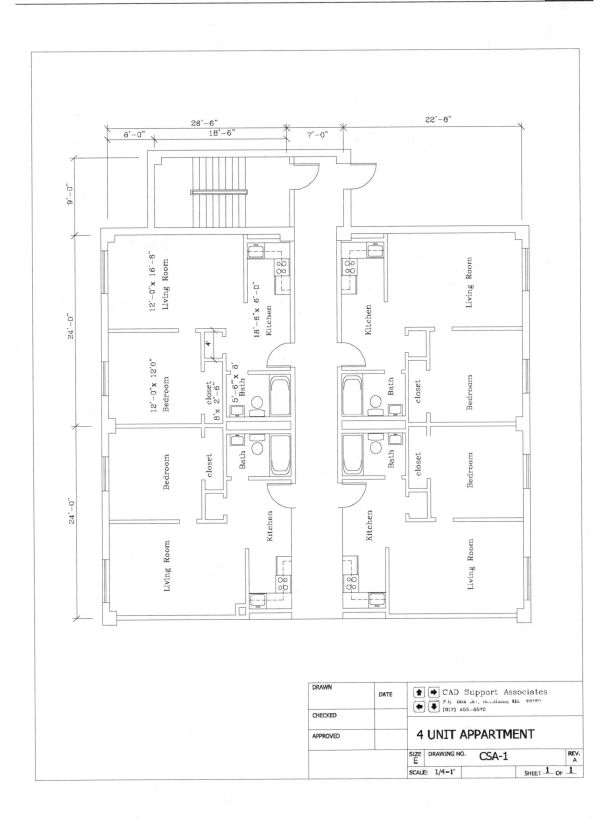

DRAWN		⬆ ➡ CAD Support Associates		
	DATE	P.O. BOX 311, Needham, MA 98100		
CHECKED		⬅ ⬇ (817) 455-8570		
APPROVED		**4 UNIT APPARTMENT**		
		SIZE E	DRAWING NO. CSA-1	REV. A
		SCALE: 1/4=1'		SHEET 1 OF 1

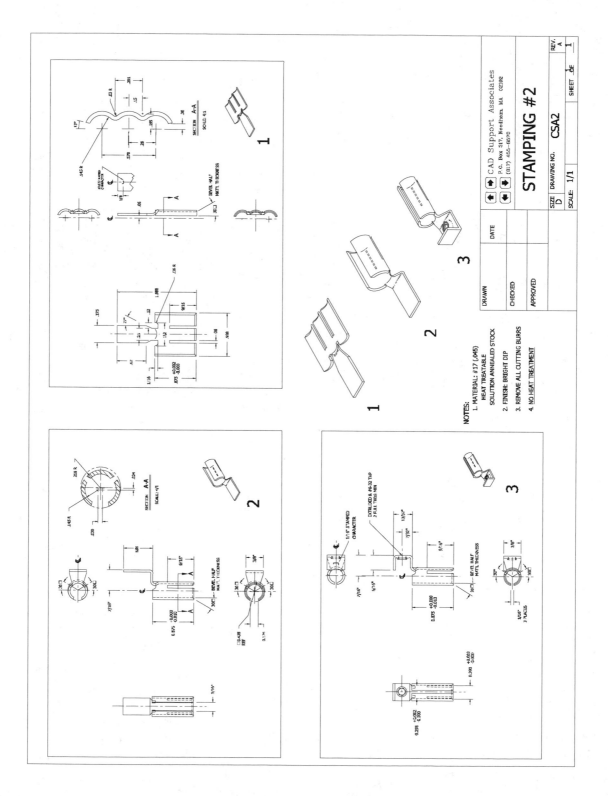

STAMPING #2

CAD Support Associates
P.O. Box 317, Needham, MA 02192
(317) 455-8670

DRAWING NO. CSA2

SIZE D   SCALE: 1/1

REV. A

SHEET OF

DRAWN
CHECKED
APPROVED
DATE

NOTES:
1. MATERIAL: #17 (.045)
   HEAT TREATABLE
   SOLUTION ANNEALED STOCK
2. FINISH: BRIGHT DIP
3. REMOVE ALL CUTTING BURRS
4. NO HEAT TREATMENT

SECTION A-A
SCALE 4/1

BEVEL HALF
MAT'L THICKNESS

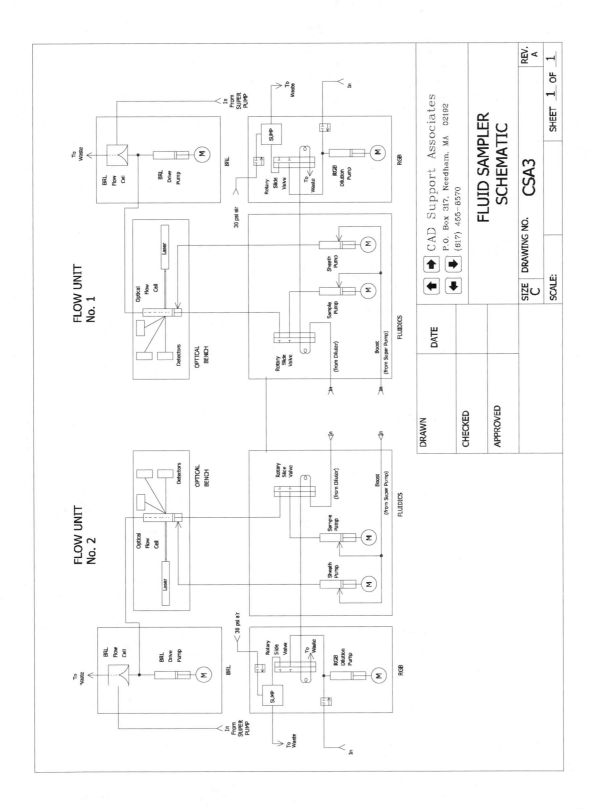

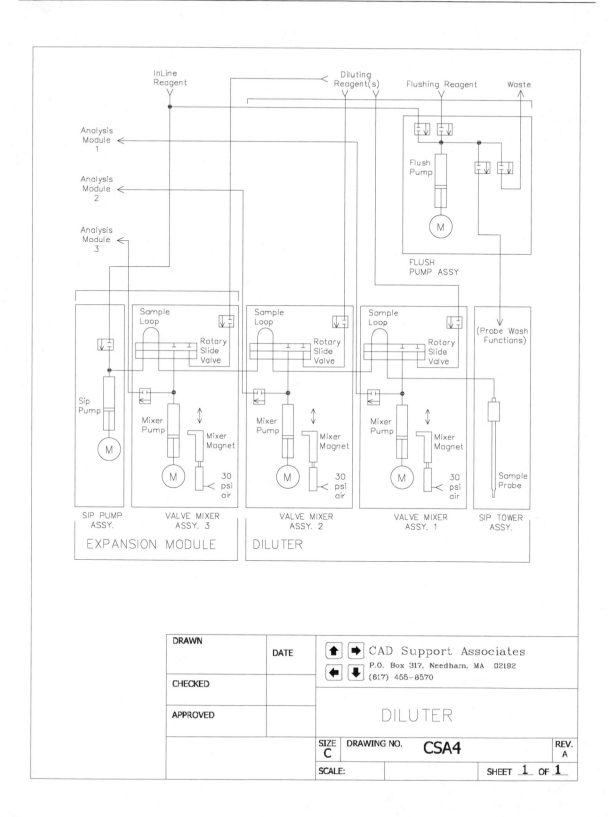

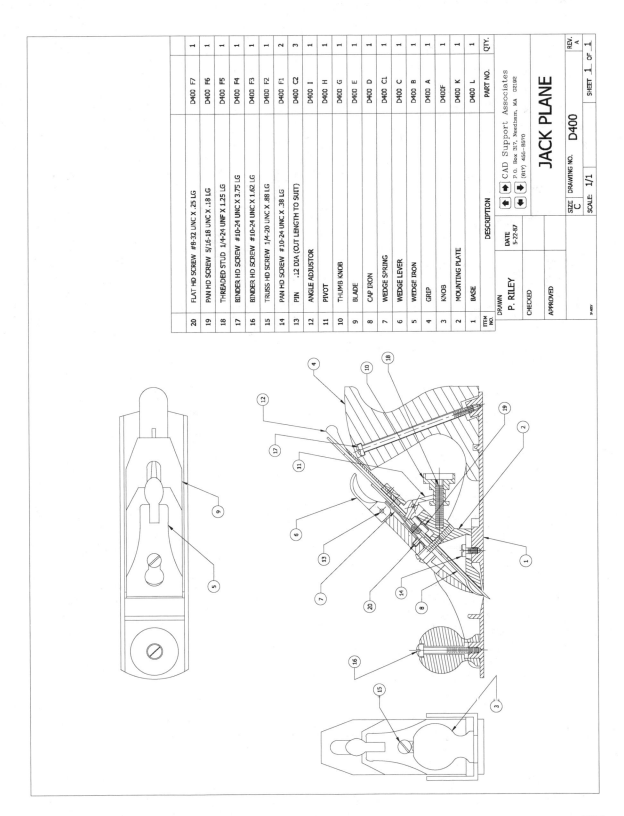

ITEM NO.	DESCRIPTION	PART NO.	QTY.
20	FLAT HD SCREW #8-32 UNC X .25 LG	D400 F7	1
19	PAN HD SCREW 5/16-18 UNC X .18 LG	D400 F6	1
18	THREADED STUD 1/4-24 UNF X 1.25 LG	D400 F5	1
17	BINDER HD SCREW #10-24 UNC X 3.75 LG	D400 F4	1
16	BINDER HD SCREW #10-24 UNC X 1.62 LG	D400 F3	1
15	TRUSS HD SCREW 1/4-20 UNC X .88 LG	D400 F2	1
14	PAN HD SCREW #10-24 UNC X .38 LG	D400 F1	2
13	PIN .12 DIA (CUT LENGTH TO SUIT)	D400 C2	3
12	ANGLE ADJUSTOR	D400 I	1
11	PIVOT	D400 H	1
10	THUMB KNOB	D400 G	1
9	BLADE	D400 E	1
8	CAP IRON	D400 D	1
7	WEDGE SPRING	D400 C1	1
6	WEDGE LEVER	D400 C	1
5	WEDGE IRON	D400 B	1
4	GRIP	D400 A	1
3	KNOB	D400F	1
2	MOUNTING PLATE	D400 K	1
1	BASE	D400 L	1

DRAWN P. RILEY	DATE 5-22-87	CAD Support Associates
CHECKED		P.O. Box 317, Needham, MA 02192
APPROVED		(617) 455-8670

JACK PLANE

SIZE C	DRAWING NO. D400	REV. A
SCALE: 1/1		SHEET 1 OF 1

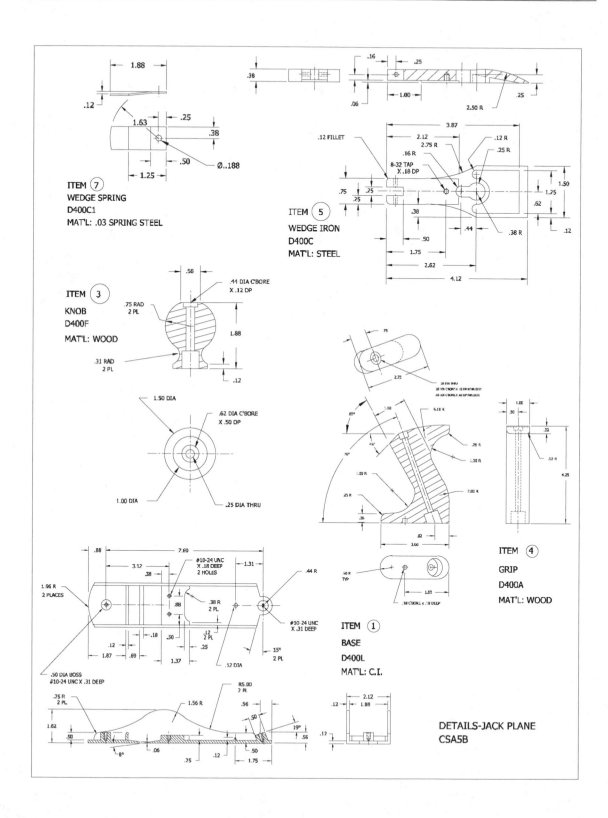

ITEM (7)
WEDGE SPRING
D400C1
MAT'L: .03 SPRING STEEL

ITEM (5)
WEDGE IRON
D400C
MAT'L: STEEL

ITEM (3)
KNOB
D400F
MAT'L: WOOD

ITEM (4)
GRIP
D400A
MAT'L: WOOD

ITEM (1)
BASE
D400L
MAT'L: C.I.

DETAILS-JACK PLANE
CSA5B

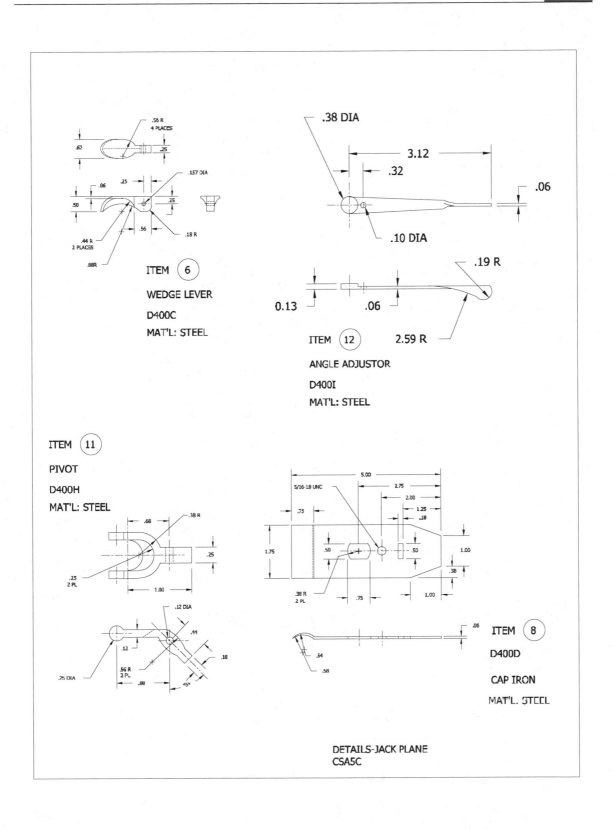

ITEM 6
WEDGE LEVER
D400C
MAT'L: STEEL

.38 DIA
3.12
.32
.06
.10 DIA
.19 R
0.13 .06
ITEM 12 2.59 R
ANGLE ADJUSTOR
D400I
MAT'L: STEEL

ITEM 11
PIVOT
D400H
MAT'L: STEEL

ITEM 8
D400D
CAP IRON
MAT'L. STEEL

DETAILS-JACK PLANE
CSA5C

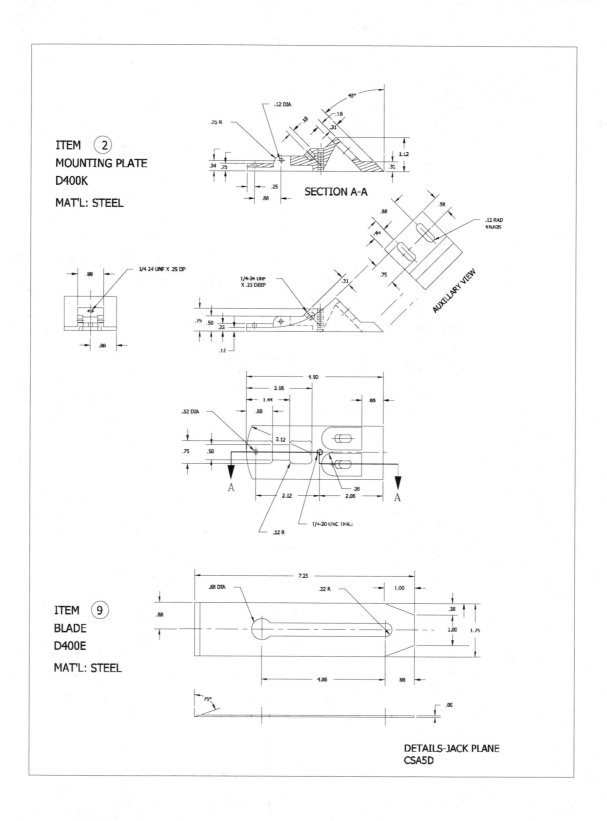

ITEM ②
MOUNTING PLATE
D400K

MAT'L: STEEL

SECTION A-A

AUXILIARY VIEW

ITEM ⑨
BLADE
D400E

MAT'L: STEEL

DETAILS-JACK PLANE
CSA5D

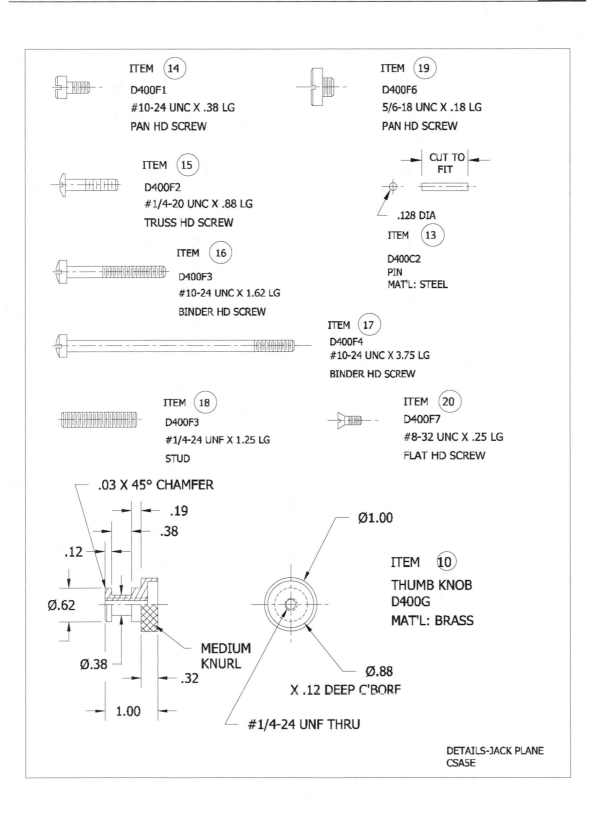

ITEM (14)
D400F1
#10-24 UNC X .38 LG
PAN HD SCREW

ITEM (19)
D400F6
5/6-18 UNC X .18 LG
PAN HD SCREW

ITEM (15)
D400F2
#1/4-20 UNC X .88 LG
TRUSS HD SCREW

CUT TO
FIT

.128 DIA

ITEM (13)
D400C2
PIN
MAT'L: STEEL

ITEM (16)
D400F3
#10-24 UNC X 1.62 LG
BINDER HD SCREW

ITEM (17)
D400F4
#10-24 UNC X 3.75 LG
BINDER HD SCREW

ITEM (18)
D400F3
#1/4-24 UNF X 1.25 LG
STUD

ITEM (20)
D400F7
#8-32 UNC X .25 LG
FLAT HD SCREW

.03 X 45° CHAMFER

.19
.38
.12
Ø.62
Ø.38
.32
1.00

MEDIUM
KNURL

Ø1.00

ITEM (10)
THUMB KNOB
D400G
MAT'L: BRASS

Ø.88
X .12 DEEP C'BORE

#1/4-24 UNF THRU

DETAILS-JACK PLANE
CSA5E

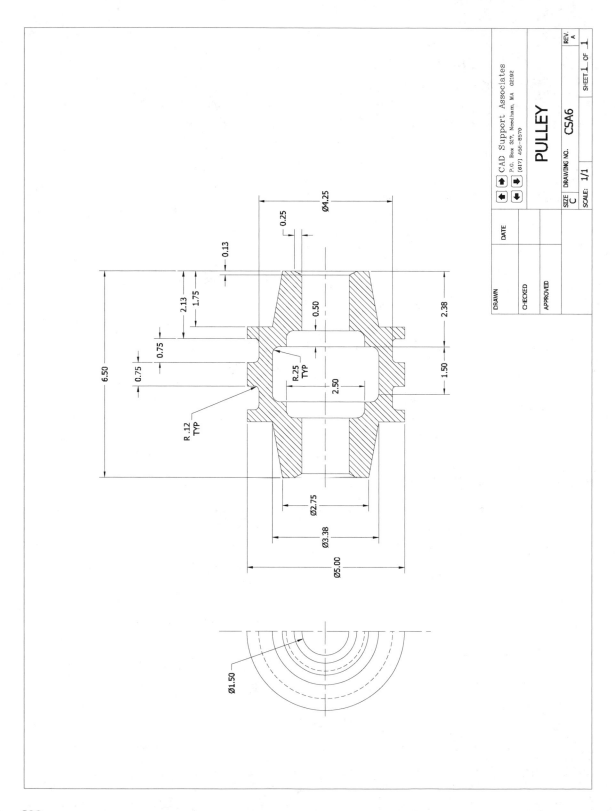

692

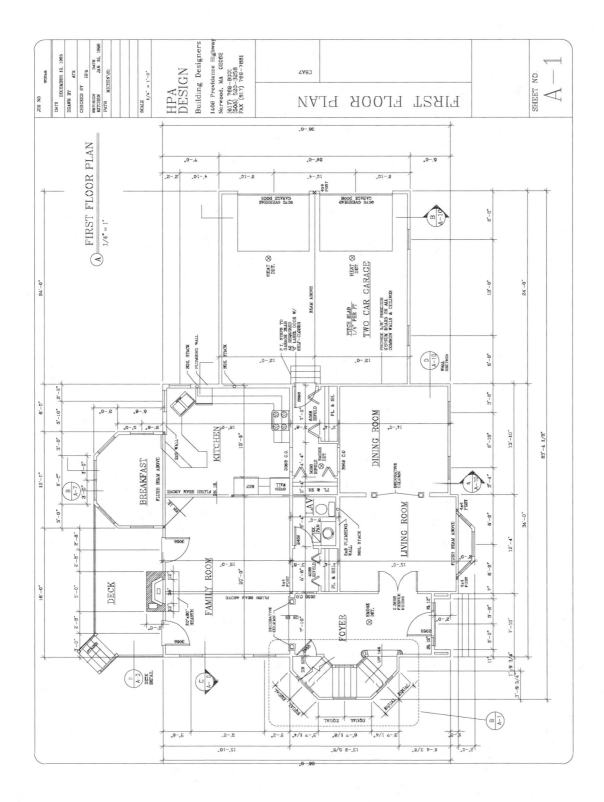

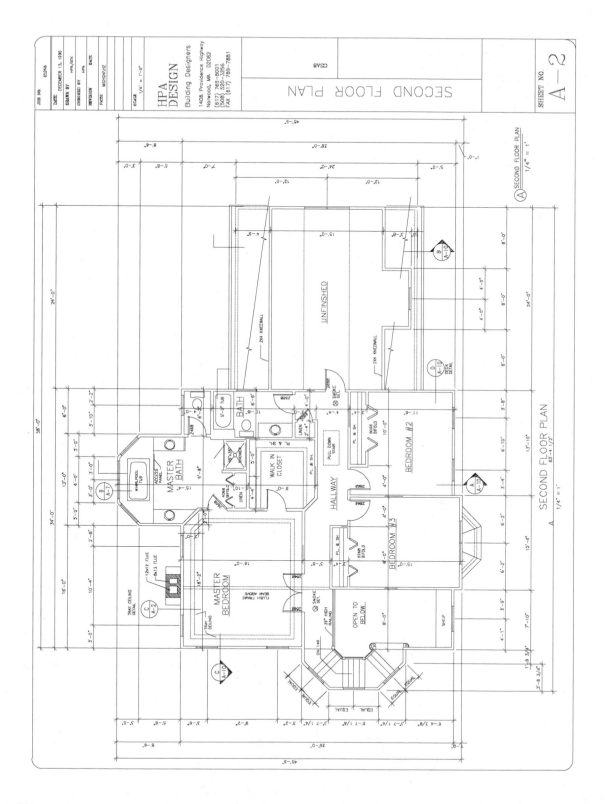

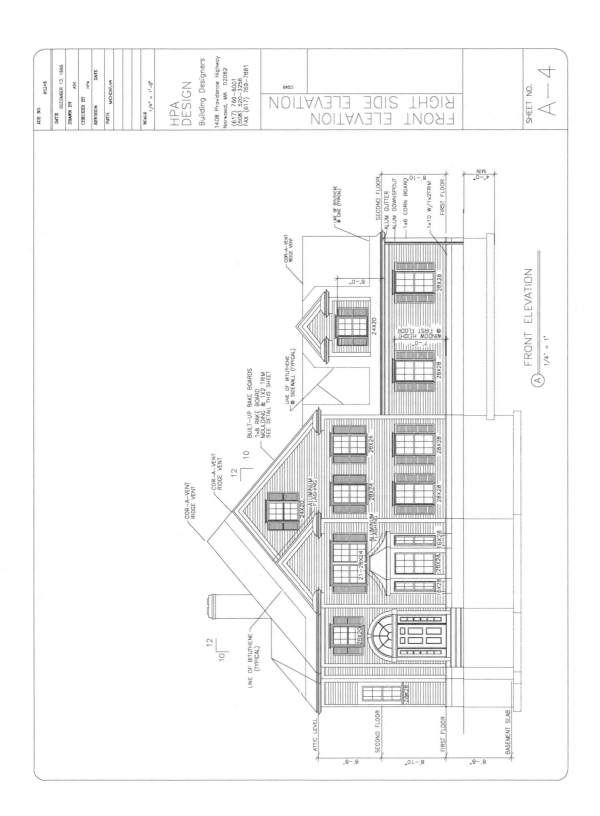

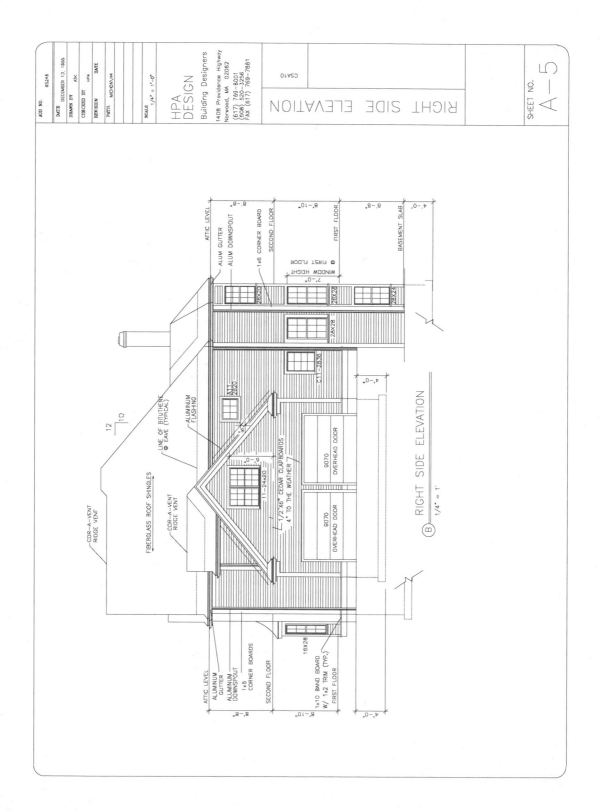

RIGHT SIDE ELEVATION

(B) RIGHT SIDE ELEVATION
1/4" = 1'

FIBERGLASS ROOF SHINGLES
COR-A-VENT RIDGE VENT
ATTIC LEVEL
ALUMINUM GUTTER
ALUMINUM DOWNSPOUT
1x6 CORNER BOARDS
SECOND FLOOR
1x10 BAND BOARD W/ 1x2 TRIM (TYP.)
FIRST FLOOR
16X28
8'-8"
8'-10"
4'-0"

COR-A-VENT RIDGE VENT
LINE OF BITUTHENE (TYPICAL) @ EAVE
ALUMINUM FLASHING
1/2"X6" CEDAR CLAPBOARDS 4" TO THE WEATHER
11-24X20
2X30
A11
9070 OVERHEAD DOOR
9070 OVERHEAD DOOR
6'-0"
6'-0"

12
10

ATTIC LEVEL
ALUM GUTTER
ALUM DOWNSPOUT
1x6 CORNER BOARD
SECOND FLOOR
WINDOW HEIGHT @ FIRST FLOOR
FIRST FLOOR
BASEMENT SLAB
28X20
28X28
28X28
28X28
C11-28X36
28X28
7'-0"
8'-8"
8'-10"
5'-8"
4'-0"
4'-0"

HPA DESIGN
Building Designers
1408 Providence Highway
Norwood, MA 02062
(617) 769-8001
(508) 520-3256
FAX (617) 769-7881

JOB NO. 95245
DATE DECEMBER 13, 1995
DRAWN BY ATK
CHECKED BY HPA
REVISION DATE
PATH. MICHON\H4
SCALE 1/4" = 1'-0"

CS410

SHEET NO. A-5

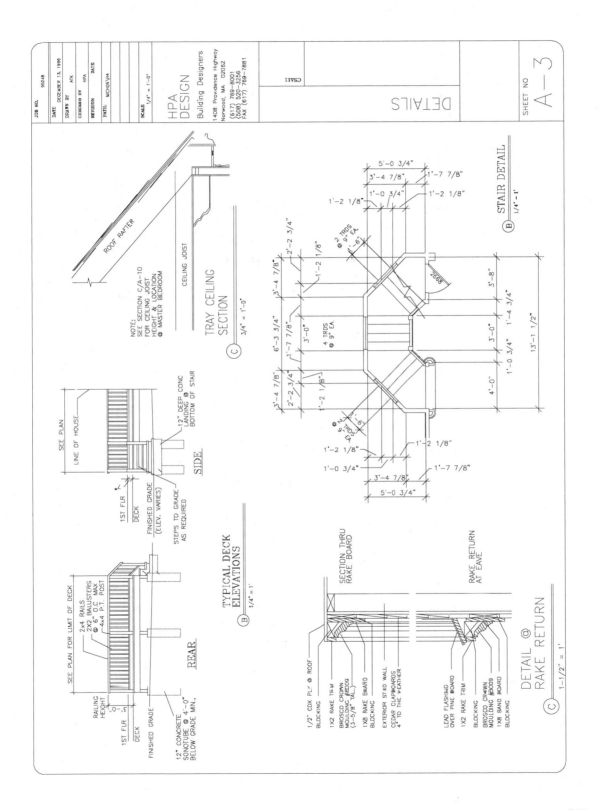

TRAY CEILING
SECTION
C 3/4" = 1'-0"

ROOF RAFTER

CEILING JOIST

NOTE:
SEE SECTION C/A-10
FOR CEILING JOIST
HEIGHT & LOCATION
@ MASTER BEDROOM

STAIR DETAIL
B 1/4" = 1'

SEE PLAN

LINE OF HOUSE

1ST FLR
DECK

FINISHED GRADE
(ELEV. VARIES)

STEPS TO GRADE
AS REQUIRED

12" DEEP CONC
LANDING @
BOTTOM OF STAIR

SIDE

TYPICAL DECK
ELEVATIONS
B 1/4" = 1'

SEE PLAN FOR LIMIT OF DECK

2x4 RAILS
2X2 BALUSTERS
@ 6" O.C. MAX
4x4 P.T. POST

RAILING
HEIGHT

3'-0"

1ST FLR
DECK

FINISHED GRADE

12" CONCRETE
SONOTUBE @ 4'-0"
BELOW GRADE MIN.

REAR

SECTION THRU
RAKE BOARD

1/2" CDX PL' @ ROOF
BLOCKING
1X2 RAKE TRIM
BROSCO CROWN
MOULDING #E009
(3-5/8" TALL)
1X8 RAKE BOARD
BLOCKING
EXTERIOR STUD WALL
CEDAR CLAPBOARDS
4" TO THE WEATHER

RAKE RETURN
AT EAVE

LEAD FLASHING
OVER PINE BOARD
1X2 RAKE TRIM
BLOCKING
BROSCO CROWN
MOULDING #E009
1X8 BAND BOARD
BLOCKING

DETAIL @
RAKE RETURN
C 1-1/2" = 1'

HPA
DESIGN
Building Designers
1408 Providence Highway
Norwood, MA. 02062
(617) 769-8001
(508) 520-3256
FAX (617) 769-7881

CSA11

DETAILS

SHEET NO
A-3

JOB NO.   96248
DATE: DECEMBER 13, 1995
DRAWN BY   ATK
CHECKED BY   HPA
REVISION   DATE
DATE: NICHON V.H4
SCALE   1/4" = 1'-0"

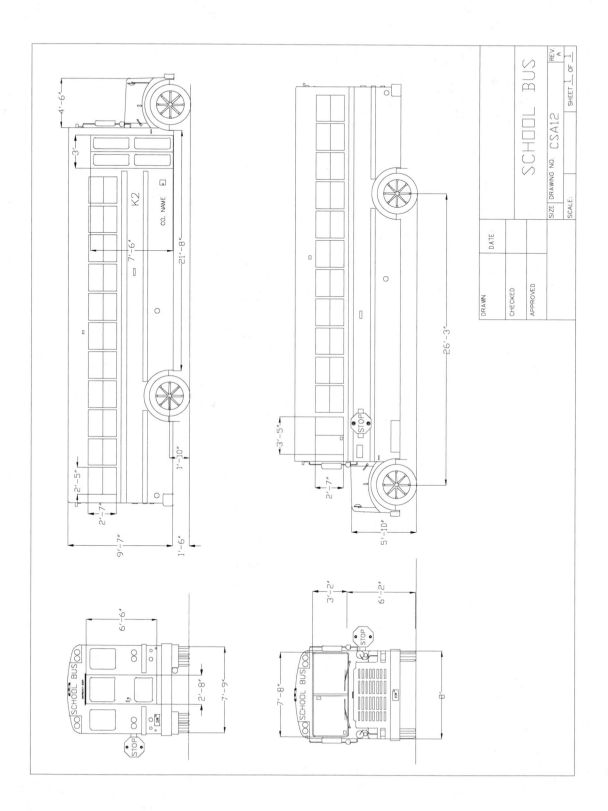

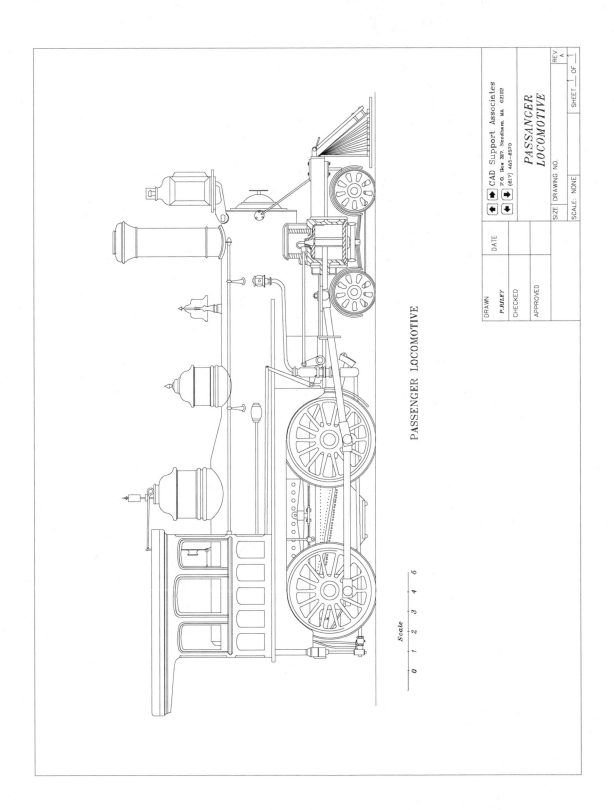

PASSENGER LOCOMOTIVE

Scale
0 1 2 3 4 5

Drawing Courtesy of: Brian Tufts

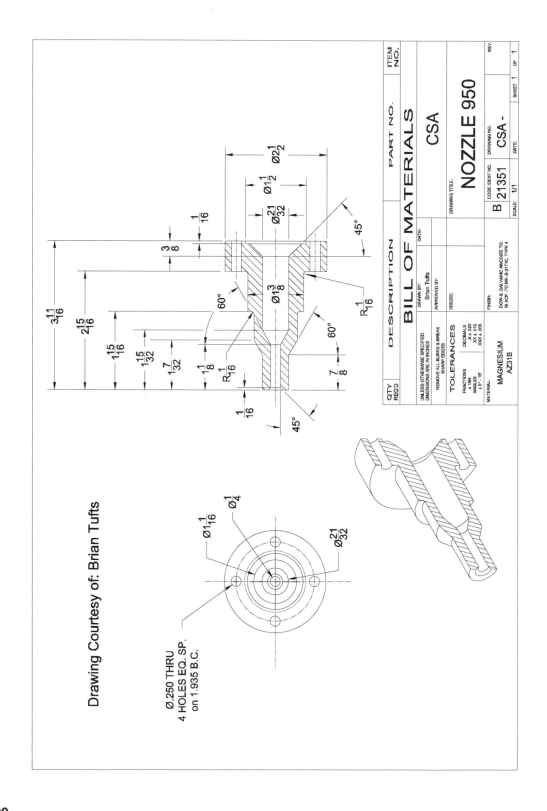

700

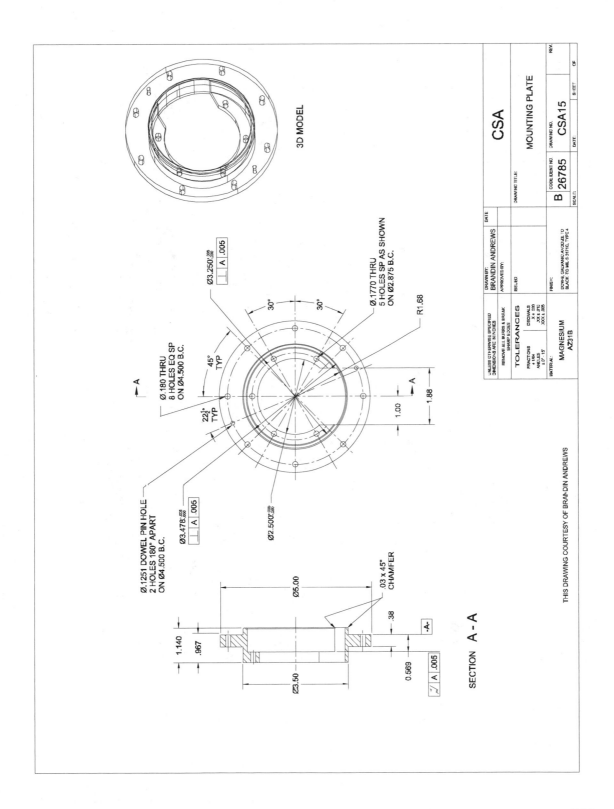

3D MODEL

Ø.180 THRU
8 HOLES EQ SP
ON Ø4.500 B.C.

Ø.1251 DOWEL PIN HOLE
2 HOLES 180° APART
ON Ø4.500 B.C.

Ø3.250⁺·²⁰⁵/·²⁰⁰ ⟂ | A | .005

Ø.1770 THRU
5 HOLES SP AS SHOWN
ON Ø2.875 B.C.

R1.68

30°
30°
45°
TYP
22½°
TYP

Ø3.478⁺·⁰⁰⁵/·⁰⁰⁰ ⟂ | A | .005

Ø2.500⁺·⁰⁰⁵/·⁰⁰⁰

1.00

1.88

A

A

Ø5.00
Ø3.50
.03 x 45°
CHAMFER
.38

1.140
.967

0.569

-A-

⟋ | A | .005

SECTION A - A

THIS DRAWING COURTESY OF BRANDIN ANDREWS

UNLESS OTHERWISE SPECIFIED
DIMENSIONS ARE IN INCHES

REMOVE ALL BURRS & BREAK
SHARP EDGES

TOLERANCES

FRACTIONS	DECIMALS
±1/64	X ± .005
ANGLES	XX ± .010
1.0°-15'	XXX ± .005

MATERIAL:
MAGNESIUM
AZ31B

DRAWN BY:
BRANDIN ANDREWS

APPROVED BY:

ISSUED

FINISH:
DOW9, GALVANIC ANODIZE TO
BLACK TO MIL-S-3017IG, TYPE 4

DATE:

DRAWING TITLE:

CSA

MOUNTING PLATE

CODE IDENT NO | DRAWING NO | REV.
B 26785 | CSA15

SCALE: | DATE: | SHEET: | OF:

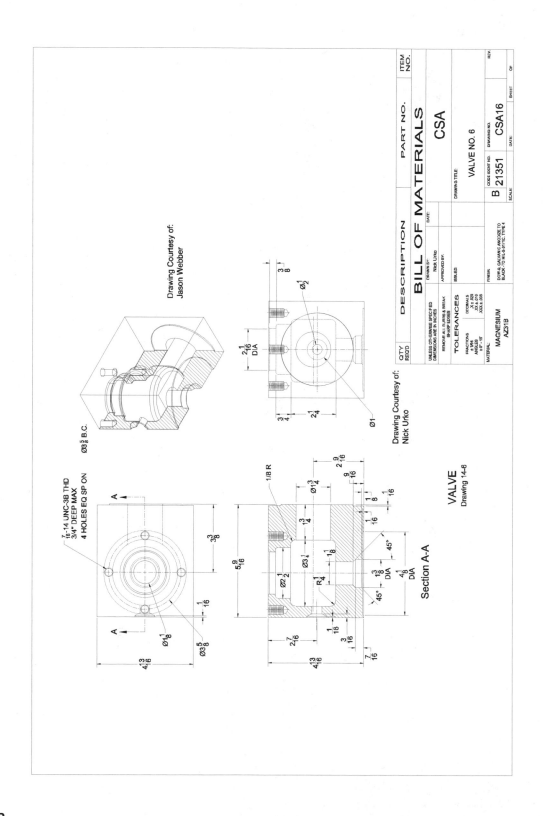

Drawing Courtesy of:
Jason Webber

Drawing Courtesy of:
Nick Urko

VALVE
Drawing 14–6

Section A-A

QTY REQ'D	DESCRIPTION		PART NO.	ITEM NO.

BILL OF MATERIALS

UNLESS OTHERWISE SPECIFIED DIMENSIONS ARE IN INCHES

REMOVE ALL BURRS & BREAK SHARP EDGES

TOLERANCES

FRACTIONS ± 1/64
ANGLES ± 0° - 15'

DECIMALS
.X ± .020
.XX ± .010
.XXX ± .005

MATERIAL:
MAGNESIUM
AZ31B

FINISH:
DOW-9 GALVANIC ANODIZE TO BLACK - TO MIL-S-3171C, TYPE 4

DRAWN BY: Nick Urko
APPROVED BY:
ISSUED:

DRAWING TITLE:
VALVE NO. 6

CODE IDENT NO. 21351

DRAWING NO. CSA16

PART NO. CSA

B   DATE: REV.

SCALE: SHEET: OF

702

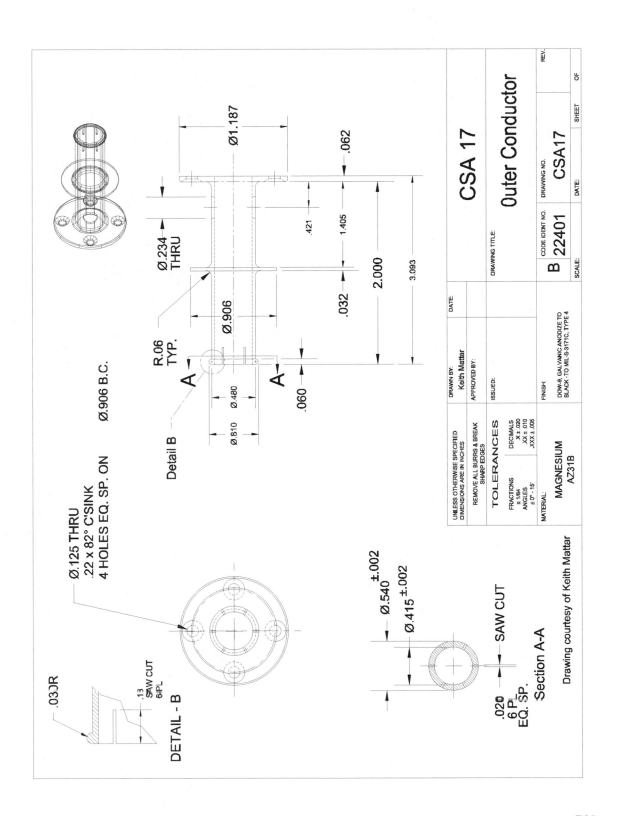

Ø1.187

.062

Ø.234
THRU

.421

1.405

R.06
TYP.

Ø.906

.032

2.000

3.093

A

A

Ø.480

.060

Ø.810

Detail B

Ø1.187

Ø.125 THRU
.22 x 82° C'SINK
4 HOLES EQ. SP. ON   Ø.906 B.C.

.033R

.13
SAW CUT
6 PL

DETAIL - B

Ø.540 ±.002

Ø.415 ±.002

.020
6 P
EQ. SP.

SAW CUT

Section A-A

Drawing courtesy of Keith Mattar

UNLESS OTHERWISE SPECIFIED DIMENSIONS ARE IN INCHES		DRAWN BY: Keith Mattar	DATE:		CSA 17		REV.
REMOVE ALL BURRS & BREAK SHARP EDGES		APPROVED BY:					
TOLERANCES	DECIMALS X ± .020 XX ± .010 XXX ± .006	ISSUED:		DRAWING TITLE:	Outer Conductor		
FRACTIONS ± 1/64 ANGLES ± 0° - 15'				CODE IDENT NO.	DRAWING NO.		
MATERIAL: MAGNESIUM AZ31B		FINISH: DOW-9, GALVANIC ANODIZE TO BLACK - TO MIL-S-31710, TYPE 4		B 22401	CSA17		
				SCALE:	DATE:	SHEET	OF

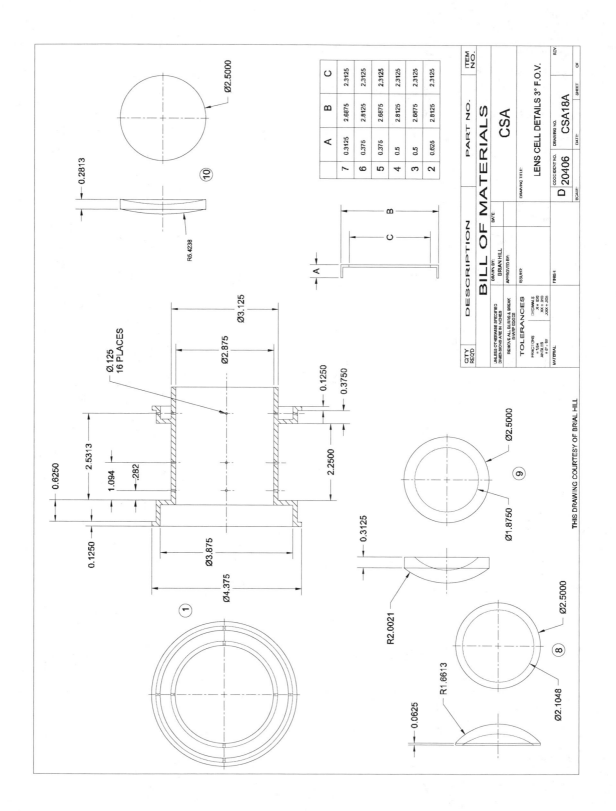

THIS DRAWING COURTESY OF BRIAL HILL

	A	B	C
7	0.3125	2.6875	2.3125
6	0.375	2.8125	2.3125
5	0.376	2.6875	2.3125
4	0.5	2.8125	2.3125
3	0.5	2.6875	2.3125
2	0.626	2.8125	2.3125

BILL OF MATERIALS

PART NO.

CSA

DRAWING TITLE:

LENS CELL DETAILS 3° F.O.V.

CODE IDENT NO. 20406   DRAWING NO. CSA18A

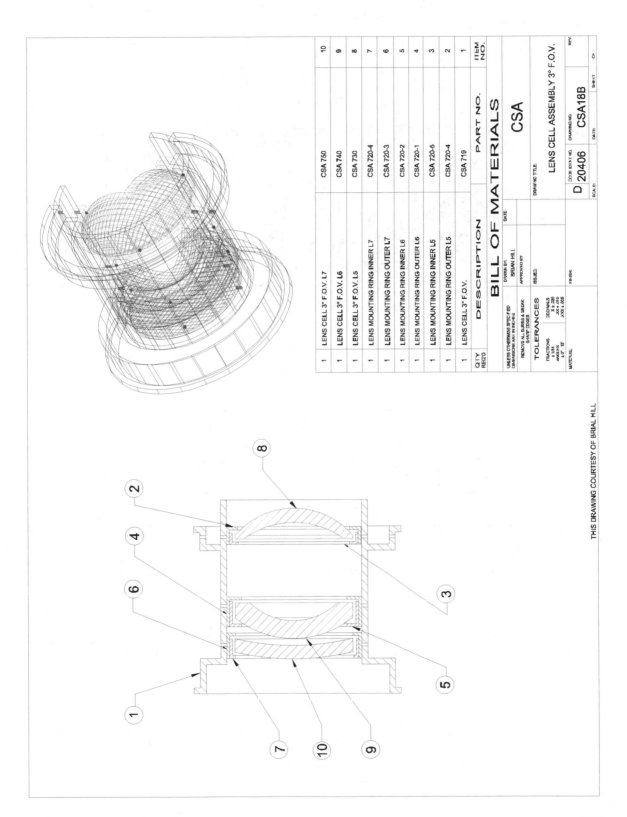

BILL OF MATERIALS

QTY REQ'D	DESCRIPTION	PART NO.	ITEM NO.
1	LENS CELL 3° F.O.V. L7	CSA 750	10
1	LENS CELL 3° F.O.V. L6	CSA 740	9
1	LENS CELL 3° F.O.V. L5	CSA 730	8
1	LENS MOUNTING RING INNER L7	CSA 720-4	7
1	LENS MOUNTING RING OUTER L7	CSA 720-3	6
1	LENS MOUNTING RING INNER L6	CSA 720-2	5
1	LENS MOUNTING RING OUTER L6	CSA 720-1	4
1	LENS MOUNTING RING INNER L5	CSA 720-5	3
1	LENS MOUNTING RING OUTER L5	CSA 720-4	2
1	LENS CELL 3° F.O.V.	CSA 719	1

DRAWING TITLE:

CSA

LENS CELL ASSEMBLY 3° F.O.V.

DRAWN BY: BRIAN HILL

APPROVED BY:

ISSUED:

FINISH:

UNLESS OTHERWISE SPECIFIED
DIMENSIONS ARE IN INCHES
REMOVE ALL BURRS & BREAK
SHARP EDGES

TOLERANCES

FRACTIONS ± 1/64
ANGLES ± 1° - 15'

DECIMALS
.X ± .030
.XX ± .010
.XXX ± .005

MATERIAL:

CODE IDENT NO. 20406 DRAWING NO. CSA18B

D SCALE: DATE: SHEET OF

Appendix

B

Creating Customized Toolbars

This appendix and the next are provided to give you an introduction to some of the many ways in which AutoCAD can be customized to more efficiently fit the needs of a particular industry, company, or individual user. In Chapter 10 you learned how to create customized tool palettes. Tool palettes give you easy access to libraries of frequently used blocks, symbols, and commands. You can also create customized toolbars to store sets of frequently used commands or commands that have been modified to suit your preferences. Creating your own customized toolbars is a simple and powerful feature that also gives you some idea of the more complex customization options discussed in Appendix C.

This appendix takes you through the procedure of creating your own toolbar and modifying the behavior of some basic commands. On completing this exercise, you will have added a simple toolbar to your own system and have the knowledge necessary to create other toolbars of your own design.

There are two levels to the creation of a customized toolbar. At the first level, you simply create the toolbar, give it a name, and add whatever commands you wish to put there. This can be very handy for putting together sets of tools that would otherwise be located on different toolbars and menus. At the second level, you actually modify the function of a command, then alter its name and the look of its toolbar button so that it functions differently from the standard AutoCAD command. In this exercise, we begin by creating a toolbar with five commands and then we show how to alter three of these commands.

> **Note:** The ability to create and customize toolbars is a powerful feature. We strongly discourage you from making changes in the standard AutoCAD set of toolbars. Adding, removing, or otherwise changing standard commands can lead to confusion and to the need to reload the AutoCAD menu. You create less confusion if you customize only new toolbars that you create yourself.

B.1 Adding Tools to a Customized Toolbar

GENERAL PROCEDURE

1. Open the View menu and select Toolbars.
2. Right-click on Toolbars.
3. Highlight New and click Toolbar.
4. Give the new toolbar a name by overtyping in the Customizations in ALL CUI Files list.
5. Select a Category from the Command List.
6. Find tools on the Commands List and drag them up to the name of the new toolbar in the Customizations in ALL CUI Files list.
7. Click OK to exit the dialog box.

⊕ You can begin this exercise in any AutoCAD drawing.

⊕ Open the View menu and select Toolbars.

This opens the Customize User Interface (CUI) dialog box, shown in Figure B-1. This is a centralized location for customizing various elements of

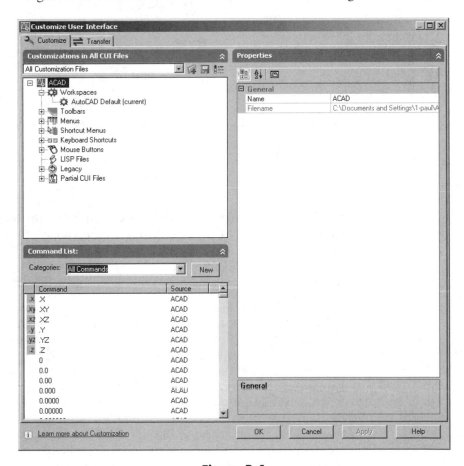

Figure B-1

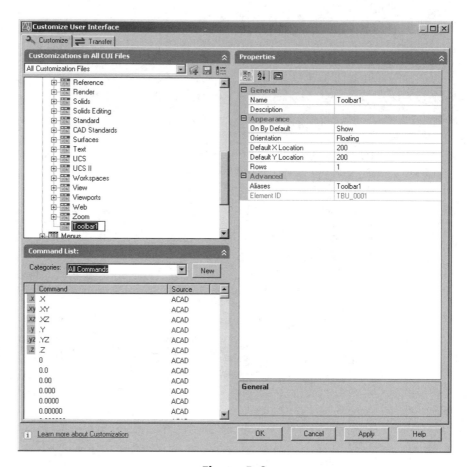

Figure B-2

the AutoCAD interface. Elements that can be customized are listed in the Customizations in ALL CUI Files list on the upper left. You can learn more about CUI files in Appendix C.

✦ Right-click the word Toolbars on the Customizations in ALL CUI Files list on the left.

✦ Highlight New and click Toolbar.

This opens a Properties window on the right side of the CUI dialog box and adds a new toolbar to the bottom of the list in the list of toolbars on the left, as in Figure B-2. The default name is Toolbar1 (or Toolbar2 if someone has already created a Toolbar1 on your system). This is fine for our purposes. Feel free to type in a different name if you like. Next we add commands to the new toolbar.

The procedure for adding commands to a toolbar is simple. You select a category from the Categories list and then drag individual commands up to the name of the toolbar. For our purposes, we bring together five very common commands. These commands are available elsewhere, of course, but bringing them together in one place on a small toolbar that doesn't get in the way on the screen can be useful.

The Categories list includes all of the standard pull-down menu titles, but there are commands within each of these categories that are not on the pull-down menus and there are also commands you might want that you will not find in these default lists. We get to this issue in a moment. For now, let's begin with the LINE command.

⊕ Click the arrow to open the drop-down list next to Categories in the Command List window at the bottom left of the dialog box.

You see a list beginning with All Commands and ending with Legacy.

⊕ In the categories list, highlight Draw.

This opens a list of Drawing commands in the Command List below Categories.

⊕ Scroll down the list until you see the Line command and tool.

From here, it is a simple matter of dragging the tool up to the new toolbar name.

⊕ Left-click on the Line tool, hold down the pick button, and drag the tool up just to the left of "Toolbar1."

When you are in the correct position, there will be a small blue arrow to the right of Toolbar1.

⊕ With the blue arrow showing, drop the command by releasing the pick button.

You see a Button Image and a Properties window for this command on the right, and the Line command is added to Toobar1 in the Customizations in ALL CUI Files box, as shown in Figure B-3.

⊕ To see your new toolbar so far, right-click Toolbar1 in the Customizations in ALL CUI Files box.

This calls up a Preview, as shown in Figure B-4. Your new toolbar now has one tool and a close button. We add one more tool from the Draw category and then move on to other categories. When we are done, your new toolbar will resemble Figure B-5.

The common Draw toolbar has the Circle command with the radius option as the default. It might be useful to have the command with the diameter option as the default on our toolbar. You can find this option on the Command List in the dialog box.

⊕ Scroll up the Command List and find Center Diameter next to the Circle tool.

⊕ Drag the Circle Center Diameter up to Toolbar1.

Your new toolbar now has two tools.

Let's move on to the Edit category and add the Erase tool to our toolbar.

⊕ Open the Categories list and highlight Edit.

⊕ Drag the Erase tool up to Toolbar1.

Your customized toolbar now has three tools. You can check out the Preview anytime by right-clicking Toolbar1. We add two more tools to complete the first level of this exercise. First, we add the Linear tool. There is nothing new in this procedure.

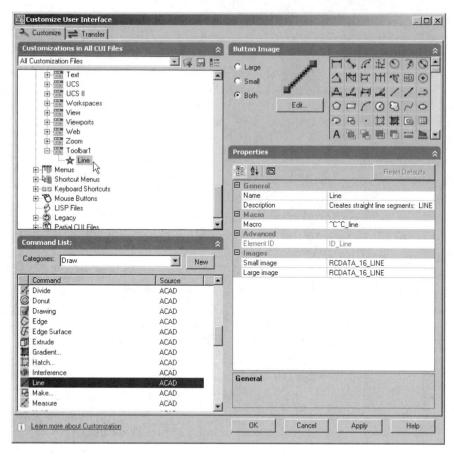

Figure B-3

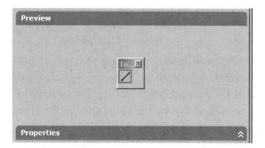

Figure B-4

Figure B-5

⊕ Highlight Dimension in the Categories list.
⊕ Drag the Linear tool up to Toolbar1.

    The last tool we add is the Distance command tool. If you are not familiar with DIST, see Chapter 2 (Section 2.9). DIST is an inquiry command. As you can see, Inquiry is not on the Categories list. Where will we find the Distance tool?

⊕ Scroll down to the bottom of the Categories list.
⊕ Highlight All Commands in the Categories list.
⊕ Scroll down the Command List until you see the Distance tool.
⊕ Drag the Distance tool up to Toolbar1.

    Your new toolbar is now complete and should resemble Figure B-5, shown previously.

B.2   Creating Customized Tools

GENERAL PROCEDURE

1. With the Customize User Interface dialog box open, highlight a tool on a customized toolbar.
2. In the Properties panel, give the command a new name.
3. Edit the command macro associated with the tool button.
4. Edit the button image.
5. Assign the button image location to the tool reference.
6. Check to see that the tool works the way you want it to.

In this section, we offer a very simple introduction to the possibilities of customization through the use of customized toolbar buttons. In Section B.1, you created a new toolbar with five tools selected from different categories. In this section, we show you how to customize three of these tools so they function differently from standard AutoCAD commands.

⊕ You should be in an AutoCAD drawing with the customized toolbar created in B.1 open on your screen.
⊕ If necessary, open the View menu and select Toolbars.

    This opens the Customize User Interface dialog box.

⊕ With the Customize User Interface dialog box open, left-click to open Toolbar1 and then highlight Line in your newly created toolbar.

    This automatically opens the Properties panel shown in Figure B-6. This is a very powerful and interesting place in the AutoCAD system. Here you can change the command name associated with this tool, change the appearance of the toolbar button, and edit the macro that determines, to an extent, how the command functions. Note that you are not actually creating a new command, but have the ability to determine default options that are

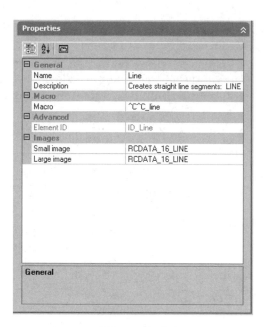

Figure B-6

entered automatically as part of the command procedure. For example, it might be nice to have a version of the LINE command that draws only one line segment and then returns you to the command prompt. This is easily accomplished with a little knowledge of AutoCAD macro language. Macros are automated key sequences. By automatically entering an extra press of the Enter key after drawing a single line segment, we can complete the command sequence as desired.

First, though, let's give this tool button a name to differentiate it from the standard Line tool.

⊕   Click in the Name edit box under Properties and add a 1 to the name so that it reads Line1.

This is a good descriptive name and it also associates it with Toolbar1, if you have used this as your toolbar name.

Next, we modify the macro so that the command is complete after one line segment is drawn. For the purposes of this exercise, you only need to know two items of AutoCAD macro language. The semicolon (;) is the macro language equivalent to pressing Enter. When AutoCAD sees a semicolon in a macro, it acts as if the user has pressed Enter or the spacebar. The backslash character (\) is the pause for user input character. When AutoCAD reads a backslash in a macro, it waits for something to be entered through the keyboard or the pointing device.

⊞ Click in the box next to Macro and add ;\\; to the macro, so that the complete macro reads ^C^C_line;\\;

It is very important that this be entered exactly as shown, without extra spaces. Macro language, like any programming language, is very fussy.

Let's analyze what these characters do.

^C^C	The macro equivalent of typing Ctrl+C (or the Esc button) twice, which cancels any command in progress before entering the LINE command.
Line	Types Line at the command prompt
;	Like pressing Enter after typing the command
\	Waits for user to specify the first point
\	Waits for user to specify a second point
;	Like pressing Enter or the spacebar, ends the command sequence.

In a moment, we try this, but first let's change the button image to show that the command sequence for this customized tool is different from the standard LINE command.

⊞ Click Edit in the Button Image panel.

This opens the Button Editor dialog box illustrated in Figure B-7. This box provides simple graphics tools for creating or editing button images. The four tools include a drawing "pencil" for drawing individual grid cells, a line tool, a circle tool, and an erase tool. In addition, there is a grid and a color palette. We simply shorten the Line button image to differentiate it from the regular Line tool.

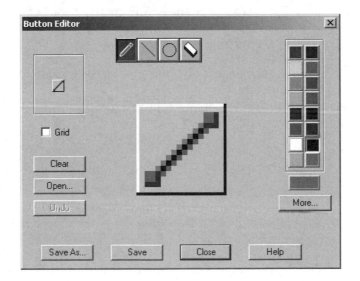

Figure B-7

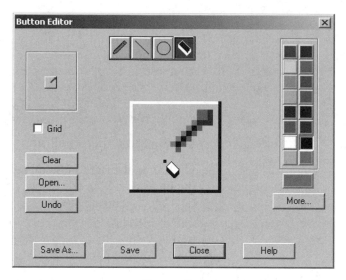

Figure B-8

Click the Erase tool at the top right and use it to erase the lower left half of the Line button image, as shown in Figure B-8.

⊕ Click Save.

This opens a Create File dialog box. It should automatically open to the correct location. Button image files are BMP files and must be saved in the same folder as the CUI file with which they are associated. Typically that file will be in C:\Documents and Settings\<owner>\Application Data\Autodesk\ AutoCAD 2006\R16.2\enu\Support

⊕ Type Line1 for the name of the tool button.

Notice that there will now be two aspects of this modified Line command in the CUI file: the Line1 command, which is the Line command modified by the additional macro characters, and the tool button image stored as a BMP file. We refer to both of them as Line1.

⊕ Click Save in the Create File dialog box.
⊕ Click Save in the Button Editor box.
⊕ Click Close in the Button Editor box to return to the Customize User Interface dialog box.

There is one last step to complete the creation of Line1 on your new tool-bar. You must associate the button image with the modified command. This is done in the Properties Panel to the right of the words Small image and Large image. Right now you will see "RCDATA_16_LINE" in both of these locations. This refers to the standard button image of the Line command. We replace this with the modified image you just created.

⊕ Click in the edit box to the right of Large image.

This opens a Select Image File dialog box with RCDATA_16_LINE as the default file. In the window above this you should see Line1, along with several folders and any other BMP files that may have been created and placed in this location.

⊕ Highlight Line1.

You should see Line1 in the File name edit box.

⊕ Click Open.

This brings you back to the Customize User Interface (CUI) dialog box with the new location and BMP file listed next to Large image.

⊕ Repeat this procedure for the Small image:

1. Click in the edit box to the right of Small image.
2. If necessary, highlight Line1 in the Select Image File dialog box.
3. Click Open.

You should now have the Line1 bitmap image referenced in both image size edit boxes.

⊕ Click Apply to execute the changes to your customized tool button.

⊕ Click on Line1 in the list of Toolbar1 tools on the left.

Notice that the image in the Preview changes.

Now, let's close the CUI dialog box and try our new tool.

⊕ Click OK.

⊕ Select the Line1 tool from your customized toolbar.

Note: If for any reason your Toolbar1 is not showing, you can open it as you would any toolbar. Right-click any toolbar to open the toolbar list and select Toolbar1 from the list.

⊕ Select a first point anywhere in your drawing area.

⊕ Select a second point.

You should be back to the command prompt. If this did not happen, check the syntax on the macro for your Line1 tool.

Next, we return to the CUI dialog box and make similar changes in two more tools. We customize the Erase tool so that it erases a single object and then exits the command, and we customize the Linear tool so that it defaults to dimensioning an object.

⊕ Open the View menu and select Toolbars.

⊕ Double-click Toolbars from the list on the left.

⊕ Double-click Toolbar1.

⊕ Double-click Erase.

⊕ Add a 1 in the Name edit box so that it reads Erase1.

⊕ In the macro associated with this button, add ;\; after erase.

The macro should read

$$\wedge C \wedge C\_erase;\backslash;$$

Consider how this macro works. After canceling any other command, it types erase and then the first semicolon enters the ERASE command. The \ tells Auto-CAD to wait for input. After the user points to one object, the second semicolon completes the command and returns to the command prompt.

Figure B-9

✦ Click Edit in the Button Image window to open the Button Editor.
✦ Use the Erase tool and the Pencil tool to create the button image shown in Figure B-9.

> This image shows the eraser head over a single object.

✦ Save the modified image as Erase1.
✦ Click Close to close the Button Editor.
✦ In the CUI dialog box, double-click next to Small and Large images and open Erase1 to associate the button image with the tool reference.
✦ Click Apply to apply changes to the Erase1 tool.

> The Erase1 tool is now complete with a modified button image.

After one more sequence of modifications, our work will be complete.

✦ Select Linear in the list under Toolbar1 button.
✦ Add a 1 in the Name edit box, so that the name reads Linear1.

> We use this tool to default to object selection as the method for creating a single linear dimension.

✦ Add ;;\ to the macro associated with this button.

> The macro should read

$$\wedge C \wedge C\_dimlinear;;\backslash$$

The first semicolon enters the command. The second enters the Select object option. The backslash creates a pause for object selection. After this there is no further instruction, so AutoCAD waits for further input. After the dimension position is selected, the command terminates. There is no need for a semicolon at the end because returning to the command prompt after dimension placement is normal procedure in this command.

✦ Click Edit to open the Button Editor.
✦ Using the Crayon tool, draw a short line segment below the Dimension icon, as shown in Figure B-10.
✦ Save the modified button image as Linear1.
✦ Close the Button Editor.
✦ Assign the Linear1 button to the Small and Large button images for the Linear1 command.
✦ Click Apply and then OK to close the CUI dialog box.

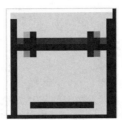

Figure B-10

Finally, to complete this exercise, use your customized toolbar to do the following:

1. Use the Line1 tool to draw a single line segment.
2. Use the Linear1 tool to dimension the line.
3. Use the Erase1 tool to erase the line.
4. Use the Erase1 tool again to erase the dimension.

Be aware that pressing the spacebar to repeat one of these commands repeats the regular AutoCAD command, not the macro you created for your customized toolbar.

Menus, Macros, and the CUI Dialog

When you begin to look below the surface of AutoCAD as it is configured straight out of the box, you find a whole world of customization possibilities. This open architecture, which allows you to create your own menus, commands, toolbars, tool palettes, and automated routines, is one of the reasons for AutoCAD's success. It is characteristic of all AutoCAD releases and has made room for a vast network of third-party developers to create custom software products tailoring AutoCAD to the particular needs of various industries and tasks.

The Customize User Interface dialog box, new in AutoCAD 2006, brings a major change to the way customization is handled. In previous versions of AutoCAD, many of the customizable elements in the CUI dialog were accessible through different means. The largest single resource for customizing elements was the menu system. The standard acad menu (which addressed much more than pull-down menus) was contained in a file with an .mnu extension. This file could be accessed and edited in a word processing program. In AutoCAD 2006, the mnu and related files have been replaced by the XML-based CUI file, and the elements formerly accessible through word processing can now be modified directly through the single interface of the CUI dialog box. In this appendix we will further explore the vocabulary of AutoCAD macro language and show how it is used with the elements in the CUI dialog. The intention of this discussion is not to make you an AutoCAD developer, but to give you a taste of what is going on in the CUI system. After reading this, you should have a sense of what elements are readily available for customization.

C.1 The CUI Dialog Box

If you have worked through Appendix B, you have already gotten a taste of what is available in the CUI dialog box and how it works. The beauty of the system is that all elements are customized in the same way. Like toolbars, all elements are represented by starred entries in the tree view on the left and Properties panels on the right. Some elements also have Button Image panels. Following is a list of the elements in the tree view with a brief discussion of each. In Section C.2 you will find further discussion of AutoCAD macro language characters.

⊕   To view the CUI dialog box, open the View menu and select Toolbars, or open the Tools menu, highlight Customize, and select Interface.

The tree view is in the top left panel and includes nine elements: Workspaces, Toolbars, Menus, Shortcut Menus, Keyboard Shortcuts, Mouse Buttons, LISP Files, Legacy, and Partial CUI Files. Following is a brief description of each.

Workspaces: Workspaces are a simple form of customization. Workspaces consist of open toolbars, menus, palettes, and dockable windows. By opening or closing toolbars and selecting elements to add or remove from the drawing area, you can create unique and customized configurations. These can be saved as workspaces and then opened together as named Workspace from the Window pull-down menu. The AutoCAD default workspace includes all of the elements you are used to seeing. A simple example of a customized workspace would be to open the Dimension and Text toolbars and then save this configuration as an "Annotation" workspace. Then whenever you want to be in this workspace you open the Window menu, highlight Workspace, and select Annotation.

Toolbars: Toolbars can be created and added to the tree view list of toolbars. Everything you need to know about toolbar creation is in Appendix B. You can also modify existing toolbars using the same techniques used to create new ones. We do not recommend modifying the AutoCAD toolbars.

Menus: These are the standard pull-down menus you see at the top of your drawing area. If you open Menus in the tree view, you see the list from File to Help. If you open File, you see the list of commands on the File pull-down menu, beginning with New and proceeding down to Exit. Most entries on pull-down menus refer to commands and they work exactly like the tool button entries on toolbars. For example, click New on the list and you will see the Button Image for the New command on the top right and the Properties panel below that. The macro for this line on the menu is ^C^C_new. If you are not familiar with the Properties panel, read Appendix B.

Shortcut Menus: Here you will find a list of standard shortcut menus. Under Grips Cursor Menu, for example you will see familiar grip modes and options that appear when you right-click while in the grip editing system.

Keyboard Shortcuts: This list is a good place to explore the complete keyboard shortcuts available. For example, open the tree view, then the Shortcut keys list and look under New. You will find that this is the place where Ctrl+N is established as the keyboard shortcut for entering the New command. There are 30 keyboard shortcuts defined here, including many you've probably never noticed. The Temporary Overrides list shows key combinations that will temporarily override a setting without changing it. Most of these use the Shift key in combination with another key.

Mouse Buttons: The options with a standard two-button mouse are pretty limited, but this list gives you a place for customizing pointing devices with more than the two buttons.

LISP Files: AutoCAD allows you to create customized routines in other languages, in addition to the macro language presented here. AutoLISP is a programming language based on LISP. LISP is a standard list processing language. You see AutoLISP statements in place of some macros in the Properties panel. LISP statements are enclosed in parentheses.

Legacy: Legacy refers to elements of the drawing area that are no longer in common use but are still supported for those who like to use them. This includes screen menus, tablet menus, and image tile menus. You do not need to know about these unless you are working on a system that uses legacy features.

Partial CUI Files: The way to create customized user interface files is to add partial files to the standard file. This way you do not lose the original and can go back to it at any time. If you open this entry you will see that there is currently one Partial CUI file defined under the name CUSTOM. It contains all the elements of the standard file, but there are no entries under the main element headings. To create your own partial CUI file you can start with CUSTOM and add commands and macros to any of the elements.

This completes the tour of the CUI dialog box. In the next section you will find additional macro characters and their meanings.

C.2 What Characters Are Used in AutoCAD Macros?

The following table lists some menu and macro characters you find in many elements of the CUI file.

Most Common AutoCAD Macro Characters

&	Placed before a letter that can be used as an alias. The letter will be underlined on the menu.
;	Same as pressing Enter while typing.
^	Ctrl.
^C	Ctrl+C, same as pressing Esc.
^C^C	Double cancel; cancels any command, ensures a return to the Command: prompt before a new command is issued.
POPn	Section header, where *n* is a number between 1 and 16, identifying one of the 16 possible pull-down menu areas. POP0 refers to the cursor menu.
[ ]	Brackets enclose text to be written directly to the screen or pull-down menu area. Eight characters are printed on the screen menu. The size of menu items on the pull-down menu varies.
[–]	Writes a blank line on a pull-down menu.
_	English-language flag.
'	Transparent command modifier.

( )	Parentheses enclose AutoLISP and DIESEL expressions.
\	Pause for user input. Allows for keyboard entry, point selection, and object selection. Terminated by pressing Enter or pick button.
~	Begins a pull-down menu label that is unavailable. Can be used to indicate a function not currently in use.
*^C^C	This set of characters causes the menu item to repeat.

Appendix

D | Data Exchange Formats

AutoCAD has the capacity to recognize and create files in a number of common file exchange formats. These allow you to translate AutoCAD drawings for use with other software and to bring drawings from other programs into AutoCAD. Following is a list of available drawing file types, listed by extension with descriptions of the purpose of each, followed by the commands used to import and export them:

FILE EXTENSION	PURPOSE
3DS	3D Studio. 3DS files are used by Autodesk's 3D Studio software. 3D Studio is an Autodesk rendering program with advanced lighting and material capabilities. EXPORT, 3DSOUT, 3DSIN
BMP	Bitmap. Bitmap files use a pixel-by-pixel digital representation of screen images. BMPOUT, PASTECLIP
DWF	Drawing Web Format. For publishing drawings on the World Wide Web. DWF files can be viewed on the Internet by others who have a Web browser and the AutoCAD plug-in WHIP! DWF files are created for viewing and publishing; they are not read by AutoCAD for editing and information exchange, as regular DWG files would be. DWFOUT, ePLOT
DXB	Drawing Exchange Binary. A binary-coded format used by AutoSHADE. DXBIN
DXF	Data Exchange Format. A text file format for exchanging drawings between different CAD programs. AutoCAD reads and writes DXF files for exchange with other systems. SAVEAS
EPS	Encapsulated Postscript. For printing and plotting on machines with postscript capability. PSOUT, PSIN
SAT	ACIS (*.sat extension) files capture regions, solids, and NURB (NonUniform Rational B-spline) surfaces in an ASCII format for exchange with other modeling software. ACISOUT, ACISIN
STL	Stereolithograph Apparatus. For translating solid object data into a format compatible with a Stereolithograph machine.

	Stereolithography is a technology that creates actual physical models from CAD solid model data. STLOUT
WMF	Windows Metafile. For saving objects in a raster or vector image format for use with other Windows programs. EXPORT, WMFOUT, WMFIN

In addition to these file types, also remember that images can be transferred among Windows applications using the clipboard (Chapter 10) and that raster images can be attached in a manner similar to external references (Chapter 10). The clipboard makes use of the CUTCLIP, COPYCLIP, and COPYLINK commands for exporting and PASTECLIP, PASTELINK, and PASTESPEC for importing. When importing through the clipboard, AutoCAD automatically recognizes and uses the most efficient format among its options of DWG, WMP, and BMP files. Raster images are attached using the IMAGEATTACH command, which supports a large number of image file types. See the *AutoCAD User's Guide* for additional information on raster images and image file types.

D.1 Creating Export Files

Although the file formats that AutoCAD can export vary widely and are used for quite different purposes, the procedure for creating them is identical. As long as you know what type of file you want to create, all you need to do is open the Export dialog box from the File menu (Figure D-1), give the export file a name,

Figure D-1

and select the type of file you want to save it as. To create a 3DS (3D Studio file), for example, follow this procedure:

1. Open the File menu and select Export.
2. In the Export Data dialog box, type a name for the file.
3. Open the Save As Type list and select 3D Studio (*.3ds).
4. Click Save.

For other drawing exchange formats, follow the same procedure, selecting the file type you want from the Save As Type file list. DWF files are created using the ePLOT feature of the PLOT dialog box.

D.2 Importing Files in Other Formats

Many of the drawing file types listed previously can be imported into AutoCAD as well. Importing most drawing file types is handled through the Insert menu. In most cases, you will select a file type, select a file, and open it. An example of an import procedure for a WMF follows:

1. Open the Insert menu and select Windows Metafile.
2. In the Import WMF file dialog box, select the name of a WMF file to insert.
3. Select Open.
4. Specify an insertion point and scale factors, just as you would when inserting a block with the INSERT command.

Different types of files require different insertion specifications, as shown in their respective Import dialog boxes. File types on the Insert menu are shown in Figure D-2. DXF files are opened using the OPEN command, selecting DXF from the Files of type list.

Figure D-2

Appendix E

Additional Tools for Collaboration

This book is designed primarily as a tutorial for a single user at a computer workstation or a student in a class with access to a workstation. In order to stay true to this goal it has been necessary to leave certain very important aspects of CAD practice alone. In addition to the programming and customizing tools introduced in Appendixes B and C, there are numerous tools that are only encountered in collaborative environments, where the work space extends beyond the individual and the individual computer. In this appendix, we briefly introduce a few of these tools, so that readers may enter a collaborative environment with some understanding of these processes. These tools are not necessary for the completion of any drawing in this book, but they belong in your repertoire of techniques.

E.1 CAD Standards

The CAD Standards feature is important in work environments where drawings from one organization might be used in other organizations or departments. Using CAD Standards files allows quick checking and modifying of drawings to ensure that externally created or outsourced drawings use standards compatible with standards in place for drawings created in-house. AutoCAD's CAD Standards feature requires the use of a drawing standards file. This can be any drawing that uses the desired standards, including layer definitions and properties, dimension styles, text styles, and linetypes. To understand the issues involved, imagine that in Your Company, Inc. all drawings have a standard layer, we'll call it Layer1, that is red. In order to support this practice, a certain Drawing A has been defined as a CAD Standards file (saved with a .dws extension). Your Company receives Drawing B from Their Company. Drawing B and Drawing A both have a layer called Layer1, but in Their Company, Layer1 is yellow. As a Your Company's CAD expert, you must ensure that Drawing B complies with Your Company's standards. You proceed as follows:

⊕   Open Drawing B.

⊕ Open the Tools menu, highlight CAD Standards, and select Configure. This opens the Configure Standards dialog box.

⊕ Select Drawing A as the CAD Standards file.

⊕ In the same dialog box click Check Standards. This opens a dialog box that shows you any discrepancies between Drawing A and Drawing B.

⊕ Click the Fix button to alter Layer1 in Drawing B to match the standard of Drawing A.

Now that Drawing A is defined as a Standards file for Drawing B, anytime you try to change a property in Drawing B so that it does not match a standard, you will get a Standards Violation notification in the lower right corner of your screen. You can use the blue link to run a standards check and fix the problem or you can ignore and close the message.

E.2 Layer Translation

Layer translation is closely related to CAD Standards checking. It works similarly, but only addresses layers and it allows you to adjust the layers in any drawing to match layers in another drawing. You are not restricted to using drawings that have been defined as standards files, but can use any drawing to shape any other drawing. Properties that can be matched are all the properties that define layers. To translate Layer1 properties in Drawing A to Layer1 properties in Drawing B:

⊕ Open Drawing B.

⊕ Open the Tools menu, highlight CAD Standards, and select Layer Translator.

This opens the Layer Translator. Layers in the current drawing are shown in the Translate From panel. There is nothing in the Translate To panel until we load a drawing.

⊕ Click Load.

This opens a Select Drawing File dialog box. You can select a drawing, a template drawing, or a CAD Standards drawing file.

⊕ Navigate to the folder where Drawing A is located.

⊕ Select Drawing A.

Notice that this can be any drawing. It does not have to be a .dws drawing.

⊕ Click Open.

Layers from Drawing A are now listed in the Translate To panel.

⊕ Highlight Layer1 in both panels.

⊕ Click Map.

The proposed translation shows in the Layer Translations Mapping panel.

⊕ Click Translate.

⊕ Click Yes to save or No to eliminate the old layer information in Drawing B.

E.3 Management of Named Objects

When managing multiple drawings from different sources, you are likely to encounter the problem of duplicate definitions. For example, what happens when a drawing that is externally referenced or block-inserted has layers, linetypes, text styles, dimension styles, blocks, or views with names that are the same as those in the current drawing? Good question. In the case of blocked drawings, name definitions in the current drawing override those in the inserted block, regardless of its origin. In the case of XREFed drawings, named objects are given special designations that eliminate the duplication. For example, if Drawing B is attached to Drawing A and both have a layer called FLOOR, a new layer is created in A called B|FLOOR.

E.4 Sheet Set Management

Most industrial design projects involve not one drawing but a set of drawings detailing different views or different aspects of a single design. When a design project is to be communicated to a client or a consultant it is likely to be represented by a whole set of related drawings. Sets of drawings like these, called Sheet Sets, may be created manually by saving particular layouts from individual drawings and then assembling all the relevant layouts and views in a single location. This process can become quite complex, especially when the individual drawings are on different computers and rely on external references, font files, plot files, and so on that may reside in different locations. To facilitate the creation of Sheet Sets, AutoCAD includes a system called the Sheet Set Manager. Through this interface, layouts from individual drawings are collected into a new drawing. Here, layouts can be easily organized into categories and subsets so that the Sheet Set presents a coherent design concept. One sheet of the set may be designated as the title sheet and this may display a table showing the organizational hierarchy of the complete Sheet Set. Sheets in the Sheet Set are given numbers and designations shown in standard symbol blocks that update automatically if the number and organization of the Sheet Set changes. Consider the following work flow:

- Create drawings in model space.
- In each drawing, create layouts presenting a design image.
- Using the Sheet Set Manager, collect layouts from all relevant drawings into a single set.
- Create a title sheet listing all layouts (sheets) and showing how they are organized.
- Create a Sheet Set package that contains the Sheet Set and all files required to view the set, all organized through the Sheet Set Manager.
- Archive the Sheet Set.
- eTransmit the Sheet Set to a client or consultant.

INDEX